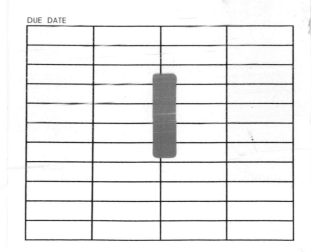

JUN   1991

914.95
Bel   Bell, Robert E.

         Place-names in
         classical mythol-
         ogy

DUE DATE

Place-Names in Classical Mythology: Greece

Place-Names in Classical Mythology: Greece

Robert E. Bell

ABC-CLIO

Santa Barbara, California
Oxford, England

Library of Congress Cataloging-in-Publication Data

Bell, Robert E.
   Place-names in classical mythology : Greece / Robert E. Bell.
   Bibliography: p.
   Includes index.
   1. Greece—Gazetteers.   2. Mythology, Greek—Dictionaries.
I. Title.
DF16.B45 1988   914.95′0014—dc19   88-16870

ISBN 0-87436-507-4 (alk. paper)

10 9 8 7 6 5 4 3 2

This book is Smyth-sewn and printed on acid-free paper ∞ .
Manufactured in the United States of America

Contents

Introduction

This place-name dictionary is a logical extension of *A Dictionary of Classical Mythology: Symbols, Attributes, and Associations* (ABC-Clio, 1982) and, in fact, was originally intended to be a part of that work. However, since such a cumulation would have made the earlier volume far too cumbersome and perhaps confusing, it was decided to make the place-name dictionary a companion work complete in itself.

Places provide another perspective for examining mythological beings. The circumstances surrounding their beginnings and adventures are important in understanding how mythic dynasties developed, how religious worship spread, and why migrations took place. This book covers roughly one thousand place-names. The length of each entry depends on the importance of the place and information available from ancient writers. In some cases, a sentence or two is sufficient if a place merely has been named for a mythological being. In other cases, an entry may run for pages because of the great importance of the place in mythological and religious history. Thebes, for example, not only was the birthplace of Dionysus and Heracles but saw also the rise and fall of the house of Oedipus, from Oedipus' abandonment as an infant to the two wars of the Seven against Thebes and the Epigoni.

The purpose of this work is to organize into one book the geography of classical mythology. For the most part no attention is paid to historical events or individuals unless there are mythological associations (such as religious phenomena, foundation of temples, etc.). No single work exists devoted exclusively to this purpose. There are several, of course, that refer to mythological backgrounds, but they fail to go into the kind of detail I feel is required for this fascinating subject. The great Pauly-Wissowa *Realencyclopadie der Altertumswissenschaft* might eventually provide such detail, but it would require enormous patience and linguistic ability to pursue a subject through this labyrinthine work.

The *Princeton Encyclopedia of Classical Sites,* while tremendously useful for geographical purposes, treats mythological backgrounds as incidental information, which is, of course, in keeping with the nature of the work. Catherine Avery's *New Century Handbook of Classical Geography* is meant to be no more than a quick reference to places in the ancient world; in it mythological references are exceedingly brief. The mythological content of modern travel guides ranges from the accurate and brief (e.g., Stuart Rossiter's *Blue Guides: Greece*) to the incorrect and very sketchy. One heavily used modern guide, for example, calls the Gulf of Argolis the Gulf of the Acropolis and in one edition identified the city of Argos as the point of origin of the famous voyage of the Argonauts.

The consideration of guidebooks brings up an additional purpose of this volume. I have travelled rather extensively in Greece, alone and on organized tours. On the tours, people have wanted to know more about what happened in mythology in such and such a place, and the otherwise well-informed guides have not been very helpful. One guide's rendition of the Oedipus legend was a masterpiece of invention, scarcely approaching any of the commonly accepted versions, but it succeeded in turning the whole bus against the gods. And once, sitting at a table on the tree-lined street of Kardamili in the Mani, I knew that nobody else, including the guide, knew that Cardamyle was one of the seven cities promised by Agamemnon to Achilles if he would reenter the battle at Troy. It would have been nice for them to know.

But this volume is not to be thought of as a guidebook. Its purpose is the enhancement of mythological interest by putting the hundreds of small and large legends and cycles into geographical context. In Greece the past and present coexist. Nowhere else can one feel so intensely the infusion of the ancient with the modern. Nowhere else can one feel so strongly the role that place has played in the development of the old, often sorrowful stories. One has only to drive up the mountain slope to Davlia (ancient Daulis) to recapture the brooding sense of tragedy that surrounded Procne and Philomela fleeing before the ax of Tereus. With this sense of place in mind, I have often described the setting of a place, perhaps too generously in some cases. Very often physical setting has played a vital part in the stories (e.g., the citadel at Argos in the account of the mass murder of the Danaid bridegrooms, the walls of Tiryns in the murder of Iphicles by Heracles, the gates of Thebes in the war of the Seven). I have visited a large number of the places listed and for the descriptions of these have drawn on personal observation. In other cases I have relied on the descriptions of others. The mid–nineteenth century work by William Smith, *Dictionary of Greek and Roman Geography*, in many cases provided a very good scaffolding on which to build the updated accounts because he did an excellent job of pulling together the original sources. His accounts, however, abound in errors and had to be thoroughly checked. Many of his accounts speculated on locations subsequently uncovered by archaeological investigation. His Athenian agora, for example, is placed to the south of the Areiopagus. The *Princeton Encyclopedia*, the *Blue Guide*, and Dorothy Leekley's volumes on excavations in Greece were extremely useful in identifying ancient names with modern ones and putting monuments in the right places.

The geographical scope of this book is the political boundaries of modern Greece. It was tempting to include Ionia, Italy, Sicily, Cyprus, and North Africa, but again the book would have become unwieldy. I have in mind a further volume on classical place-names beyond Greece. Meanwhile, the ancient places of Greece itself are listed alphabetically with the modern name, if known, in parentheses. In very many cases, the modern name is merely the modern Greek spelling of the ancient name; in some cases there is no change at all. In many other cases, the name is changed altogether. In certain instances I have used the nearest place from which the remains of an ancient city can be located (e.g., Exarhos for both Abae and Hyampolis). When no modern name appears in parentheses, either the site is still unknown or I was not able to verify a modern name. In respect to modernized spellings, I have not invented my own system of transliteration but have relied on the Greek National Tourist Organisation since travelers will be using the good maps that it provides. Even with the GNTO there are minor inconsistencies (e.g., Olympia instead of Olimbia). It should be stated that an attempt for consistency in the whole business of modern place-names and transliteration is exasperating. For example, the Athenian port city appears on selected current maps with the following spellings: Peiraieus, Piraeus, Pireas, Pireefs. Piraievs,

Peiraeus. According to the U.S. Board on Geographic Names, the famous Pythian oracle is located not at Delphi or Delfi (GNTO) but at a place called Dhirfis. Therefore, it seemed wise to adopt the spellings provided by the GNTO, particularly since highway directional signs and site identifications, when transliterated, follow the same system.

There is no single map or atlas that can show all the places covered in this volume. I used a variety of cartographic resources in identifying and verifying place-names. Most of these I acquired in Athens either from the Greek National Tourist Organisation or from bookstores (for specific references to these maps see the Bibliography). I found Kummerly and Frey's "Griechenland" to be the best overall map of modern Greece. The maps in the *Blue Guides: Greece* are also helpful, but the *Guide's* main value is the detail in the text that establishes distances between towns, even the smallest ones, and that points out adjacent ruins of ancient places. Volume 5 of the *Loeb Classics* edition of Pausanias is useful for location of ancient cities in relation to each other and for location of other topographical features such as mountains and rivers.

For ancient names I have followed the transliterations in the *Loeb Classical Library*, although various translators have not always agreed. If a name appears in the *Loeb* translation of Pausanias, I have usually used that spelling because Pausanias is the most frequently cited author in this work. The *Loeb Classical Library* is less consistent with personal names, the Pausanias translation using the ending *-eia* and the Apollodorus *-ia*. I have again followed Pausanias. In one or two cases I have made a small departure from consistency for the sake of common usage, such as *Medea* and *Jason* instead of *Medeia* and *Iason;* for the same reason in a few common words, like *Nike,* I have departed from my usual practice of spelling a kappa in an ancient word as the letter *c*. In referring to the citadels of cities, I have used acropolis in lower case. The only exception is in Athens, where it is capitalized.

Citations to ancient works are confined to those works for which there is a *Loeb* edition. Most libraries have this series, and readers can refer to the original texts and their translations. Statements from writers and commentators for whom there is no *Loeb* edition have no citations. I have included some of these sources in the bibliography. Citations are in standard bibliographical format for classical works, and a table of abbreviations is provided.

See references and the occasional *See also* references point the reader to entries where more information on the same subject is available. Short entries (ACIS was an earlier name of the island of SIPHNOS) also act as *See* references, directing the reader to the entry for the upper-case place-name at the end of the statement (SIPHNOS in this example).

The compilation of this volume has been a rewarding experience. In the course of the project I have made three trips to Greece (added to five earlier ones). Working on this project has given me a keen appreciation of Greek geography, and it has been exciting to bring life to a pile of stones in some remote town. I would like to thank Susan McGregor, Nikolaos Kokkinos, and especially Mark Hanrahan, who helped me find and explore some of these places. My deepest gratitude goes to Dr. Anna Strataridakis for her expert knowledge of Greece and its language and people and for the continuing inspiration and support she gives me as a friend and fellow writer.

Guide to Citation Abbreviations

Aelianus (Aelian.)
  De Natura Animalium (De Nat. Anim.)
  Varia Historia (V.H.)
Aeschylus (Aeschyl.)
  Agamemnon (Agam.)
  Choephori (Choeph.)
  Eumenides (Eum.)
  Persae (Pers.)
  Prometheus Vinctus (Prom.)
  Septem Contra Thebas (Sept.)
Alciphron (Alciph.)
  Epistulae (Ep.)
Apollodorus (Apollod.)
Apollonius Rhodius (Apollon. Rhod.)
Aratus (Arat.)
Aristophanes (Aristoph.)
  Acharnenses (Acharn.)
  Aves (Av.)
  Lysander (Lys.)
  Plutus (Plut.)
  Ranae (Ran.)
  Thesmophoriazusae (Thes.)
  Vespae (Vesp.)
Aristotle (Aristot.)
  Historia Animalium (H.A.)
  Meteorologica (Meteor.)
  Politica (Polit.)
Athenaeus (Athen.)
Augustine (August.)
  De Civitate Dei (De Civ. Dei)
Callimachus (Callim.)
  Fragmenta (Frag.)
  Hymnus in Apollinem (Hymn. in Apoll.)
  Hymnus in Cererem (Hymn. in Cer.)
  Hymnus in Delum (Hymn. in Del.)
  Hymnus in Dianam (Hymn. in Dian.)
  Hymnus in Jovem (Hymn. in Jov.)
  Lavacrum Palladis (Lav. Pall.)

Catullus (Catull.)
Cicero (Cic.)
  De Divinatione (De Div.)
  De Finibus (De Fin.)
  De Legibus (De Leg.)
  De Natura Deorum (De Nat. Deor.)
  Post Reditum in Senatu (Post Redit. in Senat.)
  Tusculanae Disputationes (Tusc.)
Claudian (Claud.)
  *Epithalamium de Nuptiis Honorii Augusti et
    Maria (De Nupt. Mar.)*
  Gigantomachia (Gigantom.)
  In Rufinum (In Rufin.)
Clemens Alexandrinus (Clem. Alex.)
  Stromateis (Strom.)
Demosthenes (Dem.)
  De Corona (De Cor.)
  De Falsa Legatione (De Fals. Leg.)
Dio Cassius (Dio Cass.)
Diodorus Siculus (Diod.)
Diogenes Laertius (Diog. Laert.)
Dionysius Halicarnassensis (Dionys.)
Euripides (Eurip.)
  Andromache (Androm.)
  Bacchae (Bacch.)
  Cyclops (Cycl.)
  Electra (Elect.)
  Hercules Furens (Herc. Fur.)
  Hippolytus (Hippol.)
  Ion (Ion)
  Iphigenia Aulidensis (Iphig. Aul.)
  Iphigenia Taurica (Iphig. Taur.)
  Medea (Med.)
  Orestes (Orest.)
  Rhesus (Rhes.)
  Supplices (Suppl.)
  Troades (Troad.)
Gellius (Gell.)

Herodotus (Herod.)
Hesiod (Hes.)
    Fragmenta (Frag.)
    Opera et Dies (Op. et D.)
    Scutum Herculis (Scut. Herc.)
    Theogonia (Theog.)
Homer (Hom.)
    Iliad (Il.)
    Odyssey (Od.)
Homeric Hymns
    Hymnus Homericus ad Apollinem (Hymn. Hom. ad Apoll.)
    Hymnus Homericus ad Cererem (Hymn. Hom. ad Cer.)
    Hymnus Homericus ad Mercurium (Hymn. Hom. ad. Mer.)
    Hymnus Homericus ad Panem (Hymn. Hom. ad Pan.)
    Hymnus Homericus ad Venerem (Hymn. Hom. ad Ven.)
Horace (Hor.)
    Carmina (Carm.)
Julian (Jul.)
    Orationes (Orat.)
Juvenal (Juv.)
Livy (Liv.)
Lucan (Lucan)
Lucian (Lucian)
    Amores (Amor.)
    De Morte Peregrini (De Mort. Per.)
    De Saltatione (De Salt.)
    Dei Marini (Dei Marin.)
    Demonax (Demon.)
    Dialogi Deorum (Dial. Deor.)
    Dialogi Meretricii (Dial. Meret.)
    Dialogi Mortuorum (Dial. Mort.)
    Timon (Tim.)
Lycophron (Lycoph.)
Martial (Mart.)
Moschus (Mosch.)
Nonnus (Nonn.)
    Dionysiaca (Dionys.)
Ovid (Ov.)
    Ars Amatoria (Ars Am.)
    Epistulae ex Ponto (Ep. ex Pont.)
    Fasti (Fast.)
    Heroides (Her.)
    Ibis (Ib.)
    Metamorphoses (Met.)
    Tristia (Trist.)
Pausanias (Paus.)
Philostratus (Philostr.)
    Vita Apollonii (Vit. Apoll.)

Pindar (Pind.)
    Isthmian Odes (Isth.)
    Nemean Odes (Nem.)
    Olympian Odes (Ol.)
    Pythian Odes (Pyth.)
Plato (Plat.)
    De Re Publica (De Re Pub.)
    Gorgias (Gorg.)
    Leges (Leg.)
    Phaedrus (Phaedr.)
Pliny (the Elder) (Plin.)
Plutarch (Plut.)
    Moralia:
        Amatoriae Narrationes (Amat. Narr.)
        Apophthegmata Laconica (Apophth.)
        De Cohibenda Ira (De Cohib. Ir.)
        De Defectu Oraculorum (De Def. Or.)
        De E apud Delphos (no abbrev.)
        De Garrulitate (De Garrul.)
        De Genio Socratis (De Gen. Socr.)
        De Iside et Osiride (De Is. et Osir.)
        De Pythiae Oraculis (De Pyth. Or.)
        Parallela Graeca et Romana (Paral. Gr. et Rom.)
        Quaestiones Graecae (Quaest. Gr.)
        Quaestiones Romanae (Quaest. Rom.)
        Quaestionum Convivalium (Quaest. Conviv.)
        Septem Sapientium Convivium (Sept. Sapient. Conviv.)
    Vitae Parallelae:
        Alexander (Alex.)
        Aratus (Arat.)
        Aristides (Aristid.)
        Camillus (Camil.)
        Cimon (Cim.)
        Demetrius (Demetr.)
        Lycurgus (Lyc.)
        Lysander (Lys.)
        Pelopidas (Pelop.)
        Pericles (Per.)
        Pyrrhus (Pyrr.)
        Solon (Sol.)
        Sulla (Sull.)
        Themistocles (Them.)
        Theseus (Thes.)
Polybius (Polyb.)
Propertius (Propert.)
Ptolemaeus (Ptol.)
Sophocles (Soph.)
    Ajax (Aj.)
    Electra (Elect.)
    Oedipus Coloneus (Oed. Col.)

Oedipus Tyrannus (Oed. Tyr.)
Philoctetes (Phil.)
Trachiniae (Trach.)
Statius (Stat.)
    Achilleis (Achill.)
    Silvae (Silv.)
    Thebias (Theb.)
Strabo (Strab.)
Suetonius (Suet.)
    Divus Augustus (Div. Aug.)
Tacitus (Tacit.)
    Annales (Ann.)
Theocritus (Theocrit.)
Theophrastus (Theophrast.)
    Historia Plantarum (Hist. Pl.)

Thucydides (Thuc.)
Valerius Flaccus (Val. Flacc.)
Varro (Varr.)
    De Re Rustica (De Re Rus.)
Virgil (Virg.)
    Aeneid (Aen.)
    Eclogues (Ecl.)
    Georgics (Georg.)
Vitruvius (Vitruv.)
Xenophon (Xenoph.)
    Anabasis (Anab.)
    De Vectigalibus (De Vectig.)
    Hellenica (Hellen.)

Place-Names in
Classical Mythology: Greece

ABAE (EXARHOS)　　an ancient town of Phocis, near the frontiers of the Opuntian Locrians, was said to have been built by Abas, twelfth king of Argos, son of Lynceus and Hypermnestra and grandson of Danaus (Paus. 10.35.1). Near the town and on the road toward Hyampolis was an ancient temple and oracle of Apollo, who from it derived the surname of Abaeus (Herod. 8.33). So celebrated was this oracle that it was consulted both by Croesus and Mardonius. Before the Persian invasion the temple was richly adorned with treasures and votive offerings. It was twice destroyed by fire: the first time by the Persians in their march through Phocis (480 B.C.) and a second time by the Boeotians in the Sacred or Phocian War (346 B.C.). Hadrian caused a smaller temple to be built near the ruins of the former one. In the temple there were three ancient statues in bronze of Apollo, Leto, and Artemis, which had been dedicated by the Abaei and had perhaps been saved from the former temple. There are remains of the walls, which formed the enclosure of the temple (Herod. 1.46, 8.134; Diod. 16.58). The site is 2.5 km west of Exarhos village in the upper reaches of a tributary of the Cephissus. The village is 18 km west and then south from Atalanti.

ABANTIS　　was an ancient name of EUBOEA.

ABDERA (AVDIRA)　　was a town upon the south coast of Thrace on Cape Bulustra (Akra Karasou), about 17 km northeast of the point at which the Nestus River flows into the sea. According to mythology, it was founded by Heracles in honor of his favorite, Abderus, a son of Hermes of Opus. Diomedes, a son of Ares and Cyrene, was king of the Bistones in Thrace. He owned several mares, which he fed with human flesh, and the

eighth labor of Heracles was to fetch these mares to Mycenae. With several companions he made an unexpected attack on those who guarded the horses in their stables, took the animals, and conducted them to the seacoast. Here he was overtaken by the Bistones and, during the ensuing fight, he entrusted the mares to his friend Abderus, who was killed and eaten by them. Heracles defeated the Bistones and killed Diomedes, whose body he fed to the mares. He then built the town of Abdera in honor of his unfortunate friend and returned to Mycenae with the mares, which had become tame after eating the flesh of their master (Apollod. 2.5.8; Diod. 4.15). According to some, Abderus was a servant of Diomedes and was killed by Heracles together with his master and his four man-devouring horses.

The complete outline of the walls has been excavated. A building with courts was probably part of the agora. Artifacts from the excavation are on exhibit in the museum of Kavala. The ruins are located on the coast 7 km from the modern town of Avdira.

ABIA (AVIA)　　was a town in Messenia on the Messenian Gulf and a little above the valley of Choerius, which formed the boundary between Messenia and Laconia in the time of Pausanias. It is said to have been the same town as the Ira of the *Iliad* (9.292), one of the seven towns that Agamemnon offered to Achilles. It derived its name from Abia, the nurse of Hyllus, a son of Heracles. She had built a temple of Heracles at Ira, for which the Heraclid Cresphontes afterward honored her in various ways, notably by changing the name Ira to Abia (Paus. 4.30.1). The modern town is about 15 km south along the gulf from Kalamata.

1

ABYDON (See AMYDON)

ACACESIUM was a town of Arcadia in the district of Parrhasia, at the foot of a hill of the same name and about 7 km on the road from Megalopolis to Phigalia. It is said to have been founded by Acacus, son of Lycaon; and, according to some traditions, Hermes was brought up at this place by Acacus, thereby deriving the surname Acacesius (Callim. *Hymn. in Dian.* 143). Upon the hill there was a statue in stone, in the time of Pausanias, of Hermes Acacesius, and three-quarters of a kilometer from the town was a celebrated temple of Despoena (Paus. 8.36.10). This temple probably stood on the hill on which are now the remains of the church of Agios Elias. Pan also had a temple near Acacesium, where a perpetual fire burned. He also had an ancient oracle there at which the nymph Erato had been the priestess (Paus. 8.37.11).

ACADEMIA (AKADEMIA) was located in the greater Athens area. It was originally owned by Academus, an Attic hero. When Castor and Polydeuces invaded Attica to liberate their sister Helen, Academus betrayed to them that she was kept concealed at Aphidna. For this reason the Tyndarids always showed him much gratitude, and whenever the Lacedaemonians invaded Attica, they always spared the land belonging to Academus, which lay on the Cephissus (Plut. *Thes.* 32). This piece of land abounded in plane and olive plantations. Twelve sacred olive trees, supposed to be from Athena's tree on the Acropolis, grew here. The Academy was traditionally founded by Academus (Hekademos). An early Helladic dwelling excavated here might be the house of Academus since it is near a large shrine from the seventh or eighth century. The area is reached by following Odos Plataion for 2.5 km from the northwest corner of the Keramikos.

ACARNANIA (AKARNANIA) the most westerly province of Greece, was bounded on the north by the Ambracian Gulf, on the northwest by Amphilochia, on the west and southwest by the Ionian Sea, and on the east by Aetolia. At one time the Achelous River formed the boundary between Acarnania and Aetolia. The name of Acarnania is derived from Acarnan, one of the Epigoni, son of Alcmaeon and Callirrhoe and brother of Amphoterus. After slaying his father's murderer, he and his brother fled Phegeus' relatives and arrived eventually at Delphi at the request of Achelous, their grandfather. Here they left the necklace and robe of Harmonia. Then they went to Epeirus, where Acarnan founded the state called after him Acarnania (Apollod. 3.7.5–7; Thuc. 2.102; Strab. 10.2.26).

One of the Acarnanian dynasties began with Icarius, the son of Perieres and grandson of Aeolus. His brothers were Aphareus, Leucippus, and Tyndareus. Hippocoon, a bastard son of Perieres, expelled his two brothers, Tyndareus and Icarius, from Lacedaemon. They fled to Thestius at Pleuron and dwelt beyond the river Achelous. Subsequently, when Heracles had slain Hippocoon and sons, Tyndareus returned to Sparta, while Icarius remained in Acarnania. While in Acarnania, Icarius became the father of Penelope, Alyzeus, and Leucadius. After the death of Icarius, Alyzeus and Leucadius reigned over Acarnania, and Alyzeus founded the town of Alyzia there (Strab. 10.2.10).

Apart from these Laconian and Argive colonies, the Teleboans, descendants of Teleboas, son of Pterelaus and grandson of Lelex, were believed to have settled in Acarnania (Strab. 7.7.2, 10.2.20).

Apollo Carneius was worshipped in Acarnania. The origin of the name was by some derived from Carnus, an Acarnanian soothsayer, whose murder by Hippotes provoked Apollo to send a plague into the army of Hippotes while he was on his march to Peloponnesus. Apollo was afterward propitiated by the introduction of the worship of Apollo Carneius (Paus. 3.13.3). The chief priest of the temple of Apollo at Actium, a promontory in Acarnania, seems to have been a person of high rank; and either his name or that of the *strategus*, the chief magistrate, was employed for official dates. The Acarnanians formed their towns into a league, which first met at Stratus, their chief town.

ACESA was a name given by Philoctetes to the island of LEMNOS.

ACHAIA (AHAIA) originally called Aegialus or Aegialeia, a province of the northern Peloponnesus, extended along the Corinthian Gulf from the river Larissus, a little south of the promontory of Araxus, which separated it from Elis, to the river Sythas, which separated it from Sicyonia. On the south it was bordered by Arcadia and on the southwest by Elis. It is only a narrow strip of country lying along the slope of the north range of Arcadia, from which extend numerous ridges running into the sea. The plains at the foot of these mountains are watered by several streams, most of which are dry in summer. The highest mountain in Achaia is situated behind Patras and is called Mount Panahaiko.

There are three conspicuous promontories on the coast: (1) Drepanum, the name of which is connected by Pausanias (7.23.4) with the sickle of Cronus; (2) Rhium, opposite the promontory of Antirrhium on the borders of Aetolia and Locris; on the Rhium was a temple of Poseidon (Thuc. 2.86); and (3) Araxus.

The rivers of Achaia, from east to west, are: (1) Sythas, forming the boundary between Achaia and Sicyonia; Pausanias (2.7.8) says that at the festival of Apollo there was a procession of children from Sicyon to the Sythas and back again to the city; (2) Crius; (3) Crathis; (4) Buraicus; (5) Cerynites; (6) Selinus;

(7) Maganitas; (8) Phoenix; (9) Bolinaeus, named from an ancient town Bolina, which had disappeared in the time of Pausanias (7.24.4); (10) Selemnus; (11) Charadus; (12) Meilichus; (13) Glaucus; (14) Peirus, also called Achelous; and (15) Larissus, forming the boundary between Achaia and Elis.

The original inhabitants of Achaia are said to have been Pelasgians and were called Aegialeis, or "coast-men" from Aegialus, the ancient name of the country. Some writers, however, said the origin was mythological, derived from Aegialeus, a king of Sicyonia (Herod. 7.94; Paus. 7.1.1). Aegialeus was a son of Inachus and the Oceanid Melia. According to Sicyonian tradition, he was an autochthon, brother of Phoroneus and first king of Sicyon, to whom the foundation of Aegialus was ascribed (Paus. 2.5.6). The Ionians subsequently settled in the country.

Ion, the fabulous ancestor of the Ionians, is described as a son of Apollo by Creusa, the daughter of Erechtheus and wife of Xuthus (Apollod. 1.7.3). The most celebrated story about him is that which forms the subject of the *Ion* of Euripides. Apollo had visited Creusa in a cavern below the Propylaea, and when she gave birth to a son, she exposed him in the same cave. Apollo, however, had the child conveyed to Delphi and there had him educated by a priestess. When the boy had grown and Xuthus and Creusa came to consult the oracle about the means of obtaining an heir, the answer was that the first human being which Xuthus met on leaving the temple should be his son. Xuthus met Ion and acknowledged him as his son; but Creusa, imagining him to be a son of her husband by a former lover, caused a cup to be presented to the youth that was filled with the poisonous blood of a dragon. Her intention was discovered when Ion, before drinking, poured out a libation to the gods and a pigeon that drank of it died on the spot. Creusa in panic fled to the altar of the god. Ion dragged her away and was on the point of killing her when a priestess intervened, explaining the mystery and showing that Ion was the son of Creusa. Mother and son thus became reconciled, but they did not share the knowledge with Xuthus. Xuthus, however, was satisfied, for he, too, received a promise that he should become a father, a promise fulfilled when Dorus and Achaeus were born.

The inhabitants of Aegialus were likewise Ionians, and among them there was a tradition that Xuthus, when expelled from Thessaly, went to Aegialus. After his death Ion was on the point of marching against the Aegialeans when their king, Selinus, gave him his daughter Helice in marriage. After the death of Selinus, Ion succeeded to the throne, and thus the Aegialeans received the name Ionians; the town of Helice was built in honor of Ion's wife (Paus. 7.1.4; Apollod. 1.7.3).

The Ionians remained in possession of the country till the invasion of Peloponnesus by the Dorians, when the Achaians, who had been driven out of Argos and Lacedaemon by the invaders, marched against the Ionians in order to obtain new homes for themselves. Under the command of their king, Tisamenus, the son of Orestes, they defeated the Ionians in battle. The Ionians shut themselves up in Helice where they sustained a siege for a time, but they finally left the country and sought refuge in Attica. Tisamenus himself was slain by the Heracleidae (Apollod. 2.8.3). The Achaians thus became masters of the country, which was called after them Achaia (Herod. 1.145). The Achaians regarded Achaeus, a son of Xuthus and Creusa and brother of Ion, as the author of their race, and they derived from him their own name as well as that of Achaia.

There were twelve independent cities recognized in Achaia, and they formed a confederation. These cities continued to be governed by the descendants of Tisamenus down to Ogygus, after whose death they abolished kingly rule and established a democracy. In the time of Herodotus (1.145) the twelve cities were: Pellene, Aegeira, Aegae, Bura, Helice, Aegium, Phypes, Patrae, Pharae, Olenus, Dyme, Tritaea. The bond of confederacy among these cities was very loose, and their connection was of a religious rather than of a political nature. Their original place of meeting was at Helice, where they offered a common sacrifice to Poseidon, the guardian divinity of the place; but after Helice had been destroyed by a tidal wave in 373 B.C., they transferred their meetings to Aegium, where they sacrificed to the Panachaean Demeter and to Zeus Homagyrius, or Homarius (Paus. 7.24.2,3). This surname of Zeus referred to him as god of the assembly or league, and he was most likely invoked at Aegium when Agamemnon assembled the Greek chiefs to deliberate on the war against Troy.

ACHAIA   was a district in the south of Thessaly, in which Phthia and Hellas were situated. It appears to have been the original abode of the Achaians, who were thus called Phthiotan Achaians to distinguish them from the Achaians in Peloponnesus. According to tradition, Achaeus, the son of Xuthus and Creusa and brother of Ion, was regarded as the ancestor of all the Achaians. He is thus the eponymous founder of both Thessalian Achaia and Peloponnesian Achaia, which was formerly called Aegialus. When his uncle Aeolus died in Thessaly, Achaeus returned there and made himself master of Phthiotis, which received from him the name of Achaia (Paus. 7.1.3; Strab. 8.7.1; Apollod. 1.7.3).

It was from this part of Thessaly that Achilles came, and Homer (*Il.* 2.684) says that the subjects of this hero were called Myrmidons and Hellenes and Achaians. This district continued to retain the name of Achaia in the time of Herodotus (7.173, 197), and the inhabitants of Phthia were called Phthiotan Achaians till a still later period (Thuc. 8.3).

ACHARNAE (AHARNES)   the largest deme of Attica, belonging to the tribe Oeneis, was situated 11 km north of Athens and consequently not far from the foot of Mount Parnes in the general neighborhood of the modern villages of Aharnes and Ano Liossia. The weight of evidence suggests Aharnes as the most likely site of Acharnae. The population was rough and warlike. They possessed sanctuaries or altars of Apollo Agyieus (Protector of Streets and Public Places), of Heracles, of Athena Hygieia ′ (as identified with Hygieia, goddess of health, when her role is extended to include mental health), of Athena Hippia, of Dionysus Melpomenus (the Singer), and of Dionysus Cissus, so called because the Acharnians said that ivy first grew in this deme (Apollod. 1.31.6).

ACHELOUS (AHELOOS)   is the largest and most celebrated river in Greece, rising in the Pindos range near Mount Lakmos and entering the plain of Akarnania and Etolia near Stratos. It flows into the Ionian Sea near the ancient Acarnanian site of Oeniadae. It once formed the boundary between Acarnania and Aetolia and at various times has been assigned as a part of one or the other province. It has been called by other names: Aspropotamo, Thoas, Axenus, and Thestius. In summer it is divided into five or six rapid streams and in its wanderings through the plain, anciently called Paracheloitis, it is difficult often to trace its course. At its mouth its alluvium has formed a number of small islands, which belong to a group called the Echinades in antiquity. The chief tributaries were: Campylus, Cyathus, Petitarius, and Anapus. The Achelous was regarded as the ruler and representative of all fresh water in Hellas.

Achelous, the god of the river, was a son of Oceanus and Tethys, or Gaea. When Achelous on one occasion lost his daughters, the Sirens, and in his grief invoked his mother Gaea, she received him to her bosom, and on that very spot she caused the river bearing his name to gush forth. When he and Heracles fought for possession of Deianeira, Achelous first attacked Heracles in the form of a serpent, and on being cornered, changed into a bull. The hero wrenched off one of his horns, which became a cornucopia, or horn of plenty (Soph. *Trach.* 9; Ov. *Met.* 9.8; Apollod. 2.7.5). When Theseus returned home from the Calydonian chase, he was hospitably received by Achelous, who related to him how he had created the islands called Echinades (Ov. *Met.* 8.547).

Alcmaeon, son of Amphiaraus, having become insane after he murdered his mother, went to Psophis for purification, but Psophis was visited by famine for harboring a matricide. An oracle advised him to go to a country that had been formed subsequent to the murder of his mother, and was therefore under no curse. The country thus pointed out was a tract of land recently formed at the mouth of the river Achelous. Apollodorus (3.7.3–5) gives a detailed account of Alcmaeon's wanderings until he reached Achelous, who gave him his daughter Callirrhoe in marriage.

Strabo (10.2.19) proposes a very ingenious interpretation of the legends about Achelous, all of which, according to him, arose from the nature of the river itself. It resembled a bull's voice in the noise of its water. Its windings gave rise to the story about his forming himself into a serpent. His contest with Heracles referred to the embankments by which Heracles confined the river to its bed; the large tracts of land thus gained for cultivation are expressed by the horn of plenty. From the earliest times he was considered to be a great divinity throughout Greece (Hom. *Il.* 21.194) and was invoked in prayers, sacrifices, upon taking oaths, etc. The contest of Achelous with Heracles was represented on the throne of Amyclae (Paus. 3.18.16), and in the treasury of the Megarians at Olympia there was a cedar and gold statue of him made by Dontas (Paus. 6.19.12). On several coins of Acarnania the god is represented as a bull with the head of an old man.

ACHERON (AHERON)   a river of Epeirus in Thesprotia, passes through the lake Acherusia and, after receiving the river Cocytus (Kokitos), flows into the Ionian Sea south of the promontory Cheimerium. On the Acheron, Hades, the king of the lower world, is said to have reigned and to have retained Theseus as a prisoner; and on its banks was an oracle called Necromanteion (Herod. 5.92.7), which was consulted by evoking the spirits of the dead. When Epeirus subsequently became better known, the Acheron or the entrance to the lower world was transferred to other more distant parts, and at last the Acheron was placed in the lower world itself. Thus we find that Homer (*Od.* 10.513) describes the Acheron as a river of Hades, into which the Pyriphlegethon and Cocytus are said to flow. Virgil (*Aen.* 6.297) describes it as the principal river of Tartarus, from which the Styx and Cocytus sprang.

According to later traditions, Acheron had been a son of Helios and Gaea or Demeter and was changed into the river bearing his name in the lower world because he had refreshed the Titans with drink during their contest with Zeus. Some sources further state that Ascalaphus was a son of Acheron and Orphne or Gorgyra. In late writers the name Acheron is used in a general sense to designate the whole of the lower world (Virg. *Aen.* 7.312; Cic. *Post Redit. in Senat.* 10). Cerberus, the many-headed dog that guarded the entrance of Hades, was said to have kept watch, according to some, at the mouth of the Acheron.

The Acheron may be seen today from the highway crossing the river near the ruins of the Nekromanteion, about halfway between Preveza and Igoumenitsa.

ACHERUSIA (AHEROUSIA)   was the name of several lakes, which like the various rivers of the name of Acheron, were believed to be connected with the lower world. At last the Acherusia came to be considered in the lower world itself. The most important of these lakes was the one in Thesprotia, through which the Acheron flowed. There was also a small lake by this name near Hermione in Argolis (Paus. 2.35.10), and it, too, was thought to be connected with the underworld.

ACHNE   was an earlier name of the island of CASUS.

ACIDALIUS   was a fountain near Arcadian Orchomenus, in which Aphrodite bathed with the Charites. She derived the surname Acidalia from this well (Virg. *Aen.* 1.720).

ACIDUSA   was a fountain in Boeotia, named for Acidusa, wife of Scamander (Plut. *Quaest. Gr.* 4).

ACIS   was an earlier name of the island of SIPHNOS.

ACONTIUM   a town in Arcadia, derived its name from Acontes or Acontius, a son of Lycaon (Apollod. 3.8.1).

ACRAEA   a mountain in Argolis opposite the Heraion, or great temple of Hera near Mycenae, was named for Acraea, a daughter of the river-god Asterion. Acraea with her sisters Euboea and Prosymna acted as nurse to Hera (Paus. 2.17.2).

ACRAEPHNIUM, ACRAEPHIA, ACRAEPHIUM, or ACRAEPHNIAE (AKREFNIO)   was a town of Boeotia on the slope of Mount Ptoum on the east bank of Lake Copais. Acraephnium is said to have been founded by Athamas or Acraepheus, son of Apollo; and according to some writers it was the same as the Homeric Arne. It contained a temple of Dionysus (Paus. 9.23.5). The church of Agios Giorgios seems to have been erected on the site of this temple. At the distance of 3 km from the town, on the right of the road and upon Mount Ptoum, was a celebrated sanctuary and oracle of Apollo Ptous. This oracle was consulted by Mardonius before the battle of Plataea and is said to have answered his emissary, who was a Carian, in his own language. The name of the mountain was derived by some from Ptous, a son of Apollo and Euxippe. Both Acraephnium and the oracle belonged to Thebes. There was no temple as such of the Ptoan Apollo; Plutarch (*Pelop.* 16) mentions a tholos, but other writers speak only of shrine-like monuments

(Herod. 8.135). The oracle ceased after the capture of Thebes by Alexander, but the sanctuary still continued to retain its celebrity. There is evidence that a festival was celebrated in honor of the Ptoan Apollo every four years. The ruins of Acraephnium are situated at a short distance to the south of the modern village of Akrefnio. The remains of the acropolis are visible on an isolated hill above Lake Copais, and at its foot on the north and west are traces of the ancient town. Active excavation of the city itself has not yet taken place, but it is known that an altar dedicated to Zeus Soter, the city's chief divinity, stood in the agora. In his honor were held the Soteria festivals with gymnastic and musical contests. The ruins near the fountain probably belong to the sanctuary of the Ptoan Apollo. Apollo also received the surname Acraephius from his worship here.

ACRIAE or ACRAEAE   was a town of Laconia, on the east side of the Laconian bay, 5.5 km south of Helos. Strabo (8.3.12, 8.5.1) describes the Eurotas as flowing into the sea between Acriae and Gythium. Acriae possessed a sanctuary and statue of the mother of the gods, which was said by the inhabitants of the town to be the most ancient in Peloponnesus.

Pausanias (6.21.10) lists Acrias among the suitors of Hippodameia and says that he was killed by her father Oenomaus. Acrias was a Lacedaemonian, according to Pausanias, and the founder of Acriae.

ACROCORINTHUS (AKROKORINTHOS)   (See CORINTH)

ACTE   was the original name of ATTICA.

ACTIUM (AKTIO)   is a promontory in Acarnania at the entrance of the Ambracian Gulf (Gulf of Arta) off which Augustus gained his celebrated victory over Antony and Cleopatra in 31 B.C. There was a temple of Apollo on this promontory, which Thucydides (1.29) mentions as situated in the territory of Anactorium. This temple was of great antiquity, and Apollo derived from it the surnames Actius and Actiacus. There was also an ancient festival named Actia celebrated here in honor of the god. Augustus after his victory enlarged the temple and revived the ancient festival, which was thereafter celebrated every five years with musical and gymnastic contests and horse races (Dio Cass. 51.1; Suet. *Div. Aug.* 18). The chief priest of the temple was called *Hierapolos,* and his name was employed in official documents to mark the date. Strabo (7.7.6) says that the temple was situated on a hill and that below was a plain with a grove of trees and a dockyard; in another passage (10.2.7) he describes the harbor as situated outside the gulf. On the opposite coast of Epeirus, Augustus founded the city of Nicopolis in honor of his victory. Actium was properly not a town, though it is sometimes described as such; but after the foundation of Nicopolis, a few buildings sprang up around the temple, and it served as a kind of suburb to Nicopolis. According to one tradition, Aeneas, after the taking of Troy, stayed in Thrace the first winter and then sailed with his companions to various towns and islands throughout Greece. Among the places he visited was Actium.

ACYTON　　was another name given to the island of MELOS.

ADRIATIC SEA　　was the name given both by Greek and Latin writers to the inland sea still called the Adriatic, which separates Italy from Albania, Dalmatia and Epeirus and is connected at its south end with the Ionian Sea. It appears to have been at first regarded by the Greeks as a mere gulf or inlet of the Ionian Sea. The navigation of the Adriatic was much dreaded on account of the frequent and sudden storms to which it was subject; its evil character on this account is repeatedly alluded to by Horace (*Carm.* 1,3,15,33, etc.).

Aristaeus was an ancient divinity worshipped in various parts of Greece, as in Thessaly, Ceos, and Boeotia, but especially in the islands of the Aegean, Ionian, and Adriatic Seas. Aristaeus is one of the most beneficent divinities in ancient mythology: he was worshipped as the protector of flocks and shepherds, of vine and olive plantations; he taught men to hunt and keep bees.

The Adriatic figured in certain of the heroic expeditions of mythology. One of the most important was the expedition of the Argonauts. Scarcely any other adventure in the ancient stories of Greece has been so differently related by poets of all kinds. The most striking differences occur in countries or seas through which the Argonauts returned home. Apollonius Rhodius and Apollodorus make them sail from the Euxine into the rivers Ister and Eridanus into the western ocean or the Adriatic. Also concerned with the Adriatic is Antenor, a Trojan, son of Aesyetes and Cleomestra. After the Trojan War, according to some accounts, he went with the Heneti to Thrace and from there to the western coast of the Adriatic, where the foundation of many towns is ascribed to him (Liv. 1.1; Strab. 13.1.50).

AEDEPSUS (LOUTRA EDIPSOU)　　was a town on the northwest coast of Euboea, 30 km from Cynus on the opposite coast of the Opuntian Locri. It contained warm baths sacred to Heracles, which were used by the dictator Sulla for relief from gout (Plut. *Sull.* 26). These warm baths are still found in the neighborhood of Loutra Edipsou, the site of Aedepsus. Very little excavation has taken place here because of proximity to the modern resort, so little is known of the public buildings described by ancient writers.

AEGAE (AKRATA)　　a town of Achaia and one of the twelve Achaian cities, was situated upon the river Crathis and inland from the coast between Aegeira and Bura. It took its name from a local goat, which suckled the infant Zeus. It is mentioned by Homer (*Il.* 8.203) and was celebrated in the earliest times for its worship of Poseidon. Demeter Panachaea (Goddess of All the Achaians) was worshipped at Aegae (Paus. 7.24.2). It was afterward deserted by its inhabitants, who removed to the neighboring town of Aegeira. All traces of Aegae have disappeared, but it probably occupied the site of Akrata, which is situated upon a commanding height rising from the left bank of the river Crathis. The tiny village of Eges, about 7 km inland from Mavra Litharia on the coast, may have been the site of ancient Aegae, but Akrata seems better to fit the description of the ancient city.

AEGAE (EDESSA)　　a town in Emathia in Macedonia and the burial place of the Macedonian kings, is probably the same as Edessa, though some writers make them two different towns. Archelaus, a son of Temenus, a Heraclid, fled to king Cisseus in Macedonia when he was expelled by his brothers. Cisseus promised him the succession to his throne and the hand of his daughter if he would assist him against his neighboring enemies. Archelaus performed what was asked of him; but when, after the defeat of the enemy, he sought the fulfillment of the promise, Cisseus had a hole dug in the earth, filled it with burning coals, and covered it over with branches, planning that Archelaus might fall into it. The plot was discovered, and Cisseus himself was thrown into the pit by Archelaus, who then fled. At the command of Apollo, he built the town of Aegae on a spot to which he was led by a goat. According to some accounts, Alexander the Great was a descendant of Archelaus. The name of the present city of Edessa is the same as the ancient name, which alternated at times with the name Aegae, a common name in Greek geography. It was the first capital of the Macedonians until King Archelaus (413–399 B.C.) transferred the royal seat to Pella. Because of the continuous occupation of the city, none of the monuments referred to by ancient writers has been discovered.

AEGAE (LIMNI?)　　was a town in Euboea on the western coast north of Chalcis and a little south of Orobiae. Strabo (9.2.13) says that it was 120 stadia (22 km) from Anthedon in Boeotia. It is mentioned by Homer, but had disappeared in the time of Strabo. It was celebrated for its worship of Poseidon from the earliest times; and Poseidon's temple, situated on a lofty mountain, still existed when Strabo wrote. Aegaeus was a surname Poseidon derived from the town (Virg. *Aen.* 3.74). Poseidon was also said to have a palace in the depths of the sea near Aegae (Hom. *Il.* 13.21, *Od.* 5.381) where he kept his horses with bronze hoofs and golden manes. Strabo also derived the name of the Aegean Sea from this town. It is supposed that Aegae stood near the modern town of Limni, but so far nothing has been unearthed to substantiate this idea.

AEGAEAE   (See AEGIAE)

AEGEAN SEA (EGEO PELAGOS)   is part of the Mediterranean. It is bounded on the north by Macedonia and Thrace, on the west by Greece, and on the east by Asia Minor. At its northeast corner it is connected with the Propontis by the Hellespont. Its extent was differently estimated by the ancient writers, but the name was generally applied to the whole sea as far south as the islands of Crete and Rhodes. Its name was variously derived by the ancient writers either from the town of Aegae in Euboea or from Aegeus, the father of Theseus, who threw himself into it; or from Aegaea, the queen of the Amazons, who perished there; or from Aegaeon, who was represented as a marine god living in the sea; or, lastly, from *aigis,* a squall, on account of its storms.

A list of the most important beings identified with the Aegean follows.
(1) Poseidon, the god of the sea, was said to have his palace in the depth of the sea near Aegae in Euboea (Hom. *Il.* 13.27, *Od.* 5.381), where he kept his horses with bronze hoofs and golden manes. With these horses he rode in a chariot over the waves of the sea, which became smooth as he approached; the monsters of the deep would recognize him and play around his chariot (Hom. *Il.* 13.27; Virg. *Aen.* 5.817; Apollon. Rhod. 3.1240).
(2) Aegaeon was a son of Uranus by Gaea. He and his brothers, Gyges and Cottus, are known by the name Uranids (Hes. *Theog.* 502) and are described as huge monsters with one hundred arms and fifty heads (Apollod. 1.1.1; Hes. *Theog.* 149). Most writers mention the third Uranid under the name of Briareus instead of Aegaeon, a circumstance explained by Homer (*Il.* 1.403), who says that men called him Aegaeon, but the gods Briareus. Some writers represented Aegaeon as a son of Gaea and Pontus and as living as a marine god in the Aegean Sea.
(3) Aegeus was a son of Pandion II, king of Athens. He begot Theseus by Aethra. When Theseus went to Crete to deliver Athens from the tribute it had to pay to Minos, he promised his father that on his return he would hoist white sails as a signal of his safety. When he approached the coast of Attica, however, he forgot his promise. His father, who was watching from a rock on the seacoast, saw the black sail, thought that his son had perished, and threw himself into the sea, which, according to some

traditions, received from this event the name Aegean (Plut. *Thes.* 22; Diod. 4.61; Paus. 1.22.5).
(4) Daedalus, after being exiled from Athens, went to Crete where he obtained the friendship of Minos. He made the well-known wooden cow for Pasiphae; and when Pasiphae gave birth to the Minotaur, Daedalus constructed the labyrinth at Cnossus in which the monster was kept (Ov. *Met.* 8). For his part in the affair, Daedalus was imprisoned by Minos, but Pasiphae released him, and, as Minos had seized all the ships on the coast of Crete, Daedalus procured wings for himself and his son Icarus (or made them of wood) and fastened them on with wax. Daedalus himself flew safely over the Aegean, but, as Icarus flew too near the sun, the wax melted, and he dropped down and was drowned in that part of the Aegean which was called after him the Icarian Sea. According to a more prosaic version of the story, Pasiphae furnished Daedalus with a ship in which he fled to an island of the Aegean, where Icarus was drowned in a hasty attempt to land.

The Aegean was dangerous to ancient navigation on account of its numerous islands and rocks and also on account of the Etesian or northerly winds, which often blow with great fury. To the storms of the Aegean the poets frequently allude.

The Aegean Sea was divided into: (1) *Mare Thracium,* the northern part of the Aegean washing the shores of Thrace and Macedonia; (2) *Mare Myrtoum,* the part of the Aegean south of Euboea, Attica, and Argolis, which derived its name from the small island Myrtus (and ultimately from Myrtilus, who though he helped Pelops win Hippodameia was treacherously drowned by him in this part of the Aegean); (3) *Mare Icarium,* the southeastern part of the Aegean along the coasts of Caria and Ionia, which derived its name from the island of Icaria (and ultimately from Icarus); and (4) *Mare Creticum,* the most southerly part of the Aegean, north of the island of Crete. (See also ICARIAN SEA and MYRTOAN SEA.)

The Aegean contains numerous islands. Of these the greatest number are in the southern part of the sea and are divided into two principal groups: the Cyclades, lying off the coasts of Attica and Peloponnesus, ánd the Sporades, lying along the coasts of Caria and Ionia. In the northern part of the sea are the larger islands of Euboea, Thasos, and Samothrace, and off the coast of Asia Minor those of Samos, Chios, and Lesbos. The many legends associated with individual islands will be treated separately, but certain beings were associated with the islands in general. Aristaeus, an ancient agricultural divinity, was worshipped in various parts of Greece but especially in the islands of the Aegean, Ionian, and Adriatic seas, which had once been inhabited by Pelasgians. The Amazons, a warlike race of females who figure prominently in several of the adventures of Greek mythology, came from the country about the Caucasus and are said to have at different times invaded Thrace, Asia Minor, the islands of the Aegean, and Greece itself.

AEGEIRA (EGIRA)   a town of Achaia and one of the twelve Achaian cities, situated between Aegae and Pellene, was located on hills about 1.5 km from the sea and near a river. This river was probably the Crius, which flowed into the sea a little to the west of the town. According to Pausanias, the upper city was twelve stadia (2 km) from its port and seventy-two stadia (13 km) from the oracle of Heracles Buraicus (Paus. 7.26.1). Pausanias relates that Aegeira occupied the site of the Homeric Hyperesia (*Il.* 2.573, 15.254) and that it changed its name during the occupation of the country by the Ionians. He adds that the ancient name still continued in use. On the decay of the neighboring town of Aegae, its inhabitants were transferred to Aegeira (Strab. 8.7.4). The most important of the public buildings of Aegeira was a temple of Zeus, which has been excavated. A colossal head of Zeus from a statue has also been found. It also contained a very ancient temple of Apollo and temples of Artemis Agrotera (Huntress) and of Aphrodite Urania (Heavenly), who was worshipped in the town above all other divinities. Tyche, the personification of chance or luck, was also worshipped at Aegeira, where she was represented with the horn of Amaltheia and a winged Eros by her side (Paus. 7.26.3). The port of Aegeira has been placed at Mavra Litharia (Black Rocks), to the left of which on the summit of a hill are some vestiges of an ancient city, which must have been Aegeira.

AEGEUM   was a mountain of Crete, according to Hesiod (*Theog.* 484). Cronus was in the habit of swallowing all the children born to his wife, Rhea. When she was about to give birth to Zeus, Rhea applied to Uranus and Gaea, her parents, for advice about how the child might be saved. Before the hour of birth came, Uranus and Gaea sent Rhea to Lyctos in Crete, requesting her to bring up her child there. Rhea accordingly concealed her infant in a cave on Mount Aegeum and gave Cronus a stone wrapped up in cloth, which he swallowed in the belief that it was his son. Aegeum appears to be a part of the Dictaean mountain system since Hesiod (*Theog.* 482) places it in proximity to Lyctos.

AEGIAE or AEGAEAE (EGIES)   was a town of Laconia about 5.5 km from Gythium, supposed to be the same as the Homeric Augeiae (*Il.* 2.583). It possessed a temple and lake of Poseidon. Its site is probably Egies, which seems to fit the distance.

AEGIALEIA   was an earlier name of SICYON.

AEGILA   was a town of Laconia with a temple of Demeter, of uncertain site, but placed by some on the gulf of Skutari (Paus. 4.17.1).

AEGINA (EGINA)   is an island in the Saronic Gulf surrounded by Attica, Megaris, and Epidaurus, from each of which it is about 20 km. In spite of its small size, Aegina was one of the most celebrated islands in Greece, both in the mythical and historical periods. It is said to have been called originally Oenone or Oenopia and to have received the name of Aegina from Aegina, the daughter of the river-god Asopus, who was carried to the island by Zeus and there bore him a son, Aeacus. In some traditions Aegina was not yet inhabited at the time of Aeacus's birth and Zeus changed the ants (*myrmikes*) of the island into men, the Myrmidons, over whom Aeacus ruled. Ovid (*Met.* 7.520), on the other hand, supposes that the island was inhabited at the time of the birth of Aeacus. He states that during the reign of Aeacus, Hera, jealous of Aegina, ravaged the island by sending a plague or a fearful dragon, by which nearly all its inhabitants were carried off and that Zeus restored the population by changing the ants into men. These legends are a mythical account of the colonization of Aegina, which seems to have been originally inhabited by Pelasgians and afterward received colonists from Phthiotis, the seat of the Myrmidons, and from Phlius on the Asopus. Aeacus, while he ruled in Aegina, was renowned in all Greece for his justice and piety and was frequently called upon to settle disputes, not only among men but even among the gods themselves (Pind. *Isth.* 8.48; Paus. 1.39.6).

A legend preserved in Pindar (*Ol.* 8.39) relates that Apollo and Poseidon took Aeacus as their assistant in building the walls of Troy. When the work was completed, three dragons rushed against the wall, and the two dragons that attacked the parts of the wall built by the gods fell dead. The third forced its way into the city through the part built by Aeacus, and Apollo prophesied that Troy should fall through the hands of the Aeacidae. Aeacus was also believed by the Aeginetans to have surrounded their island with high cliffs to protect it against pirates (Paus. 2.29.6). Several other incidents connected with Aeacus are mentioned by Ovid (*Met.* 7.506, 9.435). By Endeis he had two sons, Telamon and Peleus, and by Psamathe a son, Phocus, whom he preferred to the other two. The older brothers killed Phocus during a contest and had to flee the island. The tomb of Phocus was shown in Aegina (Paus. 2.29.9) and today may be the circular structure northwest of the temple of Apollo in the town of Aegina.

After his death Aeacus became one of the judges in Hades (Ov. *Met.* 13.25), and, according to Plato (*Gorg.* 523), especially for the shades of Europeans. In works of art he was represented bearing a scepter and the keys of

Hades (Apollod. 3.12.6; Pind. *Isth.* 8.47). Aeacus had sanctuaries in Athens and Aegina (Paus. 2.29.6), and the Aeginetans regarded him as the guardian deity of their island (Pind. *Nem.* 8.22). They afterwards built a sanctuary on their island called the Aeaceion, which was a square place enclosed by walls of white marble. Aeacus was believed in later times to be buried under the altar in this sacred enclosure (Paus. 2.29.9). In the town of Aegina to the southeast of the temple of Apollo is a square edifice that is possibly the Aeaceion.

Aeacus was so favored by the gods that when Greece was visited by a drought in consequence of a murder (Diod. 4.60.61), the oracle of Delphi declared that the calamity would not cease unless Aeacus prayed to the gods that it might. Aeacus showed his gratitude for divine favor by erecting a temple to Zeus Panhellenius on Mount Panhellenion (Paus. 2.30.4). Zeus Panhellenius (God Common To or Worshipped By All the Hellenes or Greeks) occurred first as a name of the Dodonaean Zeus, whose worship had been transplanted by the Hellenes in their emigration from Thessaly to Aegina. Subsequently, when the name Hellenes was applied to all the Greeks, the meaning of the god's name likewise became more extensive. It was derived from the sacrifice which Aeacus was said to have offered on behalf of all the Greeks at the command of the Delphic oracle in order to avert a famine (Paus. 1.44.9). On that occasion Aeacus designated Zeus as the national god of all the Greeks (Pind. *Nem.* 5.19; Herod. 9.7). In Aegina a festival, the Panhellenia, was also celebrated. The worship of Zeus was firmly established on the island, but it appears that at an early time it vied with the worship of Poseidon since there is a story that the two gods once disputed possession of Aegina (Plut. *Quaest. Conviv.* 9.6).

The chief town in the island is called Aegina and is situated on the northwest side. The most important building there was the Aeaceion. Near the shore there was a theater as large as that at Epidaurus. Behind it was a stadium and numerous temples. The city had two harbors, the principal one located near the temple of Apollo and the other, called the secret harbor, near the theater. The temple of Apollo (or possibly Poseidon) is near Cape Kolonna (named for the single column left standing from the temple). Southeast of the temple is located the already mentioned Aeaceion. North of the temple is a round structure, possibly the tomb of Phocus. Xenophon (*Hellen.* 5.1.10) mentions a Heracleion, or temple of Heracles. There is preserved in the museum of Aegina a statue of Heracles, but it is from the temple of Apollo (formerly attributed to Aphrodite). All that remains of the temple is a lone column without its capital and some scattered foundations.

On the hill at the northeast end of the island are the remains of the temple of Aphaea, the Aeginetan equiv-

alent of the Cretan goddess Britomartis. It is of the Doric order, and many of the columns are still standing. The temple was explored in 1811 and again in 1894 and in 1901. Seventeen beautiful sculptures of Parian marble that occupied the tympana of the pediment were found buried under the ruins of the temple. They were restored by Thorvaldsen in Rome and then sent to Munich where they remain. There are also casts of them in the British Museum. The subject of the eastern pediment appears to be the expedition of the Aeacidae or Aeginetan heroes against Troy under the guidance of Athena. The sculptures of the western pediment probably represent the contest of the Greeks and Trojans over the body of Patroclus. Parts of a third group have been located and are in the National Archaeological Museum in Athens. The temple had been regarded originally as that of Zeus Panhellenius and from 1826 till the end of the century as that of Athena. In 1951–1953 and again in 1966–1969 renovation and restoration of the temple took place.

Britomartis appears originally to have been a Cretan divinity of hunters and fishermen. She not only was worshipped in Crete but also appeared to the inhabitants of Aegina and was there called Aphaea. A sailor, Andromedes, carried her from Crete to Aegina. When they landed there, he tried to rape her and she fled to the sanctuary of Artemis. The Aeginetans built a sanctuary, later a temple, to her and worshipped her as a goddess. She was strongly identified with Artemis.

In the interior of the island was a town called Oea, about 3.5 km from the city of Aegina. It contained statues of Auxesia and Damia (Herod. 5.83; Paus. 2.30.4). The position of Oea has not yet been determined, but its name suggests a connection with Oenone, the ancient name of the island. Therefore it has been supposed that it was originally the chief place of the island, at a time when national security required an inland location for the capital and when the commerce and naval power that drew population to the coastal site had not yet begun.

Auxesia and Damia were two Cretan maidens who were stoned to death during an insurrection at Troezen and later paid divine honors. The Athenians contributed olive wood for statues of them, as directed by an oracle, on condition that the Epidaurians should every year offer up sacrifices to Athena Agraulos and Erechtheus. But when Aegina separated itself from Epidaurus, the Aeginetans, who had their sacred objects in common with the Epidaurians, took away the two statues and erected them in Oea, where they offered sacrifices and celebrated mysteries. When the Epidaurians, in consequence of this, ceased to perform the sacrifices at Athens and when the Athenians heard of the statues being carried to Aegina, they demanded them from the Aeginetans. The islanders refused, and the Athenians threw ropes around the sacred statues to drag them away by force. But thunder and earthquakes ensued, and the Athenians engaged in the work were seized with madness, in which they killed one another. The Aeginetan legend added that the statues, while the Athenians were dragging them down, fell upon their knees and remained permanently in this position (Herod. 5.82–86; Paus. 2.30.5).

A final note is that Aegina was the last port touched by the Argonauts on their way home to Iolcus from Crete.

AEGIUM (EGIO)   one of the twelve cities of Achaia, was situated upon the coast west of the river Selinus, 5.5 km from Rhypae and 7.5 km from Helice. It stood between two promontories in the corner of a bay, which formed the best harbor in Achaia next to that of Patrae. It is said to have been formed out of a union of seven or eight villages. It is mentioned by Homer (*Il.* 2.574) as a part of the domain of Agamemnon. Some traditions say that Zeus was born and brought up here. The Achaian League convened here, and the meetings were held in a grove near the sea called Homagyrium or Homarium, sacred to Zeus Homagyrius or Homarius. Close to this grove was a temple of Athena Panachaea. The words *homagyris* (assembly) and *Homarion,* a precinct of Aegium, have reference to those meetings, though in later times they were explained as indicating the spot where Agamemnon assembled the Grecian chiefs before the Trojan War. There were several temples, statues, and public buildings at Aegium, among which were a statue of Eileithyia, goddess of birth, with the head, hands, and feet uncovered; her statues were usually covered head to toe. There was also a temple of Asclepius, god of healing (Paus. 7.23.7).

Egio, which occupies the site of the ancient Aegium, is a place of some importance. It is a small commercial port and has several fountains and attractive parks. It stands on a hill, which becomes a cliff at the sea. Remains of the ancient town have been discovered on a hill to the east of Egio, but the modern city has obliterated most traces of ancient sanctuaries and buildings mentioned by Pausanias (7.23.5–24.4).

AEGLE   was an earlier name of the island of SYME.

AEGOSTHENA (EGOSTHENA or PORTO GERMENO)   was a town in Megaris on the Corinthian Gulf at the foot of Mount Cithaeron and on the borders of Boeotia. It possessed a sanctuary and statue of the seer Melampus, in whose honor an annual festival was celebrated there (Paus. 1.44.5). Melampus was a son of Amythaon by Eidomene, Aglaia, or Rhodope. He was looked upon by the ancients as the first mortal who had been endowed with prophetic powers, as the first who practiced the medical arts and as the one who established the worship of Dionysus in Greece (Apollod. 2.2.2). Very few monumental remains have been discovered, but the fortifications are the best preserved examples of military architecture in Greece.

AEMONIA (HAEMONIA)   was an earlier name of THESSALY.

AEMUS   (See HAEMUS)

AENEIA   a town of Chalcidice in Macedonia, was situated, according to Livy, opposite Pydna and 25 km from Thessalonica on the Thermaic Gulf. It appears to have stood on the promontory which forms the northwest corner of the peninsula of Chalcidice. It was said to have been founded by Aeneas the first winter after the taking of Troy (Liv. 40.4, 44.32).

AENOS (ENOS)   is a mountain 1,600 meters high on the island of Kefalonia. Zeus had a temple on this mountain and was consequently worshiped here as Zeus Aeneius or Aenesius.

AEOLIS   was an earlier name of THESSALY.

AEPEIA (PETALIDI)   was one of the seven Messenian towns offered by Agamemnon to Achilles. It was identified with CORONE by Pausanias (4.34.5).

AEPY (PLATANA?)   a town in Elis, so called from its lofty locations, is mentioned by Homer and is probably the same as the Triphylian town Epeium, which stood between Macistus and Heraea. It has been placed about 10 km in direct distance southeast from Olympia. Men of Aepy accompanied Nestor to the Trojan War (Hom. *Il.* 2.592). The town, which was also called Aepium, Epium, or Epeium, was ultimately taken over by the Eleans and demolished. Among its ruins (near Platana) are remains of a theater and several temples.

AERIA   was an earlier name of the island of THASOS.

AESON or **AESONIS** (SESKLO?)   was a town of Magnesia in Thessaly, the name of which is derived from Aeson, the father of Jason (Apollon. Rhod. 1.411). Ruins near Sesklo may be the site of the ancient town.

AETHALEIA   was an earlier name of the island of LEMNOS.

AETHALIA   was an earlier name of the island of CHIOS.

AETHRA   was an earlier name of the island of THASOS.

AETHRAEA   was an earlier name of the island of RHODES.

AETOLIA (ETOLIA)   is a district of Greece, the boundaries of which have varied at different periods. In the time of Strabo it was bounded on the west by Acarnania, from which it was separated by the river Achelous, on the north by the mountainous country inhabited by the Athamanes, Dolopes, and Dryopes, on the northeast by Doris and Malis, on the southeast by Locris, and on the south by the entrance to the Corinthian Gulf. The country between the Achelous and the Euenus Rivers appears in tradition as the original abode of the Aetolians.

The mountains of Aetolia mentioned by ancient writers were: Tymphrestus, Bomi, Corax, Taphiassus, Chalcis, Aracynthus, Panaetolium, Myenus, Macynium, and Curium. The two chief rivers were the Achelous and Euenus. The Campylus and Cyathus were tributaries of the Achelous.

Of several lakes the most important were Trichonis and Hyria. From Hyria issued the river Cyathus. Near Lake Hyria there is a ravine which Ovid (*Met.* 7.371) calls "Cycneia Tempe" because Cycnus was said to have been here changed into a swan by Apollo. In the lower plain of Aetolia were several smaller lakes or lagoons: Cynia, Uria, and a large lake near Calydon.

The original inhabitants of Aetolia are said to have been Curetes, who, according to some accounts, had come from Euboea (Strab. 10.3.6). They inhabited the plains between the Achelous and the Euenus, and the country in consequence was eponymously named Curetis. Besides them we also find mention of the Leleges and the Hyantes. These three peoples probably belonged to the great Pelasgic race and were not Hellenes. The first great Hellenic settlement in the country is said to have been that of the Epeans, led by Aetolus, six generations before the Trojan War. Aetolus was a son of Endymion and the nymph Neis, or Iphianassa (Apollod. 1.7.6). He was married to Pronoe, by whom he had two sons, Pleuron and Calydon. His father compelled him and his two brothers, Paeon and Epeius, to decide by a contest at Olympia which of them would succeed him in his kingdom of Elis. Epeius gained the victory and occupied the throne after his father; upon his death, he was succeeded by Aetolus. During the funeral games that were celebrated in honor of Azan, Aetolus ran with his chariot over Apis, the son of Jason or Salmoneus and killed him. He was therefore expelled by the sons of Apis (Paus. 5.1.8). After leaving Peloponnesus, he went to the country of the Curetes between the Achelous and the Corinthian Gulf, where he slew Dorus, Laodocus, and Polypoetes, the sons of Helios and Phthia and gave to the country the name of Aetolia. Aetolus founded the town of Calydon, which he called after his son and which became the capital of his dominions. The Curetes continued to reside at their ancient capital Pleuron at the foot of Mount Curium, and for a long time carried on war with the inhabitants of Calydon.

At the time of the Trojan War, Pleuron as well as Calydon were governed by the Aetolian chief Thoas, son of Andraemon. Since Pleuron appeared in the later period of the heroic age as an Aetolian city, it was represented as such from the beginning in some legends. Pleuron, like Calydon, is said to have derived its name from a son of Aetolus (Apollod. 1.7.7); and at the very time that some legends represent it as the capital of the Curetes and engaged in war with Oeneus, king of Calydon, others relate that it was governed by his own brother, Thestius. Thestius figures in the period prior to the Trojan War. Tyndareus, heir to the throne of Sparta, was expelled by his step-brother and fled to Thestius in Aetolia. While there he assisted him in his wars against his neighbors. In Aetolia he married Leda, the daughter of Thestius, and afterwards he was restored to his kingdom of Sparta by Heracles.

Aetolia was celebrated in the heroic age of Greece on account of the hunt of the Calydonian boar and the exploits of Tydeus, Meleager, and the other heroes of Calydon and Pleuron. The Aetolians also took part in the Trojan War under the command of Thoas; they came in forty ships from Pleuron, Calydon, Olenus, Pylene, and Chalcis (Hom. *Il.* 2.638). Diomedes was a son of Tydeus and the successor of Adrastus in the kingdom of Argos, though he was descended from an Aetolian family (Apollod. 1.8.5). He was one of the most renowned heroes in the Trojan War. Upon his return to Argos, he met with an evil reception, for his wife was living in adultery. He therefore quitted Argos either of his own accord or was expelled by the adulterers, and went to Aetolia. His going to Aetolia and the subsequent recovery of Argos are placed in some traditions immediately after the war of the Epigoni, and Diomedes is said to have gone with Alcmaeon to assist his grandfather Oeneus in Aetolia against his enemies. During the absence of Diomedes, Agamemnon took possession of Argos; but when the expedition against Troy was decided upon, Agamemnon from fear invited Diomedes and Alcmaeon back to Argos and asked them to take part in the projected expedition. Diomedes alone accepted the proposal and thus recovered Argos (Apollod. 1.8.6; Paus. 2.25.2). According to other traditions, Diomedes did not go to Aetolia till after his return from Troy when he was expelled from Argos. It is said that he went first to Corinth; but when he was informed there of the distress of Oeneus, he hastened to Aetolia to assist him. Diomedes conquered and slew the enemies of his grandfather and then took up his residence in Aetolia.

Sixty years after the Trojan War some Aeolians, who had been driven out of Thessaly along with the Boeotians, migrated into Aetolia and settled in the country around

Pleuron and Calydon, which was then called Aeolis after them (Strab. 10.3.4). Twenty years afterward occurred the great Dorian invasion of Peloponnesus under the command of the descendants of Heracles. The Aetolian chief Oxylus took part in this invasion and conducted the Dorians across the Corinthian Gulf. In return for his services he received Elis after the conquest of Peloponnesus (Aristot. *Polit.* 6.25; Strab. 8.1.2).

There were three main divisions of the Aetolians—the Apodoti, Ophionenses, and Eurytanes. The last, who were the most numerous of the three, spoke a language unintelligible to others and were in the habit of eating raw meat (Thuc. 3.102). They dwelt north of the Ophionenses, as far, apparently, as Mount Tymphrestus, at the foot of which was the town of Oechalia, which Strabo describes as a place belonging to this people. They are said to have possessed an oracle of Odysseus.

At the time of their greatest power, the Aetolians were masters of the whole of western Acarnania, of the south of Epeirus and Thessaly, and of Locris, Phocis, and Boeotia. They likewise assumed the entire control of the Delphic oracle and of the Amphictyonic Assembly (Plut. *Demetr.* 40; Polyb. 4.25).

AGAMEDE   a town in Lesbos, was believed to have derived its name from Agamede, a daughter of Macaria.

AGANIPPE   on Mount Helicon was a sacred grove of the Muses, to which Pausianias ascended from Ascra. On the left of the road, before reaching the grove of the Muses, was the celebrated fountain of Aganippe, which was believed to inspire those who drank of it, and from which the Muses were called Aganippides (Paus. 9.29.5; Catull. 61.26). Aganippe, the nymph of the fountain, was a daughter of the river-god Permessus. Near Mount Helicon, Ephialtes and Otus were said to have offered the first sacrifices to the Muses; and in that place was a sanctuary with their statues. The sacred wells Aganippe and Hippocrene were located there. On Mount Libethrias, which is connected with Mount Helicon, there was a sacred grotto of the Muses. It seems rather certain that Aganippe is the fountain that issues from the left bank of the stream on Mount Pirgaki. It is near the chapel of Agios Nikolaos and a ruined monastery. Around this fountain can be observed numerous building stones and in the neighboring fields are remains of dwelling places.

AGRAE   a town on the Ilissus in Attica, was said to have been the first place Artemis hunted after her arrival from Delos. She had a temple there with a statue carrying a bow (Paus. 1.19.6), and she was worshipped under the name Artemis Agrotera (Huntress).

ALAGONIA (KAMBOS)   was a town of Laconia near the Messenian frontier, belonging to the Eleuthero-

Lacones, containing temples of Dionysus and Artemis. This site was occupied in medieval times by the fortress of Zarnata, south of the modern village of Kambos. The town was 5.5 km from Gerenia, the modern Keries (Paus. 3.21.7, 26.11). It was named for Alagonia, a daughter of Zeus and Europa.

ALALCOMENAE (ALALKOMENES)   an ancient town in Boeotia, was situated at the foot of Mount Tilphossium, to the northeast of Coroneia and near Lake Copais. According to some, Athena was born there and is therefore called Alalcomeneis in Homer. Some claim that the surname of the goddess was derived from Alalcomenes, a Boeotian autochthon, who was believed to have brought up Athena and to have been the first to introduce her worship (Paus. 3.33.5). According to some writers, he advised Zeus to have a figure of oak dressed in bridal attire and carried about accompanied by hymeneal songs in order to change the anger of Hera into jealousy. The name of the wife of Alalcomenes was Athenais and that of his son Glaucopus, both of which refer to the goddess Athena. Athena also had the surname Trito or Tritogeneia from the stream Triton near Alalcomenae (Paus. 9.33.7).

The temple of the goddess stood a little distance from the town on the Triton, a small stream flowing into Lake Copais. Beyond the modern village of Alalkomenes, the site of Alalcomenae, are some foundations, apparently those of a temple. Both the town and the temple were plundered by Sulla, who carried off the statue of the goddess (Hom. *Il.* 4.8; Paus. 9.33.6).

ALCIMEDON   was an Arcadian plain named for Alcimedon, an Arcadian hero. He was the father of Phillo, by whom Heracles begot a son, Aechmagoras, whom Alcimedon exposed but Heracles saved (Paus. 8.12.2).

ALEA (ALEA)   was a town of Arcadia between Orchomenus and Stymphalus. It is said to have been founded by Aleus, a son of Apheidas and grandson of Arcas. He was king of Tegea in Arcadia, married to Neaera, and said to have founded the first temple of Athena at Tegea (Paus. 8.23.1; Apollod. 3.9.1). In the time of Pausanias, Alea contained temples of the Ephesian Artemis, of Athena Alea, and of Dionysus. Every other year a festival, called the Sciereia, was celebrated in honor of Dionysus. At this festival women were flogged, just as Spartan youths were, before the image of Artemis Orthia. The town of Alea appears to have been situated in the territory either of Stymphalus or Orchomenus. The ruins are about 5 km from the modern village of Alea (formerly Bouiati), which is located in Argolis near the Arcadian border. Alea was never a town of importance, but some writers have, though inadvertently, placed at this town the celebrated temple of Athena Alea, which was situated at Tegea.

ALESIAEUM   called Aleision by Homer (*Il.* 2.617), was a town of Pisatis, situated upon the road leading across the mountains from Elis to Olympia. Its site is unknown.

ALIPHERA (ALIFERA)   a town of Arcadia in the district of Cynuria, was situated upon a steep hill 7.5 km south of the Alpheius and near the boundaries of Elis. It was built by Alipherus, one of the sons of Lycaon killed by Zeus with a flash of lightning for their impiety (Apollod. 3.8.1). A large number of its inhabitants moved to the newly founded Megalopolis in 371 B.C., but it still continued to be a place of some importance. It contained temples of Asclepius and Athena and a celebrated bronze statue of Athena, who was said to have been born there. Zeus Lecheates (Protector of Childbed), who, as the father of Athena, was worshipped there (Paus. 8.26.6).

In addition, Myiagrus or Myiodes (Fly-catcher) is the name of a hero invoked at Aliphera, at the festival of Athena, as the protector against flies (Paus. 5.14.1). There are still considerable remains of this town on the hill called Nerositsa. In 1932–1935 the whole acropolis was uncovered. Excavation of the temple of Athena disclosed bases of dedicatory statues and a large base probably belonging to the huge bronze statue of Athena mentioned above. The sanctuary of Asclepius is located west of the acropolis. The lower city contained the fountain of Tritonis. The site of modern Alifera (formerly Rangozio) is about 15 km northwest of Andritsena.

ALMONES   (See OLMONES)

ALMOPIA   a district in Macedonia inhabited by the Almopes, is said to have been conquered by the Temenidae of Argos. According to some it is the same country now called Moglena, which bordered upon the ancient Edessa to the northeast. Ptolemy (3.13.24) assigns to the Almopes three towns—Horma, Europus, and Apsalus. Almopia and its inhabitants, the Almopes, were believed to have derived their name from Almops, a giant, the son of Poseidon and Helle.

ALOIUM   a town of Thessaly, was founded by the Aloeidae. Aloeidae is a patronymic from Aloeus, but is used to designate the two sons, Otus and Ephialtes, of his wife Iphimedeia by Poseidon. The Aloeidae were renowned in the earliest stories of Greece for their extraordinary strength and daring spirit. When they were nine years old, each of their bodies measured four meters in breadth and twelve in height. At this early age they threatened the Olympian gods with war and attempted to pile Mount Ossa upon Mount Olympus and Mount Pelion upon Mount Ossa. They would have accomplished this object, says Homer (*Od.* 11.305), had they been allowed to grow to the age of manhood; but Apollo destroyed them before their beards began to appear.

ALOPE   a town of Phthiotis in Thessaly, was placed by some between Larissa Cremaste and Echinus. There is a question as to whether this town was the same as the Alope in Homer (*Il.* 2.682; Strab. 9.4.9). Alope, a daughter of Cercyon, was beloved of Poseidon on account of her great beauty and became by him the mother of a son, whom she exposed immediately after his birth. However, a mare came and suckled the child until he was found by shepherds, who quarrelled over the elegant attire of the boy. The case was brought before Cercyon, who recognized by the dress whose child the boy was. He ordered Alope put to death and her child exposed again. The boy was fed and found in the same manner as before, and the shepherds called him Hippothoon. The body of Alope was changed by Poseidon into a well, which bore the same name (Aristoph. *Av.* 533). The town of Alope was believed to have derived its name from her. There was a monument of Alope on the road from Eleusis to Megara, on the spot where she was believed to have been killed by her father (Paus. 1.39.3).

ALOPECE (AMBELOKIPI)   a deme of Attica, was situated only about 3.5 km from Athens and not far from Cynosarges (Herod. 5.63). It was therefore east of Athens near the modern suburb of Ambelokipi, east of Lycabettus. It possessed a temple of Aphrodite and also, apparently, one of Hermaphroditus (Alciph. *Ep.* 3.37). There are some remains of an ancient building in the church at Ambelokipi, which may be those of the temple of Aphrodite.

ALPHEIUS (ALFIOS)   is the largest river of Peloponnesus. It rises in the southeast of Arcadia close to the source of the Eurotas River on the frontiers of Laconia, flows in a westerly direction through Arcadia and Elis, and after passing Olympia falls into the Ionian Sea. The Alpheius, like several other rivers and lakes in Arcadia, disappears more than once into the limestone mountains of the country and then emerges again, after flowing some distance underground. At the mouth of the river was a temple and grove of Artemis Alpheionia.

Alpheius, the god of the river Alpheius, was a son of Oceanus and Tethys (Pind. *Nem.* 1.1; Hes. *Theog.* 338). According to Pausanias (5.7.2), Alpheius was a passionate hunter and fell in love with the nymph Arethusa, but she fled from him to the island of Ortygia near Syracuse and metamorphosed herself into a well. Thereupon Alpheius became a river that flowed from Peloponnesus under the sea to Ortygia and there united its waters with those of the well Arethusa. This story is related somewhat differently by Ovid (*Met.* 5.572). Once while bathing in the river Alpheius, Arethusa was surprised and pursued by the god, but Artemis took pity upon her and changed her into a spring, which flowed under the earth to the island of Ortygia. The poet calls Arethusa Alpheias. According to other stories, Artemis was also the object of the love of Alpheius. Once when pursued by him, she fled to Letrini in Elis, and here she covered her face and those of her nymph companions with mud so that Alpheius could not discover or distinguish her (Paus. 6.22.9). This occasioned the building of a temple of Artemis Alphaea at Letrini. According to another version, the goddess fled to Ortygia, where she likewise had a temple under the name of Artemis Alphaea. An allusion to Alpheius' love of Artemis is evidenced in the fact that at Olympia the two divinities had one altar in common (Paus. 5.14.6). These accounts probably originated in the popular belief that there was a natural subterranean connection between the Alpheius River and the fountain of Arethusa. Among several other things, it was believed that a cup thrown into the Alpheius would make its reappearance in the fountain of Arethusa in Ortygia (Strab. 6.2.4, 8.3.12). One account is given which is altogether unconnected with those mentioned above. It says that Alpheius was a son of Helios and killed his brother Cercaphus in a contest. Haunted by despair and the Erinyes, he leapt into the river Nyctimus, which afterward received the name Alpheius.

The Alpheius River is also connected with other events and beings in mythology. One event has to do with Heracles and one of his labors. Eurystheus imposed upon Heracles the task of cleaning the stables of Augeas in one day. Augeas was king of Elis and extremely rich in cattle. Heracles, without mentioning the command of Eurystheus, went to Augeas, offering in one day to clean his stables, if he would give him one-tenth of his cattle or a part of his territory. Augeas, believing that Heracles could not possibly accomplish what he proposed, agreed, and Heracles took Phyleus, the son of Augeas, as his witness. He then diverted the rivers Alpheius and Peneius through the stables, which were thus cleaned within the time fixed upon. But Augeas, who learned that Heracles had undertaken the work at the command of Eurystheus, withheld the reward, denied his promise, and declared that he would have the matter decided by a judicial verdict. Phyleus then testified against his father, who exiled him from Elis. Eurystheus declared that he would not accept the work thus performed as one of the promised labors because Heracles had negotiated separate payment for it (Apollod. 2.5.5). At a later time Heracles marched with an army of Argives and Tirynthians against Augeas to take revenge on him. In a narrow gorge in Elis Heracles was taken by surprise by Cteatus and Eurytus, nephews of Augeas, and lost a great number of his warriors. Later, however, Heracles slew Cteatus and Eurytus, invaded Elis, and killed Augeas and his sons. After this victory, Heracles marked out the sacred ground on which the Olympian games were to be

celebrated, built altars, and instituted the Olympian festival games (Apollod. 2.7.2; Pind. *Ol.* 10.55).

Melampus, a son of Amythaon, was looked upon by the ancients as the first mortal endowed with prophetic powers and other divine gifts. He acquired the power of prophesying from the victims that were offered to the gods, and, after having met with Apollo on the banks of the Alpheius he became a most renowned soothsayer (Apollod. 1.9.11).

Apomyius (Driving Away the Flies) was a surname of Zeus at Olympia. On one occasion when Heracles was offering a sacrifice to Zeus there, he was annoyed by hosts of flies. After he offered a sacrifice to Zeus Apomyius, the flies withdrew across the river Alpheius. From that time the Eleans sacrificed to Zeus under this name (Paus. 5.14.1). Asclepius was sometimes called Asclepius Demaenetus, a title derived from the name of a temple of his on the Alpheius (Paus. 6.21.4). Finally, Virgil (*Aen.* 10.179) gives the epithet Alpheae to the Etruscan city of Pisae because the place was said to have been founded by colonists from Pisa in Elis, near which the Alpheius flowed.

ALTHEPIA   was a name for the territory of Troezen. Althepus was a son of Poseidon and Leis, a daughter of Orus, king of Troezen. The territory of Troezen was called Althepia after him. In his reign, Pallas and Poseidon disputed the possession of the country with each other (Paus. 2.30.6).

ALUS   (See HALUS)

ALYCUM   (See PHALYCUM)

ALYZIA (KANDILA)   was a town on the west coast of Acarnania. It was 3 km from the sea, on which it possessed a harbor and a sanctuary, both dedicated to Heracles. In this sanctuary were some works of art by Lysippus, representing the labors of Heracles, which a Roman general caused to be removed to Rome on account of the remoteness of the place. The remains of Alyzia are still visible in the valley of Kandila. The island immediately opposite was called Carnus (modern Kalamos). Alyzia is said to have derived its name from Alyzeus, a son of Icarius and brother of Penelope and Leucadius. After his father's death, he reigned in conjunction with his brother over Acarnania and is said to have founded the town of Alyzia there.

AMARYNTHUS (AMARINTHOS)   was a town on the coast of Euboea only 1.33 km from Eretria, to which it belonged. It possessed a celebrated temple of Artemis, surnamed Amarynthia or Amarysia, in whose honor there was a festival of this name celebrated both in Euboea and Attica (Strab. 10.1.10; Paus. 1.31.5). Votive inscriptions mentioning Leto, Apollo, and Artemis have been found on a hill about 2 km east of the modern village of Amarinthos and that site has been identified as the location of the temple. Others place Amarynthus closer to Eretria at a yet undiscovered site. The town was believed to have derived its name from Amarynthus, a hunter of Artemis.

AMBRACIA (ARTA)   was an important city to the north of the Ambracian Gulf, which derived its name from this place. It was situated on the east bank of the river Arachthus 16 km from the gulf. It stood on the west side of a rugged hill, and the acropolis occupied the east summit of this hill. It was about 5 km in circumference, and, in addition to its strong walls, was well protected by the river and the heights which surrounded it. It is generally described as a town of Epeirus, of which it was the capital under Pyrrhus and subsequent monarchs.

According to tradition, Ambracia was originally a Thesprotian town founded by Ambrax, son of Thesprotus and grandson of Lycaon. Some say it was named for Ambracia, daughter of Augeas. Aeneas, after the fall of Troy, wintered in Thrace and later sailed around Greece, founding cities and erecting temples to his mother. One of the places he touched was Ambracia; from there he set out to Dodona, where he met the Trojan Helenus. One of the churches in the modern city incorporates porphyry columns thought by some to be from a temple of Aphrodite. Livy (38.5) mentions a temple of Asclepius at Ambracia, and Plutarch (*Quaest. Rom.* 59) says that the Muses possessed a temple here which was adorned with their statues. The modern name of Ambracia is Arta, which is probably a corruption of the name of the Arahthos River, upon which it stands.

AMBRYSUS or AMBROSSOS (DISTOMO)   a town of Phocis, was situated 11 km from Stiris, northeast of Anticyra, at the southern foot of Mount Cirphis in a fertile valley, which produced wine and a variety of berry used for scarlet dye. Ambryssus was the mythical founder of the town (Paus. 10.36.3). The site of Ambrysus is fixed at the modern village of Distomo by an inscription found there. The remains of the ancient city are few and inconsiderable. Some guide books call the ancient city Ambrossos.

AMNISUS (AMNISOS)   a town in the north of Crete, and the harbor of Cnossus in the time of Minos, was situated on a low hill at the mouth of a river of the same name (modern Karteros). The modern town of Amnisos is about 7 km east of Iraklio. Amnisus possessed a cave sanctuary of Eileithyia, the goddess of birth, who was believed to have been born in a cave in the territory of Cnossus. The nymphs of the river, called Amnisiades or Amnisides, were sacred to this goddess and were also connected with the worship of Artemis (Hom. *Od.* 19.188; Apollon. Rhod. 3.877). A cult of Zeus Thenatas had a sanctuary here near the shore on the west side of the hill. Idomeneus is supposed to have sailed from here to Troy.

AMPHE   was an earlier name of the island of CASUS.

AMPHICLEIA or AMPHICAEA (AMFIKLIA)   was a town in the north of Phocis, 11 km from Lilaea and about the same distance from Tithorea. Herodotus calls it Amphicaea, and it also bore for some time the name of Ophiteia. It seems that a certain chief suspected that his enemies were trying to kill his baby son, so he hid the child in a safe place. A wolf came and attempted to seize the baby but was prevented from doing so by a serpent. The father returned and, thinking that the serpent was going to harm the child, threw a javelin that killed both the snake and the baby. The father built a common pyre for the serpent and his son. It was reported that the town resembled a burning pyre (Paus. 10.33.10). The place was celebrated in the time of Pausanias for the worship of Dionysus. Dionysus as the god of wine is also both an inspired and an inspiring god, that is, a god who has the power of revealing the future to man by oracles. Since prophetic power most often is combined with the art of healing, Dionysus, like Apollo, was called Iatros or Hygiatis, and at his oracle of Amphicleia he cured diseases by revealing the remedies to the sufferers in their dreams (Paus. 10.33.11).

AMPHIGENEIA   one of the towns belonging to Nestor (Hom. *Il.* 2.593), was placed by some ancient critics in Messenia and by others in Macistia, a district in Triphylia. Strabo (8.3.24) assigns it to Macistia near the river Hypsoeis, where in his time stood a temple of Leto. Its site is not known.

AMPHILOCHIA   was a small district at the east end of the Ambracian Gulf, bounded on the north by Ambracia and on the south by the territory of the Agraei. It did not extend far inland. It is a mountainous district with cliffs along the coast. The Amphilochi were a non-Hellenic tribe, although they were supposed to have derived their name from the Argive Amphilochus, the son of Amphiaraus. The only town in their country was Argos, surnamed Amphilochicum. The modern town of Amfilohia (formerly Karavassaras) is the supposed site of ancient Limnaea, but neither place has any mythological association.

AMPHIPOLIS (AMFIPOLI)   was a town in Macedonia, situated on a hill on the east bank of the Strymon River about 4.5 km from the sea. The Strymon flowed almost around the town, which gave the town its name. Its position was one of the most important in this part of

Greece. It stood in a pass that crosses the mountains around the Strymonic Gulf; and it commanded the only easy access from the coast of that gulf into the great Macedonian plains. It was originally called Ennea Hodoi (Nine Ways) from the many roads which met at this place. It belonged to the Edonians, a Thracian people.

The deity worshipped at Amphipolis appears to have been Artemis Tauropolis or Artemis Brauronia (Diod. 18.4; Liv. 44.44), whose head frequently appears on the coins of the city. The surname Tauropolis identified Artemis with the Taurian goddess to whom bulls were sacrificed. Brauronia was a surname from the deme of Brauron in Attica, where Orestes and Iphigeneia landed on their flight from Taurus with the image of Artemis. A temple of Clio, the Muse of history, was uncovered here in 1959–1960. The famous lion statue is from the period of Alexander the Great. The site of ancient Amphipolis is adjacent to the modern village of Amfipoli. There are still a few remains of the ancient city.

AMPHISSA (AMFISSA) was the chief town of the Locri Ozolae, situated in a pass at the head of the Crissaean plain and surrounded by mountains, from which circumstance it is said to have derived its name. The distance between Delphi and Amphissa is about 14 km. According to tradition, Amphissa was called after a nymph of this name, the daughter of Macar and granddaughter of Aeolus, who was beloved of Apollo. Her memory was perpetuated by a splendid monument (Paus. 10.38.5). In a passage from Pausanias (10.38.7) he speaks of a temple of the Anakes Paides at Amphissa. This epithet was used to designate the Dioscuri, thus characterized as rulers of the world. Pausanias further states that it was a doubtful point whether the deities were the Dioscuri, the Curetes, or the Cabeiri; and from this circumstance a connection between Amphissa and Samothrace has been suggested. Pausanias saw a temple of Athena on the acropolis here and a bronze statue, which was said to have been brought back from Troy by Thoas, the son of Andraemon. There was also evidence of a cult of Asclepius.

Upon the invasion of Greece by Xerxes, many Locrians removed to Amphissa (Herod. 8.32). At a later period the Amphictyons declared war against the town because its inhabitants had dared to cultivate the Crissaean plain, which was sacred to Apollo, and had molested the pilgrims who came to consult the oracle at Delphi. The walls of the ancient acropolis are almost the only remains of the ancient city. The tomb of Andraemon and his wife Gorge was seen at Amphissa in the time of Pausanias (10.38.5). Andraemon was the son-in-law of Oeneus, king of Calydon, and was given the kingdom by Diomedes when Oeneus became too old to govern.

AMPHRYSUS a small river in Thessaly, rising in Mount Othrys and flowing near Alus into the Pagasaean Gulf, is celebrated in mythology as the river on the banks of which Apollo fed the flocks of King Admetus (Apollon. Rhod. 1.54). The epithet Amphrysius is often used in reference to Apollo.

AMPHRYSUS a town in Phocis. (See AMBRYSUS.)

AMYCLAE (AMIKLES) was an ancient town of Laconia situated on the right or east bank of the Eurotas River 3.5 km south of Sparta. It was one of the most celebrated cities of Peloponnesus in the heroic age. It is said to have been founded by the Lacedaemonian king Amyclas, son of Lacedaemon and Sparta and father of Hyacinthus, and to have been the home of Tyndareus and the birthplace of Castor and Polydeuces. The legend of Hyacinthus tells us that he was extraordinarily beautiful and was beloved by Thamyris and Apollo, who unintentionally killed him during a game of discus (Apollod. 1.3.3). Some traditions relate that he was beloved also by Zephyrus, the west wind (or Boreas, the north wind), who, from jealousy of Apollo, caused the god's discus to strike and kill the youth (Lucian *Dial. Deor.* 14). From the blood of Hyacinthus there sprang the flower of the same name, on the leaves of which there appeared the exclamation of woe, "*AI, AI,*" or the letter *Y* (upsilon) being the initial of (H)Yacinthus. He was worshipped at Amyclae as a hero, and a great festival, the Hyacinthia, was celebrated in his honor.

Amyclae is mentioned by Homer (*Il.* 2.584), and it continued to maintain its independence as an Achaian (in the Homeric sense) town long after the conquest of Peloponnesus by the Dorians. According to the common tradition, which represented that conquest as effected in one generation by the descendants of Heracles, Amyclae was given by the Dorians to Philonomus as a reward for his having betrayed to them his native city Sparta. Philonomus is further said to have peopled the town with colonists from Imbros and Lemnos. Despite this tradition, there can be no doubt that the ancient Achaian population maintained themselves in the place independent of Sparta for many generations. It was only shortly before the first Messenian war that the town was conquered by the Spartan king Teleclus (Paus. 3.2.6). After its capture by the Lacedaemonians, Amyclae became a village and was only memorable because of the festival of the Hyacinthia celebrated annually and because of the temple and colossal statue of Apollo, surnamed Amyclaeus. Pausanias (3.19.2) estimated the size of the statue at 30 cubits (13.5 meters) in height. It appears to have been very ancient, for with the exception of the head, hands, and feet, the whole resembled more a bronze pillar than a statue. This figure of the god wore a helmet, and in his hands he held a spear and bow. Every year the women of Amyclae made a new chiton for the god, and the place where they made it was also called the Chiton (Paus. 3.16.4). The throne on which this statue was placed was a celebrated work of art and was constructed by Bathycles of Magnesia. It was crowned with a great number of bas-reliefs, of which Pausanias (3.18.9–19.5) gives a full account: Amphitrite, wife of Poseidon and goddess of the Mediterranean; Anaxias and Mnasinus, the sons of Castor, on horseback; Atlas bearing heaven on his shoulders and holding in his hands the golden apples of the Hesperides; Bellerophon in his contest with the Chimaera; Cephalus being carried off by Hemera or Eos; Cheiron, the wisest and most just of the Centaurs; Demodocus, the famous bard of the Odyssey, playing at the dance of the Phaeacians; Lycurgus, who took part in the battle of the Seven Against Thebes, engaged in a contest with Amphiaraus; Memnon, the son of Eos, in battle against Achilles; and Titys, the giant son of Gaea, being felled by the arrows of Artemis and Apollo for trying to rape Leto.

Among other individuals associated with Amyclae were Agamemnon and Cassandra. According to Pindar (*Pyth.* 11.48), the murder of Agamemnon took place at Amyclae, and Pausanias (2.16.6) states that the inhabitants of this place disputed with those of Mycenae the possession of the tomb of Cassandra, whose statue was at Amyclae. In later times statues of Agamemnon were erected in several parts of Greece, and he was worshipped as a hero at Amyclae and Olympia (Paus. 3.19.6, 5.25.9). Deiphobus, son of Hippolytus, purified Heracles at Amyclae after the murder of Iphitus (Apollod. 2.6.2; Diod. 4.31). Sparta, the wife of Lacedaemon and mother of Amyclas, was represented on a tripod at Amyclae (Paus. 3.18.8).

In addition to Apollo and the Dioscuri, other gods were worshipped here. Artemis Leucophryne, whose surname was derived from Leucophrys, a town in Phrygia, had a splendid temple there, as well as at Magnesia on the Maeander. There was a statue of Artemis at Amyclae that had been dedicated by the Magnesian Bathycles (Paus. 3.18.8). Zeus Messapeus had a sanctuary between Amyclae and Mount Taygetus; his surname was said to have been derived from a priest by the name of Messapeus (Paus. 3.20.3). Dionysus was worshipped as Dionysus Psilax (Giver of Wings or Unbearded) (Paus. 3.9.6).

Excavation of Amyclae has been mostly confined to the hill of Agia Kiriaki, located between Amikles and Sparta and about three-quarters of a kilometer from the Eurotas. In 1889–1890 Tsountas located the foundation of the throne of Apollo Amyclaeus. The shrine of Alexandra-Cassandra and Agamemnon with its statue of Clytemnestra mentioned by Pausanias (3.19.6) has so far not been found, but thousands of votive offerings to Alexandra-Cassandra have been excavated in the area of Agia Paraskevi.

AMYDON was a town in Macedonia on the Axius, from which Pyraechmes led the Paeonians to the assistance of Troy where he was killed by Patroclus (Hom. *Il.* 2.848, 16.287). The place is called Abydon by others.

AMYMONE was a river in the Argive plain. The grove of Lerna, which consisted for the most part of plane trees, extended from Mount Pontinus to the sea and was bounded on one side by the Pontinus River and on the other by the Amymone River. The second labor of Heracles was the fight against the Lernean Hydra. This monster was the offspring of Typhon and Echidna and was brought up by Hera. It ravaged the country of Lerna near Argos and dwelt in a swamp under a palm tree at the source of the Amymone. The numerous heads of the water-snake may perhaps have been suggested by the numerous sources of this river. Amymone is frequently mentioned by the poets. It is said to have derived its name from one of the daughters of Danaus. When Danaus arrived in Argos, the country was suffering from a drought. Poseidon was indignant at the river-god Inachus because Inachus had voted against him in his contest with Hera for possession of Argos. Danaus sent Amymone to fetch water, and she wandered a fairly long way from Apobathmi, where the Danaids had landed. Meeting a stag, she shot at it, but hit a sleeping satyr, who rose and pursued her. Poseidon appeared and rescued the maiden from the satyr but appropriated her for himself; he then showed her the wells at Lerna (Apollod. 2.1.4). According to another form of the tradition, Amymone fell asleep on her expedition in search of water, and was surprised by a satyr. She invoked Poseidon, who appeared and cast his trident at the satyr, who escaped when the trident struck into a rock. Poseidon, after ravishing the maiden, bade her draw the trident from the rock. When she did, a threefold spring gushed forth immediately, which was called after her the well of Amymone. Her son by Poseidon was called Nauplius (Lucian *Dei Marin.* 6; Paus. 2.8.2).

AMYRUS (KASTRI?) a town in Thessaly, was situated on a river of the same name flowing into Lake Boebeis. It is mentioned by Strabo (9.5.22), quoting Hesiod, as the "vine-bearing Amyrus." The surrounding country was called the Amyric plain. Some have thought that ruins at Kastri are those of ancient Amyrus. Amyrus was a son of Poseidon, and it was believed that the town and river Amyrus derived their name from him (Val. Flacc. 2.11).

ANAGYRUS (VARI) was a deme of Attica belonging to the tribe Erechtheis, situated southeast of Athens near the promontory Zoster. Pausanias (1.31.1) mentions at this place a temple of the mother of the gods, which so far has not been found. The ruins of Anagyrus have been found near Vari.

ANAPHE (ANAFI)   is one of the Cyclades, a small island east of Thira. It is said to have been originally called Membliarus from Membliarus, who came with others to the island in search of Europa. He was a son of Poecilus, a Phoenician, and a relation of Cadmus. Cadmus left him at the head of a colony in the island of Thera or Calliste (Herod. 4.147; Paus. 3.1.7). Anaphe was celebrated for the temple of Apollo Aegletes (Radiant God), the foundation of which was ascribed to the Argonauts. During a night voyage from Corcyra in the direction of Crete, they were overtaken by a storm. Apollo sent brilliant flashes of lightning that enabled them to discover a neighboring island raised by him out of the sea, which they called Anaphe. Here they erected an altar to Apollo, and solemn rites were instituted, which continued to be observed down to very late times (Apollon. Rhod. 4.1706; Apollod. 1.9.26). There are still considerable remains both of this temple on the eastern side of the island, and also of the ancient city, which was situated nearly in the center of Anaphe on the summit of a hill. Several important inscriptions have been discovered. The island is mountainous, of little fertility, and cultivated to its detriment. It contains a vast number of partridges, which flourished there in antiquity also. Athenaeus (9.400) relates that a native of Astypalaea let loose a brace of these birds upon Anaphe, where they multiplied so rapidly that the inhabitants were almost obliged to abandon the island in consequence.

ANAPHLYSTUS (ANAVISSOS)   was a deme of Attica belonging to the tribe Antiochis. It was situated on the west coast of Attica opposite the island of Eleussa and a little north of the promontory of Sunium. It was a place of some importance. Xenophon recommended the erection of a fortress here for the protection of the mines of Sunium (Xenoph. *De Vectig.* 4.43). Strabo (9.1.21) places a sanctuary of Aphrodite Colias in the neighborhood of Anaphlystus. He also speaks of a Paneion (Grotto of Pan) in the neighborhood of Anaphlystus. It is no doubt the same as the very beautiful and extensive cavern above Mount Elymbo in the Paralian range, of which the western portion bears the name of Pani.

ANAURUS   was a small river in Magnesia in Thessaly, flowing past Iolcus into the Pagasaean Gulf, in which Jason is said to have lost one of his sandals (Apollon. Rhod. 1.8; Apollod. 1.9.16). Jason was the son of Aeson. After the death of Cretheus, the founder of Iolcus and father of Aeson, Pelias, who was the nephew, or, according to others, a brother of Jason, ruled at Iolcus. Pelias was told by an oracle that he should be killed by a

descendant of Aeolus and therefore put to death all the Aeolidae; but Jason, whose grandfather, Cretheus, had been the eldest son of Aeolus and who was on that account likewise destined to die, was saved by his own relatives, who lamented over him as though he were dead and entrusted him to Cheiron the Centaur to be educated (Pind. *Nem.* 3.94). Pelias was now advised by an oracle to be on his guard against a man with only one shoe. Once when Pelias offered up a sacrifice to Poseidon, Jason was among those invited. He arrived with only one sandal, having lost the other in crossing the river Anaurus, on the banks of which he had lived as a peasant. Another tradition represents Jason as coming in Magnesian costume from Mount Pelion (Pind. *Pyth.* 4.140; Apollod. 1.9.16). Instead of the river Anaurus, others mention the Euenus or Enipeus. They add that Hera, being in love with Jason, assumed the appearance of an old woman, stood on the bank of the river, and requested him to carry her across; and that Jason in so doing lost one of his sandals. In any case, Pelias, on learning the identity of Jason, arranged to get rid of him by sending him on the quest for the Golden Fleece.

ANCHESMUS (TOURKOVOUNI)   was a hill in the environs of Athens. Zeus Anchesmius derived his surname from this hill, on which, as on several Attic hills, there was a statue of the god (Paus. 1.32.2). The modern name of this hill is Tourkovouni, and it can be seen on the left of Leoforos Kifissias on the way from Athens to Kifissia.

ANCHISIA   was a mountain north of Mantineia in Arcadia adjacent to the plain of Alcimedon. A tradition preserved in Pausanias (8.12.8) states that Anchises, the father of Aeneas, died in Arcadia and was buried there by his son at the foot of a hill, which received from him the name of Anchisia.

ANDANIA (FILIA)   was an ancient town of Messenia and the capital of the kings of the race of the Leleges. It was situated on the road leading from Messene to Megalopolis. Its ruins, according to some, are situated upon a hill near the village of Filia. The Homeric Oechalia is identified by Strabo with Andania, but by Pausanias with Carnasium, which was only 1.5 km from Andania (Paus. 4.2.2).

Lycus was a son of Pandion and brother of Aegeus, Nisus, and Pallas. He was expelled by Aegeus and took refuge in the country of the Termili with Sarpedon. That country was afterward eponymously called Lycia (Herod. 1.173, 7.92). He was honored at Athens as a hero, and the Lyceum derived its name from him (Paus. 1.19.4; Aristoph. *Vesp.* 408). He is said to have raised the mysteries of the Great Goddesses to greater celebrity and to have introduced them from Attica to Andania (Paus. 4.1.4). He is sometimes also described as an ancient prophet, and the family of the Lycomedae at Athens traced their name and origin to him. This family was intimately connected with the Attic mysteries and possessed chapels in the deme of Phylae and at Andania (Paus. 1.19.3, 4.1.6–9).

ANDREIS   was a district neighboring Orchomenus in Boeotia and was named for Andreus, a son of the river-god Peneius in Arcadia.

ANDROS (ANDROS)   is the most northerly and one of the largest islands of the Cyclades, southeast of Euboea, 35 km long and 13 broad. According to tradition, it derived its name from Andreus, a son of the river-god Peneius in Arcadia. He was also responsible for the naming of Andreis, a district around Orchomenus in Boeotia. Pausanias also speaks of Andreus (it is, however, uncertain whether he means the same man as the former) as the person who first colonized Andros. According to Diodorus (5.79), Andreus was one of the generals of Rhadamanthys, from whom he received the island, afterward called Andros, as a present.

The present population of Andros is about 12,000. Its soil is fertile, and its chief products are silk and wine. It was also celebrated for its wine in antiquity, and the whole island was regarded as sacred to Dionysus. There was a tradition that, during the festival of this god, a fountain flowed with wine (Plin. 31.13,16; Paus. 6.26.2). We are told that the island also possessed a fountain of Zeus and temples of Apollo, Hestia, and Athena. A statue of Hermes was uncovered here in the early nineteenth century, but on the whole Andros has so far produced few classical remains.

ANEMOREIA   a town of Phocis mentioned by Homer, (*Il.* 2.521) was situated on a height on the borders of Phocis and Delphi and is said to have derived its name from the gusts of wind which blew over the place from the two summits of Mount Parnassus (Strab. 9.3.15).

ANIGRUS   was the name of a small river in the Triphylian Elis called Minyeius by Homer (*Il.* 11.721), which rose in Mount Lapithas and near Samicum ran into marshland. Its water had an offensive smell, and its fish were not edible. This was ascribed to the Centaurs having washed in the water after they had been wounded by the poisoned arrows of Heracles. Near Samicum were caverns sacred to the nymphs of the river, the Nymphae Anigrides. On the coast of Elis, not far from the mouth of the river, there was a grotto sacred to them, which was visited by persons afflicted with cutaneous diseases. They were cured here by prayers and sacrifices to the nymphs and by bathing in the river (Paus. 5.5.11; Strab. 8.3.19).

ANTHANE   was a town in Laconia. The derivation of its name is uncertain. Anthas was a son of Poseidon and Alcyone, the daughter of Atlas. He was king of Troezen and believed to have built the town of Antheia, and, according to a Boeotian tradition, the town of Anthedon also. Anthes is probably another form of Anthas. One writer called him the founder of Anthane; another says that the island of Calaureia was originally named for him Anthedonia (Plut. *Quaest. Gr.* 19).

ANTHEDON (LOUKISSIA)   a town of Boeotia and one of the cities of the League, was situated on the Strait of Euripus or the Euboean Sea at the foot of Mount Messapius, 13 km from Chalcis and 30 from Thebes. Anthedon is mentioned by Homer (*Il.* 2.508) as the most distant town of Boeotia. Anthas, a son of Poseidon, was king of Troezen and believed to have built the town of Anthedon. Other accounts state that Anthedon derived its name from a nymph Anthedon (Paus. 9.22.5).

The inhabitants derived their origin from the sea-god Glaucus, who is said to have been originally a native of the place. Glaucus was a fisherman and had the good luck to gain immortality by eating a part of the divine herb that Cronus had sown (Athen. 7.48; Claud. *De Nupt. Mar.* 10.158). His parentage is different in the different traditions, which are enumerated by Athenaeus; some called his father Copeus, others Polybus, the husband of Euboea, and others again Anthedon or Poseidon. He was further said to have been a clever diver, to have built the ship Argo, and to have accompanied the Argonauts as their steersman. In the naval battle of Jason against the Tyrrhenians, Glaucus alone remained unhurt. He sank to the bottom of the sea, where he was invisible to everyone except Jason. From this moment he became a marine deity and was of service to the Argonauts. The story of his sinking or leaping into the sea was variously modified in the different traditions. There was a belief in Greece that once in every year Glaucus, accompanied by marine monsters, visited all the coasts and islands and gave his prophecies (Paus. 9.22.6). Fishermen and sailors paid him particular reverence and watched his oracles, which were believed to be very trustworthy. He was represented as a man whose hair and beard were dripping with water, with bristly eyebrows, his breast covered with seaweed, and the lower part of the body ending in the tail of a fish.

We learn from Pausanias that there was a sacred grove of the Cabeiri in the middle of Anthedon, surrounding a temple of those deities, and near it a temple of Demeter. The Cabeiri were mystic divinities who occur in various parts of the ancient world. The worship of the Cabeiri occurred chiefly in Samothrace, Lemnos, and Imbros. Outside the walls there was a temple of Dionysus and a spot called "the leap of Glaucus." A small temple discovered southeast of the city in 1889 may be that of Dionysus. The gymnasium at Anthedon was sacred to

Zeus. Near Anthedon was the tomb of the Aloeidae. These were the two sons, Otus and Ephialtes, of Poseidon and Iphimedeia. They are renowned in the earliest stories of Greece for their extraordinary strength and daring spirit. Varios stories recount their fabled energy and impiety against the gods. They were worshipped in various places. Sepulchral monuments of the Aloeidae were seen in the time of Pausanias (9.22.5) near Anthedon. Here also was the tomb of Iphimedeia, a daughter of Triops and wife of Aloeus. Being in love with Poseidon, she often walked by the sea and collected its waters in her lap, by which means she became by Poseidon the mother of the Aloeidae. Once she and her daughter Pancratis were carried off by pirates and were delivered by the Aloeidae.

The wine of Anthedon was celebrated in antiquity. The ruins of the town are situated 2.5 km from Loukissia.

ANTHEDONIA was the original name of CALAUREIA.

ANTHEIA (ANTHIA) was a town in Messenia mentioned by Homer (*Il.* 9.151), who calls it "deep-meadowed," supposed by later writers to be the same as Thuria, though some identified it with Asine (Strab. 8.4.5; Paus. 4.31.1). The modern town of Anthia is near the ruins of the ancient site. (See THURIA.)

ANTHEIA was a town in Argolis near Troezen. It was said to have been founded by Anthas, a son of Poseidon and king of Troezen (Paus. 2.30.8).

ANTHELA (ANTHILI) was a town in Phthiotis. Near the united streams of the Phoenix and the Asopus, Mount Oeta approached so close to the marsh of the gulf that it left a very narrow space for vehicles or individuals to pass. In the immediate vicinity of the pass was the town of Anthela, celebrated for the temples of Amphictyon and the Amphictyonic Demeter, containing seats for the Amphictyonic Council, who held here their autumnal meetings. At Anthela, Mount Oeta recedes a little from the sea, leaving a plain a little more than three-quarters of a kilometer in breadth. Amphictyon was a son of Deucalion and Pyrrha, the famous survivors of the Flood, or, according to others, an autochthon. He was regarded as the founder of the amphictyony of Thermopylae, and in consequence of this belief a sanctuary of Amphictyon was built in the village of Anthela, which was the most ancient place of meeting of this amphictyony (Herod. 7.200). Demeter Amphictyonis was worshipped at Anthela, and sacrifices were offered to her at the opening of every meeting of the amphictyons of Thermopylae (Strab. 9.4.17). The modern town of Anthili is adjacent to the ancient site. It is just off the National Road in the vicinity of the Thermopylae monument.

ANTHEMUS was an earlier name of the island of SAMOS.

ANTICYRA (ANTIKIRA) was a town in Phocis located on a peninsula on a bay (Sinus Anticyranus) of the Corinthian Gulf. It owed its importance to the excellence of its harbor on this sheltered gulf and to its convenient situation for communications with the interior. It is said to have been originally called Cyparissus, a name mentioned by Homer (*Il.* 2.519; Paus. 10.36.5). On the approach to the town there was a sanctuary of Artemis Dictynnaea with an image of black stone. In the harbor was a sanctuary of Poseidon, which had an image of bronze with one foot resting on a dolphin. Here were buried the sons of Iphitus, Epistrophus and Schedius. Another temple, possibly of Athena, was discovered in 1954. Anticyra was chiefly celebrated for the production and preparation of the best hellebore in Greece, the chief remedy in antiquity for madness.

ANTICYRA was a town in Thessaly in the district Malis at the mouth of the Spercheius (Herod. 7.198). According to some, the best hellebore was grown at this place, and one of its citizens showed the medicine to Heracles, when during one of his episodes of insanity he had entered this neighborhood.

ANTICYTHERA (ANDIKITHIRA) is an island about 38 km southeast of Cythera and nearly halfway between there and Crete. The chief city of classical Anticythera was Aegileia, the remains of which are 1.5 km from the modern hamlet of Potamos. It is surprising that no mythological accounts refer to this island. But Apollo Aegileus was worshipped here, as attested by discovery of a statue base and a temple in 1889.

ANTRON was a town of Thessaly in the district of Phthiotis at the entrance of the Maliac Gulf and opposite Oreus in Euboea. It is mentioned in the *Iliad* (2.697) as one of the cities of Protesilaus. It was under the protection of Demeter. It probably owed its long existence to the quality of its rocks, which produced some of the best millstones in Greece, as a result of which it was often called Petreis. Off Antron was a sunken rock called Onus Antronus (Millstone of Antron) (Strab. 9.5.14). The name of the modern village Molos suggests a connection with the ancient commercial importance of the place.

ANYGRUS was a fountain in Attica. Icarius was an Athenian who lived in the reign of Pandion and hospitably received Dionysus upon his arrival in Attica. The god showed him his gratitude by teaching him the cultivation of the vine and giving him bags filled with wine. Icarius now rode about in a chariot and distributed the precious gifts of the god. Some shepherds, mistaking intoxication for poisoning, slew Icarius and threw his body into the well Anygrus, or buried it under a tree.

AONIA   was the ancient name of Boeotia. The Aones were some of the most ancient inhabitants of Boeotia, who derived their origin from Aon, a son of Poseidon. They appeared to have dwelt chiefly in the rich plains about Thebes, a portion of which was called the Aonian plain in the time of Strabo (9.2.31). Both by the Greek and Roman writers Boeotia is frequently called Aonia, and the adjective Aonius is used as a synonym for Boeotian (Callim. *Hymn. in Del.* 75; Gell. 14.6). Hence the Muses, who frequented Mount Helicon in Boeotia, are called Aonides and Aoniae Sorores (Ov. *Met.* 5.333; Juv. 7.58).

Menippe was a daughter of Orion and sister of Metioche. After Orion was killed by Artemis, Menippe and Metioche were brought up by their mother. Athena taught them the art of weaving, and Aphrodite gave them beauty. Once the whole of Aonia was visited by a plague, and the oracle of Apollo Gortynius, when consulted, ordered the inhabitants to propitiate the two Erinyes by the sacrifice of two maidens, who were to offer themselves to death of their own accord. Menippe and Metioche offered themselves; they thrice invoked the infernal gods and then killed themselves with their shuttles (Ov. *Met.* 13.694). Persephone and Hades metamorphosed them into comets. The Aonians erected to them a sanctuary near Orchomenus, where a propitiatory sacrifice was offered to them every year by youths and maidens. The Aeolians called these maidens Coronides.

APESAS (FOKAS)   was a mountain in Peloponnesus above Nemea in the territory of Cleonae, where Perseus is said to have been the first person who sacrificed to Zeus Apesantius (Paus. 2.15.3). The remains of the altar of Zeus are located near the eastern part of the summit. The Nemean lion was said to have hunted there. The modern name of the mountain is Fokas.

APHETAE (AGIA KIRIAKI)   was a port of Magnesia in Thessaly, said to have derived its name from the departure of the Argonauts from it (Apollon. Rhod. 1.591). Aphetae has been identified with the modern harbor of Trikeri at Agia Kiriaki or with a harbor on the island of Palea Trikeri.

APHIDNA or APHIDNAE (AFIDNES)   one of the twelve ancient towns of Attica (Strab. 9.1.20), is celebrated in the mythological period as the place where Helen was confined for a period of time. Theseus, aided by his friend Peirithous, carried off Helen from Sparta while she was still a girl and placed her at Aphidna under the care of Aethra, his mother. He further entrusted both of them to the care of his friend Aphidnus, telling him to guard them in absolute secrecy. Meanwhile, he assisted Peirithous in his ill-fated attempt to carry off Persephone from the lower world. Helen's brothers, Castor and Polydeuces, the Dioscuri, were understandably upset by this kidnapping and set about organizing a rescue mission. They were accompanied by Cnageus, a Laconian, and Alycus, a son of Sciron. While Theseus was absent from Attica and Menestheus was endeavoring to usurp the government, the Dioscuri marched into Attica and ravaged the country round the city. Some say that the inhabitants of Deceleia told the Lacedaemonians where Helen was concealed, but the usual story is that Academus, an Attic hero, betrayed her location to them. For this reason the Tyndarids always showed him much gratitude, and whenever the Lacedaemonians invaded Attica they always spared the land belonging to Academus, which lay on the Cephissus near Athens (Plut. *Thes.* 32). The Dioscuri took Aphidna by assault. Unfortunately Alycus, their ally, was killed at Aphidna but buried in Megara at a place which was named for him. Cnageus, another ally, was taken prisoner, sold as a slave, and taken to Crete, where he served in the temple of Artemis. He later escaped with a priestess of the goddess who carried her statue to Sparta (Paus. 3.18.3). The Dioscuri carried away their sister Helen, and Aethra was made their prisoner. Menestheus then opened to them the gates of Athens, and Aphidnus adopted Castor and Polydeuces as his sons, in order that, according to their wishes, they might become initiated in the Eleusinian mysteries. They felt that they had as close a connection with the city as Heracles, and this privilege was granted to them. Aphidnus more than likely was the founder of Aphidna or one of a line of kings of the city bearing his name. Later the Athenians paid divine honors to the Dioscuri (Plut. *Thes.* 31; Lycoph. 499). According to some, Theseus did not carry off Helen but instead had promised Idas and Lynceus that he would guard her for them, and he kept her at Aphidna.

Modern Afidnes (formerly Kiorka) is near the hill Kotroni on which there are some ancient walls that might be identified with the ancient town. Both are about 26 km from Athens.

APHRODISIAS   was a town in the south of Laconia on the Boeatic Gulf, said to have been founded by Aeneas (Paus. 8.12.8). Boeus, a son of Heracles, was said to have led colonists from Aphrodisias to Boeae, the Laconian town which he founded.

APHYTIS (AFITOS)   was a town on the east side of the peninsula Pallene in Macedonia, a little below Potidaea (Herod. 7.123; Thuc. 1.64). Xenophon (*Hellen.* 5.3.19) says that it possessed a sanctuary of Dionysus and the Nymphs, to which the Spartan king Agesipolis desired to be removed before his death; but it was more celebrated for its temple of Zeus Ammon, whose head appears on its coins (Plut. *Lys.* 20; Paus. 3.18.3).

APIA   was named for Apis, a son of Telchis and father of Thelxion. He was king at Sicyon and is said to have been such a powerful prince that previous to the arrival of Pelops, Peloponnesus was called Apia after him (Paus. 2.5.7). (See PELOPONNESUS.)

APOBATHMI (KIVERI)   a small place in Argolis near the frontiers of Cynuria, was said to have been so called from Danaus landing at this spot (Paus. 2.38.4). Danaus was a son of Belus and Anchinoe and a grandson of Poseidon and Libya. He was brother of Aegyptus, and father of fifty daughters, and the mythical ancestor of the Danai (Apollod. 2.1.4). Having reason to believe that his brother's sons were plotting against him in northern Africa, he heeded the advice of an oracle, built a ship, and set off with his daughters. He landed first at Rhodes and then sailed to Peloponnesus, where he landed at a place near Lerna, which was afterwards called from this event Apobathmi (Landing Place). The modern town is called Kiveri.

APOLLONIA   was a city on the Ionic Gulf whose citizens dedicated a group of statues of Trojan heroes at Olympia. These were by the great sculptor Lycius. Euenius was a seer of Apollonia and father of Deiphonus. He was one of the most distinguished citizens of Apollonia. One night when he was tending the sheep of Helios, which the noble Apolloniatae had to do by turns, the flock was attacked by wolves, and sixty sheep were killed. Euenius said nothing of the occurrence but intended to purchase new sheep and thus to make up for the loss. But the loss became known and Euenius was brought up for trial. He was deprived of his office, and his eyes were put out as a punishment for his carelessness and negligence. Hereupon the earth ceased to produce fruit, and the sheep of Helios ceased to produce young. Two oracles were consulted and responded that Euenius had been punished unjustly because the gods themselves had sent the wolves among the sheep and that the calamity under which Apollonia was suffering should not cease until Euenius should have received all the reparation he might desire. A number of citizens accordingly waited upon Euenius and, without mentioning the oracles, asked him in the course of their conversation what reparation he would demand if the Apolloniatae should be willing to make any. Euenius, in his ignorance of the oracles, merely asked for two acres of the best land in Apollonia and the finest house in the city. The deputies then said that the Apolloniatae would grant him what he asked for, in accordance with the oracles. Euenius was indignant when he heard how he had been deceived; but the gods gave him a compensation by bestowing on him the gift of prophecy (Herod. 9.92–95).

The sheep had been the property of Helios. Temples of Helios seem to have existed in Greece at a very early time (Hom. *Od.* 12.346), and in later times we find his worship established in various places—in Apollonia (Herod. 9.93), for example.

APTERA (APTERA)   was a city of Crete, situated to the east of Polyrrhenia and 15 km from Cydonia (Strab. 10.4.13). Here was placed the scene of the legend of the contest between the Sirens and the Muses. The Sirens were beings who were believed to have the power of enchanting and charming by their song anyone who heard them. Late poets represent them with wings, which they are said to have received at their own request in order to be able to search after Persephone (Ov. *Met.* 5.552), or as a punishment from Demeter for not having assisted Persephone, or from Aphrodite because they wished to remain virgins (Aelian. *De Nat. Anim.* 17.23; Apollon. Rhod. 4.896). Once, however, they allowed themselves to be prevailed upon by Hera to enter into a contest with the Muses, and, being defeated, they were deprived of their wings (Paus. 9.34.3). From this circumstance came the name Aptera (Wingless). However, some contend that an artist named Pteras provided the name (Paus. 10.5.10). After the victory of the Muses, the Sirens lost the feathers of their wings from their shoulders. Having thus become white, they cast themselves into the sea. The name of the neighboring islands, Leucas, alludes to their whiteness. In some representations the Muses are seen with feathers on their heads, alluding to their contest with the Sirens, for when the Sirens were deprived of the feathers of their wings, the Muses put them on as an ornament.

Aptera was one of the largest ancient cities of Crete. The city flourished in classical and Roman times. Remains of monuments to be seen at the site, still called Aptera, include a small Doric temple of Apollo, a temple of Demeter and Persephone, and others. Artemis Aptera was also worshipped there. Its port is Kalives. To the west of Aptera is Mount Berecynthus (Mount Malaxa). This mountain has been identified with the discovery of bronze and iron and their gift to man by the Idaean Dactyls.

ARACYNTHUS (ARAKINTHOS)   was a range of mountains in Aetolia running in a southeast direction from the Achelous River to the Euenus and separating the lower plain of Aetolia near the sea from the upper plain above the lakes Hyria and Trichonia (Strab. 2.10.4). This mountain is located north of Pleuron. According to some, there was a mountain of the name of Aracynthus both in Boeotia and in Attica, or perhaps on the frontiers of the two countries. The mountain is connected with the Boeotian hero Amphion both by Propertius (3.13.42) and by Virgil (*Ecl.* 2.24). Aphrodite Aracynthias derived her surname from Mount Aracynthus, the position of which is a matter of uncertainty, and on which she had a temple.

ARAETHYREA   the ancient capital of Phliasia, is said by Pausanias to have been originally named Arantia, after Aras, its founder, and to have been called Araethyrea after a daughter of Aras of this name. Araethyrea had a brother called Aoris, and is said to have been fond of the chase and warlike pursuits. When she died, her brother called the country of Phliasia Araethyrea after her (Hom. *Il.* 2.571; Strab. 8.6.24). She was the mother of Phlias, from whom the town of Phlius and the territory of Phliasia derived their names. The monuments of Araethyrea and her brother, consisting of round pillars, were still extant in the time of Pausanias; and before the mysteries of Demeter commenced at Phlius, the people always invoked Aras and his two children with their faces turned toward these monuments (Paus. 2.12.4–6). The name of its founder was retained in the time of Pausanias in the hill Arantius, on which it stood. Its inhabitants quitted Araethyrea and founded Phlius 5.5 km from the former town. It has been supposed that the ruins on Mount Polyfengo are those of Araethyrea.

ARAINUS (AGERANOS)   was a small place in Laconia on the west side of the Laconian Gulf, containing the monument of Las, who founded a town called Las after himself. The natives claimed that Las was killed by Achilles when he came to their country to ask Tyndareus for the hand of Helen. Achilles is mentioned nowhere else as a suitor of Helen, but he more than likely accompanied his friend Patroclus, who was a suitor of Helen and who probably killed Las (Paus. 3.24.10). Arainus has been placed at modern Ageranos.

ARANTIA   was the original name of ARAETHYREA.

ARANTINUS   (See ARAETHYREA)

ARBIUS   was a mountain in Crete from which Zeus received the surname Arbius because he was worshipped there.

ARCADIA (ARKADIA)   the central area of Peloponnesus, is bounded on the east by Argolis, on the north by Achaia, on the south by Messenia and Laconia. Next to Laconia it is the largest division in Peloponnesus. Its greatest length is about 83 km, and its breadth varies from 60 to 70 km. It is surrounded on all sides by mountains, forming a kind of natural wall, which separate it from the other Peloponnesian states.

In the western region of Arcadia the mountains are high and bleak and possess small, not very fertile valleys. The mountains are covered with forests and abound in game. It is drained by the Alpheius River and its tributary streams. This part of Arcadia in ancient times was thinly populated, and its inhabitants were considered among the crudest of the Greeks. They obtained a living by hunting and the raising and feeding of cattle.

The eastern region is intersected by mountains of lower elevation, between which there are several small and fertile plains, producing oil, grain, and wine. These plains are so completely encompassed by mountains that the streams that flow into them from the mountains only find outlets by natural chasms in the rocks. Many of these streams, after disappearing beneath the ground, rise again. In these mountain-enclosed plains were situated almost all the chief cities of Arcadia—Tegea, Mantineia, Orchomenus, Stymphalus, and Pheneus, whose territories extended along the whole eastern frontier of Arcadia, from the borders of Laconia to those of Sicyon and Pellene in Achaia.

The principal mountains of Arcadia are: Cyllene, in the northeast corner of the country, known also as Crathis, Araonius, and Erymanthus; Lampeia and Pholoe, both of them a southerly continuation of Erymanthus; Lyrceius, Artemisium, Parthenium, and the range of mountains separating Arcadia from Argolis and connected with the northern end of Taygetus; and Maenalus and Lycaeus.

The chief river of Arcadia, which is also the principal river of Peloponnesus, is the Alpheius. It rises near the southern frontier, flows in a northwest direction, and receives many tributaries. Besides these, the Styx, Eurotas, and Erasinus also rise in Arcadia. All these rivers were represented as mythological beings, with Alpheius the most prominent. Of the numerous small lakes on the eastern frontier of Arcadia, the most important was Stymphalus, near the town of that name.

The Arcadians regarded themselves as the most ancient inhabitants of Greece and called themselves Proselenai, as though laying claim to an antiquity higher than that of the moon. They derived their name from an eponymous ancestor Arcas, the son of Zeus. The Greek writers call them indigenous and Pelasgus is said to have been their first sovereign. Shut up within their mountains the Arcadians experienced fewer changes than most of the inhabitants of Greece. They had a reputation among the Greeks for hospitality, kindness, and piety. We know that music formed an important part of their education; and they were celebrated throughout antiquity both for their love of music and for the success with which they cultivated it. The lyre is said to have been invented in their country by Hermes. The syrinx, also, which was the musical instrument of shepherds, was the invention of Pan, the principal god of Arcadia. The simplicity of the Arcadian character was exaggerated by the Roman poets into an ideal excellence; and its shepherds were represented as living in a state of innocence and virtue.

The religion of the Arcadians was such as might have been expected from a nation of shepherds and huntsmen. Atlas, according to some accounts, resided at first in Arcadia. His daughter Maia became by Zeus the mother of Hermes, who was born in a cave on Mount Cyllene. Hermes was called Atlantiades from this ancestry and Cyllenius from his birthplace. Shortly after birth he stole the cattle of Apollo and drove them to Pylos. Then he returned to Cyllene, where he invented the lyre and plectrum from a tortoise shell. The principal feature in the traditions about Hermes consists of his being the herald of the gods, and in this capacity he appears even in the Homeric poems; his original character of an ancient Pelasgian, or Arcadian divinity of nature, gradually disappeared in the legends. He was especially worshipped by shepherds, and this feature in the character of Hermes is a remnant of the ancient Arcadian religion, in which he was the fertilizing god of the earth, who conferred his blessings on man. The most ancient seat of his worship is Arcadia, the land of his birth, where Lycaon, the son of Pelasgus, is said to have built the first temple to Hermes. From Arcadia his worship was carried to Athens and ultimately spread throughout Greece.

The most prominent deity worshipped by the Arcadians was Pan, the son of Hermes. Pan was the great god of flocks and shepherds. He was brought up by the nymphs. From one of these, Sinoe, he derived the surname Sinoeis (Paus. 8.30.2). The principal seat of his worship was Arcadia and from there his name and his worship spread over other parts of Greece; at Athens his worship was not introduced till the time of the battle of Marathon (Paus. 8.26.2; Virg. *Ecl.* 10.26). In Arcadia he was the god of forests, pastures, flocks, and shepherds; he dwelt in grottoes (Ov. *Met.* 14.515) and wandered on the summits of mountains and rocks, or in valleys, either amusing himself with the chase or leading the dances of the nymphs (Aeschyl. *Pers.* 448; *Hymn. Hom. ad Pan.* 20). As the god of flocks, both of wild and tame animals, it was his province to increase them and guard them (Ov. *Fast.* 2.271,277; Virg. *Ecl.* 1.33); but he was also a hunter, and hunters owed their success—or lack thereof—to him. In Arcadia hunters used to scourge his statue if they hunted in vain (Theocrit. 7.107); during the heat of midday he used to slumber and was very indignant when anyone disturbed him (Theocrit. 1.16). As god of flocks, bees also were under his protection, as well as the coast where fishermen carried on their pursuit (Theocrit. 5.15). As the god of everything connected with pastoral life, he was fond of music and was the inventor of the syrinx or shepherd's flute, which he not only played but also taught to others. Pan, like other gods who dwelt in forests, was dreaded by travellers to whom he sometimes appeared, and whom he startled with a sudden awe or terror (Eurip. *Rhes.* 36). Thus when Pheidippides, the

Athenian, was sent to Sparta to solicit aid against the Persians, Pan accosted him and promised to terrify the barbarians if the Athenians would worship him (Herod. 6.105). He is said to have had a terrific voice (Val. Flacc. 3.31) and by it to have frightened the Titans in their fight with the gods. He was also believed to be possessed of prophetic powers and to have instructed Apollo in that art (Apollod. 1.4.1). While roaming the forests he fell in love with the nymph Echo, by whom he became the father of Iynx. He also lusted after Syrinx, whom he pursued into the river Ladon, her father, who changed her into reeds. From some of these Pan made a flute that he named for her. Fir trees were sacred to him, as the nymph Pitys, whom he loved, had been metamorphosed into that tree (Propert. 1.18.20). The sacrifices offered to him consisted of cows, rams, lambs, milk, and honey (Theocrit. 5.58). Sacrifices were also offered to him in common with Dionysus and the nymphs (Paus. 2.24.7). Sanctuaries and temples of Pan are frequently mentioned, especially in Arcadia, as at Heraea, on the Nomian Hill near Lycosura, on Mount Parthenium (Paus. 8.26.2), and at Megalopolis (8.30.2), near Acacesium. At Megalopolis a perpetual fire burned in his temple and at the same time there was an ancient oracle, at which the nymph Erato had been his priestess (8.37.11). In works of art Pan is represented as a voluptuous and sensual being, with horns, pug nose, and goat's feet, sometimes in the act of dancing and sometimes playing the syrinx.

Another ancient Arcadian divinity was Artemis, who presided over the chase and who appears to have been originally a goddess different from Artemis, the sister of Apollo, though the two were afterward syncretized. The Arcadian Artemis was a goddess of the nymphs and was worshipped as such in Arcadia in very early times. Her sanctuaries and temples were more numerous in this country than in any other part of Greece. In Arcadia she hunted with her nymphs on Taygetus, Erymanthus, and Maenalus; twenty nymphs accompanied her during the chase, and with sixty others, daughters of Oceanus, she held her dances in the forests of the mountains. Her bow, quiver, and arrows were made by Hephaestus, and Pan provided her with dogs. Her chariot was drawn by four stags with golden antlers (Callim. *Hymn. in Dian.* 13.81.90; Apollod. 2.5.3; Pind. *Ol.* 3.51). Her temples and sanctuaries in Arcadia were usually near lakes or rivers, whence she was called Limnatis or Limnaea (Paus. 8.53.11). In the precincts of her sanctuaries there were often sacred springs. As a nymph Artemis also appears in connection with river-gods, as with Alpheius, and thus it is understandable why fish were sacred to her (Diod. 5.3).

The worship of Zeus, surnamed Lycaeus, was also very ancient in Arcadia and was celebrated with human sacrifices even down to the Macedonian period, a fact which proves that the Arcadians still retained much of their rude and savage character. The Arcadian Zeus was born, according to the legends of the country, in Arcadia, either on Mount Parrhasium (Callim. *Hymn. in Jov.* 7.10) or in a district of Mount Lycaeus, which was called Cretea (Paus. 8.38.2; Callim. *Hymn. in Jov.* 14). He was brought up there by the nymphs Theisoa, Neda, and Hagno; the first of these gave her name to an Arcadian town, the second to a river, and the third to a fountain (Paus. 8.38.3). Lycaon, a son of Pelasgus, who built the first and most ancient town of Lycosura, called the god Zeus Lycaeus, erected a temple, and instituted the festival of the Lyceia in honor of him; he further offered to Zeus bloody sacrifices, among others his own son, in consequence of which he was metamorphosed into a wolf (Paus. 8.2.3,38.1; Callim. *Hymn. in Jov.* 4). No one was allowed to enter the sanctuary of Zeus Lycaeus on Mount Lycaeus, and there was a belief that any person who entered it would die within twelve months, and that in the sanctuary neither human beings nor animals cast a shadow (Paus. 8.38.6). Those who entered it intentionally were stoned to death, unless they escaped by flight; those who got in by accident were sent to Eleutherae (Plut. *Quaest. Gr.* 39). On the highest summit of Mount Lycaeus there was an altar of Zeus, in front of which, toward the east, there were two pillars bearing golden eagles. The sacrifices there were kept secret (Paus. 8.38.5; Callim. *Hymn. in Jov.* 68).

Despoena was the name under which Persephone was worshipped in Arcadia, where she was called a daughter of Poseidon Hippius and Demeter. She was said to have been brought up by the Titan Anytus. In a temple near Acacesium his statue stood by the side of Despoena's (Paus. 8.37.5). Persephone Soteira (Saving Goddess) was also worshipped in Arcadia (Paus. 8.31.1).

Apollo Nomius was originally a local divinity of the shepherds of Arcadia, but later he was transformed into and identified with the Dorian Apollo. The conquest of Peloponnesus by the Dorians raised Apollo to the rank of principal divinity in the peninsula. Athena Tritonis was also worshipped in Arcadia. The connection of Athena with Triton and Tritonis caused afterward the various traditions about her birthplace, so that wherever there was a river or a well of that name, as in Arcadia, the inhabitants of those districts asserted that Athena was born there. Aristaeus, the ancient agricultural divinity, was worshipped in Arcadia as protector of flocks and bees (Virg. *Georg.* 1.14.4). The Moirae, or Fates, along with Zeus Moiragetes (Leader of the Fates), were represented in the temple of Despoena near Acacesium. The mystical worship of the Cabeiri is said to have begun in Arcadia. It seems that Dardanus, son of Zeus and grandson of Atlas, ruled in Arcadia but left with one of his sons, Idaeus, on account of the flood and ensuing calamities. Taking with

them the Palladium from the temple of Pallas, they went first to Samothrace and then to Phrygia, where Dardanus founded the town that eventually became Troy. Deimas, another son of Dardanus, remained behind in Arcadia. Even the Roman Penates were sometimes considered as identical with the Cabeiri, and some thought that the Penates were carried by Dardanus from the Arcadian town of Pheneus to Samothrace and that Aeneas brought them from there to Italy. The Camenae, also Roman divinities, were ancient prophetic nymphs, whom later traditions represent as having been introduced into Italy from Arcadia. One of these was Carmenta or Carmentis, and some state that her original name was Nicostrate and that she was called Carmentis (Oracular) from her prophetic powers (Dionys. 1.15,32). According to these traditions, she was the mother of Euander, the Arcadian, by Hermes, and after having endeavored to persuade her son to kill Hermes, she fled with him to Italy, where she gave oracles. It is also said that she changed the fifteen characters of the Greek alphabet, which Euander introduced into Latium, into Roman ones.

Argus Panoptes (All-Seeing) was another half-divine being associated with Arcadia. He derived his surname from his one hundred eyes, some of which were always awake. He was of superhuman strength, and after he had slain a fierce bull that ravaged Arcadia, a satyr who robbed and violated persons, the serpent Echidna that rendered the roads unsafe, and the murderers of Apis, Hera appointed him guardian of the cow into which Io had been metamorphosed. Zeus commissioned Hermes to carry off the cow, and Hermes accomplished the task, according to some accounts, by stoning Argus to death, or, according to others, by lulling him to sleep with his flute and then cutting off his head. Hera transplanted his eyes to the tail of the peacock, her favorite bird (Apollod. 2.1.2; Ov. *Met.* 1.264).

The mythological history of Arcadia is mostly a recital of a long line of kings and major events that took place during their reigns. It appears from the genealogy of these kings that the Arcadians were, from an early period, divided into several independent states. The most ancient division appears to have been into three separate bodies. This was a few generations after the appearance of the mythical ancestor Pelasgus. According to Arcadian tradition, he was either an autochthon or a son of Zeus. By Meliboea, Cyllene, or Deianeira he became the father of Lycaon. He was, consequently, the first king of Arcadia, and Lycaon was the second. The traditions about Lycaon place him in different lights: according to some he was a barbarian who even defied the gods (Ov. *Met.* 1.198), while others describe him as the first civilizer of Arcadia, who built the town of Lycosura and introduced the worship of Zeus Lycaeus. It is added that he sacrificed a child on the altar of Zeus and that during the sacrifice he was changed by Zeus into a wolf (Paus. 8.2.3). By several wives Lycaon became the father of a large number of sons, some say fifty; but neither their number nor their names are the same in all accounts. The sons of Lycaon are said to have been notorious for their insolence and impiety, and so Zeus visited them in the disguise of a poor man, intending to punish them. They invited him to a repast, and at the suggestion of one of them, Maenalus, they mixed the entrails of a boy whom they had murdered into one of the dishes. According to Ovid (1.220–239), Zeus was recognized and worshiped by the Arcadian people, but Lycaon, after a vain attempt to kill the god, resolved to try him with the dish of human flesh. However, Zeus pushed away the table that bore the horrible food, and the place where this happened was afterward called Trapezus, from the Greek word "table." Lycaon and all his sons, with the exception of the eldest, Nyctimus, were killed by Zeus with a flash of lightning, or, according to others, were changed into wolves. Some say that the Deucalion flood occurred in the reign of Nyctimus as a punishment for the crimes of the Lycaonids. The sons of Lycaon had prior to this been responsible for founding a large number of cities, most of them named eponymously: Pallantium, founded by Pallas; Phigalia, by Phigalus; Tricoloni, by Tricolonus; Mantineia, by Mantineius; Maenalus, by Maenalus; and so on. Some of them founded cities far beyond Arcadia. One of them, Oenotrus, founded Oenotria in Italy. Three other sons, Daunus, Iapyx, and Peucetius, set up colonies at Daunia, Peucetia, and Messapia in Italy under the tribal name of Iapygians.

Nyctimus had a sister, Callisto. She was a huntress and a companion of Artemis. Zeus, however, had intercourse with her; and in order that the deed might not be known to Hera, he metamorphosed her into a she-bear. But, notwithstanding the precaution, Callisto was slain by Artemis during the chase, through the contrivance of Hera. Arcas, the son thus born to Callisto, was given by Zeus to Maia, the mother of Hermes, to be brought up, and Callisto was placed among the stars under the name of Arctos (Apollod. 3.8.2). The Arcadians showed the tomb of Callisto 5.5 km from the spring Cruni near Tricoloni; it was on a hill planted with trees, and on the top of the hill there was a temple of Artemis Calliste or Callisto (Paus. 8.35.8). After the death of Nyctimus, Arcas became the fourth king of Arcadia and gave to the country, which until then had been called Pelasgia, the name of Arcadia. He taught his subjects the arts of making bread and weaving. He was married to the nymph Erato, by whom he had three sons, Elatus, Apheidas, and Azan, among whom he divided his kingdom. The tomb of Arcas was shown at Mantineia, where his remains had been carried from Mount Maenalus at the command of the Delphic oracle (Paus. 8.9.3).

Azan acquired Azania, and his son, Cleitor, who inherited the kingship of that part of Arcadia, died childless. Elatus had acquired Mount Cyllene. Later he went to Phocis on an expedition and founded Elateia. After his death, the reign of this part of Arcadia—and Azania as well—went next to Aepytus, one of his four sons. A statue of Elatus was shown at Tegea (Paus. 8.48.6). Aepytus had originally ruled over Phaesana on the Alpheius River. When his cousin Cleitor died, Aepytus succeeded him as well, and the total part of Arcadia ruled by him was called Aepytis (Paus. 8.4.4). Aepytus was killed during a hunt on Mount Sepia by the bite of a poisonous snake. His tomb was shown in the time of Pausanias, who was anxious to see it since it was mentioned in Homer (*Il.* 2.604). Afterward the reign passed to his brother Stymphalus. Through Stymphalus the rule passed, apparently separate from the Tegean line established by Apheidas, to the third son of Arcas. Apheidas had acquired the kingship of Tegea, and the reign passed to his son Aleus, during whose reign the sanctuary of Athena Alea was established at Tegea. One of his sons was Lycurgus, and he became king, but the rule moved back and forth between his heirs and those of Cepheus, his brother. Lycurgus had four sons, all of whom died before Lycurgus did but not without distinction. Ancaeus, for example, was an Argonaut and later was killed in the Calydonian boar hunt. The rule moved from Lycurgus, then, to his grand-nephew Echemus, during whose reign the first Dorian invasion took place. During the invasion Echemus succeeded in slaying in single combat Hyllus, the son of Heracles (Paus. 8.5.1, 45.3). After the fall of Hyllus, the Heracleidae were obliged to promise not to repeat their attempts upon Peloponnesus within the next fifty or one hundred years. According to one writer, Echemus accompanied the Dioscuri on their expedition to Attica to recover Helen. On his death the reign moved back to Lycurgus' grandson, Agapenor, who commanded the Arcadians at Troy and founded Paphos in Cyprus after the Trojan War. With Agapenor the Tegean line seems to have run out, and the Arcadian rule converged in the line of Elatus, where it had been passed down through Stymphalus.

During the reign of Stymphalus, Pelops, designated by some as an Arcadian, had tried to conquer Stymphalus but could not. He finally had murdered him by stratagem and cut his body in pieces. For this crime Greece was visited by a famine, which was averted only by the prayer of Aeacus (Apollod. 3.12.6). The reign had then gone to Stymphalus' son, Agamedes, then to Cercyon, and finally to Hippothous, who had taken up residence at Trapezus instead of Tegea. Hippothous' son was Aepytus, and during his rule, Orestes, in consequence of an oracle, moved to Arcadia from Mycenae. Aepytus met an unhappy fate by entering the sanctuary of Poseidon at

Mantineia, an action forbidden to any human being. He was blinded because of this impiety and died soon after. His son Cypselus then became king, and during this time the Dorians returned. He made an alliance through the marriage of his daughter Merope with the Dorian Cresphontes, and this began a series of hostilities between the Tegeatans and Laconians. The rule passed from father to son: Holais to Bucolion to Phialus (who changed the name Phigalia to Phialia) to Simus (during whose reign the statue of the Demeter Melaenis was consumed by fire, thus presaging his own death) to Pompus (who formed a strong alliance with Aeginetan merchants and even named his son Aeginetes as a mark of friendship). The son of Aeginetes was Polymestor, and during his reign came the Laconian invasion of Tegea under Charillus. The rule next moved to Aichnis, the nephew of Polymestor, and during his reign came the Laconian war against Messenia. Aichnis' son Aristocrates, though king, was stoned to death for raping a priestess in the sanctuary of the Artemis Hymnia. His son Hicetas became king and named his own son Aristocrates. This Aristocrates was also stoned to death for treason, taking bribes from Laconia. Thus ended the mythological line of the Arcadian kings.

Arcadia was associated with the lives and experiences of many famous mortals in Greek myth. One of these was Atalanta. She was described as the daughter of Iasius, who, disappointed that she was not a boy, exposed her at birth on the Parthenian hill. She was suckled by a bear, the symbol of Artemis, and after she had grown up, she lived as a virgin, slaying the two Centaurs, Hylaeus and Rhoetus, who pursued her. She also took part in the Calydonian boar hunt and the games celebrated in honor of Pelias. Afterward, her father recognized her as his daughter; and when he desired her to marry, she made it the condition that every suitor who wanted to win her should first of all contend with her in a footrace. If the suitor conquered her, he was to be rewarded with her hand in marriage; if not, he was to be put to death by her. This she did because she was the most swift footed among all mortals and because the Delphic oracle had cautioned her against marriage. Meilanion, one of her suitors, conquered her by dropping one after another three golden aples, which Aphrodite had given him. Their beauty charmed Atalanta so much that she could not refrain from gathering them. Thus she was conquered and became the wife of Meilanion. Later the two profaned the sanctity of the sacred grove of Zeus by having sexual intercourse there and they were both metamorphosed into lions.

Alcmaeon was buried at Psophis. He had fled there from Argos after killing his mother. He in turn was murdered by his brothers-in-law, Temenus and Axion, the sons of Phegeus, when he returned from Acarnania to try to recover the fatal necklace of Harmonia from his first wife Alphesiboea, daughter of Phegeus, for his second wife Callirrhoe. His tomb at Psophis was unremarkable except that it was surrounded by huge cypresses reaching to such a height that even the mountain by Psophis was overshadowed by them. The inhabitants of Psophis would not cut them down since they considered them sacred to Alcmaeon. Anchises, the father of Aeneas by Aphrodite, is also said to have been buried in Arcadia. Aeneas was said to have buried him at the foot of a hill, which received from him the name of Anchisia. Areithous, a Pylian king surnamed the Club-Man because he fought exclusively with a club, was killed by cunning by Lycurgus, who lured him into a narrow defile at Pheia so that he could not swing his club. Areithous was buried at Phoezon, a place in Arcadia not yet identified. According to some traditions, Oicles, the father of Amphiaraus, who accompanied Heracles in the first expedition against Troy, returned home and lived in Arcadia. He was visited there by his grandson Alcmaeon and later died and was buried near Megalopolis (Paus. 8.36.6). The remains of Orestes were originally at Tegea. He had died from a snake bite in Arcadia and was buried there. Later, during a truce in a war between the Lacedaemonians and Tegeatans, the Lacedaemonian Lichas found the remains of Orestes at Tegea and took them to Sparta, which according to an oracle could not gain the victory unless it possessed the remains of Orestes (Herod. 1.67; Paus. 8.54.4).

Heracles has surprisingly little connection with Arcadia. He did father Telephus by Auge, daughter of Aleus. Telephus was reared by a hind and educated by King Corythus in Arcadia. After the Trojan War he was worshipped as a hero on Mount Parthenium in Arcadia (Paus. 8.54.6; Apollod. 1.8.6), and on the temple of Athena Alea in Tegea, he was represented as fighting with Achilles (Paus. 8.45.7). There was a well-known wooden statue of Heracles, attributed to Daedalus, located near Phaedrias on the borders of Messenia and Arcadia (Paus. 8.35.2). Buphagus was an Arcadian hero who received the wounded Iphicles, brother of Heracles, into his house and took care of him until he died. Buphagus was afterward killed by Artemis for having pursued her (Paus. 8.14.9,27.17).

Finally, Arcadia, continuing an unsavory reputation begun in the time of Lycaon, was the location of still other criminal types. Clymenus, a son of Caenus and a minor king of Arcadia, was married to Epicaste, by whom he had a daughter Harpalyce. He had an incestuous love for his daughter and after having had sex with her, he gave her in marriage to Alastor. Later he took her away from Alastor and again lived with her. Harpalyce, in order to avenge her father's crime, killed her younger brother, or, according to others, her own son by Clymenus, and placed his flesh prepared in a dish before her father. She herself was thereupon changed into a bird, and Clymenus hanged himself. Menephron, another Arcadian, is said to have lived incestuously with his mother Blias and his daughter Cyllene (Ov. *Met.* 7.386). Phineus, the blind soothsayer, was said by some to have been a king in Arcadia. He had been blinded because he had blinded his own sons and half-buried them in the earth because of their alleged attempted seduction of his deceitful second wife Idaea. The genesis of the feud between the Dioscuri and Idas and Lynceus took place in Arcadia, when the four stole a herd of oxen from Arcadia. Idas divided up the booty by cutting a bull into four parts; he declared that whichever of them should first succeed in eating his share should receive half the oxen and the second should have the other half. Idas, thereupon, not only ate his own quarter but devoured that of his brother, in addition, and then drove the whole herd to his home in Messenia (Pind. *Nem.* 10.60; Apollod. 3.11.2).

AREIOPAGUS   (See ATHENS)

ARENE   was a town mentioned by Homer (*Il.* 2.591, 11.723) as belonging to the dominions of Nestor and situated near the spot where the Minyeius flows into the sea. In the Homeric *Hymn to Apollo* (423) it appears in conjunction with other towns on the western coast of Peloponnesus. According to Pausanias (4.2.4,3.7), it was built by Aphareus, who called it after Arene, both his wife and half-sister. It was commonly supposed in later times that Arene occupied the site of Samicum in Triphylia, near the mouth of the Anigrus, which was believed to be the same as the Minyeius (Strab. 8.3.19; Paus. 5.6.2).

ARGEIA   (See ARGOLIS)

ARGISSA   in Homer (*Il.* 2.738) was a town in Pelasgiotis in Thessaly on the Peneius River and near Larissa. Later called Argura, the distance between this place and Larissa was so small as to explain the remark of one commentator that the Argissa of Homer was the same as Larissa. The site of ancient Argissa has been placed by some at the mound at a little distance from Larissa, extending 1.5 km from east to west (Strab. 9.5.19). It was on the left bank of the Peneius about 7 km from Atrax. Polypoetes, a son of Peirithous and Hippodameia, was one of the Lapiths, who joined the Greeks in the Trojan War, commanding the men of Argissa, Gyrtone, Orthe, Elone, and Oloosson (Hom. *Il.* 2.738). At the funeral games of Patroclus he gained the victory in throwing the iron ball (*Il.* 23.836). After the fall of Troy, Polypoetes and Leonteus are said to have founded the town of Aspendus in Pamphylia.

ARGOLIS (ARGOLIS).   The territory of Argos was called Argolis by Herodotus (1.82) but more frequently Argeia by other Greek writers (Thuc. 5.75; Strab. 8.6.8). By these words the Greek writers signified only the territory of the city of Argos, which was bounded on the north by the territories of Phlius, Cleonae, and Corinth; on the west by that of Epidaurus; on the south by the Argolic Gulf and Cynuria; and on the east by Arcadia.

The Argeia, or Argolis proper, extended from north to south from the frontiers of Phlius and Cleonae to the frontiers of Cynuria, in direct distance about 40 km. It was separated from Arcadia on the west by Mounts Artemisium and Parthenium and from the territory of Epidaurus on the east by Mount Arachnaeum. Lessa was a town on the borders of Epidauria (Paus. 2.26.1), and from this town to the border of Arcadia the direct distance was about 47 km. The plain in which the city of Argos is situated is one of the largest plains in Peloponnesus, being from 10 to 20 km in length and from 7 to 8 km in width. It is shut in on three sides by mountains and only open on the fourth to the sea. This plain was very fertile in antiquity and was famous for its excellent horses. The southwest part of the plain has a large number of springs, which make it quite marshy. It was here that the marsh of Lerna and the fathomless Alcyonian pool lay, where Heracles is said to have conquered the Hydra. It has been well observed by a modern writer that the victory of Heracles over this fifty-headed water-snake may be understood as a successful attempt by the ancient rulers of the Argive plain to bring its marshy extremity into cultivation by draining its sources and embanking its streams.

The two chief rivers in the plain of Argos are the Inachus and the Erasinus. The Inachus rises in Mount Artemisium on the borders of Arcadia. It flows east of the city of Argos into the Argolic Gulf. The Erasinus is the only river in the plain of Argos that flows during the whole year. It issues from rocks at the foot of Mount Chaon to the southwest of Argos in several large streams, forming a river of considerable size that flows directly across the plain into the Argolic Gulf.

In the time of the Peloponnesian War, the whole of Argeia was subject to Argos, but it originally contained several independent cities. Of these the most important were Mycenae and Tiryns, which in the heroic days were more celebrated than Argos itself. Argos is situated about 6 km from the sea. Mycenae is about 15 km north of Argos; and Tiryns about 10 km southeast of Argos. Nauplia, the port of Argos, is about 3 km beyond Tiryns.

Many roads converged at Argos. One narrow pass through Mount Treton led to Nemea. It was the haunt of the Nemean lion later slain by Heracles. Another ascended Mount Artemisium, on whose summit was the temple of Artemis near the sources of the Inachus. Another led to Tegea and Sparta, and another branched from the Tegean road to reach Apobathmi (the landing place of Danaus) and south to the plain of Thyrea. Still another road led to Nauplia, the harbor of Argos. On this road was a small village called Temenium, which derived its name from the Doric hero Temenus, who was said to be buried there. There was also, of course, a road leading directly from Argos to the Heraion, or temple of Hera.

The mythological history of Argolis, the territory, is discussed in conjunction with that of Argos, the city, following.

ARGOS (ARGOS)   was situated about 6 km from the sea in the Argolid plain. Its citadel, called Larisa or Larissa, the Pelasgic name for a citadel (Paus. 2.24.1; Strab. 8.6.7) was most impressive, being built on an isolated mountain of 275 meters in height. A little to the east of the town flowed the river Charadrus, a tributary of the Inachus.

According to the general testimony of antiquity, Argos was the most ancient city of Greece. It was originally inhabited by Pelasgians and is said to have been built by the Pelasgic chief Inachus. Inachus was a river-god, described as a son of Oceanus and Tethys. By a Melian nymph or by his sister Argeia he became the father of Phoroneus and Aegialeus, to whom others add Io, Argus Panoptes, and Phegeus (Apollod. 2.1.1,3). Inachus is the most ancient god or hero of Argos. Inachus the river is said to have received its name from the fact that Inachus the man threw himself into it when Zeus, enraged at the reproaches that Inachus made on account of the treatment of Io, sent a Fury to pursue him. The river had before him borne the name of Carmanor or Haliacmon; and as Inachus was the first ruler and priest at Argos, the country is frequently called the land of Inachus (Eurip. *Orest.* 932). In the dispute between Poseidon and Hera over the possession of Argos, Inachus decided in favor of Hera, and consequently it was said that Poseidon deprived him and the two other judges, the river-gods Asterion and Cephissus, of their water, so that they became dry except in rainy seasons (Paus. 2.15.5; Apollod. 2.1.4). The ancients themselves made several attempts to explain the stories about Inachus. Sometimes they looked upon him as a native of Argos who, after the flood of Deucalion, led the Argives from the mountains into the plains and confined the waters within their proper channels. At other times they regarded him as an immigrant who had come across the sea as the leader of an Egyptian or Libyan colony and had united the Pelasgians, whom he found scattered on the banks of the Inachus.

Others describe Phoroneus, the son of Inachus, as the founder of Argos (Paus. 2.15.5). Phoroneus is said to have been the first to offer sacrifices to Hera at Argos and to unite the people, who until then had lived in scattered habitations, into a city that was called after him the City of Phoroneus (Paus. 2.15.5). He is further said to have

discovered the use of fire (Paus. 2.19.5). His tomb was shown at Argos, where offerings were brought to him as a hero (2.20.3).

Phoroneus had a son, Apis, and a daughter, Niobe. Apis became king of Argos, established a tyrannical government, and renamed the Peloponnesus Apia after himself; but he was killed in a conspiracy headed by Thelxion, his son, and Telchin, another relative (Apollod. 1.7.6, 2.1.1). He is said, after his death, to have been worshipped as a god under the name Serapis; and this statement shows that Egyptian myths are intermingled with the story of Apis. This confusion is still more manifest in the tradition that Apis gave up his kingdom of Argos and went to Egypt, where he reigned for several years afterward (August. *De Civ. Dei* 18.5). Apis is spoken of as one of the earliest lawgivers among the Greeks. Meanwhile, Niobe was impregnated by Zeus and became the mother of Argus, the third (or fourth) king of Argos. It is from Argus that the country afterward was called Argolis and all Peloponnesus derived the name of Argos (Paus. 2.16.1). By Euadne, or by Peitho, he became the father of Iasus, Peiranthus (or Peiras), Epidaurus, Criasus, and Tiryns. Pausanias mentions only two sons— Peirasus (or Peiranthus or Peiras) and Phorbas.

Phorbas was succeeded by his son Triopas, and Triopas was the father of Iasus and Agenor. Iasus was king, and his famous daughter was Io (although she is commonly described as a daughter of Inachus, the founder of the worship of Hera at Argos). In any case, the chronological tables of the priestesses of Hera at Argos placed Io at the head of the list of priestesses under the name of Callirrhoe or Callithyia. Zeus had her as a mistress, but on account of Hera's jealousy he metamorphosed Io into a white cow. Hera knew this and asked for the cow as a present from Zeus. She then placed the cow under the guard of the hundred-eyed giant Argus Panoptes, who tied her to an olive tree in the grove of Hera at Mycenae. But Hermes was commissioned by Zeus to deliver Io and carry her off. Hermes lulled Argus to sleep with flute music, slew him with a stone, and then decapitated him. Hera then sent a gadfly that tormented Io and pursued her through the whole earth, until at length she found rest on the banks of the Nile (Apollod. 2.1.2). A peculiar and mournful festival was celebrated in honor of Io at Argos. There are other places besides Argos where we find legends of Io, but they are probably importations from Argos, either transplanted with the worship of Hera or through colonies sent by Argos. The Greeks residing in Egypt maintained that Io had been in Egypt, where she was said to have given birth to Epaphus and to have introduced the worship of Isis. Epaphus became the founder of a family from which sprang Danaus, who subsequently returned to Argos. This part of the story seems to have arisen from certain resemblances of religious notions that subsequently even gave rise to the identification of Io and Isis. Herodotus (1.1, 2.41) tells us that Isis was represented like the Greek Io in the form of a woman with cow's horns. The ancients believed Io to be the moon, and there is a tradition that the Argives called the moon Io.

Concerning the brothers of Iasus, not a great deal is known. Pelasgus was the mythical ancestor of the Pelasgians, the earliest inhabitants of Greece who established the worship of the Dodonaean Zeus, Hephaestus, the Cabeiri, and other divinities that belong to the earliest inhabitants of the country. In Argos, Pelasgus, son of Triopas by Sois, was said to have founded the city of Argos, to have taught the people agriculture, and to have received Demeter on her wanderings at Argos, where his tomb was shown in later times (Paus. 1.14.2, 2.22.2). Xanthus, son of Triopas by Oreasis, was a king of the Pelasgians and afterward settled in the island of Lesbos (Diod. 5.81; Callim. *Hymn. in Del.* 41).

Agenor, the other son, had no particular distinction except that the rule of Argos passed to his son Crotopus next after Iasus, Agenor's brother. Crotopus was the father of Sthenelas and a daughter, Psamathe. Psamathe became by Apollo the mother of Linus, the personification of a dirge or lamentation. When Psamathe had given birth to Linus, she exposed the child out of fear of her father. He was found by shepherds who brought him up, but the child was afterward torn to pieces by dogs. Psamathe's grief at the occurrence betrayed her misfortune to her father, who condemned her to death. Apollo, in his indignation at the father's cruelty, visited Argos with a plague; when his oracle was consulted about the means of terminating the plague, he answered that the Argives must propitiate Psamathe and Linus. This was attempted by means of sacrifices, and matrons and virgins sang dirges called *linae*. The pestilence did not cease until Crotopus quitted Argos and settled at Tripodiscus in Megaris (Paus. 1.43.9). Of the son, Sthenelas, nothing is known except that the rule of Argos passed from him next to his son, Gelanor.

Meanwhile, the line from Io continued. Her son Epaphus in Egypt married Memphis, and their daughters were Lysianassa and Libya. By Poseidon Libya became the mother of Agenor, Lelex, and Belus. Agenor went to Phoenicia to start the line that produced Cadmus; Lelex was the ancestor of the Leleges, and Belus by Anchinoe became the father of Aegyptus and Danaus. Belus had given Aegyptus the land of Arabia and Danaus that of Libya. Aegyptus became the father of fifty sons and Danaus of fifty daughters. Danaus had reason to believe that the sons of his brother were plotting against him, and either fear or the advice of an oracle induced him to build a large ship and to embark with his daughters. They stopped first at Rhodes and then came to Peloponnesus,

landing at a place near Lerna, which was afterward called from this event Apobathmi (Paus. 2.38.4). At Argos a dispute arose between Danaus and Gelanor, the reigning monarch, about the government. After many discussions the people deferred the resolution of the dispute until the next day. At its dawn, a wolf rushed among the cattle and killed one of the oxen. This occurrence was to the Argives an omen which seemed to announce to them how the dispute should terminate, and Danaus was accordingly made king of Argos. Out of gratitude he now built a sanctuary of Apollo Lycius, who, as be believed, had sent the wolf (Paus. 2.19.3). Danaus also erected wooden statues of Zeus and Artemis and dedicated his shield in the sanctuary of Hera (Paus. 2.19.6). He is further said to have built the acropolis of Argos and to have provided the place with water by digging wells (Strab. 8.6.9). The sons of Aegyptus in the meantime had followed their uncle to Argos; they assured him of their peaceful sentiments and sued for the hands of his daughters. Danaus still mistrusted them and remembered the cause of his flight from his country; however, he gave his daughters (the Danaids) to his nephews by lot. All the brides with the exception of Hypermnestra murdered their husbands by the command of their father. In after times the Argives were called Danai. Whether Danaus died a natural death, or whether he was killed by Lynceus, his only surviving son-in-law, is a point on which the various traditions are not agreed, but he is said to have been buried at Argos, and his tomb in the agora of Argos was shown there as late as the time of Pausanias (2.20.4; Strab. 8.6.9).

Hypermnestra was punished by her father with imprisonment but was afterward restored to her husband. The Danaids buried the corpses of their victims and were purified of the crime by Hermes and Athena at the command of Zeus. Danaus afterwards found it understandably difficult to obtain husbands for his daughters, and so he invited men to public contests, in which his daughters were given as prizes to the victors (Pind. *Pyth.* 9.117). Notwithstanding their purification mentioned in earlier writers, later poets relate that the Danaids were punished for their crimes in Hades by being forever compelled to pour water into a vessel full of holes (Ov. *Met.* 4.462, *Her.* 14). Others relate that Danaus or the Danaids provided Argos with water and for this reason certain of the Danaids were worshipped at Argos as divinities; and this may possibly be the foundation of the story about the punishment of the Danaids. Ovid calls them by the name Belides from their grandfather Belus; and Herodotus (2.171), following the tales of the Egyptians, says that they brought the mysteries of Demeter Thesmophoros from Egypt to Peloponnesus and that the Pelasgian women there learned the mysteries from them.

Lynceus succeeded Danaus on the throne of Argos (Apollod. 2.1.5, 2.1; Paus. 2.16.1). The cause of Hypermnestra's sparing Lynceus is not the same in all accounts. It is said that she assisted her husband in his escape from the vengeance of Danaus, that he fled to Lyrceia (Lynceia), and that from there he gave a sign with a torch that he had safely arrived. Hypermnestra returned the sign from the citadel of Argos, and in commemoration of this event the Argives celebrated a festival with torches every year (Paus. 2.25.4). When Lynceus received the news of the death of Danaus from his son Abas, Lynceus gave to Abas the shield of Danaus, which had been dedicated in the temple of Hera, and instituted games in honor of Hera, in which the victor received a shield as his prize. According to some, Lynceus slew Danaus and all the sisters of Hypermnestra in revenge for his brothers. Lynceus and his wife were revered at Argos as heroes and had a common sanctuary. Their tomb was shown there not far from the altar of Zeus Phyxius (Paus. 2.21.2) and their statues stood in the temple at Delphi as a present from the Argives (Paus. 10.10.5).

Abas, the son of Lynceus and Hypermnestra, then became the twelfth king of Argos. He married Ocaleia, who bore him twin sons, Acrisius and Proetus. He is described as a successful conqueror and as the founder of the town of Abae in Phocis (Paus. 10.35.1) and of the Pelasgic Argos in Thessaly (Strab. 9.5.6). The fame of his warlike spirit was so great that even after his death, when the people whom he had subdued revolted, they were put to flight by the simple act of showing them his shield (Virg. *Aen.* 3.286). It was from this Abas that the kings of Argos were called by the patronymic Abantiads.

Acrisius, son of Abas, is said to have quarrelled with his twin, Proetus, even in the womb. When Abas died and Acrisius had grown up, he expelled Proetus from his inheritance; but, supported by his father-in-law, Iobates the Lycian, Proetus returned. Acrisius was compelled to share his kingdom with his brother by giving up Tiryns to him, while he retained Argos for himself. An oracle had declared that Danae, the daughter of Acrisius, would give birth to a son who would kill his grandfather. For this reason Acrisius kept Danae shut up in a subterranean apartment or a brazen tower. But here, notwithstanding the precautions of her father, she became mother of Perseus by Zeus, who visited her in the form of a shower of gold. Perseus is sometimes referred to by the surname Inachis because he was born at Argos, the city of Inachus. Acrisius ordered mother and child to be exposed on the sea in a chest; but the chest floated to the island of Seriphos, where both were rescued by Dictys, the brother of King Polydectes (Apollod. 2.2.1, 4.1). The oracle was subsequently fulfilled, and Perseus succeeded to the throne of Argos.

After Proetus had acquired Tiryns, along with the Heraion, Midea, and the coast of Argolis (Paus. 2.16.2), he had Tiryns fortified by the Cyclopes. The Cyclopes were regarded as skillful architects from a Thracian tribe that derived its name from a King Cyclops. They were expelled from their homes in Thrace and went to the Curetes (Crete) and to Lycia. From there they followed Proetus back to Argos to protect him, and they built gigantic walls against Acrisius. The grand fortifications of Argos, Tiryns, and Mycenae were in later times regarded as their works (Apollod. 2.1.2; Strab. 8.6.11). Such walls, commonly known as Cyclopean walls, still exist in various parts of Greece and Italy and consist of unhewn, polygonal stones, which are sometimes sixty or ninety meters in breadth. Proetus was married to Anteia, the daughter of his Lycian protector Iobates. The hero Bellerophon, in order to be purified from murder, fled to Proetus, and Anteia fell in love with him. When her offers were rejected by him, she accused him of having tried to seduce her and insisted that he be put to death. Proetus, unwilling to kill with his own hands, sent him to Iobates in Lycia with a sealed letter that requested that the young hero be killed. Iobates accordingly sent him on a mission that was certain to be fatal—slaying the Chimaera.

Megapenthes was the son of Proetus. After Perseus had accidentally slain Acrisius, his grandfather, he was ashamed because of the gossip about the homicide, and on his return to Argos, he induced Megapenthes to exchange kingdoms with him. Megapenthes thus became king of Argos and Perseus of Tiryns. There was a tradition that Megapenthes later killed Perseus. The son of Megapenthes was Argeus, and Argeus was the father of Anaxagoras. It was during the reign of Anaxagoras that the women of the kingdom were seized with madness and roamed about the country in a frantic state. Melampus, the famous seer, was eventually summoned and was able to cure the women on condition that he and his brother Bias should receive an equal share with Anaxagoras in the kingdom of Argos (Paus. 2.18.4; Diod. 4.68). Thus a parallel rule was established. The Biantidae continued to rule in Argos for four generations, but ended with Cyanippus, who died childless. The rule of the descendants of Melampus continued for six generations, ending with Amphilochus, son of Alcmaeon, when he migrated to Amphilochia on the Ambracian Gulf.

The story of the two royal houses begun by Bias and Melampus is a tempestuous one, with one or another family member involved in the greatest adventures of the heroic age. Melampus' son was Antiphates, and Antiphates' son was Oicles, or Oicleus. Oicles accompanied Heracles on his expedition against Laomedon of Troy and was slain in battle there (Apollod. 2.6.4; Diod. 4.32). According to others, he returned home from the expedition and dwelt in Arcadia, where he was visited by his grandson Alcmaeon, and where in later times his tomb was shown (Apollod. 3.7.5; Paus. 8.36.6). His son was Amphiaraus. The son of Bias was Talaus. He was married to Lysimache and was father of Adrastus, Parthenopaeus, Pronax, Mecisteus, Aristomachus, and Eriphyle. He occurs among the Argonauts (Apollon. Rhod. 1.118), and his tomb was shown at Argos (Paus. 2.21.2). Adrastus for a time reigned at Argos in common with Amphiaraus, his cousin, but after a feud broke out between them, Adrastus fled to Sicyon, where he succeeded Polybus on the throne. Afterward, however, Adrastus became reconciled to Amphiaraus, gave him his sister Eriphyle in marriage, and returned to his kingdom of Argos. During the time he reigned there, it happened that Tydeus of Calydon and Polyneices of Thebes, both fugitives from their native countries, met at Argos near the palace of Adrastus and exchanged first words and then blows. On hearing the noise, Adrastus came out and separated the combatants, in whom he immediately recognized the two men that had been promised him by an oracle as the future husbands of two of his daughters; for one bore on his shield the figure of a boar, and the other that of a lion, the two creatures the oracle had stated that his daughters would marry. Adrastus thereupon gave his daughter Deiphyle to Tydeus and his daughter Argeia to Polyneices. At the same time he promised to lead each of these princes back to his own country. Adrastus now prepared for war against Thebes.

Meanwhile, Amphiaraus and Eriphyle had produced four children—Alcmaeon, Amphilochus, Eurydice, and Demonassa. On marrying Eriphyle, Amphiaraus had sworn that he would abide by her decision on any point of disagreement with Adrastus. When, therefore, Adrastus called on him to join the expedition of the Seven against Thebes, Amphiaraus, although he foresaw its unfortunate outcome and at first refused to take any part of it, was nevertheless persuaded by his wife to join his friends. Eriphyle had been enticed to induce her husband by the famous necklace of Harmonia, which Polyneices had given her. As he left Argos, Amphiaraus enjoined his sons to avenge his death on their heartless mother (Apollod. 3.6.2; Diod. 4.65; Hom. *Od.* 15.247). On their way to Thebes the heroes instituted the Nemean games. During the war against Thebes, Amphiaraus fought bravely but still could not suppress his anger at the whole undertaking. When Adrastus and Amphiaraus were the only heroes who survived, the latter was pursued by Periclymenus and fled toward the river Ismenus. Here, before he was overtaken by his enemy, the earth opened and swallowed up Amphiaraus together with his chariot and his charioteer, Baton. Zeus then made him immortal (Pind. *Nem.* 9.57, *Ol.* 6.21). Henceforth Amphiaraus was worshipped as a hero, first at Oropus and afterward in all Greece (Paus. 1.34.2; Liv. 45.27). He had a sanctuary at Argos as did Baton; both were represented on the chest of Cypselus and both had statues, side by side at Delphi, which had been dedicated by the Argives.

Adrastus was the only survivor of the Seven against Thebes, and he lived to organize the successful war of the Epigoni, or sons of the original seven. He died at Megara on his way home from Thebes. He was worshipped as a hero in several parts of Greece.

When the Epigoni prepared for a second expedition against Thebes to avenge the deaths of their fathers, the oracle promised them success and victory if they chose Alcmaeon as their leader. He was at first reluctant to undertake the command since he had not yet taken vengeance on his mother, as he had promised his father. But she, who had now received from Thersander, the son of Polyneices, the robe (*peplos*) of Harmonia in addition to the necklace, induced him to join the expedition. Alcmaeon distinguished himself greatly in the war. When, after the fall of Thebes, he learned the reason for which his mother had urged him to take part in the expedition, he followed the advice of an oracle of Apollo and slew her. For this deed he became mad and was haunted by the Erinyes. He eventually went to Phegeus in Psophis, and, being purified by him, he married his daughter Alphesiboea, to whom he gave the necklace and robe of Harmonia. But the country in which he now resided was visited by a famine in consequence of his being the murderer of his mother. The oracle advised him to go to a country that had been formed subsequent to the murder and was therefore under no curse. The country thus pointed out was a tract of land recently formed at the mouth of the river Achelous. When he reached the mouth of the Achelous, the river-god gave him his daughter Callirrhoe in marriage. Callirrhoe desired to possess the necklace and robe of Harmonia, and Alcmaeon, to gratify her wish, went to Psophis to get them from Phegeus, under the pretext that he intended to dedicate them at Delphi in order to be freed from his madness. Phegeus complied with his request, but when he heard that the treasures had been fetched for Callirrhoe, he sent his sons Temenus and Axion in pursuit. They killed Alcmaeon at Delphi, and Callirrhoe's sons in turn took bloody vengeance on them. Alcmaeon after his death was worshipped as a hero. He was represented in a statue at Delphi and on the chest of Cypselus (Paus. 10.10.4, 5.17.7).

Amphilochus, Alcmaeon's brother, was according to some traditions one of the Epigoni and also a participant in the murder of Eriphyle. He is mentioned as one of the suitors of Helen and as having taken part in the Trojan War. On the return from the war he together with Mopsus, who like himself was a seer, founded the town of Mallos in Cilicia. From here he proceeded to his native place, Argos. But he was not satisfied with the state of affairs there and returned to Mallos. When Mopsus refused to allow him any share in the government of their common colony, the two seers fought a single combat in which both were killed. Their tombs, which were placed in such a manner that the one could not be seen from the other, existed as late as the time of Strabo near Mount Margasa, not far from Pyramus (Strab. 14.5.15). Thucydides (2.68) claims that Amphilochus returned from Troy to Argos, but being dissatisfied there, he emigrated and founded Argos Amphilochium on the Ambracian Gulf. It is more likely that this was Amphilochus, his nephew, son of Alcmaeon (Apollod. 3.7.7). In any case, this migration ended the rule of the Amythaonidae (Bias and Melampus and their descendants) in Argos, since the Biantid line had proceeded from Adrastus to Aegialeus and then to Cyanippus, who died without issue.

The rule begun by Danaus and reaching down to Anaxagoras, when Melampus and Bias intervened, fared only slightly better. Continuing to rule in conjunction with the Amythaonidae, the Danaid rule went next to Alector, son of Anaxagoras. Alector had no particular distinction except that he did advise Polyneices about the manner in which Amphiaraus might be compelled to take part in the expedition against Thebes, i.e., by bribing Eriphyle with the fatal necklace of Harmonia. Others say it was Iphis, the son of Alector, who advised Polyneices. The children of Iphis were Laodice, Eteocles, and Euadne, who married Capaneus, son of Hipponous and Laodice. Capaneus was one of the Seven against Thebes, and because of his blasphemy, Zeus struck him with lightning while trying to scale a wall during the siege. Capaneus is one of those heroes whom Asclepius was believed to have called back to life (Apollod. 3.10.3). At Delphi there was a statue of Capaneus dedicated by the Argives (Paus. 10.10.3).

Sthenelus, both grandson and great-grandson of Iphis, next came to the throne of Argos. He was one of the Epigoni and commanded the Argives under Diomedes in the Trojan War, being the faithful friend and companion of Diomedes (Hom. *Il.* 2.564, 4.367, 23.511). He was one of the Greeks concealed in the wooden horse, and at the distribution of the booty, he was said to have received an image of a three-eyed Zeus, which was in aftertimes shown at Argos (Paus. 2.24.3, 8.46.2). His own statue and tomb also were believed to exist at Argos (2.20.5). His son, Cylarabes, next succeeded to the throne, but the line begun by Danaus ended with him because he died without an heir.

Before going on with what happened next in the succession of kings, it is necessary to pause and introduce the question of Diomedes, the Trojan War hero and later colonizer, and his somewhat ambiguous role in the history of Argos. He was the son of Tydeus and Deiphyle, daughter of Adrastus. Tydeus had been one of the Seven against Thebes and was killed during the expedition. Upon reaching adulthood, Diomedes married Aegialeia, daughter of Adrastus (or more likely daughter of

Aegeialeus, the son of Adrastus). He then marched with the Epigoni and razed Thebes. When he returned to Argos, he went at once with Alcmaeon, leader of the Epigoni, to Calydon to avenge his grandfather Oeneus on the sons of his brother Agrius, who had usurped the throne. They restored Oeneus to power but had to assign the kingdom to Andraemon, Oeneus' son-in-law, since Oeneus was too old to rule. Diomedes took his grandfather with him to Argos, where Oeneus died and was buried at Oenoe. Diomedes had been a suitor of Helen and was required by the oath taken of all her suitors to join the Trojan War. With Sthenelus and Euryalus he led eighty ships from Argos, Tiryns, Hermione, Asine, Troezen, Eione, Epidaurus, Aegina and Mases (Hom. *Il.* 2.559). In the army of the Greeks before Troy, Diomedes was, next to Achilles, the bravest among the heroes; and, like Achilles and Odysseus, he enjoyed the special protection of Athena, who assisted him in special crises (5.826, 6.98, etc.). With Odysseus he carried away the Palladium, which guaranteed the fall of Ilium. According to some, he carried the Palladium with him to Argos, where it remained until Ergiaeus, one of his descendants, took it away with the assistance of the Laconian Leagrus, who conveyed it to Sparta (Plut. *Quaest. Gr.* 48). On his return from Troy, he had to suffer much from the enmity of Aphrodite, but Athena still continued to protect him. Arriving in Argos, he met with an evil reception that had been prepared for him by Aphrodite: his wife Aegialeia was living in adultery with Cometes at the instigation of Nauplius of Euboea (in revenge for Diomedes' role in the treacherous slaying of Palamedes, Nauplius' son). In any case, he assumed a role in governmental affairs, and there is doubt about what this role was. Although he was Adrastus' son-in-law (or grandson-in-law), he had less claim to the throne than Cyanippus, who was in direct line of descent through his father Aegialeus, Adrastus' son, who had been killed in the campaign of the Epigoni. Diomedes and Euryalus, cousins to Cyanippus, acted more or less as regents to the boy king. When the king died childless, the throne reverted to the older Argive family, and Sthenelus' son Cylarabes became full monarch, integrating the parts of the kingdom previously held by the descendants of Bias and Melampus. Because of the adulterous affair of his wife, Diomedes left Argos or was expelled and went to Aetolia and finally to Italy, where he married the daughter of Daunus, king of Apulia, and founded the city of Argyripa. The worship and service of gods and heroes was spread by Diomedes far and wide; in and near Argos he caused temples of Athena to be built (Paus. 2.24.2).

There is a story that immediately after the war of the Epigoni and during Diomedes' absence in Aetolia, Agamemnon took possession of Argos; but when the expedition against Troy was resolved upon, Agamemnon from fear invited Diomedes and Alcmaeon back to Argos and asked them to take part in the projected expedition. Diomedes alone accepted the proposal and thus recovered Argos (Strab. 10.2.25; Apollod. 1.8.6).

Orestes, son of Agamemnon and Clytemnestra, next entered the line of kings. He was to have been killed when Agamemnon was assassinated, but he was spirited away and saved. When he attained manhood, he returned to avenge his father, coming first to Argos. After he killed Clytemnestra and Aegisthus and received expiation, he then returned and took possession of his father's kingdom at Mycenae. Later when Cylarabes of Argos died without leaving an heir, Orestes also became king of Argos. He married Hermione, daughter of Menelaus and Helen, and became by her the father of Tisamenus.

Tisamenus was king for quite a short time for he was deprived of his kingdom when the Heracleidae invaded Peloponnesus (Apollod. 2.8.2). He was slain in a battle against the Heracleidae, and his tomb was afterward shown at Helice, from where at a later time his remains were removed to Sparta by command of an oracle (Paus. 7.1.8).

Temenus, a son of Aristomachus and one of the Heracleidae, was the father of Ceisus, Cerynes, Phalces, Agraeus, and Hyrnetho. He was one of the leaders of the Heracleidae into Peloponnesus, and, after the conquest of the peninsula he received Argos as his share (Apollod. 2.8.4). Temenus openly preferred Deiphontes, son of Antimachus, over his own sons, both as a general in war and as an advisor. Even before this he had made him his son-in-law by marrying him to Hyrnetho, his favorite daughter. He was accordingly suspected of intending to place Deiphontes on the throne and for this reason his sons plotted against him. The tomb of Temenus was shown at Temenium near Lerna (Paus. 2.38.1). His descendants, the Temenidae, being expelled from Argos, are said to have founded the kingdom of Macedonia, whence the kings of Macedonia called themselves Temenidae (Herod. 8.138; Thuc. 2.99).

From the earliest times, says Pausanias (2.19.2), the Argives loved freedom and self-government and thus limited the authority of their kings so that to Medon, son of Ceisus, and to his descendants was left a kingdom that was such only in name. Meltas, the son of Lacedas, the tenth descendant of Medon, was condemned by the people and deposed altogether from the kingship. Thus ended the Heraclid line of kings and the whole succession of dynasties of ancient Argos.

Even after the Doric conquest, Argos appears as the first state in Peloponnesus, Sparta being second, and Messene third. Herodotus (1.82) states that in ancient times the whole eastern coast of Peloponnesus down to Cape Malea, including Cythera and the other islands, belonged to Argos, the superiority of which is also indicated by the legend, which makes Temenus the eldest of the three Heracleidae. The power of Argos, however, was not derived exclusively from her own territory but also from her role as head of a league of several other important Doric cities. Cleonae, Phlius, Sicyon, Epidaurus, Troezen, Hermione, and Aegina were all members of this league, which, while organized for religious purposes, really gave Argos a political advantage. This league, like others of the same kind, was called an Amphictyonia (Paus. 4.5.2); and its patron god was Apollo Pythaeus. There was a temple to this god in each of the confederated cities, while his most holy sanctuary was on the Larissa, or acropolis of Argos. This religious supremacy continued till a later time; and in the Peloponnesian War the Argives still claimed offerings from the confederate states to the temple of Apollo Pythaeus on the Larissa (Thuc. 5.53).

Few towns in Greece paid more attention to the worship of the gods than Argos. Hera was the deity whom they revered above all others. This goddess was an Achaean rather than a Dorian divinity and appears in the *Iliad* as the guardian deity of the Argives; but her worship was adopted by the Dorian conquerors and was celebrated for a very long time.

The chief temple of this goddess, called the Heraion, was situated between Argos and Mycenae. Its remains were discovered for the first time in 1831 by General Gordon, the commander of the Greek forces in Peloponnesus. Its ruins are about 10 km from Argos. The hill on which the ruins are situated is an irregular triangular platform with its apex pointing towards Mount Euboea and its base towards Argos.

In the heroic age, when Mycenae was the chief city in the Argeia, the inhabitants of this city probably had the management of the temple. The vestibule of the temple contained ancient statues of the Charites, the bed of Hera, and a shield which Menelaus had taken at Troy from Euphorbus. (Pythagoras confirmed in his own mind his belief that he had been Euphorbus in a previous life when he recognized the shield in the temple.) The sitting colossal statue of Hera in this temple, made of gold and ivory, was the work of Polycletus. She wore a crown on her head adorned with the Charites and Horae; in one hand she held a pomegranate and in the other a scepter headed with a cuckoo (Paus. 2.17.4; Stat. *Theb.* 1.383). In the historical age the temple belonged to the Argives, who had the exclusive management of its affairs. The high priestess of the temple held her office for life; and the Argives counted their years by the date of her office (Thuc. 2.2). Once in four years, probably in the second year of every Olympiad, there was a magnificent procession from Argos to this temple, in which almost the whole population of the city took part. The priestess rode in a chariot drawn by two white oxen (Herod. 1.31; Cic.

Tusc. 1.47). A famous story is told of Cydippe, one of these priestesses, and her sons Biton and Cleobis. During the festival of Hera, when Cydippe had to ride to the temple in a chariot and when the oxen did not arrive in time, the two sons dragged the chariot with their mother a distance of 8 km to the temple. The priestess, moved by the filial love of her sons, prayed to the goddess to grant them what was best for mortals. After the solemnities of the festival were over, the two brothers went to sleep in the temple and never rose again. The Argives made statues of the brothers and sent them to Delphi, where they still may be seen. Pausanias (2.20.3) saw a relief in stone at Argos representing Cleobis and Biton drawing the chariot with their mother.

Another priestess, Admete, daughter of Eurystheus and Antimache, was reported to have fled with the image of the goddess to Samos. Pirates were engaged by the Argives to fetch the image back, but the enterprise did not succeed because the ship, when laden with the image, could not be made to move. The men took the image back to the coast of Samos and sailed away. When the Samians found it, they tied it to a tree, but Admete purified it and restored it to the temple of Samos. This story seems to be an invention of the Argives, by which they intended to prove that the worship of Hera in their place was older than in Samos.

In the city itself there were also two temples of Hera, one of Hera Acraea on the ascent to the acropolis (Paus. 2.24.1) and the other of Hera Antheia in the lower part of the city (Paus. 2.22.1). Before the temple of Hera Antheia (Blooming or Friend of Flowers) was a mound under which the women were buried who had come with Dionysus from the Aegean islands and had fallen in a contest with the Argives and Perseus. Hera also derived a surname from the city of Argos and was thus referred to as Hera Argeia (Paus. 3.13.8).

But the temple of Apollo Lyceius is described by Pausanias (2.19.3) as by far the most celebrated of all the temples in Argos. Tradition ascribed its foundation to Danaus. It stood on one side of the agora (Thuc. 5.47), which Sophocles therefore calls "the Lyceian agora of the wolf-slaying god" (Soph. *Elect.* 6). There was also a temple of Apollo Pythaeus on the acropolis, which, as we have already seen, was a common sanctuary for the Dorian states belonging to the ancient Argive confederacy (Paus. 2.24.1; Thuc. 5.53). The statue in this temple was of bronze and was called Apollo Deiradiotes because the citadel was called Deiras (Ridge).

Demeter was worshipped here, and her worship consisted in great measure of orgiastic mysteries. She had a temple between Argos and Mycenae under the name of Demeter Mysia, said to have been derived from an Argive Mysius, who received her kindly during her wanderings and built a sanctuary to her (Paus. 2.18.3,35.4). She also

had a temple at Argos under the name of Demeter Pelasga or Pelasgis (Pelasgian Woman or Goddess). This surname was probably derived from Pelasgus, the son of Triopas, who had founded her sanctuary (Paus. 2.22.2).

Dionysus, after proving to the Thebans that he was the god of wine, went to Argos. As the people there also refused to acknowledge him, he made the women mad to such a degree that they killed their own babies and devoured their flesh (Apollod. 3.5.2). According to another statement, Dionysus with a host of women came from the islands of the Aegean to Argos, but was conquered by Perseus, who slew many of the women (Paus. 2.20.4,22.1). Afterwards, however, Dionysus and Perseus became reconciled, and the Argives adopted the worship of the god and built temples to him. One of these was called the temple of Dionysus Cresius because the god was believed to have buried on that spot Ariadne, his beloved, who was a Cretan (Paus. 2.23.8).

Zeus Mechaneus (Skilled in Inventing) was worshipped at Argos (Paus. 2.22.2). Zeus Meilichius (God Who Can Be Propitiated or Gracious One) was used as a surname of Zeus seen as the protector of those who honored him with propitiatory sacrifices. Altars were erected to Zeus Meilichius at Argos (Paus. 2.20.1; Plut. *De Cohib. Ir.* 9). Zeus Nemeius (Nemean) had a sanctuary at Argos with a bronze statue, the work of Leucippus, and where games were celebrated in his honor (Paus. 2.20.3,24.2). Zeus Soter (Savior) occurs at Argos where the sacrifices offered to him were called *soteria* (Plut. *Arat.* 53). Finally, the temple of Zeus Larissaeus crowned the summit of the Larissa, or acropolis at Argos (Paus. 2.24.3).

Artemis was called Artemis Pheraea here, where she had a temple (Callim. *Hymn. in Dian.* 259; Paus. 2.10.7,23.5). Athena Oxyderces (Sharp-sighted) had a sanctuary on the acropolis. It adjoined the temple of Apollo Pythaeus and had been dedicated by Diomedes. Remains of both the Apollo and Athena temples have been found. Here Athena also had the surname Salpinx (War Trumpet). When the Dorians marched against Argos, they used a trumpet, which had been invented by Tyrsenus and given to them by Hegeleos, his son (Paus. 2.21.3).

A sepulchral monument of Castor existed in the temple of the Dioscuri at Argos. (This sepulcher betrayed the mortality of Castor.) Anaxias, or Anaxis, was a son of Castor and Elaeira and cousin of Mnasinus, with whom he is usually mentioned. The temple of the Dioscuri contained also the statues of these two sons of the twins (Paus. 2.22.5).

Asclepius, the god of healing, had a shrine at Argos (Paus. 2.23.4). He shared this sanctuary with his daughter, Hygieia, the goddess of health. The worship of Helios, the sun god, was established at Argos (Paus. 2.18.3). So was that of the Horae, or goddesses of the seasons (Paus. 2.20.4). The worship of Britomartis, the Cretan divinity of hunters and fishermen, existed here for a time. Hymenaeus, the god of marriage, was from Argos. According to an Argive tradition, while sailing along the coast of Attica, he delivered a number of Attic maidens from the violence of some Pelasgian pirates and was afterward praised by them in their bridal songs, which were called, after him, hymeneal songs.

Poseidon, having lost his bid for control of Argos, had little else to do with the area except in the case of Amymone, one of the daughters of Danaus. When Danaus arrived in Argos, a drought afflicted the country, according to the wish of Poseidon, who was indignant at Inachus for reasons already given. Danaus sent Amymone out to fetch water. Meeting a stag, she shot at it but hit a sleeping satyr, who rose and pursued her. Poseidon appeared and rescued the maiden but promptly accomplished what the satyr had tried to do. He then showed her the wells at Lerna as a source of water (Apollod. 2.1.4). According to another form of the tradition, Amymone fell asleep on her expedition and was surprised by a satyr. She invoked Poseidon, who appeared and cast his trident at the satyr. Poseidon's trident, however, struck into a rock instead, and the satyr escaped. After ravishing the maiden, Poseidon bade her draw the trident from the rock, from which a threefold spring gushed forth, and it was called after her the spring of Amymone. Her son by Poseidon was called Nauplius (Lucian *Dei Marin.* 6; Paus. 2.38.2).

In addition, certain heroes other than those of the royal houses have connections with the history of Argos. Nauplius, the son of Poseidon and Amymone, did not rule at Argos, even though he was of royal blood. He was a famous navigator and is said to have discovered the constellation of the great bear (Strab. 8.6.2). He also was the eponymous founder of Nauplia.

The majority of poets and mythographers relate that Heracles was born at Thebes, but Diodorus (4.10) says that Amphitryon was not expelled from Tiryns till after the birth of Heracles, and Euripides (*Herc. Fur.* 18) describes Argos as the native country of the hero. His mother Alcmena was from nearby Mycenae. Licymnius, her brother and Heracles' uncle, was buried in Argos. The second labor of Heracles was the fight against the Lernean Hydra, which ravaged the country of Lerna near Argos. After his labors he journeyed to Troy to fetch the horses that Laomedon had promised but refused him. On his return from Troy, he was cast, through the influence of Hera, onto the coast of Cos, but Zeus carried him safely to Argos (Hom. *Il.* 14.249, 15.18). Soon after his return to Argos he marched against Augeas to punish him for his breach of promise.

Helenus, a son of Priam and Hecuba, according to an Argive tradition, was buried at Argos (Paus. 2.23.5).

Epeius, who sailed with thirty ships from the Cyclades to Troy, was called the artist, and it was he who built the wooden horse. There were at Argos carved images of Hermes and Aphrodite, which were believed to be the works of Epeius (Paus. 2.19.6). Talthybius was the herald of Agamemnon at Troy. He was worshipped as a hero at Sparta and Argos, where sacrifices also were offered to him (Paus. 3.12.7; Herod. 7.134). Tantalus, son of Thyestes, was married to Clytemnestra before Agamemnon (Paus. 2.22.3) and is said by some to have been killed by Agamemnon. His tomb was shown at Argos.

Finally, some minor figures with interesting stories are associated in one way or another with Argos. Chloris was a daughter of Amphion and Niobe. According to an Argive tradition, her original name was Meliboea, and she and her brother Amyclas were the only children of Niobe not killed by Apollo and Artemis. But the terror of Meliboea at the death of her brothers and sisters was so great that she turned completely white and was therefore called Chloris. She and her brother built the temple of Leto at Argos, which contained the statue of Chloris also (Paus. 2.21.10).

Clymenus, son of Caenus or Schoenus, a minor king in Argolis, was married to Epicaste, by whom he had, among other children, a daughter Harpalyce. He loved her incestuously and after ravishing her, he first gave her in marriage to Alastor, son of Neleus and Chloris, but afterward reclaimed her and lived with her. Harpalyce, in order to avenge her father's crime, slew her younger brother, or, according to others, her own son and placed his flesh on a dish before her father. She was thereupon changed into a bird, and Clymenus hanged himself.

According to reports, the remains of Pyrrhus were deposited in the temple of Demeter, where he died, and his shield was affixed above the entrance (Paus. 2.21.4). A street named Coele (Paus. 2.23.1) appears to have led from the agora to the Larissa, the ascent to which was by the ridge of the Deiras. At the foot of the hill Deiras was a subterranean building, which is said to have once contained the bronze chamber in which Danae was confined by her father Acrisius (Paus. 2.23.7). The gymnasium, called Cylarabis from the son of Sthenelus, was situated outside the city, at a distance of less than three hundred paces, according to Livy (34.26; Paus. 2.22.8). The gate that led to it was called Diamperes. It was through this gate that Pyrrhus entered the city on the night of his death (Plut. *Pyrrh.* 32). The king fell near the sepulcher of Licymnius in a street leading from the agora to the gymnasium (Plut. *Pyrrh.* 34; Paus. 2.22.8).

The principal gates of Argos appear to have been: (1) the gate of Eileithyia, so called from a neighboring temple of this goddess, leading to Mycenae and Cleonae (Paus. 2.18.3); (2) the gate of Deiras, leading to Mantineia (Paus. 2.25.1); (3) the gate leading to Tegea (Paus.

2.24.5); (4) the gate leading to Temenium; (5) the gate Diamperes leading to Tiryns, Nauplia, and Epidaurus; and (6) a gate leading to the Heraion.

Of the two streams between which the Heraion stood, the northwestern one was the Eleutherion and the southeastern the Asterion. Pausanias says that the river Asterion had three daughters—Euboea, Prosymna, and Acraea. Euboea was the mountain on the lower part of which the Heraion stood; Acraea, the small mountain which rose across from it; and Prosymna the region below it.

Nauplia was the harbor of Argos.

ARGOS AMPHILOCHICUM (KRIKELLOS) was the chief town of Amphilochia, situated at the eastern extremity of the Ambracian Gulf on the river Inachus. Its territory was called Argeia. Its inhabitants claimed that their city had been colonized from the celebrated Argos in Peloponnesus, though the legends of its foundation differed. According to one tradition, Amphilochus, son of Amphiaraus, being dissatisfied with the state of things in Argos on his return from Troy, emigrated from his native place and founded a city of the same name on the Ambracian Gulf. According to another tradition, it was founded by Alcmaeon, who called it after his brother Amphilochus (Thuc. 2.68). Still another account attributes the founding to Amphilochus, son of Alcmaeon. The site of Argos Amphilochicum has been a subject of dispute. Thucydides (3.105) says that it was situated on the sea. Polybius (22.13) describes it as 180 stadia (33 km) and Livy (38.10) 22 miles (36.5 km) from Ambracia. It is generally accepted that ruins of the ancient city lie adjacent to the town of Krikellos on the east shore of the Ambracian Gulf.

ARGOS ORESTICUM, the chief town of the Orestae, was said to have been founded by Orestes when he fled from Argos after the murder of his mother (Strab. 7.7.8). The site of Argos Oresticum is uncertain, but a modern writer places it near Ambracia (Arta), since the Orestae have been thought to be a Molossian people.

ARGOS PELASGICUM was probably employed by Homer (*Il.* 2.681) to signify the whole of Thessaly. Some have thought that by Pelasgic Argos the poet alluded to a city, and that this city was the same as the Thessalian Larissa. Abas, the twelfth king of Argos, the son of Lynceus and Hypermnestra and father of Proetus and Acrisius by Ocaleia, is described as a successful conqueror and the founder of the town of Abae in Phocis (Paus. 10.35.1) and of the Pelasgic Argos in Thessaly. On the other hand, Pelasgus, son of Poseidon and Larissa, was described as the founder of the Thessalian Argos.

ARGURA (See ARGISSA)

ARGYPHEA was a place mentioned in the Homeric *Hymn to Apollo* (432) along with Arene, and therefore it was probably a town in Triphylia.

ARISBA (ARISVI) was a town in Lesbos, which Herodotus (1.151) speaks of as being taken over by the Methymnae. Pliny (5.39.139) says it was destroyed by an earthquake. Arisbe was a daughter of Macareus and wife of Paris, and the town of Arisba derived its name from her. The remains of the acropolis of ancient Arisba are northeast of the market town of Kaloni and north of the village of Arisvi.

ARISTAEON was a town in Thrace near Mount Haemus. It was named for Aristaeus, an ancient divinity worshipped in various parts of Greece. After many travels during which he conferred many benefits on mankind, he at last went to Thrace, where he became initiated in the mysteries of Dionysus. After having lived for some time near Mount Haemus, where he founded the town of Aristaeon, he disappeared.

ARISTONAUTAE (See PELLENE)

ARMENIUM (ARMENIO) a town of Pelasgiotis in Thessaly, situated between Pherae and Larissa near Lake Boebeis, was said to have been the birthplace of Armenius. Armenius was one of the Argonauts who was believed to have been born a native of Rhodes or of Armenium in Thessaly and to have settled a country called Armenia after him (Strab. 11.14.12). The mound at the village of Armenio is over 1 km in circumference and has some appearance of having been surrounded with walls.

ARNE was a town of Boeotia mentioned by Homer (*Il.* 2.507) as one of the Boeotian cities led to the Trojan War by captains Peneleos and Leitus. It was described as "rich in vines." It was probably founded by the Boeotians after their expulsion from Thessaly. Some of the ancients identified this Boeotian Arne with Chaeroneia (Paus. 9.40.5), others with Acraephnium (Strab. 9.2.34); and others again supposed that it had been swallowed up by the waters of Lake Copais. The town was believed to have derived its name from Arne, a daughter of Aeolus. Others say that Arne was named for Arne, the nurse of Poseidon. When Cronus searched after his son to devour him, Arne declared that she did not know where he was. Areithous was king of Arne and husband of Philomedusa. In the *Iliad* (7.8) he is called Corynetes (Club-Bearer) because he fought with no other weapon but a club. In a war in Peloponnesus to which the passage in the *Iliad* refers, he fell by the hand of the Arcadian Lycurgus, who drove him into a narrow gorge, where he could make no use of his club. The tomb of Areithous was shown at Phoezon in

Arcadia as late as the time of Pausanias (8.11.4) but it remains lost in modern times. Menesthius, a son of Areithous and Philomedusa, was slain at Troy by Paris (Hom. *Il.* 7.9,136). (See CHAERONEIA and ACRAEPHNIUM.)

ARNE (MATARANGA)   was the chief town of the Aeolian Boeotians in Thessaly, which was said to have derived its name from Arne, a daughter of Aeolus (Paus. 9.40.5). The town was said to have been founded three generations before the Trojan War (Diod. 4.67). According to Thucydides (1.12), the Aeolian Boeotians were expelled from Arne by the Thessalians sixty years after the Trojan War and settled in the country called Boeotia after them; but other writers represent the Thessalian Arne as founded by Boeotians who had been expelled from their country by the Pelasgians (Strab. 9.2.3,2.34). The Aeolian Boeotians are thought to have occupied the center of Thessaly and nearly the same district as the Thessaliotis of later times. When Cierium was discovered, many concluded that it and Arne were identical. The site of ancient Arne, then, along with the ruins of Cierium is placed at the modern town of Mataranga between the Enipeas and a tributary of that river, probably the ancient Curalius.

ARNE   or "Lamb's Well" in the neighborhood of Mantineia was believed to have derived this name from Arne, nurse of Poseidon. When Cronus searched after Poseidon to devour him, Arne is said to have declared that she did not know where he was. Others derive the name from the circumstance that Rhea, after giving birth to Poseidon, hid him among a flock of lambs. She did so to prevent Cronus from devouring him. She claimed she had given birth to a horse, and Cronus devoured it instead of Poseidon (Paus. 8.8.2).

AROTRIA   was an earlier name of ERETRIA in Euboea.

ARTEMISIUM (ARTEMISI)   was a mountain forming the boundary between Argolis and Arcadia with a temple of Artemis on its summit (Paus. 2.25.3). It is 1,772 meters in height.

The third labor of Heracles consisted of his catching alive the Ceryneian stag in Arcadia. He pursued it in vain for a whole year. At length it fled from Oenoe to Mount Artemisium and from there to the river Ladon in Arcadia.

ARTEMISIUM (ARTEMISSIO)   was the name of a promontory on the northwest coast of Euboea immediately opposite the Thessalian Magnesia, so called from the temple of Artemis Proseoa, belonging to the town of Histiaea. The site of the temple lies near the modern village of Artemissio. The famous bronze statue of

Poseidon, now in the National Museum at Athens, was found off Cape Artemissio in 1928.

ASCRA (ASKRA)   was a town of Boeotia on Mount Helicon and in the territory of Thespiae, from which it was forty stadia (7 km), according to Strabo (9.2.25). Some have placed Ascra near the village of Neohori, 4 km west of Thespiae, others at Xironomi, a village 10 km southwest of Thespiae. But the likeliest site is at the modern village of Askra, where there are ruins, so far little excavated. Ascra was said to have been founded by Otus and Ephialtes, the sons of Aloeus. Actually the Aloeidae were sons of Poseidon by Iphimedeia, wife of Aloeus. Pausanias (9.29.1) relates that they were believed to have been the first of all men who worshipped the Muses on Mount Helicon, and to have consecrated this mountain to them; but they worshipped only three Muses—Melete, Mneme, and Aoide. It is reported that in conjunction with the Aloeidae, Oeoclus, a son of Poseidon by Ascra, built the town of Ascra (Paus. 9.29.1), which was named for his mother.

ASEA (KATO ASEA)   was a town of Arcadia in the district of Maenalia, situated near the frontier of Laconia on the road from Megalopolis to Pallantium and Tegea. The city was in ruins in the time of Pausanias, who mentions its acropolis. About 1 km from the city on the road to Pallantium were the sources of the Alpheius River and near them those of the Eurotas. Near the sources of the Alpheius was a temple of the Mother of the Gods, roofless and with two lions made of stone. North of Asea on the road to Pallantium and on the summit of Mount Boreium was a temple of Athena Soteira (Saving Goddess) and Poseidon, said to have been founded by Odysseus on his return from Troy (Paus. 8.3.4, 44.4). This sanctuary was excavated in 1910, 1917, and 1958. The remains of Asea are to be seen on the height that rises above the copious spring of water called Frangovrisi, the source of the Alpheius.

ASINE (TOLO)   a town on the coast of Argolis, is mentioned by Homer (*Il.* 2.560) as one of the places subject to Diomedes. It is believed to have been founded by the Dryopes, who originally dwelt on Mount Parnassus. Eratus, a son of Heracles by Dynaste, was a king in Argos and made a successful expedition against Asine, which was besieged and taken (Apollod. 2.7.8; Paus. 2.36.5). In an early war between the Lacedaemonians and the Argives, the Asineans allied themselves with the Lacedaemonians, and as soon as the Lacedaemonians returned home, the Argives laid siege to Asine and razed it to the ground, sparing only the temple of the Apollo Pythaeus (ca. 800 B.C.). The Asineans escaped by sea; and the Lacedaemonians gave to them, after the end of the first Messenian war, a portion of the Messenian territory, where they built a new town. Nearly ten centuries after the destruction of the city its ruins were visited by Pausanias, who found the temple of Apollo still standing (Paus. 2.36.5). The ruins of Asine are at Tolo, where there are some Hellenic remains. The city extended to the slope of Mount Barbouna opposite Asine to the north. The temple of Apollo was probably atop this hill.

ASINE   was a name by which LAS in Laconia was known.

ASINE   in Messenia (See ANTHEIA)

ASOPIA   was the name of a plain of Sicyonia. It was called Asopis or Asopia because of the Peloponnesian river Asopus, which flowed through Sicyonia into the Corinthian Gulf. Aloeus, a son of Helios by Circe or Antiope, received from his father the sovereignty over the district of Asopia (Paus. 2.1.6, 3.10).

ASOPUS (PLITRA)   was a town of the Eleuthero-Lacones in Laconia, on the east side of the Laconian Gulf and 11 km south of Acriae. It possessed a temple of the Roman emperors and on the citadel a temple of Athena Cyparissia. Two kilometers above the town there was a temple of Asclepius (Paus. 3.22.9). Strabo speaks of Cyparissia and Asopus as two separate places, but some think that Asopus was the later name of Cyparissia. Pausanias says that at the foot of the acropolis of Asopus were the ruins of the city of the Paracyparissian Achaeans. Strabo (8.5.2) describes Cyparissia as a town with a harbor, situated upon a promontory, which corresponds to the site of Plitra. This modern town is on the high, rocky peninsula of Akra Xilis, east of which there is a deep inlet of the sea and a good harbor. The acropolis of Cyparissia or Asopus must have occupied the summit of Akra Xilis. There is a modern town Assopos 9 km inland from Plitra, but it is probably a recent commemorative name.

ASOPUS (ASOPOS)   is a river of Peloponnesus rising in the mountains south of Phlius and flowing through Sicyonia into the Corinthian Gulf. It flows past the city of Sicyon on the east and joins the sea a little eastward of a round height in the plain (Strab. 8.6.24; Paus. 2.5.2). Asopus, the god of the river Asopus, was a son of Oceanus and Tethys. He was married to Metope, the daughter of the river-god Ladon, by whom he had two sons and twelve or, according to others, twenty daughters. Several of these daughters were carried off by gods, stories which are commonly believed to reflect the historical circumstance of colonies established by the people from the banks of the Asopus that transferred the name Asopus to rivers in the countries where they settled. In Greece there were two rivers of this name, the one in Achaia in

Peloponnesus and the other in Boeotia, and the legends of the two are frequently confused with each other. The more celebrated of the two is that of Peloponnesus. When Zeus had carried off Asopus' daughter Aegina and Asopus had searched after her everywhere, he was at last informed by Sisyphus of Corinth that Zeus was the guilty party. Asopus then revolted against Zeus and wanted to fight with him, but Zeus struck him with his thunderbolt and confined him to his original bed. Pieces of charcoal, which were found in the bed of the river in later times, were believed to have been produced by the lightning of Zeus (Apollod. 3.12.6).

The surname of Nemesis Adrasteia is derived by some writers from Adrastus, who is said to have built the first sanctuary of Nemesis on the river Asopus (Strab. 13.1.13).

ASOPUS   is a river of Boeotia that flows through the southern part of the country in an easterly direction and empties into the Euboean Gulf in Attica near Oropus. Its principal sources are near the ruins of Eutresia. In the upper part of its course it forms the boundary between the territories of Thebes and Plataeae, flowing through a plain called Parasopia (Strab. 9.2.24). It forces its way through a rocky ravine into the plain of Tanagra and then enters the maritime plain of Oropus. It got its name from the Asopus River of Sicyonia.

ASPLEDON   also called Spledon, was an ancient city of Boeotia mentioned by Homer (*Il.* 2.510), located 4 km from Orchomenus. The river Melas flowed between the two cities. Pausanias (9.38.9) relates that it was abandoned in his time from want of water. This ancient Minyan town is said to have derived its name from Aspledon, a son of Poseidon and the nymph Mideia. The site of Aspledon is uncertain.

ASPROPOTAMO   (White River) was another name of the river ACHELOUS.

ASTACUS (ASTAKOS)   was a Megarian colony located in Acarnania on a west coast promontory called Crithote. Remains of a temple of Zeus Caraos and inscriptions from it have been reported.

ASTERIA   was the original name of the island of DELOS.

ASTERIA   was an earlier name of RHODES.

ASTERION   was a small stream in Argos flowing on the southeast side of the Heraion, or temple of Hera, the waters of which are said by Pausanias to disappear in a chasm. No trace of this chasm has been found; but it was observed that its waters were absorbed into the earth at a

small distance from the temple (Paus. 2.17.2). Asterion
was god of the river Asterion in Argos. In the dispute
between Poseidon and Hera over the possession of Argos,
Asterion decided in favor of Hera, and as a consequence it
was said that Poseidon deprived him and the two other
judges, the river-gods Inachus and Cephissus, of their
water, so that they became dry except in rainy seasons
(Paus. 2.15.4; Apollod. 2.1.4). Acraea was a daughter of
Asterion. She and her sisters, Euboea and Prosymna,
acted as nurses to Hera. A hill Acraea opposite the temple
of Hera near Mycenae derived its name from the goddess
(Paus. 2.17.2).

ASTERIS   was an island between Ithaca and
Cephallenia, where the suitors lay in wait for Telemachus
on his return from Peloponnesus (Hom. *Od.* 4.846). This
island gave rise to considerable dispute among ancient
commentators. Some maintained that it was no longer in
existence; but this was denied by Apollodorus, who stated
that it contained a town called Alalcomenae (Strab.
10.2.16). Some modern writers identify Asteris with a
rocky islet, now called Dyscallio; but as this island lies at
the northern extremity of the strait between Ithaca and
Cephallenia, it would not have answered the purpose of
the suitors as a place of ambush for a vessel coming from
the south.

ASTERIUM (VLOHOS)   was a town of Thessaly mentioned by Homer (*Il.* 2.735) as one of the Thessalian
cities whose men were led by Eurypylus, son of Euaemon,
in forty ships to the Trojan War. Asterium, according to
some, was named for the white, crystalline limestone of
the hill on which it was built. Others identified the name
with Asterius, son of Cometes, one of the Argonauts who
came from the town of Peiresiae. It was located on the
west bank of the Enipeus, south of Vlohos and has been
identified with the ancient city of Peiresiae. The modern
town is 7.5 km south of the midpoint on the highway
between Trikala and Larissa.

ASTRABE   was a former name of the island of
CASUS.

ASTRAEUS   was an earlier name of the CAICUS
River.

ASTYPALAEA (ASTIPALEA)   is an island in the
Aegean Sea, one of the Dodekanissia, lying between Anafi
and Kos. Astypalaea was described as about 146 km in
circumference. The island consists of two large, rocky
masses, united in the center by an isthmus. On the north
and south the sea enters two bays between the two halves
of the island; and the town, which had the same name as
the island, stood on the west side of the southern bay. To
the south and east of this bay lie several waterless,

deserted islands. Towards the east may be seen Kos,
Nisiros, and Tilos, and toward the south in clear weather
Kasos, Karpathos, and Kriti (ancient Crete). The ruins of
the ancient city of Astypalaea had sanctuaries of Athena,
Asclepius, and Apollo and Artemis. Coins from here
featured heads of Perseus, Medusa, Dionysus, Athena,
and Asclepius.

Astypalaea was said to have been originally called
Pyrrha when the Carians possessed it, then Pylaea, next
Theon Trapeza (Table of the Gods) on account of its
fertility, and finally Astypalaea from the mother of
Ancaeus (Paus. 7.4.1). Astypalaea was a daughter of
Phoenix and Perimede, the daughter of Oeneus. She was a
sister of Europa and became by Poseidon the mother of
both the Argonaut Ancaeus and Eurypylus, king of the
island of Cos. We are told that Astypalaea was a colony of
the Megarians, and Ovid (*Met.* 7.461) mentions it as one
of the islands subdued by Minos.

The modern town has fewer than 1,500 inhabitants.
The many churches are built to a large extent from ruins
of temples, and they contain numerous inscriptions. The
favorite hero of the island was Cleomedes. He was an
athlete, of whom the following legend is recorded. In the
seventy-second at the Olympic games; the judges decided
that he had been guilty of unfair play and punished him
with the loss of the prize. Stung to madness by the
disgrace, he returned to Astypalaea, and there in a blind
fury he shook down the pillar that supported the roof of a
boys' school, crushing all who were in it beneath the
ruins. The Astypalaeans tried to stone him, but he fled for
refuge to the temple of Athena where he got into a chest.
His pursuers, having vainly attempted to open the chest,
at length broke it to pieces; but no Cleomedes was there.
They sent accordingly to consult the Delphic oracle and
received the following answer: "Last of heroes is
Cleomedes of Astypalaea; honor him with sacrifices as
being no longer a mortal." From that time the
Astypalaeans paid honors to Cleomedes as to a hero.

It is related that a couple of hares were brought into
Astypalaea from Anaphe, and their progency so overran
the island that the inhabitants were obliged to consult the
Delphic oracle. The oracle advised the Astypalaeans to
hunt the hares with dogs, and in this way more than six
thousand were caught in one year (Athen. 9.400). This
tale is a counterpart to the one about the brace of
partridges introduced from Astypalaea into Anaphe. The
island is said to be the only one in the Aegean that is free
from snakes.

ATABYRIA   was an earlier name of Rhodes.

ATABYRIS (ATAVIROS)   is a mountain in Rhodes.
Rhodes is crossed from north to south by a chain of
mountains, the highest point of which was called Atabyris
or Atabyrion in ancient times. It is 1,215 meters above sea

level. On top of it stood a temple of Zeus Atabyrius. Althaemenes was a son of Catreus, king of Crete. In consequence of an oracle that Catreus would lose his life by one of his children, Althaemenes fled from Crete with his sister, Anemosyne, in order to avoid becoming the instrument of his father's death. He landed in Rhodes at a place he called Cretenia, and in remembrance of the god of his own native island, he erected on Mount Atabyris an altar to Zeus Atabyrius, high enough that he could see his native land. Scanty remains of the temple can still be seen at the site. Votive offerings left at the shrine can be seen in the Rhodes Museum. Upon this mountain there were, it is said, brazen bulls that roared when anything extraordinary was going to happen.

ATHAMANIA   was a region in the southeast of Epeirus between Mount Pindus and the river Arachthus. The river Achelous flowed through this narrow district. Its chief towns were Argithea, Tetraphylia, Heracleia, and Theodoria; of these Argithea was the capital. The Athamanes were a rude people and the last of the Epirot tribes to obtain political power. They extended their dominions as far as Mount Oeta (Strab. 9.4.10). They were subsequently subdued by the Macedonians, and in the time of Strabo (9.4.17) had ceased to exist as a separate people. The region is named for Athamas, a son of Aeolus and Enarete. After he had been seized by madness and had killed his own son Learchus, Ino, his wife, threw herself with another son, Melicertes into the sea. Athamas, as the murderer of his son, was obliged to flee from Boeotia. He consulted an oracle about where he should settle. The answer was that he should settle where he would be treated hospitably by wild beasts. After long wanderings, he at last came to a place where wolves were devouring sheep. When he came up, they ran away, leaving their prey behind. Athamas recognized the place alluded to by the oracle, settled there, and eponymously called the country Athamania. He then married Themisto, who bore him several sons (Apollod. 1.9.1). There is a mountain in the Pindos range still today called Athamanon, and there is a town near it called Theodoriana.

ATHAMANTIUS CAMPUS   was a plain in Boeotia between Acraephnium and Lake Copais, where Athamas was said to have once lived (Paus. 9.24.1). This was also the name of a plain in Phthiotis in Thessaly, close to the city Halus or Alus, so called from Athamas, the founder of Halus (Apollon. Rhod. 2.514).

ATHENA AETHYIA   was a rock on the coast of Megara. Pandion, a son of Cecrops and Metiadusa, was a king of Athens. Being expelled from Athens by the Metionidae, he fled to Megara, and there he married Pylia, the daughter of King Pylas. When Pylas, as a result

of having committed a murder, fled to Peloponnesus, Pandion came to the throne of Megara. He became the father of Aegeus, Pallas, Nisus, Lycus, and a bastard son, Oeneus, and also a daughter, who was married to Sciron (Apollod. 3.15.1). His tomb was shown in the territory of Megara near the rock of Athena Aethyia on the seacoast (Paus. 1.5.3), and at Megara he was honored with a shrine (1.41.6).

ATHENAE   was an ancient town of Boeotia on the Triton River and near Lake Copais, which, together with the neighboring town of Eleusis, was destroyed by a flood (Paus. 9.24.2). Cecrops, the early king of Attica, is said to have founded these two towns. He had a shrine at Haliartus. There was also a town in Euboea called Athenae, also founded by Cecrops. From these traditions it appears that Cecrops must be regarded as a hero of the Pelasgian race; and it has been remarked that the different mythical persons of this name connected with the town in Boeotia and Euboea are all the same hero, whose name and story were transferred from Attica to other places.

ATHENAE DIADES   was a town in Boeotia near the promontory Cenaeum, founded by the Athenians (Strab. 10.1.5), or according to some by Dias, a son of Abas.

ATHENS (ATHINA)   the capital of Attica, is situated between 6.5 and 8 km from the seacoast in the central plain of Attica, which is enclosed by mountains on every side except the south, where it is open to the sea. This plain is bounded on the northwest by Mount Parnes, on the northeast by Mount Pentelicus, on the southeast by Mount Hymettus, and on the west by Mount Aegaleos. Of the hills that rise in the southern part of the plain the most prominent is a high, isolated mountain called Lycabettus. Southwest of Lycabettus there are four hills of moderate height. About 1.5 km from Lycabettus is the Acropolis, or citadel of Athens, a square, craggy rock rising abruptly to a height of about 46 meters. The Acropolis has a flat summit about 305 meters long from east to west by 152 meters broad from north to south. Immediately west of the Acropolis is a second hill of irregular form, the Areiopagus. To the southwest there rises a third hill, the Pnyx, on which assemblies of the citizens were held; and to the south of the Pnyx is a fourth hill known as the Museion. On the east and west sides of the city there are two small streams, both of which are completely dry most of the year. In ancient times the stream on the east, called the Ilissus, was joined by the Eridanus close to the Lyceum outside the walls and then flowed in a southwest direction through the south quarter of the city. The stream on the west, named the Cephissus, ran due south at a distance of about 2.5 km from the walls. South of the city were the harbors of Athens, located on the Saronic Gulf.

The original city on the Acropolis was said to have been built by Cecrops and was called Cecropia even in later times (Strab. 9.1.20; Eurip. *Suppl.* 658). Cecrops was the first king of Attica, which had previously been called Acte (Apollod. 3.14.1). He was an autochthon, or son of Gaea, as were Actaeus and Cranaus, who therefore might, in a sense, be regarded as his brothers or half-brothers. Actaeus has been called the earliest king of Attica, and Cecrops married his daughter Agraulos, with whom he had four children: Agraulos, Herse, Pandrosos and Erysichthon. Cecrops is described as having an upper body of human appearance and a lower body of a serpent. In his reign Poseidon with his trident called forth a well on the Acropolis, which was known in later times by the name of the Erechthean well, from its being enclosed in the temple of Erechtheus (Paus. 1.26.5; Herod. 8.55). The marine god now wanted to take possession of the country; but Athena, who entertained the same desire, planted an olive tree on the Acropolis and called Cecrops to witness the act. That olive tree continued to be shown down to the latest times. When Poseidon, who had no witness to attest that he had created the well, disputed the possession of Attica, Cecrops decided in favor of the goddess. Cecrops is represented in Attic legends as the author of the first elements of civilized life (e.g., marriage, the political division of Attica into twelve communities) and also as the introducer of a new mode of worship, inasmuch as he abolished the bloody sacrifices, which had until then been offered to Zeus, and substituted cakes in their stead (Paus. 8.2.2,3).

The offspring of Cecrops were interesting. Erysichthon died without issue during his father's lifetime. This happened on his return from Delos, whence he brought to Athens the ancient image of Eileithyia, the goddess of childbirth. Herse was beloved of Hermes and the mother of Cephalus, who was carried away by Eos, the goddess of dawn, and became by her the father of Tithonus. At Athens sacrifices were offered to her, and the maidens called Arriphorae carried the vessels containing the libation (Paus. 1.27.4). Pandrosos was also worshipped at Athens, along with Thallo, and had a sanctuary there near the temple of Athena Polias (Apollod. 2.14.2,6; Paus. 1.2.5,27.3). Pandrosos was probably represented in one of the pediments of the Parthenon. According to some accounts, she was by Hermes the mother of Ceryx.

Agraulos, however, was the most important of all in early legends about Athens. According to Pausanias (1.18.2), Athena gave to her and her sisters a chest with the express command not to open it. But Agraulos and Herse could not control their curiosity, opened it, and found Erichthonius inside. They were seized with madness at the sight of Erichthonius and threw themselves

from the steep rock of the Acropolis, or into the sea. According to Ovid (*Met.* 2.710), Agraulos and Herse survived their opening of the chest, and Agraulos, who had persuaded her sister to open it, was punished in this manner. Hermes came to Athens during the celebration of the Panathenaea and fell in love with Herse. Athena made Agraulos so jealous of her sister that she even attempted to prevent the god from entering Herse's house. Indignant at such an outrage, Hermes changed Agraulos into a stone. Another legend represents her in a totally different light. Athens was at one time involved in a seemingly endless war, and an oracle declared that it would cease if someone would voluntarily be sacrificed for the good of the country. Agraulos came forward and threw herself down the Acropolis. The Athenians in gratitude for this built her a temple on the Acropolis, in which the young Athenians who were receiving their first suit of armor customarily took an oath that they would always defend their country to the last. The Attic deme of Agraule derived its name from this heroine, and a festival and mysteries were celebrated at Athens in her honor. The Cecropian line was continued through Alcippe, her daughter by Ares.

Meanwhile, Cranaus, the third autochthon in the ancestry of Attic kings, had married Pedias, the daughter of Mynes of Lacedaemon. He is said to have reigned at the time of the flood. His children by Pedias were three daughters—Cranae, Cranaechme, and Atthis, from the last of whom Attica was believed to have derived its name. He was deprived of his kingdom by Amphictyon, the husband of Cranae. Amphictyon was a son of Deucalion and Pyrrha, and after usurping the throne he ruled twelve years until he himself was expelled by Erichthonius. He was married to Chthonopatra, by whom he had a son Physcus, the father of Locrus. According to others, Aetolus was his son and Physcus his grandson. Amphictyon was believed to have been the first to introduce the custom of mixing wine with water and to have dedicated two altars to Dionysus Orthos and the nymphs. Dionysus of Halicarnassus (4.25), who calls him a son of Hellen, Pausanias (10.8.1), and others regard him as the founder of the amphictyony of Thermopylae, and in consequence a sanctuary of Amphictyon was built in the village of Antheia on the Asopus, which was the most ancient place of the meeting of this amphictyony (Herod. 7.200). Locrus, his grandson, became by Cabya the father of Locrus, the mythical ancestor of the Ozolian Locrians (Plut. *Quaest. Gr.* 15).

Nothing is known of Cranaechme, but Atthis or Attis, the third daughter, is believed to have been the source of the name Attica (Paus. 1.2.6). When the goddess Athena repulsed the advances of Hephaestus, the god of fire, his semen fell on the ground and he became by Gaea or by Atthis the father of a son who had either completely or only half the form of a serpent. This was Erichthonius, or Erechtheus I. Athena reared this being without the knowledge of the other gods, had him guarded by a dragon, and then entrusted him, concealed in a chest, to the daughters of Cecrops who were forbidden to open the chest. Their curiosity overcame them, and, on viewing the child in the form of a serpent or entwined by a serpent, they went mad and killed themselves. The serpent escaped into the shield of Athena and was protected by her (Apollod. 3.14.6; Paus. 1.18.2). When Erichthonius had grown up, he expelled Amphictyon and usurped the government of Athens, and his wife Pasithea bore him a son Pandion. Erichthonius is said to have introduced the worship of Athena, to have instituted the festival of the Panathenaea, and to have built a temple of Athena on the Acropolis. When Athena and Poseidon disputed about the possession of Attica, Erichthonius declared in favor of Athena (Apollod. 3.14.1). He was further the first to use a chariot with four horses, for which reason he was placed among the stars as Auriga (Virg. *Georg.* 1.205, 3.113); and lastly he was believed to have made the Athenians acquainted with the use of silver, which had been discovered by the Scythian king Indus. He was buried in the temple of Athena, and his worship on the Acropolis was connected with that of Athena and Poseidon (Apollod. 3.14.6). His famous temple, the Erechtheion, stood on the Acropolis. In it were three altars, one of Poseidon (on which sacrifices were offered to Erechtheus also), the second of Butes, and the third of Hephaestus (Paus. 1.26.5).

Pandion, son of Erichthonius, was married to Zeuxippe, by whom he became the father of Procne and Philomela and the twins Erechtheus and Butes. In a war against Labdacus, king of Thebes, he called upon Tereus of Daulis in Phocis for assistance, and afterward rewarded him by giving him his daughter Procne in marriage. The tragic story of Tereus, Procne, and Philomela is related elsewhere. (See DAULIS). It was in the reign of Pandion that Dionysus and Demeter were said to have come to Attica (Apollod. 3.14.6). Butes, Athenian shepherd, ploughman, and warrior, became after the death of Pandion a priest of Athena and of the Erechtheian Poseidon. The Attic family of the Butadae or Eteobutadae derived their origin from him. In the Erechtheion on the Acropolis there was an altar dedicated to him, and the walls were decorated with paintings representing scenes from the history of the family of the Butadae (Paus. 1.26.5).

Erechtheus II, after Pandion's death, succeeded his father as king of Athens and was regarded in later times as one of the Attic eponymi. He was married to Praxithea, by whom he became the father of Cecrops II, Pandoros, Metion, Orneus, Procris, Creusa, Chthonia or Otionia, and Oreithyia. Merope is also usually considered one of his daughters. These daughters, whose names and whose stories differ very much in the different traditions, agreed among themselves to die all together if one of them was to die. When Eumolpus, the son of Poseidon, who assisted the Eleusinians in the war against the Athenians, had been killed, Poseidon (or an oracle) demanded the sacrifice of one of the daughters of Erechtheus. When one was drawn by lot, the others voluntarily accompanied her in death, and Erechtheus himself was killed by Zeus with a flash of lightning at the request of Poseidon (Apollod. 3.15.4; Plut. *Paral. Gr. et Rom.* 20). In his war with the Eleusinians, Erechtheus is also said to have killed Immaradus, the son of Eumolpus (Paus. 1.5.2). According to Diodorus Siculus (1.29), Erechtheus was an Egyptian, who brought grain to Athens during a famine and who also instituted the worship of Demeter and the Eleusinian mysteries.

The children of Erechtheus figured in a series of famous stories and lineages associated with Athens and Attica. Orneus was the father of Peteos and grandfather of Menestheus. From him the town of Orneae was believed to have derived its name (Hom. *Il.* 2.571; Paus. 2.25.5). Peteos was expelled from Athens by Aegeus and is said to have gone to Phocis, where he founded the town of Stiris (Hom. *Il.* 2.552, 4.338; Apollod. 3.10.8). Menestheus led the Athenians against Troy and surpassed all other mortals in arranging the war steeds and men for battle (Hom. *Il.* 2.552, 4.327). With the assistance of the Tyndarids he is said to have driven Theseus from his kingdom and to have died at Troy (Plut. *Thes.* 32,35; Paus. 1.17.6).

Pandoros founded a colony in Euboea (Apollod. 3.15.1). Procris was married to Cephalus, a son of Deion of Phocis, by whom she became the mother of Archius, the father of Laertes. Their fateful romance is elsewhere described. (See PHOCIS.) Otionia gave herself for a sacrifice to aid her father, Erectheus II, in his war with the Eleusinians. Chthonia, if there was another daughter of this name, married her uncle Butes. Oreithyia once strayed beyond the river Ilissus and was carried off by Boreas, the god of the north wind, by whom she became the mother of Cleopatra, Chione, Zetes and Calais (Apollod. 3.15.1). Zetes and Calais of Argonaut fame are seen elsewhere. (See TENOS.)

Creusa, another daughter of Erechtheus, was married to Xuthus and her son Ion, the fabulous ancestor of the Ionians, was said to be her son by Apollo. Apollo had visited Creusa in a cave below the Propylaea of the Acropolis, and when she gave birth to a son, she exposed him in the same cave. The god, however, had the child conveyed to Delphi and there had him educated by a priestess. Other traditions represent Ion as a king of Athens between the reigns of Erechtheus II and Cecrops for it is said that the Athenians called for his assistance in their war with the Eleusinians and that he conquered Eumolpus. Then he became king of Athens and fathered four sons—Geleon (Teleon), Aegicores, Argades, and Hoples. He divided the Athenians into four classes, each one named for one of his sons. Creusa went on to produce two other sons by Xuthus—Dorus and Achaeus, the eponymous ancestors of the Dorians and Achaeans. Teleon was father of the Argonaut Butes (Apollon. Rhod. 1.95). From him the Teleonites in Attica derived their name (Eurip. *Ion* 1579).

Metion and Merope were brother and sister. Metion married Alcippe, who, for lack of evidence to the contrary, was a relative considerably older than he from the Cecropian line. His sons, the Metionidae, expelled their cousin Pandion from the kingdom of Athens but were themselves afterward expelled by the sons of Pandion (Apollod. 3.15.1, 5,6,8; Paus. 1.5.3). He also had a son, Eupalmus, who, in the family tradition, apparently married his aunt Merope and produced three children, Daedalus, Perdix, and Metiadusa. Under the name of Daedalus the Greek writers personified the earliest development of the arts of sculpture and architecture. Ancient writers generally represent Daedalus as an Athenian of the royal race of the Erechtheidae (Paus. 7.4.5; Plut. *Thes.* 18). He devoted himself to sculpture and made great improvements in that art. He instructed his nephew Calos, (or Talos or Perdix), son of his sister Perdix, who soon came to surpass him in skill and ingenuity. The inventions ascribed to Calos were the saw, the chisel, the compass, and the potter's wheel. Daedalus killed him through envy by throwing him headlong from the temple of Athena on the Acropolis, but the goddess caught him in his fall and changed him into a bird, the perdix, or partridge (Ov. *Met.* 8.241). Pausanias (1.21.4, 26.5) states that he was buried on the road leading from the theater to the Acropolis. Daedalus was condemned to death by the Areiopagus for the murder but escaped to Crete. Among the ingenious works attributed to him was a folding seat in the temple of Athena Polias at Athens (Paus. 1.27.1). The style of architecture which he employed continued down to the beginning of the fifth century B.C.; the artists of that period were called Daedalids and claimed an actual descent from Daedalus. The most important of the Daedalids included Endoeus of Athens. A deme of the Athenian tribe Cecropis bore the name of Daedalidae. Feasts called Daedaleia were kept in different parts of Greece.

The most important offspring of Erechtheus was Cecrops II since through him the royal succession continued. He married Metiadusa, the sister of Daedalus and Perdix, and their son was Pandion II, who became king of Athens. Being expelled from Athens by the Metionidae, he fled to Megara and there married Pylia, the daughter of King Pylas. Pandion later obtained the government of Megara and became the father of Aegeus, Pallas, Nisus, Lycus, Oeneus, and a daughter (Apollod. 3.15.1; Paus. 1.5.3). A statue of him stood at Athens on the Acropolis among those of the eponymous heroes (Paus. 1.5.3). The Pandionidae, or sons of Pandion, after their father's death, returned from Megara to Athens and expelled the Metionidae. Aegeus, the eldest among them, obtained the supremacy, Lycus the east coast of Attica, Nisus Megaris, and Pallas the south coast (Apollod. 3.15.6; Paus. 1.5.4).

Aegeus first married Meta and then Chalciope, neither of whom bore him any children. He ascribed his misfortune to the anger of Aphrodite, and in order to conciliate her introduced her worship at Athens (Paus. 1.14.6). Meanwhile, Aegeus expelled Lycus, who took refuge in the country afterward called Lycia. Lycus was honored at Athens as a hero, and the Lyceum derived its name from him (Paus. 1.19.4; Aristoph. *Vesp.* 408). He is said to have raised the mysteries of the Great Goddesses to greater celebrity and to have introduced them from Attica to Andania in Messenia (Paus. 4.1.7,8). He is sometimes also described as an ancient prophet (Paus. 4.20.4), and the family of Lycomedae at Athens traced their name and origin to him. This family was intimately connected with the Attic mysteries and possessed chapels in the deme of Phylae and at Andania. Nisus apparently helped maintain peaceful relations between Megaris and Attica. He married Abrote, and their daughter was Scylla. Although he was ruler at Megara, his tomb was shown at Athens behind the Lyceum (Paus. 1.19.4). The celebrated family of the Pallantidae at Athens traced its origin to Pallas (Apollod. 3.15.5; Paus. 1.22.2).

Aegeus became the father of Theseus by Aethra, daughter of Pittheus, king of Troezen. When he reached maturity, Theseus, by his mother's directions, left for Athens with the sword and sandals, tokens left by Aegeus. Eager to emulate Heracles, he went by land, displaying his prowess by destroying robbers and monsters that infested the country. Periphetes, Sinis, Phaea the Crommyonian sow, Sciron, Cercyon, and Procrustes fell before the invincible hero. Arriving at Cephisus, he was purified by the Phytalidae. At Athens he was immediately recognized by Medea, who spent some time at Athens after her return from Corinth to Colchis and is said to have become mother of a son, Medus, by Aegeus (Apollod. 1.9.28). Medea plotted to poison Theseus at a banquet. By means of the sword that he carried, Theseus was recognized by Aegeus, acknowledged as his son, and declared his successor. The sons of Pallas, thus disappointed in their hopes of succeeding to the throne, attempted to secure the succession by violence and declared war; but, being betrayed by the herald Leos, they were destroyed.

The capture of the Marathonian bull was the next exploit of Theseus. It was the same enterprise in which

Androgeus, the son of Minos, perished. When the time had come for the Athenians to send to Minos their compensatory tribute of seven youths and seven maidens, Theseus voluntarily offered himself as one of the youths, planning to slay the Minotaur, the fearful bull-headed monster to whom the youths and maidens were fed. In Crete Ariadne, Minos' daughter, fell in love with Theseus and assisted him in killing the Minotaur. For one or another reason he abandoned her at Naxos on the return trip. As the vessel in which he sailed approached Attica, he neglected to have a white sail hoisted, which was to have been the signal that the expedition had been successful. The neglect led to the death of Aegeus, who in despair threw himself into the sea from the rock on which he waited. From this event the sea was called the Aegean Sea (Plut. *Thes.* 22; Diod. 4.61). Aegeus was one of the eponymous heroes of Attica, one of the Attic tribes (Aegeis) deriving its name from him (Paus. 1.5.2). His grave, called the heroon of Aegeus, was believed to be at Athens (Paus. 1.22.6), and Pausanias mentions two statues of him, one at Athens and the other at Delphi, the latter of which had been made of the tithes of the booty taken by the Athenians at Marathon (Paus. 1.5.2).

The fateful ship that carried Theseus to Athens was believed to have been in existence well into historical times. This vessel was sent every year to Delos with sacred envoys. Soon after Theseus landed on his return from Crete, he instituted the festival called the Oschophoria. The origin of the Pyanepsia and the reinstitution of the Isthmian games were also ascribed to him.

One of the most renowned of the adventures of Theseus was his expedition against the Amazons. He is said to have assailed them before they had recovered from the attack of Heracles and to have carried off their queen, Antiope. The Amazons in their turn invaded Attica and penetrated into Athens itself. The final battle, in which Theseus overcame them, was fought in the very midst of the city. In support of the historical truth of this, Plutarch (*Thes.* 27) finds evidence in the names of the localities and the tombs of the fallen Amazons. By Antiope Theseus had a son named Hippolytus, and after her death he married Phaedra, the daughter of Minos of Crete and Ariadne's sister. By Phaedra he was the father of Acamas and Demophon. Phaedra fell in love with her stepson Hippolytus, and he rejected her advances. Therefore she accused him of attempted seduction. Theseus cursed his son and prayed to Poseidon to destroy him. Thereafter, when Hippolytus was riding in his chariot along the sea coast, Poseidon sent a bull forth from the sea. The horses were frightened, upset the chariot, and dragged Hippolytus till he was dead. Theseus afterward learned that his son was innocent and Phaedra, in despair, killed herself. Asclepius, the god of healing, restored Hippolytus to life,

according to some. There was a monument of Hippolytus in front of the temple of Themis at Athens (Paus. 1.22.1).

Theseus figures in many other ancient heroic undertakings. With his friend Peirithous he abducted the very young Helen of Sparta and secreted her at Aphidna under the protection of his mother Aethra. When Helen's brothers, the Dioscuri, rescued her, they took Aethra as a slave, and later Aethra accompanied Helen to Troy. Theseus also went with Peirithous to Hades in an attempt to carry off Persephone. The venture failed, and only Theseus was able to escape eternal imprisonment. Peirithous was worshipped at Athens as a hero (Paus. 1.30.4; Apollod. 1.8.2). Eventually Menestheus endeavored to incite the people against Theseus, who found himself unable to reestablish his authority after returning from his adventures. He retired to Scyros where he met with a treacherous death. The departed hero was believed to have appeared to aid the Athenians at the battle of Marathon. In 469 B.C. a skeleton of large size was found by Cimon in Scyros and brought to Athens. It was believed to be that of Theseus, in whose honor a temple was erected, in which the bones were deposited. This temple has never been found, but for many years an Athenian landmark was mistakenly called the Theseion. A festival in honor of Theseus was celebrated on the eighth day of each month, especially on the eighth of Pyanepsion. Connected with this festival were two others: the Connideia, in memory of Connidas, the guardian of Theseus; and the Cybernesia, which referred to his voyage.

Although Theseus must be viewed as a legendary hero king, the Athenians in later times regarded him as the author of the great political change that took place in Athens near the time of the Trojan War. Before his time Attica had been made up of about a dozen petty, independent states or townships that acknowledged no head and were connected only by a kind of feudal union. Theseus, through a combination of persuasion and force, abolished separate political jurisdictions and made Athens the capital of a single commonwealth. The festival of Synoecia was celebrated in commemoration of this change in government. The Athenian festival was reinstituted under the name of Panathenaea (Thuc. 2.15). Theseus established a constitutional government, retaining for himself only certain powers. He organized the citizenry into three classes—the Eupatridae (nobles), Geomori (farmers), and Demiurges (artisans) (Plut. *Thes.* 24–26). This revolution did indeed take place at some time, but Theseus' role must be questioned unless we assign him quasi-historical status. There are several connections that lend him credibility as the mythological representative of an Ionic migration into Attica, a migration that might have added to the strength of Ionian settlers already in the country and that might have led to the political union with which Theseus was individually credited.

Writers have tended to confuse Acamas and Demophon, sons of Theseus by Phaedra. Previous to the expedition of the Greeks against Troy, Acamas and Diomedes were sent to demand the surrender of Helen, but during his stay at Troy Acamas won the affection of Laodice, daughter of Priam, and begot by her a son, Munitus. This child was brought up by the grandmother of Acamas, Aethra. Acamas was said to be one of the Greeks concealed in the wooden horse. On his return from Troy he was killed by a fall from a horse in Cyprus. The Attic tribe Acamantis derived its name from him. Demophon also accompanied the Greeks against Troy (although Homer does not mention him), and there effected the liberation of his grandmother Aethra, who was with Helen as a slave (Paus. 10.25.8). On Demophon's return from Troy, Phyllis, the daughter of the Thracian king Sithon, fell in love with him, and he consented to marry her. But before the nuptials were celebrated, he went to Attica to settle his affairs at home, and as he tarried longer than Phyllis had expected, she began to think that she was forgotten and put an end to her life. Afterward, when Diomedes, returning from Troy, was thrown onto the coast of Attica and began to ravage the country, Demophon marched out against the invaders; he took the Palladium from them, but had the misfortune to kill an Athenian in the struggle. For this murder he was summoned by the people of Athens before the court—the first time that a man was tried by that court (Paus. 1.28.9). According to some, Demophon assisted the Heracleidae against Eurystheus, who fell in battle, and the Heracleidae received from Demophon settlements in Attica, which were called the tetrapolis. Orestes, too, came to Athens to seek the protection of Demophon. He arrived during the celebration of the Anthesteria and was kindly received; the precautions that were taken so that he might not pollute the sacred rites gave rise to the second day of the festival, which was called Choes (Athen. 10.437; Plut. *Quaest. Conviv.* 2). Demophon was painted in the Lesche at Delphi together with Helen and Aethra, meditating how he might liberate Aethra (Paus. 10.25.7). Acamas, his brother, was in the Lesche as well, and there was also a statue of him at Delphi (Paus. 10.10.1, 26.2).

Athens owes much of the preservation of its religious and mythological heritage to several of its rulers. Peisistratus and his sons (560–514 B.C.) founded the temple of Apollo Pythius and began construction on the gigantic temple of the Olympian Zeus. They also began work on the theater of Dionysus of the southeast slope of the Acropolis. Under Cimon both the Theseion and the Stoa Poikile, which was adorned with paintings of Polygnotus, Micon, and others, were built. Pericles,

however, made the greatest contribution with both the Parthenon and the Erechtheion. During his time the theater of Dionysus was also completed. Julius and Augustus Caesar contributed to the erection of the portico of Athena Archegetis. But it was Hadrian who contributed most of all to the architectural splendor of the city. He completed the temple of Zeus Olympius and erected temples, a library, and a stoa.

The gates of Athens were: (1) Dipylum—to Thria and Eleusis; (2) Sacred Gate—to Eleusis; (3) Peiraic—to Peiraeus; (4) Melitian—to Melite; (5) Itonian—to Phalerum (with a monument of Antiope the Amazon standing just within the gate); (6) Diochares—to the Lyceum; (7) Diomeian—to Cynosarges; (8) Herian—to the outer Cerameicus; (9) Acharnian—to Acharnae; (10) Equestrian; and (11) the Gate of Aegeus.

Pausanias, father of all Baedekers, travelled through Greece about A.D. 160 and described it in his *Periegesis,* or *Tour.* His books were for tourists, of which Greece had many even in the second century. His description of Athens gives us a most thorough picture of the city and many of its still existing and, at that time, even recent monuments and art works. Moving about the city he described buildings and objects that have been viewed ever since by literally millions of people. His *Tour* succeeded beyond his wildest dreams, beyond anything he could have imagined. Various things he wrote about have disappeared over the centuries, but much remains. The modern tourist crosses and recrosses his ancient itinerary. It is probably just as well not to try to follow his steps. The following account organizes the ancient remains and known but vanished buildings and monuments by general areas, with the Acropolis as the focus.

West of the Acropolis: The favorite but not the most direct way from Peiraeus led through the Ceramic Gate. The Cerameicus was actually a deme. The brook Eridanus flowed across it. The area was said to have taken its name from Ceramos, a supposed son of Dionysus and Ariadne. In the Outer Cerameicus lay the Peribolos of Artemis Calliste as well as that of Artemis Soteira, a precinct long attributed to the worship of Hecate. From the gate to the Cerameicus extended colonnades. One of them contained sanctuaries of the gods, a gymnasium of Hermes, and a house consecrated to Dionysus Melpomenus, in which some of the noblest Athenians are said to have imitated the Eleusinian mysteries. Here were also statues of Athena Paeonia, of Zeus, of Mnemosyne, of the Muses, and of Apollo. Here also was the demigod Acratus, one of the companions of Dionysus, whose face was the only thing seen projecting from the wall. A relief showed Amphictyon, king of the Athenians, entertaining Dionysus and other gods. The most impressive building in the Inner Cerameicus was the Pompeion. Here were kept those items necessary for the processions. It can still be seen today.

The Cerameicus was adjacent to Melite, a deme of the tribe Cecropis. Its boundaries cannot be determined, but it probably included the hills of the Nymphs, the Pnyx, and the Museion. It also encompassed two separate demes. Melite is said to have been named from a wife of Heracles. It was one of the most populous parts of the city and contained several temples as well as houses of distinguished men. In Melite were the Hephaestion, the Eurysaceion, the Colonus Agoraeus, the temple of Heracles Alexicacus, the Melanippeion (in which Melanippus, the son of Theseus was buried), the temple of Athena Aristobula, and private homes of noted persons of the past.

Still in Melite, between the Pompeion and the Stoa of Zeus lay the Sanctuary of Demeter, Kore, and Iacchus with statues of them by Praxiteles (Paus. 1.2.4). A damaged monumental base signed by Praxiteles was found built into a wall north of the railway and today is in the National Museum. Since Heracles is said to have been initiated into the Lesser Eleusinian mysteries in Melite, it is likely that Demeter's sanctuary is the one in which the initiation took place. It was probably for this reason that a temple was also built to Heracles in Melite, in which at the time of the plague there was dedicated the celebrated statue of Heracles Alexicacus.

The two demes incorporated in the area of the more extensive Melite were Scambonidae and Collytus. Scambonidae belonged to the tribe of Leontis. Its connection with the deme Melite is intimated in the legend that Melite derived its name from Melite, a daughter of Myrmex and wife of Heracles and that this Myrmex gave his name to a street in Scambonidae. The deme of Collytus belonged to the tribe Aegeis. We are told that Collytus was the father of Diomus, the favorite of Heracles. This deme might have been between the hills of Pnyx and Museion. The Pnyx was the meeting place of the Ecclesia, or Assembly. The Museion derived its name from Musaeus, the poet successor of Orpheus, according to tradition, but the name probably came from the Muses, who may have had a shrine there. To the north of the Pnyx rises the so-called Hill of the Nymphs to a height of 104 meters. The name is a modern one, derived from the dedication to the Nymphs that was carved on a rock in the garden of the observatory. On a rock below the Church of Agia Marina is an inscription written from right to left marking the boundary of the Precinct of Zeus.

On the immediate west of the Acropolis is the Areiopagus. The Areiopagus, or Hill of Ares, was so called because Ares was brought to trial here before the assembled gods by Poseidon on account of his murdering Halirrhothius, a son of Poseidon. Here Aeschylus placed the camp of the Amazons (*Eum.* 681–706). He also described the trial of Orestes on the Areiopagus for the murder of his mother. There are still sixteen steps leading up to the hill from the area adjacent to the Acropolis. About forty-five meters southeast from the top of the steps there is a wide chasm in the rocks leading to a recess. This was the sanctuary of the Eumenides, commonly called by the Athenians the Semnae (Venerable Goddesses) (Paus. 1.28.6). Within this sacred enclosure was the tomb of Oedipus (Paus. 1.28.7), the possession of which was long regarded as essential to the safety of Athens. Between the sanctuary of the Semnae and the lowest gate of the Acropolis stood the shrine of Hesychius, to whom a ram was burned before the sacrifices to the Eumenides. His descendants, the Hesychidae, were the hereditary priests of these goddesses. The precinct of the cave was a recognized sanctuary for murderers and fugitive slaves. Persons acquitted by the court of the Areiopagus usually sacrificed at the cave as well.

Beyond the Outer Cerameicus was the Academy. The road to the Academy (Academia), which was about 1 or 1.5 km from the Dipylum Gate, ran through the Outer Cerameicus. It was called the most beautiful suburb of the city. The Academy is said to have belonged originally to the hero Academus and was afterward converted into a gymnasium. It was surrounded by a wall and was adorned with walks, groves, and fountains. The beauty of the plane trees and olive plantations was particularly celebrated (Plin. 12.1.5). In front of the entrance were a statue and an altar of Eros, and within the enclosure were a temple of Athena and altars of the Muses, Prometheus, Heracles, etc. (Paus. 1.30.2). It was from the altar of Prometheus that the race of the Lampadephoria started. Near the temple of Athena in the Academy were the Moriae, or sacred olives, which were derived from the sacred olive in the Erechtheion. This was the first olive tree planted in Attica, and one of the Moriae was shown to Pausanias as the second. They were under the guardianship of Zeus Morius. A little way beyond the Academy was the hill of Colonus, immortalized by the tragedy of Sophocles. This hill, known today as the hill of Colonus Hippios, the refuge of Oedipus (*Oed. Col.* 688–719), is fifty-six meters in height and lies to the east of Odos Lenorman, enveloped by the city. The name of Academia is still attached to this area of the city.

North of the Acropolis: To the North of the Acropolis lay the center of the ancient city. The Agora was the assembly where the Athenians met daily for all aspects of community life. In 1970 excavations uncovered the Stoa Basileius, or Royal Colonnade, in which the Archon Basileus held his court. Upon the roof of the Stoa Basileius were statues of Theseus throwing Sciron into the sea and of Hemera carrying away Cephalus. Near the Portico of the Stoa were statues of Athenian generals and

Zeus Eleutherius. A number of sockets for hermae, or phallic monuments, may be seen at the north end. The Epilenaia, a drama festival, was possibly held in front of the Royal Stoa. To the east is the Leocoreion. Pausanias did not mention this monument, which commemorates the daughters of Leos, who were sacrificed to save Athens from a plague.

Behind the Portico of Zeus Eleutherius is the Stoa of Zeus Eleutherius, which stands alongside the Stoa Basileius. The foundations of this stoa extend to the railway, the construction of which destroyed the north wing. The stoa was built by unknown architects about 430 B.C. to honor Zeus as savior of the Athenians from the Persians.

Near the Stoa Basileius was the Temple of Apollo Patrous, the same deity as the Pythian Apollo but worshipped at Athens as a guardian under the name of Patrous (Dem. *De Cor.* 274). The statue of Apollo that stood inside is probably the one now in the Stoa of Attalos. Apollo Patrous (Father) was specially worshipped as the father of Ion by the Athenians, who counted themselves of Ionian descent. He was patron deity of state administration; before him magistrates were sworn and citizens registered. Adjoining are the remains of the Temple of Zeus Phratrius and Athena Phratria, the deities of the ancestral religious brotherhoods, or phratries.

South of these buildings was the Metroon, a Temple of the Mother of the Gods, whose statue was made by Pheidias. Here public records were kept. In front of the Metroon is a row of foundations for monuments. Here has been reerected a headless statue of Hadrian. It is identified by the decoration of the corset, which includes a crowned Athena standing upon the wolf suckling Romulus and Remus.

Near the Metroon was the Bouleuterion, or Council House of the Five Hundred, in which were sanctuaries of Zeus Boulaeus and Athena Boulaea and an altar of Hestia Boulaea. Suppliants placed themselves under the protection of these deities, and oaths were taken upon their altars (Xenoph. *Hellen.* 2.3.52; Diod. 14.4).

The Tholos, or more properly the Prytanicon, stood immediately south of the Bouleuterion. It was a circular building and was covered with a dome built of stone. It contained some small silver images of the gods and was the place where the fifty Prytanes, the presidential committee, took their common meals and offered their sacrifices (Dem. *De Fals. Leg.* 419). Discovered in 1934, it provided the first certain fixed point for relative locations within the Agora. In ancient times the building became the headquarters of Athenian government.

Going back toward the north one finds remains of the Peribolos of the Eponymous Heroes, in which stood statues of the ten legendary heroes chosen by the Delphic oracle as "founders" of the original ten tribes. After these were the statues of Amphiaraus and of Eirene, bearing Plutus as her son. Situated on the side of the Panathenaic Way was an altar, thought to be that of Eleos (Pity). It was also used as the point from which distances were measured, and it was a place of sanctuary. Next was the Temple of Ares, in which were two statues of Aphrodite, one of Ares by Alcamenes, an Athena by Locrus of Paros, and a statue of Enyo by the sons of Praxiteles. Around this temple there stood statues of Heracles, Theseus, and Apollo. The site of the Temple of Ares has been marked. North of this was an altar supposed to be that of Aeacus. To the extreme north of this range of buildings and monuments was the Peribolos of the Twelve Gods, much of which is obscured by the railway.

Going south along the Panathenaic Way, one comes to the ruins of the Odeion, or concert hall, which looked north to the Stoa of the Giants. This stoa was destroyed and rebuilt and destroyed again by fire. About A.D. 400 a gymnasium was built on the site. The Odeion seated about 1,000 people, but only a few marble seats are preserved. In the Odeion was also a statue of Dionysus. The Giants, two of which are in fact Tritons, were reused in the facade of the fifth century gymnasium. Near the Odeion and gymnasium was a fountain called Enneacrunus (Nine Pipes) since it was so constructed by Peisistratus. Today we can see remains of its presence known as the Fountain House. Beyond the fountain was a temple dedicated to Demeter and Kore. A statue of Triptolemus stood inside another temple, outside of which was an ox of bronze. Still farther was the temple of Eucleia.

Overlooking the Agora is the temple of Hephaestus, the so-called Theseion. The misnomer "Theseion" is not likely to be easily displaced from popular usage. The Hephaestion, as it should rightly be called, was mistaken in the Middle Ages for the shrine erected in 475 B.C. to house the bones of Theseus recovered from Scyros. The mistake was partially due to the metopes on the east of the temple that depict eight exploits of Theseus. The ten metopes of the east front show nine of the twelve labors of Heracles. The true Theseion, which ancient sources locate on the north slope of the Acropolis, has not yet been found.

Near the Hephaestion was the Eurysaceion, or shrine of Eurysaces. He and his brother Philaeus had given up Salamis to the Athenians and had been given property in Attica. The property of Eurysaces was in the deme of Melite (Plut. *Sol.* 10). Also near the Hephaestion was a sanctuary of Aphrodite Urania. Pausanias visited another stoa in the Agora area. It was the Stoa Poikile, on the approach to which was a bronze Hermes, surnamed Agoraeus. This was the Stoa from which the Stoic philosophers obtained their name (Lucian *Demon.* 14). It had three walls covered with paintings, thus the name *poikile,* meaning "painted" or "adorned." On one wall was the battle of Oenoe in Argolis. On the center wall was a picture of the Athenians under Theseus fighting against the Amazons and another representing the rape of Cassandra by Ajax. On a third wall was a painting of the battle of Marathon. These paintings, probably executed on wooden plaques, were very celebrated. The paintings had disappeared before A.D. 402. The remains of the Stoa Poikile have not yet been located but have been supposed to be under the north side of Odos Adrianou.

Pausanias' account of buildings in the Agora ignores the Stoa of Attalos, which today is a principal tourist site in Athens. Erected by Attalos II, king of Pergamum (159–138 B.C.), it was used for all manner of public events and for buying and selling. On the ground floor beneath the portico are displayed various sculptures, bases, and reliefs. Among these are the Apollo Patrous by Euphanor, a base for statues of Demeter and Kore, the *Iliad* and *Odyssey* personified, Aphrodite, a Nereid, Athena, and Nike (Victory). In the Exhibition Gallery are vases with mythological subjects, e.g., a kylix depicting Achilles and Memnon in combat, paintings showing the introduction of Heracles to Olympus and Greeks and Trojans fighting for the body of Patroclus, and a replica of the Apollo Lyceius of Praxiteles.

At the south end of the Stoa of Attalos was the Library of Pantainos. Titus Flavius Pantainos had this built before A.D. 102 and dedicated it to Athena Polias. On along the Panathenaic Way, the site of the Eleusinion has been identified by the discovery of reliefs, inscriptions, and pottery relating to the worship of Demeter and Kore. Diagonally across from the Library of Pantainos are the remains of a Nymphaion and a fountain-house.

South of the Odeion and across from the south end of the Stoa of Attalos was the Gymnasium of Ptolemy, which contained hermae of stone and a few historical statues. Pausanias describes the temple of Theseus, which he placed near the Gymnasium. As mentioned earlier, this temple has never been found. After leaving the Thesion, Pausanias went to the temple of the Dioscuri, frequently named the Anaceion because the Dioscuri were called the Anaces, or *Anacoi,* by the Athenians (Plut. *Thes.* 33). He did not, however, mention the distance from the Theseion to the Anaceion or the direction which he took. He only adds that above the temple of the Dioscuri was the sacred enclosure of Agraulos. The latter was situated on the north side of the Acropolis immediately under the Erechtheion. Near the Agraulion, says Pausanias, was the Prytaneion. The site of the Prytaneion, which was the official center of the city where the sacred flame was kept burning, has not yet been found.

North of the Acropolis are other monuments. Of these, two of the most celebrated are the Portico of Athena Archegetis and the Horologium of Andronicus Cyrrhestes. The former is the main entrance to the Roman market. It has an outer portico with four columns, which support a pediment. A worn inscription records the dedication of the building to Athena Archegetis and states that its erection was due to the generosity of Julius and Augustus Caesar. Beyond the Portico outside the market stands the Tower of the Winds, properly the Horologium of Andronicus Cyrrhestes. It was built in the first century B.C. by the astronomer Andronicus of Cyrrhos as a sundial, waterclock, and weathervane. On the octagonal structure each face marks a cardinal point and is decorated with a relief representing the wind blowing from that direction. The tower, according to Vitruvius (1.6.4), originally featured a revolving bronze Triton holding a wand, which pointed out the face coinciding with the wind direction at the time. The eight figures are represented as winged and floating almost horizontally through the air.

East of the Acropolis: Pausanias went straight from the Prytaneion to the Olympieion, between which buildings he noticed the Temple of Serapis, the meeting place of Theseus and Perithous, and the Temple of Eileithyia.

The Arch of Hadrian, which is still extant, is opposite the Olympieion and provided one entrance to the temple. This arch, once adorned with Corinthian columns, was inscribed on both sides, describing the arch as dividing "Athens, the ancient city of Theseus" from the "City of Hadrian."

The Sanctuary of Olympian Zeus is on a terrace surrounded by a retaining wall, which has been mostly restored. In the center stand the majestic remains of the Olympieiom, or Temple of the Olympian Zeus, the largest temple in Greece. It took seven hundred years to build. The task was completed finally by Hadrian, who dedicated the temple on his second visit to Athens *ca.* A.D. 130 and set up within it a chryselephantine statue of the god (a copy of that by Pheidias at Olympia), along with a colossal statue of himself. Scanty remains of a small, early shrine have been discovered with an exit through a subterranean passage to the Ilissus. This rather supports a tradition that a temple was founded here by Deucalion over the chasm through which the waters receded after the flood. Pausanias relates that in commemoration of this event an annual sacrifice of flour mixed with honey was thrown into the cleft. The ruins of the Olympieion are popularly known as Kolonnaes; the columns are floodlit in summer.

After describing the Olympieion, Pausanias mentions the temples of Apollo Pythius and Apollo Delphinius. The Phythion was one of the most ancient sanctuaries in Athens. It was separated from the Temple of Zeus by a wall, upon which was the altar of Zeus Astrapaeus. The Delphinion was apparently near the

Python. It was also a temple of great antiquity, having been founded, so it was said, by Aegeus. In its neighborhood sat one of the courts for the trial of homicides. A temple of Hera and Zeus Panhellenius and a sanctuary common to all the gods were also in the area. These had been constructed by Hadrian. Nearby the remains associated with the precinct of Cronus and Rhea can be seen today.

The Ilissus flows from two sources on the slopes of Hymettus, one at Kaisariani and the other at Agios Ioannis Theologos. The united branches, either underground or canalized, flow on the south side of the city, passing on the south side of the Museion, and eventually emptying into the Bay of Falero. The area extending outside the south wall of the city along the river bank was in ancient times known as *Kepoi* (Gardens). In this locality was a temple of Aphrodite; the statue of this goddess by Alcamenes, called Aphrodite in the Gardens, was one of the most famous pieces of statuary in all Athens (Plin. 36.5).

Here also was the Callirrhoe Spring, the only source of good drinkable water in Athens. It was employed in all the more important services of religion and by women prior to their nuptials (Thuc. 2.15). The waters of the fountain were made to pass through small pipes pierced in the face of the rock, through which they descended into the pool below. Of these orifices seven are still visible. The fountain also received a supply of water from the cistern in the Olympieion. Near the spring an eroded statue of Pan can be found in a space cut into the rock.

There were several other buildings in this area. On the banks of the Ilissus River were the altar of Boreas, who carried off Oreithyia from those banks, and the altar of the Ilissian Muses (Herod. 7.189). The altar of Boreas is described by Plato (*Phaedr.* 6) as opposite the temple of Artemis Agrotera. On the other side of the Ilissus, Pausanias entered the district Agrae or Agra, in which was the temple of Artemis Agrotera. On the south side of the Arditos highway near Odos D. Koutoula are the remains of a temple wall known as the Temple by the Ilissus. It may be the temple of Artemis Agrotera.

The Cynosarges and Lyceum were both situated outside the walls. This was the district known as Diomeia. Cynosarges was a sanctuary of Heracles and a gymnasium. It is said to have derived its name from a white dog, which carried off part of the victim, when sacrifices were first offered by Diomus to Heracles (Herod. 5.63, 6.116). The Lyceum, a gymnasium dedicated to Apollo Lyceius, was also situated in this area (Paus. 1.19.3). It was the chief of the Athenian gymnasia and was adorned by Peisistratus, Pericles, and Lycurgus. In the vicinity of the Lyceum was a fountain of the hero Panops.

The Panathenaic Stadium was also situated on the south side of the Ilissus. The Stadium was constructed *ca.*

350 B.C., but it had been used previously for the athletic contests of the Panathenaic games. It was capable of accommodating forty thousand persons on the marble seats that were eventually built.

The most prominent landmark east of the Acropolis is Lycabettus (Likavitos). This is the lofty, isolated mountain overhanging the city on its northeast side. This hill was identified by the ancient geographers with Anchesmus, which is described by Pausanias (1.32.2) as a small mountain with a statue of Zeus Anchesimus. According to Attic legend, Athena went to Pallene, a deme to the northeast of Athens in order to procure a mountain to serve as a bulwark in front of the Acropolis; returning with the mountain, she was told by a crow of the birth of Erichthonius and dropped Mount Lycabettus on the spot where it still stands.

South of the Acropolis: At the immediate east end of the base of the Acropolis ran a street that led to the Lenaion or sacred enclosure of Dionysus. The position is marked by the existing Choragic Monument of Lysicrates. This elegant monument was dedicated by Lysicrates in 335–334 B.C. The frieze of the monument represents the destruction of the Tyrrhenian pirates by Dionysus. It was the practice of the victorious leaders of the choruses to dedicate to Dionysus the tripods they had gained in the contests in the theater. Many of these tripods were placed upon small temples, which were erected either in the precincts of the theater or in the street that ran along the east side of the Acropolis from the Prytaneion to the Lenaion. This street was near the theater and was called the Street of the Tripods (Paus. 1.20.1). High above this street in a cavern in the middle of the rocks at the east end of the Acropolis was the Eleusinion, which has been identified by the discovery of reliefs, inscriptions, and cult pottery.

The Lenaion, which contained two temples of Dionysus and which was close to the theater, was situated in the district called Limnae. It was here that the Dionysiac festival called Lenaea was celebrated (Thuc. 2.15).

On the south of the Acropolis rock, the modern visitor crosses the line of wall that once bounded the sacred enclosure of Dionysus Eleuthereus. Traces of the wall survive to the east, but the main entrance to the precinct from the Street of the Tripods has not been excavated. The worship of Dionysus Eleuthereus was introduced into Athens in the sixth century B.C. from Eleutherae in Boeotia. The earliest festival was called Lenaea (Winepress) but was supplanted by the Dionysia, which was characterized by competing choruses dressed like satyrs, who danced round the altar of the god and sang their "goat songs." These poetic and musical contests anticipated Greek tragedy.

Inside the sacred area are the foundations of a small fourth century temple built to house the chryselephantine statue of Dionysus by Alcamenes. Its base can still be seen. An older temple is nearer the theater. The stone theater of Dionysus was started in 500 B.C. but not finished for another 150 years. This theater lay beneath the south wall of the Acropolis near its east end. Sixty front-row seats remain, including the elaborate throne of the priest of Dionysus Eleuthereus. The reliefs in the orchestra portray scenes from the life of Dionysus. Above the theater is a grotto that was converted into a small temple by Thrasyllus, a victorious chorus director. Inside the cavern were statues of Apollo and Artemis destroying the children of Niobe. Upon the face of the temple was a colossal figure of Dionysus, now in the British Museum.

West of the theater was the Tomb of Calos, or Talos, below the steep height of the Acropolis, from which Daedalus is said to have hurled him down. There is no evidence today of such a tomb. Next came the Asclepieion or Sanctuary of Asclepius, which stood immediately above the Odeion of Herodes Atticus (which had not been constructed in Pausanias' time). Its site is determined by the statement that it contained a fountain celebrated as the one at which Ares slew Halirrhothius, the son of Poseidon. The Asclepieion, or Sanctuary of Asclepius in the City, was dedicated in 418 B.C. The worship of Asclepius, which spread from Epidaurus, was introduced into Athens on the occasion of the plague of 429 B.C. The cure of patients followed a ritual: they washed in the sacred spring, offered sacrifices at an altar, and then retired to await dreams, through which Asclepius was supposed to reveal his cure.

To the south of the Odeion, on either side of the modern entrance stairway, are remains of various dates including a sanctuary of the nymphs, excavated in 1955–1959. Next to the Asclepieion on the ascent to the Acropolis was the temple of Themis (with the tomb of Hippolytus in front of it), the temple of Aphrodite Pandemos and Peitho, and the temple of Gaea Curotropos and Demeter Chloe. All these sanctuaries have disappeared except for fragments belonging to the shrine of Aphrodite Pandemos. The proximity of this temple to the tomb of Hippolytus is alluded to in Euripides (*Hippol.* 29). The temple of Gaea and Demeter was probably situated beneath the temple of Athena Nike.

The Acropolis: The Acropolis served as the fortress, the sanctuary, and the museum of the city. At the time of the Persian Wars it had ceased to be inhabited as the city itself and was used exclusively for the worship of Athena and the other guardian deities of the city. It was one immense sanctuary. Every four years the Panathenaic festival took place, and a great procession accompanied the peplos, or embroidered robe, of Athena to her temple

on the Acropolis. There were three manifestations of Athena on the Acropolis. The most ancient was Athena Polias (Protector of the City), made of olive wood and said to have fallen from heaven; her sanctuary was the Erechtheion. The second was the Athena Parthenos (Virgin) a statue of ivory and gold, the work of Pheidias. The third was the Athena Promachus (Champion) a colossal statue of bronze, also the work of Pheidias, standing erect with helmet, spear, and shield. This Athena was also called the "Bronze" or the "Great Athena" (Dem. *De Fals. Leg.* 428). Since it stood in the open nearly opposite the Propylaea, it was one of the first things seen upon entering. It was of gigantic size. It was taller even than the Parthenon, and the point of its spear and the crest of its helmet were visible off the promontory of Sunium to ships approaching Athens (Paus. 1.28.2). With its pedestal it must have stood about twenty-one meters high. The peplos of the Panathenaic procession was carried to the ancient statue of Athena Polias and not to the Athena of the Parthenon.

Being a citadel, the Acropolis was fortified and had been since the time of the ancient Pelasgians, who are said to have built a wall around it called the Pelasgic Wall (Herod. 5.64). The rocks along the north side of the Acropolis were called the Long Rocks.

The Cave of Apollo and Pan, more usually called the Cave of Pan, lay at the base of the northwest angle of the Acropolis, a little below the Propylaea, near a spring of water. Here Apollo is said to have had sexual intercourse with Creusa, who became the mother of Ion. The worship of Pan in this cave was introduced after the battle of Marathon because of the services he rendered to the Athenians on that occasion. The fountain near the cave was called Clepsydra from its being supposed to have had a subterranean communication with the harbor of Phalerum.

The sanctuary of Agraulos, one of the three daughters of Cecrops, was also a cavern situated on the north face of the Acropolis. The Agraulion was in part of the Long Rocks, which ran east of the grotto of Pan. It was at this spot that Agraulos and her sister Herse threw themselves from the rocks of the Acropolis after opening the chest that contained Erichthonius (Paus. 1.18.2). According to one tradition, Agraulos leapt from the Acropolis as a sacrifice to save her country; and it was probably on this account that the Athenian ephebi took the oath of patriotism already mentioned. There was an opening from the cave to the floor of the citadel. An ancient flight of stairs found near the Erechtheion led into the cavern.

The road up the west slope of the Acropolis led from the Agora and was paved with slabs of Pentelic marble. At the summit of the rock is the Propylaea, one of the masterpieces of Athenian art. The Propylaea is made up of a central hall with a doorway and two wings. The entrances had massive wooden gates. Adjacent to the north wing was a room called the Pinakotheke, which was a picture gallery. In the south wing a small enclosure was a precinct of the Graces, associated probably with the worship of Hecate of the Tower, who had a triple image located nearby. Near the enclosure of Artemis Brauronia, which abutted on the Propylaea, was a bronze statue of the Trojan horse from which Menestheus, Teucer, and the sons of Theseus were represented looking out. From other authorities we learn that spears projected from this horse and also that it was of colossal size (Aristoph. *Av.* 1128).

On the west front of the south wing stood the small temple of Nike Apteros (Wingless Victory) (Paus. 1.22.4). From here the Saronic Gulf is visible, and it was here that Aegeus is said to have watched the return of Theseus from Crete (Paus. 1.22.4). From this part of the rock he threw himself when he saw the black sail on the mast of the ship bringing Theseus home. The temple of Nike Apteros, built entirely of Pentelic marble, is nearly square, with an entrance having four Ionic columns on each end. Athena may be distinguished on the east frieze by her shield; next to her appears to be Zeus. At the south corner are Peitho, Aphrodite, and Eros. Inside was a marble statue of Athena holding in her right hand a pomegranate and in her left hand the helmet of the Athena Areia. Nike Apteros was identified with Athena and was called Nike Athena. The reliefs, which date from *ca.* 410 B.C., represented a band of winged Victories attendant upon Athena and included the famous Victory adjusting her sandal. Standing as she did at the exit from the Acropolis, her protection was sought by persons starting on hazardous missions.

A flight of steps to the left of the Propylaea probably was a secret staircase used every year by the *Arrephoroi.* These were two (or four) girls of noble birth between the ages of seven and eleven, chosen to perform a special service in honor of Athena. They wove and carried the peplos, but by an underground passage they also carried down to the sanctuary of Aphrodite in the Gardens (not yet located) some sort of ritual object. This they exchanged for another mysterious object that they brought back.

The Parthenon derived its name from its being the temple of Athena Parthenos (Virgin). It was built under the administration of Pericles, and its architects, according to Plutarch, were Callicrates and Ictinus. The general superintendence of the erection was entrusted to Pheidias.

At the west front of the Parthenon is a flight of nine steps cut in the rock and seven more, in fragments, continue upward. Before the steps stood the bull set up by the Council of the Areiopagus. Below the steps was the entrance court, closed on the south side by the Chalcothece, or magazine of bronzes. To the west of this was the sanctuary of Artemis Brauronia. Within this area, which was really a small stoa, is the pedestal (two marble blocks) of a colossal bronze figure of the Trojan Horse. At the corner of the Propylaea is the round pedestal of a statue to Athena Hygieia. During the building of the Propylaea one of the workmen fell and was badly hurt. Pericles was told by Athena in a dream how to cure him, and in gratitude set up a bronze image of the goddess (Plut. *Per.* 13).

Between the Propylaea and the Parthenon were many statues. A few paces in front of the Propylaea may be seen some foundations on which stood the colossal statue of Athena Promachos by Pheidias. It was a monument to Athenian valor in the Persian Wars. The goddess was represented standing with her right arm leaning on her spear and holding in her left a shield with figures in relief of the battle of the Lapiths and Centaurs. North of the Parthenon is a rock-carved dedication to Gaea Carpophoros. Here stood a personification, rising apparently from the ground, of Earth praying to Zeus for rain.

The Parthenon was designed to provide a new sanctuary exclusively for Athena Polias. Here her statue might be suitably housed and the Athenian treasure stored. It was erected in 447–438 B.C. as the tallest building on the Acropolis and situated on its highest part. Pheidias supervised, if he did not actually design, all of the sculptures. He was, however, solely responsible for the creation of the chryselephantine statue of Athena. The name Parthenon, meaning the Virgin's Apartment, originally applied to one room in the temple. The statue of Athena Polias became popularly though unofficially known as Athena Parthenos.

We know from Pausanias (1.24.5) that the subject of the sculptures on the east pediment was the birth of Athena, but there is little left of them. What we actually see are a part of a statue of Helios, four heads of the horses of his chariot rising from the sea, the reclining figure of Dionysus (or Theseus), and a head of Selene's horse, with original, battered remains of two other horseheads. These are a combination of casts and originals, most of the originals being part of the Elgin Marbles in the British Museum. The west pediment represented the contest of Athena and Poseidon for the possession of Attica. What we see are Cecrops seated and his daughter Pandrosos kneeling with her arm about his shoulders. All these are originals except for part of the serpent on which Cecrops is seated; this also is in the British Museum. The metopes were originally ninety-two in number. Only forty-one remain but for the most part they are so battered as to be unrecognizable. The metopes in the British Museum and the Louvre are all from the south side and depict the contest of the Lapithae and Centaurs.

Those of the east front remain in position; they represent the Gigantomachia. The subject of the metopes of the west front appears to be an Amazonomachia.

The statue of Athena Polias, popularly called Athena Parthenos, was of gold plate over a wooden frame and stood, with the pedestal, nearly twelve meters high. The face, hands, and feet were of ivory. The pupils of the eyes were of precious stones. The goddess stood upright, clad in a dress that reached to her feet; on her breast was the head of Medusa wrought in ivory; in her right hand she held a crowned Victory nearly two meters high, and in the other a spear. On her helmet was a sphinx flanked by griffons in relief. On her sandals was chiselled the battle of the Centaurs and Lapiths. At her feet was a shield, on the outside of which was carved in relief the battle of the Amazons with the Athenians. On the inside was a representation of the Gigantomachia. Near the base of the spear was a serpent, perhaps Erichthonius. On the pedestal in relief was the birth of Pandora. The dress and other ornaments were all of solid gold and weighed over 1,000 kilograms.

Around the outer walls of the enclosure and seven meters above the floor ran a continuous Ionic frieze. Existing parts of it in Athens and in the British Museum give a reasonably good idea of its content. It represented the procession of celebrants at the Great Panathenaic Festival. The Greater Panathenaia was founded by Erichthonius and renewed by Theseus. It occurred on every fourth anniversary of Athena's birthday, in the month of Hecatombaeon (August). Athletic, musical, and equestrian contests were held, and the victors received Panathenaic prizes of vases of olive oil from the sacred olive trees. In the Procession, the new embroidered robe (*peplos*) of Athena Polias was borne in state through the streets of Athens on a ship on wheels. The robe was probably woven by the *Arrephoroi*, the maids in waiting on Athena. The celebration ended with a sacrifice, after which the robe was deposited in the Erechtheion.

The Erechtheion stands near the north end of the Acropolis, about halfway between the east and west ends. It was designed to succeed the old temple of Athena (the foundations of which lie between the Erechtheion and the Parthenon). It is a rectangle with a projecting porch on either side. In one chamber of the Erechtheion were the altars of Poseidon-Erechtheus, of Hephaestus, and of the hero Butes. In the other cella was the highly venerated olive-wood statue of Athena Polias, not to be confused with the Athena Polias in the Parthenon. The goddess held a round shield on which was carved the head of Medusa (Eurip. *Elec.* 1254–57). The sacred robe, renewed every four years at the Panathenaic Festival, was woven to adorn her shrine. In front of the statue was a golden lamp tended by elderly widows. In other parts of the cella were a wooden Hermes, said to have been presented by

Cecrops, and a folding chair made by Daedalus. Beneath the antechamber was the Erechtheian "sea." This was a well, presumably covered with marble tiles. Near it were markings believed to have been left by Poseidon's trident, which caused the well to appear. When the south wind blew, the well gave forth the sound of waves.

Near the colonnaded north portico stood the altar of the Thyechoos, a priest who offered sacrifices of honey cakes to Zeus Hypatus. An opening from here leads into the basement of the temple, where lived the sacred serpent for whom the honey cakes served as food.

In an outer court below the north portico was the Pandroseion, or sacred enclosure of Pandrosos, which contained a small temple. Here grew the Sacred Olive of Athena, which was reported to have sprouted again after being burned by the Persians. The temple more than likely contained a statue of Pandrosos and an altar of Thallo, one of the Horae, to whom the Athenians paid divine honors along with Pandrosos (Paus. 9.35.2). More to the south was the Cecropion. The foundations of the Erechtheion were modified at the southwest corner to avoid disturbing an earlier structure, the presumed Tomb of Cecrops, which was covered by a single huge block of stone.

The south portico, or Porch of the Caryatids, formerly had six statues of maidens, rather more than life-size. The four surviving Caryatids are presently housed in the Acropolis Museum to prevent further deterioration. They originally stood four in front and two behind, their tunics made to resemble column flutings.

The Erechtheion was surrounded on most sides by a *temenos*, or sacred enclosure, separated from the rest of the Acropolis by a wall. In the *temenos* there were several statues, including the colossal figures in brass of Erechtheus and Eumolpus, ready to engage in combat; some ancient wooden statues of Athena; Cycnus fighting with Heracles; Theseus finding the sandals and sword of Aegeus under the rock; and Theseus and the Marathonian bull. Of the frieze of the temple only a little over one hundred fragments have been recovered, mostly in bad condition; they are in the Acropolis Museum.

The Acropolis Museum, with the exception of the bronzes and the bases (now in the National Museum) contains all the portable objects discovered on the Acropolis since 1834. Among items in the Museum with direct mythological reference are: the oldest known relief from the Acropolis showing Heracles and the Hydra, with Iolaus driving his chariot, and the crab sent by Hera to harass the hero; part of an early pediment representing Iris introducing Heracles to Zeus, Hera, and Athena after his apotheosis; pedimental figures of the Gigantomachia from the old temple of Athena (*ca.* 525 B.C.); fragments from the Parthenon pediments and metopes of Oreithyia, the contest of Athena and Poseidon, the birth of Athena, and a Centaur carrying off a Lapith woman; and the parapet of the temple of Athena Nike with the well-known Victory adjusting her sandal.

Elsewhere in Athens. Other objects of mythological interest can be found throughout Athens. On the corner of Euripidou and Menandrou streets is the chapel of Agios Ioannis Stin Kolona built around a Roman column with a Corinthian capital that projects through the roof. The column, probably from a gymnasium dedicated to Apollo, has a reputation for being able to cure fevers. In the Benaki Museum, Room BB contains objects from ancient Greece, notably a bronze Heracles from the sanctuary of Apollo Ptous in Boeotia (490–480 B.C.). There is a charming marble Pan at the left of the entrance to the Zappeion. This is a modern piece by Georgios Demetriades. In the Proto Necrotaphion Athenon, the principal cemetery of Athens, is buried Heinrich Schliemann (1822–1890), the archaeologist; Trojan scenes in bas-relief decorate his mausoleum. The nearby tomb of Adolf Furtwaengler (1853–1907) bears a marble copy of a sphinx he unearthed at Aegina. In front of the Hellenic Academy are the colossal figures of Athena and Apollo by the Greek sculptor Drosos; they occupy two tall and uninspiring Ionic columns.

The National Archaeological Museum is so vast and has such a staggering quantity of objects relating to mythology that it is necessary to refer viewers to the catalogs of the Museum. Not to be missed, however, are the gold mask of (according to Schliemann) Agamemnon, the powerful bronze statue of Poseidon (or Zeus), the relief from Eleusis, the Finlay Crater of Marsyas retrieving the double flute discarded by Athena, the Myrrhine Lekythos depicting Hermes Psychopompos leading Myrrhine to the river Acheron, and scores of heads, torsos, altars, and reliefs depicting gods and heroes brought from sites all over Greece.

Although the Athenians had particular deities and heroes to whom they paid special tribute, they accepted representations of other gods and mythological beings from all over Greece. Some of these had been brought by tribes who migrated to Athens. For example, the death and return to life of Adonis were celebrated in annual festivals, the Adonia, at Athens. Aeacus, the famed king of Aegina and later a judge in Hades, had a sanctuary at Athens. Acratopotes, the drinker of unmixed wine, was a hero worshipped in Munychia in Attica. According to Pausanias (1.2.5), who calls him simply Acratus, he was one of the divine companions of Dionysus. Pausanias saw his image at Athens in the house of Polytion, where it was fixed in the wall. Ajax the Greater was worshipped as an eponymous hero, one of the Attic tribes (Aeantis) being called after him (Plut. *Quaest. Conviv.* 1.10). After Heracles was raised to the rank of a god, his mother, Alcmena, and his sons feared Eurystheus and fled to

Athens. When Hyllus later cut off the head of Eurystheus, Alcmena satisfied her revenge by picking out its eyes (Apollod. 2.8.1). At Athens she was worshipped as a heroine, and an altar was erected to her in the temple of Heracles (Paus. 1.19.3). Amphiaraus, the celebrated hero of the expeditions against Thebes by the Seven and the Epigoni, was worshipped as a hero in all Greece; he had a statue at Athens (Paus. 1.8.2). So did Amphilochus, his son (Paus. 1.34.2).

The great Olympian gods were represented in Athens by a variety of temples, sanctuaries, statues, and festivals. Athena, of course, was the great divinity of Athens. She was protectress of the phratries and houses that formed the basis of the state. The festival of the Apaturia had a direct reference to this particular point in the character of the goddess. She was believed to have instituted the ancient court of the Areiopagus, and in cases where the votes of the judges were equally divided, she cast the pivotal vote in favor of the accused (Aeschyl. *Eum.* 753; Paus. 1.28.5). The two great festivals already discussed—the Panathenaea and Arrhephoria—were celebrated in her honor. She was frequently represented in works of art, and the three statues of her by Pheidias represented the highest ideal of perfection. The first was the celebrated, colossal, chryselephantine statue on the Acropolis; the second was a still greater bronze statue made out of the spoils taken by the Athenians in the battle of Marathon; the third was a small bronze statue called the Beautiful or the Lemnian Athena because it had been dedicated at Athens by the Lemnians. Athena Areia (Warlike) was worshipped at Athens. Her statue, together with those of Ares, Aphrodite, and Enyo, stood in the temple of Ares (Paus. 1.8.4). Her worship under this name was instituted by Orestes after he had been acquitted by the Areiopagus of the murder of his mother (Paus. 1.28.5). It was Athena Areia who gave the deciding vote in his case since the Areiopagites were equally divided. Athena had other surnames at Athens, such as Hippia (Paus. 1.30.4), Paeonia (Paus. 1.2.5), Pallenis (Herod. 1.62), Polias (Paus. 1.27.1), and Poliuchos. The Palladium was an image of Pallas Athena, generally an ancient one, which was kept hidden and secret and was revered as a pledge of the safety of the town or place where it existed. After the sack of Troy, several cities claimed the honor of possessing the ancient Trojan Palladium. Athens was one because it was believed that Diomedes, on his return from Troy, landed on the Attic coast at night and, without knowing where he was, began to plunder. But Demophon, who hastened to protect the country, took the Palladium from Diomedes (Paus. 1.26.9). This Palladium at Athens, however, was different from another image of Pallas there, which was also called Palladium and stood on the Acropolis.

Apollo was a popular god at Athens as everywhere else. Under the surname of Alexicacus (Averter of Evil), he was worshipped by the Athenians because he was believed to have stopped the plague that raged at Athens in the time of the Peloponnesian War (Paus. 1.3.4). Apollo Boedromius (Helper in Distress), was another name under which the Athenians worshipped him. According to some, the god was thus called because he had assisted the Athenians in the war with the Amazons, who were defeated on the seventh of Boedromion, the day on which the Boedromia were afterward celebrated (Plut. *Thes.* 27). According to others, the name arose from the circumstance that in the war of Erechtheus and Ion against Eumolpus, Apollo had advised the Athenians to rush upon the enemy with a war cry (*boi*) if they wanted to conquer (Callim. *Hymn. in Apoll.* 69). Under the names Delphinius and Pythius he had temples at Athens. He was also worshipped under the name of Apollo Lyceius (Paus. 1.19.4), a surname not altogether clear as to derivation but probably from the Athenian Lyceum. A statue of Apollo Parnopius (Expeller of Locusts) was on the Acropolis (Paus. 1.24.8).

Artemis, one of the great divinities of the Greeks and one with a large number of attributes and identifications, was variously worshipped at Athens. The Greeks identified the Taurian goddess with Artemis, and when Iphigeneia and Orestes returned from Tauris with the Taurian image, they landed at Brauron in Attica. From this place the goddess derived the name of Brauronia (Paus. 1.23.7, 33.1). The Brauronian Artemis had a temple on the Acropolis. Artemis was also worshipped at Athens under the names Agrotera (Huntress), Ariste (Best), Aristobule (Best Adviser), Calliste (Fairest), Delphinia, Leucophryne (from a town in Phrygia where Themistocles, who erected a statue of Artemis Leucophryne on the Acropolis, had once ruled), Lysizona (Goddess Who Loosens the Girdle), and Orthia.

Zeus, of course, as the supreme deity, was worshipped widely in Athens, notably at the vast temple of the Olympian Zeus. An altar of Zeus Hypatus existed in front of the Erechtheion, where it was allowed to offer up to him neither anything alive nor libations, but only cakes (Paus. 1.26.5). Zeus Maemactes (Stormy) named the Attic month Maemacterion. In that month the Maemacterion was celebrated at Athens (Plut. *De Cohib. Ir.* 9). Zeus Meilichius (Gracious), the god who can be propitiated, was the protector of those who honored him with propitiatory sacrifices. At Athens cakes were offered to him every year at the festival of the Diasia (Thuc. 1.126; Xenoph. *Anab.* 7.7.4). Altars were erected to Zeus Meilichius on the Cephissus (Paus. 1.37.4). Zeus Polieus (Protector of the City) had an altar on the Acropolis. Upon this altar barley and wheat were strewn, which were consumed by the bull about to be sacrificed to the god.

The priest who killed the victim threw away the ax as soon as he had struck the fatal blow, and the ax was then brought before a court of justice (Paus. 1.24.4, 28.11).

Demeter, the center of whose worship was at Eleusis, had many altars and statues at Athens, several of them in conjunction with Persephone. Some of her names and associations were a result of migrations of her worshippers to Athens from other places. For example, Demeter Achaea was worshipped at Athens by the Gephyraeans who had emigrated there from Boeotia (Herod. 5.61; Plut. *De Is. et Osir.* 378). Demeter Chloe (Blooming) was a name of Demeter as protectress of the green fields. Under this name she had a sanctuary at Athens jointly with Gaea Curotropos (Paus. 1.22.3). A festival called Chloeia was held in her honor. Thesmophoros (Lawgiver) was a surname of Demeter and Persephone, in honor of whom the Thesmophoria were celebrated at Athens in the month of Pyanepsion (Herod. 2.171, 6.16; Aristoph. *Thes.* 303), and to whom sanctuaries were also erected in other places. The Eleusinian mysteries belonged to Demeter and Persephone in common, but to Persephone alone were dedicated the mysteries celebrated at Athens in the month of Anthesterion. Triptolemus must also be mentioned in connection with Demeter. He was the Eleusinian upon whom Demeter bestowed the responsibility of spreading the cultivation of grain throughout Greece. He established the worship of Demeter and instituted the Thesmophoria (Dionys. 1.12; Ov. *Fast.* 4.507). He had temples and statues at both Eleusis and Athens. Mecon was the name of an Athenian whom Demeter loved and who was metamorphosed into a poppy plant (Callim. *Hymn. in Cer.* 45).

Dionysus was widely worshipped in Athens. Pegasus, a priest of Eleutherae, was believed to have introduced the worship of Dionysus at Athens (Paus. 1.2.5), but there is another version of the introduction of the god's worship into Attica. Icarius, also called Icarus or Icarion, was an Athenian who lived in the reign of Pandion and hospitably received Dionysus upon his arrival in Attica. The god showed him his gratitude by teaching him the cultivation of the vine and giving him bags filled with wine. Icarius now rode about in a chariot and distributed the precious gifts of the god; but some shepherds, whom their friends intoxicated with wine and who thought that they were poisoned by Icarius, slew him and threw his body into the well Anygrus. Other accounts maintain that the body was buried under a tree. His daughter Erigone (for he was married to Phanothea, the inventor of the hexameter) (Clem. Alex. *Strom.* 1.366), or, as some call her, Altis, searched for a long time and was finally conducted to his grave by his faithful dog Maera. In her grief his daughter hanged herself on the tree under which he was buried. Zeus or Dionysus placed her, together with Icarius and his cup among the stars; Erigone became the

Virgin, Icarius Bootes or Arcturus, and Maera the dog star. The god then punished the ungrateful Athenians with a plague or a mania, in which all the Athenian maidens hung themselves as Erigone had done (Gell. 15.10). The oracle, when consulted, answered that Athens should be delivered from the calamity as soon as Erigone should be propitiated and her own and her father's bodies should be found. The bodies were not discovered, but a festival was instituted in honor of Erigone, and fruits were offered up as a sacrifice to her and her father. The *ascoliasmos* or dancing on a leather bag filled with air and smeared with oil at the festivals of Dionysus was likewise traced to Icarius, who was said to have killed a ram for having injured the vines, made a bag of his skin, and then performed a dance. Dionysus Amphietes or Amphieterus was one of the names of the god at Athens, and since the Dionysiac festivals were held here annually, the name probably signifies yearly. Dionysus Antheus (Blooming) was another name he bore at Athens (Paus. 1.31.2). Dionysus Limnaea (Lake-Dwelling) was still another name (Thuc. 2.16; Aristoph. *Ran.* 216). Dionysus Melanaegis (Armed with a Black Aegis) also was known at Athens (Paus. 2.35.1). Still another manifestation was Dionysus Melpomenus (Singer) (Paus. 1.2.5). In the temple of the Horae at Athens there was an altar of Dionysus Orthos (Athen. 2.38). Iacchus was the solemn name of the mystic Bacchus at Athens and Eleusis. At Athens a statue of Iacchus bearing a torch in his hand was seen by the side of those of Demeter and Kore (Paus. 1.2.4). At the celebration of the great Eleusinian mysteries in honor of Demeter, Persephone, and Iacchus, the statue of the last divinity, carrying a torch and adorned with a myrtle wreath, was carried on the sixth day of the festival (the twentieth of Boedromion) from the temple of Demeter across the Thriasian plain to Eleusis. The statue of Iacchus was accompanied by a large, riotous procession of the initiated, who sang the Iacchus, carried mystic baskets, and danced amid the sounds of cymbals and trumpets (Plut. *Them.* 15, *Camil.* 19; Herod. 8.65). Finally should be mentioned the painting in the sanctuary of Dionysus at Athens of Lycurgus, the king of the Thracian Edones, who persecuted Dionysus and his worshippers. For this impiety he was blinded, and this punishment was depicted in the painting (Paus. 1.20.3).

Aphrodite had both temples and statues at Athens. The best known of these was the sanctuary of Aphrodite Pandemos (Common to All the People). In the sense that the surname applied to Aphrodite as uniting all the inhabitants of a country into one social or political body, she was worshipped at Athens, and her worship was said to have been instituted by Theseus at the time when he united the scattered townships into one great body of citizens (Paus. 1.22.3). According to some writers, it was Solon who erected the sanctuary of Aphrodite Pandemos,

either because her image stood in the agora or because the hetairae had to pay the costs of its erection (Athen. 13.569). A festival in honor of her is mentioned by Athenaeus (14.659). The sacrifices offered to her consisted of white goats (Lucian *Dial. Meret.* 7). The Sanctuary of Aphrodite in the Gardens has been previously mentioned in conjunction with the ritual performed by the Arrephoroi in the Panathenaea ceremony. Aphrodite's son, Eros, was also worshipped at Athens, where he had an altar at the entrance of the Academy (Paus. 1.30.1).

Ares, the god of war, was one of the great Olympian gods. According to a late tradition, he slew Halirrhothius, the son of Poseidon, as Halirrhothius was on the point of raping Alcippe, the daughter of Ares. Poseidon accused Ares in the Areiopagus, where the Olympain gods were assembled in court. Ares was acquitted, and this event was believed to have given rise to the name Areiopagus (Paus. 1.28.5; Apollod. 3.14.2). At Athens he had a temple containing a statue made by Alcamenes (Paus. 1.8.4). Enyo, the goddess of war, had a statue made by the sons of Praxiteles that stood in the temple of Ares (Paus. 1.8.4).

Hephaestus had temples and festivals in Athens in common with Athena. There was the famous statue of him by Alcamenes, in which his lameness was slightly indicated (Cic. *De Nat. Deor.* 1.30). His temple, the Hephaestion, has been described above.

Hades, the god of the underworld, had a temple at Athens in the grove of the Erinyes.

Poseidon was not a popular god in Athens except through his identification with Erechtheus. When Poseidon and Athena quarrelled over which of them should name the capital of Attica, the gods decided that the new city should take its name from the one who should bestow upon mankind the most useful gift. Poseidon then created the horse, and Athena called forth the olive tree. Earlier Poseidon had tried to take possession of Attica by thrusting his trident into the ground on the Acropolis thereby calling forth a well of salt water. Attica, however, was assigned to Athena. When he lost, Poseidon inundated all of the surrounding country (Apollod. 3.14.1).

Hestia, the goddess of the hearth, was regarded as one of the great gods. At Athens, as elsewhere in Greece, she had her special sanctuary under the name of Prytanitis with a statue and sacred hearth.

The more ancient gods were variously represented at Athens. The worship of Gaea, the personification of the earth, appears to have been universal among the Greeks. She had a temple at Athens and also a statue (Paus. 1.24.3). There was a temple of Rhea, the mother of the gods, in the *peribolos* (enclosure) of the Olympieion (Paus. 1.18.7), and the Athenians are said to have been the first among the Greeks who adopted her worship (Jul. *Orat.* 5). Mnemosyne, the goddess of memory, one of the Titans and mother of the Muses, had a statue at Athens (Paus. 1.2.5). Prometheus had a sanctuary in the Academy, from where a torch race took place in honor of him (Paus. 1.30.2). Themis, the personification of the order of things, was worshipped at Athens (Paus. 1.22.1). The Horae, personifications of the seasons and later regarded as the goddesses of order in general and of justice, were also worshipped at Athens. Two Horae, Thallo (Spring) and Carpo (Autumn) were worshipped from very early times (Paus. 9.35.2; Athen. 14.636). The Athenian youths, on becoming ephebi, mentioned Thallo, among other gods, in the oath they took in the temple of Agraulos. The temple of the Horae also contained an altar of Dionysus Orthus (Athen. 2.38). The Eumenides (Gracious Ones) were usually called by euphemistic names, because people dreaded to call these fearful goddesses, the Erinyes (Furies), by their real name; the name Eumenides was first given to them after the acquittal of Orestes by the court of the Areiopagus when their anger had become soothed (Soph. *Oed. Col.* 128). It was by a similar euphemism that at Athens the Erinyes were called *Semnai Theai* (Venerable Goddesses) (Paus. 1.28.6). At Athens there were statues of only two of them, although they are usually conceived of as three in number. They were worshipped at Athens, where they had a sanctuary and a grotto, as described, on the Areiopagus. Their statues were not formidable (Paus. 1.28.6), and a festival, the Eumenidcia, was celebrated at Athens in their honor. The Charities (Graces) were usually three in number, but the Athenians worshipped only two—Auxo and Hegemone—and had statues of them.

Other personifications of human characteristics had altars and statues at Athens. Eirene was the goddess of peace. After the victory of Timotheus over the Lacedaemonians, altars were erected to her at Athens at the public expense (Plut. *Cim.* 13). Her statue at Athens stood beside that of Amphiaraus, carrying in its arms Plutus, the god of wealth (Paus. 1.8.2); another stood near that of Hestia in the Prytaneion (Paus. 1.18.3). Eleos, the personification of pity or mercy, had an altar in the Agora. Those who implored the assistance of the Athenians, such as Adrastus and the Heracleidae, approached the altar of Eleos as suppliants (Apollod. 2.8.1, 3.7.1).

Eucleia was a divinity worshipped at Athens and to whom a sanctuary was dedicated there out of the spoils that the Athenians had taken in the battle of Marathon (Paus. 1.14.5). The goddess was a personification of glory. Her name was also used at Athens as a surname of Artemis, and her sanctuary was of an earlier date. Plutarch remarks that many mistook Eucleia for Artemis and thus made her the same as Artemis Eucleia, but that others described her as a daughter of Heracles and Myrto, a daughter of Menoetius. He adds that Eucleia died as a maiden and was worshipped in Boeotia and Locris where she had an altar and a statue in every marketplace, on which persons about to marry used to offer sacrifices to her. Whether a connection existed between the Attic and Boeotian Eucleia (and if it did exist, what its nature was) is unknown. It is probable, however, that the Attic divinity was, as stated above, a personification and consequently quite independent of Eucleia, the daughter of Heracles.

Athenians also worshipped Hebe, Horme, Nike, Aedos, Pheme, and Tyche. Hebe, the personification of youth, had an altar in the Cynosarges, near one of Heracles (Paus. 1.19.3). Horme, the personification of effort, also had an altar in the agora at Athens (Paus. 1.17.1). Nike, the goddess of victory, has already been discussed in connection with her temple on the Acropolis. Aedos, the personification of modesty, and Pheme, the personification of rumor or report, both had altars at Athens (Paus. 1.17.1). Tyche, the goddess of chance or luck, was worshipped there also.

Additionally, several minor gods, including those whose worship was focused in other parts of Greece, were given recognition in Athens. The Dioscuri, Castor and Polydeuces, sons of Zeus, had an altar here. Theseus had carried off their sister Helen from Sparta and kept her in confinement at Aphidna. The Dioscuri marched into Attica and took Aphidna by assault. Menestheus, who was trying to usurp the government while Theseus was absent, opened the gates of Athens to them, and the Athenians paid them divine honors (Plut. *Thes.* 31). Eileithyia, also called Eleithyia, Eilethyia, or Eleutho, was goddess of childbirth. Her worship seems to have started in Crete, but it spread over Delos and Attica. She had a sanctuary in Athens containing three carved images of the goddess, which were covered all over down to the toes. Two were believed to have been presented by Phaedra, and the third by Erysichthon from Delos (Paus. 1.18.5). Eileithyia Lysizona (Goddess Who Loosens the Girdle) was a surname at Athens (Theocrit. 17.60). The Gamelii were divinities presiding over marriage (although the name in this context also pertained to nearly all the gods, particularly Zeus, Hera, Aphrodite, Peitho, Artemis, and the Moirae). The Athenians called their month Gamelion (January/February) after these divinities. There was also a festival of the Gamelia. The Muses were usually nine in number, but eight was the number first recognized at Athens (Plat. *De Re Pub.* 116). At length, the number nine seems to have become established in all Greece. In Athens there was, as mentioned, a temple of the Muses in the Academy (Paus. 1.30.2). Pan, the great god of flocks and shepherds had his principal seat of worship in Arcadia, but his worship afterward spread over other parts of Greece. At Athens his worship was not introduced till the time of the battle of Marathon (Paus. 8.26.2; Virg. *Ecl.* 10.26) and eventually he had a shrine there. When Pheidippides the Athenian was sent to Sparta to solicit its aid against the Persians, Pan accosted him and promised to terrify the barbarians if the Athenians would worship him (Herod. 6.105; Paus. 1.28.4). Peitho (Persuasion) was worshipped in conjunction with Aphrodite Pandemos. The Venti (Winds) had the remarkable monument erected by Andronicus Cyrrhestes. Boreas, the north wind, also had a temple on the river Ilissus (Herod. 7.189; Paus. 8.27.9), and Zephyrus, the west wind, had an altar on the sacred road to Eleusis. Cotys or Cotytto was a Thracian goddess, whose festival, the Cotyttia, resembled that of the Phrygian Cybele and was celebrated on hills with riotous proceedings. In later times her worship was introduced at Athens and was connected, like that of Dionysus, with licentious frivolity.

Heroes and heroines were part of Athenian mythological history. Alcon was a son of Erechtheus and father of Phalerus the Argonaut. He was represented as such a skillful archer that once when a serpent had entwined his son, he shot the serpent without hurting the child. Androgeus, the son of Minos, has already been mentioned in the account of Theseus. He came from Crete to the games of the Panathenaea at Athens and conquered all his opponents in the games. This good luck became the cause of his destruction. According to some, Aegeus, the king of Athens, feared Androgeus and sent him to fight against the Marathonian bull, which killed him. According to others, he was assassinated by his defeated rivals on the road to Thebes, where he was going to take part in a solemn contest. According to Diodorus Siculus (4.60), Aegeus himself had Androgeus murdered near Oenoe on the road to Thebes because he feared lest Androgeus should support the sons of Pallas against him. To avenge the death of his son, Minos made war on the Athenians and exacted the gruesome tribute of seven maidens and seven youths for recurrent sacrifice to the Cretan Minotaur. Androgeus was worshipped in Attica as a hero; an altar was erected to him in the port of Phalerus (Paus. 1.1.2,4), and games, the Androgeonia, were celebrated in his honor every year in the Cerameicus.

Codrus, the son of Melanthus, reigned as king of Athens, according to tradition, some time after the conquest of Peloponnesus by the Dorians. Once when the Dorians invaded Attica from Peloponnesus, they were told by an oracle that they should be victorious if the life of the Attic king was spared. Accordingly, the Dorians took the greatest precautions not to kill the king. When Codrus was informed of the oracle, he resolved to sacrifice himself and thus to deliver his country. In the disguise of a common man he entered the camp of the enemy. There he began quarrelling with the soldiers and was slain in the ensuing struggle. When the Dorians discovered the death

of the Attic king, they abstained from further hostilities and returned home. Tradition adds that because no one was thought worthy to succeed such a high-minded and patriotic king, the kingship was abolished, and instead a responsible archon was appointed for life.

Among other heroes and heroines at Athens, Pausanias mentions Cyamites, Deucalion, Pandora, and Hippothoon. Cyamites (Hero of Beans) was a mysterious cult figure who had a small sanctuary on the road from Athens to Eleusis. No particulars are known about him, but Pausanias (1.37.3) says that those who were initiated into the mysteries or had read the so-called Orphica would understand the nature of the hero. There was a tradition that Deucalion, survivor of the great flood, had lived at Athens, and the sanctuary of the Olympian Zeus there was regarded as his work. His tomb was shown in the neighborhood of the sanctuary (Paus. 1.18.8). Pandora, the first woman on earth, was represented on the pedestal of the statue of Athena in the Parthenon (Paus. 1.24.7). And Hippothoon was an Attic hero, a son of Poseidon and Alope. He had a shrine at Athens, and one of the Attic *phylae* (tribes) was called after him Hippothoontis (Paus. 1.5.2).

Eumolpus was a Thracian who migrated to Attica. The Eleusinians, who were involved in a war with Athens, called upon Eumolpus for assistance. Eumolpus came with a large band of Thracians but was slain by Erechtheus. According to some, the Eleusinians under Eumolpus attacked the Athenians, but were defeated, and Eumolpus and his two sons, Phorbas and Immaradus, were slain (Thuc. 2.15). Pausanias, however, relates that in the battle Erechtheus and Immaradus fell and that thereupon peace was concluded on the condition that the Eleusinians should be subject to Athens in all respects save these: that they alone should have the celebration of their mysteries and that Eumolpus and the daughters of Celeus should perform the customary sacrifices. The tomb of Eumolpus was shown both at Eleusis and Athens (Paus. 1.38.2).

Athenian tradition related that Eurysaces, the son of the Telamonian Ajax, and his brother Philaeus had given up to the Athenians the island of Salamis and that the brothers received in return property in Attica. One of the brothers then settled at Brauron and the other at Melite. Eurysaces, like his father, was honored at Athens with an altar (Plut. *Sol.* 10; Paus. 1.35.2).

Hyacinthus was a Lacedaemonian who is said to have gone to Athens and, in compliance with an oracle, to have caused his daughters to be sacrificed on the tomb of the Cyclops Geraestus. This sacrifice delivered the city from the famine and plague under which it was suffering during the war with Minos. His daughters, who were sacrificed either to Athena or Persephone, were known in Attic legend as the Hyacinthides (Apollod. 3.15.8). Some traditions make them the daughters of Erechtheus and relate that they received their name from the village of Hyacinthus, where they were sacrificed at the time when Athens was attacked by the Eleusinians, Thracians, or Thebans. Those traditions in which they are described as the daughters of Erechtheus confound them with Agraulos, Herse, and Pandrosos.

Heracles is also associated with Athens. *Index* (Indicator or Denouncer) is the Latin translation of *Menytes,* a Greek surname by which the hero was known there. Once a golden vessel had been stolen from the temple of Heracles. The hero repeatedly appeared to Sophocles in a dream until the poet informed the Areiopagus of the theft and the thief was arrested and confessed his crime. From this circumstance the temple was afterward called the temple of Heracles Menytes, or Heracles Index (Cic. *De Div.* 1.25). A companion of Heracles was Iolaus, a son of Iphicles. He was especially celebrated for his attachment to the descendants of the hero, even after his death. He is said to have come to their assistance from the lower world when Eurystheus demanded of the Athenians the surrender of the children of Heracles, who had been kindly received. Iolaus, who was already dead, begged the gods of the lower world for permission to return to life in order to assist the children of his master. The request being granted, he returned to the upper world, slew Eurystheus, and then went to rest again (Pind. *Pyth.* 9.137).

Pausanias also mentions Thymoetes, Sciron, and Polyxena. Thymoetes, an Athenian hero, was believed to have been the king of Attica and a son of Oxyntas (Paus. 2.18.9). One of the Attic demes, Thymoetiadae, derived its name from him. Sciron was the famous robber who haunted the frontier between Attica and Megaris. He was slain by Theseus. In the pediment of the royal Stoa there was a group of figures of burnt clay, representing Theseus in the act of throwing Sciron into the sea (Paus. 1.3.1). Polyxena, the daughter of Priam and Hecuba of Troy, was sacrificed by Neoptolemus on the tomb of his father, Achilles. The sacrifice of Polyxena was represented in the Pinakotheke on the Acropolis (Paus. 1.22.6).

The Amazons represent a mysterious chapter in the mythological account of Athens. Antiope was either a sister or daughter of Hippolyte, who married Theseus. Diodorus Siculus (4.16) states that Theseus received her as a present from Heracles. When Attica subsequently was invaded by the Amazons, Antiope fought with Theseus against them and died by his side the death of a heroine. Molpadia, another Amazon, was said to have killed Antiope and was afterward slain herself by Theseus. Her tomb was shown at Athens (Plut. *Thes.* 26,27; Paus. 1.2.1). Hippolyte was queen of the Amazons. When her army marched to Attica and was conquered, she fled to Megara where she died of grief and was buried. In some

accounts Theseus is said to have been married to Hippolyte instead of Antiope. Euripides in his *Hippolytus* makes her the mother of Hippolytus. According to one writer, Antiope was a daughter of Ares and was killed by Theseus himself in consequence of an oracle.

When the Epidaurians, to end a famine, were directed by an oracle to erect statues to Auxesia and Damia, two Cretan maidens who had been stoned to death at Troezen, they asked permission of the Athenians to cut down an Attic olive tree. The request was granted, on the condition that every year the Epidaurians should offer up sacrifices to Athena Agraulos and Erechtheus. When the condition was complied with, the country of Epidaurus again bore fruit as before. Now when again Aegina separated itself from Epidaurus, which had till then been regarded as its metropolis, the Aeginetans, who had had their own objects of worship in common with the Epidaurians, took away the two statues of Auxesia and Damia, and erected them in a part of their own island called Oea, where they offered sacrifices and celebrated mysteries. When the Epidaurians, in consequence of this, ceased to perform the sacrifices at Athens, and the Athenians heard of the statues being carried to Aegina, they demanded that the Aeginetans return them. The islanders refused, and the Athenians threw ropes round the sacred statues to drag them away by force. But thunder and earthquakes ensued, and the Athenians engaged in the work were seized with madness, in which they killed one another. Only one of them escaped to carry back to Athens the sad tidings. The Aeginetans added to this legend that the statues, while the Athenians were dragging them down, fell upon their knees and that they remained in this attitude ever after (Herod. 5.12–86; Paus. 2.30.4; *Hymn Hom. ad Cer.* 122).

Finally, two stories about ordinary mortals round out this mythological description of Athens. First is the love of Acontius of Ceos for Cydippe of Athens. (See CEOS.) Less fortunate was Meles, an Athenian who was beloved by Timagoras. Meles refused to accept him and instead ordered him to leap from the rock of the Acropolis. Timagoras, who was only a *metoikos* (emigrant) at Athens, did as he was bid; but Meles, repenting of his cruel command, likewise threw himself from the rock. The Athenians from that time are said to have worshipped the god Anteros as the avenger of Timagoras (Paus. 1.30.1).

ATHMONUM (MAROUSSIO)   a deme of Attica, was situated on the site of the village Maroussio, formerly Amarousion, which is 2.5 km from Kifissia on the road to Athens. The name of the modern village has been derived from Amarysia, a surname of Artemis, who was worshipped under this designation at Athmonum (Paus. 1.35.5). The cult of Artemis Amarysia had its origin in Euboea. Athmonum also possessed a very ancient temple of Aphrodite Urania (Paus. 1.14.7), possibly identified with a nearby Phoenician settlement. Inscriptions also refer to Amarysian games.

ATHOS (ATHOS)   is the tall mountain at the tip of the long peninsula that runs out into the sea from Halkidiki in Macedonia between the Singitikos Gulf and the Aegean. This peninsula was initially called Acte (Thuc. 4.109), but the name Athos was given both to it and to the mountain (Herod. 7.22). The length of the peninsula is 66.5 kilometers, and its average width about 6.5 kilometers.

Zeus Athous was a name derived from Mount Athos, on which the god had a temple (Aeschyl. *Agam.* 270). Athos is first mentioned by Homer (*Il.* 14.229), who represents Hera as resting on its summit on her flight from Olympus to Lemnos. Deucalion, after his ship had been floating for about nine days, landed, according to common tradition, on Mount Parnassus; others made him land on Mount Athos.

In the peninsula were five cities: Dium, Olophyxus, Acrothoum, Thyssus, and Cleone. To these some add Charadriae, Palaeorium, and Apollonia. The tip of the peninsula, above which Mount Athos rises abruptly, is called Akra Pinnes (ancient Nymphasium).

ATRAX   was a town in Thessaly, situated above the river Peneius about 16.5 km from Larissa (Liv. 32.15). Atrax has been placed on the right bank of the Peneius about 23 km west of Larissa. A few miles west are ruins that may have been a temple of Poseidon, identified by inscriptions with Atrax. Atrax, from whom the town was believed to have derived its name, was a son of Peneius and Bura. He was the father of Hippodameia and Caenis, the latter of whom by the will of Poseidon was changed into a man and named Caenus (Ov. *Met.* 12.190).

ATTICA (ATTIKI)   is one of the political divisions of Greece. The name Attica is probably derived from the Greek word *acte* (headland, promontory) because its land is a projecting peninsula; in like manner the peninsula of Mount Athos was originally called Acte. Attica would thus be a corruption of Actica, which would be regularly formed from *Acte.* Strabo (9.1.3) and Pliny (4.7.11) both state that the country was originally called Acte. Its name, however, was usually derived by the ancient writers from the autochthon Actaeus or Actaeon, or from Atthis, daughter of Cranaus, who is represented as the second king of Athens (Paus. 1.2.6; Apollod. 3.14.5).

Ancient Attica was bounded on the east by the Aegean Sea, on the west by Megaris and the Saronic Gulf, and on the north by Boeotia. Modern Attiki includes the old region of Megaris and is bordered by Korinthia. Quite recently the nome of Pireas was created, which embraces

the area of Pireas itself, the Saronic islands, the area of ancient Troezenia on the Peloponnesian mainland, and even Kithira off the southern tip of Greece. Attica is separated from Boeotia by a range of high mountains, which extend from the Corinthian Gulf to the channel of Euboea. The most important part of this range was called Cithaeron (Kithero), and its two branches were called the Onean and Parnes Mountains. The Onean range ends at the Scironian Rocks and the Parnes end above the promontory of Rhamnous. These mountains effectively protected the peninsula of Attica from the rest of Greece. There were three principal passes through the range of the Cithaeron and Parnes, all of which were of great importance in ancient times for the protection of Attica. One ran from Thebes and Plataea to Eleusis; the central one was the pass of Phyle, through which was the direct road from Thebes to Athens; and the eastern one was the pass of Deceleia, leading from Athens to Oropus and Delium.

The Athenian plain is bounded on the west by Mount Aegaleos. Through this range the modern highway follows the old pass leading from the Eleusinian into the Athenian plain. It is now called the pass of Dafni; through it the Sacred Way from Eleusis to Athens formerly ran. On the west the Athenian plain is bounded by Mount Pentelicus (Pendeli) and Mount Hymettus (Imitos), which terminates in the promontory of Zoster (Vouliagmeni).

Northeast of the Athenian plain between Parnes, Pentelicus, and the sea, is a district known as Diacria in antiquity. The only level part of this district is the small plain of Marathon, open to the sea. Southeast of the Athenian plain, beyond Pentelicus and Hymettus, is a district anciently called Mesogaea or the Midland district. Paralia or Paralus, i.e., the Seacoast district, included the whole of the south of Attica, extending from the promontory Zoster on the west and from Brauron on the east to Sunium.

The rivers of Attica are almost dry in summer and only full in winter or after heavy rains. The Athenian Plain has two rivers, the Cephissus and the Ilissus. The Cephissus flows southwards from Mount Parnes on the west side of Athens and empties into the Phaleric bay. The Ilissus rises at the north end of Hymettus and joins the Eridanus near the Lyceum on the east side of Athens. In the wet season it is channelled to carry the runoff, and in the dry season it all but disappears. There are three or four rivulets elsewhere in Attica, mainly on the east coast, but they are insignificant.

The mountains of Attica produced fine marble, especially Mount Pentelicus, which supplied inexhaustible materials for the public buildings and statues of Athens. Hymettus also produced excellent marble. Blue or black marble was found at Eleusis. The hilly district of Laurium, above the promontory of Suniun, contained valuable silver mines.

Attica was known for a variety of comestibles. The olive tree was regarded as the gift of Athena, and its cultivation was always under the special care and protection of the goddess. From the olive tree that grew in the temple of the goddess on the Acropolis there came the Moriae, or sacred olive trees in the Academy, and from these again all the other olive trees that grew in temple areas and the plantations of private persons. The fig tree was under the protection of Demeter. Like the sacred olive tree on the Acropolis, there was a sacred fig tree at Eleusis, which the goddess Demeter is said to have produced. The most celebrated wine of Attica was produced at Icaria, where Dionysus is said to have been welcomed. Generally, though, the Attican wine was not superior. The honey, however, was particularly fine, especially that from Mount Hymettus.

The mythical history of Athens can be said, for the most part, to be the mythical history of Attica. As earlier stated, Actaeus, son of Gaea, was said to be the earliest king of Attica. He was succeeded by Cecrops, who married his daughter Agraulos. Others claim that Cecrops was the first king of Attica (Apollod. 3.14.1). Still others speak of Periphas, an Attic autochthon previous to the time of Cecrops, who was a priest of Apollo. On account of his virtues he was made king; but as he was honored to the same extent as Zeus, the god wished to destroy him. At the request of Apollo, however, Zeus metamorphosed him into an eagle and his wife likewise into a bird (Ov. *Met.* 7.400). There was also a tradition of the Athmonians that Porphyrion was the most ancient king of Attica, reigning before Actaeus and introducing into Attica the worship of Aphrodite (Paus. 1.2.5, 14.7).

Cecrops, if we follow Apollodorus (3.14.1), was the first king of Attica, which derived from him its name Cecropia, having previously borne the name of Acte. He is described as an autochthon and also as having the upper body of a human and the lower body of a serpent. He was married to Agraulos, the daughter of Actaeus, by whom he had a son Erysichthon and three daughters, Agraulos, Herse, and Pandrosos (Apollod. 3.14.1; Paus. 1.2.6). In his reign Poseidon called forth with his trident a well on the Acropolis and disputed the possession of Attica with Athena. (See ATHENS.) Cecrops is represented in the Attic legends as the author of the first elements of civilized life, such as marriage, and the political division of Attica into twelve communities. He also introduced a new mode of worship, inasmuch as he abolished the bloody sacrifices that had until then been offered to Zeus and substituted cakes in their stead (Paus. 8.2.2). The name of Cecrops occurs also in other parts of Greece. Later writers describe Cecrops as having migrated into Greece with a band of colonists from Sais in Egypt (Diod. 1.29).

Cranaus, an autochthon, was king of Attica at the time of the flood. He was married to Pedias, by whom he became the father of Cranae, Cranaechme, and Atthis, from whom Attica was believed to have derived its name. He was deprived of his kingdom by Amphictyon, his son-in-law, and after his death he was buried in the deme of Lamprae, where his tomb was shown as late as the time of Pausanias (1.2.5,31.2). Amphictyon, son of Deucalion and Pyrrha, ruled for twelve years. He was believed to have been the first who introduced the custom of mixing wine with water and to have dedicated two altars to Dionysus Orthos and the nymphs.

Other kings, heroes, and beings were interwoven into the ancient legendary history of Attica. The Amazons, the mysterious, warlike race of females from the country around the Caucasus Mountains and the Thermodon River, invaded Greece from time to time. In the reign of Theseus they came as far south as Attica, trying to recapture the kidnapped Antiope, one of their tribe (Plut. *Thes.* 31,33). According to some writers Diomedes was robbed of the Palladium by Demophon in Attica, where he landed one night on his return from Troy, without knowing where he was (Paus. 1.28.9). There was mention of an Ogygian flood in Attica. This Ogygus was the father of the Attic hero, Eleusis. The sisters Procne and Philomela, wives of the terrible Tereus, were said to have escaped to Attica, where they eventually wept themselves to death (Paus. 1.41.9).

The major gods worshipped in Attica are the same as those of Athens but with often broader application. The worship of Athena was introduced into Attica at a very early period, where she became the great national divinity of the city and the country. Here she was afterward regarded as the Thea (Goddess) Soteira, Hygieia, and Paeonia. The serpent, symbol of perpetual renovation, was sacred to her (Paus. 1.23.5). Among the other things sacred to her are mentioned the owl, the cock, and the olive tree. Her well-known contest with Poseidon over the possession of Attica has been noted. Athena loved an Attic maiden by the name of Myrmex. When the goddess invented the plow, Myrmex boastfully pretended to have made the discovery herself, whereupon she was metamorphosed into an ant. According to some, Myrmex was a man and the father of Melite, from whom the Attic deme of Melite derived its name.

Demeter, the goddess of agriculture, was worshipped particularly in Attica. The most prominent theme in the myths of Demeter is the kidnapping of her daughter Persephone by Hades. Some traditions place this event in Attica, either at Erineus on the Cephissus, in the neighborhood of Eleusis, or at Colonus. Demeter, after wandering far and wide and deliberately causing the land to become infertile, finally prevailed on the other gods to restore Persephone. Hermes is said to have delivered her daughter at Eleusis. When Demeter restored fertility to the earth, she also instructed Triptolemus, Diocles, Eumolpus, and Celeus, all from Attica, in the mode of her worship and in the mysteries. This was in response to the kindness shown to her in her wandering search by Metaneira and Celeus, the parents of Triptolemus. Demeter had attempted to confer immortality on their other son, Demophon, by placing him in fire, but one night she was observed by Metaneira, who screamed, causing the spell to be broken and the child to be consumed by flames. The extravagant hilarity displayed at the festivals of Demeter in Attica was traced to Iambe, a Thracian woman. She was the daughter of Pan and Echo, and a slave of another Metaneira, the wife of Hippothoon. It is said that when Demeter in her wanderings came to Attica, Iambe cheered the mournful goddess by her jokes (*Hymn. Hom. ad Cer.* 202). She was believed to have given the name to iambic poetry. Not all stories about Demeter ended as well. She wandered to the house of Misme, where she was received hospitably, and Misme gave her something to quench her terrible thirst. As the goddess emptied the vessel at one draught, Ascalabus, the son of Misme, laughed at her and ordered a whole cask to be brought. Demeter, indignant at his conduct, sprinkled the few remaining drops from her vessel upon him and changed him into a lizard (Ov. *Met.* 5.447).

Apollo was sometimes identified with the Egyptian Horus and in this relationship was thought of as the god of the burning sun. Those who adopt this view derive Apollo from Egypt and regard the Athenian Apollo Patrous as the god who was brought to Attica by the Egyptian colony under Cecrops. Others view the original and essential feature of Apollo's character to be his role as "Averter of Evil." He is originally a divinity peculiar to the Doric race, and the most ancient seats of his worship are Tempe and Delphi. From there it was transplanted to Crete, the inhabitants of which spread it over the coasts of Asia Minor and parts of Greece, including Attica. Apollo Zosterius was worshipped in Attica on the slip of land stretching into the sea between Phaleron and Sunium.

Artemis Amarynthia or Amarysia was a name of Artemis derived from the Euboean hero, Amarynthus, or the town of Amarynthus, where she was worshipped. She was also worshipped under this name in Attica (Paus. 1.31.4). Erigone was a daughter of Aegisthus and Clytemnestra. It was related that Orestes wanted to kill her, as he had her mother, but that Artemis removed her to Attica and there made Erigone her priestess.

There were a few minor deities widely worshipped in Attica. Auxo was an ancient divinity worshipped together with Hegemone under the name of Charites. Thallo was one of the Attic Horae, who was believed to grant prosperity to the young shoots of plants and was also invoked in the political oath that the citizens of Athens had to take (Paus. 9.35.2).

Among the heroes worshipped in Attica were Androgeus and Adrastus. Androgeus, a son of Minos, is said to have conquered all his opponents in the games of the Panathenaea. This caused him to be killed, even though events are related differently. Minos made war on Attica in consequence. Androgeus was worshipped in Attica as a hero, and an altar was erected to him in the port of Phaleron (Paus. 1.1.4), and games, Androgeonia, were celebrated in his honor every year in the Cerameicus. He was also worshipped under the name of Eurygyes, which referred to ownership of broad fields, and from this name it can be assumed that originally Androgeus was worshipped as the introducer of agriculture into Attica. Adrastus, son of Talaus, was a principal figure in the expedition of the Seven against Thebes and the war of the Epigoni. After his death he was worshipped in several parts of Greece, including Attica (Paus. 1.30.4).

As earlier stated, the oldest political division of Attica is said to have been made by Cecrops, who divided the country into twelve independent communities, which were afterward united into one state by Theseus. The names of these communities were: Cecropia, Tetrapolis, Epacria, Deceleia, Eleusis, Aphidna, Thoricus, Brauron, Cytherus, Sphettus, Cephisia, and Phalerus.

Cecrops also divided the people of Attica into four *phylae* (tribes), which existed from the earliest times—Cecropis, Autochthon, Actaea, and Paralia. In the reign of Cranaus these names were changed into Cranais, Atthis, Mesogaea, and Diacris. The names continued to change and finally disappeared before the time of the Ionic tribes of Geleontes, Hopletes, Argades, and Aegicores. Cleisthenes (510 B.C.) abolished the four ancient Ionic tribes and formed ten new tribes, deriving their names from Attic heroes: Erechtheis, Aegeis, Pandionis, Leontis, Acamantis, Oeneis, Cecropis, Hippothoontis, Aeantis, Antiochis. Two hundred years later, two tribes were added and their names were changed from time to time for diplomatic purposes. Finally, in the reign of Hadrian, the number of tribes was increased to thirteen by the addition of Hadrianis, in honor of the emperor.

Each tribe was subdivided into a certain number of demes (*demoi*), or townships. The whole territory of Attica was parcelled out into these demes, in one or other of which every citizen was enrolled. Their number was reported as high as 174 in the third century B.C. (Strab. 9.1.16). The demes assigned to each tribe were not always adjoining. For example, five of the demes that made up Athens belonged to five different tribes. Descendants always remained in the deme in which their ancestors were originally enrolled. If persons moved to another deme they were not enrolled in the new deme. The larger demes had a town or village as their center, but the smaller ones sometimes had only a common temple or place of assembly.

The names of most of the demes are preserved. Public documents usually added to the name of a person the name of the deme to which he belonged. It is not always possible to ascertain the location of many of them, since they were not mentioned in history.

In this work only those demes having some role in mythological or religious history are described. The demes of Athens, with the exception of Peiraeus and Phalerum, are considered along with the city. There are separate entries for others. (See ACHARNAE, ALOPECE, ANAGYRUS, ANAPHLYSTUS, APHIDNA, ATHENS, ATHMONUM, BRAURON, CEPHALE, COLONUS, CORYDALLUS, DECELEIA, ELEUSIS, HALAE ARAPHENIDES, HALIMUS, HECALE, ICARIA, IPHISTIADAE, LAMPTRA, MARATHON, MELAENAE, MYRRHINUS, OENOE, PALLENE, PEIRAEUS, PHALERUM, PHILAIDAE, PHYLA, POTAMUS, PRASIAE, RHAMNUS, SPHETTUS, SUNIUM, THORICUS, TIIRIA, THYMOETADAE, XYPETE.)

AUGEIAE   was a town of Laconia, mentioned by Homer (*Il.* 2.583), probably the same as the later Aegiae.

AUGEIAE   was a town of Locris Epicnemidia, near modern Skarfia, mentioned by Homer (*Il.* 2.53). It had disappeared by the time of Strabo (9.4.5).

AULIS (VATHI)   a town of Boeotia, was named for Aulis, a daughter of Ogygus and Thebe (Paus. 9.19.6). Other traditions call her a daughter of Euonymus, the son of Cephissus. She was one of the goddesses who watched over oaths under the name of Praxidicae. Aulis was situated on the Euripus, the strait between Euboea and the mainland, and celebrated as the place at which the Grecian fleet assembled when they were about to sail against Troy. Aulis was located 5 km from Chalcis. It stood upon a rocky height, just as suggested by Homer (*Il.* 2.303). This height was situated between two bays, the one to the south called the Bay of Vathi. The town Vathi on this bay is adjacent to the site of Aulis. The area was originally famous for pottery, but modern Vathi is involved in shipbuilding.

Aulis was in the territory of Tanagra. In the time of Pausanias it had only a few inhabitants, who were potters. Its temple of Artemis was said to have been founded by Agamemnon (Paus. 9.19.6). The ruins of the temple were discovered during the building of a road in 1941.

After two years of preparation, the Greek army and fleet assembled in the port of Aulis. After they had arrived, they witnessed a marvelous omen: when a sacrifice was offered under the boughs of a tree, a serpent crawled from under it and devoured a nest of eight young birds and their mother. Calchas interpreted the sign to indicate that the Greeks would have to fight against Troy for nine years but that in the tenth the city would fall (*Il.* 2.303). Another fateful incident occurred while the Greeks were assembled at Aulis. Agamemnon, it is said, killed a stag sacred to Artemis, and in addition provoked the anger of the goddess by irreverent words. Some say he had boasted that the goddess herself could not hit better. Others say that in the year in which Iphigeneia was born, he had vowed to sacrifice the most beautiful thing produced in that year but had afterward neglected to fulfil his vow. Artemis in return visited the Greek army with a plague and produced a perfect calm so that the Greeks were unable to leave the port. Then the seer Calchas declared that the anger of the goddess could not be soothed unless Iphigeneia were offered to her as an atoning sacrifice. Agamemnon at first resisted the command, but the entreaties of Menelaus at length caused him to relent, and he consented to having Iphigeneia brought by Odysseus and Diomedes, under the pretext that she was to be married to Achilles. When Iphigeneia had arrived and was on the point of being sacrificed, Artemis carried her off in a cloud to Tauris, where she was made to serve the goddess as her priestess; a stag was substituted in her place and sacrificed (Eurip. *Iphig. Taur.* 10–30,783, *Iphig. Aul.* 1540). According to some, Iphigeneia was saved in a peal of thunder by the voice of Artemis and the interference of Achilles, who had been won over by Clytemnestra; Achilles then sent Iphigeneia to Scythia. Another writer even states that Achilles was actually married to her and became by her the father of Pyrrhus. After this the calm ceased, and the army sailed to the coast of Troy.

AULON   was a valley in the northwest of Messenia on the border of Elis and Messenia. Pausanias speaks of a temple of Asclepius Aulonius, which he places near the Neda River; but whether there was a town of the name of Aulon is uncertain. Some suppose that there was a town of this name near the entrance of the gorge that leads from Cyparissia to the mouth of the Neda and believe that its position is marked by some ruins near the sea on the right bank of the river Cyparissus (Strab. 8.3.25; Xenoph. *Hellen.* 3.2.25; Paus. 4.36.7). There is a modern village Avlonas near the Neda, but no connection has been established between it and the ancient name.

AXENUS   was another name by which the ACHELOUS River was called.

AXIUS (AXIOS)   is the principal river of Macedonia and was the eastern boundary of the kingdom before the reign of Philip. It rises in Yugoslavia, flows in a southeastern direction through Macedonia, and empties into the Thermaic Gulf. The Axius has frequently changed its course. In earlier times it flowed into the sea between Chalastra and Thessalonica. In the Middle Ages it was called Bardarium, from which came the modern name of Vardar in Yugoslavia. The Axius is a deep and rapid river in winter and is nearly 3 km wide before reaching the sea.

Axius was a Paeonian river-god, who begot by Periboea, the daughter of Acessamenus, a son named Pelegon, the father of Asteropaeus.

AXUS (AXOS)   was a city of Crete situated on a river, which, according to some, gave its name to Axus. The city was also referred to as Oaxes or Oaxus. According to one tradition, the Theraean Battus was the son of Phronima, the daughter of Etearchus, king of this city. Etearchus had married a second wife when the girl's mother died. The new wife hated Phronima and tortured her. Finally she accused the girl of fornication, and her father tricked a friend, a Theraean merchant, into promising to throw the girl into the sea on his way back to Thera. The merchant, Themison, was greatly angered by this request and did keep his promise. He put the girl into the sea with a rope, pulled her back aboard, and sailed home to Thera. Phronima became the mistress of a wealthy Theraean, Polymnestus, and soon gave birth to Battus, who founded Cyrene in Libya.

The ancient city was discovered in the modern village of Axos, near Mount Ida. The river Axos flows past the village. Above the village is the ancient acropolis, where remains of Cyclopean walls, along with bronzes and coins, were found. The coins of Axus show representations of Zeus and Apollo, as might be expected in a city situated on the slopes of Mount Ida. Apollo by Acacallis or Anchiale was the father of Axus, who was believed to have founded the city. Some votives were excavated from a temple of Demeter in 1914.

AZANIA   was a district of Arcadia. Azan, a son of Arcas and the nymph Erato, was the brother of Apheidas and Elatus, and father of Cleitor. The part of Arcadia that he received from his father was eponymously called Azania. After his death, funeral games, which were believed to have been the first in Greece, were celebrated in his honor (Paus. 8.4.2,3).

AZORUS (VOUVALA)   was a town in Thessaly, situated at the foot of Mount Olympus. Azorus, with the two neighboring towns of Pythium and Doliche, formed a Tripolis (Liv. 42.53, 44.2). Azorus was the helmsman of the ship Argo and is said to have built the town that bears his name. The ruins of Azorus are southwest of the village of Vouvala. This village is a few kilometers from Elassona. Vouvala is not on many maps, so local directions might be necessary.

BAEA   was the name of a mountain on the island of Cephallenia. It probably derived its name from Baeus, the helmsman of Odysseus (Lycoph. 964). Baeus is said to have died during the stay of Odysseus in Sicily.

BARNICHIUS   was a later name of the ENIPEUS River.

BASILIS   a town of Arcadia in the district Parrhasia, on the Alpheius, was said to have been founded by the Arcadian king Cypselus. Cypselus was a son of Aepytus, father of Merope and father-in-law of Cresphontes. Basilis contained a temple of the Eleusinian Demeter (Paus. 8.29.5). There are a few remains of Basilis near Kiparissia.

BASSAE   (See PHIGALIA)

BERMIUS (VERMIO)   is a range of mountains in Macedonia, between the Haliacmon (Aliakmon) and Ludias (Loudias) Rivers, at the foot of which stood the city of Beroea. Herodotus (8.138) relates that this mountain was impassable on account of the cold and that beyond it were the gardens of Midas, in which roses spontaneously grew. Midas was the wealthy king of Phrygia and a promoter of the worship of Dionysus. A story is related about him and Silenus, the ancient, inebriated follower of Dionysus. During the expedition of Dionysus from Thrace to Phrygia, Silenus had gone astray in a state of intoxication and was caught by country people in the rose gardens of Midas. He was bound in wreaths of flowers and led before the king. These gardens were near Mount Bermius, where Midas was king of the Briges, with whom he afterward migrated to Asia, where their name was changed to Phryges (Herod. 7.83, 8.138). Midas received Silenus kindly, conversed with him, and after having treated him hospitably for ten days, he led him back to Dionysus. In his gratitude the god offered to grant Midas a favor. Midas requested that all things he touched should be changed into gold. His wish was granted, but since even the food he touched was changed into gold, he implored the god to take back his favor. Dionysus accordingly ordered him to bathe in the source of the Pactolus River near Mount Tmolus in Lydia. This bath saved Midas, and the river from that time had an abundance of gold in its sand (Ov. *Met.* 11.90).

BEROEA (VERIA)   was a city in Macedonia in the north part of the province in the district called Emathia (Imathia), situated on a tributary of the Haliacmon River and upon the lower east slope of Mount Bermius. According to a Macedonian legend, Beroea was one of the daughters of the mythological king Beres, the other two being Mieza and Olganos. Beroea had historical but little mythological importance. Inscriptions have revealed that Heracles Cynagidas, Asclepius, Hermes, and Zeus Hypsistus had cults here. There also was a sanctuary of the Mother of the Autochthonous Gods nearby on Mount Bermius. A colossal head of Medusa was found by the east gate of the city wall. More remains might have been uncovered but for the fact that Veria has been continuously occupied since classical times. The modern city has numerous churches, is a handicraft center, and serves as a base for tourist expeditions to nearby Vergina, the site of the royal Macedonian tombs.

BESSA was a town in Locris, so called from its situation in a wooded glen, mentioned by Homer (*Il.* 2.532), but which had disappeared by the time of Strabo (9.4.5). It was located in proximity to Scarpheia, Thronium, and Thermopylae.

BIENNUS (ANO VIANOS) was a small city of Crete that has been placed at some distance from the sea, midway between Hierapytna and Leben, the most eastern of the two parts of Gortyna. The contest of Otus and Ephialtes with Ares is said to have taken place near this city. In this instance the Aloeidae put Ares in chains and kept him imprisoned in a bronze jar for thirteen months. The god would have perished had not Hermes been informed of his imprisonment by Eriboea, the mother, according to one tradition, of the giants, and liberated him (Hom. *Il* 5.385). From this violent conflict the city is said to have derived its name. Biennus, being near Mount Dicte, was among the places in Crete that were particularly sacred to Zeus. The highest part of the village of Vianos is the site of Biennus. In nearby Kato Simi there has been found a sanctuary dedicated to Hermes and Aphrodite.

BODONE was a town in Thessaly, which derived its name from Bodon, an ancient hero. Only one writer mentioned this town but gave no particulars about its location.

BOEAE (NEAPOLI) was a town in the south of Laconia, situated between the promontories Malea and Onugnathos, in the bay called after it Boeaticus Sinus. The town is said to have been founded by Boeus, one of the Heracleidae, who led colonists here from the neighboring towns of Etis, Aphrodisias, and Side (Paus. 3.22.11). From Pallene in Thrace, where Aeneas stayed the winter after the taking of Troy, he sailed with his companions to Delos, Cythera, and Boeae (whence he built Etis and Aphrodisias) (Paus. 3.22.11). Boeae afterwards belonged to the Eleuthero-Lacones and was visited by Pausanias, who mentioned a temple of Apollo in the forum and temples of Asclepius and of Serapis and Isis elsewhere. There were ruins of a temple of Asclepius and Hygieia 1.5 km from the town. Artemis Soteira (Saving Goddess) was worshipped at Boeae (Paus. 3.22.13). The remains of Boeae may be seen at the head of the gulf, now called Viatikos. This location places Boeae in the neighborhood of the modern town Neapoli.

BOEBE (KANALIA) was a town of Magnesia in Thessaly. Mentioned by Homer, it was situated on the east side of the lake called Boebeis after it (Hom. *Il.* 2.712; Herod. 7.129). The town was named for Boebus, a son of Glaphyrus. Ancient writers frequently mentioned the lake but rarely name the town. The ancient lake, about 25 km long and 8 km wide, received the rivers Onchestus, Amyrus, and several smaller streams, but had no outlet. Athena is said to have bathed her feet in its waters. The lake is now a much smaller body of water and is controlled and drained by a tunnel. The reclaimed land is used for various crops such as cotton. The town of Boebe occupied a height on the slope of Mount Kanalia near the town of Kanalia, and its acropolis may be traced on the summit.

BOEOTIA (VIOTIA) was one of the political divisions of Greece, lying between Attica and Megaris on the south and Locris and Phocis on the north, and bounded on the other two sides by the Euboean Sea and the Corinthian Gulf respectively. It was a large, hollow basin, shut in on the south by Mounts Cithaeron and Parnes, on the west by Mount Helicon, on the north by the slopes of Mount Parnassus and the Opuntian mountains, and on the east by a continuation of the Opuntian range along the Euripus as far north as the mouth of the Asopus. This basin is divided into two distinct portions by Mounts Ptoum and Phoenicium. The northernmost of these two divisions is drained by the Cephissus and its tributaries, the waters of which form Lake Copais; the southernmost is drained by the Asopus, which empties into the Euboean Sea. Streams flowing into north Boeotia could only find an outlet through subterranean channels called *katavothra* in the limestone mountains.

These *katavothra* were not sufficient to carry off the waters of the lake, which consequently often inundated the surrounding plain. The tradition of the Ogygian deluge probably recalls such an inundation; and it is also related that the Pelasgian towns of Athenae and Eleusis were also destroyed by a similar calamity (Paus. 9.24.2). To guard against this danger, the ancient inhabitants of the district constructed at a very early period two artificial tunnels, the direction of which may still be traced. These two great works are among the most striking monuments of what is called the heroic age; they are further said to have been built by the Minyae of Orchomenus and to have accounted for its wealth. These tunnels are said to have been stopped up by Heracles, who by this means inundated the lands of the Minyae of Orchomenus (Diod. 4.18; Paus. 9.38.7). It is probable that with the decline of the power of the Minyae these tunnels were neglected and thus became gradually choked up.

Lake Copais was in more ancient times called Cephissus (Hom. *Il.* 5.709; Strab. 9.2.20) from the river of this name. It finally was designated as Copais because Copae, the town, stood on the northeast extremity, which was the deepest part.

The mountains of Boeotia were: (1) Hyphanteium, on the north end of Lake Copais; (2) Ptoum, at the southeast end of the lake, where there was a celebrated sanctuary of Apollo Ptous (Paus. 9.23.6; Herod. 8.135); (3) Phoenicium, the mountain connecting Mount Ptoum with the range of Helicon; this mountain rose immediately above Lake Copais, and on its upper slope was a huge stone resembling a woman's head looking into the lake; this stone gave rise to a legend that the Sphinx threw her victims into the lake (Paus. 9.26.2); (4) Tilphossium, on the south side of Copais; at the foot of the hill was the small fountain Tilphossa or Tilphussa, where the seer Teiresius is said to have died; (5) Leibethrias, a part of Mount Helicon; (6) Laphystium, another part of Mount Helicon about 3.5 km from Coroneia and the location of a sacred precinct of Zeus Laphystius; according to the Boeotians, Heracles is said to have dragged Cerberus into the upper world at this spot; and (7) Thurium, which separated the plains of Lebadeia and Chaeroneia.

The principal pass into northern Boeotia was along the valley of the Cephissus, which entered the plain of Chaeroneia from Phocis through a narrow gorge formed by a ridge of Mount Parnassus. There was also a pass crossing the mountains from Chaeroneia by way of Panopeus to Daulis and from there to Delphi (Paus. 10.4.1). To the east Boeotia was connected with Locris by a road leading across the mountains from Orchomenus to Abae and Hyampolis, and from there to Opus on the Euboean Sea (Paus. 10.35.1). Southern Boeotia was divided by Mount Teumessus into two distinct parts, the plain of Thebes and the valley of the Asopus.

In the northern part of the plain of Thebes was Lake Hylica, now called Iliki. There was a small lake to the east of Hylica, now called Paralimni. Its ancient name is uncertain, although some believe it was called Schoenus, the name of the river upon which the town of Schoenus stood. It was thus named eponymously after Schoeneus, son of Athamas and king of Boeotia, who was the father of the Boeotian Atalanta.

The only notable streams in the plain of Thebes were the Ismenus and Dirce, upon which Thebes stood. The northwest portion of the plain of Thebes was called the Teneric Plain. To the west of Thebes were the plains of Thespiae and Leuctra. Apart from the Asopus, the only other rivers in the extreme south of Boeotia were the Oeroe and the Thermodon. Southwest of Thebes was the plain of Plataea.

Vineyards flourished on the sides of the mountains, and it was in Boeotia that the vine is said to have been first planted by Dionysus, whom the legends represent as a native of Thebes (Paus. 9.25.1). Boeotia also produced reeds for flutes. These grew in the marshes of Lake Copais.

Boeotia was originally inhabited by various barbarous tribes, chief among which were the Minyae, dwelling at Orchomenus, and the Cadmeans at Thebes. According to mythology, the Boeotians as a race got their name from Boeotus, who was a son of the nymph Melanippe and Itonus, the son of Amphictyon (Paus. 9.1.1). Earlier there had been a hero, Aon, the son of Poseidon, from whom the Aonians and Aonia (the ancient name of Boeotia) had derived their names (Paus. 9.5.1; Stat. *Theb.* 1.34). The ruling line was passed from Boeotus to Itonus, his son, who was the father of Hippalcimus, Electryon, Archilochus, and Alegenor. Hippalcimus was the father of Peneleos by Asterope. Peneleos was an Argonaut and also participated in the Trojan War, in which he was killed. His son, Opheltes, was the father of Damasichthon, who was king of Thebes. The story of the royal succession of Boeotia as a whole is interwoven with the stories of individual cities and can be found in the entries for those cities. We know that the Boeotians as a nation went against Troy under the leadership of Arcesilaus, Clonius, and Prothoenor, who sailed in ten ships. All three were slain. The remains of Arcesilaus were brought back to Boeotia, where a monument was erected to his memory in the neighborhood of Lebadeia.

According to Thucydides, sixty years after the Trojan War an important change took place in the population of Boeotia. The Boeotians, an Aeolian people, who had up till then lived in the southern part of Phthiotis in Thessaly on the Pagasaean Gulf and whose chief town was Arne, were driven from their homes by the Thessalians, who are said to have come from Thesprotia. These dispossessed Boeotians then migrated to the south and occupied the land then called Cadmeia, to which they gave their own name of Boeotia (Thuc. 1.12). The Minyans and Cadmeans partly withdrew from their cities and partly intermarried with the conquering race. An enigma surrounds the time of this Boeotian migration. In referring to the Seven against Thebes and the Epigoni, Homer (*Il.* 4.385, 5.804, 23.680) always calls the inhabitants of the beleaguered city Cadmeones. At the time of the Trojan War, however, the inhabitants of the same country are always called Boeotians, and their leaders, Peneleos, Leitus, Arcesilaus, Prothoenor, and Clonius, are connected, both by genealogy and legends, with the Aeolic Boeotians who came from Thessaly. Consequently, the migration of the Aeolian Boeotians ought to be placed between the time of the Epigoni and that of the Trojan War. It is likely that the account in Thucydides adheres to the genuine legend and that Homer only numbers the Boeotians in the great military coalition of the Greeks to satisfy the inhabitants of that country in his time. In deference to Homer, Thucydides does suggest that some of the Aeolian Boeotians had settled in Boeotia prior to the war and that the ones who sailed against Troy were the displaced Thessalians.

In any case, at the beginning of the historical period all of the cities in Boeotia were inhabited by Boeotians. The Minyans and other ancient races had almost entirely vanished. The most important of these cities formed a political confederacy under the leadership of Thebes. Of these greater cities, which had smaller towns dependent upon them, there appear to have been originally fourteen. Some have identified them as: Thebes, Orchomenus, Lebadeia, Coroneia, Copae, Haliartus, Thespiae, Tanagra, Anthedon, Plataea, Ocaleae, Chalia, Onchestus, and Eleutherae. The religious festival of the league, the Pamboeotia, was held at the temple of Athena Itonia in the neighborhood of Coroneia (Paus. 9.34.1).

In Boeotia, along with the rest of Greece, Athena was a principal divinity. Most of the traditions relate that she was born from the head of Zeus, who was worshipped in Boeotia as Zeus Carius. Some relate that Prometheus, Hermes, or Palacmon assisted Zeus in giving birth to Athena and mention the river Triton as the place where the event took place (Apollod. 1.4.6). The connection of Athena with Triton caused the various traditions about her birthplace: wherever there was a river or a well called Triton (as in Crete, Thessaly, Boeotia, Arcadia, and Egypt), the inhabitants of that district asserted that Athena had been born there. The connection of Athena with Triton suggests that we must look for the most ancient seat of her worship in Greece to the banks of the river Triton in Boeotia, which emptied into Lake Copais and on which there were two ancient Pelasgian towns, Athenae and Eleusis, which were, according to tradition, swallowed up by the lake. Athena was worshipped in all parts of Greece, and from the ancient towns on Lake Copais her worship was introduced at a very early period into Attica, where she became the great national divinity of the city and the country.

The worship of Apollo, though originating in northern Greece, spread from there to Crete and then back to Boeotia and Attica. He was reported to have carried off Sinope, a daughter of Asopus, from Boeotia to Paphlagonia, where she gave birth to Syrus and where the town of Sinope was named after her. Aristaeus, the ancient divinity who conferred many benefits on man, was worshipped in Boeotia, where he is said to have gone when he grew up to learn healing and prophecy from Cheiron the Centaur. According to some statements he married Autonoe, the daughter of Cadmus, who bore him several sons, Charmus, Calaicarpus, Actaeon, and Polydorus (Hes. *Theog.* 975).

The Telchines and Cabeiri were worshipped in Boeotia. The mysterious Telchines, originally from Crete and Rhodes, were cultivators of the soil and ministers of the gods. As such they came to Boeotia, and one, at least, went to Teumessus, where the worship of Athena Telchinia was established. The no less mysterious Cabeiri, although usually connected with Samothrace, were worshipped elsewhere as well, such as Thebes and Anthedon, where they had sanctuaries. Pelarge, the daughter of Potneus and wife of Isthmiades, was said to have instituted the orgies of the Boeotian Cabeiri (Paus. 9.25.7). These Cabeiri possessed the power of averting dangers and increasing prosperity.

Eucleia was described as a daughter of Heracles and Myrto. She died a virgin and was worshipped in Boeotia and Locris, where she had an altar and a statue in every marketplace. Persons about to marry used to offer sacrifices to her. Whether or not a connection existed between the Attic and Boeotian Eucleia is unknown, though it is probable that the Attic divinity was a surname of Artemis and quite independent of Eucleia, the daughter of Heracles.

Finally, according to one story, the Pleiades, virgin companions of Artemis, were pursued, together with their mother Pleione, by the hunter Orion in Boeotia. Their prayer to be rescued from him was heard by the gods, and they were metamorphosed into doves and placed among the stars (Pind. *Nem.* 2.17).

BOMYCAS   was an earlier name of the EUROTAS River.

BOTACHIDAE or POTACHIDAE   was a deme at Tegea. It was believed to have derived its name from Botachus, a son of Iocrites and grandson of Lycurgus.

BRASIAE   (See PRASIAE)

BRAURON (VRAONA)   was one of the twelve ancient cities of Attica. It was situated on or near the east coast of Attica between Steiria and Halae Araphenides near the river Erasinus (Strab. 8.6.8, 9.1.22). Its name is preserved in the village called Vraona (with its adjacent Paleo Vraona) situated south of the Erasinus River. It was named for Brauron, an ancient hero. A later hero connected with Brauron was Eurysaces. He was a son of the Telamonian Ajax and Tecmessa and had been named after the broad shield of his father (Soph. *Aj.* 575). An Athenian tradition related that Eurysaces and his brother Philaeus had given up to the Athenians the island of Salamis, which they inherited from their grandfather, and that the two brothers received in return two districts in Attica. Eurysaces settled at Brauron and Philaeus at Melite. Eurysaces was honored, like his father, at Athens with an altar (Plut. *Sol.* 10; Paus. 1.35.3).

Brauron is famous because of the worship of Artemis Brauronia, in whose honor a festival was celebrated in this place (Herod. 6.138). According to Greek legend, there was in Tauris a goddess whom the Greeks for some reason identified with their own Artemis and to whom all strangers that were thrown on the coast of Tauris were sacrificed (Eurip. *Iph. Taur.* 36). At the time of the Trojan War, Iphigeneia, who had been rescued by Artemis from being sacrificed at Aulis, was serving Artemis as priestess in Tauris. Meanwhile, her brother Orestes, on the advice of an oracle, planned to steal the image of Artemis in Tauris, which was believed once to have fallen from heaven, and to carry it to Attica (Eurip. *Iph. Taur.* 79). When Orestes accompanied by Pylades arrived in Tauris, they were seized, as were all strangers, and were about to be sacrificed in the temple of the goddess. But Iphigeneia recognized her brother and fled with him and the statue of the goddess. They carried the statue to Brauron, whence the goddess derived the name Brauronia (Paus. 1.23.9). Under this name she also had a sanctuary on the Acropolis at Athens, which contained a statue of her made by Praxiteles. Her image at Brauron, however, was believed to be the more ancient and the one that Orestes and Iphigeneia had brought with them from Tauris. Iphigeneia is said to have died in Brauron as a priestess of Artemis Brauronia. The goddess of the sanctuary was particularly connected with childbirth and was worshipped especially by women. Servants in the temple were young girls between the ages of five and ten years, who were called *arctoi* (bears). Only the foundation of the temple remains. Nearby is the sacred spring, from which offerings were recovered. The most striking building at the site is the stoa, much of which has been restored. A new museum houses finds from the site.

Artemis Orthia also had a temple at Brauron. It was at the altar of Artemis Orthia that Spartan boys had to undergo the *diamastigosis,* a brutal scourging ritual.

BRISA was a mountain in Lesbos. Dionysus Brisaeus derived his surname from this mountain, or from a nymph Brisa, who was said to have brought up the god.

BRUSIS was a portion of Macedonia. It was said to have derived its name from Brusus, a son of Emathius.

BRYSEAE (SKLAVOHORI) was a town of Laconia, southwest of Sparta, at the foot of Mount Taygetus. Its name occurs in Homer (*Il.* 2.583) but Bryseae was only a small village in the time of Pausanias, who mentions, however, a temple of Dionysus at the place. Only women were permitted to enter the temple, in which they performed the sacred rites. The site of Bryseae was discovered near the village of Sklavohori.

BUDEIUM was a town of Thessaly mentioned by Homer (*Il.* 16. 572), called Budeia by later writers, and described as a town of Magnesia (Lycoph. 359). Budeia was a Boeotian woman, the wife of Clymenus and mother of Erginus, from whom the town derived its name. Others derived the name from Budeois, an Argive hero. Another hero, Epeigeus, was a Myrmidon and son of Agacles, who was obliged to flee from Budeium after killing his father. He took refuge in the house of Peleus, who sent him with Achilles to Troy, where he was killed by Hector.

BULIS was a town of Phocis on the boundary of Boeotia. It was situated upon a hill 1.33 km from the Crissaean Gulf. It was founded by the Dorians under the leadership of Bulon (Paus. 10.37.2). In the time of Pausanias, more than half of the population was employed in fishing for the murex, a snail that yielded a purple dye. The harbor of Bulis was Mychus.

BUPORTHMUS was the name of a promontory of Argolis running out into the sea near the town of Hermione. On it was a temple of Demeter and her daughter and another of Athena Promachorma (Protectress of the Bay) (Paus. 2.34.9)

BUPRASIUM a town of Elis and the ancient capital of the Epeii, was situated near the left bank of the Larissus on the frontiers of Achaia. Buprasium is frequently mentioned by Homer (*Il.* 2.615).

BURA was a town of Achaia, one of the twelve Achaean cities. It was situated on a height 7.5 km from the sea and southeast of Helice. Some said it derived its name from Bura, a daughter of Ion and Helice (Paus. 7.25.5). Others said the town derived its name from the large stables for oxen possessed at Bura by Dexamenus the Centaur. Bura was swallowed up by an earthquake and all the inhabitants destroyed. The rebuilt city was visited by Pausanias, who mentions its temples of Demeter, Aphrodite, and Eileithyia. A little to the east of Bura was the river Buraicus and on the banks of this river between Bura and the sea was a statue and an oracular cavern of Heracles Buraicus (Herod. 1.145; Paus. 7.25.8). Persons who visited this oracle first prayed before the statue and then threw four dice upon a table. These dice were marked with certain characters, the meaning of which was explained with the help of a painting that hung in the cave (Paus. 7.25.10). Gaea, the personification of the earth, was also worshipped here. Her worship appears to have been universal among the Greeks and she had temples in various places, including Bura. The ruins of Bura occupy a hilltop to the east of the entrance of the Vouraikos Gorge south of Diakofto.

BYBLIS was another name by which the island of MELOS was called.

CABARNIS was another name by which the island of PAROS was called.

CABEIRAEA (KABIRIO) was a sanctuary of the Cabeiri located in Boeotia about 8 km west of Thebes. The Cabeiri were mysterious divinities whose main shrine was in Samothrace but who were worshipped all over Greece and even in Egypt. Their parentage was variously given, and no one was even sure about their names and number. Speculation was inhibited, since the names of the Cabeiri could not be uttered with impunity. Therefore, they were many times euphemistically called the "Great Gods." Pausanias (9.25.5), on leaving Thebes, came to the area of this city. He spoke of a grove of Demeter Cabeiraea and Kore and said that only the initiated could enter it. After adding that the sanctuary of the Cabeiri was about seven stadia (1.33 km) beyond, he begged to keep his silence about the nature of the Cabeiri and their ritual. However, he did describe the origin of the ritual. Once there was in this place a city, he said, and Demeter became acquainted with both Prometheus, one of the Cabeiri, and his son Aetnaeus and she gave something into their keeping. Pausanias speculates that this was the sacred rites. When the Epigoni invaded this area, the rites had to be transferred to another place. However, one Telondes later transferred them back. The wrath of the Cabeiri was violent and implacable. There are stories of individuals in historical times, such as Mardonius the Persian and some men of Alexander the Great, who entered this sanctuary and were either driven to madness or were destroyed by lightning. The Cabeiri were thought to be guardians of vineyards and the fertility of flocks.

This sanctuary was discovered in 1887–1888 but no excavation began until 1955. Remains of a temple have been found, as well as some other buildings thought to be used in the rituals. The sanctuary of the Cabeiri at nearby Anthedon was thought to be connected with this one.

CADISTUS is a mountain of Crete belonging to the ridge of the Lefka Ori. Its position has been fixed at Akra Spanda, the most northerly point of the whole island. The mass of mountain of which the cape was composed bore the double names of Cadistus and Dictynnaeus (Plin. 4.12.60). Cadistus was the original name of the promontory and mountain, while Dictynnaeus was an epithet afterward given and derived from the worship and temple of Dictynna.

CADMEIA was the original name of ancient THEBES.

CADMUS was an earlier name of the ISMENUS River at Thebes.

CAENO (AGIOS NIKOLAOS) was a city of Crete in the neighborhood of Tarrha and Elyrus. The Cretan goddess Britomartis, the daughter of Zeus and Carma and granddaughter of Carmanor, was said to have been born at Caeno. The site has been fixed near the harbor town of Agios Nikolaos, a fashionable and very popular resort.

CAERATUS was the original name of CNOSSUS.

CAICUS was a river in Macedonia. Aelianus (*De Nat. Anim.* 15.1) speaks of a river Astraeus flowing between Thessalonica and Beroea. Some conjecture that "Astraeus" in Aelianus is a false reading for "Axius." The Astraeus was named for a youth Astraeus, who unwittingly had sexual intercourse with his sister Alcippe. When he learned what he had done, he threw himself into the river. It was renamed Caicus from another youth, Caicus, son of Hermes and Ocyrrhoe, who for unknown reasons threw himself into the Astraeus.

CALAUREIA (POROS) was the name of a small island in the Saronic Gulf opposite Pogon, the harbor of Troezen. It possessed an ancient temple of Poseidon that was considered an inviolable asylum. Poseidon is said to have received the island from Apollo in exchange for Delos, which he had owned in common with Gaea. An ancient amphictyony, consisting of the representatives of the seven cities of Hermione, Epidaurus, Aegina, Athens, Prasiae, Nauplia, and Orchomenus of Boeotia met in this temple. It was also in this temple that Demosthenes committed suicide by poison. The Calaureians erected a statue to the great orator within the temple and paid divine honors to him (Strab. 8.6.14; Paus. 2.33.3).

Calaureia was about 10 km in length and was separated from the mainland by a strait of three-quarters of a kilometer wide. Pausanias mentions a second island in the immediate vicinity named Sphaeria, afterwards Hiera, containing a temple of Athena Apaturia and separated from the mainland by a strait so narrow and shallow that there was a passage over it on foot. At present there is only one island, but it may be assumed from the shape of the land that two original islands have later joined. The sole island is now called Poros (Ford) because the narrow strait is fordable, as it was in ancient times.

The remains of the temple of Poseidon were discovered in 1765 near the city of Kalavria in the center of the island. Here was found a small Doric temple reduced to a heap of ruins. Subsequent excavation has uncovered a complex of buildings associated with the maritime amphictyony.

Plutarch (*Quaest. Gr.* 19) says that the island of Calaureia was originally called Anthedonia after Anthes. Anthes was probably an alternative form of Anthas, a son of Poseidon and Alcyone. Plutarch also gives two other early names by which the island was called. One was Eirene from the daughter of Poseidon and Melanthea. The other was Hypereia from Hyperes, a king of Troezen and son of Poseidon and Alcyone. The island was also called Hyleesa.

CALLIARUS was a town in eastern Locris mentioned by Homer (*Il.* 2.531). It was uninhabited in Strabo's time (9.4.5). Calliarus, from whom the town derived its name, was a son of Odoedocus and Laonome.

CALLICHORUM was a spring in Eleusis. It was located close to the northeast corner of the Great Propylaea of the sacred precinct. It was called the Well of the Fair Dances, for here the Eleusinian women instituted a dance and sang in honor of Demeter. Demo was a daughter of Celeus and Metaneira, who, together with her sisters, kindly received Demeter at the well Callichorum (*Hymn. Hom. ad Cer.* 109).

CALLIRRHOE was the name of a spring at Calydon not far from the harbor. It was named for a maiden of Calydon, who, when she was loved by Coresus, a priest of Dionysus, rejected all the offers he made to her. At length, he implored his god to punish the cruel girl. Dionysus now brought a plague of madness on the people of Calydon. The Dodonaean oracle, which was consulted about a means of averting the calamity, answered that Dionysus must be propitiated and that Callirrhoe (or someone in her stead) must be sacrificed to him. The maiden endeavored in vain to escape her fate; but when she was led to the altar, Coresus, instead of carrying out the sacrifice, felt his love for her revive so strongly that he sacrificed himself. Overcome by pity, Callirrhoe cut her throat near a spring that derived its name from her (Paus. 7.21.1).

CALLISTE was the original name of the island of THERA.

CALLIUM or CALLIPOLIS the chief town of the Callienses, was situated on the eastern boundaries of Aetolia on one of the heights of Mount Oeta and on the road from the valley of the Spercheius to Aetolia. It lay on the road from Pyra (the summit of Oeta, where Heracles was supposed to have burned himself) to Naupactus, and it was divided by Mount Corax from lower Aetolia (Liv. 30.31).

CALYDON (KALIDONA) the most celebrated city of Aetolia in the heroic age, was founded by Aetolus in the land of the Curetes and was called Calydon after one of his sons. Aetolus was a son of Endymion and the nymph Neis. He was married to Pronoe, by whom he had two sons, Pleuron and Calydon. He earlier had succeeded to the throne of the kingdom of Elis, but having accidentally killed Apis, the son of Iason, he was expelled by the sons

of Apis. After leaving Peloponnesus, he went to the country of the Curetes, between the Achelous River and the Corinthian Gulf, where he slew Dorus, Laodocus, and Polypoetes, the sons of Helios and Phthia, and gave the country the name of Aetolia (Paus. 5.1.6; Apollod. 1.7.6). Some say that Calydon was founded by Calydon himself, who was married to Aeolia and the father of Epicaste and Protogeneia. His brother Pleuron, who founded the neighboring town of Pleuron, had a son Agenor, who married Episcaste, his cousin, and became by her father of Porthaon and, according to some, Thestius. Porthaon became king of Pleuron and Calydon and married Euryte, who bore him sons, Laocoon, Leucopeus, Agrius, Alcathous, Melas, Oeneus, and a daughter Sterope. Oeneus became king of Calydon and Pleuron and married Althaea, daughter of Thestius and sister of Leda and Hypermnestra. Oeneus had by her Troxeus, Thyreus, Periphas, Clymenus, Agelaus, Meleager, Gorge, Mothone, Melanippe, Eurymede, and Deianeira, and, according to some, Tydeus. According to others, Tydeus was born to his second wife Melanippe; still others claim that Tydeus was the result of an incestuous relationship with Gorge, his daughter. Oeneus was deprived of his kingdom by the sons of Agrius, who imprisoned and mistreated him. But he was later avenged by Diomedes, who slew Agrius and his sons, except Thersites, and restored the kingdom either to Oeneus himself or (as Oeneus was too old to rule) to his son-in-law Andraemon. Diomedes took his grandfather with him to Peloponnesus, but some of the sons who lay in ambush slew the old man near the altar of Telephus in Arcadia. Diomedes buried his body at Argos and named the town Oenoe after him (Apollod. 1.8.5; Diod. 4.65).

Tydeus, the son of Oeneus and father of Diomedes, was one of the princes who joined Polyneices in the expedition of the Seven against Thebes. Tydeus was obliged to flee from his country because of a murder he had committed. Writers disagree on the victim, some saying he killed his father's brother Melas, Leucopeus, or Alcathous; others that he slew Thoas or Aphareus, his mother's brother; others that he slew his brother Olenias; and still others that he killed the sons of Melas, who had revolted against Oeneus. He fled to Adrastus at Argos, who purified him of the murder and gave him his daughter Deipyle in marriage. With Adrastus he went against Thebes, where he was seriously wounded and died.

But the greatest event in the history of Calydon and its greatest hero were connected with one of the most famous adventures in Greek mythology, the Calydonian boar hunt. Oeneus, the king of Calydon, had once neglected to offer up a sacrifice to Artemis, in consequence of which the angry goddess sent a monstrous boar into the fields of Calydon, which were ravaged by the beast. No one had the courage to hunt it. Oeneus asked for help from other cities and offered the boar's skin as a trophy for the one who killed the brute. The cities sent their finest heroes; even the Curetes, the traditional enemies of the Calydonians, joined the hunt. The list of hunters varies, but one usually finds the names of the following heroes: Amphiaraus, son of Oicles; Amyntor, a son of Ormenus; Ancaeus, an Arcadian, a son of Lycurgus; Deucalion of Crete, son of Minos and Pasiphae; the Dioscuri; Dryas, a son of Ares; Peleus, father of Achilles; Telamon, brother of Peleus; Idas and Lynceus, sons of Aphareus; Laertes, father of Odysseus; Jason, the leader of the Argonauts; Nestor, son of Neleus, from Pylos; Theseus, son of Aegeus of Athena; and his friend Peirithous, son of Ixion from Larissa; and Heracles, the most renowned of all Greek heroes. Also among the hunters was the Arcadian huntress Atalanta. Some of the other hunters at first refused to hunt with a woman, but Meleager, the leader of the hunt, who was in love with her, forced them to accept her.

The hunt started, and Ancaeus and a few other hunters were killed by the boar. Peleus also accidentally killed his friend Eurytion. Atalanta is said to have first wounded the animal, but it was Meleager who killed the beast and was awarded its skin. He gave the skin to Atalanta, but the sons of Thestius took it from her. For this act Meleager made the fatal mistake of slaying them. These were the brothers of his mother, Althaea, and she pronounced a curse upon him, in consequence of which he became indignant and stayed at home from battles between the Calydonians and Curetes. Without him the victorious Curetes threatened to overpower Calydon. The old men of the town promised him the most extravagant rewards if he would again join in the fight, and his own friends begged him to relent, but all in vain. Finally, however, he yielded to the prayers of his wife, Cleopatra; he put the Curetes to flight but never returned home because the Erinyes, the goddesses of retribution, who had heard the curse of his mother, overtook him (Hom. *Il.* 9.527–600). The post–Homeric account gives a different cause of his death. When Meleager was seven days old, the Moirae (Fates) appeared, declaring that the boy should die as soon as the piece of wood that was burning on the hearth should be consumed. When Althaea heard this, she extinguished the piece and concealed it in a chest. Meleager thus became invulnerable; but after he had killed his mother's brothers, she lighted the piece of wood, and Meleager died. Following this, Althaea and Cleopatra, his mother and his wife, hanged themselves (Apollod. 1.8.2; Diod. 4.34; Ov. *Met.* 8.450). The sisters of Meleager wept unceasingly after his death, until Artemis changed them into guinea hens. Two of them, Gorge and Deianeira, through the mediation of Dionysus, were not metamorphosed. The story of Meleager, his hunt

of the Calydonian boar, his contest with the sons of Thestius, and other scenes of his life, were frequently represented by ancient artists. He usually appears as a robust hunter with curly hair, the Aetolian *chlamys* (mantle), and a boar's head.

Heracles, as stated, is said to have taken part in the Calydonian boar hunt. After a number of punitive expeditions following his labors, he proceeded to Calydon, where he demanded Deianeira, the daughter of Oeneus, for his wife. He had to fight with Achelous, the river-god, for possession of Deianeira. He had been married to her for nearly three years, when, at a repast in the house of Oeneus, he accidently killed the boy Eunomos, the son of Architeles. The father of the boy pardoned the murder, as it had not been committed intentionally; but Heracles, in accordance with the law, went into exile with Deianeira. She later became the unwitting cause of his death and hanged herself.

The kingly line of Calydon was continued through Meleager's sister Gorge, who married Andraemon. As already stated, Diomedes gave the kingdom to Andraemon because of the advanced age and infirmity of Oeneus. After a long reign he, too, died, and his tomb, together with that of Gorge, was seen at Amphissa in the time of Pausanias (10.33.3). The son of Andraemon and Gorge was Thoas, and after Andraemon's reign he succeeded to the throne of Calydon and Pleuron. He went against Troy with forty ships (Hom. *Il.* 2.638).

Thoas had a son Haemon, about whom nothing is known, except that he was the father of Oxylus. When the Dorians invaded Peloponnesus, they, in accordance with an oracle, chose Oxylus as one of their leaders. He afterward became king of Elis, which he conquered (Paus. 5.3.6; Aristot. *Polit.* 6.2.5). He became the father of Aetolus and Laias by Pieria. Aetolus died in Elis while very young, and the line which had begun in Elis with his ancestor Aetolus had gone full circle.

Another hero associated with Calydon was Bellerophon, who was hospitably received by Oeneus and given a costly belt (Hom. *Il.* 6.216). Still another was Cycnus, a son of Apollo by Hyria. He was a handsome hunter living in the district between Pleuron and Calydon, and, although beloved by many, he rejected all his lovers. Only one, Phyllius, persevered in his love. Cycnus at last imposed upon him three labors: to kill a lion without weapons, to catch alive some monstrous vultures that devoured men, and with his own hand to lead a bull to the altar of Zeus. Phyllius accomplished all these tasks, but, on the advice of Heracles, he refused to give to Cycnus the bull that he had received as a prize. Cycnus was furious at the refusal and leaped into Lake Canope, which was from that time called after him the Cycnean lake. His mother Hyria followed him, and both were metamorphosed by Apollo into swans. Ovid (*Met.* 7.371), who relates the same story, makes the Cycnean lake arise from Hyria melting away in tears at the death of her son.

Callirrhoe was a maiden of Calydon, who, when she was loved by Coresus, a priest of Dionysus, rejected all the offers he made to her. At length, he implored his god to punish the cruel maid. Dionysus consequently brought a plague of madness on Calydon. The Dodonaean oracle ruled that Callirrhoe had to be sacrificed. When she was led to the altar, Coresus, feeling his passion for her return, sacrificed himself in her stead. But she also now killed herself near a spring which derived its name from her (Paus. 7.21.1).

Calydon and Pleuron are said by Strabo (10.2.3) to have been once among the finest cities of Greece but to have sunk in his time into insignificance. Calydon was situated in a fertile plain near the Euenus and 12.5 km from the sea, according to Pliny (4.2.6). It is frequently mentioned by Homer, who gives it the epithets "rocky" and "steep," but he probably meant the district and not the city itself. Homer also celebrates the fertility of the plain of the "lovely" Calydon (*Il.* 2.640). In the earliest times the inhabitants of Calydon appear to have been engaged in incessant hostilities with the Curetes, who continued to reside in their ancient capital Pleuron and who endeavored to expel the invaders from their country. A vivid account of one of the battles between the Curetes and Calydonians is given in an episode of the *Iliad* (9.529).

Calydon was the headquarters of the worship of Artemis Laphria, and when, in the historic period, the inhabitants of the town were removed to Nicopolis, Augustus gave to Patrae in Achaia the statue of this goddess, which had belonged to Calydon (Paus. 4.31.7, 7.18.7). Her worship had previously been introduced at Naupactus and Patrae from Calydon. The name Laphria was traced back to a hero, Laphrius, son of Castalius, who was said to have instituted her worship at Calydon. There was also a statue of Dionysus Calydonius at Patrae that had been removed from Calydon (Paus. 7.21.1). Near Calydon there was a temple of Apollo Laphrius (Strab. 10.2.21).

The ruins of Calydon lie just to the north of the main highway running from Antirio to Messolongi, the marked exit just after crossing the Euenus River heading west. The city was located on a hill with two low summits and extended into the valley below. There are a few remains of the walls dating from the third century B.C. The perimeter was about 4 km. The acropolis was to the northwest and was well fortified by a double gate with two towers. From the gate a road led to Stratos, the ancient capital of Acarnania. Another road left the west gate for Laphrium, the sacred precinct, which was dedicated to the worship of Artemis and Apollo.

In the precinct there were two temples, one dedicated to Artemis and the other to Apollo. In the sixth century these temples were remodelled, and the temple to Apollo was painted with mythological figures. The temple of Artemis was decorated with sphinxes and metopes depicting the labors of Heracles. In the fourth century the area was again remodelled. A portico was built, and a new temple of Artemis erected. Within the temple was a chryselephantine statue of Artemis mentioned by Pausanias (7.18.10). Other buildings and artifacts have been uncovered in the area, notably a hero shrine called the Leonteion. Its walls are decorated with carved medallions featuring scenes of heroes and gods in the history of Calydon. Many of the finds can be seen in the National Museum of Athens.

CALYMNA (KALIMNOS)   is one of the Dodekanissa, lying off the coast of what was ancient Caria between Leros and Cos. It appears to have been the principal island of the group that Homer calls Calydnae (*Il.* 2.677).

The island was originally inhabited by Carians and was afterward colonized by Aeolians from Thessaly or Dorians under Heraclid leaders. It also received an additional colony of Argives, who are said to have been shipwrecked on the island after the Trojan War (Diod. 5.54; Hom. *Il.* 2.675). It produces figs, grapes, barley, oranges, and olives. Ancient Calymna was famed for its honey, which rivalled the honey of Attica.

Its ancient towns were Coos, Notium, Nisyrus, and Mendeterus. Near the southwest promontory of the island is the Cave of Kefalas, which was discovered to have been a sanctuary of Zeus Olympius. On the west side of the island have been found ruins believed to have been part of a temple of Apollo Calydneus.

CAMEIRUS (KAMIROS)   was one of the three most ancient towns of the island of Rhodes, the other two being Lindus and Ialysus. These were believed to have been founded by three grandsons of the Heliad Ochimus—Cameirus, Lindus, and Ialysus. According to others, Cameirus was founded by the Heraclid Tlepolemus (Diod. 4.58, 5.57). The town of Cameirus is said to have derived its name from Cameirus, a son of Cercaphus and Cydippe and a grandson of Helios. Others say that Tlepolemus built the towns of Lindus, Ialysus, and Cameirus and gave them the names of three Danaids. Danaus, it will be remembered, first landed at Rhodes on his flight with his daughters from Egypt. Tlepolemus was a son of Heracles by Astyoche, the daughter of Phylas (Hom. *Il.* 2.658; Apollod. 2.76) or by Astydameia, the daughter of Amyntor, king of the Dolopians in Thessaly (Pind. *Ol.* 7.41). Tlepolemus was king of Argos, but after slaying his uncle Licymnius, he was obliged to take flight, and, obeying the command of an oracle, settled in Rhodes where he built the three cities. From here he joined the Greeks in the Trojan War with nine ships (Hom. *Il.* 2.65).

The city of Cameirus is connected also with the mysterious Telchines. These were a family, a class of people, or a tribe, said to have been descended from Thalassa or Poseidon (Diod. 5.55; Nonn. *Dionys.* 14.40). The accounts of the Telchines are very few and very scanty, and in them the deities appear in different roles. For example, they appeared as cultivators of the soil and ministers of the gods; as such they came from Crete to Cyprus and from there to Rhodes, or they proceeded from Rhodes to Crete and Boeotia. Rhodes (and likewise the three towns of Cameirus, Ialysus, and Lindus) was abandoned by them because they foresaw that the island would be inundated. From there they scattered in different directions. At Cameirus they worshipped Hera, from which circumstances she was known as Hera Telchinia.

These three towns, together with Cos, Cnidus and Halicarnassus, formed what was called the Doric hexapolis, which had its common sanctuary on the Triopian headland on the coast of Caria. Apollo was the patron deity of the confederation (Herod. 1.144). Cameirus, called ""chalky" by Homer (*Il.* 2.656), was rediscovered in 1859 and excavated in 1929. The ruins of Cameirus are rather extensive, with remains of an agora, colonnades, and temples. Behind the stoa to the south are ruins of a temple of Athena.

CAMIRUS was an earlier name of HIERAPYTNA in Crete.

CANETHUS was the name of a hill in Chalcis, the chief town of Euboea. When Alexander crossed over into Asia, the Chalcidians strengthened the fortifications of their city by enclosing within their walls a hill on the Boeotian side called Canethus, which thus formed a fortified bridgehead. Canethus, which is also mentioned by Apollonius Rhodius (1.77) is probably the hill that rises immediately above the modern bridge and is the citadel of the present town. This hill is named for Canethus, the son of Atlas and father of Canethus in Euboea (Apollod. 3.8.1).

CANOPE was a lake in the vicinity of Pleuron and Calydon. Cycnus, a son of Apollo by Hyria, was a handsome hunter who rejected all lovers. One of them, Phyllius, persisted and Cycnus gave him impossible tasks to accomplish. Phyllius did the tasks but eventually refused to yield to Cycnus a bull that he had received as a prize. Cycnus, exasperated at the refusal, leaped into Lake Canope, which was thereafter called the Cycnean lake. His mother followed him, and both were metamorphosed into swans. Ovid (*Met.* 7.371) makes the Cycnean lake arise from Hyria melting away in tears at the death of her son.

CAPHAREUS or CAPHEREUS (KAFIREUS) is a rocky and dangerous promontory, forming the southeastern extremity of Euboea, once called Kavo Doro but renamed Kafireus to recall the ancient name. It was off this promontory that the Grecian fleet was wrecked on its return from Troy (Eurip. *Troad.* 90; Herod. 8.7; Paus. 2.23.1). Nauplius, the father of Palamedes, is said to have lighted torches to misdirect the returning heroes in revenge for the murder of his son on a false charge of treason.

Ajax the Lesser was the son of Oileus, king of the Locrians. After the taking of Troy, it is said, he rushed into the temple of Athena where Cassandra had taken refuge and was embracing the statue of the goddess as a suppliant. Ajax dragged her away with violence and led her to the other captives (Virg. *Aen.* 2.403; Eurip. *Troad.* 70). According to some statements, he even raped her in the temple. Others said this charge of impiety was invented by Agamemnon, who wanted Cassandra for himself. Ajax was to be stoned to death but saved himself by establishing his innocence by an oath (Paus. 10.26.1,31.1). But whether true or not, Athena had sufficient reason for being indignant, as Ajax had dragged a suppliant from her temple. On his voyage homeward a storm on the Capharean Rocks wrecked his ship; he himself was killed by Athena with a flash of lightning, and his body was washed upon the rocks, which after this were called the Rocks of Ajax.

CAPHYAE (HOTOUSSA) was a town of Arcadia situated in a small plain northwest of the lake of Orchomenus. It was protected against flooding from this lake by a levee raised by the inhabitants of Caphyae. The city is said to have been founded by Cepheus, who was the son of Aleus and Neaera or of Cleobule and an Argonaut from Tegea, of which he was king. He had twenty sons and two daughters, and nearly all his sons perished in an expedition that they undertook with Heracles. The town of Caphyae was also believed to have derived its name from Cepheus (Paus. 8.23.3). The remains of the walls of Caphyae are visible upon a small hill of the modern village of Hotoussa, which stands near the edge of the lake. Pausanias (8.23.3) speaks of a mountain in the neighborhood of the city named Cnacalus, on which the inhabitants celebrated a yearly festival to Artemis Cnacalesia.

Artemis is also connected with the history of Caphyae in another way. Artemis Apanchomene (Strangled Goddess) was a name of the goddess at Caphyae, and its origin is related by Pausanias (8.23.6,7). In the neighborhood of Caphyae in a place called Condylea, there was a sacred grove of Artemis Condyleatis. Once while some boys were playing in this grove, they put a string around the goddess' statue and stated that they were strangling Artemis. Some of the inhabitants of

Caphyae were outraged by this impiety and stoned the boys to death. Subsequently all the women of Caphyae had premature births, and all the children were born dead. This curse did not cease until the boys were honorably buried and an annual sacrifice for them was observed in accordance with the command of an oracle of Apollo. The surname Condyleatis was then changed to Apanchomene.

CARDAMYLE (KARDAMILI) was a town of Messenia and one of the seven places offered by Agamemnon to Achilles (Hom. *Il.* 9.150,292). It was situated on a strong, rocky height 1.33 km from the sea and 11 km from Leuctra (Paus. 3.26.7; Strab. 8.4.4). Pausanias mentions at Cardamyle sanctuaries of Athena and of Apollo Carneius; and in the neighborhood of the town a sanctuary of the Nereids. Nereids (*Nereides*) is a patronymic applied to the daughters of Nereus and Doris, who were regarded by the ancients as marine nymphs of the Mediterranean. They were worshipped in several parts of Greece, but more especially in seaport towns, such as Cardamyle. There are considerable ruins 1 km northeast of the town about 1,300 meters from the sea.

CARIA was the name of the acropolis of Megara. It derived its name from Car, a son of Phoroneus and king of Megara (Paus. 1.39.4,40.5). His tomb was shown as late as the time of Pausanias (1.44.9) on the road from Megara to Corinth.

CARNASIUM was a city sometimes identified with OECHALIA.

CARNEATES was an earlier name of PHLIUS.

CARPATHUS (KARPATHOS) is an island in the sea between Crete and Rhodes, which gave its name to the Carpathian Sea. Carpathus is 50 km in length and 12 km wide at its widest point. The island consists for the most part of lofty, bare mountains full of ravines and hollows, and the coast is generally steep and inaccessible. The principal mountain, Lastros, which is in the center of the island, is 1,121 meters in height.

Carpathus is said to have been subject to Minos and afterward colonized by Argive Dorians (Diod. 5.54). It always remained a Doric country. The dialect of the modern inhabitants retains many ancient Doric words. At the time of the Trojan War it is mentioned along with Nisyrus, Casus, and Cos (Hom. *Il.* 2.676). Antiphus, a son of Thessalus, and his brother Pheidippus joined the Greeks with thirty ships and commanded the men of these islands. At a later period Carpathus was under the rule of the Rhodians.

Proteus was the prophetic old man of the sea. Virgil (*Georg.* 4.387) mentions the island of Carpathus as his place of residence. Anyone wishing Proteus to foretell the future was obliged to catch hold of him at midday. He had the power of assuming every possible shape in order to escape the necessity of prophesying; but whenever he saw that his endeavors were of no avail, he resumed his usual appearance and told the truth. When he had finished his prophecy, he returned into the sea. He is sometimes represented as riding through the sea in a chariot drawn by seahorses (Virg. *Georg.* 4.389).

There are considerable ruins on Carpathus, but few that have been identified with mythological beings or ancient worship. Near Volada an inscription was found that mentioned a temple of Apollo at the city of Carpathus.

CARTHAEA (POLES) was situated on the southeast side of the island of Ceos at the foot of deep gorges descending from the heights. There are still considerable ruins of this town, among which are temples of Athena and Apollo.

Epeius was a son of Panopeus, called the artist, who went with thirty ships from the Cyclades to Troy. About the close of the Trojan War he built the wooden horse under the protection and with the assitance of Athena (Hom. *Od.* 8.492, 11.523; Paus. 2.29.4). In the Homeric poems he appears as a mighty and gallant warrior, whereas later traditions assign to him an inferior place among the heroes at Troy. One writer called him the water bearer of the Atreidae, and as such he was represented in the temple of Apollo at Carthaea.

CARYAE (KARIES?) was a town of Laconia upon the boundary of Arcadia. It was originally an Arcadian town belonging to Tegea but was conquered by the Spartans and annexed to their territory (Paus. 8.45.1). Caryae was celebrated for its temple of Artemis Caryatis and for the annual festival of this goddess. The statue of the goddess stood in the open, and Lacedaemonian virgins used to perform a traditional dance there (Paus. 3.10.7; Lucian *De Salt.* 10). In the second Messenian war, Aristomenes is said to have carried off the Lacedaemonian virgins who were dancing at Caryae in honor of Artemis (Paus. 4.16.9). It was, perhaps, from this ancient dance of the Lacedaemonian maidens that the Greek artists gave the name *Caryatides* to the female figures employed in architecture instead of pillars.

The exact position of Caryae is not known. It is evident from the account of Pausanias (3.10.7) that it was situated on the road from Tegea to Sparta, and the modern village of Karies would seem to satisfy both that description and also the condition of its being near the frontier of Arcadia. The similarity in name (Kariai on some maps) would further suggest some connection.

CARYSTUS (KARISTOS) was a town of Euboea situated on the south coast of the island at the foot of

Mount Oche. It is mentioned by Homer (*Il.* 2.539) and is said to have been founded by Dryopes (Thuc. 7.57; Diod. 4.37). Its name was derived from Carystus, the son of Cheiron and Chariclo. Carystus was the home of Epipole, a daughter of Trachion. In the disguise of a man she went with the Greeks against Troy; but when Palamedes discovered her sex, she was stoned to death by the Greek army.

Carystus was celebrated for its greenish marble, which was in much demand at Rome. Strabo places the quarries at Marmarium, a place upon the coast near Carystus, opposite Halae Araphenides in Attica. There are very few remains of ancient Carystus.

CASSOPE (ZALONGO)   was the chief town of the Cassopaei, a people of Epeirus. It stood a short distance from the sea on the road from Pandrosia to Nicopolis. The ancient city was not less than 5 km in circumference, and its ruins, which were discovered in 1951–1955, are quite extensive. The ruins include a vaulted hero shrine in the southwest corner of the city and a temple of Aphrodite outside the east wall. The city was abandoned with the founding of Nicopolis. The ruins may be seen at the village of Zalongo.

CASSOTIS   was a spring at Delphi named for Cassotis, a Parnassian nymph. This well provided the water that gave the priestess the power of prophecy (Paus. 10.24.5). Above the tomb of Neoptolemus was the stone that Cronus was said to have swallowed instead of his son Zeus, and afterward to have vomited up. Pausanias saw this stone, which was not very far from the fountain Cassotis; access to the stone was through a small wall built near the fountain. He further said that the Cassotis flowed into the adytum of the temple of Apollo. The Cassotis has been identified with the spring Kerna, which flows between the ruins of the theater and the stadium.

The name Cassotis occurs only in Pausanias, but the fountain itself is mentioned by other ancient writers. In the Homeric *Hymn to Apollo* (300) it is referred to as a beautifully flowing fountain, where Apollo slew the serpent. Euripides (*Ion* 112) alludes to it as watering the sacred grove surrounding the temple. This sacred grove consisted of laurel trees and myrtles, but one laurel tree in particular was called specifically the Pythian laurel, and branches of it were used for sacred purposes within the temple.

CASTALIA   is a spring at Delphi. Castalia, the nymph of the spring, was thought to be a daughter of Achelous (Paus. 10.8.5) and to have thrown herself into the water when pursued by Apollo. Some derived the name of the Castalian well from one Castalius, who was either a simple mortal or a son of Apollo and father of Delphis, who came from Crete to Crissa and there founded the worship of the Delphian Apollo. Another account makes Castalius a son of Delphus and father of Thyia (Paus. 7.18.6, 10.6.2). The Muses are sometimes called Nymphae Castalides (Castalian nymphs) because the Castalian spring was sacred to them (Theocrit. 7.148; Mart. 7.11).

The gorge between the two summits of Parnassus is the bed of a stream, which in the rainy season forms a waterfall about sixty meters in height. At the lower end of the dry bed of the stream where it emerges from between the cliffs, is the Castalian spring. It flows through a hollow dell down to the Pleistus River, passing by the monastery of the Panaghia on its left, or east side.

The Castalia supplied the holy water of the Delphian temple. All persons who came to consult the oracle, wished to pray to the god before engaging in the Pythian games, or visited Delphi for any religious object whatsoever, were obliged to purify themselves at this sacred fountain (Pind. *Pyth.* 4.290, 5.39; Plut. *Arist.* 20). Even the servants of the temple used the water for this purpose (Eurip. *Ion* 94). The chief form of the purification seems to have involved washing the hair, but those who visited Delphi for the purpose of being purified from murder bathed their whole bodies in the Castalian spring. There are still steps leading down to remains of a bath cut out of the rock that received the waters of the spring. It is called by some the Bath of the Pythian Pilgrims. Beside the spring Apollo is said to have planted a sprig of laurel he brought from Tempe. The base of a statue of Gaea, the goddess of the earth, suggests that the spring was very early a site of Chthonic cult worship.

In later times the Castalian spring was said to impart poetic inspiration to those who drank of it. But this is an invention of the Roman poets, who appear to have attributed to the spring this power because Apollo was the protector of the Muses.

CASTHANAEA (NTAMOUHARI)   was a town of Magnesia in Thessaly at the foot of Mount Pelion. In the town was a temple of Aprhodite Casthanitis. The town has been placed at some ruins near a small port named Ntamouhari 6 km from Tsangarada. From this town the chestnut tree, which still abounds on the east side of Mount Pelion, derived its name in Greek and the modern languages of Europe (Herod. 7.183,184; Plin. 4.9.16).

CASUS or CASSOS (KASSOS)   an island between Carpathus and Crete in the Carpathian Sea is 13 km from Carpathus. It has an overall length of 19 km, most of which is precipitous and inaccessible. It is said to have been formerly called Amphe, Achne, or Astrabe. The remains of the ancient town, which was also called Casus, were found in the interior of the island at the village of Polio, the former capital. The ancient port town was at Emporeion (modern Emboreio); among the ancient ruins discovered there were sepulchral chambers partly built in the earth. Antiphus, a son of Thessalus, and his brother Pheidippus joined the Greeks with thirty ships and commanded the men of Carpathus, Casus, Cos, and other islands in the Trojan War (Hom. *Il.* 2.675).

CAUS was a town in Arcadia. Pausanias (8.25.1) found in it ruins but noted a sanctuary of Asclepius Causius, who took the surname from the town. It was about 7.5 km from Thelpusa.

CEA (See CEOS)

CECROPIA was an earlier name of ATHENS.

CELAENAE (See MELAENAE)

CENAEUM (LIHADA) was a promontory of Euboea, forming the northwest extremity of the island and opposite the Malic Gulf. On this promontory was a temple of Zeus Cenaeus (Thuc. 3.93). This temple was founded by Heracles. After the hero took Oechalia and slew Eurytus and his sons and carried off his daughter Iole as a prisoner, he landed at Cenaeum and erected an altar to Zeus Cenaeus. Here also he sent his companion Lichas in search of a wedding garment, which would prove Heracles undoing. Despite searches for the sanctuary, no remains of a temple have been found.

CENCHREAE (KEHRIES) the port of the Saronic Gulf, was a center for trade with Asia and about 11 km from Corinth. This port was not an artificial one like that of Lechaeum. It was a bay protected by two promontories on the north and south, extended by breakwaters. There are still remains of these moles. Pausanias (2.2.3) writes that a bronze Poseidon stood upon a rock in the sea and that to the right of the entrance was a temple of Aphrodite and to the left were sanctuaries of Asclepius and of Isis. Cenchreae was one of the locales Apuleius describes in his *Metamorphoses.*

Cenchreae is now deserted, but it retains its name in the form of Kehries. The ancient town stood upon the slopes of the hill above the town, as proven by the numerous remains of its foundations. Between this hill and the heights to the right and the left there were two small plains; through one plain ran the road leading to Schoenus and through the other the road leading to Corinth. Pausanias (2.2.3) mentions certain lukewarm salt springs flowing from a rock into the sea in the direction of Cenchreae and called the Bath of Helen.

Cenchrias, a son of Poseidon and Peirene, was killed accidentally by Artemis. He and his brother Leches were believed to have given their names to Cenchreae and Lechaeum, the two port towns of Corinth (Paus. 2.2.3,3.3,24.8).

CEOS or CEA (KEA or TZIA) an island in the Aegean Sea and one of the Cyclades, is situated about 21 km southeast of the promontory of Sunium in Attica. The island is 23 km in length from north to south and 16 km in width from east to west. Ceos was originally called Hydrussa because of its plentiful water supply. It was said to have been inhabited by nymphs, who were frightened away from the island by a lion and crossed over to Carystus; from this circumstance a promontory of Ceos was called Leon. It is also claimed that the city of Naupactus founded a colony on Ceos. The island once possessed four towns: Iulis, Carthaea, Coressia, and Poeeessa. In the time of Strabo, however, the last two had ceased to exist, the inhabitants of Coressia having been transferred to Iulis and those of Poeeessa to Carthaea (Strab. 10.5.6). Between Poeeessa and Coressia there were temples of Apollo Smintheus and Athena Nedusia. Nestor on his way from Troy was said to have founded the temple of Athena. On the promontory of Agia Irini there was a temple of Dionysus.

Cyparissus, a youth of Ceos, a son of Telephus, was beloved by Apollo and Zephyrus or Silvanus. When he inadvertently killed his favorite stag, he was seized with immoderate grief and metamorphosed into a cypress (Ov. *Met.* 10.120).

Another beautiful youth of the island was Acontius. On one occasion he came to Delos to celebrate the annual festival of Artemis and fell in love with Cydippe, the daughter of a noble Athenian. When he saw her sitting in the temple attending to the sacrifice she was offering, he threw before her an apple upon which he had written the words "I swear by the sanctuary of Artemis to marry Acontius." Cydippe read aloud what was written upon it and then threw the apple away. But the goddess had heard her vow, as Acontius had wished. After the festival was over he went home and waited to see what would happen. After some time, when Cydippe's father was about to give her in marriage to another man, she fell ill just before the wedding was to begin. This same situation was repeated three times. Acontius, hearing of the occurrences, hurried to Athens. The Delphic oracle, which was consulted by the maiden's father, declared that Artemis by the repeated illnesses was punishing Cydippe for her perjury. The girl then revealed the whole affair to her mother, and her father was finally persuaded to give his daughter to Acontius.

Aristaeus was an ancient divinity worshipped in various parts of Greece but especially in the islands of the Aegean, Ionian and Adriatic Seas, which had once been inhabited by Pelasgians. According to some, he married Autonoe, the daughter of Cadmus, who bore him several sons: Charmus, Calaicarpus, Actaeon, and Polydorus. After the unfortunate death of Actaeon, he left Thebes and went to Ceos, whose inhabitants he delivered from a destructive drought by erecting an altar to Zeus Icmaeus. This gave rise to an identification of Aristaeus with Zeus in Ceos. The benefits that he conferred upon mankind differed in different places according to their especial wants. Ceos, which was much exposed to heat and droughts, received through him rain and refreshing winds.

CEPHALE (KERATEA)   was a deme of Attica belonging to the tribe of Acamantis. Keratea, a town 19 km north of ancient Sunium, has been identified by inscriptions as the site of Cephale. Cephale possessed a temple of the Dioscuri, who were here called the Great Gods (Paus. 1.31.1). Sanctuaries of Hera and Asclepius are thought to have existed there, and an altar of Aphrodite presumably existed between Keratea and Kaki Thalassa.

CEPHALLENIA (KEFALONIA)   opposite the Corinthian Gulf and the coast of Acarnania, is the largest island in the Ionian Sea. Along the northern half of the east coast of Cephallenia lies the small island of Ithaca, which is separated from it by a narrow channel about 5 km in width. The island is 52 km from tip to tip. Its width is very unequal, varying from 13 to 26 km.

Homer (*Od.* 4.671) describes Cephallenia as "rugged," referring to the mountain ridge which crosses the island from northwest to southeast. The highest summit of this range, which rises to the height of about 1,219 meters, was called Aenus, and upon it was a temple of Zeus Aenesius. There is also a mountain called Baea said to have been named after the pilot of Odysseus. The principal plain in Cephallenia is that of Same on the east side of the island.

The island is called Same or Samos in Homer. Its earliest inhabitants appear to have been Taphians, as was the case on neighboring islands (Strab. 10.2.24). It is said to have derived its name from Cephalus, a son of Deion, the ruler of Phocis, and Diomede. He was married to Procris. After Cephalus had accidentally killed his wife, he went out with Amphitryon against the Teleboans. After the conquest of the Teleboans, Amphitryon rewarded him with the island, which he eponymously named Cephallenia (Apollod. 2.4.7; Strab. 10.2.14). The inhabitants of the island are called Cephallenes and are described as the subjects of Odysseus as early as Homer (*Il.* 2.631, *Od.* 20.210, 24.355); but Cephallenia, as the name of the island, first occurs in Herodotus (9.28).

Cephallenia was a tetrapolis, containing the four states of Same, Pale, Cranii, and Proni. This division of the island appears to have been a very ancient one since a legend derived the names of the four cities from the names of the four sons of Cephalus. Of these states Same was probably the most ancient, as it is mentioned by Homer (*Od.* 20.288).

Britomartis originally was a Cretan divinity of hunters and fishermen. According to one tradition, she migrated from Phoenicia (her mother, according to this tradition was Carme, daughter of Phoenix) to Argos, to the daughters of Erasinus, and thence to Cephallenia, where she received divine honors from the inhabitants under the name of Laphria.

CEPHISSUS (KIFISSOS)   is a river in Attica near Athens. It flows southward from Mount Parnes on the west side of Athens and empties into the Phaleric bay. Today the Cephissus is mainly canalized in the city and located farther west than its ancient bed.

Academus was an Attic hero, who, when Castor and Polydeuces invaded Attica to liberate their sister Helen, betrayed to them that she was kept concealed at Aphidna. For this reason the Tyndarids always showed him much gratitude, and whenever the Lacedaemonians invaded Attica, they always spared the land belonging to Academus, which lay on the Cephissus, 1 km from Athens (Plut. *Thes.* 32). This piece of land was subsequently devoted to olive plantations (Plut. *Cim.* 13) and was called Academia from its original owner.

Zeus Meilichius is protector of those who honored him with propitiatory sacrifices. At Athens cakes were offered to him every year at the festival of the Diasia (Thuc. 1.126; Xenoph. *Anab.* 7.7.4). Altars were erected to Zeus Meilichius on the Cephissus (Paus. 1.37.3). Today the medieval church of Agios Savas stands on the site of a temple of Demeter built to commemorate her meeting with Phytalus, who received her hospitably. On this spot she gave him the first fig tree. After Theseus had overcome the Isthmian monsters he arrived at the Cephissus and was purified by the Phytalidae, descendants of Phytalus.

CEPHISSUS (KIFISSOS)   is one of the two small streams of the Eleusinian plain in Attica. It is also called the Sarandaforo. It rises in Mount Cithaeron and crosses the narrow plain of Eleutherae before it descends into that of Eleusis.

Procrustes (Stretcher) is a name given to the famous robber Polypemon or Damastes. He used to force all strangers who fell into his hands to lie in a bed that was either too small or too large, and then he had their limbs stretched by force or cut off until they died. He was slain by Theseus on the Cephissus. The bed of Procrustes is used proverbially even in the present day (Plut. *Thes.* 11; Paus. 1.38.5; Ov. *Met.* 7.438).

CEPHISSUS (KIFISSOS)   is a river in Boeotia, which in ancient times flowed into Lake Copais. Today it spreads out in a vast area of irrigated land, and the overflow falls into Lake Iliki.

Cephissus, the divinity of the river Cephissus, is described as a son of Pontus and Thalassa and the father of Diogeneia and Narcissus. He had an altar in common with Pan, the nymphs, and Achelous in the temple of Amphiaraus near Oropus (Paus. 1.34.2). The worship of the Charites was believed to have been first introduced into Boeotia by Eteoclus or Eteocles, the son of Cephissus, in the valley of that river (Paus. 9.35.1; Theocrit. 16.104; Pind. *Ol.* 14).

The story of the beautiful youth Argynnus is connected with this river. Agamemnon loved Argynnus, having seen him swimming in the Cephissus River, in which he later drowned. Agamemnon buried him and founded there a temple of Aphrodite Argynnis (Athen. 13.603).

CERAMEICUS (KERAMIKOS)   was the name of two demes that made up the area of greater ATHENS.

CERIADAE   was a deme west of Pnyx outside the city walls of ATHENS.

CERINTHUS (MANDOUDI)   a town upon the northeast coast of Euboea and near the small river Budorus, was said to have been founded by the Athenian Cothus. It is mentioned by Homer (*Il.* 2.538) and was still extant in the time of Strabo (10.1.5), who speaks of it as a small place (Apoll. Rhod. 1.79).

Elephenor was a son of Chalcodon and prince of the Abantes in Euboea, whom he led against Troy in forty ships. Cerinthus was one of the cities whose inhabitants followed him to war (Hom. *Il.* 2.538).

CERYNEIA (MAMOUSIA)   was a town of Achaia. In the time of Strabo, Ceryneia was dependent upon Aegium. It was situated inland upon a lofty height west of the river Cerynites and a little south of Helice. Its ruins have been discovered on the height, which rises above the left bank of the Cerynites where it emerges from the mountains into the plain (Paus. 7.25.5). It was held that the wine of Ceryneia produced abortion.

The third labor of Heracles was fetching the stag of Ceryneia alive to Mycenae. This animal had golden antlers and brazen feet. It had been dedicated to Artemis by the nymph Taygete because the goddess had saved her from the pursuit of Zeus. The pursuit took place in Argolis and Arcadia, but the name of the stag came from the name of this town.

CESTRINE (FILIATES)   was a district of Epeirus in the south of Chaonia. It was separated from Thesprotia by the river Thyamis. It is said to have received its name from Cestrinus, son of Helenus and Andromache; it was previously called Cammania (Paus. 1.11.1, 2.23.6). The principal town of this district is called Cestria by Pliny

(4.1.4), but its more usual name appears to have been Ilium or Troja in memory of the Trojan colony of Helenus. The remains are still visible near the town of Filiates, a modern market town about 20 km from the Albanian border.

CHAERONEIA (HERONIA)   was a town of Boeotia, situated near the Cephissus River on the border with Phocis. The town itself does not appear to have been of much importance, but it became renowned because of the battles fought in its vicinity. Its position, which commanded the entrance from Phocis into Boeotia, made it strategically important in protecting Boeotia from an invading force. It was situated at the head of the plain, shut in by a high, projecting rock, which formed in ancient times the citadel of the town and was called Petrachus or Petrochus (Paus. 9.41.6). The town lay at the foot of the hill. It is said to have derived its name from Chaeron, the son of Apollo and Thero, who was the daughter of Phydas.

Chaeroneia is not mentioned by Homer; but some ancient writers suppose it to be the same town as the Boeotian Arne (Hom. *Il.* 2.507). Arne, from whom the town was believed to have derived its name, was a daughter of Aeolus (Thuc. 1.12; Paus. 9.40.5). In the historical period it was dependent upon Orchomenus.

Chaeroneia stood upon the site of the modern village Heronia (formerly Kapraina). There are not many remains of the ancient city upon the plain. Some ruins of the citadel may be seen upon the projecting rock already described; and on the face of the rock fronting the plain are traces of the ancient theater. In the theater have been found dedications to Apollo Daphnephorus and Artemis Soodina. Nearby, on the side of Mount Thourion, the chapel of Agia Paraskevi is built on the site of a temple of Heracles. In the church of the Panagia in the village are several remains of ancient art and inscriptions, one of which indicates that Serapis was worshipped in the town. No trace of a sanctuary has so far been found. Pausanias (9.41.6) states that the principal object of worship in his time was the scepter of Zeus once borne by Agamemnon and considered to be the undoubted work of the god Hephaestus. Some traditions claim that Rhea gave birth to Zeus at Chaeroneia.

The most striking object at Heronia is a historical one. The famous Lion of Chaeroneia, discovered in 1818, is believed to be the funeral monument of the Sacred Band of Thebans, for buried beneath it were found 254 skeletons. The Lion stands 5.5 meters high on a foundation 3 meters high and is made of five blocks of marble. It is well worth the short trip north from Livadia.

CHALCIA or CHALCE (HALKI)   is a small island about 17 km off the northwest coast of Rhodes. It had a small town of the same name, a temple of Apollo, and a harbor (Strab. 10.5.15). The island was probably subject to Rhodes. Today it is bare and hilly and has fewer than five hundred inhabitants. There is no reason to visit to see classical remains.

CHALCIS (HALKIDA) is the chief town of Euboea, separated from the coast of Boeotia by the narrow strait of the Euripus, which is at this spot only thirty-seven meters across. In antiquity, as today, a bridge connected Chalcis with the Boeotian coast. It was said to have derived its name from Chalcis, one of the daughters of Asopus and Metope. According to others, Chalcis was the mother of the Curetes and Corybantes, the former of whom were the earliest inhabitants of Chalcis (Strab. 10.1.9).

Chalcis was a city of great antiquity and continued to be an important place from the earliest to the latest times. It is said to have been founded before the Trojan War by an Ionic colony from Athens under the leadership of Pandoros, the son of Erechtheus (Strab. 10.1.8). It is mentioned by Homer (*Il.* 2.537). After the Trojan War, Cothus settled in the city another Ionic colony from Athens. Chalcis soon became one of the greatest of the Ionic cities and at an early period carried on an extensive trade with almost all parts of the Hellenic world. It gave its name to the peninsula of Chalcidice in consequence of the large number of cities that it founded in this district. There are few remains of the ancient city. We read, however, that the ancient city was richly endowed with public buildings and sanctuaries, including that of Apollo Delphinius. There was also a temple of Zeus Olympius, according to an inscription.

Amphidamas was a king of Chalcis, who was honored after death with funeral games given by his sons. In one of these, a poetry contest, Hesiod won a prize of a golden tripod, which he dedicated to the Muses of Helicon (Hes. *Op. et D.* 654).

Chalcodon was a son of Abas, king of the Chalcidians in Euboea. He was slain by Amphitryon in a battle against the Thebans (Paus. 8.15.6–7).

Linus was a personification of the dirge or lamentation and therefore described as a son of Apollo by a Muse (Calliope or Urania, or by Psamathe or Chalciope) (Apollod. 1.3.2; Paus. 1.43.7, 2.19.8). Linus died in Euboea, and Chalcis boasted of possessing his tomb, the inscription of which is preserved by Diogenes Laertius (*Prooem.* 4): "Here Theban Linus, whom Urania bore,/ The fair-crowned Muse, sleeps on a foreign shore."

Phalerus, a son of Alcon and grandson of Erechtheus or Eurysthenes, was one of the Argonauts and the founder of Gyrton. He is said to have emigrated with his daughter Chalciope or Chalcippe to Chalcis and when his father demanded that he should be sent back, the Chalcidians refused to deliver him up.

CHAONIA was a district of Epeirus. The Chaones, who were at one time the most powerful of the three major Epirot tribes and who are said to have ruled over the whole country (Strab. 7.7.5), inhabited in historical times the district upon the coast from the Ceraunian mountains to the river Thyamis, which separated them from the Thesprotians (Thuc. 1.46). Chaonia lay partially in what today is Albania.

The earliest inhabitants of Epeirus are said to have been Pelasgians. Dodona is represented as an oracle of the Pelasgians, and Chaonia is also called Pelasgian. The Chaones are said to have been interpreters of the oracle of Zeus.

After the fall of Troy, Andromache, wife of Hector, fell to the share of Neoptolemus, son of Achilles, who took her to Epeirus, and to whom she bore three sons, Molossus, Pielus, and Pergamus. Here she was found by Aeneas. After the death of Neoptolemus, or, according to others, after his marriage to Hermione, the daughter of Menelaus and Helen, Andromache became the wife of Helenus, a brother of Hector, who is described as a king of Chaonia, a part of Epeirus, and by whom she became the mother of Cestrinus (Virg. *Aen.* 3.295).

CHARADRA was a town in Messenia of uncertain site, said to have been built by Pelops (Strab. 8.4.4).

CHARISIA was a town in Arcadia lying between Parrhasia and Maenalia. Its location is unknown. Charisius was a son of Lycaon, to whom tradition ascribed the foundation of Charisia (Paus. 8.3.2).

CHERSONESUS (HERSONISSOS) was the port of the city Lyctus, with a temple of Britomartis (Strab. 10.4.13), 26 km from Cnossus. Lyctus was 15 km inland, and the port was the best on the north coast of Crete between Cnossus and Olus. Later Chersonesus became a more important city than Lyctus itself. The site of the temple of Britomartis is on a small promontory about 1 km east of Hersonissos.

Britomartis was originally a Cretan divinity who presided over sports and hunting. On the introduction of the worship of Artemis into Crete she became identified with her. Later accounts say that she was a daughter of Zeus and Carme and was loved and pursued by Minos. To escape him she leaped into the sea and was changed by Artemis into a goddess.

CHIOS (HIOS) is an island of the Aegean 8 km off the coast of Turkey and about halfway between Lesvos and Samos. Chios was the name of two mythical personages, each of whom is said to have given the island its name (Paus. 7.4.8). Earlier names of the island were Aethalia, Macris, and Pityussa, or "Pine Island" from its pine forests (Strab. 13.1.18).

Chios is about 50 km in length with its greatest width about 30 km, its narrowest about 13 km. The harbor of its chief town, Chios, was capable of holding eighty ships. The city of Emporios had a megaron and temple of Athena, of which there are some remains. At Phanae was a temple of Apollo, the ruins of which can still be seen near the town of Olimbi. Because of its remarkably good soil and climate it produces a variety of crops— citrus, olives, almonds, mastic, and grapes. In antiquity Chian wine was famous, and the people of the island claimed to be the discoverers of the art of making wine.

The town or the island of Chios was one of the places that claimed to be the birthplace of Homer, and the natives showed a place on the north coast of the island, at some distance from the town, which they called the Stone Homer. It was probably a shrine connected with the worship of Cybele.

The oldest inhabitants of the island were said to be Pelasgians. Myth assigns the beginnings to three sons of Poseidon, who were born on the island. Two of these sons were Angelos and Melas, whose mother was a Chian nymph. Then came Oenopion and his sons from Crete, who were followed by Carians, and then Abantes from Euboea. Other settlers came from Histiaea in Euboea under Amphiclus. Hector, the fourth in descent from Amphiclus, fought with the Abantes and Carians, killed some of them, and made terms with the rest for their leaving the island. After this, Hector decided that the people of Chios ought to join the Ionians in their religious festival at Panionium (Paus. 7.4.8). Whoever may have been the earliest settlers, Chios was by tradition colonized by the Ionians. The younger sons of Codrus, king of Athens, after a dispute over succession to the throne, came to Chios 140 years after the Trojan War, settling both the island and the west coast of Asia Minor. This historical account helps explain the affiliation of Chios with the mainland confederation.

Zeus Aethiops (Burnt-Face) was worshipped on the island (Lycoph. 537). Dionysis Omadius (Flesh-Eater) was a manifestation of Dionysus, to whom human sacrifices were offered in Chios and Tenedos.

Oenopion was a son of Dionysus and husband of the nymph Helice, by whom he became the father of Thalus, Euantes, Melas, Salagus, Athamas, and Merope. From Crete he emigrated with his sons to Chios, which Rhadamanthys had assigned to him (Paus. 7.4.8; Diod. 5.79). While he was king of Chios, he received a visit from Orion, the very handsome giant and hunter, son of Hyrieus in Boeotia. For a long time Orion sued for the hand of Merope, with whom he had fallen in love. Meanwhile he cleared the island of wild beasts and brought the spoils of the chase as presents to his beloved. Oenopion continued to defer the marriage, so that Orion one day became intoxicated and forced his way into the

house and raped Merope. Oenopion now implored the assistance of Dionysus, who caused Orion to be thrown into a deep sleep during which Oenopion blinded him. Orion was told by an oracle that he should recover his sight if he would go toward the east and expose his eyes to the rays of the rising sun. Orion, following the sound of a Cyclops' hammer, went to Lemnos, where Hephaestus gave Cedalion to him as his guide. When he afterward recovered his sight, Orion returned to Chios to take vengeance. Since Oenopion had been concealed by his friends, Orion was unable to find him and so proceeded to Crete, where he lived as a hunter with Artemis (Apollod. 1.4.3). The tomb of Oenopion was shown at Chios and was seen by Pausanias (7.5.13).

CHITONE was an Attic town where a festival, the Chitonia, was celebrated in honor of Artemis Chitona or Chitonia. This surname represented her as a huntress with her chiton fastened up to allow for hunting. Others declared that the clothes of newly-born children were sacred to Artemis (Callim. *Hymm. in Dian.* 225). Still others derived the name from the village of Chitone itself. It was more likely that the village derived its name from the festival.

CHLAMYDIA was an early alternative name of the island of DELOS.

CHRYSE was the most celebrated of the several small islands near Lemnos. Here Philoctetes was said to have been abandoned by the Greeks. According to Pausanias (8.33.4), this island was afterward swallowed up by the sea, and another, which was given the name Hiera, appeared in its stead. We cannot know what happened to Hiera, but submarine research in 1960 located in the Charos Reef, about 16.5 km offshore, slabs of marble belonging to the temple of Apollo that stood on the ancient island of Chryse.

Philoctetes, a son of Poeas and Demonassa, was the most celebrated archer in the Trojan War. He led the warriors from Methone, Thaumacia, Meliboea, and Olizon against Troy in seven ships. But on the voyage his men left him behind on the island of Lemnos because of the stench from a wound he had received from the bite of a snake on the neighboring island of Chryse. This misfortune happened to him as he was showing to the Greeks the altar of Athena Chryses and approached too near the serpent that was guarding the temple of the goddess (Soph. *Phil.* 1327). Other traditions say he was bitten while he was looking at the tomb of Troilus in the temple of Apollo Thrymbraeus, or as he was showing to his companions the altar of Heracles, or during a sacrifice offered by Palamedes to Apollo Smintheus.

CHRYSE was an early name of the island of THASOS.

CICHYRUS was a later name of the town of EPHYRA in Epeirus.

CIERIUM (PIRGOS) was a town in Thessaly that some identified with Arne, the chief town of the Aeolian Boeotians in Thessaly, from which they migrated to Boeotia. The site of Cierium was first discovered when inscriptions and coins found on the spot proved that it stood adjacent to Pirgos near the modern village of Mataranga between the Enipeus River and one of its tributaries. The identification of Cierium and Arne is strongly suggested by an inscription that mentions Poseidon Cuerius, a name most probably connected with the river Cuarius or Coralius in Boeotia (Strab. 9.2.29). The expelled Boeotians gave this name to the river and built beside it a temple of Athena Itonia in memory of their former home in Thessaly. It seems evident that the river upon which Cierium stood was called Cuerius, Cuarius or Curalius, since Strabo (9.5.17) mentions a river Curalius in Thessaly that flowed past the temple of Athena Itonia into the Peneius. Pausanias (1.13.2) also appears to speak of this temple of Athena Itonia since he describes it as situated between Pherae and Larissa, which is sufficient to indicate the site of Cierium. (See also Thessalian ARNE.)

CIRRHA was the harbor of Delphi after having been earlier the harbor of Crissa. It was named for Cirrha, a nymph (Paus. 10.37.5). Crisus or Crissus was a son of Phocus and husband of Antiphateia, by whom he became the father of Strophius. He is called the founder of Crissa and Cirrha (Paus. 2.19.4).

The town was built at the head of the Crissaean Gulf and rose to the status of a town from being the port of Crissa. Crissa was built upon a hill at some distance from the sea for purposes of security from attack, especially by sea. Eventually, the town grew to power, and a second place sprang up on the coast and became in turn the port of the inland town. Cirrha was situated at the mouth of the river Pleistus (Paus. 10.8.8) and at the foot of Mount Cirphis (Strab. 9.3.3). Ruins of the most ancient Cirrha have not been found but are thought to be between Itea and the modern town of Kirra at a short distance from the Pleistus.

Two plains lay between Crissa and Cirrha. The Cirrhaean plain was the small one, near the town of Cirrha and extending from the sea as far as the modern village of Kirra. The more fertile Crissaean plain stretches as far as modern Hriso and Amfissa. After the destruction of Cirrha, the small Cirrhaean plain on the coast was dedicated to Apollo.

In course of time the seacoast town of Cirrha increased at the expense of Crissa. Also, the sanctuary of Pytho grew into the town of Delphi, which eventually claimed to be independent of Crissa. Thus Crissa declined as Cirrha and Delphi rose in importance. The power of Cirrha aroused the jealousy of the Delphians, particularly since the inhabitants of Cirrha commanded the approach to the temple by sea. In addition, the Cirrhaeans exacted exorbitant tolls from the pilgrims who landed at the town on their way to Delphi. The inhabitants of Cirrha also were said to have mistreated the suppliants on their return from the temple (Strab. 9.3.3); Athen. 13.560). In consequence of these outrages, the Amphictyons declared war against the Cirrhaeans about 595 B.C.; at the end of ten years they succeeded in taking the city, which was razed to the ground. The spoils of Cirrha were employed by the Amphictyons in founding the Pythian games.

Cirrha later was rebuilt as the port of Delphi. In the time of Pausanias it contained a temple common to Apollo, Artemis, and Leto, in which were statues of Attic work. What are believed to be ruins of this temple may be seen today on a mound north of the town of Kirra.

CISSUS was the name of a mountain in Macedonia. There was a town of the same name not far from the Rhaecelus, which appears to have been the name of the promontory where Aeneas founded his city, Aeneia (Lycoph. 1236). Cissus, along with Aeneia and Chalastra helped to provide population for Thessalonica (Dionys. 1.49).

CITHAERON (KITHERO) is a range of mountains separating Boeotia from Megaris and Attica. It and its two branches, the Oenean Mountains and the Parnes, completely protect the peninsula of Attica from the rest of Greece. Its pine woods are still celebrated for game. The principal pass opens from the south onto the great Boeotian plain. Cithaeron is said to have derived its name from Cithaeron, a mythical king of Plataea. One of the times Hera was angry with Zeus, the god sought the counsel of Cithaeron. Cithaeron advised him to dress a wooden statue so that it resembled Plataea, the daughter of Asopus, and to take it with him in his chariot. Zeus followed this advice, and when he rode along with his pretended mistress, Hera, in a jealous frenzy, ran up to the chariot and tore the clothing from the figure. Upon discovering that it was a statue, she became reconciled to Zeus (Paus. 9.1.2,3.1.2). As a result, the summit was sacred to the Cithaeronian Zeus, and here was celebrated the festival called Daedala, commemorating the event of the mistaken identity.

Cithaeron was also sacred to Dionysus, the god of wine. Dionysus wandered far and wide from his native Thebes but returned later to the area and caused the women to leave their homes and to celebrate Bacchic festivals on Mount Cithaeron. When Semele, the sister of Agave, was destroyed by the sight of Zeus in his splendor and prematurely delivered Dionysus, Agave and her sisters spread the rumor that Semele had only pretended that Zeus was the father of her child in order to conceal her guilt and that her destruction was just punishment for her falsehood. For this slander Agave was severely punished. During one of the Dionysiac festivals on Mount Cithaeron, Pentheus, the king of Thebes and the son of Agave, wished to halt these riotous proceedings and went himself to Mount Cithaeron, where he climbed a tree to witness the secret revelry of the Bacchic women. He was discovered and torn to pieces by his mother, who in her frenzy believed him to be a wild beast (Apollod. 3.5.2; Ov. *Met.* 3.725).

Cithaeron was the scene of several other well-known legends. One had to do with the metamorphosis of Actaeon. He was a son of Aristaeus and Autonoe, a daughter of Cadmus. He was trained in the art of hunting by Cheiron, the Centaur, and was afterward torn to pieces by his own fifty hounds on Mount Cithaeron. The usual account is that he had seen Artemis while she was bathing, so that the angry goddess changed him into a stag, in which form he was torn to pieces by the dogs (Ov. *Met.* 3.155; Callim. *Lav. Pall.* 110).

Another legend concerned Amphion and Zethus and their mother Antiope. According to some, Antiope was the wife of Lycus and was seduced by Epopeus, king of Sicyon. She was thrown out by her husband, after which time she was visited by Zeus. Dirce, the second wife of Lycus, was jealous of Antiope and had her put in chains, but Zeus helped her escape to Mount Cithaeron, where she gave birth to twin sons, Amphion and Zethus. Her sons grew up among the shepherds and did not know their descent. When the truth was discovered, Dirce was killed by Amphion and Zethus. Her body was changed by Dionysus, in whose service she had been engaged, into a spring on Mount Cithaeron.

Oedipus was exposed on Mount Cithaeron. Laius, his father, was foretold by an oracle that his newborn son would be his death, so Laius had the infant's feet pierced and bound together, and the child was left to die on Mount Cithaeron. There he was found by a shepherd of King Polybus of Corinth.

The tragedy of Niobe was said by some to have taken place, in part, on this mountain. She and her husband Amphion had twelve children. Being proud of the number, she boasted that she was superior to Leto, who had given birth to only two children. Apollo and Artemis, indignant at her presumption and the insult to their mother, slew all but two of her children. According to Apollodorus (3.5.6), the sons were killed by Apollo during the chase on Mount Cithaeron.

The forest that covered Cithaeron abounded in game; and at a very early period, lions and wolves were said to have been found there. The Cithaeronian lion, slain by Alcathous, was celebrated in mythology (Paus. 1.41.3). Alcathous was a son of Pelops and Hippodameia,

brother of Atreus and Thyestes. Pausanias (1.41.4) relates that after Euippus, the son of King Megareus, was destroyed by the Cithaeronian lion, Megareus offered his daughter Euaechme and his kingdom to anyone who should kill the lion. Alcathous undertook the task, conquered the lion, and thus obtained Euaechme for his wife and afterward became the successor of Megareus. In gratitude for this success he built at Megara a temple of Artemis Agrotera and Apollo Agraeus. Another Cithaeronian lion was the prey of Heracles. His first great adventure while he was still watching the oxen of his father was his fight against and victory over the Cithaeronian lion. The animal caused great havoc among the flocks of Amphitryon and Thespius, king of Thespiae, and Heracles promised to deliver the country from the monster. Thespius, who had fifty daughters, rewarded Heracles by making him his guest so long as the chase lasted and gave up his daughters to him, each for one night (Apollod. 2.4.10). Heracles slew the lion and afterward wore its skin as his ordinary garment and its mouth and head as his helmet; others related that the lion's skin of Heracles was taken from the Nemean lion.

Teiresias, the famous blind soothsayer of antiquity, was, according to one account, made blind by coming upon two serpents coupling on Mount Cithaeron. With his staff he struck at them and killed the female. Instantly he became a female and lived for seven years in that state. At the end of that time, he came upon the serpents and this time killed the male, whereupon he again became a male. So, when Zeus and Hera argued about whether men or women get the greatest pleasure from sexual intercourse, they called on Teiresias, who was, after all, an authority. He ruled that women get more satisfaction, so Hera, having lost the argument, struck him blind. Zeus compensated by giving him the power of prophecy and a long life.

Finally, a class of prophetic nymphs on Mount Cithaeron was given the surname Sphragitides. They had a grotto here called Sphragidion (Plut. *Arist.* 9, *Quaest. Conviv.* 1.10).

CLADEUS (KLADEOS)   was a river flowing west of the valley of Olympia. It flows north to south along the west side of the Sacred Grove and falls into the Alpheius River. This river rises at Lalas in Mount Foloi. The Sacred Grove, or Altis, was adorned with trees. This space of the Altis was measured out by Heracles and was surrounded by this hero with a wall (Pind. *Ol.* 11.44).

Oenomaus, a son of Ares and Harpinna, was married to the Pleiad Sterope, by whom he became the father of Hippodameia. He was king of Pisa in Elis. He refused to surrender his daughter to a suitor unless he could defeat him in a chariot race. Oenomaus invariably won and thereupon killed the suitor. Pelops won by deceit, and Oenomaus was thrown into the river Cladeus (Paus. 6.21.3).

CLEITOR (KATO KLITORIA) was a town in Arcadia, the name of which was derived by some from its being situated in an enclosed plain. It occupied a small territory called Cleitoria, bounded on the east by the territory of Pheneus, on the west by that of Psophis, on the north by that of Cynaetha and Achaia, and on the south by the territories of Caphyae, Tripolis, and Thelpusa. The river Cleitor ran south of the town.

Cleitor is said to have been founded by a hero of the same name, the son of the Arcadian king Azan (Paus. 8.4.5,21.3). The territory of Cleitoria formed an important part of the Azanian district. The Cleitorian fountain was regarded as one of the curiosities of Azania; and the Aroanian Mountains, on the summit of which the daughters of Proetus wandered in their madness, are called the Azanian Mountains. Proetus was a son of Abas and twin brother of Acrisius. By Anteia or Stheneboea he became the father of Lysippe, Iphinoe and Iphianassa. When these daughters arrived at the age of maturity, they were striken with madness for one or another reason, and in this state they wandered through Peloponnesus. Melampus promised to cure them if Proetus would give him one-third of his kingdom. Proetus would not accept the terms, and the madness spread to other Argive women. Eventually Proetus capitulated, and Melampus and Bias cured the women and married two of his daughters. The place where this cure was effected was, according to some, the spring of Cleitor (Ov. *Met.* 15.325). It was later claimed that whoever drank from this fountain forever lost his taste for wine. A spring of water gushing forth from the hill on which the ruins stand is usually supposed to be this miraculous fountain.

The Cleitorians were renowned among the Peloponnesians for their love of liberty. An instance of this occurred even from mythical times in the brave resistance they offered to Sous, king of Sparta (Plut. *Lyc.* 2, *Apophth.* 234). Their power was increased by the conquest of Lusi, Paus, and other towns in their region. In commemoration of these conquests they dedicated at Olympia a bronze statue of Zeus (Paus. 5.23.7).

Pausanias (8.21.4) gives only a brief description of Cleitor. He says that its three principal temples were those of Demeter, Asclepius, and Eileithyia; that about three-quarters of a kilometer from the city the Cleitorians possessed a temple of the Dioscuri; and that on the summit of a mountain, 5.5 km from the city, there was a temple of Athena Coria. The ruins of Cleitor are about 5 km from Kato Klitoria, a village that still bears the name of the ancient town.

Besides the famous fountain of Cleitor there was another marvel in the territory of Cleitor. This was the singing fish of the river Aroanius. These fish, which were called *poikiliae* (many-colored), were said to sing like thrushes.

CLEONAE (ARHEES KLEONES) was a city of Peloponnesus described by Roman writers as part of Argolis. Cleonae was situated on the road from Argos to Corinth, at a distance of 22 km from Argos and 18 from Corinth. There was a narrow pass through the mountains from Argos called Tretus. Cleonae stood in a small plain upon the Langeia River flowing into the Corinthian Gulf a little west of Lechaeum. In its territory was Mount Apesas, now called Foukas, connected with the Acrocorinthus by a rugged range of hills.

Cleonae possessed only a small territory. It derived its chief importance from the Nemean games that were celebrated in its territory in the grove of Nemea between Cleonae and Phlius. Heracles is said to have slain Eurytus and Cteatus, the sons of Actor, near Cleonae. These brothers were often called Moliones from their mother, Molione. They were nephews of Augeas, king of the Epeians. When Heracles marched against Augeas to punish him for refusing to give the reward he had promised, Augeas entrusted the conduct of the war to the Moliones; but Heracles, who in the meantime was taken ill and concluded peace with Augeas, was then himself attacked and beaten by them. In order to take vengeance, he afterward slew them near Cleonae on the frontiers of Argolis, as they had been sent from Elis to sacrifice on behalf of the town at the Isthmian games (Apollod. 2.7.2; Pind. *Ol.* 11.33; Paus. 8.14.9). The Eleians demanded that the Argives atone for this murder; but as the latter refused, and were not excluded from the Isthmian games, Molione, the mother of the brothers, cursed all Eleians who should ever again take part in those games (Paus. 5.2.2). Heracles, on the other hand, dedicated six altars at Olympia in honor of his victory and was instituted special honors at Nemea for the 360 Cleonaeans who had died while assisting him. The tomb of Eurytus and Cteatus was shown in later times at Cleonae (Paus. 2.15.1). Diodorus Siculus (4.33) mentions a temple of Heracles erected in the neighborhood in memory of that event.

On his way to kill the Nemean lion Heracles came to Cleone, where he was hospitably received by a poor man called Molorchus. This man was about to offer a sacrifice, but Heracles persuaded him to wait for thirty days until he should return from his fight with the lion. In that way, he said, they might together offer sacrifices to Zeus Soter; he added, however, that if he himself should not return, the man should offer a sacrifice to him as a hero. The thirty days passed, and as Heracles did not return, Molorchus prepared to sacrifice to the hero. But at that moment Heracles arrived in triumph over the monster, and both sacrificed to Zeus Soter.

Cleone is said to have derived its name either from Cleones, the son of Pelops, or from Cleone, the daughter of the river-god Asopus (Paus. 2.15.1). It was conquered by Dorians, whereupon some of its inhabitants, together with those of the neighboring town of Phlius, are said to have founded Clazomenae in Asia Minor (Paus. 7.3.9). In the Dorian conquest Cleonae formed part of the lot of Temenus and in early times was one of the confederated allies or subordinates of Argos.

The existing ruins are scanty. In 1912 a Doric temple, perhaps of Heracles, was excavated. There are also traces of a temple of Athena.

CLEPSYDRA was a fountain in Messenia. Ithome and Neda were Messenian nymphs. According to Messenian tradition, they nursed Zeus and bathed the infant in the Clepsydra fountain (Paus. 4.33.1) after he was stolen by the Curetes to prevent his being devoured by his father. On the ascent to the summit of Ithome, which is the Messenian acropolis, is a spring called Clepsydra. It is said to have been named this because of the theft of the infant Zeus by the Curetes. Water was carried every day from the spring to the sanctuary of Zeus of Ithome. The statue there of Zeus was the work of Ageladas, the master of Pheidias, and was made originally for the Messenian settlers in Naupactus. The priest was chosen annually and kept the image in his house. There was an annual festival, the Ithomaea, and originally a musical contest was held.

CNESIUS was the name of a mountain in Arcadia. Ares Aphneius (Giver of Food or Plenty) had a temple on this mountain near Tegea. Aerope, the daughter of Cepheus, became by Ares the mother of a son, Aeropus, but she died at the moment she gave birth to the child. Ares, wishing to save the child, caused him to derive food from the breast of his dead mother. This wonder gave rise to the surname Aphneius (Paus. 8.44.8).

CNOSSUS or GNOSSIS (KNOSSOS) was the royal city of Crete, situated to the north of the island about 5 km south of the modern port of Iraklio. It originally was called Caeratus from the small river of that name that flowed beneath its walls (Strab 10.4.8). Tritta was a name that had been sometimes applied to it. It was said to have been originally inhabited by Titans, who were hostile to Zeus but were driven away by Pan with the fearful sounds of his shell trumpet (*Hymn. Hom. ad Apoll.* 336; Diod. 3.57, 5.66).

The foundation of Cnossus was attributed to Minos, who made it his chief residence (Hom. *Od.* 19.178). The city and its neighborhood was peculiarly connected with Zeus. At the nearby river Theren, according to tradition, the marriage of Zeus and Hera was celebrated (Diod. 5.72). The most common traditions assigned the birthplace of Zeus to this locality. Crete is called the island or nurse of Zeus, and his worship there appears to have been very ancient. Among the places in the island that were particularly sacred to the god, we must mention the district about Mount Ida, especially Cnossus, which was said to have been built by the Curetes, and where Minos had ruled and conversed with Zeus (Hom. *Od.* 19.172; Diod. 5.70). Crete was also undoubtedly the earliest seat of worship of Rhea, the mother of Zeus. Diodorus Siculus (5.66) saw the site where her temple had once stood in the vicinity of Cnossus.

The well-known Cretan labyrinth was located at Cnossus. It was described as a building erected by Daedalus and the abode of the Minotaur. Daedalus, being condemned to death by the Areiopagus for the murder of his nephew, went to Crete, where the fame of his skill obtained for him the friendship of Minos. He made the well-known wooden cow for Pasiphae; and when Pasiphae gave birth to the Minotaur, Daedalus constructed the labyrinth at Cnossus, in which the monster was kept (Ov. *Met.* 8). The Minotaur was a monster with a human body and a bull's head. He was shut up in the labyrinth and fed with the bodies of the youths and maidens whom the Athenians at fixed times were obliged to send to Minos as tribute. The monster was slain by Theseus.

For his part in this affair, Daedalus was also confined in the labyrinth; but Pasiphae released him. Since Minos had seized all the ships on the coast of Crete, Daedalus fashioned wings for himself and his son Icarus and fastened them on with wax. Daedalus himself flew safely over the Aegean, but, as Icarus flew too near the sun, the wax melted, and he fell and was drowned in that part of the Aegean called after him the Icarian Sea. According to a more prosaic version of the story, Pasiphae furnished Daedalus with a ship in which he fled to an island of the Aegean, where Icarus was drowned in a hasty attempt to land.

The rule of Cnossus passed eventually to Idomeneus, who was the son of Deucalion and grandson of Minos and Pasiphae. He is sometimes called Lyctius or Cnosius from the Cretan towns of Lyctus and Cnossus. In conjunction with Meriones, the son of his half-brother Molus, he led the Cretans in eighty ships against Troy and was one of the bravest heroes in the Trojan War. His tomb was shown at Cnossus where he and Meriones were worshipped as heroes (Diod. 5.79).

Apart from Zeus and Rhea, other deities worshipped at Cnossus were Aphrodite Antheia (Blooming or Friend of Flowers), Apollo Delphinius, and Eileithyia, the goddess of birth. Apollo received his surname from his having shown the Cretan colonists the way to Delphi while riding on a dolphin or metamorphosing himself into a dolphin. Under this name Apollo had a temple at Cnossus. The worship of Eileithyia appears to have first established among the Dorians in Crete, where she was believed to have been born in a cave in the territory of Cnossus. From there her worship spread over Delos and Attica.

The excavations of Sir Arthur Evans in 1900 gave a new perspective to the old legends because the vast palace at Knossos with its multitude of chambers, corridors, stairways, and storage areas did indeed resemble a labyrinth. The fresco and carvings of bull leapers gave credibility to the study of the contests with the Minotaur. The restored palace is today one of the most impressive sites in Crete. Near the palace is the Villa Dionysus, a Roman building with mosaics depicting a Dionysiac cult.

COCCYGIUM   was a later name of Mount THORNAX in Argolis.

COELE   lay southwest of the Pnyx and was one of the demes that made up the area of greater ATHENS.

COLIAS   Promontory (See ATHENS)

COLLYTUS   was one of the demes that made up the area of greater ATHENS.

COLONIDES   was a town in the southwest of Messenia, described by Pausanias as standing upon a height at a short distance from the sea and 7.5 km from Asine. The inhabitants affirmed that they were not Messenians but a colony from Athens founded by Colaenus. Colaenus was a mythical king of Attica who was believed to have resigned even before the time of Cecrops (Paus. 1.31.5). The site is uncertain. It has been placed upon the Messenian Gulf north of Koroni, where are some remains of ancient buildings, but some suppose it to have stood on the bay of Finiki, northwest of the promontory Akritas.

COLONUS   celebrated as the deme of Sophocles and the scene of one of the poet's tragedies, was situated about 2 km from the gate of the city of Athens called Dipylum, near the Academy and the Cephissus River (Thuc. 8.67; Cic. *De Fin.* 5.1). It derived its name from two small but conspicuous heights, which rise from the plain a little to the north of the Academy. It was under the special care of Poseidon and is called by Thucydides (8.67) the shrine of this god. It is frequently called Colonus Hippius to distinguish it from the Colonus Agoraeus in Athens. In additon to the temple of Poseidon it had a sacred enclosure of the Eumenides, altars of Athena Hippia, Demeter, Zeus, and Prometheus, together with sanctuaries of Peirithous, Theseus, Oedipus, and Adrastus (Paus. 1.30.4).

CONDYLEA   (See CAPHYAE)

COPAE (KASTRO)   a town of Boeotia, was situated upon the northern shore of Lake Copais, which derived its name from this town. It is mentioned by Homer (*Il.* 2.502); but it was a small place, and its name rarely occurs in Grecian history. One of the eleven Boeotian districts, it was still in existence in the time of Pausanias (9.24.1) who mentions here the temples of Demeter, Dionysus, and Serapis. The modern village of Kastro (formerly Topolia) occupies the site of Copae. It once stood upon a promontory in the lake that was connected with the mainland by only a narrow causeway. Today it stands on dry ground near the intersection of the highway from Orhomenos with the National Road. No excavations have been conducted.

COPAIS   (See BOEOTIA)

CORCYRA or CORFU (KERKIRA)   is an island in the Ionian Sea, opposite the coast of Epeirus. It is known by most modern travellers by the name of Korfu, which is an Italian corruption of the Byzantine name Korypho, one of the peaks on which the citadel of the chief town was built. The channel by which the island is separated from the mainland is narrowest at the north entrance, being only about 3 km in width; it then expands into an open gulf between the two coasts, being in some places 23 km across. The length of the island from north to south is about 63 km; its width varies from 5 to 33 km.

Four promontories are mentioned by ancient writers: Cassiope, the northeast point; Phalacrum, the northwest point; Leucimme or Leucimna, a low sandy point on the east coast; and Amphipagus, the southern extremity. The island is generally mountainous. It was celebrated for its fertility in antiquity. This attribute is no less true today: it has citrus crops, tomatoes, figs, and four million olive trees.

The most ancient name of the island is said to have been Drepane, apparently from its resemblance in shape to a scythe (Apollon. Rhod. 4.983). It is further said that its next name was Scheria, which Homer describes as a fertile and lovely island, inhabited by the Phaeacians, an enterprising, seafaring people, who had originally colonized the island under the leadership of Nausithous. He was a son of Poseidon and Periboea and had led the Phaeacians from Hypereia in Thrinacia to Scheria in order to escape from the Cyclopes (Hom. *Od.* 7.56).

Alcinous was a son of Nausithous and grandson of Poseidon. His name is celebrated in the story of the Argonauts and still more in that of Odysseus. In the former, Alcinous is represented as living with his queen Arete on the island of Drepane. The Argonauts, returning from Colchis, came to the island and were hospitably received. When the Colchians, in their pursuit of the Argonauts likewise arrived in Drepane and demanded that Medea be delivered to them, Alcinous declared that if she was still a virgin she should be restored to them, but that if she was already the wife of Jason he would protect her and her husband against the Colchians. The Colchians were obliged, by the contrivance of Arete, to depart without their princess, and the Argonauts continued their voyage homewards after they had received costly gifts from Alcinous (Apollon. Rhod. 4.990–1225; Apollod. 1.9.25,26). According to one tradition, Absyrtus was not taken by Medea and dismembered but was sent by his father in pursuit of her. He overtook her in Corcyra, where she had fled and had been kindly received by King Alcinous, who refused to surrender her to Absyrtus. When he overtook her a second time on the island of Minerva, he was slain by Jason.

According to Homer (*Od.* 6.12), Alcinous was the happy ruler of the Phaeacians in the island of Scheria and had by Arete five sons and one daughter, Nausicaa. The description of his palace and his dominions, the manner in which Odysseus was received, the entertainments given to him, and the stories he related to the king about his own wanderings, occupy a considerable portion of the Odyssey and form one of its most charming parts. The leading character in the rendering of these stories was Demodocus, the famous bard of the Odyssey, who according to the fashion of the heroic age delighted the guests of King Alcinous during their repast by singing about the feats of the Greeks at Troy. Later writers said that Nausicaa eventually became the wife of Telemachus, Odysseus' son, and mother by him of Perseptolis and Ptoliporthus.

In Corcyra, the capital of the island, we find mention of temples of Zeus, Hera, Dionysus, the Dioscuri, and Alcinous (Thuc. 3.70,75,81). At the beginning of the eighth century B.C. there was established a large sanctuary probably dedicated to a tutelary divinity of Corcyra and mainland areas. As time went on, small temples were established by cults that grew up around the sanctuary. Among these were temples to Apollo, Hermes, and Aphrodite. Another Apollo temple was discovered in 1822 near the Kardaki spring in the capital city. But the most impressive monument of Kerkira is the sanctuary of Artemis discovered near the area of Garitza in the capital. Several slabs of the pediment of the temple can be seen in the museum of Kerkira. A gigantic Gorgon, flanked with her offspring Chrysaor and Pegasus, is central, and on the sides are groups, including Priam being killed by Neoptolemus and Zeus battling a giant. A fragmented metope shows Achilles and Memnon. At Kanoni, the discovery of a figure of Artemis leads to speculation that another sanctuary was dedicated here to the goddess. Near the cloister of Panagia Kassiopitra there are traces of a temple of the sixth century possibly dedicated to Poseidon. On the northeast end of the island was the city of Cassiope (Kassiopi). It was celebrated for its temple of Zeus Cassius, or Casius, at whose altar Nero sang. The head of

the god with the epigraph Zeus Casius frequently occurs on coins.

CORESSA or CORESSIA   (See CEOS)

CORFU   (See CORCYRA)

CORINTH (KORINTHOS)   was one of the most important cities of ancient Greece. It stood upon the Isthmus, which connected the northern division of Greece with Peloponnesus. On either side of the Isthmus, which is a rocky and sterile plain, rise the mountains of northern Greece and Peloponnesus respectively. The mountains to the north, which bear the name of Gerania, extend across the Isthmus from sea to sea. There are only three passes through them, the most celebrated of which is the shortest road between Corinth and Megara. It is upon the shore of the Saronic Gulf and still bears the name of the Skironides Petrai, or Scironian Rocks. The mountains to the south were called the Oneian Ridge, from their resemblance to an ass's back. The lofty rock, the Acrocorinthus, which formed the citadel of Corinth, is part of the Oneian Ridge but is separated from it by a ravine. Seen from the north the ridge appears to be an isolated mountain, but it extends eastward as far as the Saronic Gulf. The Acrocorinthus does not reach the sea to the west, but there is a narrow, level space between the foot of the mountain and the sea. This level space was protected by the two long walls connecting the city with its port town of Lechaeum. East of the city there were two passes, one through the ravine, which separated the Acrocorinthus and the Oneian Mountains, and the other along the shore at Cenchrae (Xenoph. *Hell.* 6.5.51). Thus Corinth completely commanded the three passes, which alone led from the Isthmus to Peloponnesus.

The Phoenicians, the great sailors and traders of the ancient world, had first noted Corinth's favorable position for commerce, and there was a Phoenician colony there at an early period. These colonists occupied the Acrocorinthus, and the city thereafter had special characteristics that identified it with them. The worship of Aphrodite there had a certain oriental character, and a Phoenician goddess identified with Athena was also worshipped. The mark of the colonists was also left in the name of the Corinthian mountain called Phoenicaeum.

Thucydides (4.42) mentions Aeolians as the inhabitants of Corinth at the time of the Dorian invasion, but Ionians also formed a considerable part of the population in the earliest times since Ionians were in possession of the coasts on either side of the Isthmus, and on the Isthmus itself was the most revered seat of Poseidon, the chief deity of the Ionic race. Still, the earliest rulers of Corinth are always represented as Aeolians.

The most ancient name of the city was Ephyra, derived from Ephyra, a daughter of Oceanus. It is not known when the name was changed to Corinth. Homer (*Il.* 2.570, 6.152,210, 13.664) uses both names interchangeably. According to the Corinthians themselves Corinthus, from whom the city derived its name, was a son of Zeus. According to another legend, the gods Poseidon and Helios contended for the possession of the Corinthian land. Briareus, one of the Uranids, or huge, hundred-armed monsters, was chosen as arbitrator in the dispute. Under his decision Poseidon obtained the Isthmus and Helios both the rock, afterward called Acrocorinthus, and Ephyra.

Helios had two sons, Aeetes and Aloeus. He gave Ephyra to Aeetes and Asopia (Sicyon) to Aloeus. Aeetes, deciding to go to Colchis, left his country under the rule of Bunus, a son of Hermes. Upon the death of Aloeus and Bunus, Epopeus, the son of Aloeus, obtained Ephyra as well as Asopia. Marathon, the son of Epopeus, who had left the country during his lifetime, returned at his death and divided his territory between his sons Corinthus and Sicyon, from whom the two towns obtained their names. When Corinthus died without heirs, the Corinthians invited Medea from Iolcus, as the daughter of Aeetes to take over the government, and thus her husband Jason obtained the sovereignty of Corinth.

According to the common account, after Jason the Argonaut and Medea went from Iolcus to Corinth, they lived happily there for a period of ten years until Creon, king of Corinth, betrothed his daughter Glauce to Jason, and thus led him to desert Medea. Medea invoked the gods by whom Jason had sworn to be faithful to her, and sent Glauce a poisoned garment and diadem. When Glauce put on the garment, she, together with her father, was consumed by the poisonous fire that issued from the vestment. Creon's reign at Corinth poses a mystery. There is no provision for his reign in the royal line. He might have been an interim ruler after the death of Corinthus until the arrival from Iolcus of Jason and Medea. His father's name was Lycaethus, but nothing else is known of him. In any case, Medea followed this violent act by an even more violent one. She killed her own children by Jason, Mermerus and Pheres, and then fled to Athens in a chariot drawn by winged dragons, the gift of Helios. Pheres apparently was old enough to have fathered a son for, according to Homer (*Od.* 1.260), Mermerus, the son of Pheres and grandson of Jason, was the father of Ilus and Ephyra and skilled in the art of preparing poison. Medea's younger children she placed, previous to her flight, as suppliants on the altar of Hera Acraea, but the Corinthians took them away and put them to death (Apollod. 1.9.16; Ov. *Met.* 7). According to Diodorus Siculus (4.54), Medea set a fire in the royal palace at Corinth in which Creon and Glauce were burnt, but Jason escaped. Further, she had three sons, Thessalus, Alcimenes, and Thersander, the two last of whom were

killed. They were buried by Jason in the sanctuary of Hera at Corinth (Diod. 4.54,55). Thessalus, who escaped, was educated at Corinth and afterward succeeded Acastus on the throne of Iolcus. The earliest accounts we have do not mention Medea's murder of her children, but represent her as a priestess of Corinth, where she was killed by the Corinthians (Aelianus *V.H.* 5). Pausanias (2.3.11) relates that after the death of Corinthus, Medea was invited from Iolcus and ruled over Corinth, her lawful paternal inheritance, in conjunction with Jason. Medea concealed her children in the temple of Hera, hoping thereby to make them immortal; but Jason, indignant at this conduct, deserted her and returned to Iolcus. Medea afterward returned to Iolcus, leaving the throne to Sisyphus, with whom she is said to have been in love.

Sisyphus was a son of Aeolus and Enarete, brother of Cretheus, Athamas, Salmoneus, Deion, Magnes, Perieres, Canace, Alcyone, Peisidice, Calyce, and Perimede. He was married to Merope, a Pleiad, and became by her the father of Glaucus, Ornytion, Thersandrus, and Halmus. Merope was a daughter of Atlas. After her death she and her sisters were placed in the heavens as the constellation Pleiades. She is the seventh and least visible star, because she is ashamed of having been married to a mortal man (Apollod. 1.9.3,3.10.1; Ov. *Fast.* 4.175). Sisyphus, according to one writer, was also the father of Odysseus. He claims that previous to her marriage to Laertes, Anticleia lived on intimate terms with Sisyphus (Eurip. *Iphig. Aul.* 524). Sisyphus is said to have built the town of Ephyra, afterward known as Corinth (Hom. *Il.* 6.153; Apollod. 1.9.3), though, according to another tradition, Medea, on leaving Corinth, gave him the government of that city. As king of Corinth he promoted navigation and commerce, but was fraudulent, avaricious, and altogether of bad character; his whole house was in as bad repute as he himself (Hom. *Il.* 6.153). He is said to have found the body of Melicertes on the coast of Corinth, to have buried it on the Isthmus, and to have founded the Isthmian games in honor of him. Melicertes, it will be remembered, was a son of Ino and Athamas and therefore a nephew of Sisyphus. Ino, driven mad by Hera, leapt into the sea with Melicertes in her arms. Melicertes' body washed ashore and was found, but meanwhile the boy had become a sea deity under the name of Palaemon.

The wickedness of Sisyphus during his lifetime was severely punished in the lower world where he had to roll uphill a huge marble block, which as soon as it reached the top always rolled down again (Ov. *Met.* 4.459). The special reasons for this punishment are given variously. Some say that it was because he had betrayed the designs of the gods. Others say that he attacked travellers and killed them with a huge block of stone. He was slain, according to some, by Theseus. Other traditions relate that Sisyphus lived in enmity with his brother Salmoneus and consulted the oracle about how he might get rid of him. Apollo answered that if he begot sons by Tyro, the wife of his brother, they would avenge him. Sisyphus indeed became the father of two sons by Tyro, but she killed them immediately after their birth, and Sisyphus took cruel revenge on her. Another tradition states that when Zeus had carried off Aegina, the daughter of Asopus, from Phlius, Sisyphus betrayed the matter to Asopus and was rewarded by him with a well on Acrocorinthus (Apollod. 1.9.3, 3.12.6; Paus. 2.5.1). Others, again, say that Zeus, to avenge his treachery, sent Death to Sisyphus, who, however, succeeded in putting Death in chains, so that no man died until Ares delivered Death, whereupon Sisyphus himself also expired. Before he died he desired his wife not to bury him. She complied with his request. Then Sisyphus in the lower world complained of being neglected and asked Pluto, or Persephone, to allow him to return to the upper world to punish his wife. When this request was granted, he refused to return to the lower world until Hermes carried him off by force; this piece of treachery is said to be the cause of his punishment. His punishment was represented by Polygnotus in the Lesche at Delphi (Paus. 10.31.2). He was believed to have been buried on the Isthmus, but very few even among his contemporaries knew the exact place (Paus. 2.2.2).

Under the sway of Sisyphus and his descendants Corinth became one of the richest and most powerful cities in Greece. As mentioned, Sisyphus had two sons, Glaucus and Ornytion. From Glaucus sprang the celebrated hero Bellerophon, who was worshipped with heroic honors at Corinth, and whose exploits were a favorite subject among the Corinthians down to the latest times. Therefore we constantly find upon the coins of Corinth and her colonies the figure of the winged horse Pegasus, which Bellerophon caught at the fountain of Peirene on the Acrocorinthus. Bellerophon's proper name was Hipponous, and he is said to have received the name Bellerophon from having slain the noble Corinthian, Bellerus. Others related that he had unintentionally slain his own brother, Deliades, Peiren, or Alcimenes (Apollod. 2.3.1). In order to be purified from one or the other of these murders he fled to Proetus at Argos, where Anteia, the wife of Proetus, fell in love with him. Even though he did not reciprocate, he was forced to leave the kingdom. Proetus sent him to Iobates in Lycia with a letter requesting that he be put to death. Iobates accordingly sent him to kill the monster Chimaera, which he did with the help of the winged steed Pegasus. Pegasus had sprung from the blood from the severed head of Medusa, and no one had ever been able to catch him. Bellerophon tried long and hard to gain possession of Pegasus and finally had to consult the soothsayer Polyidus at Corinth. Polyidus advised him to spend a night in the temple of

Athena, and, as Bellerophon was sleeping, the goddess appeared to him in a dream, commanding him to sacrifice to Poseidon and giving him a golden bridle. When he awoke he found the bridle, offered the sacrifice, and caught Pegasus, who was drinking at the well Peirene (Pind. *Ol.* 13.90). According to some, Athena herself tamed and bridled Pegasus and surrendered him to Bellerophon (Paus. 2.4.1), or Bellerophon, as some believed, received Pegasus from his own father Poseidon. For her role in helping tame Pegasus to the bridle, Athena earned the surname Chalinitis, and under this name she had a temple at Corinth (Paus. 2.4.1).

It is believed that Bellerophon was not an absolute king but was subject to Proetus and the Argives. When Bellerophon migrated to Lycia, it appears that the Corinthians continued to be subjects of the kings of Argos or Mycenae. By themselves they provided no leader for the campaign against Troy, but shared in the expedition as part of the forces, Mycenaean and others, led by Agamemnon.

The descendants of Ornytion, the other son of Sisyphus, continued to rule at Corinth. Ornytion had two sons, Phocus and Thoas. Phocus migrated to the region to which he gave the name Phocis. Upon the death of Ornytion, Thoas became king of Corinth. Thoas was succeeded by his son Damophon, then by Damophon's son Propodas. The sons of Propodas appear to have ruled jointly, and it was during their reign that the Dorians took Corinth, under the leadership of Aletes, the son of Hippotas, the son of Phylas, the son of Antiochus, the son of Heracles.

It is said that the Dorian conquest (and the beginning of the historical era) was not effected till the generation after the return of the Heracleidae into Peloponnesus. When the Heracleidae were on the point of crossing over from Naupactus, Hippotas slew the prophet Carnus, in consequence of which he was banished for ten years and not allowed to take part in the enterprise. His son Aletes, who derived his name from his long wanderings, was afterward the leader of the Dorian conquerors of Corinth and the first Dorian king of the city (Paus. 2.4.3). Doridas and Hyanthidas, the sons of Propodas, gave up the kingship to Aletes and remained at Corinth, but the Corinthian people were conquered and expelled (Paus. 2.4.3). The family of Aletes, sometimes called the Aletidae, maintained themselves at Corinth down to the time of Bacchis (Paus. 2.4.3, 5.18.2; Pind. *Ol.* 13.17).

Aletes himself and his descendants reigned for five generations to Bacchis, the son of Prumnis. The Bacchidae, named for him, reigned for five more generations to Telestes, the son of Aristodemus. Telestes was assassinated, thus ending the rule of kings; but *prytanes,* chosen from the Bacchidae and ruling for one year each, continued the administration of the government until

Cypselus, the son of Eetion, became tyrant and expelled the Bacchidae in 665 B.C.

The patron goddess of the city was Aphrodite, who had a splendid temple on the Acrocorinthus, where there were kept more than one thousand sacred female slaves for the service of strangers. In no other city of Greece do we find this institution of sacred prostitution as a regular part of the worship of Aphrodite. It is rather certain that it was introduced into Corinth by the Phoenicians. Aphrodite was represented in this temple as the victorious goddess in arms. Under the summit was a small fountain of Peirene. Below the Peirene was the Sisypheion, where remains of a white marble palace were shown.

Aphrodite Melaenis (Dark) was also worshipped in Corinth, along with many other gods and goddesses of varying rank. Artemis had a sanctuary here in conjunction with a sacred spring (Paus. 2.3.5). Demeter's worship was carried from here by colonists to Sicily. Persephone had a temple, and the Moirae (Fates) had a sanctuary. Deima, the personification of terror, was represented in the form of a fearful woman on the tomb of Medea's children (Paus. 2.3.6). The worship of Hera was very ancient at Corinth. The Horae, goddesses of the seasons and of order in general, were worshipped here, as were the Muses, to whom the spring of Peirene was sacred. Poseidon, it will be remembered, disputed with Helios the sovereignty of Corinth and gained the lower city and the Isthmus. Heracles was represented by a wooden statue ascribed to Daedalus (Paus. 2.4.5). Hygieia, the goddess of health, had a sanctuary in conjunction with her father Asclepius.

Athena Hellotia was worshipped at Corinth. According to some, her surname was derived from Hellotia, one of the daughters of Timander. When Corinth was burned by the Dorians, Hellotia fled into the temple of Athena with her sister Eurytione where they died. Soon after, a plague broke out in Corinth, and the oracle declared that it would not cease until the souls of the maidens were propitiated and a sanctuary erected to Athena Hellotia. Dionysus Lysius (Deliverer) was also worshipped here, where there was a carved image of the god, the body of which was gilded and the face painted red (Paus. 2.2.5). Finally, in later times the worship of Cotys was introduced at Athens and Corinth. Cotys was a Thracian divinity, whose festival, the Cotyttia, resembled that of the Phrygian Cybele and was celebrated on hills with riotous proceedings and licentious frivolity.

Several other heroes and individuals of lesser importance were connected with the mythological history of Corinth. Actaeon was a son of Melissus and grandson of Abron, who had fled from Argos to Corinth for fear of the tyrant Pheidon. Archias, a Corinthian, enamored with the beauty of Actaeon, endeavored to carry him off; but in the struggle between Melissus and Archias, Actaeon was killed. Melissus brought his complaints forward at the Isthmian games, and, praying to the gods for revenge, he threw himself from a rock. Almost at once Corinth was visited by a plague and drought, and the oracle ordered the Corinthians to propitiate Poseidon and avenge the death of Actaeon. Archias wasted no time and fled to Sicily, where he founded the town of Syracuse (Plut. *Amat. Narr.* 772; Paus. 5.7.2).

Arion, an ancient Greek bard, was, according to some, the son of Poseidon. On one occasion he was sailing from Sicily to Corinth. The sailors coveted the prizes he had won at a musical contest and planned his murder. Apollo revealed the plot in a dream, and Arion, after invoking the gods on his cithara, threw himself overboard. Music-loving dolphins had heard the song and took him to land, and he returned to Corinth. The sailors, arriving later, were arrested and punished.

The Homeric hero Diomedes, after his return from Troy, was, according to some, expelled from Argos, from where he went first to Corinth; but being informed there of the distress of Oeneus, his grandfather, he hastened to Aetolia to assist him. After conquering his enemies, he took up residence there.

Polyidus was a son of Coeranus, a grandson of Abas, and a great-grandson of Melampus. He was, like his ancestor, a celebrated soothsayer at Corinth and is described as the father of Euchenor, Astycrateia, and Manto. After Alcathous had murdered his own son Callipolis at Megara, he was purified by Polyidus.

Tantalus was a son of Zeus and father of Pelops, Broteas, and Niobe. All traditions agree that he was a wealthy king, but there is disagreement about his kingdom. Some state that it was in Asia, others that it was in Argos or Corinth. He is celebrated in ancient story for the severe punishment inflicted on him in the lower world after his death. For one reason or another, he was punished by being placed in the midst of a lake where the waters receded each time he bent to drink. Branches laden with fruit hung over his head but withdrew when he reached for the fruit. Over his head there was suspended a huge rock ever threatening to crush him.

Finally, Polybus, Neleus, and Melas each have connections with Corinth. Polybus, a king of the city, was said to have brought up Oedipus. He was the husband of Periboea or Merope (Apollod. 3.5.7). He, like Creon, does not fit into the royal line of Corinth. Pausanias (2.6.3) makes him king of Sicyon and describes him as a son of Hermes and Chthonophyle. Neleus was an Aeolid, son of Cretheus, brother of Pelias, and father of Nestor. Pausanias (2.2.2) says that Neleus died at Corinth. Melas was a son of Antassus at Gonusa near Sicyon. He joined the Dorians on their march against Corinth. His services were at first declined, but he was afterward allowed to fight in the ranks of the Dorians. He was the ancestor of the family of Cypselus (Paus. 2.4.4, 5.18.7).

Corinth was one of the earliest seats of Grecian art. It possessed some of the finest paintings in Greece, and statuary flourished there, works of bronze being particularly celebrated. The most elaborate order of architecture was named Corinthian. One of the earlier works of Corinthian art, which retained its celebrity in later times, was the famous chest of Cypselus; it was made of cedar and adorned with figures from mythology. It was dedicated at Olympia, where it was seen by Pausanias (5.17.5–19.10), who gives a minute description of it. The Corinthian vases of terra cotta, commonly decorated with animals and monsters, were among the finest in Greece.

The city of Corinth lay at the northern foot of the Acrocorinthus. It did not stand in the plain but upon a broad, level rock, which is nearly seventy-seven meters in height above the plain that separates it from the bay of Lechaeum.

The road leading to the city from Cenchreae was lined with sepulchral monuments; and on either side of the road was a grove of cypress trees adorned with temples of Bellerophon and Aphrodite and other monuments. Upon entering Corinth through the gate that probably bore the name of Cenchreae, one proceeded to the agora where the greatest number of temples stood.

Pausanias (2.2.6,7) mentions a statue of Artemis Ephesia, two wooden statues of Dionysus, a temple of Tyche, a temple sacred to all the gods, a fountain issuing from a dolphin at the foot of a bronze Poseidon, and statues of Apollo Clarius, Aphrodite, Hermes, and Zeus. In the middle of the agora was a bronze Athena, on the base of which were the figures of the Muses in relief.

From the agora four principal streets branched off, one leading to Cenchreae, the second to Lechaeum, the third to Sicyon, and the fourth to the Acrocorinthus.

On leaving the agora along the road to Lechaeum, one passed throgh the Propylaea, on which stood two gilded chariots, one bearing Phaethon and the other Helios. A little beyond, to the right of the road, was the fountain of Peirene. This fountain was adorned with white marble; the water from it flowed into certain artificial caverns into an open receptacle. It was at the fountain of Peirene that Bellerophon is said to have caught Pegasus. As Pegasus was in some legends represented as the horse of the Muses, Peirene was regarded by the Roman poets as a fountain sacred to these goddesses. Peirene, the nymph of the fountain, was the mother of Cenchrias, for whom the port was named. The fountain was supposed to have arisen out of the tears she shed in her grief over the death of her son.

Farther along the road to Lechaeum there was a statue of Apollo, then a statue of Hermes with a ram, and statues also of Poseidon, Leucothea, and Palaemon upon a dolphin. Farther on was the most remarkable of all the fountains in Corinth: Bellerophon mounted on Pegasus, through whose hoof the water flowed (Paus. 2.3.5).

On the road to Sicyon there were in succession the temple of Apollo with a bronze statue of the god; the fountain of Glauce; the tomb of Medea's children; the temple of Athena Chalinitis, so called because she gave Bellerophon the bridle by which he secured Pegasus; the temple of Jupiter Capitolinus; and the ancient gymnasium with nearby temples sacred to Zeus and Asclepius. On the road leaving the city by the Teneatic Gate was a temple of Eileithyia.

On the ascent to the Acrocorinthus there were altars of Helios and a sanctuary of Necessity and Force, which no one was allowed to enter; a temple of the Mother of the Gods, containing a pillar and a throne, both made of stone; a temple of Juno Bunaea, named from Bunus, the third king of Corinth, the son of Hermes and Alcidameia; and upon the summit the temple of Aphrodite, to whom the whole mountain was sacred (Paus. 2.4.7).

Excavations at Corinth were started in 1896. Among the buildings uncovered was the peribolos of Apollo, an open court surrounded by a marble Ionic colonnade. In the center are heavy foundations that most likely supported the bronze statue of the god mentioned by Pausanias. The fountain of Peirene with its chamber-like grottoes is immediately south of the peribolos (but a shrine of Artemis possibly lay between the two). On a small, isolated hill to the west of the peribolos is the temple of Apollo, one of the oldest temples in Greece. Seven Doric columns remain standing. On the west side of the forum were a row of Roman shops, immediately in front of which were temples of Venus Fortuna, Heracles, Poseidon, the Clarian Apollo, and a pantheon.

The museum houses several works of art having mythological interest: a crater with a scene of Heracles and the Centaurs, a head of a fallen Amazon, a painted sphinx, a statue of Aphrodite, heads of Artemis and Tyche, a relief of dancing Maenads, and a head of Dionysus. In the center courtyard of the museum are frieze reliefs of the labors of Heracles, a gigantomachia, and Enyo, the goddess of war. In the museum is also a room housing finds from an Asclepieion, which was located north of the museum near the city wall.

North of the museum is the so-called fountain of Glauce, which was built over a reservoir. To the east of the fountain is a colonnaded area in which a temple, probably of Hera Acraea, stood. Connected to it was the fountain of Lerna, which provided water for use by the Asclepieion. Near it was an additional water supply, a fountain known as the Baths of Aphrodite. To the west lay a sanctuary of Zeus, still not located, but from architectural fragments believed to be greater in size than any temple in Corinth or even in Peloponnesus.

On the lower slopes of modern Akrokorinthos can be seen a sanctuary of Demeter and Kore, which has been excavated since 1968. On Akrokorinthos one finds the upper Peirene spring. The remains of the temple of Aphrodite there are quite meager.

CORINTHIAN ISTHMUS (ISTHMIA)   was the most important part of the territory of Corinth and one of the most important parts of Greece. The Isthmus was a land route from north to south and from the eastern to the western sea. More especially it was hallowed by the celebration of the Isthmian games. The designation of Corinthian Isthmus was applied to the entire area lying between the two gulfs, to the narrowest part of the Isthmus, and especially to the vicinity of the Poseideion and the locality of the Isthmian games. The Corinthians built a series of walls across the Isthmus, the first in 1200 B.C. and the last in the reign of Justinian.

The only town on the Isthmus in ancient times was Schoenus on the Saronic Gulf. Situated at the narrowest part of the Isthmus, it was the port of the Isthmian sanctuary. This harbor is now called Kalamaki.

The sanctuary lay about 1 km southeast of Schoenus. Today the Corinthian canal separates Kalamaki from Isthmia. The sanctuary was roughly quadrangular in form, containing the temple of Poseidon Isthmius and other sanctuaries; it was surrounded on all sides by a strong wall, which still can be clearly traced. Pausanias briefly points out the stadium and theater, both constructed of white marble and both outside the sacred enclosure. Here the Isthmian games were celebrated. The main gate of the sanctuary appears to have been in the east wall. The road leading from this gate to the temple of Poseidon was lined on one side by the statues of conquerors in the Isthmian games and on the other side by pine trees. Upon the temple, which was not large, stood Tritons, probably serving as weather vanes. In the pronaos, the front porch of the temple, Pausanias (2.1.7) saw two statues of Poseidon and by their side statues of Amphitrite, his wife, and Thalassa, a personification of the Mediterranean Sea. Inside the temple was a statuary group of four gilded horses with ivory hooves, drawing the chariot of Poseidon, Amphitrite, and Palaemon. The chariot stood on a base, on which was a bas-relief of Thalassa with her child Aphrodite; on either side were Nereids, the marine nymphs of the Mediterranean. Foundations of the temple and the altar may be seen still.

Within the sacred enclosure, to the west, was the Palaemonion, consisting of two sanctuaries, one above ground, containing images of Poseidon, Leucothea, and Palaemon; and a subterranean sanctum, where Palaemon was said to have been buried. This sanctum was the most sacred spot in the Isthmus since the Isthmian festival originally honored Palaemon. In the temple was a statue of Palaemon lying on a dolphin. Palaemon was a son of Athamas and Ino, originally called Melicertes. When his mother went mad, she leapt into the sea with him. His body was washed by the waves (or carried on the back of a dolphin) into the port of Schoenus on the Corinthian Isthmus, or to that spot on the coast where subsequently the altar of Palaemon stood. There the body was found by his uncle Sisyphus, king of Corinth, who ordered it to be carried by Donacinus and Amphimachus to Corinth, and on the command of the Nereids instituted the Isthmian games and sacrifices of black bulls in honor of the deified Palaemon. In works of art Palaemon is represented as a boy carried by marine deities or dolphins. Poseidon was subsequently substituted for this local divinity as the patron god of the festival; but Palaemon continued to receive special honor, and in his sanctum the most sacred oaths were sworn. Pausanias (1.44.9) also mentions an ancient sanctuary called the altar of the Cyclopes. Sisyphus and Neleus were said to have been buried here, but the site of their graves was unknown. Car, son of Phoroneus and king of Megara was also buried nearby. As late as the time of Pausanias his tomb was shown on the road from Megara to Corinth. Glaucus, the son of Sisyphus, was said to have haunted the Corinthian Isthmus. His shade frightened the horses during the races, and a certain spot at which they shied was called Taraxippus (Paus. 6.20.19).

There were several other buildings besides. Most of these were erected by Publius Licinus Priscus Juventianus, high priest for life at Roman Corinth. Beside the Palaemonion he erected the sacred avenue, the temple of Helios, the peribolos of the Sacred Grove and within it temples of Demeter, Kore, Dionysus, and Artemis with their statues. He repaired the temple of Eueteria, of Kore, and of Pluto which had fallen into decay from earthquakes and age.

In the Corinthian territory north of the Isthmus was a district called Peraea. There were three forts on this promontory, one of them called Heraion from its being the site of the temple and oracle of Hera Acraea (Xenoph. *Hell.* 4.5.5). The fortress consisted of the temple itself, which stood upon the extremity of the promontory and was surrounded with strong walls, of which the remains are still extant. A little way inland is a chapel of Agios Nikolaos, also surrounded with walls and probably the site of an ancient sanctuary; perhaps it was the temple of Poseidon, who is frequently represented by Agios Nikolaos. A lake near the Heraion is a salt lake surrounded by mountains except on the side open to the sea. It is conjectured that it is the lake Eschatiotis mentioned by Curtius. Gorgo, the daughter of Megareus and wife of Corinthus, is said to have plunged into this lake upon learning of the murder of her children. In consequence of this, the lake received the name of Gorgopis.

Between the flat ground of the Isthmus and the Scironian Rocks there are three plains upon the coast. The chief town in this district was Crommyon, and the name Crommyonia was sometimes given to the whole country between Megara and Schoenus. Between Crommyon and Schoenus was the village of Sidus. To the east of Crommyon, at the west end of the Scironian Rocks, was a temple of Apollo Latous, which marked the boundaries of the provinces of Corinthia and Megaris in the time of Pausanias (1.44.14). This temple must have been near the modern village of Kineta, a little above which the road leads over the Scironian Rocks to Megara.

Alcyoneus was a giant, who possessed the Isthmus at the time when Heracles drove away the oxen of Geryon. The giant attacked the hero's party, crushing twelve wagons and twenty-four men with a huge block of stone. Heracles himself warded off the stone with his club and slew Alcyoneus. The block with which the giant had threatened Heracles was shown on the Isthmus down to a very late period (Pind. *Nem.* 4.44). Telamon, son of Aeacus, was said to have been a great friend of Heracles and to have assisted him against Alcyoneus.

Theseus is well remembered for his experiences on the Isthmus. When he went from Troezen to Athens to claim his heritage, he travelled by way of the Isthmus so that he could emulate Heracles. During this trip he overcame robbers and monsters, which infested the country. One of these was Sinis, a son of Polypemon, Pemon, or Poseidon by Sylea, the daughter of Corinthus. He was also called according to some, Pitycamptes. He dwelt on the Isthmus as a robber, destroying the travellers whom he had conquered by fastening them to the tops of fir trees and then letting the trees spring apart, thereby tearing the victim in half. He himself was killed in this manner by Theseus. When Theseus accomplished this, he caused himself to be purified by Phytalus at the altar of Zeus Meilichius because Theseus himself was related to Sinis (Paus. 1.37.3), or, according to others, he propitiated the spirit of Sinis by instituting in his honor the Isthmian games. Theseus also killed Phaea, the colossal sow of Crommyon, which ravaged the neighborhood.

CORIUM was a town in Crete, near which was a temple of Athena and a lake. The site is 15 km south of the village of Thronos, site of the ancient city of Sybrita. There is evidence of destruction by fire. On the acropolis there are remains of the temple.

CORMANOR was an earlier name of the INACHUS River.

CORONE (PETALIDI) was a town of Messenia situated upon the west side of the Messenian Gulf. According to Pausanias (4.34.5), it was built on the site of the Homeric Aepeia and named after the Boeotian city of Coroneia by its founder Epimelides, a native of the older city. This name was changed by the Messenians to Corone. According to others, Corone corresponded to the Homeric Pedasus (Strab. 8.4.5).

Pausanias (4.34.4) says that Corone was situated at the foot of a mountain called Mathia. The present name of the mountain is Likodimo, at the foot of which stands Petalidi, on the site of Corone, in a small but fertile plain. In the mid–nineteenth century settlers restored the ancient name to the place. The modern town of Koroni, however, which is situated upon a promontory some distance south of Petalidi, occupies the site of Asine. It is probable that the inhabitants of Corone migrated at some period to Asine, carrying with them their ancient name.

On the acropolis of the city was a bronze statue of Athena, who became the patron deity of Corone in consequence of her worship at Coroneia. This statue bore a crow in its hand (Paus. 4.34.3). In the agora there was a statue of Zeus Soter. In the lower city were temples of Artemis, of Dionysus, and of Asclepius. The latter two temples featured marble statues of the gods.

There are considerable remains of Corone. Five Doric columns suggest a temple to one of the divinities mentioned above. Fifteen km south of Corone, near the coast, was the temple of Apollo Corythus, and remains indicate that four successive temples were built on the site, the location of the present village of Longa. It is likely that Apollo was worshipped here as a warlike god.

CORONEIA (AGIOS GEORGIOS) was a town described by Strabo (9.2.29) as situated upon a height near Mount Helicon. It stood upon an isolated hill at the entrance of a valley leading southward to Mount Helicon. From this hill one could see Lake Copais. On either side of the hill flowed two streams, one on the east side called Coralius or Cuarius, and the other on the west named Phalarus. Coroneia is said to have been founded by the Boeotians from Arne in Thessaly after they had been driven out of their original homes by the Thessalians; and they appear to have called it Coroneia after the Thessalian town of that name. Pausanias (9.34.5) says that it was founded by and named for Coronus, as son of Thersander and grandson of Sisyphus. At the time of the founding they also built in the plain in front of the city a temple of Athena Itonia, named after the one in Thessaly. They also transferred the name of the Thessalian river Cuarius or Curalius to the one that flowed by the temple. In this temple was held the festival of the Pamboeotia (Paus. 9.34.1).

Coroneia is mentioned by Homer (*Il.* 2.503) in conjunction with Haliartus. Pausanias (9.34.2) says that the most remarkable objects in Coroneia were altars of Hermes Epimelius and of the winds, and a little below them the temple of Hera. The principal remains of the ancient city are those of the theater, the temple of Hera, and the agora. These remains are located about 4 km south of the modern village of Agios Georgios, which itself is a short distance south of the main highway from Thebes to Livadia. On an adjacent road there is a modern village undoubtedly named for the ancient town, but the ruins are closer to Agios Georgios.

The twelfth labor of Heracles was fetching Cerberus from the underworld. The place where he appeared with the monster was said by some to be Coroneia.

COROPE (KOROPI) was a city in Thessaly and the site of the shrine and oracle of Apollo Coropaeus. This sanctuary was in existence from the archaic period, and the oracle was still consulted into Roman times. The site is located on the right bank of a small river about 20 km south of modern Volos on the east shore of a gulf, the Kolpos Pagassitikos. The modern village of Koropi occupies the site, which was discovered in 1882 but not excavated until 1906.

CORYCIUM (KALIVIA) is the celebrated cave about 11.5 km northeast of Delfi and about the same distance northwest of Arahova. It is situated in the mountain on the north side of the valley. It was named for Corycia, a nymph who became by Apollo the mother of Lycorus or Lycoreus. It was sacred to Pan and the nymphs, which is attested by an inscription found inside. Pan and the nymphs were regarded as the companions of Dionysus, whose orgies were celebrated upon these heights. The Thyiads, or Delphic Bacchants, held a biennial festival here by torchlight. The cave is now called Sarantavli (Forty Chambers). It has been used historically as a place of refuge by the inhabitants of Delfi and neighboring towns.

CORYDALLUS (KORIDALOS) was a deme of Attica at the foot of the mountain of the same name. It was placed by Strabo (9.1.14) between Thria and Peiraeus near the straits of Salamis. Diodorus Siculus (4.59) concurred with this location in his narration of the journey of Theseus to Athens. After the contest of Theseus and Cercyon, which took place to the west of Eleusis, Theseus next killed Procrustes, who dwelt in Corydallus. (See CEPHISSUS.)

CORYMBIA was an earlier name of RHODES.

CORYPHASIUM (KORIFASIO) is the Messenian promontory said to be the location of the harbor of ancient Pylos. Athena Coryphasia derived her name from this promontory on which she had a sanctuary (Paus. 4.36.2). On the north slope of this neck of land is also located the so-called Grotto of Nestor. The entrance is 9 meters wide and 3.6 high. The cave itself is about 18 meters long and 12 high. The stalactites resemble animals and hanging hides and thus gave rise perhaps to the story that Neleus and Nestor kept their cattle here. The cave is also identified with the place in which Hermes hid the cattle he stole from Apollo.

CORYPHUM was the name of a mountain in the territory of Epidaurus, on the summit of which was a temple of Artemis Coryphaea (Goddess of the Peak). On the road up the mountain was a twisted olive tree, and it was thought that Heracles gave it this shape by bending it, possibly to mark the boundary between Epidaurus and Asine. Coryphum is thought to be a hill in the southwest of the valley (Paus. 2.28.2).

COS (KOS) is an island in the Aegean Sea. One of its earlier names was Meropis (Thuc. 8.41); another was Nymphaea (Plin. 5.31.36). Its location is nearly opposite the Gulf of Halicarnassus, and it is separated by a narrow strait from Cnidus and the Triopian promontory. Its principal city is Kos. The creation of Cos was connected with the story of the contest between the gods and giants. Polybotes was a giant, who was pursued by Poseidon across the sea as far as the island of Cos. There Poseidon tore away a part of the island (which was afterward called Nisyrion), threw it upon the giant, and buried him under it (Apollod. 1.6.2; Paus. 1.2.4).

Tradition connects the earliest Greek inhabitants of Cos with a migration from Epidaurus, and the common worship of Asclepius seems to have maintained a link between the two for a long period of time. Merops, the father of Eumelus, was king of the island, which he called Cos after his daugher, while the inhabitants were called Meropes after the king himself. His wife, the nymph Ethemea, was killed by Artemis because she had neglected to worship that goddess and was carried by Persephone to the lower world. Merops, in grief for his wife, tried to kill himself but Hera changed him into an eagle, which she placed among the stars.

Eurypylus, a son of Poseidon and Astypalaea, was a later king of Cos. He was killed by Heracles who landed in Cos on his return from Troy and, being taken for a pirate, was attacked by the Coans (Apollod. 2.7.1,8). According to another tradition, Heracles attacked the island in order to obtain possession of Chalciope, the daughter of Eurypylus, whom he loved. Heracles himself was wounded by Chalcodon but was saved by Zeus. After he had ravaged Cos, he left. Telamon, the lover of Heracles, had accompanied the hero in his expedition against Troy and also assisted him in the fight against the Meropes. Thessalus was the offspring of the union between Heracles and Chalciope, and he became the father of Pheidippus and Antiphus (Hom. *Il.* 2.679; Apollod. 2.7.8).

In Homer (*Il.* 2.677,867) we find the people of the island fighting against the Carians. Antiphus, the son of Thessalus, was one of the Greek heroes at Troy. He and his brother Pheidippus joined the Greeks with thirty ships and commanded the men of Carpathus, Casus, Cos, and other islands (Hom. *Il.* 2.675).

The city of Kos has continued till our time. Excavations were begun in the early part of the century. In the city a sanctuary attributed to Aphrodite Pandemos was found. Near it was a temple of Heracles. In the ancient agora an altar of Dionysus has been identified. Several mosaics have been discovered in the houses of the ancient city, notably of Europa, Silenus, Orpheus, and the judgment of Paris. Near the city is the sanctuary of Asclepius. Originally this had been a sanctuary of Apollo Cyparissius. After the death of the most famous citizen of Cos, Hippocrates, the construction of the Asclepieion was begun. The area included a temple, a bath, an altar, a building to house the priests, and other buildings with special functions in this healing sanctuary. A school of physicians had been attached to the sanctuary, and its great collection of votive models made it almost a museum of anatomy and pathology. In the southern part of the island excavations in the grotto of Aspripetri have revealed the existence of a cult of Pan and the nymphs. Near Kardamena ruins have been identified with a sanctuary of Apollo. At Pili a hero shrine has been described as that of Charmylos. Between Pili and Asfendiou is a sanctuary of Demeter and Kore with a small Hellenistic temple.

Aphrodite Anadyomene (Goddess Rising out of the Sea) was a name of Aphrodite that alluded to her having been born from the foam of the sea. This name did not have much celebrity before the time of Apelles, but his famous painting in which the goddess was represented as rising from the sea and drying her hair with her hands at once drew great attention to this poetical idea and excited the emulation of other artists, painters and sculptors alike. The painting was made for the inhabitants of Cos, who set it up in their temple of Asclepius. Its beauty induced Augustus to have it removed to Rome, and the Coans were indemnified by a reduction in their taxes of 100 talents. In the time of Nero the greater part of the picture had become effaced, and it was replaced by the work of another artist (Plin. 35.36.12,15).

Icarius was an Athenian who tried to introduce the worship of Dionysus but was killed by shepherds who mistook intoxication for poisoning. Some say the murderers fled to Cos, which was therefore seized with a drought, during which the fields were burned and epidemics prevailed. Aristaeus prayed to his father, Apollo, for help, and Apollo advised him to propitiate Icarius with many sacrifices and to beg Zeus to send the winds called

Etesiae, which Zeus in consequence made blow at the rising of the dog star for forty days (Apollod. 3.14.7).

Finally, there is a charming story about a maiden of Cos named Ctesylla, who was loved by Hermochares. It is identical to the story of Cydippe and Acontius. (See CEOS.)

CRANAE (MARATHONISI) was the name of an island in the Laconian Gulf opposite Gythium, to which Paris carried Helen from Sparta. Their marriage was consummated here (Paus. 3.22.1). The little rocky islet, now called Marathonisi, is connected by a causeway to the mainland. The ruined foundation of a temple supports at present a chapel (Hom. *Il.* 3.442; Paus. 3.22.1).

CRANEION a suburb of Corinth, was the aristocratic quarter of the city and the favorite place of residence of wealthy Corinthians. Hence it was the chief promenade of Corinth. Bellerophon, the Corinthian hero, had a sanctuary here in a cypress grove (Paus. 2.2.4).

CRANNON (DOXARAS) known originally as Ephyra, was one of the most important cities of Thessaly, being the seat of the Scopadae, kinsmen of the powerful Aleuadae of Larissa, from which it was distant about 25 km. One of the eight leading Thessalian cities, it issued coins as early as 480 B.C. There were temples of Athena and Asclepius, where the state archives were said to be kept. There are ruins of the temple of Asclepius, which was built on the bank of a still-flowing stream. There are also two Mycenaean tholos tombs.

CRATHIS (KRATHIS) is a river in Achaia. It rises in a mountain of the same name in Arcadia and empties into the Corinthian Gulf near Aegae. It is one of the few streams of Achaia that does not dry up in summer. The Styx, which rises in the Arcadian mountain of Aroania, is a tributary of the Crathis. Gaea Eurysternos (the Goddess with the Broad Chest) had a sanctuary on the Crathis near Aegae with a very ancient statue (Paus. 7.25.8).

CREMNIA was an earlier name of GORTYN.

CRENIDES was the original name of PHILIPPI.

CRETE (KRITI) an island situated in the Aegean basin of the Mediterranean Sea, is 267 km long and 60 km wide. The interior is a very mountainous, woody, and interspersed with fertile valleys. A continuous mass of high land runs its whole length, about the middle of which is Mount Ida. To the west it is connected with a chain called the White Mountains; to the east it extends to the ridge of Mount Dicte. There are several rivers, mostly torrents, usually dry in summer. There are, however, many springs. Mount Ida, connected in ancient story with metallurgy, was covered with forests, the wood of which was used extensively in forging and smelting. Crete was celebrated for its medicinal herbs, wines, and honey. The island was free from dangerous wild beasts, a blessing it owed to Heracles (Diod. 4.17). The favorable climate makes Crete today an agricultural center, and it produces a large variety of crops.

The Dorians first appeared in Crete during the heroic age; the Homeric poems mention different languages and different races of men—Eteocretes, Cydonians, Dorians, Achaians, and Pelasgians, as all coexisting on the island. The island was described as populous and as having ninety cities (Hom. *Od.* 19.174).

At the beginning of things there was an autochthonous king of Crete named Melisseus. He became by Amaltheia the father of the nymphs Adrasteia and Ida, to whom Rhea entrusted the infant Zeus to be reared in the Dictaean grotto. Rhea put Zeus under the care of the nymphs because Cronus, her husband, is said to have devoured all his children by Rhea. When she was on the point of giving birth to Zeus, she, by the advice of her parents, went to Lyctus in Crete. When Zeus was born, she gave to Cronus a stone wrapped up like an infant, and the god swallowed it as he had swallowed his other children (Hes. *Theog.* 446; Apollod. 1.1.5; Diod. 5.70). The worship of the Cretan Rhea later became confused with the Phrygian worship of the mother of the gods. Crete was undoubtedly the earliest seat of Rhea's worship. Diodorus Siculus (5.66) saw the site where her temple had once stood in the neighborhood of Cnossus.

The nymphs fed Zeus with milk of the goat Amaltheia, and the bees of the mountain provided him with honey (Apollod. 1.1.6; Diod. 5.70). Amaltheia the goat was rewarded for this service by being placed among the stars. According to other traditions, Amaltheia was a nymph or a daughter (and wife) of Melisseus, king of Crete, and is said to have fed Zeus the milk of a goat. When the goat once broke off one of her horns, Amaltheia filled it with fresh herbs and fruits and gave it to Zeus, who placed it together with the goat among the stars (Ov. *Fast.* 5.115). According to other accounts, Zeus himself broke off one of the horns of the goat Amaltheia, gave it to the daughters of Melisseus and endowed it with such powers that the possessor of it could have it filled instantly with whatever he or she might wish. In nursing the infant god the nymphs were assisted by the Curetes (Callim. *Hymn. in Jov.* 47). Apollonius Rhodius (3.132) relates that Adrasteia gave to the infant a beautiful globe to play with, and on some Cretan coins Zeus was represented sitting upon a globe.

According to some, Aega was another daughter of Melisseus and was chosen to suckle the infant Zeus, but as she was found unable to do so, the service was performed by the goat Amaltheia. According to others, Aega was a daughter of Helios and of such dazzling brightness that the Titans in their attack upon Olympus became frightened and requested their mother Gaea to conceal her in the earth. She was accordingly confined in a cave on Crete, where she became the nurse of Zeus. In the fight with the Titans Zeus was commanded by an oracle to cover himself with her skin (*aegis*). He obeyed the command and then raised Aega among the stars.

Crete is thus called the island or nurse of the great Zeus, and his worship there appears to have been very ancient. Among the places in the island particularly sacred to the god we must mention: (1) the district about Mount Ida, especially Cnossus, which was said to have been built by the Curetes and where Minos had ruled and conversed with Zeus (Hom. *Od.* 19.172; Plat. *Leg.* 1.1; Cic. *De Nat. Deor.* 3.21); (2) Gortyn, where the god, in the form of a bull, landed when he had carried off Europa from Phoenicia and where he was worshipped under the surname Hecatombaeus; and (3) the towns about Mount Dicte, such as Lyctus, Praesus, Hierapytna, Biennus, Eleuthernae, and Oaxus. Zeus is said to have fathered a son by a nymph from Mount Ida. This was Cres, from whom Crete was believed to have derived its name (Paus. 8.53.3). According to Diodorus Siculus (5.64), Cres was an Eteocretan, i.e., a Cretan autochthon.

Europa was a daughter of the Phoenician king Agenor and sister of Cadmus, Phoenix, and Cilix. Zeus became enamored of her and decided to kidnap her. To do this he changed himself into a beautiful bull, and Europa while playing on the beach came and rode on the back of the bull. The bull suddenly plunged into the sea and swam to Crete. Once there, Zeus assumed his regular form and by Europa had three sons, Minos, Rhadamanthys, and Sarpedon. After this, Zeus departed, and Europa was left with her sons. The continent of Europe is believed to have received its name from Europa. Hellotis was her surname in Crete, where also a festival, Hellotia, was celebrated in her honor.

Asterius was king, inheriting the throne from his father Tectamus, or Teutamus, a son of Dorus and a great-grandson of Deucalion, who had come to Crete with an Aeolian and Pelasgian colony. Teutamus had married a daughter of Creteus, the king at that time. Zeus came to Crete with Europa in the reign of Creteus.

Minos and Sarpedon quarreled over the kingdom, but Minos won out. Their enmity had started earlier, when they both fell in love with Miletus, the son of Apollo and the Cretan nymph Areia. Miletus preferred Sarpedon and fled with him to Caria, where he later built a town named after himself (Apollod. 3.1.2; Paus. 7.2.3). Sarpedon could not return to Crete, so he took refuge with Cilix, his uncle in Cilicia, whom he assisted against the Lycians. Afterward he became king of the Lycians, and Zeus granted him the privilege of living three generations

(Herod. 1.173; Apollod. 3.1.2). Rhadamanthys, meanwhile, from fear of Minos fled to Ocaleia in Boeotia and there married Alcmena, the mother of Heracles. In consequence of his justice throughout life he became after his death one of the judges of Hades and took up his abode in Elysium (Apollod. 3.1.2; Hom. *Od.* 4.564, 7.323; Pind. *Ol.* 2.137).

Minos succeeded Asterius and married Itone, daughter of Lyctius. According to some he married Crete, a daughter of Asterius. As king he is said to have established many useful laws. After his death he became one of the judges of the shades in Hades. By Itone he became the father of Lycastus; Lycastus became by Ida the daughter of Corybas, the father of another Minos, whom, however, some called a son of Zeus.

Minos II, having become king, was also a renowned lawgiver. He possessed a powerful navy. He was married to Pasiphae, a daughter of Helios and Perseis (but some say his wife was Crete) (Apollod. 3.1.2), and by her he was father of Creteus, Deucalion, Glaucus, Androgeus, Acalle, Xenodice, Ariadne, and Phaedra (Apollod. 2.1.3). He aimed at the supremacy of Crete and declared that it was destined to him by the gods. In proof of this he said that anything he prayed for was granted. Accordingly, as he was offering up a sacrifice to Poseidon, he prayed that a bull might come forth from the sea and he promised to sacrifice the animal to the god. A bull appeared, and Minos was confirmed as king. But he admired the beauty of the bull and did not sacrifice it, substituting another in its place. Poseidon therefore caused Pasiphae to conceive an unnatural and unendurable passion for the animal. She concealed herself in an artificial cow made by the genius craftsman Daedalus and thus became by the bull the mother of the Minotaur, a monster that had the body of a man but the head of a bull. Minos shut the monster up in the labyrinth that Daedalus had been ordered to construct. Apollodorus (3.1.4), who tells the story, calls the Minotaur Asterius. Daedalus for his part in the affair was imprisoned. Pasiphae released him, but Daedalus was unable to leave the island because of carefully guarded harbors. Daedalus fashioned wings for himself and his son Icarus and thus escaped Crete. Icarus flew too near the sun and fell into the sea, but Daedalus flew safely to Sicily.

Minos divided Crete into three parts, each of which contained a capital, and is said to have ruled nine years (Hom. *Od.* 19.178). The Cretans traced their legal and political institutions to Minos, and he is said to have been instructed in the art of lawgiving by Zeus himself; the Spartan, Lycurgus, was believed to have taken the legislation of Minos as his model (Paus. 3.2.4). In his time Crete was a powerful maritime state, and Minos not only checked the piratical pursuits of his contemporaries but made himself master of the Greek islands of the Aegean

(Thuc. 1.48). The most ancient legends describe Minos as a just and wise lawgiver, whereas later accounts represent him as an unjust and cruel tyrant (Philostr. *Vit. Apoll.* 3.25). In support of the latter case, we can look at the story regarding his son, Androgeus. Androgeus went to Athens once to the Panathenaic festival and conquered all his opponents in the games. This extraordinary good luck, however, became the cause of his destruction. Androgeus was killed, and various accounts are given as the how, the most widely accepted being that Aegeus, king of Athens, sent him to fight against the Marathonian bull, which killed him. All accounts of his death involve an element of treachery. In consequence, Minos made war on the Athenians. Androgeus was worshipped in Attica as a hero, and games, Androgeonia, were celebrated in his honor every year in the Cerameicus. He was also worshipped under the name Eurygyes (Owner of Extensive Fields) from which it has been inferred that originally Androgeus was worshipped as the introducer of agriculture into Attica. Somewhere along the way, Androgeus had managed to father two sons, Alcaeus and Sthenelus.

In any case, in order to avenge the wrong done to his son, Minos made war on the Athenians and Megarians. He subdued Megara and compelled the Athenians at intervals to send him as a tribute seven youths and seven maidens, who were devoured in the labyrinth by the Minotaur (Apollod. 3.15.8; Paus. 1.27.9; Plut. *Thes.* 15).

On one of the occasions when the Athenians had to send to Minos their tribute of seven youths and maidens, Theseus, the king's son, offered himself as one of the youths, with the plan of slaying the Minotaur. When the intended victims arrived in Crete, Ariadne, the daughter of Minos, fell in love with Theseus and provided him with a sword, with which he slew the Minotaur, and a ball of twine by which he found his way out of the labyrinth. Having effected his object and rescued the band of victims, Theseus set sail for home, carrying Ariadne with him. Most accounts say that he abandoned her on the island of Naxos. Years later he married Phaedra, the younger sister of Ariadne. Phaedra thereby became stepmother to Hippolytus. When Theseus learned that she had tried unsuccessfully to seduce his son, causing his exile and subsequent death, Phaedra killed herself. Ariadne was said to have been found on Naxos by the god Dionysus, who fathered by her sons Oenopion and Staphylus. Oenopion by the nymph Helice fathered many children, among them Merope. He later migrated to Chios. There he blinded Orion, who had raped Merope while he was courting her. Orion was later cured of his blindness and returned for vengeance. But Oenopion hid and thus escaped. Orion then went to Crete, where he ended his days.

Glaucus was another son of Minos by Pasiphae. When yet a boy, while he was playing at ball or pursuing a mouse, he fell into a cask of honey and died in it. Minos searched for him in vain and eventually retained Polyidus, a soothsayer from Argos. Polyidus, led by an owl and bees, found the body of Glaucus, and Minos demanded that Polyidus restore him to life. When Polyidus said he could not do this, Minos had him entombed alive with the body of Glaucus. In the vault he saw a serpent approach the dead body and killed it. Soon another serpent came carrying an herb that it placed on the dead snake. The dead serpent regained life, so Polyidus placed the herb on Glaucus, who rose to life again. Minos richly rewarded him and sent him back to Argos.

Catreus (or Creteus or Crateus) was another son of Minos by Pasiphae. His children were Aerope, Clymene, Apemosyne, and Althaemenes. When Catreus inquired of the oracle how his life should end, the answer was that he would die by the hand of one of his children. The son Althaemenes learned of the oracle and was afraid that he might be the murderer, so he left Crete with his sister Apemosyne. They landed at a place in Rhodes, and Catreus took possession of it, naming it Cretenia. The god Hermes fell in love with Apemosyne and pursued her, catching her and raping her by spreading fresh, slippery hides on the path along which she fled from him. She told her brother what had happened, but he did not believe her and kicked her to death. To further protect his father from the oracle's prediction he gave his other sisters, Aerope and Clymene, to Nauplius to sell into foreign lands. Aerope became the wife of Pleisthenes, who became by her the father of Agamemnon and Menelaus. Clymene became the wife of Nauplius himself and thereby mother of Oeax and Palamedes. Later, in declining years, Catreus wanted to pass the kingdom to his son Althaemenes and so sought him in Rhodes. He landed with his retainers on a deserted coast, and they were mistaken for pirates by cowherds, who fought them. During this time Althaemenes arrived and killed Catreus with a javelin. When he learned that he had, after all, fulfilled the old prophecy, he prayed to the gods and was swallowed up by the earth (Apollod. 3.2.1).

Still another son of Minos ws Deucalion. He was an Argonaut and one of the Calydonian hunters. He became the father of Idomeneus and Crete and a bastard son Molus. Idomeneus was a man of great beauty and is mentioned among the suitors of Helen. His half-brother Molus met an unhappy end. It was said that he attempted to rape a nymph and was afterward found without a head. At a certain festival in Crete they showed the image of a man without a head who was called Molus. The son of Molus was Meriones. He and his uncle Idomeneus led the Cretans in eighty ships against Troy, and they both were among the bravest of heroes in the Trojan War. After the fall of Troy, Idomeneus returned home in safety, though once in a storm he vowed to Poseidon to sacrifice to the god whatever he should meet first on landing, if the god would grant him a safe return. The first person he met on landing was his own son, whom he accordingly sacrificed. Crete was thereupon visited with a plague, and the Cretans expelled Idomeneus. He went to various places and eventually settled at Colophon, but his tomb was shown at Cnossus, where he and Meriones were worshipped as heroes (Diod. 5.79). Meriones also returned safely from Troy, although some traditions state that he was thrown on the coast of Sicily by a storm and was received by the Cretans who had settled there. Most accounts say he reached Crete safely and was buried there.

Minos had other sons by nymphs. By Paria he had Eurymedon, Nephalion, Chryses and Philolaus, and by Dexithea he had Euxanthius. Apparently his sons by Paria banded together and formed a colony on Paros. When Heracles landed there on his way to gain the girdle of Hippolyte, two of his crew were killed by the sons of Minos, and he in turn slew them. In addition he laid siege to the settlement so that they offered replacements to the murdered crew members. These were Alcaeus and Sthenelus, sons of Androgeus and therefore grandsons of Minos.

Nothing is known of Euxanthius. Nor do we know anything further about Xenodice, another daughter of Minos and Pasiphae. We do know about the remaining daughter, Acacallis. Carmanor, a Cretan of Tarrha, was said to have received and purified Apollo and Artemis after they had slain the monster Python. It was in the house of Carmanor that Apollo met and fell in love with Acacallis. He begot by her a son Miletus, whom, for fear of her father, Acacallis exposed in a forest. However, wolves watched and suckled the child, until he was found by shepherds who brought him up. According to Cretan tradition, Acacallis, or Acalle as she is sometimes called, also became the mother by Hermes of Cydon, the ancestor of the Cydonians. The Tegeatans claimed, however, that Cydon was a son of Tegeates and emigrated to Crete from Tegea (Paus. 8.53.4).

As for Minos, he remained obsessed with tracking down the escaped Daedalus. He went from place to place, presenting an intricately whorled conch to be threaded through its labyrinthine interior for a reward. Finally in Sicily, the puzzle was solved and Minos knew he had found Daedalus for nobody else could possibly have the genius to accomplish this task. However, before Minos could confront his quarry, the daughters of King Cocalus murdered him.

As can be seen, the descendants of Minos all seem to have colonized other places, and the royal line appears to have disappeared from Crete itself just after the Trojan War. Up till this time, the island had figured prominently in heroic events and communication with other states and cities. The Argonauts, for example, had attempted to land in Crete but were prevented by the monster Talos. This Talos was a man of brass, the work of Hephaestus. This wonderful being was given to Minos by Zeus or Hephaestus and watched the island of Crete by walking around the island thrice every day. Whenever he saw strangers approaching, he made himself red-hot with fire and then embraced the strangers when they landed. He had in his body only one vein, which ran from head to ankles and was closed at the top with a nail. When he attempted to keep the Argonauts from Crete by throwing stones at them, Medea by her magic powers threw him into a state of madness, or, according to others, under the pretence of making him immortal she took the nail out of his vein and thus caused him to bleed to death. Others again related that Poeas killed him by wounding him with an arrow in the ankle (Apollod. 1.9.26; Apollon. Rhod. 4.2636).

Heracles, omnipresent in heroic histories of places, had to come to Crete in connection with his seventh labor, the capture of the Cretan bull. According to some, this bull had been sent out of the sea by Poseidon so that Minos might sacrifice him to the god of the sea. But Minos was so charmed by the beauty of the animal that he kept it and sacrificed another in its place. (This version obviously parallels the Pasiphae story up to this point.) Poseidon punished Minos by making the bull go mad and cause great destruction in the island. Heracles was ordered to catch the bull, and Minos was happy to give permission. Heracles accomplished this and brought the bull home on his shoulders, but he then set the animal free again. The bull now roamed about and at last came to Marathon. Heracles came to Crete again in conjunction with his tenth labor. He collected a large fleet there and sailed against Chrysaor, the wealthy king of Iberia, and his three sons, one of which was Geryones, who owned the cattle that were the object of the labor. The Cretan Heracles, one of the Idaean Dactyls, was believed to have founded the temple of Zeus at Olympia. The traditions about him resemble those of the Greek Heracles, but it is said that he lived at a much earlier period and that the Greek hero only imitated him. He was worshipped with funeral sacrifices and was regarded as a magician, like the other ancient daemons of Crete (Cic. De Nat. Deor. 3.16; Diod. 5.64).

Crete and Troy had distant connections. Teucer was the son of Scamander and first king of Troy. According to some, Scamander and Teucer immigrated into Troas from Crete, bringing with them the worship of Apollo Smintheus (Strab. 13.1.48). Dardanus, son of Zeus and Electra, was said by some to have been born in Crete. He was the mythical ancestor of the Trojans. Erichthonius, a son of Dardanus and Bateia, is mentioned among the kings of Crete (Hom. Il. 20.220; Apollod. 3.12.2).

Zeus was the principal deity of Crete. Various stories are connected with his birth and worship in the island. One had to do with Cretan robbers—Laius, Aegolius, Celeus, and Cerberus—who entered the sacred cave of bees in Crete in order to steal honey. They succeeded in their crime but perceived the cradle where the infant Zeus had lain, and that instant their brazen armor broke to pieces. Zeus thundered and wanted to kill them by a flash of lightning, but the Moirae (Fates) and Themis, goddess of laws, prevented the god because no one was allowed to kill anything on that sacred spot. And so the thieves were metamorphosed into birds (Plin. 10.60,79). Another story was about a golden dog. This dog had been made by Hephaestus. Rhea caused the infant Zeus and his nurse to be guarded in Crete by this dog, whom subsequently Zeus appointed guardian of his temple in Crete. Pandareos, a son of Merops of Miletus, stole this dog and, carrying it to Mount Sipylus in Lydia, gave it to Tantalus to care for. When Pandareos returned for it, Tantalus refused to give it up. Pandareos was changed into stone, and Tantalus was cast into the lower world to undergo the punishment that has become proverbial.

Other major deities worshipped on Crete were Apollo, Artemis, Athena, Demeter and Persephone, and Dionysus. The original and essential feature in the character of Apollo is that of "Averter of Evil"; he was originally a divinity peculiar to the Doric race, and the most ancient seats of his worship were the Thessalian Tempe and Delphi. From there it was transplanted to Crete, the inhabitants of which spread it over the coasts of Asia Minor and parts of Greece, such as Boeotia and Attica. With the Cretans he was also regarded as the god with the bow and darts. Apollo Delphinius was a name derived from the god's having shown the Cretan colonists the way to Delphi while riding on a dolphin or meta-morphosing himself into a dolphin. Under this name he had a temple at Cnossus. Castalius was a son of Apollo and father of Delphis, who came from Crete to Crissa and there founded the worship of the Delphinian Apollo. The Castalian spring at Delphi is said to have been named for him. Pteras, the mythical artist of Delphi, who is said to have built the second temple of Apollo at Delphi, is said to have given his name to the city of Aptera in Crete (Paus. 10.5.10).

The worship of Artemis was universal in Greece, and it had a special importance in Crete, mainly because of the identification of the goddess with Britomartis. Britomartis appears to have originally been a Cretan divinity of hunters and fishermen. After the introduction of the worship of Artemis into Crete, Britomartis, between whom and Artemis there were several points of resemblance, was placed in some relation to her. Artemis, who loved her, assumed her name and was worshipped under it, and in the end, the two divinities became completely syncretized. Originally, however, she was a daughter of Zeus and Carme, the daughter of Eubulus. She was a nymph, took great delight in wandering about hunting, and was beloved by Artemis. Minos, who likewise loved her, pursued her for nine months, but she fled from him and at last threw herself into the nets that had been set by fishermen, or leaped from Mount Dictynnaeum into the sea, where she became entangled in the nets but was saved by Artemis, who now made her a goddess. She was worshipped in Crete under the surname Dictymna or Dictynna. The temple of Artemis Britomartis in Crete was ascribed to Daedalus, as was a wooden statue of the same goddess at Olus. Procris, the wife of Cephalus, when she was induced by her disguised husband and his brilliant gifts to break her marriage vows and then recognized him, fled to Crete and sought the help of Artemis. Cnageus was a Laconian who accompanied the Dioscuri in their war against Aphidna and was made prisoner. He was sold as a slave and carried to Crete, where he served in the temple of Artemis; but he escaped from there with a priestess of the goddess, who carried her statue to Sparta (Paus. 3.18.4). Orion, when he was unable to take vengeance on Oenopion in Chios, went to Crete and lived as a hunter with Artemis (Apollod. 1.4.3). The cause of his death, which took place in Crete or Chios, is differently stated, but most versions involve Artemis.

Athena, while not a principal deity in Crete, was nevertheless widely acknowledged by the Cretans as having been born there. Her surname Tritonis gave rise to various traditions about her birthplace, so that wherever there was a river or a spring of that name, as in Crete, the inhabitants asserted that the goddess had been born there. A wooden statue of her at Cnossus was said to have been made by Daedalus.

Demeter was worshipped in Crete, and as elsewhere her worship consisted in large measure of orgiastic mysteries. Crete was mentioned as one of the places from which Persephone was abducted by Hades. Finally, Crete was mentioned, among other places, as the birthplace of Dionysus.

Some lesser divinities were also connected with Crete. Auxesia was a Cretan maiden, who, along with a companion named Damia, was stoned to death during an insurrection at Troezen. Later, divine honors were paid them, and a festival was instituted in their honor. The Harpies, the famous winged monsters, were said by some to live in a cave in Crete (Apollon. Rhod. 2.298). And finally, there were the Telchines, a strange class of beings about whom many stories were told. As cultivators of the soil and ministers of the gods they came from Crete to Cyprus and then to Rhodes, or they proceeded from Rhodes to Crete and Boeotia. Strabo (10.3.19) states that the Rhodian Telchines accompanied Rhea to Crete and there brought up the infant Zeus. On Crete they were called Curetes.

CRETEA (KRAMVONOS)   was a district east of Mount Lycaeus in Arcadia, where, according to some accounts, Zeus was born. Near this place was a sanctuary and grove of Apollo Parrhasius (Paus. 8.38.8). Remains of an archaic temple at Kramvonos on the road from Isoma Kario to Ano Karies have been identified with Cretea and the sanctuary. Objects from the area are in the National Museum at Athens.

CRETENIA   was a place in Rhodes where Althaemenes, son of Catreus or Creteus, landed when he fled Crete with his sister in order to avoid fulfilling the oracle that said Catreus would be killed by one of his children. Here he erected on Mount Atabyrius an altar to Zeus Atabyrius. Years later Catreus, eager to know his son, sailed to Rhodes, where he and his companions were attacked by shepherds, who thought they were pirates. During the struggle, Althaemenes came to the protection of his subjects and killed his father with a javelin. When he became aware of what he had done, he prayed to the gods and was swallowed up by the earth (Apollod. 3.2.1). The Rhodians subsequently worshipped him as a hero.

The scant remains of ancient Cretenia are on the coast road a few kilometers southwest of Kamiros. The modern inland village of Kritinia farther along the same road is not connected with the ancient place.

CRISSA (HRISO)   a town of Phocis, was situated inland a little southwest of Mount Parnassus. It was said to have been founded by Crisus or Crissus, a son of Phocus (Paus. 2.19.4). Others say that Icadius, a Cretan, guided by a dolphin, came to Mount Parnassus and there gave Delphi and Crissa their names. Its ruins may still be seen at a short distance from the modern village of Hriso. The ruins consist of very ancient polygonal walls, still as high as three meters in some places. The ancient town of Crissa gave its name to the bay above which it stood, and the name was extended from this bay to the whole of the Corinthian Gulf, which was called Crissaean in the most ancient times. Crissa was regarded as one of the most ancient cities in Greece. It was mentioned in the catalog of the *Iliad* (2.520) as the "divine Crissa." According to Homer (*Hymn. Hom. ad Apoll.* 438), it was founded by a colony of Cretans, who were led to the spot by Apollo himself and whom the god had chosen to be his priests in the sanctuary he had intended to establish at Pytho. One of these Cretans was Castalius, who was either a simple mortal or a son of Apollo and father of Delphis. At Crissa he founded the worship of the Delphinian Apollo. The name of Crissa became identified with Delphi in much the way Pisa did with Olympia. In the course of time Cirrha, the port of Delphi, increased at the expense of Crissa. Tolls were levied on pilgrims, which, along with other circumstances, caused the older city to decline. Delphi grew very important and Crissa slipped into insignificance.

CROCEAE (KROKEES)   was a village of Laconia on the road from Sparta to Gythium and celebrated for its marble quarries. There was a marble statue of Zeus Croceatas at the entrance to the village, and at the quarries bronze statues of the Dioscuri (Paus. 3.21.4). These quarries were discovered 3 km southeast of Krokees, and near the village were found some blocks of marble, probably the remains of the statue of Zeus Croceatas. A memorial of the worship of the Dioscuri at this place still exists in a bas-relief representing the two gods with their horses; beneath is a Latin inscription. The modern town is on the road from Sparta to Monemvassia, just beyond its intersection with the Sparti-Githio highway.

CROMMYON (AGII THEODORI)   was a village of the Corinthian district on the Saronic Gulf, but originally it was the last town of Megaris. It was the chief place between the Isthmus and Megara; from its name the whole of this coast was called Crommyonia. Crommyon was 22 km from Corinth and appears to have occupied the site of the ruins near Agii Theodori. The modern village is noted for its crystallized fruits. Crommyon is said by some to have derived its name from Crommus, the son of Poseidon. It is celebrated in mythology as the haunt of the wild sow destroyed by Theseus (Paus. 2.1.3; Plut. *Thes.* 9).

CRUNI   was a spring near Tricoloni, reached by a steep ascent from the town. Descending from Cruni for about 5.5 km, one comes to the grave of Callisto, a high mound of earth, where many trees grew. On the top of the mound was a sanctuary of Artemis Calliste (Most Beautiful) (Paus. 8.35.8).

CTIMENE (KATO KTIMENI)   was a town of Thessaly on the borders of Dolopia and Phthia near Lake Xynias (Apollon. Rhod. 1.67). A tradition was held that Ctimene had been given by Peleus to Phoenix. Phoenix was a son of Amyntor by Cleobule and was king of the Dolopes. He took part in the Calydonian boar hunt and also is said to have accompanied Achilles to Troy (Ov. *Her.* 3.27; Apollod. 3.13.8). His father Amyntor took for himself a mistress, and Cleobule persuaded Phoenix to seduce her rival. Amyntor cursed him for this and prayed that he would never have children. At last Phoenix fled to Peleus, who made him king of the Dolopes on the frontiers of Phthia and made him guardian and teacher of his son,

Achilles (Hom. *Il.* 9.447). The site of Ctimene is probably at Kato Ktimeni, the only place in the region having evidence of occupation from the Mycenaean period. The sanctuary of Omphale was near the boundary between Ctimene and Angeia, which replaced Ctimene as the chief Dolopian city.

CURETIS   was a region in Aetolia. The original inhabitants of Aetolia are said to have been Curetes, who, according to some accounts, had come from Euboea (Strab. 10.3.6). They inhabited the plains between the Achelous and the Evenus Rivers, and the country received in consequence the name of Curetis. Laodocus, a son of Helios and Phthia, a brother of Dorus and Polypoetes, was killed in Curetis by Aetolus (Apollod. 1.7.6), who colonized the area known as Aetolia. The Curetes will also be remembered for their involvement in the story of the Calydonian boar hunt. The kingdom of Calydon was adjacent to Curetis. (See CALYDON.)

CYCHREIA   was an earlier name of the island of SALAMIS.

CYCLADES (KIKLADES)   are a group of islands in the Aegean, lying to the south of Attica and Euboea and so called because they lie in a circle around Delos, the smallest but the most important of them. Ancient geographers disagreed on some of them, but generally they were listed as: Ceos, Cythnos, Seriphos, Siphnos, Paros, Naxos, Delos, Pheneia, Myconos, Syros, Tenos, Andros. Today the Kiklades constitute a political division, which includes around thirty islands all lying in proximity to those listed above.

According to Thucydides (1.4), the Cyclades were originally inhabited by Carians, who were expelled by Minos. The islands were afterward colonized by Ionians and Dorians.

CYDONIA (HANIA)   was one of the most ancient and important cities of Crete. Cydon was its eponymous founder. According to a tradition of Tegea, he was a son of Tegeates or of Hermes by Acacallis, the daughter of Minos; others described him as a son of Apollo by Acacallis (Paus. 8.53.4). Homer (*Od.* 3.292) speaks of the Cydonians who dwelt about the river Iardanus, whom Strabo (10.4.7) considers to be indigenous, but nowhere mentions a city Cydonia. Herodotus (3.44,59) assigns its foundation to the Samians who established themselves there, and during their five-year residence in it built the temple of Dictynna and later temples. The city had a very good harbor, which could be closed, and was adjacent to a fertile plain. The site of Cydonia is Hania, the capital of Crete. Among ancient remains there are very few with mythological content. There is, however, a handsome mosaic depicting Poseidon and Amymone.

The quince tree derived its name from the Cretan Cydonia, in the district of which city it was indigenous and was thence transported into other countries. Athena Cydonia had a temple at Phrixia in Elis, which was said to have been built by Clymenus of Cydonia (Paus. 6.21.6).

CYLLENE (KILINI)   was the seaport town of the city of Elis, from which it was 22 km in distance. Cyllene was an ancient place and is mentioned by Homer (*Il.* 15.518) as one of the towns of the Epeians. Some said that it was the port from which the Pelasgians sailed to Italy. Strabo (8.3.4) described Cyllene as an inconsiderable village having an ivory statue of Asclepius by Colotes, a contemporary of Pheidias. This statue is not mentioned by Pausanias (6.26.5), who speaks, however, of temples of Asclepius and Aphrodite. The site of Cyllene is modern Kilini. The ruins are mainly medieval, but there are traces of classical remains.

CYLLENE (KILLINI)   is a high mountain in the northeast corner of Arcadia upon the Achaian border. It was celebrated as the birthplace of Hermes. Hermes, the son of Zeus and Maia, was born in a cave on this mountain. Consequently, Cyllenius frequently occurs as an epithet of Hermes. There was a temple of Hermes Cyllenius upon the summit of Mount Cyllene, which in the time of Pausanias had fallen to ruin. The name of the mountain was said to have come from Cyllen, the son of Elatus (Paus. 8.4.4,17.1). Elatus, a son of Arcas, was king of Arcadia. He lived on Mount Cyllene and later went to Phocis to help protect Delphi against the Phlegyans. The ruins of the temple are no longer found on the summit.

The ancients regarded Cyllene as the highest mountain in Peloponnesus, but one of the summits of Taygetus rises higher. The summit of Cyllene was supposed to be so high above the wind and clouds that the ashes of the victims sacrificed there to Hermes remained undisturbed from one year's festivals to another.

Toward the north Cyllene sends out a projecting ridge, called in ancient times Chelydorea because Hermes was said to have found here the tortoise shell that he converted into a lyre (Paus. 8.17.5).

CYNAETHA (KALAVRITA)   was a town in the north of Arcadia, situated on the north slope of the Araonian Mountains. Through the valley in which it was located flowed the Erasinus (or Buraicus) River. About a half a kilometer from the town was a fountain called Alyssus, which was said to cure hydrophobia. This fountain is still flowing today. The Cynaethaeans were noted for their independence, cruelty, and wickedness. In the agora were altars of the gods, including a statue of Zeus Olympius. Kalavrita, the modern city, is a summer resort because of its pleasant mountain coolness and impressive scenery.

CYNTHUS (KINTHOS)   is a hill on the island of Delos. Mount Cynthus, from which Apollo, Artemis, and Leto so often take surnames, is a bare rock not more than 113 meters high. It was probably the acropolis of the ancient town and seems to have been surrounded by a wall. In antiquity two flights of steps led up to the summit of the mountain, one on the north, and the other on the west side. On the south summit are the remains of a little sanctuary of Zeus Hypsistus and other gods. To the east has been excavated a sanctuary of Artemis Locheia, with the foundations of a temple having a doorway in the middle of the south side. Ruins of several other sanctuaries are found along the north descent. On its sides are many architectural fragments of white marble, and on its summit stood the sanctuary of Cynthian Zeus and Athena.

CYNTHUS   was an alternate name of DELOS.

CYNURIA (KINOURIA)   was a district on the east coast of Peloponnesus between Argolis and Laconia, so called from the Cynurians, one of the most ancient tribes in the peninsula. Cynurus, a son of Perseus, was said to have led colonists from Argos into Cynuria (Paus. 3.2.1). Upon the conquest of Peloponnesus by the Dorians, the Cynurians were subdued by the Argives, whose territory at one time extended along the east coast of Peloponnesus down to Cape Malea.

The Thyreatis, or territory of Thyrea, which is the only district that can be definitely assigned to Cynuria, is one of the most fertile plains in Peloponnesus. Two streams, the Tanus, or Tanous, and the Charadrus, run through the valley. The bay between the two rivers was called the Thyreatic Gulf (Paus. 2.38.7).

CYNUS (LIVANATES)   the principal seaport of the Locri Opuntii, was situated on a cape at the northern extremity of the Opuntian Gulf, opposite Aedepsus in Euboea and 11 km from Opus (Paus. 10.1.1). Cynus was a son of Opus and father of Hodoedocus and Larymna, and Cynus was named for him (Paus. 9.23.4). It was an ancient town, being mentioned in the Homeric catalog (*Il.* 2.531) and reported to have been the residence of Deucalion and Pyrrha. The tomb of Pyrrha was shown there (Strab. 9.4.2). After the flood, Deucalion was said to have built his first residence in Cynus, but most say the site was Opus. The site of the town is about 1.5 km to the south of the village of Livanates.

CYPARISSIA (KIPARISSIA)   was a town on the west coast of Messenia a little south of the Cyparissus River, upon the bay to which it gave the name Cyparissian Gulf. Cyparissia was the only town of importance on the west coast of Messenia between Pylos and Triphylia. It is mentioned in the Homeric catalog (*Il.* 2.593) and appears to have been inhabited from the earliest to the latest times. It was beautifully situated upon the side of one of the branches of a ridge of mountains that run along this part of the Messenian coast. Upon the narrow summit of the rocks stand the ruins of the acropolis, which was connected with Mount Psikro. In the town was a temple of Apollo and one of Athena Cyparissia. On the south side a stream rushes out of the rock and flows into the sea, and a little above is an ancient structure forming the fountain sacred to Dionysus.

CYPARISSIA was an earlier name of the island of SAMOS.

CYPARISSUS was an ancient town of Phocis in the vicinity of Delphi. It is mentioned in the Homeric catalog (*Il.* 2.519) along with Pytho (Delphi). It was placed by Strabo (9.3.3) below Lycoreia, which was situated on one of the heights of Parnassus. Pausanias (10.36.3), however, says Cyparissus was an earlier name of Anticyra and that it was called by that name even in Homer's time. Cyparissus was named after the cypress trees that grew there, according to some, but others said that it was named for Cyparissus, the brother of Orchomenus. Chalcon, the shield bearer of Antilochus, was from Cyparissus. He was in love with the Amazon Penthesileia; hastening to her assistance, he was killed by Achilles, and the Greeks nailed his body to a cross. (See ANTICYRA.)

CYPHANTA (KIPARISSI) was a town on the east coast of Laconia, belonging to the Eleuthero-Lacones. It was in ruins at the time of Pausanias, but according to earlier writers it must have been a place of some importance (Paus. 3.24.2); Polyb. 4.36). Pausanias describes it as situated the equivalent of 1 km from Zarax and 2 km inland; and others speak separately of the port town and the city. Pausanias (3.24.2) adds that Cyphanta contained a temple of Asclepius and a fountain issuing from a rock, said to have been produced by a blow from the lance of Atalanta. Atalanta was a daughter of Iasus and Clymene. Her father, who had wished for a son, was disappointed at her birth and exposed her on the Parthenian hill by the side of a well and at the entrance of a cave. Modern Kiparissi is a possible site of ancient Cyphanta since it is at once a port, has a fountain, and accords with some ancient distance measures.

CYPHUS was a town of Perrhaebia in Thessaly, which supplied twenty-two ships for the Trojan War. Gouneus led the Perrhaebians and Enienes in these ships. Cyphus is placed by Strabo (9.5.20) at the foot of Mount Olympus (Hom. *Il.* 2.748).

CYRBA was an early name of HIERAPYTNA in Crete.

CYRTONES (PAVLOS?) anciently called Cyrtone, was a city of Boeotia, east of Lake Copais and 3.5 km from Hyettus. It was situated upon a mountain, after crossing which the traveller arrived at Corseia. Cyrtones contained a grove and temple of Apollo, in which were statues of Apollo and Artemis. There was also a fountain, at the source of which was a chapel of the nymphs (Paus. 9.24.4). Cyrtones has been placed on a hill between the villages of Pavlos and Loutsi. These villages are within 10 km northwest of Kastro, the site of ancient Copais. It is reported that here a festival was celebrated every spring, and this has been regarded as the remains of the ancient festival of Apollo and Artemis.

CYTHERA (KITHIRA) is an island lying off the southeast tip of Laconia. Its northern promontory, Platanistus (modern Spathi) was 7.5 km from Onugnathus (modern Elafonissi), from where persons usually crossed over to the island. Cythera is of an irregular oval shape, about 34 km in length from north to south and about 17 km wide. It is very rocky and contains only a few valleys. The stormy Cape Malea and Cythera formed the jumping off place for ancient mariners since the waters beyond had far fewer islands and different winds and currents. The Phoenicians had an ancient settlement on the island, which was the headquarters of their murex fishery off the Laconian coast. For this reason the island was also called Porphrusa or Porphyria. Cythera was said to have derived its name from Cytherus, the son of Phoenix. It was from Cythera that the worship of the Syrian goddess Aphrodite was introduced into Greece, possibly by Phoenicians who developed the purple dye industry. Consequently in Greek legends this island is said to have been the spot that received the goddess after her birth from the foam of the sea. About 5 km above the port of Avlemonas are the ruins of an ancient town in which stood the ancient temple of Aphrodite. In this temple her statue was dressed as the victorious goddess in arms (Paus. 3.23.1). In one account, Aeneas founded a temple of Aphrodite in Cythera during his wanderings after the fall of Troy.

Homer mentions two natives of Cythera. Lycophron, a son of Mastor, was obliged to quit his native Cythera because of a murder he had committed. He accompanied Telamonian Ajax against Troy, where he was slain by Hector (Hom. *Il.* 15.430). Amphidamas was one of the recipients of the famed helmet of Meriones, which he brought to Scandia in his native Cythera before passing it on to Molus (Hom. *Il.* 10.266).

CYTHERUS according to Pausanias (6.22.7) was a river in Elis, next to the village Heracleia, about 9 km from Olympia. A spring flowed into the river, and there was a sanctuary of nymphs near the spring. Individually the names of the nymphs were Calliphaeia, Synallasis, Pegaea, and Iasis, but their common patronynic was Ionides. Those who bathed in the spring were cured of all sorts of aches and pains. They say that the nymphs were named after Ion, the son of Gargettus, who migrated here from Athens.

DARDANIA   was an earlier name of the island of SAMOTHRACE.

DAULIS (DAVLIA)   was a very ancient town of Phocis near the frontier of Boeotia and on the road from Orchomenus and Chaeroneia to Delphi. It is said to have derived its name from the nymph Daulis, a daughter of Cephissus (Paus. 10.4.7). Daulis is mentioned as a Phocian town along with Crissa and Panopeus (Hom. *Il.* 2.520). It is celebrated in mythology as the residence of the Thracian king Tereus, son of Ares, who married Procne, the daughter of Pandion, king at Attica. They had a son named Itys, after which time Tereus concealed Procne somewhere in the country so that he could marry Pandion's other daughter, Philomela. He told Philomela that Procne was dead. At the same time he cut out Philomela's tongue. Philomela, however, soon discovered the truth and wove the story into a garment and sent it to Procne. Procne then came to Philomela and killed her own son Itys. Tereus had been cautioned by an oracle that his son would be killed, and he suspected his brother Dryas, whom he killed. Procne took further vengeance by placing the flesh of her child in a dish before Tereus, after which she and Philomela fled. Tereus pursued them with an ax. When they were overtaken, they prayed to the gods to change them into birds. Procne, accordingly, became a nightingale, Philomela a swallow, and Tereus a hoopoe (Ov. *Met.* 6.424–675). According to some, Procne became a swallow, Philomela a nightingale, and Tereus a hawk. According to the Megarian tradition, Tereus, being unable to overtake the women, killed himself. The Megarians showed the tomb of Tereus in their country, and an annual sacrifice was offered to him. Procne and Philomela were believed to have escaped to Attica, where they wept themselves to death (Paus. 1.41.9). In any case, the woody district around the town is still a favorite haunt of the nightingale, called by the poets the Daulian bird.

Pausanias (10.4.7) relates that the inhabitants of Daulis were few in number but surpassed all the other Phocians in stature and strength. The only building in the town mentioned by him was a temple of Athena. In the nearby district called Tronis there was a shrine of a founder hero by the name of Xanthippus; others call him Phocus, son of Ornytion, son of Sisyphus (Paus. 10.4.10).

The name of Daulis is still preserved in that of the modern village of Davlia. It is situated in a narrow valley, through which flows a branch of the Cephissus called Platania. Located here are the ruins of the ancient church of Agios Theodoros, found within the enclosure of the ancient acropolis. An inscription in the church mentions the worship of Athena Soteira.

DECELEIA (DEKELIA)   a deme of Attica, was situated near the entrance of the east pass across Mount Parnes, which leads from the northeast part of the Athenian plain to Oropus and from there forks to Tanagra in one direction and to Delium and Chalcis in the other. It was originally one of the twelve cities that gave up their autonomy in the reign of Theseus (Strab. 9.1.20). It was situated about 22 km from Athens and the same distance from the borders of Boeotia. It was visible from Athens and from its heights might be seen the ships entering the harbor of Peiraeus (Thuc. 7.19; Xenoph. *Hell.* 1.1.25).

DELIUM (DILESSI)   a village with a celebrated temple of Apollo, was situated on the coast in the territory of Tanagra in Boeotia and about 1.5 km from the territory of Oropus. This temple, which took its name from the island of Delos, overhung the sea and was about 8 km from Tanagra. It was here that the Athenians were defeated by the Boeotians in the eighth year of the Peloponnesian War, 425 B.C. Hippocrates, the Athenian commander, had seized the temple at Delium, which he converted into a fortress. He left a garrison there and started on his march back to Athens. He had already reached the territory of Oropus about 2 km from Delium, when he met the Boeotian army advancing to cut off his retreat. In this battle the Athenians were defeated with great loss; and on the seventeenth day after the battle the Boeotians retook the temple (Thuc. 4.90). The modern village of Dilessi probably occupies the site of the ancient town. Nothing of particular interest has been discovered here.

DELIUM   (See EPIDELIUM)

DELOS (DILOS)   is one of the smallest of the Cyclades, lying in the strait between Rheneia and Myconos. It appears in the earliest times as one of the holiest spots in Greece. According to the most generally accepted tradition, Poseidon with his trident brought it from the depths to the surface of the sea. It was a floating island until Zeus fastened it by silver chains to the bottom of the sea so that it might be a secure place for Leto to give birth to Apollo and Artemis (Virg. *Aen.* 3.76; Plin. 4.12.22). Leto was a daughter of Coeus and Phoebe, sister of Asteria, and mother of Apollo and Artemis by Zeus, to whom she was married before Hera. Later she was described not as the lawful wife of Zeus but as a concubine who was persecuted by Hera during her pregnancy (Apollod. 1.4.1; Callim. *Hymn. in Del.* 61). All the world being afraid to receive her on account of Hera, she wandered till she came to Delos, which was then a floating island and bore the name Asteria (Callim. *Hymn.*

in Dian. 35,37,191). But when Leto touched Delos, it suddenly stood still upon four pillars (Strab. 10.5.2). Delos was previously called Ortygia, and Artemis derived the surname Ortygia from this early name. Asteria was also a daughter of the Titans Coeus and Phoebe and sister of Leto. She was beloved by Zeus, and in order to escape his embraces she metamorphosed into a quail, threw herself into the sea, and was here changed into the island Asteria, which for a long time lay under the surface of the sea. When Leto fled here to escape Python, she prayed for the island to rise from the sea to receive her. Leto then gave birth to Apollo, who slew Python (Ov. *Met.* 6.370). Leto was generally worshipped only in conjunction with her children. As the birthplace of Apollo, Delos became one of the chief seats of his worship, and the god is said to have obtained exclusive possession of the island by giving Calaureia to Poseidon in exchange for it (Strab. 8.6.14). In the same way, the Delphians related that Apollo gave Calaureia to Poseidon in order to obtain possession of Delphi (Paus. 10.5.6). Delos was called by various other names by the poets and mythographers. Pliny (4.12.22) mentions the names Asteria, Ortygia, Lagia, Chlamydia, Cynthus, Pyrpile, and another writer refers to Pelasgia. The name Delos was supposed by the ancient writers to have been given to the island from its becoming clear or plain (*delos*) after floating about in the sea. In consequence of its having been fastened by Zeus to the bottom of the sea, it was supposed to be immovable even by earthquakes, to which the surrounding islands were frequently subject. During the fight between the giants and the gods, Porphyrion, one of the giants, a son of Uranus and Gaea, tried to rape Hera or, according to others, attempted to throw the island of Delos against the gods. Zeus hurled a thunderbolt at him, and Heracles completed his destruction with his arrows (Apollod. 1.6.2; Pind. *Pyth.* 8.12; Hor. *Carm.* 3.4.54; Claud. *Gigantom.* 114).

An interesting alternate account of the foundation of Delos has to do with a mortal. Melus was a Delian who fled to Cinyras in Cyprus. Cinyras gave him his son Adonis as a companion and his relative Peleia in marriage. Their son, also named Melus, was brought up in the sanctuary of Aphrodite. The younger Melus, after the death of his parents, who had committed suicide when Adonis was killed, was ordered by Aphrodite to return with a colony to Delos, where he founded the town of Delos. There the sheep were called *mela* by him because he first taught the inhabitants to shear them and make cloth out of their wool.

Several places claimed to be the birthplace of Apollo, but the opinion most universally held was that he was born on Delos, together with his sister Artemis. The earliest accounts, as shown, were confused, sometimes involving the monster Python, sometimes involving the jealousy of Hera. But eventually a kind of standard version evolved. Hera in her jealousy pursued Leto from land to land, from isle to isle, and endeavored to prevent her from finding a resting place in which to give birth. At last, however, Leto arrived in Delos, where she was kindly received, and after laboring for nine days she gave birth to Apollo under a palm or an olive tree at the foot of Mount Cynthus. She was assisted by all the goddesses except Hera and Eileithyia; but Eileithyia, too, hastened to give her aid, as soon as she heard what was taking place. The island, which previously had been unsteady, either floating on or buried under the waves of the sea, now became stationary and was fastened to the roots of the world. The day of Apollo's birth was believed to have been on the seventh of the month, from which he is called Hebdomagenis (Plut. *Quaest. Conviv.* 8). According to some, he was a seven months' child. The number seven was sacred to the god; on the seventh of every month sacrifices were offered to him, and his festivals usually fell on the seventh day of a month. Immediately after his birth, Apollo was fed with ambrosia and nectar by Themis, and no sooner had he tasted the divine food then he sprang up and demanded a lyre and a bow and declared that henceforth he would declare to men the will of Zeus.

No conclusive evidence exists regarding the origin of the worship of Apollo at Delos. Some have assumed that it was introduced by the Dorians. In the earliest historical times the island was inhabited by Ionians and was represented as the center of a great periodic festival in honor of Apollo, celebrated by all the Ionic cities on the mainland as well as in the islands. The festival was conducted with great splendor, and, as at Delphi, there were musical as well as gymnastic contests. Like the Olympic and other great festivals of Hellas, it doubtless grew out of one of a more limited character, and we are informed that Delos was originally the center of an amphictyony to which the Cyclades and neighboring islands belonged (Thuc. 3.104; Strab. 10.5.2). The Athenians took part in this festival, and it was related at a later period that they instituted the festival to commemorate the safe return of Theseus from Crete and that the vessel in which the sacred embassy sailed to the festival was the same one that had carried Theseus and his companions (Plut. *Thes.* 21). The festival later fell into decay at the start of the Peloponnesian War, but in the sixth year of this war, 426 B.C., the Athenians purified Delos. They removed all the tombs from the island and declared it unlawful from that time for any living being to be born or die there, and that every pregnant woman should be carried over to the island of Rheneia in order to be delivered (Thuc. 3.104; Strab. 10.5.5). On this occasion the Athenians restored the ancient festival under the name of Delia. Four years later they decided that the removal of the Delians themselves was essential to complete the purification of the island, and they banished all the inhabitants, who obtained a settlement at Atramythium.

One of Apollo's surnames was Lyceius. This name has been explained in various ways. One was that Leto came to Delos as a she-wolf and was conducted by wolves to the river Xanthus in Lycia.

Anius was a son of Apollo by Rhoeo, daughter of Staphylus, who, when her pregnancy became known, was exposed by her angry father in a chest on the waves of the sea. The chest landed in Delos, and when Rhoeo was delivered of a boy, she consecrated him to the service of Apollo, who endowed him with prophetic powers (Diod. 5.62). Anius had by Dryope three daughters, Oeno, Spermo, and Elais, to whom Dionysus gave the power of producing at will any quantity of wine, wheat, and oil— whence they were called Oenotropae. When the Greeks on their expedition to Troy landed on Delos, Anius endeavored to persuade them to stay with him for nine years, as it was decreed by fate that they should not take Troy until the tenth year, and he promised with the help of his daughters to supply them with all they wanted during that period (Ov. *Met.* 13.623). Instead, Agamemnon wanted to carry the daughters by force with the Greeks to Troy, but they implored Dionysus for assistance, and they were accordingly metamorphosed into doves (Ov. *Met.* 13.640).

Glaucus, the mortal who was changed into a marine deity, was also associated with Delos. Aristotle stated that he lived in Delos, where, in conjunction with the nymphs, he gave oracles. His prophetic power was said by some to be even greater than that of Apollo, who is called his disciple in it.

Most accounts say that Artemis was born at the same time as Apollo, but one account says that she was born somewhat earlier so that she was able to assist Leto in giving birth to Apollo. She was, as a kind of female Apollo, worshipped all over Greece but particularly in Delos. According to some, she killed Orion, the handsome giant and hunter, in Delos. They said he was loved by Artemis, and Apollo, indignant at his sister's affection for Orion, stated that she could not hit with one of her arrows a distant point that he showed to her in the sea. She thereupon took aim and hit it, but the point was the head of Orion, who had been swimming far out in the water (Ov. *Fast.* 5.537).

Two Hyperborean maidens, Hecaerge and Hyperoche, daughters of Boreas, were sent, according to the Delian tradition, to carry to the island certain sacred offerings enclosed in stalks of wheat. In this way they can be said to have introduced the worship of Artemis to Delos (Callim. *Hymn. in Del.* 292; Paus. 1.43.4, 5.7.9). The two maidens died on Delos and were honored by the

Delians with certain ceremonies (Herod. 4.33–35). Some writers claim there were several other companions, including Laodice and Loxo. Loxo, in fact, was used as a surname of Artemis (Callim. *Hymn. in Del.* 292). Delia was also her surname, derived from her birthplace, just as Apollo's was Delius. These names are also applied, especially in the plural, to other divinities who were worshipped in Delos, e.g., Demeter, Aphrodite, and the nymphs (Aristoph. *Thes.* 333; Callim. *Hymn. in Dian.* 169).

Besides Apollo and Artemis, other divinities shared in the general sacred atmosphere of worship on Delos. Among these was the ubiquitous Demeter. Dione, the mother of Aphrodite, was also worshipped here, as was Aphrodite herself. A small wooden statue of Aphrodite was ascribed to Daedalus. He was said to have made it for Ariadne, who carried it to Delos when she fled with Theseus. After the fall of Troy, Aphrodite's son Aeneas wintered in Thrace and then traveled around Greece and various islands, founding towns and building temples to his mother. On Delos he was kindly received by Anius; and a Greek tradition stated that Aeneas married a daughter of Anius by the name of Lavinia, who was, like her father, endowed with prophetic powers, and who followed Aeneas to Italy and died at Lavinium (Dionys. 1.59).

The Charites, the personifications of grace and beauty, usually in the form of three lovely women, were represented at Delos in conjunction with the most ancient statue of Apollo, where they were carried on his hand. Brizo was a prophetic goddess of Delos, who sent dreams and revealed their meaning to mankind. The women of Delos offered sacrifices to her in vessels shaped like boats, and the sacrifices consisted of various things; but fishes were never offered to her. Prayers were addressed to her that she might grant everything that was good, but especially that she might protect ships (Athen. 8.335).

Eileithyia, the goddess of birth, was present at the birth of Apollo and Artemis, and she was worshipped in Delos. Erysichthon, a son of Cecrops and Agraulos, died without issue in his father's lifetime, on his return from Delos, from where he brought to Athens the ancient image of Eileithyia.

After the fall of Corinth in 146 B.C., Delos became the center of extensive commerce. The sanctity of the spot and its consequent security, its festival that was a kind of fair, the excellence of its harbor, and its convenient situation on the route from Italy and Greece to Asia made it a favorite resort of merchants (Strab. 10.5.4).

Delos is little more than a rock, being only 8 km in circumference. The town is described by Strabo (10.5.2) as lying in a plain at the foot of Mount Cynthus, and the only buildings that he describes are the hieron of Apollo and the temple of Leto. The town was situated on the western side of the island. Mount Cynthus, after which

Apollo and Leto are so often called, is a bare granite rock not more than 133 meters high. It was probably the acropolis of the ancient town and seems to have been surrounded by a wall.

Ancient writers speak of a little river Inopus on the island. They compare its rising and falling with the same phenomena of the Nile, and some even suppose there was a connection between it and the Egyptian river (Strab. 6.2.4; Callim. *Hymn. in Del.* 206,263; Paus. 2.5.3). We also find mention of a lake or tank called Limni Trochoeides or Trochoessa, containing the water necessary for the service of the temple of Apollo. Near this lake Leto is said to have brought forth her divine children (Aeschyl. *Eum.* 9; Eurip. *Ion* 169, *Iphig. Taur.* 1103). Others represent the birthplace as near the Inopus (*Hymn. Hom. ad Apoll.* 18; Callim. *Hymn. in Del.* 206). Leto is said to have grasped a palm tree when she bore her children, and the palm was especially revered on Delos. The identical palm tree of Leto was shown in the time of Cicero (*De Leg.* 1.1).

Delos is now a heap of ruins. Whole shiploads of columns and architectural remains were carried away centuries ago to Venice and Constantinople. Of the great temple of Apollo and of numerous other buildings there is scarcely the capital of a column or an architrave left uninjured. There are still remains of the colossal statue of Apollo dedicated by the Naxians. This statue was toppled in antiquity. The sacred area of Apollo has many buildings, chief among which are the three temples of Apollo; in one of these temples was housed the treasury of the Delian confederacy.

Excavations were begun in 1873, and a great deal of the sixth century B.C. sanctuary has been uncovered, including later additions. On the Sacred Way leading to the temples of Apollo are an Artemision, or temple of Artemis, an altar of the Hyperborean maidens Laodice and Hyperoche, and an enclosure dedicated to two others, Opis and Arge. There are foundations of a building and blocks from its frieze representing the exploits of Theseus. There is a shrine of Dionysus featuring monuments in the form of huge phalli.

The Lion Terrace and the temple of Leto remain. Foundations of the altars of the twelve gods are near this Letoon. Nearby are shrines to Roma, Poseidon, and two other divinities dedicated by the Berytians. To the east are other sanctuaries, including one devoted to the Cabeiri. At the foot of Mount Cynthus is the so-called Terrace of the Foreign Gods, which includes remains of temples to Serapis and Isis. On the summit of Cynthus are foundations of the joint sanctuary of Zeus Cynthius and Athena Cynthia. On the summit are remains of the sanctuary of Zeus Hypsistus. On the east a sanctuary of Artemis Locheia has been excavated. At the base of Mount Cynthus are foundations of the Heraion, or temple of

Hera. On the west face of the rock are the remains of a sanctuary of Tyche, the goddess of fortune. In a cleft in the rock was a sanctuary of Heracles. Near the stadium area is the sanctuary of Anius dating from the sixth century B.C. To the south of the sanctuary of Apollo is a sanctuary thought to be the Dioscureion, and farther to the south the Asclepieion. This short list does not do justice to this incredible congregation of ruins. Only a detailed guidebook could begin to do so. Apart from remains of sacred buildings, there are walls, mosaics, and courts of private houses, roads which led to them, and cisterns. Most of the finds are housed in the Delos museum.

The strait separating Delos and Rheneia (modern Rinia) is about three-quarters of a kilometer in width. On the east coast of Rheneia can be found the necropolis of the Delians. A sanctuary of Heracles has also been found on the island. In this strait are two rocks called Revmataria, of which one is probably the ancient island of Hecate.

DELPHI (DELFI)   was a town of Phocis and one of the most celebrated places in the Hellenic world in consequence of its oracle of Apollo.

The situation of Delphi is one of the most striking and sublime in all Greece. It lies in the narrow vale of the Pleistus, which is shut in on one side by Mount Parnassus and on the other by Mount Cirphis. At the foot of Parnassus is a lofty wall of rocks called Phaedriades in antiquity and rising 610 meters above the sea level. This rocky barrier faces the south, and two lower ridges drop toward the Pleistus. About the middle of the semicircular recess thus formed lies the town of Delphi. The Phaedriades are cleft in the middle into two towering cliffs. Between them gushes the Castalian spring, which flows down the hill into the Pleistus. The ancient town lay on both sides of the stream, but the greater part of it on the left, or west, bank. Above the town was the sanctuary of the god, immediately under the Phaedriades.

Delphi was shut in on all sides from the rest of the world and could not be seen by any of the numerous pilgrims who visited it until they had crossed one of its rocky barriers. Three roads led to Delphi—one from Boeotia, the celebrated Schiste, and two others from the west. Of these western two, one led from Amphissa, and the other from Crissa, the modern Hriso, which was the one taken by the pilgrims coming from Cirrha. Delphi was fortified by nature, on the north, east, and west by the Phaedriades and the two projecting ridges; it was only undefended on the south. The circumference of the city was only about 3 km. The Delphian valley, or that part of the Pleistus lying at the foot of the town, is mentioned in the Homeric *Hymn to Apollo* (284).

The town of Delphi owes its origin as well as its importance to the oracle of Apollo. According to some traditions, it had belonged to other divinities before it passed into the hands of Apollo. In Aeschylus it is represented as held in succession by Gaea, Themis, and the Titaness Phoebe, the last of whom gave it to Apollo when he came from Delos (*Eum.* 1). As the source from which arose the vapors producing divine inspiration, Gaea was also regarded as an oracular divinity. She had an altar at Delphi at a later date. Themis, another Titaness, was also a prophetic divinity. It was Themis whom Deucalion consulted at Delphi about the best means of repeopling the earth after the great flood. Phoebe was the grandmother of Apollo. Pausanias (10.5.6) says that it was originally the joint oracle of Poseidon and Gaea; that Gaea gave her share to Themis, and Themis to Apollo; and that Apollo obtained from Poseidon the other half by giving him in exchange the island of Calaureia. The proper name of the oracle was Pytho; Delphi, which was subsequently the name of the town, does not occur in Homer. In the *Iliad* (9.405) the temple of Phoebus Apollo at the rocky Pytho is already filled with treasures; and in the catalog of the ships the inhabitants of Pytho are mentioned in the same line with those of Cyparissus (Hom. *Il.* 9.405). In the *Odyssey* (8.80) Agamemnon consults the oracle at Pytho. It thus appears in the most ancient times as a sacred spot; but the legend of its foundation is first related in the Homeric *Hymn to Apollo* (287–546). In this poem, Apollo, seeking for a spot where he may found an oracle, comes at last to Crissa under Mount Parnassus. He is charmed with the solitude and sublimity of the place, and begins at once to erect a temple, which is finished under the superintendence of the brothers Trophonius and Agamedes. They were sons of Erginus, king of Orchomenus, and had distinguished themselves as architects, especially in building temples and palaces. A tradition mentioned by Cicero (*Tusc.* 1.47) states that after having built the temple, they prayed to the god to grant them for their labor what was best for men. The god promised to do so on a certain date, and when that day came, the two brothers died. Some accounts say that Agamedes was a son of Apollo and step-father of Trophonius. Apollo then slew the huge serpent, a son of Gaea, which had infested the place; and from the monster the temple was called Pytho and the god Pythian.

According to others, Parnassus, a son of Cleopompus or Poseidon and the nymph Cleodora, is said to have been the founder of Delphi, the inventor of the art of foretelling the future from the flight of birds, and to have given his name to Mount Parnassus (Paus. 10.6.1). As for the building of the temple, the one by Agamedes and Trophonius was claimed by some to be the third one. The tradition was that the first temple was made of branches of the wild laurel from Tempe. The second, designed by Pteras, an artist from Delphi, was made by bees, of wax and bees' wings.

The temple now wanted priests; and the god, beholding a Cretan ship sailing from Cnossus, meta-morphosed himself into a dolphin and brought the vessel into the Crissaean Gulf. The Cretans and their leader Icadius landed and, conducted by the god, came to Mount Parnassus and gave Delphi and Crissa their names; they also became the priests of the temple. Apollo taught them to worship him under the name of Apollo Delphinius because he had met them in the form of a dolphin. Some writers suppose that this temple was really founded by colonists from Crete and that the very name Crissa points to a Cretan origin. Crissa at first had the superintendence of the sanctuary, but as a town gradually grew up around the sanctuary, the inhabitants of Delphi claimed to administer the affairs of the temple independently of the Crissaeans.

Several mythological accounts grew up around the worship of Apollo at Delphi. Apollo Lyceius was the name of the god there, but its meaning was uncertain. Many thought it had a connection with wolves. The descendants of Deucalion, who founded Lycoreia, near Delphi, followed the howl of a wolf. Near the great altar at Delphi there stood an iron wolf with an inscription (Paus. 10.14.7).

Daphne was an Oread and an ancient priestess of the Delphic oracle, to which she had been appointed by Gaea. She was loved and pursued by Apollo. On the point of being overtaken by him, she prayed to Gaea, who opened up the earth and received her. In order to console Apollo, Gaea created the evergreen laurel tree, boughs of which Apollo made into a wreath for himself (Ov. *Met.* 1.453–568).

Branchus was a son of Apollo. His mother, a Milesian, dreamed at the time she gave birth to him that the sun was passing through her body, and the seers interpreted this as a favorable sign. Apollo loved the boy for his great beauty and endowed him with prophetic power, which he exercised at Didyma near Miletus. His descendants, the Branchidae, were priests and held in great esteem (Herod. 1.157; Strab. 14.1.5).

Among others identified with Delphi were the Charites (Graces). They were represented at Delphi as carried on the hand of the ancient statue of Apollo. Still another local figure was Manto, a daughter of the seer Teiresias. She herself was a prophetess, first of the Ismenian Apollo at Thebes and subsequently of the Delphian and Clarian Apollo. After the taking of Thebes by the Epigoni, she, with other captives, was dedicated to Apollo at Delphi. The god sent the captives to Asia, where they founded a sanctuary of Apollo not far from the place where later Colophon was built.

The Muses were always identified with Apollo. In early times there were only three of them. At Delphi their names were identical with those of the lowest, middle, and highest chord of the lyre—Nete, Mese, and Hypate (Plut. *Quaest. Conviv.* 9.14). They were also known as Cephisso, Apollonis, and Borysthenis by those who considered them daughters of Apollo. Apart from their inspirational powers was their prophetic power, which belonged to them partly because of their connection with the prophetic god of Delphi. Mount Parnassus was sacred to them as well as the Castalian spring, near which they had a temple.

Hestia, the goddess of the hearth, was, like Artemis and Athena, a maiden divinity, and when Apollo and Poseidon sued for her hand, she swore by the head of Zeus to remain forever a virgin (*Hymn. Hom. ad Ven.* 24). The connection of Hestia, Apollo, and Poseidon appears also in the temple of Delphi, where the three divinities were worshipped in common.

In addition to these beings who were involved in one way or another with Apollo, there were a few divinities who were included in seemingly independent relationships with the general climate of worship. The Celedones (Soothing Goddesses) were frequently represented by the ancients in works of art. Hephaestus was said to have made their golden images on the ceiling of the temple at Delphi (Paus. 10.5.12; Athen. 7.290; Philostr. *Vit. Apoll.* 6.11). A Sibyl was one of the prophetic women who occur in various countries at different times. There was a Delphian Sibyl—an elder Delphian, who was a daughter of Zeus and Lamia, and a younger one (Paus. 10.12.1) And finally, Baetylus was the name of a peculiar kind of conical shaped stones, which were erected as symbols of gods in remarkable places. The stone that was given to Cronus to swallow instead of the infant Zeus was called Baetylus; and a little above the temple of Delphi, on the left, there was a stone that was anointed with oil every day, and on solemn occasions covered with raw wool. Tradition said that this stone was the one that Cronus had swallowed (Paus. 10.24.6).

Meanwhile Cirrha, which was originally the seaport of Crissa, increased at the expense of the latter; and thus Crissa declined in importance as Cirrha and Delphi grew. It is probable that Crissa had already sunk into insignificance before the Sacred War in 595 B.C., which ended in the destruction of Cirrha by the order of the Amphictyonic Council, and in the dedication of the Cirrhaean Plain to the town. The spoils of Cirrha were employed by the Amphictyons in founding the Pythian games, which were after that time celebrated every four years. The first celebration of the Pythian games took place in 586 B.C. The horse races and foot races were celebrated in the plain near the site of Cirrha, but later the stadium was moved to Delphi, where the musical and poetical matches had always been held.

From the time of the destruction of Cirrha, Delphi was indisputably an independent state, whatever may have been its political condition before that time. Delphi is said to have received its name from one of two individuals named Delphus. One of them was a son of Poseidon and Melantho, a daughter of Deucalion. The other was a son of Apollo and Celaeno. He is said to have had a son Pythis, who ruled over the country around Mount Parnassus, and from whom the oracle received the name Pytho (Paus. 10.6.3). The population came from Lycoreia, a town situated upon one of the heights of Parnassus above the sanctuary. This town is said to have been founded by Deucalion, and from it the Delphian nobles derived their origin. It is related that the boat that preserved Deucalion and Pyrrha landed atop Mount Parnassus. They were not the only ones saved. The inhabitants of Delphi were said to have been saved by following the howling of wolves, which led them to the summit of Parnassus, where they founded Lycoreia (Paus. 10.6.2). According to the common tradition, Deucalion and Pyrrha went to the sanctuary of Themis at Delphi and prayed that Zeus might restore mankind. The goddess bade them cover their heads and throw the bones of their mother behind them in walking from the temple. They correctly interpreted the command as meaning the stones of the earth, and they accordingly threw stones behind them; from those thrown by Deucalion there sprang up men and from those by Pyrrha women.

The five chief priests of the god, called *hosiai,* were chosen by lot from a number of families who derived their descent from Deucalion (Paus. 10.6.2; Plut. *Quaest. Gr.* 9.380). It has been conjectured that the inhabitants of Lycoreia were Dorians, who had settled in the heights of Parnassus. At all events, a Doric dialect was spoken at Delphi; and the oracle always showed a leaning toward Greeks of the Doric race. The government of Delphi appears at first to have been in the exclusive possession of a few noble families. They had the entire management of the oracle, and from them were chosen the five *hosiai.* These priests formed a criminal court that sentenced by Pythian decision all offenders against the temple to be hurled from a precipice. The chief magistrates were chosen from the noble families. Owing not only its prosperity but even its very existence to the oracle, the government was of a theocratic nature. The god possessed large domains, which were cultivated by the slaves of the temple. In addition to this, the Delphian citizens received numerous presents from the monarchs and wealthy men who consulted the oracle, while at the same time the numerous sacrifices offered by strangers were sufficient for their support. Gyges, the founder of the last Lydian dynasty, presented valuable gifts to the god (Herod. 1.13.14); and Croesus, the last monarch of this race, was one of the greatest benefactors the god ever had. In 548 B.C. the temple was destroyed by fire (Paus.

10.5.13), but was splendidly rebuilt at a cost of 300 talents.

In 480 B.C. Xerxes sent a detachment of his army to plunder the temple. The Delphians sought safety on the heights of Mount Parnassus but were forbidden by the god to remove the treasures from his temple. Only sixty Delphians remained behind, encouraged by divine portents. The Persians, arriving from the east, began to climb the rugged path leading up to the shrine. They had already reached the temple of Athena Pronaea when suddenly thunder roared and a war cry sounded from the temple of Athena. Then two huge crags rolled down from the mountains and crushed many to death. Seized with panic, the Persians fled, pursued by two warriors of superhuman size, who (the Delphians affirmed) were the two heroes Phylacus and Autonous, whose sanctuaries were near the spot. Herodotus, when he visited Delphi, saw in the sacred enclosure of Athena Pronaea the very crags that had crushed the Persians.

In 357 B.C. the Phocians, who had been accused by the Amphictyonic Council of making use of part of the sacred land for their own profit, were persuaded by Philomelus to seize the temple of Delphi itself. The enterprise was successful, and Delphi with all its treasures passed into the hands of the Phocians. This gave rise to the celebrated Sacred Wars, which are related in all histories of Greece. When at length the wars were brought to a conclusion by Philip of Macedon and the temple restored to the custody of the Amphictyons in 346 B.C., its more valuable treasures had disappeared, though it still contained most of its works of art. The Phocians were sentenced to replace these treasures, but they were far too poor to be able to do so. In 279 B.C. the Gauls attacked the temple but were repulsed in the same supernatural manner as the Persians had been. The temple was plundered by Sulla when he also robbed those of Olympia and Epidaurus. Strabo (9.3.8) describes the temple as very poor in his time. It was again rifled by Nero, who carried off five hundred bronze statues (Paus. 10.7.1). At the same time, angry with the god, Nero deprived the temple of the Cirrhaean territory, which he distributed among his soldiers, and abolished the oracle (Dio Cass. 63.14). But in the reign of Hadrian and that of Antoninus the oracle reached greater splendor than it had enjoyed since the time of the Sacred Wars. In this condition it was seen and described by Pausanias; and we learn from Plutarch (*De Pyth. Or.* 24) that the Pythia still continued to give responses. Coins of Delphi are found down to the time of Caracalla (A.D. 188–217). Constantine carried off several of its works of art to adorn his new capital. The oracle was consulted by Julian, but in A.D. 390 it was finally silenced by Theodosius.

Upon entering the town from the east, one comes first to some temples, the principal one being that of Athena Pronaea. Actually there are two temples of Athena Pronaea, one older than the other. Here sacrifices were offered before consulting the oracle. The goddess is called Pronaea from her dwelling in front of the temple of Apollo. The gateway to the precinct was dedicated to Athena Hygieia and Athena Zosteria. Near the gate were altars of Athena Hygieia and of Eileithyia. Inside the area were altars to Athena Ergane and to Zeus Polieus and Zeus Mechaneus.

A little above the temple of Athena was the sanctuary of Phylacus, a native hero, who along with his comrade Autonous assisted the Delphians, when the Persians and the Gauls made attempts upon the temple.

In ascending from the gymnasium (adjacent to the temple of Athena) to the temple of Apollo, one passes the fountain of Castalia on the right of the road. The illustrious fountain issues from the fissure between the Phaedriades, the two summits of which were sacred to Dionysus. Above them was the Corycian cave, which also belonged to Dionysus and his attendants, the Corycian nymphs.

The fountain of Castalia was the source of the holy water of the Delphian temple. Beside it Apollo planted a sprig of laurel he brought from Tempe. All persons who came to consult the oracle, wished to pray to the god before engaging in any of the matches of the Pythian games, or visited Delphi for any religious object whatsoever were obliged to purify themselves at this sacred spring (Pind. *Pyth.* 4.290, 5.39; Plut. *Arist.* 20). Even the servants of the temple used the water for the same purpose (Eurip. *Ion* 94). There are steps leading down to remains of a bath cut out of the rock that received the waters of the spring. The base of a statue of Gaea, the goddess of the earth, suggests that the spring was very early a site of chthonic cult worship.

The aged women who were elected to the office of Pythia from the Delphian families appear never to have bathed in the spring or, at all events, only upon their consecration to their prophetic office, since they lived in the temple without coming in contact with any profane objects and consequently needed no further purification.

The road from the Castalian spring led to the principal entrance to the Pythian sanctuary. The sanctuary, which contained several other buildings besides the temple, was enclosed by a wall. Inside the enclosure the first objects seen were statues of athletes and other dedicatory offerings. As late as Pliny's time these numbered no less than three thousand. Nero, as has been stated, carried off five hundred of these. They almost completely lined the Sacred Way, which led upward to the temple.

Pausanias (10.12.1) and Plutarch (*De Pyth. Or.* 9) mention the Stone of the Sibyl, which was a rock rising above the ground and was so called because it was the seat occupied by the first Sibyl. Near the Stone were the Thesauri (Treasuries) which did not stand on a single platform as at Olympia, but were built separately around the Stone of the Sibyl as far as the great altar. They were small buildings, partly above and partly below the ground, in which were kept the more valuable offerings and those that could not be exposed without injury to the air. The most celebrated of all the treasuries was that of the Corinthians, said to have been built by Cypselus (Paus. 10.13.5; Herod. 1.14, 4.162). The stoa, built by the Athenians, also served as a treasury (Paus. 10.11.6). It apparently stood east of the Stone of the Sibyl. Its frieze depicted the feats of Heracles and Theseus.

Near the stoa of the Athenians was the Bouleuterion (Senate House) of the Delphians (Plut. *De Pyth. Or.* 9). Higher up was the sanctuary of Gaea-Themis, the site of the primitive oracle guarded by Python. A nearby rock supported a statue of Leto. Farther up to the east is a rectangular base of the chariot of Helios, dedicated by the Rhodians.

In front of the temple and under the open heaven stood the great altar of Apollo, where the daily sacrifices were offered. It is probably the same as the altar mentioned by Herodotus (2.135) as a dedicatory offering of the Chians. Near the altar stood a bronze wolf, dedicated by the Delphians themselves (Paus. 10.14.7). Between the altar and the temple are bases of other monuments; one base, large and square, perhaps bore the statue of Apollo Sitalcus.

As for the temple itself, the columns of the exterior were of the Doric order. The front was built of Parian marble, while the remainder was of ordinary stone.

One of the pediments featured statues of Artemis, Leto, Apollo, the Muses, and the setting sun; the other held statues of Dionysus and the Thyiades (Paus. 10.19.4). Dionysus, as god of wine, was regarded both as an inspired and an inspiring god, who had the power of revealing to man the future by oracles. Thus, it is said, that he had as great a share in the Delphian oracles as Apollo (Eurip. *Bacch.* 300). Thyia, a daughter of Castalius or Cephissus, became by Apollo the mother of Delphus. She is said to have been the first to have sacrificed to Dionysus and to have celebrated orgies in his honor. Consequently, the Attic women, who every year went to Mount Parnassus to celebrate the Dionysiac orgies with the Delphian Thyiades, received themselves the name Thyades or Thyiades (Paus. 10.4.3).

The subjects of the metopes of the temple reflected slaughter: Heracles and Iolaus killing the Lernaean hydra, Bellerophon killing the Chimaera, Zeus killing Mimas, Pallas killing Enceladus, and Dionysus killing another of the giants (Eurip. *Ion* 190–218). As in the Parthenon, there were gilded shields beneath the metopes, dedicated from the spoils of wars.

The interior of the temple consisted of three divisions, the pronaus (front porch), the cella (enclosed main chamber), and the adytum (innermost shrine) where the oracles were delivered. On the walls of the pronaus were inscribed in golden letters the celebrated sayings of the Seven Wise Men, such as "Know thyself," and "Nothing too much" (Plut. *De Garrul.* 17; Paus. 10.24.1). Here also was set up in wood the fifth letter of the Greek alphabet, which, according to tradition, was dedicated in common by the Seven Wise Men. It was an epsilon, a simple *E,* which in the ancient Greek writing also represented the diphthong *EI.* There were various interpretations of its meaning, of which Plutarch has given an account in his treatise upon the subject, *De E apud Delphos.*

It appears that the cella was supported by Ionic columns. Inside was an altar of Poseidon, to whom the oracle partially belonged in the most ancient times; statues of two Moirae (Fates); statues of Zeus Moiragetes and Apollo Moiragetes, leaders of the Fates; the hearth upon which the priest of Apollo killed Neoptolemus, the son of Achilles; and the iron chair of Pindar, on which he is said to have sung his hymns to Apollo (Paus. 10.24.4).

The adytum, in which the oracles were delivered, was a subterranean chamber which no one was allowed to enter except the priests or those to whom special permission was given. It is described as situated in the inmost part of the temple. In the adytum was also the *Omphalos* (Navel-Stone), which was supposed to mark the middle point of the earth (Aeschyl. *Choeph.* 1034; Eurip. *Ion* 461). According to tradition, two eagles, which had been sent by Zeus, one from the east and the other from the west, met at this point and thus determined it to be the center of the earth (Pind. *Pyth.* 4.131, 6.3). The *Omphalos* is a white stone adorned with stripes of various kinds, and upon it are pictured the two eagles. It now stands on the landing of the Museum and was found in the south wall of the temple.

In the middle of the adytum stood a tripod over a deep chasm in the earth from which arose an intoxicating vapor, which was supposed to inspire the priestess with the gift of prophecy. According to Plutarch (*De Def. Or.* 50, *De Pyth. Or.* 17), this vapor arose from a fountain, said by Pausanias (10.24.7) to have been the fountain Cassotis, which disappeared beneath the ground in the adytum. The Pythia sat upon a tripod when she gave the oracles of Apollo; the object of the tripod was to prevent her falling into the chasm (Diod. 16.26). Between the legs of the tripod was suspended a circular vessel, in which were preserved the bones and teeth of the Pythian serpent. No vapor is now found issuing from any part of the Delphian rocks.

Slightly northeast of the temple is the tomb of Neoptolemus, to whom the Delphians offered sacrifices every year (Paus. 10.24.6; Strab. 9.3.9). He was said to have been murdered in the temple near the sacred hearth. After the Trojan War, Neoptolemus went to Sparta to claim Hermione, who had been promised to him, because he had heard that she had been earlier betrothed to Orestes. Shortly after his marriage he went to Delphi, some say to plunder the temple of Apollo, who had been the cause of the death of Achilles, or to demand a reckoning for his father's death. According to others, his motives were more benign. He wanted to take offerings of the Trojan booty to the god or to consult him about the means of obtaining children by Hermione. It is owing to this uncertainty that some ancient writers distinguish between two different journeys to Delphi, where he was slain, either by the command of the Pythia or at the instigation of Orestes, who was angry at being deprived of Hermione (Eurip. *Androm.* 891, 1085; Virg. *Aen.* 3.330); and, according to others again, by the priest of the temple. His body was buried at Delphi under the threshold of the temple and remained there until Menelaus caused it to be taken up and buried within the precincts of the temple (Pind. *Nem.* 7.62; Paus. 10.24.4). He was worshipped at Delphi as a hero, as presiding over sacrificial repasts and public games. At the time when the Gauls attacked Delphi, he is said to have come forward to protect the city and from that time to have been honored with heroic worship (Paus. 1.4.4, 10.23.2).

Above the tomb of Neoptolemus was the stone that Cronus was said to have swallowed instead of his son Zeus. He afterward vomited up the stone, which was not very large. Every day the attendants of the temple anointed the stone with oil and on solemn occasions wrapped it in white wool (Paus. 10.24.6). Somewhere to the near northeast of the temple was the fountain Cassotis. This was a reservoir fed by the Delphusa spring rising from a rock farther north. The Cassotis flowed into the adytum, and the Pythia drank from this spring before prophesying. The fountain also watered the sacred grove surrounding the temple (Eurip. *Ion* 112). This sacred grove, which is frequently mentioned by ancient writers, consisted of laurel trees and myrtles, but one laurel tree in particular was called preeminently the Pythian laurel, and branches of it were used for sacred purposes within the temple.

Above Cassotis was a building with paintings by Polygnotus; it was dedicated by the Cnidians, and the Delphians called it the Lesche (Club House). The paintings were vast frescoes crowded with figures of the Trojan War and of the visit of Odysseus to the underworld. The mural of Troy showed Menelaus and his men about to set sail for the return to Greece; in the center sat Helen; and though many other women were in the picture, all appeared to be gazing at her beauty. In a corner stood Andromache, with Astyanax at her breast; in another a

little boy clung to an altar in fear; and in the distance a horse rolled around on the sandy beach. Here, half a century before Euripides, was all the drama of *The Trojan Women*. In the battle scenes, Neoptolemus is depicted as the only Greek still massacring Trojans because the whole painting was commissioned to stand above Neoptolemus' grave. The list of subjects of these paintings seems endless when they are described by Pausanias (10.25–31). Polygnotus refused to take pay for these pictures but gave them to Delphi.

The site of the theater is marked by a high wall, a little to the west of the Cassotis. This wall, which is covered by several inscriptions, was the southern wall of the theater, which, as usual with Grecian theaters, was built in a semicircle upon the slope of the hill. It appears that the theater lay within the Pythian sanctuary. In the theater the musical contests of the Pythian games were carried on from the earliest to the latest times (Plut. *De Def. Or.* 8). In this general area was found the famous bronze statue, the Charioteer, which is in the Museum.

From the theater there is a sharp ascent to the stadium. At the bottom was a statue of Dionysus. The stadium, situated in the highest part of the city, was built of Parnassian stone but was adorned with Pentelic marble by Herodes Atticus. There are still considerable remains of the stadium, and its whole length may be distinctly traced.

Much of the mythological history of Delphi has been alluded to in the discussion of the founding of the town and the establishment of the temple. So important was Delphi, however, that it figured in many stories directly or indirectly because of its oracle and its importance as a sacred precinct. A procession of heroes passed its frontiers, and its history abounds with encounters, revelations, and even assassinations. Those who did not come to Delphi in person were often memorialized there.

The Attic heroes associated with Delphi were Aegeus and Ion. There was a statue of Aegeus at Delphi made of the tithes of the booty taken by the Athenians at Marathon (Paus. 10.10.1). Ion, however, had a more direct connection. He was a son of Apollo by Creusa, the daughter of Erechtheus and wife of Xuthus. Apollo had visited Creusa in a cave below the Propylaea of the Acropolis at Athens, and when she gave birth to a son, she exposed him in the same cave. The god, however, had the child conveyed to Delphi and there had him educated by a priestess. When the boy had grown and Xuthus and Creusa came to consult the oracle about the means of obtaining an heir, the answer was that the first human being whom Xuthus met on leaving the temple should be his son. Xuthus met Ion and acknowledged him as his son; but Creusa, imagining him to be a son of her husband by a former lover, offered a cup to the youth, which was filled with the poisonous blood of a dragon. Before drinking,

Ion poured out a libation to the gods, and a pigeon that drank of it died on the spot. Ion dragged Creusa away and was on the point of killing her when a priestess interfered, explained the mystery, and revealed that Ion was the son of Creusa. Mother and son thus became reconciled, but Xuthus was not let in on the secret. At the same time, Xuthus received a promise that he should become a father (of Dorus and Achaeus). Ion, in turn, became the ancestor of the Ionians (Eurip. *Ion* passim).

The cities of Argolis had many connections with Delphi. Danaus, who had usurped the throne of Argos, had a statue there. His son-in-law Lynceus, husband of Hypermnestra, alone was spared from slaughter on the night of the wedding of the fifty sons of Aegyptus to the fifty daughters of Danaus. Lynceus and his wife were regarded at Argos as heroes, and their statues stood in the temple at Delphi as a present from the Argives. Capaneus, one of the Seven against Thebes, was killed by Zeus for impiety while scaling the walls of Thebes. There was a statue of him at Delphi dedicated by the Argives (Paus. 10.10.3). Eteoclus, a son of Iphis, according to some traditions, was one of the seven heroes who went with Adrastus against Thebes. He is said to have won a prize in the footrace at the Nemean games and to have been killed by Leades (Apollod. 3.6.4.8). His statue stood at Delphi among those of the other Argive heroes (Paus. 10.10.3). Alcmaeon, son of Amphiaraus and leader of the Epigoni against Thebes, had a statue at Delphi. When he came to Psophis to recover the celebrated necklace and robe of Harmonia, he did so under the pretext that he intended to dedicate them at Delphi in order to be freed from his madness. Euryalus, son of Mecisteus, was mentioned as among the Argonauts, one of the Epigoni, and also as a participant in the Trojan War. In the painting in the Lesche he was represented as being wounded; and there was also a statue of him at Delphi, which stood between those of Diomedes and Aegialeus (Paus. 10.10.4.25.6).

The ill-fated house of Atreus moved in and out of Delphian history. Agamemnon and Menelaus were sent by Atreus to find their uncle Thyestes, who had been banished from Mycenae. The brothers also travelled through Greece to rouse the chiefs to avenge the insult offered to a Greek prince when Helen was abducted. They visited Odysseus in Ithaca, along with whom Menelaus is said to have consulted the Delphic oracle about the expedition against Troy. And at Delphi Menelaus dedicated the necklace of Helen to Athena Pronaea.

Orestes, the son of Agamemnon and Clytemnestra, had three separate connections with Delphi. Orestes grew up in the house of Strophius and after reaching adulthood he was frequently reminded by messengers from his sister Electra that he must avenge Agamemnon's death. Eventually he consulted the oracle at Delphi, which strengthened him in his plan. His second connection was his alleged instigation of the murder of Neoptolemus in Delphi because of rivalry over Hermione. His meeting there in the company of Iphigeneia with Electra was the last connection. On receiving the false report that Orestes and Pylades had been sacrificed to Artemis in Tauris, Aletes, the son of Aegisthus, assumed the government of Mycenae; but Electra, for the purpose of learning the particulars of her brother's death, went to Delphi. On the day she reached the place, Orestes and Iphigeneia likewise arrived there, but the same messenger who had before informed her of the death of Orestes now added that he had been sacrificed by Iphigeneia. Electra, enraged at this, snatched a firebrand from the altar with the intention of putting her sister's eyes out. But Orestes made himself known to Electra. All being thus reconciled, they travelled together to Mycenae, where Orestes killed the usurper Aletes, and Electra married Pylades. Hermione, the daughter of Menelaus and Helen, was first the wife of Neoptolemus and then of Orestes. The Lacedaemonians dedicated a statue of her, the work of Calamis, at Delphi (Paus. 10.16.4).

The ubiquitous Heracles, after killing his children, sentenced himself to exile. He later visited the oracle at Delphi to ask where he should settle. The Pythia first called him by the name of Heracles—for hitherto his name had been Alcides or Alcaeus—and ordered him to live in Tiryns, to serve Eurystheus for the space of twelve years, after which time he should become immortal. After this time he killed his friend Iphitus in a fit of madness and was attacked by a severe illness in consequence. He again went to Delphi to seek a cure, but the Pythia refused to answer his questions. A struggle between Heracles and Apollo ensued, and the combatants were not separated till Zeus sent a flash of lightning between them. Heracles now heard from the oracle that he should be restored to health if he would sell himself, serve three years for wages, and surrender his wages to Eurytus, the father of Iphitus, as atonement for the murder (Apollod. 2.6.1,2; Diod. 4.31). Aristodemus, according to some, was the first Heraclid king of Lacedaemon. According to others, he was prevented from this by stopping at Delphi on his way to Peloponnesus. He had consulted an oracle of Heracles about the return of the Heraclids instead of the Delphic oracle, and Apollo shot him with an arrow (Paus. 3.1.6).

Arcas, the ancestor of the Arcadians, had a statue with other members of his family at Delphi. These statues were dedicated there by the inhabitants of Tegea (Paus. 10.9.5). Elatus was a son of Arcas. He is said to have gone from Arcadia to Phocis, where he protected the Phocians and the Delphic sanctuary against the Phlegyans and founded the town of Elateia (Paus. 8.4.4). When Alcmaeon wanted to give the celebrated necklace and robe of Harmonia to his second wife Callirrhoe, he was slain by Agenor and Pronous, his brothers-in-law from his first marriage. But when the two brothers came to Delphi, where they intended to dedicate the necklace and robe, they were killed by Amphoterus and Acarnan, the sons of Alcmaeon and Callirrhoe (Apollod. 3.7.5).

There were others who came and went in Delphian mythology. Biton and Cleobis were the famous Argive brothers who, in the absence of oxen, dragged the chariot of their priestess mother to the temple of Hera during a festival. Their mother asked the goddess for the gift that was best for mortals. Hera had them go to sleep in her temple, never to awaken. The Argives made statues of the two brothers and sent them to Delphi, where they can be seen today in the Museum. Panthous, one of the elders at Troy, was originally a Delphian, who had been carried to Troy by Antenor because of his great beauty. Xenocleia was a Delphian priestess, who refused to give an oracular response to Heracles before he was purified of the murder of Iphitus; but she was compelled by him, for he threatened to take away her tripod (Paus. 10.13.7). Teiresias was the great seer of Thebes. When the Epigoni waged a successful war against Thebes, according to some he was carried to Delphi as a captive.

Finally, we find individuals outside Greece who were honored at Delphi. Triopas was a son of Poseidon and Canace and founder of Cnidus. His statue with a horse stood at Delphi, being an offering of the Cnidians (Paus. 10.11.1). Laodocus was a Hyperborean hero, who, together with Hyperochus and Pyrrhus, came to assist the Delphians against the Gauls (Paus. 10.23.3). And it is interesting that the Greeks of Cyrenaica dedicated at Delphi a chariot with a statue of Ammon (Paus. 10.13.5).

DEMETRIAS (DIMITRIAS)   was a city of Magnesia in Thessaly situated at the head of the Pagasaean Gulf. It was founded about 293 B.C. by Demetrius Poliorcetes, who relocated to this city the inhabitants of Nelia, Pagasae, Ormenium, Rhizus, Sepias, Olizon, Boebe, and Iolcus, all of which were later considered the territory of Demetrias (Strab. 9.5.15). It soon became an important place because it was well situated for commanding the interior of Thessaly as well as the gulf and seas it overlooked. Demetrias was across a narrow bay of the Pagasaean Gulf from Iolcus, by land about 3.5 km. It was a walled city about 7 km in circumference, and there remain a great number of projecting towers along the wall.

The city was founded too late to provide a locale for stories of gods or heroes, but its ruins disclose an active worship. Near the south wall was the temple of Artemis Iolcia, and remains of its enclosing wall can still be seen. Within the walls of the temple was a so-called Sacred Market. Elsewhere there are remains of altars and shrines, so far unidentified as to the divinities they honored.

DEMETRIAS   was an early name of the island of PAROS.

DEMETRIUM   was a later name of the site of ancient PYRASUS.

DERRHIUM   was a place in Laconia on Mount Taygetus containing a statue of Artemis Derrhiatis in the open air and near it a fountain called Anonus (Paus. 3.20.7). The site of the place is unknown, but it lay on the road from Sparta to Arcadia.

DIA   was a poetic name for the island of NAXOS.

DICAEA   was a Greek port town on the coast of Thrace on Lake Bistonis in the country of the Bistones. The place appears to have declined at an early period. Its modern site has not been established, but it was located near Abdera and south of the lake. It was said to have been named for Dicaeus, a son of Poseidon.

DICTAMNUM (DIKTINAIO)   a town of Crete, also referred to as Dictynna, was one of the best known towns on the island. It was situated to the northeast of Mount Dictynnaeus and southeast of the promontory Psacum, with a temple to the goddess Dictynna. The place is located about 4 km southeast of the tip of Akra Spanda. The temple was built by the Samians at Cydonia (Herod. 3.59), but there had probably been an earlier temple on the site. The sanctuary flourished during the reign of Hadrian when a road to the sanctuary was built. The existing ruins are from the temple that Hadrian had built in the second century A.D. It was excavated by the Germans in 1942.

Dictynna was a surname of both Artemis and Britomartis. The name is taken from the word for fishing net and was applied to Britomartis and Artemis as goddesses of the hunt. One tradition said that Britomartis was so called because when she had thrown herself into the sea to escape Minos she was saved in the nets of fishermen.

DICTE (DIKTI)   the well-known Cretan mountain, was the place where, according to the story, Zeus was born to Rhea in a cave. To conceal him from Cronus she entrusted his upbringing to the Curetes and the nymphs Adrasteia and Ida, the daughters of Melisseus. They fed him with milk of the goat Amaltheia, and with honey from the bees of the mountain (Apollod. 1.1.6; Diod. 5.70). The towns about the mountain were especially sacred to him, such as Praesus, Hierapytna, Biennus, Eleutherae, and Oaxus. The area of Mount Dicte was also probably the earliest seat of worship of Rhea. Zeus Dictaeus was a name of Zeus derived from Mt. Dicte. Under this name he had a temple at Praesus on the banks of the river Pothereus. The stony slopes of the mountain rose to the southeast of Cnossus on the east side. Considerable remains of ancient walls have been found about one hundred paces from the summit. On the lower slopes was a fountain.

Dicte was a nymph from whom Mount Dicte was said to have received its name. She was beloved and pursued by Minos, but she threw herself into the sea, where she was caught up and saved in the nets of fishermen. Minos then desisted from pursuing her and ordered the district to be called the Dictaean. This story is identical with the one of Britomartis, and the two must certainly have been variations of a common account.

DICTYNNAEUS (See DICTAMNUM)

DIDYMI (DIDIMA) a town of Hermionis on the road to Asine, contained in the time of Pausanias temples of Apollo, Poseidon, and Demeter, all possessing standing statues of those divinities. Apollo was worshipped here under the surname Delphinius from his having shown the Cretan colonists the way to Delphi while riding on a dolphin or metamorphosing himself into a dolphin. The town is still called Didima. It is situated in a valley, from which rises on the northeast Mount Didimo, 119 meters high, with two summits nearly equal in height. The valley is so entirely surrounded by mountains that it has no outlet for its running waters except through the mountains themselves.

DIECTERION was a town in Samos. Near this town Athena instructed Perseus in the ways to overcome the Gorgons. She showed the head of Medusa in pictures and warned him not to stare directly at her. She said he had nothing to fear from the two immortal Gorgons, Stheno and Euryale. Medusa had once ventured to contend with Athena for a prize of beauty and had as a consequence been changed into a loathsome monster, the sight of whose head turned people to stone.

DINE was a spring or subterranean river that rose in the sea about three-quarters of a kilometer off the coast of Argolis. The location was near Genethlium, the birthplace of Theseus. In ancient times the Argives cast bridled horses into Dine as an offering to Poseidon (Paus. 8.7.2).

DIOMEIA was a deme of Attica belonging to the tribe Aegeis, consisting, like the Cerameicus, of an Outer and Inner Diomeia. The Inner Diomeia made up the east part of the city of Athens and gave its name to one of the city gates in this area. In the Outer Diomeia was situated the Cynosarges, a sanctuary of Heracles that included a gymnasium. The Outer Diomeia could not have extended far beyond the walls since the deme Alopece was close to Cynosarges and only two or so kilometers from the walls of the city (Herod. 5.63).

Diomus, a son of Colyttus, was a favorite and an attendant of Heracles, from whom this deme was believed to have derived its name.

DIONYSIAS was another name for the island of NAXOS.

DIRCE (DIRKIS) is one of the two rivers of Thebes, rising a little south of the city and flowing northward into the plain of Thebes. It runs parallel with and about 1 km from the Ismenos. Between them flows a smaller stream, the Strofia. All three streams unite in the plain below the city. Both the Ismenos and Dirkis are really torrents that are dry most of the year. The Dirkis rises from several fountains and not from a single one, like the Ismenos. A considerable quantity of the water of the Dirkis is diverted to supply the fountains of the town.

Dirce was a daughter of Helios and wife of Lycus. According to some accounts, Antiope was the first wife of Lycus and was seduced by Epopeus, king of Sicyon. She was rejected by her husband, and it was after this that she was visited by Zeus. Dirce, the second wife of Lycus, was jealous of Antiope and had her imprisoned, but Zeus helped Antiope to escape to Mount Cithaeron, where she gave birth to twin sons, Amphion and Zethus. Antiope was recaptured, however, and remained in captivity for many years, being frequently abused by Lycus and Dirce. She eventually escaped and located her sons, who had been brought up by shepherds. They went to Thebes, killed Lycus, and tied Dirce to a bull and had her dragged about until she too was killed. The river Dirce received its name from her (Paus. 9.25.3).

DIRCE was a well on Mount Cithaeron. Dirce and her husband Lycus mistreated Antiope, the first wife of Lycus. Years later, Antiope's sons by Zeus, Amphion and Zethus, tied Dirce to a bull so she was dragged to death. According to one writer, her body was changed by Dionysus, in whose service she had been engaged, into a well on Mount Cithaeron. (See also DIRCE above.)

DIUM (DION) was a city of Pieria that, though not large, was considered to be one of the leading towns of Macedonia. Dium, though situated in a most unhealthy spot, was noted for its splendid buildings and its great number of statues. Outside the town was the temple of Zeus Olympius. Dium received its name from Zeus, with which word it shared the Indo-European root *di-*, meaning "bright" and, by extension, "god." Here were celebrated the public games called Olympia instituted by Archelaus in honor of Zeus and the Muses (Diod. 17.17). The theater and stadium, for which remains have been found, served doubtlessly for that celebration.

Another form of the legend of the death of Orpheus was found in an inscription at Dium on what was supposed to be the tomb in which the bones of Orpheus were buried. This ascribed his death to the thunderbolts of Zeus.

The town of Dion, located on a slope between the sea and Mount Olympus, is adjacent to the ancient site. The celebration of the Olympia featured drama as well as athletics, and so a theater is prominent among the ruins. There are also an odeion and a stadium. Inscriptional and other evidence points to cults of Athena, Dionysus, Cybele, Baubo, Artemis, Hermes, the Muses, and Olympian Zeus. Excavations have uncovered shrines of Demeter and Asclepius.

DIUM   was a town in the northwest of Euboea near the promontory of Cenaeum, of which Canae in Aeolis is said to have been a colony. Dium with its "steep citadel" is mentioned by Homer (*Il.* 2.538) as one of the towns of the Abantes, whose men were led to the Trojan War in forty ships by Elephenor.

DODONA (DODONI)   was a town in Epeirus celebrated for its oracle of Zeus, the most ancient in Greece. It was one of the strongholds of the Pelasgians, and the Dodonaean Zeus was a Pelasgian divinity. Dodon was a son of Zeus by Europa, from whom the oracle was believed to have derived its name. Other traditions traced the name to a nymph by the name of Dodona. The oracle, which was near Mount Tomarus, gave Zeus the surname Dodonais. Here Zeus was mainly a prophetic god, and the oak tree was sacred to him. He was said to have been reared by the Dodonaean nymphs. Others said that this office was performed by the Hyades, daughters of Atlas and Aethra. They were later appointed by Zeus to bring up Dionysus. In this capacity they are also called the Nysaean nymphs (Apollod. 3.4.3; Ov. *Fast.* 5.167, *Met.* 3.314). When Lycurgus threatened the safety of Dionysus and his companions, the Hyades, with the exception of Ambrosia, fled with the infant god to Thetis or to Thebes, where they entrusted him to Ino. Zeus showed them his gratitude by placing them among the stars.

Because of its great distance from the leading Grecian states, the oracle was subsequently supplanted to a great extent by that at Delphi; but it continued to enjoy a high reputation and was regarded in later times as one of the three greatest oracles, the other two being those of Delphi and of Zeus Ammon in Libya. When Jason was commissioned by his uncle to fetch the Golden Fleece, he ordered Argus to build a ship with fifty oars, in the prow of which Athena inserted a piece of wood from the speaking oaks in the grove at Dodona. The antiquity of Dodona is attested by several passages of Homer (*Il.* 2.748, 16.233; *Od.* 14.327, 19.296).

Aeneas, after the taking of Troy, travelled to various places on his way to Italy. He went to Dodona, where he met the Trojan Helenus. Io in her wanderings went first from Argos to Molossia and the neighborhood of Dodona and from there to the sea, which derived from her the name of the Ionian Sea. When Dionysus had grown up, Hera threw him into a state of madness, in which he wandered about through many countries. He is said to have gone first to the oracle of Dodona, but on the way he came to a lake that prevented him from proceeding further. One of two asses he met there carried him across the water, and the grateful god placed both animals among the stars; asses after that remained sacred to him.

The ancient critics believed that there were two places by the name of Dodona, one in Thessaly in the district of Perrhaebia near Mount Olympus and the other in Epeirus in the district of Thesprotia. Those critics said that the Enienes mentioned along with the Perrhaebi (Hom. *Il.* 2.748) of the river Titaresius came from the Thessalian Dodona; and that Odysseus, in order to consult the oracular oak of Zeus, after leaving the king of the Thesproti, visited the Dodona in Epeirus. The Thessalian Dodona is said to have been settled first; and from Thessalian Dodona the Thesprotian Dodona is said to have received a colony and its name.

The Selli whom Homer (*Il.* 16.234) describes as the interpreters of Zeus, "men with unwashen feet, that couch on the ground," appear to have been a tribe. Hesiod (*Frag.* 97) calls their country Hellopia and describes its rich pastures and fertile land. Aristotle (*Meteor.* 1.14) states that the flood of Deucalion took place in this district, which "was inhabited at that time by the Selli and by the people then called Graeci but now Hellenes." This disagrees with the common view that connected Deucalion, Hellen, and the Hellenes with the district in Thessaly between Mounts Othrys and Oeta.

The god at Dodona was said to dwell in the stem of an oak, in the hollow of which his statue was probably placed in the most ancient times and which was at first his only temple. The god revealed his will from the branches of the tree, probably by the rustling of the leaves, sounds of which the priests had to interpret. Consequently, we frequently read of the speaking oak or oaks of Dodona (Hom. *Od.* 14.327, 19.296). In the time of Herodotus and Sophocles the oracles were interpreted by three aged women called Peleiades or Pelaiai because pigeons were said to have brought the command to found the oracle. These priestesses were probably introduced instead of the Selli at the time when the worship of Dione was connected with that of Zeus at Dodona.

As Delphi grew in importance, Dodona was chiefly consulted by neighboring tribes, the Aetolians, Acarnanians, and Epeirots (Paus. 8.21.2); but it continued to enjoy great renown down to later times. For example, Croesus sent to inquire of the oracle (Herod. 1.46). Aeschylus (*Prom.* 829) and Sophocles (*Trach.* 1164) speak of the oracle in terms of the highest reverence and

Cicero (*De Div.* 1.43) relates that the Spartans in important matters were accustomed to ask the advice of the oracles either of Delphi, or Dodona, or Zeus Ammon. Under the Molossian kings, who gradually extended their dominion over the whole of Epeirus, Dodona probably rose again in importance. The coins of the Molossian kings frequently bear the heads of Zeus and Dione, or of Zeus alone within a garland of oak.

In 219 B.C. Dodona received a blow from which it never recovered. In that year the Aetolians, who were at war with Philip of Macedonia, destroyed the temple of the god (Polyb. 4.67). The oracle subsequently was restored, and Pausanias (1.17.6) mentions the temple and sacred oak tree as objects worthy of the traveller's notice. He also described the oak of Dodona as the oldest tree in all Hellas, next to the willow of Hera in Samos (Paus. 8.23.5).

Despite the celebrity of the oracle, we have no description of the temple of Dodona. It appears to have occupied a considerable space and to have contained several other buildings besides the sacred house or temple proper of the god. A writer named Demon states that the temple was surrounded with tripods bearing cauldrons and that these were placed so closely together that when one was struck the noise vibrated through all. It appears that the greater part of these had been contributed by the Boeotians, who were accustomed to send presents of tripods every year (Strab. 9.2.4). Among the remarkable objects at Dodona were two pillars, on one of which was a brazen cauldron and on the other a statue of a boy holding in his hand a brazen whip dedicated by the Corcyraeans. When the wind blew, the whip struck the cauldron and produced a loud noise. This appears to have been one of the means of consulting the god. Respecting the way in which the oracles were given, there are different accounts; and they probably differed at different times. The most ancient mode was by means of sounds from the trees. It is related that at the foot of the sacred oak there gushed forth a fountain, the noise of whose waters was prophetic and was interpreted by the priestesses. On some occasions the will of the god appears to have been ascertained by means of lots.

The site of Dodona was long thought to be located on the south end of the lake of Ioannina at a place named Kastritsa, but the site, identified in 1875 by Constantin Karapamos, is 22.5 km farther, off the Arta road and over a steep ridge to the enclosed valley of Tsakovitsa at the foot of Mount Tomarus. The modern village of Dodoni stands a little farther west.

Excavations have been carried out since 1944. Of the sanctuary only foundations exist. At first, worship centered around the sacred oak; fragments of the votive tripods of the eighth century B.C. have been recovered. A stone temple was not built until the fourth century; it consisted quite simply of cella and pronaos. This and the oak were then surrounded by a wall. After the burning of the sacred groves in 219 B.C., the temple was enlarged and the wall rebuilt. Near the temple of Zeus is a small temple of Aphrodite. Beyond are two successive versions of a temple of Dione and a sanctuary of Heracles. These are overlain by an early Christian basilica. The theater, with a capacity comparable to that of Epidaurus, has been completely excavated and restored.

DOLICHE   was an earlier name of the island of ICARIA.

DOLOPIA   inhabited by the Dolopes, was a mountainous district in the southwest corner of Thessaly, lying between Mount Tymphrestus and Mount Othrys. The Dolopes were an ancient Hellenic people and members of the Amphictyonic League. They are mentioned by Homer (*Il.* 9.484) as included in Phthia. Though belonging to Thessaly, the Dolopians seemed to have been virtually independent, and their country was at a later time a subject of continuing contention between the Aetolians and the kings of Macedonia. The only place in Dolopia of the slightest importance was Ctimene.

Amyntor, king of Dolopia, was a son of Ormenus and father of Crantor, Euaemon, Astydameia, and Phoenix. Phoenix was exiled by Amyntor for having seduced, at the instigation of his mother, Cleobule, his father's mistress. Amyntor took part in the Calydonian hunt; when conquered in a war by Peleus, he gave his son Crantor as a hostage (Ov. *Met.* 8.307, 12.364). His daughter Astydameia became by Heracles the mother of Tlepolemus. Others say her son by Heracles was Ctesippus (Apollod. 2.7.8).

DONUSA (DONOUSSA)   is a small island near Naxos, said to have been the island to which Dionysus carried Ariadne from Naxos when pursued by her father, Minos. This tale might have arisen from confounding the name of the island with the name of the god.

DORCEIA   was the name of a fountain and sanctuary at Sparta. Dorceus was a son of Hippocoon, who had a shrine at Sparta jointly with his brother Sebrus. The well near the sanctuary was called Dorceia and the place around it Sebrion (Paus. 3.15.2). It is probable that Dorceus is the same person as the Dorycleus in Apollodorus (3.10.5), where his brother is called Tebrus.

DORIS   was a small, mountainous district in Greece, bounded by Aetolia, southern Thessaly, Ozolian Locris, and Phocis. It lay between Mount Oeta and Mount Parnassus and consisted of the valley of the river Pindus, a tributary of the Cephissus, into which it flows. In this valley there were four towns forming the Doric tetrapolis—Erineus, Boium, Cytinium, and Pindus. There was an important mountain pass leading across Parnassus from Doris to Amphissa in the country of the Ozolian Locrians. At the head of this pass stood the Dorian town of Cytinium.

Doris is said to have been at first called Dryopis from its earlier inhabitants the Dryopes, who were expelled from the country by Heracles and the Malians (Herod. 1.56, 8.31, 43). It derived its name from the Dorians, who migrated from this district to conquer Peloponnesus. Therefore the country maintained a kinship with Sparta as the chief state of Doric origin, and on more than one occasion the Lacedaemonians sent assistance to Doris when it was attacked by the Phocians and other neighbors (Thuc. 1.107, 3.92). The Dorians were supposed to have derived their name from Dorus, the son of Hellen. According to one tradition, Dorus settled at once in the country subsequently known as Doris (Strab. 8.7.1); but other traditions represent him as settling his people in the country called Histiaeotis at the foot of Ossa and Olympus. Expelled from Histiaeotis by the Cadmeians, they settled on Mount Pindus and were called the Macedonian nation. From there they migrated to Dryopis; and, having passed from Dryopis into Peloponnesus, were called the Doric race. In Apollodorus (1.7.3), Dorus is represented as occupying the country opposite Peloponnesus on the Corinthian Gulf and calling the inhabitants Dorians after himself. By this description is evidently meant the whole country along the northern shore of the Corinthian Gulf, which included Aetolia, Phocis, and the land of the Ozolian Locrians.

The seats of the great Achaean monarchies are represented in the Homeric poems and carry no allusion to any Doric population in Peloponnesus. In the historical period the whole of the eastern and southern part of Peloponnesus were in the possession of Dorians.

DORIUM (VASILIKO)   was a town of Messenia celebrated in Homer (*Il.* 2.599) as the place where the bard Thamyris was struck with blindness. Thamyris was an ancient Thracian bard, a son of Philammon and the nymph Argiope. He was presumptuous enough to believe that he could surpass the Muses in song. In consequence of this rashness, he was deprived of his sight and the power of singing (Apollod. 1.3.3). He was represented with a broken lyre in his hand (Paus. 9.30.2).

The men of Dorium, Cyparissia, Amphigeneia, Pteleos, and Helus were led by Nestor of Gerenia to the Trojan War in ninety ships. Near the modern village of Vasiliko on the road between Kiparissia and Megalopoli are some Mycenaean ruins doubtfully identified with the Homeric Dorium. West of Vasiliko is Malthi, another village that has also been identified with Dorium, but that claim is even more doubtful.

DOTIUS CAMPUS   was the name of a plain in Pelasgiotis in Thessaly, situated south of Ossa, along the west side of Lake Boebeis. Dotis was a daughter of Elatus or Asterius, by Amphictyone, who gave her name to this plain. She was the mother of Phlegyas by Ares. Strabo (9.5.22), quoting Hesiod, speaks of "the holy Twin Hills in the plain of Dotium over against Amyrus rich in grapes," said to have been the dwelling place of Coronis, mother of Asclepius by Apollo. Apollo put her to death because she had favored Ischys, son of Elatus. There was also the story that Triopas expelled the Pelasgians from the Dotian plain but was himself obliged to migrate to Caria. He was the son of Poseidon and Canace and the father of Iphimedeia and Erysichthon.

This twin hill of Hesiod has been identified with a remarkable hill, rising like an island out of a plain, about 6.5 km in circumference and having two summits connected by a ridge. Between them there was a village called Lacereia (Pind. *Pyth.* 3.59). Its scanty remains may be seen today at the hamlet of Marmarinia, about 22 km northeast of Larissa.

DRACANUM (FARO)   in Icaria was one of the places that claimed to be the birthplace of the god Dionysus. Remains of the town lie near Faro at the east end of the island.

DREPANE   was an earlier name of the island of CORCYRA.

DREROS (KASTELLI)   was a hilltop city on one of the spurs of Mount Cadistus in Crete. Although it is scarcely mentioned in literature, it produced the earliest complete constitutional law yet found in Greece. Its chief deities were Athena Poliuchos (Protecting the City) and Apollo Delphinius. The city's coins depicted Apollo and the staff of Hermes. In the agora lie the remains of one of the earliest known temples of the Greek Iron Age. It is probably that of Apollo Delphinius. Statues of bronze-covered wood found at the site probably represent Apollo, Artemis, and Leto. The site is near Kastelli east of Neapoli.

DRIUS   was a mountain in the Phthiotian Achaia. Pancratis was a daughter of Aloeus and Iphimedeia. Once when Thracian pirates under Butes invaded that district, they carried off from Mount Drius the women who were solemnizing a festival of Dionysus. Among them was Iphimedeia and her daughter Pancratis. They were carried to Strongyle (later Naxos), where King Agassamenus made Pancratis his wife.

DRYMAEA (DRIMEA)   was a frontier town of Phocis on the side of Doris. It was across the Cephissus and about 11 km from Amphicleia. There was an ancient temple of Demeter at Drymaea, containing an upright statue of the goddess in stone, in whose honor the annual festival of the Thesmophoria was celebrated. Its more ancient name is said to have been Nauboleis, which was derived from Naubolus, an ancient Phocian hero, father of Iphitus (Hom. *Il.* 2.518). The site of Drymaea has been placed at the renamed village of Drimea on a rocky point of the mountain on the edge of the plain. At the summit is a circular acropolis, preserving the remains of an opening into the town (Herod. 8.33; Paus. 10.33.11).

DRYOPIS   was a district surrounding Mount Oeta. The Dryopes were one of the aboriginal tribes of Greece. Their earliest abode is said to have been on Mount Oeta and its adjacent valleys in the district called after them Dryopis. The Dorians settled in the part of their country that lay between Oeta and Parnassus and that was afterwards called Doris; but Dryopis originally extended as far north as the river Spercheius. The name of Dryopis was still applied to the latter district in the time of Strabo (9.5.10), who calls it a tetrapolis like Doris. Heracles with help from the Malians is said to have driven the Dryopes out of their country and to have given it to the Dorians. Theiodamas was the father of Hylas and king of the Dryopes (Apollod. 2.7.7; Apollon. Rhod. 1.131). Heracles, after killing Theiodamas, took Hylas with him when he joined the expedition of the Argonauts (Apollon. Rhod. 1.131). The expelled Dryopes settled at Hermione and Asine in the Argolic peninsula, at Styrus and Carystus in Euboea, and on the island of Cythnus. These are the five chief places in which we find the Dryopes in historical times. The name Dryopis has also been given to the country around Ambracia, so it is possible that the Dryopes extended at one time all the way to the Ambracian Gulf from Mount Oeta and the Spercheius.

DRYUSA   was an earlier name of the island of SAMOS.

DULICHIUM (MAKRI?)   was the name of an island in the Ionian Sea. Homer (*Il.* 2.265) says that Meges, son of Phyleus, led forty ships to Troy from Dulichium and the sacred islands Echinae, which are situated beyond the sea opposite Elis. Phyleus was the son of Augeas, king of the Epeians in Elis, who emigrated to Dulichium because he had incurred his father's anger. Augeas expelled him from Ephyra because he gave his evidence in favor of Heracles when Augeas refused to pay the hero for cleaning his stables. By Ctimene or Timandra, Phyleus became the father of Meges, who is often called Phyleides (Apollod. 2.5.5). In the *Odyssey,* Dulichium is frequently mentioned along with Same, Zacynthus, and Ithaca as one of the islands subject to Odysseus and it is celebrated for its fertility (Hom. *Od.* 1.245, 9.24; *Hymn. Hom. ad Apoll.* 429). It is also mentioned as the home of Nisus, a noble

and father of Amphinomus, one of the suitors of Penelope. Mulius also came from there. He was a servant and herald in the house of Odysseus (Hom. *Od.* 18.422).

The site of Dulichium has never been determined. Pausanias supports the idea that it had the ancient name of Cephallenia. But Strabo (10.2.19) thought that Dulichium was one of the Echinades and identifies it with Dolicha, an island that he describes as situated opposite Oeniadae and the mouth of the Achelous and about 18.5 km from the promontory of Araxus in Elis. Dolicha appears to be the same island as modern Makri, both names describing its long narrow form. Petala, being the largest of the Echinades and possessing two well-sheltered harbors, might also have a good claim to being considered the ancient Dulichium. There is no proof in the *Iliad* or *Odyssey* that Dulichium, although at the head of a confederacy of islands, was itself an island. It could have been a city on the coast of Acarnania opposite the Echinades and only 3 or 4 km across the channel.

DYME (KATO AHAIA)   was the most westerly of the twelve Achaean cities, from which circumstances it is said to have derived its name (Herod. 1.145; Polyb. 2.41). It was situated near the coast, according to Strabo (8.3.4) sixty stadia (11 km) from the promontory Araxus and, according to Pausanias (7.17.5), thirty stadia (5.5 km) from the river Larisus, which separated its territory from Elis. It is further said by Strabo (8.3.2) to have been formed out of the union of eight villages. Pausanias (7.17.5) says that its more ancient name was Paleia, and Strabo (8.7.5) says its name was Stratos. Its epithet Cauconis was derived probably from the Caucones, who were supposed to have originally inhabited the district (Strab. 8.3.11; Paus. 7.17.5). The city had the honor, along with Patrae, of reviving the Achaean League in 280 B.C. The remains of Dyme can be seen near the modern village of Kato Ahaia.

In the territory of Dyme near the promontory of Araxus there was a fortress called Teichos, which was said to have been built by Heracles when he made war upon the Eleans. It was probably during this time that Heracles became enamored of Sostratus, a youth of this region. Later, funeral sacrifices were offered to him in Achaia, and his tomb was shown in the neighborhood of Dyme (Paus. 7.17.8). Teichos was only 1.5 stadia (about 1.25 km) in circumference, but its walls were 13.7 meters high. Its site is perhaps occupied by the castle of Kalogria. In the territory of Dyme between the city and the frontiers of Elis lay two towns named Hecatombaeon and Langon. A temple of Asclepius was located between Dyme and Patrae (Strab. 8.7.4).

DYSPONTIUM (SKAFIDIA)   an ancient town in the territory of Pisa, said to have been founded by Dysponteus, a son of Oenomaus (Paus. 6.22.4). Strabo

(8.3.32) describes it as situated in the plain on the road from Elis to Olympia. It lay north of the Alpheius, not far from the sea and probably near the modern Skafidia.

ECHIDORUS (GALIKOS)   was the name of a small river of Macedonia that rose in the Crestonaean territory and, after flowing through Mygdonia, emptied into a lagoon close to the Axius (Herod. 7.124,127). It is now called the Galikos. Gallicum was the name of a place situated about 27 km from Thessalonica. It is probable that when the ancient name of the river fell into disuse, it was replaced by that of a town that stood upon its banks.

The eleventh labor of Heracles was the recovery of the apples of the Hesperides. In order to find the gardens of the Hesperides, Heracles went to the river Echidorus, after having killed Termerus in Thessaly. In Macedonia he killed Cycnus, the son of Ares and Pyrene, who had challenged him. He then went to Illyria.

ECHINADES (AHINADES)   are a group of numerous islands off the coast of Akarnania, several of which have become united to the mainland by the alluvial deposits of the river Aheloos. The Echinades are mentioned by Homer (*Il.* 2.625), who says that Meges, son of Phyleus, led forty ships to Troy from "Dulichium and the Echinae, the holy isles, that lie across the sea, over against Elis." He describes the Echinades as inhabited; but other writers represent them as deserted (Thuc. 2.102). One writer names a town, Apollonia, situated on one of the islands. Pliny (4.12.19) gives us the names of nine of these islands: Aegialeia, Cotonis, Thyatira, Geoaris, Dionysia, Cyrnus, Chalcis, Pinara, Mystus. Another of the Echinades was Artemita, which became united to the mainland (Strab. 1.3.18). One writer spoke of Artemita as a peninsula near the mouth of the river Achelous, and others connected it with the Oxeiae. The Oxeiae are sometimes spoken of as a separate group of islands to the west of the Echinades.

The Echinades derived their name from the echinus or the sea urchin in consequence of their sharp and prickly outlines. For the same reason they were called Oxeiae (Sharp Islands), a name some of them still retain under the slightly altered form of Oxies.

When Theseus returned home from the Calydonian chase, he was invited and hospitably received by Achelous, who related to him in what manner he had created the islands called Echinades. They were once nymphs, he said, and they had failed on one occasion to invite Achelous to a festival. In rage he created a flood and swept them out to sea, where they were changed into islands (Ov. *Met.* 8.580).

When the Harpies tormented Phineus, the Argonauts arrived on the scene. The Boreades, Zetes and Calais, routed and pursued them, and an oracle had said the losers in the chase would perish. One Harpy fell in the

Tigris, and the other reached the Echinades, according to some. Other writers call the islands the Strophades, which are far out in the sea and not to be confused with the Echinades, which, as has been pointed out, were formed by alluvial deposits near the coastline.

ECHINUS (AHINOS)   was a town of Phthiotis in Thessaly situated upon the Maliac Gulf between Lamia and Larissa Cremaste in a fertile district. It was said to have derived its name from Echion, one of the five surviving Spartoi who had grown from the dragon's teeth sown by Cadmus (Apollod. 3.4.1; Ov. *Met.* 3.126). He was married to Agave, by whom he became the father of Pentheus. He is said to have dedicated a temple of Cybele in Boeotia and to have assisted Cadmus in the building of Thebes (Ov. *Met.* 10.686). Strabo mentions Echinus as one of the Grecian cities that had been destroyed by an earthquake (Strab. 1.3.20). Its site is marked by the modern village of Ahinos. The modern village stands upon the side of a hill, the summit of which was occupied by the ancient acropolis.

ECHINUS (SPARTO?)   was a town in Acarnania said to have been founded by Echion, who sprang from the dragon's teeth sown by Cadmus. It occurs in the list of Acarnanian towns preserved by Pliny (4.1.5), who places it inland and near Heracleia (modern Vonitsa). It is probably coincidental that this location corresponds with that of a modern village named Sparto. Echinus and the others springing from the dragon's teeth were known as Spartoi (Sown Men).

EDONIS   was a district on the left bank of the Strymon River occupied by the Edones, a Thracian people. This district reached from Lake Cercinitis as far as the Nestus River. This area was associated with Dionysus and his introduction of the vine. Lycurgus, son of Dryas, was king of the Edonians and was the first to insult and expel the god. He also made prisoners of the Bacchic women and satyrs who followed Dionysus. The god, who had taken refuge in the sea, returned and caused Lycurgus to go mad. The insane king killed his son Dryas with an ax, thinking that he was cutting down a vine. While he was dismembering his son, he recovered his senses. As a result of this murder, a famine came to Edonis, and Dionysus, speaking through an oracle, proclaimed that the scarcity would be lifted only if Lycurgus were put to death. The Edonians accordingly obliged by taking him to Mount Pangaeum, where he was tied to his horses and torn apart (Apollod. 3.5.1.). The Edonians, as if to compensate for this early reception of Dionysus, became famous for their orgiastic worship of the god.

EILESIUM   a town of Boeotia, of uncertain site, was mentioned by Homer (*Il.* 2.499). Its name, according to

Strabo (9.2.17), who calls it Heilesium, indicates a marshy position.

EION (LIMENAS AMFIPOLIS) was a town and fortress situated at the mouth of the Strymon River 4.5 km from Amphipolis, of which it was the harbor. Phoenix, the son of Amyntor, king of the Dolopes, was the tutor of Achilles. Amyntor had blinded his son because Phoenix had been accused of trying to seduce Amyntor's mistress. Cheiron the Centaur cured him when he fled to Peleus, the father of Achilles. Phoenix also changed the name of Achilles' son from Pyrrhus to Neoptolemus. When Phoenix died, Neoptolemus buried him at Eion. Phoenix is one of the mythical beings to whom the ancients ascribed the invention of the alphabet.

EION or **EIONES** was a town in the Argolic peninsula mentioned by Homer (*Il.* 2.561) along with Troezen and Epidaurus. Its men were led to the Trojan War by Diomedes. It is said to have been one of the towns founded by the Dryopes when Heracles expelled them from Dryopis in northern Greece. Its position is uncertain but because Strabo (8.6.13) reported that the Mycenaeans expelled the inhabitants of Eiones and made it their seaport, it is thought to have been located in the plain of Kandia (Diod. 4.37).

EIRENA was an earlier name of CALAUREIA.

ELAEUS was a town in Argolis mentioned only by Apollodorus (2.5.2). He says that when Heracles had chopped off the immortal head of the Lernean Hydra, he buried it and put a heavy rock on it by the side of the way leading from Lerna to Elaeus.

ELATEIA (ELATIA) was a city of Phocis and the most important place in the country after Delphi. It controlled the northern route into the Cephissus valley and was therefore a post of great military importance. As a result, it was the capital of Phocis. Elateia is not mentioned by Homer. Its inhabitants claimed to be Arcadians, deriving their name from Elatus, the son of Arcas. Elatus was said to have resided on Mount Cyllene in Arcadia and to have gone from there to Phocis, where he protected the Phocians and the Delphic sanctuary against the Phlegyans and founded the town of Elateia (Paus. 8.4.4). A statue of him stood in the marketplace (Paus. 10.34.5).

Among the objects worthy of notice in Elateia, Pausanias (10.34.8) mentions the agora, a temple of Asclepius (containing a beardless statue of the god), a theater, and an ancient bronze statue of Athena. He also mentions a temple of Athena Cranaea, situated at the distance of 3.5 km from Elateia. The road to it was a very gentle ascent, but the temple stood upon a steep hill of small size. The office of priest in this temple was always held by youths below the age of puberty who served for the space of five years.

Some remains of the temple of Athena Cranaea have also been discovered. The surname of the goddess was derived from the name of the hill on which the temple stood. The ruins of Elateia are 2.5 km from the modern village of Elatia.

ELECTRIS was an earlier name of the island of SAMOTHRACE.

ELEON was one of the twenty-nine Boeotian towns that sent men to Troy under the leadership of Peneleos, Leitus, Arcesilaus, Prothoenor, and Clonius (Hom. *Il.* 2.500). It was said to have been one of the smaller places in the territory of Tanagra and to have derived its name from its marshy situation (Strab. 9.2.12). Its site is uncertain but some have placed it on the shore of Lake Paralimni, while others have placed it near Tanagra on the right bank of the Asopus. The modern village of Eleo on the old Athens-Thebes highway and near Tanagra probably only memorializes the name.

Amyntor, according to Homer (*Il.* 10.266), was a son of Ormenus of Eleon. Autolycus broke into Amyntor's house and stole a beautiful helmet, which afterward came into the hands of Meriones, who wore it in the war against Troy. Amyntor was the father of Crantor, Euaemon, Astydameia, and Phoenix. The last of these was cursed and expelled by Amyntor for having seduced his father's mistress (Hom. *Il.* 9.434).

ELEUSIS (ELEFSINA) was a deme of Attica belonging to the tribe Hippothoontis. It owed its celebrity to its being the chief seat of the worship of Demeter and Persephone and to the mysteries celebrated in honor of these goddesses. The mysteries, called Eleusinia, continued to be regarded as the most sacred of all the Grecian mysteries down to the fall of paganism.

Eleusis stood upon a hill near the sea and opposite the island of Salamis. Its location gave it three advantages: it was on the road from Athens to the Isthmus; it was in a very fertile plain; and it was at the head of an extensive bay, which was protected on the south by the island of Salamis. The town dated from the most ancient times. Some traced its name from an eponymous hero Eleusis (Paus. 1.38.7). He was a son of Hermes and Daeira, the daughter of Oceanus. Others make him a son of Ogygus of Thebes. He was married to Cothonea or Cyntinia. Daeira (Knowing) was said to be the daughter of Oceanus, but some called her a sister of Styx. Others represented her as identical with Aphrodite, Demeter, Hera, or Persephone (Apollon. Rhod. 3.847).

Eleusis was one of the twelve independent states into which Attica originally divided. It had exclusive control of the conduct of the mysteries. It coined its own money, a privilege possessed by no other town in Attica except Athens.

The history of Eleusis is part of the history of Athens. Once a year the great Eleusinian procession travelled from Athens to Eleusis along the Sacred Way. The ancient temple of Demeter at Eleusis was burned by the Persians in 484 B.C. (Herod. 9.395), and it was not until the administration of Pericles that it was rebuilt. Under the Romans Eleusis enjoyed great prosperity, as initiation into its mysteries became fashionable among Roman nobles. It was destroyed by Alaric in A.D. 396 and from that time disappeared from history.

The modern city of Elefsina is an industrial town with cement, petro-chemical, and steel plants. It also manufactures olive oil and soap and is engaged in shipbuilding. It is something of a shock to turn suddenly into the area of the ancient site, which is quite near the center of the modern city.

Pausanias (1.38.6) gives only a very brief description of Eleusis. He mentions a temple of Triptolemus, another of Artemis Propylaea, and a third of Poseidon Patros. He also mentions the spring of Callichorum and the Rharian plain. He claims that a dream forbade him to describe anything further about the sacred area.

The excavations are at the foot and on the east slopes of the acropolis and comprise most of the sanctuary of Demeter and Kore. The sanctuary was protected on three sides by the city wall and separated from the city itself on the fourth side by a dividing wall. Past the entrance the Sacred Way changes from a modern to an ancient paved road, which ends at a court in front of the city walls. Here the initiated gathered for purification before entering the sanctuary.

To the left are the remains of a fountain. Close to the northeast corner of the Greater Propylaea is the sacred spring that passed throughout classical times for the Callichoron (Well of the Fair Dances). Others have suggested that it is, in fact, the Parthenion (Well of the Maidens), mentioned as the place where Demeter sat to rest.

In the center of the court are the scanty marble remains of the Temple of Artemis Propylaea and Poseidon Patros. Nearby is an area thought to be the shrine of the hero Dolichos.

The Greater Propylaea, which faces northeast, is modeled after the one on the Acropolis at Athens. It is reached by steps, which lead past bases of columns that flanked the entrance. To the left is the Lesser Propylaea, which faces north. On its frieze are emblems of the cult.

The sacred precinct of Demeter was for two thousand years forbidden to the uninitiated on penalty of death. To the right of the entrance is the Plutonion, which encloses a cavern sacred to Pluto. From here there is an ascent to the large, square platform on which stood the Hall of the Mysteries.

The great Temple of Demeter, with its adjacent Telesterion (Hall of Initiation and the Mysteries), is an almost square chamber fifty-three by fifty-two meters, partly hewn out of the rock of the acropolis and partly built on a terrace. On all four sides were tiers of seats, some cut from the rock. The hall could hold about 3,000 people. Bases remain of most of the forty-two roof-supporting columns. In the center was the Anactoron. This was the holiest part of the entire temple complex and had occupied the same site since Mycenaean times. By the side of the Anactoron stood the throne of the hierophant (chief priest).

In the Museum are relatively few works of art, but they are interesting as examples of finds at this vastly important and enduring site. Outside the entrance is a Roman marble sarcophagus (*ca.* A.D. 190) decorated with scenes of the Calydonian boar hunt. In the Museum one can see a copy of the Niinnion Tablet, a red-figure vase now in the National Museum. The figures on it are most likely performing rites from the Mysteries; there is no other such representation known. In the center of one of the rooms is a huge amphora (seventh century B.C.) depicting Odysseus blinding Polyphemus and Perseus slaying Medusa. There is a marble stele of Demeter seated with Hecate. There is a relief of Demeter on the Mirthless Stone. There is also a headless and armless statue of Demeter. Behind it is part of a relief showing Triptolemus setting out in his chariot. A statue of Persephone is from Roman times. There is no representation of Dionysus except for a statue of Antinous posing as the youthful god. There are sculptures referring to Asclepius and Heracles. Of particular interest is a coin representing Demeter in a chariot drawn by winged snakes and holding in her hand a sheaf of grain. On the reverse is a sow, the animal usually sacrificed to Demeter.

The legendary foundation of a city at Eleusis by Eleusis, a son of Ogygus of Thebes before the fifteenth century B.C. is substantiated in date at least by existing remains of houses dated to the eighteenth or seventeenth centuries B.C. Tradition tells of wars between the Athenians and Eleusinians in heroic times, resulting in the deaths of Erechtheus and of Immaradus, son of Eumolpus. Eumolpus (Good Singer) was a Thracian, who is described as having come to Attica either as a bard, a warrior, or a priest of Demeter and Dionysus. The common tradition represents him as a son of Poseidon and Chione. Chione, after having given birth to Eumolpus, threw him into the sea. Poseidon, however, rescued him and had him brought up in Ethiopia by his daughter Benthesicyma. When he grew up, he married a daughter of Benthesicyma, by whom he had a son Ismarus (Immardus). But when he tried to seduce his wife's sister, Eumolpus and Ismarus were expelled, and they went to the Thracian king Tegyrius, whose daughter Ismarus married. But as Eumolpus drew upon himself the suspicion of Tegyrius, he was again obliged to take flight. He came to Eleusis where he formed a friendship with the Eleusinians. After the death of his son Ismarus, however, he returned to Thrace at the request of King Tegyrius. The Eleusinians, who were involved in a war with Athens, called Eumolpus to their assistance. Eumolpus came with a large army of Thracians, but he was slain by Erechtheus. The traditions about this Eleusinian war differ very much. According to some, the Eleusinians under Eumolpus attacked the Athenians under Erectheus but were defeated, and Eumolpus and his two sons Phorbas and Immaradus were slain (Thuc. 2.15). Pausanias (1.38.3) relates a tradition that in the battle between the Eleusinians and Athenians, Erechtheus and Immaradus fell and that peace concluded with these conditions: that the Eleusinians should in all respects be subject to Athens, except that they alone should have the celebration of their mysteries, and that Eumolpus and the daughters of Celeus should perform the customary sacrifices. When Eumolpus died, his younger son Ceryx succeeded him in the priestly office. According to some, Eumolpus came to Attica with a colony of Thracians to claim the country as the property of his father Poseidon. Mythology regards Eumolpus as the founder of the Eleusinian mysteries and as the first priest of Demeter and Dionysus. The goddess herself taught him, Triptolemus, Diocles, and Celeus the sacred rites, and he is therefore sometimes described as having himself invented the cultivation of the vine and of fruit trees in general (*Hymn. Hom. ad Cer.* 476). Legends also connected him with Heracles, whom he is said to have instructed in music or initiated into the mysteries (Theocrit. 24.108; Apollod. 2.5.12) The tomb of Eumolpus was shown both at Eleusis and Athens (Paus. 1.38.2).

Eumolpus was reputed to be the first celebrant of the mysteries of Eleusis. The introduction of the cult of Demeter is ascribed by some to the reign of Erechtheus (*ca.* 1409 B.C.) and by others to that of Pandion, son of Erichthonius (*ca.* 1462–1423 B.C.). The first shrine on the sanctuary site is dated by shards to 1500–1400 B.C., though there is nothing concrete to connect it with Demeter. The Homeric *Hymn to Demeter* gives the commonly accepted version of the institution of the mysteries by Demeter herself. The city seems to have been a rival of Athens until it came under firm Athenian sway about the time of Solon, who was elected archon in 594 B.C. Thereafter, its cult grew and the sanctuary was constantly enlarged.

Eleusis appears to have no clear-cut lineage of kings, and we find instead isolated references to such rulers as Eleusis and Celeus, Polyxenus (*Hymn. Hom. ad*

Cer. 154), and Cercyon. Cercyon, a son of Poseidon, came to Eleusis from Arcadia. He is notorious for his cruelty toward Alope and all who refused to fight with him, but he was in the end conquered and slain by Theseus (Paus. 1.39.3). Alope, his daughter, was beloved by Poseidon on account of her great beauty and became by him the mother of a son, whom she exposed immediately after his birth. But a mare came and suckled the child until it was found by shepherds, who fell into a dispute over who was to have the beautiful royal attire of the boy. The case was brought before Cercyon, who recognized the identity of the boy by his clothes. He ordered Alope put to death and her child exposed again. The latter was fed and found in the same manner as before, and the shepherds called him Hippothoon. The body of Alope was changed by Poseidon into a fountain, which bore the same name (Aristoph. *Av.* 533). There was a monument of Alope on the road from Eleusis to Megara, on the spot where she was believed to have been killed by her father (Paus. 1.39.3). Cercyon is the only one of these kings not connected in some way with the worship of Demeter.

We find also mention of persons peripheral to the Eleusinian mysteries, such as Dysaules. He was the father of Triptolemus and Eubuleus and a brother of Celeus. According to a tradition of Phlius, he had been expelled from Eleusis by Ion and had come to Phlius, where he introduced the Eleusinian mysteries. His tomb was shown at Celeae, which is said to have been named after his brother Celeus (Paus. 1.14.3, 2.14.2).

Cychreus was a king of neighboring Salamis, but he had a direct connection with the mysteries. He was a son of Poseidon and became king of Salamis, which was called after him Cychreia and which he delivered from a dragon. According to other traditions, Cychreus himself was called a dragon on account of his savage nature and was expelled from Salamis by Eurylochus; but he was received by Demeter at Eleusis and appointed a priest in her temple.

Others were connected with the spread of this worship, such as Caucon, Cyamites, Phytalus, and Rharus. Caucon, a son of Celaenus, was believed to have carried the orgies of the Great Goddess from Eleusis to Messene, where he was worshipped as a hero. Cyamites (Hero of Beans) was a mysterious cult figure who had a small sanctuary on the road from Athens to Eleusis. No particulars are known about him, but Pausinias (1.37.3) says that those who were initiated in the mysteries would understand the nature of the hero. Phytalus was an Eleusinian hero who is said to have kindly received Demeter on her wanderings and was rewarded by the goddess with a fig tree (Paus. 1.37.2). To him the noble Athenian family of the Phytalidae traced its origin (Plut. *Thes.* 12,22). Rharus was designated by some as the father of Triptolemus. The Rharian plain in the neighborhood of Eleusis was said to have been named for him, and from that plain Demeter derived the surname of Rharias.

We can see that while Poseidon had no direct role in the Eleusinian mysteries, he was considered an important deity at Eleusis. Not only was Eleusis next to the sea, but Poseidon had also fathered some of the important principals in the history of this sacred place. Two other mythological beings had shrines in the vicinity of Eleusis but no connection with the mysteries. One was Zarax, a hero who was believed to have been instructed in music by Apollo and had a shrine near Eleusis. The other was Zephyrus, the personification of the west wind, who had an altar on the Sacred Way from Athens to Eleusis (Paus. 1.37.2).

The Homeric *Hymn to Demeter* tells the commonly accepted story of the foundation of the mysteries at Eleusis. It involves Demeter and her daughter Persephone, also known as Kore (Maiden). While gathering flowers, Persephone was abducted by Hades (Pluto) to the underworld. The Eleusinians mentioned the Nysaean plain in Boeotia as the scene of her rape. Other traditions say she was abducted at Erineus near Eleusis (Paus. 1.38.5). In the mysteries of Eleusis, the return of Persephone from the lower world was regarded as the symbol of immortality, and thus she was frequently represented on sarcophagi. Demeter, in her quest for Persephone, came to Eleusis, where she was found resting (on what came to be known as the Mirthless Stone), disguised as an old woman, by Metaneira, wife of King Celeus. Demeter later revealed her identity and commanded Celeus to build a dwelling for her. She closed herself in and vowed that she would not allow crops to grow on earth until Persephone was recovered. Finally Zeus commanded Hades to return Persephone. However, while in the underworld, she had eaten pomegranate seeds and therefore she had to return there for part of every year. When Persephone was restored to Demeter, Hermes took her in Hades' chariot to Eleusis to her mother. At Eleusis both were joined by Hecate, who remained as attendant and companion to Persephone. The gods persuaded Demeter to return to Olympus and to restore fertility to the earth. Rhea descended to the Rharian plain near Eleusis and conciliated Demeter, who again allowed the fruits of the field to grow. But before she parted from Eleusis she instructed Triptolemus, Diocles, Eumolpus, and Celeus in the mode of her worship and in the mysteries.

Triptolemus was a son of Celeus and Metaneira or Polymnia, or, according to others, a son of King Eleusis by Cothonea (or Cyntinea or Hyona). Others again describe him as a son of Oceanus and Gaea, as a younger brother or relation of Celeus, as a son of Trochilus by an Eleusinian woman, as a son of Rharus by a daughter of Amphictyon, or, lastly, as a son of Dysaules (Paus. 1.14.3;

Hymn. Hom. ad Cer. 153). Triptolemus was the favorite of Demeter and the inventor of the plough and agriculture and of civilization, which is the result of it. He was the great hero in the Eleusinian mysteries (Callim. *Hymn. in Cer.* 22; Virg. *Georg.* 1.19). According to Apollodorus (1.5.2), Triptolemus was a son of Celeus and Metaneira. Celeus is described as the first priest of Demeter at Eleusis and his daughters as priestesses of the goddess (*Hymn. Hom. ad Cer.* 101; Paus. 1.38.3). Demeter, on her arrival at Eleusis, undertook to nurse Demophon, a brother of Triptolemus, who had just been born. In order to make the child immortal, Demeter at night put him into a fire. But Metaneira, discovering the proceeding, screamed out and the child was consumed by the flames. As a compensation for this bereavement, the goddess gave to Triptolemus a chariot with winged dragons and seeds of wheat. According to others, Triptolemus first sowed barley in the Rharian plain, and thence spread the cultivation of grain all over the earth; and in later times an altar and threshing floor of Triptolemus were shown there (Paus. 1.38.6). In the Homeric *Hymn to Demeter,* Triptolemus is described as one of the chief men of the country, who like other nobles is instructed by Demeter in her sacred worship (*Hymn. Hom. ad Cer.* 123,474); but no mention is made of any relationship between him and Celeus. In one tradition, Triptolemus, the son of Eleusis, was the boy whom the goddess wished to make immortal. Eleusis, who was watching her, was discovered by her and punished with instant death (Ov. *Trist.* 3.8.2). Triptolemus, after having received the dragon chariot, rode in it all over the earth making man acquainted with the blessings of agriculture. On his return to Attica, King Celeus wanted to kill him but by the command of Demeter was obliged to give up his country to Triptolemus, which Triptolemus now called Eleusis after his father. He now established the worship of Demeter and instituted the Thesmophoria. He had temples and statues both at Eleusis and Athens (Paus. 1.14.1,38.6). Triptolemus is represented in works of art as a youthful hero, sometimes with a broad-brimmed hat, on a chariot drawn by dragons, and holding in his hand a scepter and wheat ears.

Candidates for initiation into the mysteries were first admitted to the Lesser Eleusinia. These were held in the month of Anthesterion (February-March) at Agrae in Athens, on the banks of Ilissus. After their acceptance as initiates, the candidates were allowed to attend the Greater Eleusinia. This took place in Boedromion (September) and lasted nine days, starting out from and ending back in Athens. For the Greater Eleusinia a truce was in effect throughout Greece. These annual celebrations included public festivities open to all as well as the highly secret religious rite available only to initiates.

The public part culminated in a procession from Athens to Eleusis. The procession took place on the fifth of the month and was headed by a statue of Iacchus, the god associated with the cult, who carried a torch. Iacchus was the solemn name of the mystic Bacchus at Athens and Eleusis. The Phrygian Bacchus was looked upon in the Eleusinian mysteries as a child, and as such he is described as the son of Demeter (surnamed Deo or Calligeneia) and Zeus, and as the brother of Kore. His name was derived from the boisterous festive song likewise called Iacchus (Aristoph. *Ran.* 321,400; Herod. 8.65). From these statements it is clear that the ancients distinguished Iacchus, the son of Zeus and Demeter, from the Theban Bacchus (Dionysus), the son of Zeus and Semele. In some traditions Iacchus is called a son of Bacchus. He is also identified with the infernal Zagreus, the son of Zeus and Persephone. At Athens a statue of Iacchus bearing a torch in his hand was seen by the side of those of Demeter and Kore (Paus. 1.2.4). In some traditions Iacchus is described as the companion of Baubo or Babo, at the time when she endeavored to cheer the mourning Demeter by lascivious gestures.

The fundamental substance of the mysteries, the character of the sacred objects displayed, and the nature of the revelation experienced were never divulged. It was thought probable that a pageant was performed representing the action of the *Hymn to Demeter* (*Hymn. Hom. ad Cer.*). Initiation carried with it no further obligation but seems to have afforded spiritual pleasure.

ELEUSIS   was an ancient town of Boeotia on the Triton River and near Lake Copais, which, together with the neighboring town of Athenae, was destroyed by flooding of the river and lake (Paus. 9.24.2). Cecrops is said to have founded these two towns. He was the first king of Attica and the earliest champion of Athena since he decided in her favor in her dispute with Poseidon over the possession of Attica. We find the most ancient seat of Athena's worship in Greece on the banks of the Triton River.

ELEUTHERAE (KAZA)   was a fortified town on the pass from Attica to Boeotia between Mounts Parnes and Cithaeron. It belonged originally to Boeotia but was acquired by Athens in the fourth century B.C. The well-preserved circuit wall reaches around the summit of a hill, making an ellipse about 330 meters long and 165 meters wide. There are four gates. The towers, of which eight remain at the north, were two stories high and had doors, windows, and stairways. The ruins may be seen near the village of Kaza on the road from modern Elefsina to Thebes.

Eleuther, a son of Apollo and Aethusa, the daughter of Poseidon, was regarded as the founder of Eleutherae. He is said to have been the first to erect a statue of

Dionysus and spread the worship of the god. The birthplace of Dionysus was located by some at Eleutherae. The name Eleuthereus might have been derived from Eleutherae because of this opinion and because he was worshipped there. Dionysus Melanaegis (Armed or Clad with a Black Aegis) occurred also at Eleutherae, where he had a temple. From the east wall of Eleutherae can be seen the foundations of a temple dating from about 300 B.C. This was probably the temple of Dionysus mentioned by Pausanias (1.38.8).

When Antiope was with child by Zeus, fear of her mortal father induced her to flee to Sicyon, where she married Epopeus. Nycteus, her husband, killed himself in despair but charged his brother Lycus to avenge him on Epopeus and Antiope. Lycus accordingly marched against Sicyon, took the town, slew Epopeus and carried Antiope with him to Eleutherae. During her imprisonment there she gave birth to two sons, Amphion and Zethus, who were exposed but found and brought up by shepherds. (See CITHAERON.)

An interesting conjecture is raised in connection with Zeus Lycaeus. No one was allowed to enter the sanctuary of Zeus Lycaeus on Mount Lycaeon, and there was a belief that if anyone did he or she died within twelve months after. Those who entered it intentionally were stoned to death unless they escaped by flight; and those who got in by accident were sent to Eleutherae (Plut. *Quaest. Gr.* 39). This custom was questioned by Plutarch, who conjectured either that it was a symbolic reference: sent to "Free Town" (Eleutherae), i.e., set free, or used in relation to Eleuther, one of the sons of Lycaon, who had no share in the serving of human flesh to Zeus and who fled to Boeotia and established at Eleutherae a kind of amnesty for persons who involuntarily entered the sanctuary of Zeus Lycaeus.

ELEUTHERNA (ELEFTHERNA)   was a town of great importance in Crete, situated on the northwest slopes of Mount Ida, about 30 km from the harbor of Rethimno. Its origin was ascribed to the legendary Curetes, and it was here that Ametor or Amiton first accompanied his love songs on the cithara (Athen. 14.638). Eleutherna was in alliance with Cnossus till the people of Polyrrhenium and Lampe compelled it to break off from the confederacy (Polyb. 4.53,55). Among the places in Crete particularly sacred to Zeus were the towns around Mount Ida, such as Eleutherna. The ruins can be reached by a short walk from the center of the modern village of Eleftherna. The acropolis stands on a precipitous ridge and is reached by a narrow rock causeway.

ELIS (ILIA)   was the country on the west coast of Peloponnesus between Achaia and Messenia, extending from the promontory Araxus and the river Larissus on the north to the river Neda on the south, and bounded on the east by the Arcadian mountains and on the west by the Ionian Sea. It was made up of three regions: Elis Proper or Hollow Elis, the northern portion, which reached from the Araxus River to the promontory Ichthys; Pisatis, the middle portion, from the promontory Ichthys to the Alpheius River; and Triphylia, the southern portion, from the Alpheius River to the Neda River.

The coast of Elis is a long, sandy stretch with three promontories—Araxus, Chelonatas, and Ichthys. Along the coast are several lagoons that are separated from the sea only by narrow sandbars. This collection of stagnant water generates mosquitoes, gnats, and other insects, and in antiquity the Eleans invoked Zeus Apomyius and Heracles to protect them from the pests. These lagoons, on the other hand, provide the inhabitants with such an abundance of fish that it is necessary to export large quantities. This fishing industry was carried on in ancient times since we find Apollo Opsophagos (Fish-Eater) worshipped among the Eleans.

There were no natural barriers in Elis so the country had very little protection from attack. It had a better barrier than any natural one, however, in the sacred character of the whole land that emanated from the temple of Zeus Olympius on the banks of the Alpheius River. Its territory was regarded as inviolable by common consent, and for the most part, though its sanctity was not always respected, it enjoyed for several centuries exemption from the ravages of war. Therefore Elis had mostly unwalled villages, and the Alpheius valley had many sanctuaries and shrines. The inhabitants were prosperous because of their freedom to pursue peace instead of war and because of the spending of strangers who attended the festival of the Olympian Zeus.

Hollow Elis is larger and more fertile than the other two districts. It consists of a fertile plain drained by the Peneius River and its tributary the Ladon (not to be confused with the Arcadian Ladon). The Peneius rises in Mount Erymanthus and flows in a northwest direction till it reaches the valley. The Ladon, called Selleeis by Homer (*Il.* 2.659), rises a little more to the south; it falls into the Peneius just where it enters the broad valley. The united stream continues its course through this valley, past the town of Elis, and empties into the sea to the south of the promontory of Chelonatas. It appears that it might have had a different mouth in earlier times. The legend of Heracles cleansing the stables of Augeas by diverting the course of the Peneius would seem to show that even in ancient times the course of the stream had been changed either by artificial or by natural means.

The plain of Gastouni is still celebrated for its fertility; it produces flax, wheat, and cotton. The vine was also extensively cultivated and a festival called Thyia honored Dionysus in the city of Elis (Paus. 6.26.1). The

Peneius valley provided good grazing land for horses and cattle. One recalls the famous stables of Augeas, king of the Epeians in Elis, and horses of Elis were praised in the Homeric stories (*Od.* 4.634, 21.346).

Pisatis occupies the middle portion of Elis, the lower valley of the Alpheius. Mount Pholoe, an extension of Erymanthus, reaches across Pisatis from east to west and separates the Peneius and the Ladon from the Alpheius. It terminates in the promontory opposite the island of Zacynthus. This promontory, called Ichthys in ancient times because of its shape, now bears the name Katakolo.

Triphylia, the smallest and most southern of the three divisions of Elis, has very little level land since the Arcadian mountains reach almost to the sea in this area. These mounts run along the whole coastline. In the south part of Triphylia the principal ranges are Lapithas and Minthi, between which the Anigrus River empties into the sea. Minthi, the highest mountain (1,222 meters) in Elis, was one of the seats of the worship of Hades; and the herb from which it derived its name was sacred to Persephone. The river Neda divided Triphylia from Messenia.

The most ancient inhabitants of Elis appear to have been Pelasgians and of the same stock as the Arcadians. They were called Caucones, and their name is said to have been originally given to the whole country. Elis was easily accessible both by land and by sea, so many tribes settled there from a very early time. There were settlements from as far away as Phoenicia. Traces of Phoenician influence in the worship of Aphrodite Urania were found in the city of Elis.

The Epeians were very early inhabitants; they were closely connected with the Aetolians. According to legend, the first king of Elis was Aethlius (Paus. 5.1.2). He was a son of Zeus and Protogeneia, the daughter of Deucalion, and was married to Calyce, by whom he begot Endymion. According to some accounts, Endymion was himself a son of Zeus and first king of Elis (Apollod. 1.7.5). Other traditions again make Aethlius a son of Aeolus, who was called by the name of Zeus (Paus. 5.8.1). Endymion succeeded Aethlius. He is usually remembered for being the pretty youth beloved by Selene, the moon goddess, who put him to sleep forever and had by him in this somnolent state fifty daughters (Paus. 5.1.4). Others state that he expelled Clymenus from the kingdom of Elis and introduced into the country Aeolian settlers from Thessaly (Apollod. 1.7.5; Paus. 5.8.1). Some call him a son of Zeus by Protogeneia and others a son of Aetolus. He is said to have been married to Asterodia, Chromia (the great-granddaughter of Deucalion, just as he was Deucalion's great-grandson), Hyperippe, Neis, or Iphianassa. Aetolus, Epeius, Eurycyda, and Naxus are called his children. He caused his sons to engage in the race course at Olympia and promised to the victor the succession in his kingdom. Epeius conquered his brothers and succeeded Endymion as king of Elis. He was believed to be buried at Olympia, which also contained a statue of him in the treasury of the Metapontians (Paus. 6.19.11).

Epeius thus became the third king of Elis. He married Anaxiroe, the daughter of Coronus, and fathered Hyrmina. Hyrmina married Phorbas, the son of Lapithus, and became the mother of Actor, the father of the Molionidae, Eurytus and Cteatus.

Epeius died early and was succeeded by his brother Aetolus. Aetolus was married to Pronoe, by whom he had two sons, Pleuron and Calydon. During the funeral games celebrated in honor of Azan, he ran with his chariot over Apis, the son of Iason or Salmoneus, and killed him. Then the sons of Apis exiled Aetolus. After leaving Peloponnesus, he went to the country of the Curetes between the Achelous River and the Corinthian Gulf, where he slew Dorus, Laodocus, and Polypoetes, the sons of Helios and Phthia, and gave to the country the name of Aetolia. The rule of Elis was thus passed to his nephew. However, through Pleuron and Calydon a lineage was established that ultimately produced Oxylus, the eleventh king of Elis, who was one of the leaders of the Dorian invasion.

Thus Eleius, the son of Eurycyde, sister of Aetolus, and Poseidon, came to the throne. The name of the Eleians was supposedly derived from him, although others claimed that distinction for Eleius, a son of Tantalus. The Epeians, named for the previously mentioned Epeius, son of Endymion, were more widely spread than the Eleians. We find Epeians not only in Elis Proper but also in Triphylia and in the islands of the Echinades at the mouth of the Achelous; the Eleians, by contrast, were confined to Elis Proper. In Homer the name Eleians does not occur; and though the country is called Elis, its inhabitants are always the Epeians.

The rule next passed to Augeas, the son of Eleius, who was very rich in cattle. Augeas is remembered mainly because of his dirty stables and the labor of Heracles in cleansing them. Eurystheus imposed the labor of cleansing these stables in one day. Heracles approached Augeas and, without mentioning the command of Eurystheus, offered to cleanse the stables if Augeas would give him one-tenth of his cattle or part of his territory for the job. Augeas, believing that Heracles could not possibly accomplish this task, agreed, and Heracles took Phyleus, the son of Augeas, as his witness. Heracles then diverted the rivers Alpheius and Peneius through the stables, which were thus cleansed in the time agreed upon. But Augeas, who learned that Heracles had undertaken the work at the command of Eurystheus, refused the reward, denied his promise, and declared that he would have the matter decided by a judicial verdict. Phyleus then bore witness against his father, who exiled him from Elis. Eurystheus declared the work thus performed to be unacceptable because Heracles had stipulated with Augeas a payment for it (Apollod. 2.5.5). At a subsequent time Heracles marched with an army of Argives and Tirynthians against Augeas to take revenge for his faithlessness. In a narrow gorge in Elis Heracles was taken by surprise by Cteatus and Eurytus, and lost a great number of his warriors.

Cteatus and Eurytus, called the Moliones, were nephews of Augeas. According to Homer (*Il.* 11.709,750), the Moliones, when yet boys, took part in an expedition of the Epeians against Neleus and the Pylians. When Heracles marched against Augeas to punish him for refusing to give the reward he had promised, Augeas entrusted the conduct of the war to the Moliones; Heracles, who in the meantime was taken ill and concluded peace with Augeas, was mistakenly attacked and beaten by the brothers. In order to take vengeance, he afterward slew the Moliones near Cleonae, on the frontier of Argolis, as they had been sent from Elis to sacrifice at the Isthmian games on behalf of the town (Apollod. 2.7.2; Pind. *Ol.* 11.33; Paus. 8.14.9). The Eleians demanded that the Argives atone for this murder; but as the latter refused and were not excluded from the Isthmian games, Molione, the mother, cursed the Eleians who should ever take part again in those games (Paus. 5.2.2). Heracles, on the other hand, dedicated, on account of his victory, six altars at Olympia and instituted special honors at Nemea for the 360 Cleonaeans who had died while assisting him. The Moliones are also mentioned as conquerors of Nestor in the chariot race and as having taken part in the Calydonian hunt. Their tomb was shown in later times at Cleonae (Paus. 2.15.1). According to some, Heracles killed Augeas and his sons. After this victory, Heracles marked out the sacred ground on which the Olympic games were to be celebrated, built altars, and instituted the Olympian festival and games (Apollod. 2.7.2; Pind. *Ol.* 10.55). According to Pausanias, Heracles sacked Elis with an army. To Phyleus he gave up the land of Elis and all prisoners; he also allowed Augeas to escape punishment. When Phyleus had returned to Dulichium after organizing the affairs of Elis, Augeas died at an advanced age, and the kingdom devolved on Agasthenes, the other son of Augeas (Paus. 5.3.2,3).

Under Augeas, certain responsibility for the government of Elis came to be shared, and this joint rule was continued in the next reign. Actor and his remaining sons had a share in the kingdom. Also a certain Amarynceus, a son of Pyttius of Thessaly, was given a share in the government of Elis for his allegiance when Heracles was preparing to attack (Paus. 5.1.11). When Amarynceus died, his sons celebrated funeral games in his honor, in which Nestor, as he himself relates, took part (Hom. *Il.* 23.629).

When Agasthenes ascended the throne of Elis, he shared the government with Amphimachus and Thalpius. For the sons of Actor had married twin sisters, the daughters of Dexamenus, who was king at Olenus. Amphimachus was the son of Cteatus and Theronice, and Thalpius was the son of Eurytus and Theraphone. Amarynceus, who had shared the government with Augeas, apparently was succeeded in this administrative role by his son Diores because it is reported that the kingdom of the Epeians was divided into four states. This is borne out by the statement of Homer (*Il.* 2.620) that the Epeians had four leaders in the Trojan War—Diores, Amphimachus, Thalpius, and Polyxenus, son of Agasthenes. Collectively, they sailed in forty ships. They were highly esteemed in the war, referred to as "glorious Epeians" by Homer (*Il.* 13.686). Other leaders emerged on the field, such as Meges, son of Phyleus, and Amphion and Dracius. Of the four principal captains, however, only Polyxenus returned.

The son of Polyxenus was Amphimachus, named for his father's associate, relative, and friend, who died at Troy. Amphimachus became king and fathered a son whom he called Eleius, thus retaining another family name. While Eleius was king, the assembly of the Dorian army under the sons of Aristomachus took place, with a view to returning to Peloponnesus (Paus. 5.3.5). In accordance with an oracle, they chose Oxylus as one of their leaders. He was a son of Haemon and husband of Pieria, by whom he became the father of Aetolus and Laias. Like the ruling family, he was descended from Endymion and, in fact, was eighth in descent from Aetolus, the fourth king of Elis. Aetolus had been exiled and settled in Aetolia; Oxylus was born there. When Oxylus conquered Elis, it was fitting that he should recover the royal lineage for his branch of the family. He had three sons, Aetolus, Laias, and Andraemon. Of Andraemon nothing is known except that he married Dryope, who by Apollo became mother of Amphissus. Aetolus died while still a boy, and his parents were directed by an oracle to bury him neither inside nor outside the city of Elis. They accordingly buried him under the gate at which the road to Olympia commenced. The gymnasiarch of Elis used to offer an annual sacrifice on his tomb as late as the time of Pausanias (5.4.4). Laias succeeded his father to the throne, and at that point the line began to move into the historical period.

Great changes now followed. In consequence of the kinship of the Epeians and Aetolians, they easily coalesced into one people, who from that time appeared under the name of Eleians. They formed a powerful kingdom in the northern part of the country in the plain of the Peneius. Some writers think that an Aetolian colony was also settled at Pisa. Pisa is represented in the earliest times as the residence of Oenomaus and Pelops, who gave his name to the peninsula; subsequently Pisa disappeared altogether and was not mentioned by Homer. It was probably absorbed in the great Pylian monarchy. It regained its independence at a later time and was the head of a confederacy of eight states. After the overthrow of the Pylian monarchy, the Minyae, who had been expelled from Laconia by the conquering Dorians, took possession of Triphylia and drove out the original inhabitants of the country, the Paroreatae and Caucones (Herod. 4.148). Here they set up a state consisting of six cities, and they were strong enough to maintain their independence against the Messenian Dorians. The name Triphylia was sometimes derived from an eponymous Triphylus, an Arcadian chief (Polyb. 4.77; Paus. 10.9.1); but the name probably describes their ethnic composition from three principal tribes—the Epeians, the Minyae, and the Eleians (Strab. 8.3.3).

According to the religious traditions at Elis, Cronus was the first ruler of that country, and in the golden age there was a temple dedicated to him at Olympia. Rhea entrusted the infant Zeus to the Idaean Dactyls, who were also called Curetes, and had come from Mount Ida in Crete to Elis. Heracles contended with his brother Dactyls in a footrace and adorned the victor with a wreath of olive. In this manner he is said to have founded the Olympian games and Zeus to have contended with Cronus for the kingdom of Elis (Paus. 5.7.6). It is obvious that there has always been confusion in regard to the foundation of the games at Olympia.

The celebration of the festival of Zeus at Olympia had originally belonged to the Pisatans, in the neighborhood of whose city Olympia was situated. Upon the conquest of Pisa, the presidency of the festival passed over to their Eleian conquerors; but the Pisatans never forgot their ancient privilege and made many attempts to recover it. Over a period of four hundred years battles and alliances took place, and ultimately in 362 B.C. the Eleians had Olympia fully assigned to them along with the presidency of the festival (Xenoph. *Hellen.* 7.4.33,34).

The other major gods deserving special mention for tribute paid them in Elis were Hera, Artemis, Demeter, Hades, Dionysus, Apollo, Athena, and Aphrodite.

Hera was worshipped under the surname Ammonia since the inhabitants of Elis had from the earliest times been in the habit of consulting the oracle of Zeus Ammon in Libya (Paus. 5.15.11).

Artemis was worshipped under three surnames. The name Artemis Alphaea (Alpheaea, or Alpheiusa) she derived from the river-god Alpheius, who loved her. Artemis Cordaca was derived from an indecent dance called *cordax,* which the companions of Pelops are said to have performed in honor of the goddess after a victory they had won (Paus. 6.22.1). Artemis Orthia, at whose altar in Sparta boys had to undergo ritualistic flogging, had a temple in the city of Elis.

Chamyne was a surname of Demeter derived from one Chamynus, to whom the building of a temple of Demeter at Elis was ascribed (Paus. 6.21.1). Her son-in-law Hades had a sacred enclosure and a temple which was opened only once in every year (Paus. 6.25.2).

The temple of Apollo Acacesius was the principal temple in the city of Elis. The surname, which had the same meaning as Acestor and Alexicacus, characterized the god as the averter of evil (Paus. 6.24.6).

Dionysus was said by some to have been born in Elis. Narcaeus, a son of Dionysus and Narcaea, introduced there the worship of Dionysus (Paus. 5.16.7) and also established a sanctuary of Athena Narcaea.

There were two temples of Aphrodite. Aphrodite Urania had a chryselephantine statue by Pheidias depicting her with one foot on a tortoise. Aphrodite Pandemos (Common to All the People) was a surname at Elis. Her statue by Scopas showed her riding on a ram (Paus. 6.25.1).

In addition to these divinities may be added Helios. His worship was established in Elis later than in other parts of Greece (Paus. 6.24.6). Statues of the Charites were mentioned at Elis. Dactyli, different from the Idaean Dactyls, were named as healing divinities (Paus. 5.7.6). Tyche, the goddess of chance or luck, was worshiped in Elis (Paus. 6.25.4). Even the jovial, drunken satyr, Silenus, the constant companion of Dionysus, had a temple at Elis, where Methe (Drunkenness) stood by his side handing him a cup of wine.

ELIS (ILIS or ILIDA)   was the capital of the country of Elis. Its position was the best that could have been chosen for the capital. The point at which the Peneius emerges from the hills into the plain was a hill 152 meters in height. This hill was the acropolis of Elis and commanded the narrow valley of the Peneius. The ancient city lay at the foot of the hill and extended across the river. No remains have been found on the north bank so it is probable that all the public buildings were on the south bank of the river. On the site of the ancient city there are two or three small villages, which bear the common name of Paleopoli.

Elis is mentioned as a town of the Epeians by Homer (*Il.* 2.615); but in the earliest times the two chief towns in the country appear to have been Ephyra, the residence of Augeas, in the interior, and Buprasium on the coast. Elis first became a place of importance upon the invasion of Peloponnesus by the Dorians. Oxylus and his Aetolian followers appear to have settled on the aforementioned hill as the place best suited for ruling the country. After that time it was first the residence of the kings and later the aristocratic families who governed the country after the abolition of monarchy. Elis was the only fortified town in the country.

When Pausanias visited Elis, it was one of the most populous and splendid cities of Greece.

The gymnasium stood on the side of the river Peneius; and it is probable that the gymnasium and agora occupied the greater part of the space between the river and the citadel. The gymnasium was a vast enclosure surrounded by a wall. It was by far the largest gymnasium in Greece, since all the *athletae* in the Olympic games were obliged to undergo a month's previous training here.

The gymnasium had two principal entrances, one leading by the street called Siope (Silence) to the baths, and the other above the cenotaph of Achilles to the agora. Toward one end of this stoa was the Hellanodicaion, a building divided from the agora by a street. It was the official residence of the Hellanodicae, the presidents of the Olympic games, who received here instruction in their duties for ten months preceding the festival. The temple of Aphrodite Urania was adjacent to the stoa, as was the temple of Apollo Acacesius. Statues of Helios and Selene, a temple of the Graces, a temple of Silenus, and the tomb of Oxylus were also located here. On the way to the threater was the temple of Hades. The Nymphae Acmenes were certain nymphs worshiped at Elis, where a sacred enclosure contained their altar, together with those of other gods (Paus. 5.15.6). Near the theater was a temple of Dionysus containing a statue of the god by Praxiteles. On the acropolis was a temple of Athena containing a statue of the goddess in gold and ivory by Pheidias. Excavations, begun in 1910 and still proceeding, have so far uncovered the agora, part of the Hellanodicaion, two gymnasia, the south stoa called the Corcyraea, and the theater. The other buildings mentioned by Pausanias are still to be found.

ELLOPIA   was an earlier name of the island of EUBOEA.

ELONE   was a town of Perrhaebia in Thessaly, afterward called Leimone, according to Strabo (9.5.19). The same writer says that it was in ruins in his time and that it lay at the foot of Mount Olympus not far from the river Titaresius. Polypoetes, a son of Peirithous and Hippodameia, was one of the Lapiths, who joined the Greeks in the Trojan War, commanding the men of Argissa, Gyrtone, Orthe, Elone, and Oloosson (Hom. *Il.* 2.738), At the funeral games of Patroclus he gained the victory in throwing the iron ball (Hom. *Il.* 23.836). After the fall of Troy, Polypoetes and Leonteus are said to have founded the town of Aspendus in Pamphylia.

ELYRUS (RODOVANI)   was the most important city of southwest Crete. It had a harbor, Suia, situated on the south coast of the island. Pausanias says that he had seen at Delphi the bronze goat dedicated by the Elyrians. The goat was represented in the act of suckling Phylacis and Phylander, children of Apollo and the nymph Acacallis, whose love had been won by the youthful god at the house of Carmanor at Tarrha. The site of Elyrus was discovered south of Rodovani. There are remains of walls, the circumference of which is about 3 km. At another elevation there are other walls, thought to be an acropolis. Farther on are some massive stones, some pieces of an entablature, and several fragments of the shafts of columns, all that now remains of an ancient temple. There are also remains of a theater.

EMATHIA (IMATHIA)   was a district mentioned by Homer (*Il.* 14.226) in conjunction with Pieria. It lay between Thessaly and Paeonia and Thrace. It included the region beyond the Haliacmon and on the east side of the Olympian ridge. It was protected on all sides by mountains and marshes and was far enough from the sea to be secure from invasion. Emathus was a son of Macedon and brother of Pierus, from whom Emathia was believed to have derived its name. Pierus, an autochthon and king of Emathia, begot by Euippe or Antiope nine daughters, to whom he gave the names of the nine Muses. They afterward entered into a contest with the Muses, and, being conquered, they were metamorphosed into various birds (Paus. 9.29.1; Ov. *Met.* 5.295). The daughters of Pierus, the Pierides, are sometimes called Emathides after their uncle (Ov. *Met.* 5.669).

Part of Emathia was occupied by the Briges, who were driven out of the Temenidae, whose center of government was at Edessa. Herodotus (8.138) placed the gardens of Midas, king of the Briges, at the foot of Mount Bermius.

ENIPEUS (ENIPEAS)   one of the principal rivers of Thessaly, rises in Mount Othrys and, after flowing through the plain of Pharsalus, flows into the Peneius. Its chief tributary is the Apidanus. Enipeus was a river-god in Thessaly, who was beloved by Tyro, the daughter of Salmoneus. She was the wife of Cretheus. Poseidon was enamored of her and appeared to her in the form of Enipeus and became by her the father of Pelias and Neleus (Apollod. 1.9.8). By Cretheus she was the mother of Pheres, Amythaon, and Aeson, the father of Jason (Hom. *Od.* 11.235; Apollod. 1.9.8). When Jason came from Mount Pelion on his way to Iolcus for the first time, he lost a sandal in a river. Some say this river was the Enipeus. Hera, being in love with Jason, assumed the appearance of an old woman and, standing on the bank of the river, requested him to carry her across. In doing so Jason lost one of his sandals. Ovid (*Met.* 6.116) relates that Poseidon assumed the form of Enipeus on another

occasion and begot by Iphimedeia two sons, Otus and Ephialtes.

Enipeus was also the name of a river in Elis, about which the story of Tyro and Poseidon is likewise related. It is the more likely that the location of the story was in Thessaly than in Elis. However, the river in Elis did rise near a place called Salmone, a name that recalls the name of Tyro's father.

ENISPE (DIMITRA)   was an Arcadian town mentioned by Homer (*Il.* 2.606) in the catalog of ships along with Rhipe and Stratia. These joined other Arcadian towns under Agapenor in sixty ships, which Agamemnon had given them because of their ignorance of seafaring. The location of these three towns could never be determined, even in ancient times. Pausanias (8.25.12) contends that the notion that Enispe, Stratia, and Rhipe were islands in the Ladon was nonsense. Only as late as 1939 a claim was made that Enispe was located on a hill near the modern village of Dimitra. The name of the village was changed from Divritsi to reflect the discovery there of a temple of Demeter. The site of Dimitra seems to fit the Homeric epithet "wind-swept."

ENNEA HODOI   (See AMPHIPOLIS)

EPEIRUS (IPIROS)   was the name given to the country lying between the Ionian Sea and the Pindus range and reaching from the Acroceraunian promontory and the boundaries of Illyria and Macedonia on the north to the Ambracian Gulf on the south. The name Epeirus signified the mainland and was the name originally given to the whole of the west coast of Greece, all the way from the Acroceraunian promontory (in present day Albania) as far as the entrance of the Corinthian Gulf. In this sense the name was used from Homer's time until as late as the Peloponnesian War. Today the area, while less extensive, is still quite large, reaching from the Albanian border to the Gulf of Arta and bordering Macedonia, Thessaly, and Central Greece on the east and south. The mountains run in a general direction from north to south and have in all but recent times been the resort of semicivilized and robber tribes. The most extensive and fertile plain is that of Ioannina, near which is situated the oracle of Dodona.

Along the coast southward from the Acroceraunian promontory, a lofty and rugged range of mountains extends. Hardly any of the names of the mountains in the interior are preserved with the exception of Tomarus or Tmarus above Dodona. The most important rivers are: the Arahthus and Louros, flowing into the Ambracian Gulf; the Thiamis, flowing into the Ionian Sea near the Albanian border; and the Aheron, also flowing into the Ionian Sea.

The three chief Epeirot tribes were the Chaones, Thesproti, and Molossi. The most ancient inhabitants of

Epeirus are said to have been Pelasgians. Dodona was represented as an oracle of the Pelasgians. Chaonia was also called Pelasgian; and the Chaones were said, like the Selli at Dodona, to have been interpreters of the oracle of Zeus.

Helenus, son of Priam and Hecuba, was, like his sister Cassandra, a seer. He foretold to Pyrrhus (Neoptolemus), son of Achilles, that Troy should fall only through Pyrrhus and Philoctetes. After the destruction of the city, he revealed to Pyrrhus the sufferings that awaited the Greeks who were returning home by sea and persuaded him to return by land and settle in Epeirus. After the Trojan War, Andromache, the wife of the slain Hector, fell to the share of Pyrrhus, who took her to Epeirus and to whom she bore three sons, Molossus, Pielus, and Pergamus. Here she was found by Aeneas on his landing in Epeirus at the moment she was offering up a sacrifice at the tomb of her beloved Hector (Virg. *Aen.* 3.295). Some state that from Troy Pyrrhus first went to Molossia and from there to Phthia, where he recovered the throne that had in the meantime been taken from Peleus by Acastus. Others say that on his return to Scyros he was cast by storm onto the coast of Ephyra in Epeirus, where Andromache gave birth to Molossus. Still others say that he went to Epeirus on his own accord because he would or could not return to Phthia in Thessaly (Paus. 1.11.1; Virg. *Aen.* 3.333). In Epeirus he is also said to have carried off Lanassa, a granddaughter of Heracles, from the temple of the Dodonean Zeus and to have become by her the father of eight children. After the death of Pyrrhus (or after his marriage to Hermione), Helenus received a portion of the country called Chaonia, of which he became king. He married Andromache, who had been his dead brother's wife. By her he became the father of Cestrinus. When Aeneas came to Epeirus, he was hospitably received by Helenus, who also foretold to him the future events in his life (Virg. *Aen.* 3.245,374; Ov. *Met.* 15.438). After the death of Helenus, who left his kingdom to Molossus, Andromache followed her son Pergamus to Asia. She was supposed to have died at Pergamus, where in after times a shrine was erected in her memory (Paus. 1.11.2).

Arribas (Arrybas, Arymbas, or Tharrytas) was a descendant of Achilles and one of the early kings of the Molossians in Epeirus. When he came to the throne, he was still very young. Being the last surviving member of the royal family, his education was conducted with great care, and he had been sent to Athens to study. On his return he displayed so much wisdom that he won the affection and admiration of his people. He framed for them a code of laws and established a regular constitution. He can be regarded as one of the mythical ancestors of the Molossians, to whom they ascribed the foundation of their political institutions (Plut. *Pyrr.* 1; Paus. 1.11.1).

Two other beings connected with Epeirus were also kings. Echetus was a cruel king who was the terror of all mortals. He was a son of Euchenor and Phlogea. His daughter Metope or Amphissa, who had yielded to the embraces of her lover Aechmodicus, was blinded by her father, and Aechmodicus was emasculated. Echetus further gave iron barleycorns to his daughter, promising to restore her sight if she would grind them to flour (Hom. *Od.* 18.83, 21.307; Apollon. Rhod. 4.1093). Aidoneus was a mythical king of the Molossians, who is represented as the husband of Persephone and father of Cora. After Theseus with the assistance of Peirithous had carried off Helen, he accompanied Peirithous when Peirithous tried to carry off Cora, the daughter of Aidoneus. The king, thinking the two strangers were well-meaning suitors, offered the hand of his daughter to Peirithous on condition that he should fight and conquer his dog Cerberus. But when Aidoneus discovered that they had come with the intention of kidnapping his daughter, he had Peirithous killed by Cerberus and kept Theseus in captivity. The Athenian hero was afterward released at the request of Heracles (Plut. *Thes.* 31,35). This story is a good example of the efforts to make mythological stories historically acceptable.

EPEIUM   (See AEPY)

EPHYRA (EFIRA)
was a town of Elis, situated upon the river Selleeis. It was the ancient capital of Augeas, whom Heracles conquered (Hom. *Il.* 2.659, 15.531). Phyleus, a son of Augeas, was expelled by his father from Ephyra because he gave evidence in favor of Heracles. He then migrated to Dulichium (Hom. *Il.* 2.269, 15.530, 23.637). By Ctimene or Timandra Phyleus became the father of Meges, who is also called Phyleides (Apollod. 2.5.5). His daughter Astyoche became by Heracles the mother of Tlepolemus (Hom. *Il.* 2.658).

Strabo (8.3.5) locates Ephyra 120 stadia (22 km) from Elis on the road to Lasion and says that on its site or near it was built the town of Oenoe or Boeonoa. The site is represented by the Greek National Tourist Organisation as immediately south of the Pinios Dam and as indeed about 22 km from Ilis on the way to Agrapidohorio, the site of ancient Pylos.

EPHYRA (MESOPOTAMO)
was a town of Thesprotian Epeirus afterward called Cichyrus, according to Strabo (7.7.5) It stood near the place where the river Acheron and the Acherusian lake empty into the sea. The acropolis of the city rises north of the Necromanteion. This structure was an oracle of the dead and a sanctuary of Persephone and Hades. It bordered on the once extensive Acherusian lake, which was regarded as a principal entrance to the underworld. The whole atmosphere of this place is somber, and the labyrinthine

corridors, the windowless rooms, and evidence of gim-
mickry for special effects must have raised necromancy to
a fine art. The ruins are reached by way of Mesopotamo, a
crossroads village on the Preveza-Igoumenitsa highway.

Thesprotian Ephyra appears to be the town mentioned in two passages of the *Odyssey* (1.259, 2.328). In
the first, Odysseus went to the Thesprotian Ephyra to
fetch from Ilus, the son of Mermerus, poison for his
arrows; but as he could not get it there, he afterward
obtained it from Anchialus of Taphus. The second passage
has to do with a charge against Telemachus by one of the
wooers of Penelope. He claimed that Telemachus was
planning the death of the suitors by enlisting aid from
Pylos or acquiring poison from Ephyra to be put in their
wine. Apparently Ephyra had a reputation as supplier of
deadly drugs. Pausanias represents Cichyrus as the capital
of the ancient kings of Thesprotia, where Theseus and
Peirithous were thrown into chains by Aidoneus.
Aidoneus, it will be recalled, was a mythical king of
Epeirus, who was visited by Peirithous and Theseus when
the heroes intended to kidnap his daughter, Cora. When
Aidoneus discovered this, he had Peirithous killed by his
vicious dog Cerberus and kept Theseus in captivity until
he was released by Heracles (Plut. *Thes.* 31,35).

It will be remembered, too, that a storm cast
Neoptolemus, returning to Scyros from Molossia, onto
the coast of Ephyra. There Andromache gave birth to
Molossus, to whom the Molossian kings traced their
descent (Pind. *Nem.* 4.82, 7.54).

EPHYRA   was the ancient name of CORINTH.

EPHYRA   was the original name of CRANNON.

EPIDAURUS (ARHIA EPIDAVROS)   was a town on
the east coast of Peloponnesus in the district of Argolis.
Epidaurus, its mythical founder, was a son of Argos and
Euadne, but according to Argive legends he was a son of
Pelops; according to legends of Elis he was a son of Apollo
(Apollod. 2.1.2; Paus. 2.26.3). Throughout most of Greek
history Epidaurus was an independent state having its
own small territory (Epidauria), bounded on the west by
Argolis, on the north by Corinthia, on the south by
Troezenia, and on the east by the Saronic Gulf. Epidaurus
is situated on a small peninsula that projects from a
narrow plain, surrounded on the land side by mountains.
North of the peninsula is a well-protected harbor. The
original town was confined to the peninsula, which is
about 3 km in circumference.

Epidaurus had only a small territory, but it made up
in importance what it lacked in size. Its principal importance lay in its temple of Asclepius, which was about 8 km
from the city. Asclepius was the god of the medical arts.
Some accounts say that Coronis gave birth to him during
an expedition of her father Phlegyas into Peloponnesus in
the territory of Epidaurus and that she exposed him on
Mount Tittheion, which was before called Myrtion. Here
he was fed by a goat and watched by a dog, until at last he
was found by Aresthanas, a shepherd, who saw the boy
surrounded by a lightning-like luminescence. The truth of
the tradition that Asclepius was born in the territory of
Epidaurus was attested by an oracle that was consulted to
decide the question (Paus. 2.26.6; Cic. *De Nat. Deor.*
3.22). Asclepius was worshipped all over Greece, and
many towns claimed the honor of his birth. His temples
were usually built in healthy places, on hills outside the
town, and near springs believed to have healing powers.
These temples were not only places of worship but also
were frequented by great numbers of sick persons and
may therefore be compared to modern sanitaria.

Epidaurus lay near Aegina and the other islands of
the Saronic Gulf and nearly opposite the harbors of
Athens. One remembers the story of Theseus, who walked
the circuit of land between Troezen and Athens, destroying many monsters and outlaws en route. One of these
was Periphetes, a son of Hephaestus and Anticleia. He was
called Corynetes (Club-Bearer) and was a robber at
Epidaurus, who slew the travellers he met with an iron
club. Theseus at last slew him and took his club for his
own use (Apollod. 3.16.1; Plut. *Thes.* 8). Epidaurus was
also nearly due east of Argos, from which there was a
highway to Epidaurus, forming the chief line of communication between Argos and the Saronic Gulf.

It is generally believed that Epidaurus had been
colonized by Ionians and that they were expelled by the
Dorian invaders. Pausanias relates that at the time of the
Dorian invasion Epidaurus was governed by Pityreus, a
descendant of Ion, who surrendered the country without
a contest to Deiphontes and the Argives and then retired
to Athens with his followers (Paus. 2.26.2). Deiphontes
was a son of Antimachus and husband of Hyrnetho, the
daughter of Temenus the Heraclid, by whom he became
the father of Antimenes, Xanthippus, Argeius, and
Orsobia. When Temenus, in the division of Peloponnesus,
had obtained Argos as his share, he bestowed all his
affections upon Hyrnetho and her husband, for which he
was murdered by his sons, who thought themselves
neglected. But after the death of Temenus, the army
declared Deiphontes and Hyrnetho his rightful successors
(Apollod. 2.8.5). According to Pausanias (2.19.1), the
sons of Temenus did indeed form a conspiracy against
their father and Deiphontes; but after the death of
Temenus it was not Deiphontes who succeeded him, but
Ceisus, his eldest son. Deiphontes, on the other hand, is
said to have lived at Epidaurus, where he went with the
army that was attached to him and from where he
expelled the Ionian king, Pityreus (Paus. 2.26.2). His
brothers-in-law, however, who begrudged him the possession of their sister Hyrnetho, went to Epidaurus and

tried to persuade her to leave her husband; and when this attempt failed, they carried her off by force. Deiphontes pursued them, and after having killed one of them, Cerynes, he wrestled with the other, who held his sister in his arms. In this struggle Hyrnetho was killed by her own brother, who then escaped. Deiphontes carried her body back to Epidaurus and there erected a sanctuary to her (Paus. 2.28.3).

Whatever truth there may be in these legends, the fact is certain that the Dorians became the rulers of Epidaurus and continued to be the ruling class in the state well into the historical period. Very early Epidaurus appears to have been one of the chief commercial cities in Peloponnesus. It colonized Aegina, which was for a long time subject to it. The story is told that once during an insurrection at Troezen, two Cretan maidens, Auxesia and Damia, were stoned to death. According to an Epidaurian tradition, the country of Epidaurus was visited by famine, and the Delphic oracle advised the Epidaurians to erect statues of the maidens carved from olive wood. The Epidaurians were permitted by the Athenians to cut down an Attic olive tree on condition that the Epidaurians each year should offer up sacrifices to Athena Agraulos and to Erechtheus. When the conditions were complied with, the country of Epidaurus bore fruit as before. When the Aeginetans ceded from Epidaurus, they took the statues with them; and the Epidaurians ceased to offer sacrifices at Athens. The Athenians demanded the statues and tried to drag them away but went mad in the attempt.

Epidaurus also colonized near the coasts of Asia Minor the islands of Cos, Calydnus, and Nisyrus (Herod. 7.99). But as Aegina grew in importance, Epidaurus declined. By the sixth century B.C. almost all the commerce of the mother city had passed into the hands of the Aeginetans.

In Roman times Epidaurus was little more than the harbor of the temple of Asclepius. Pausanias (2.29.1) gives only a brief account of its public buildings. He mentions a temple of Athena Cissaea on the acropolis; temples of Dionysus, Artemis, and Aphrodite in the city; a sacred enclosure of Asclepius in the suburbs; and a temple of Hera, whose worship was very ancient at Epidaurus, on a promontory at the harbor. The foundations of the ancient walls may be traced in many parts along the cliffs of the peninsula.

The temple of Asclepius was one of the most celebrated spots in Greece. Patients came from all parts of the Hellenic world. The place functioned also as a kind of spa. The temple itself was only a small part of the sacred spot. There was a sacred enclosure that contained several public buildings. The temple of Asclepius contained a chryselephantine statue of the god. The temple was the work of Thrasymedes of Paros and was half the size of the temple of Zeus at Olympia. The god sat upon a throne holding a staff in one hand and resting the other upon the head of a serpent; a dog lay at his feet. Serpents were connected with the worship of Asclepius, especially here, where there was a species of tamed serpents that were viewed as guardians. It was believed that the god himself often appeared as a serpent.

On one side of the temple there were dormitories for those who came to consult the god. The sick who visited the various temples of Asclepius usually had to spend one or more nights in his sanctuary, during which they followed a course of recovery prescribed by the priests. The god came to them in dreams and described both the disease and the remedy. Those who were cured offered a sacrifice to the god, usually a cock or a goat, and posted in the temple their medical record. Several of these tablets are still extant. Near the temple was the tholos, a circular building of white marble built by Polycleitus of Argos; its purpose is still uncertain. In the sacred enclosure there was a theater, also built by Polycleitus. The other objects within the sacred enclosure were temples of Artemis, Aphrodite, and Themis, a stadium, a fountain covered with a roof, and several works erected by Antoninus Pius before he became emperor of Rome. The most important of these second century A.D. buildings were the bath of Asclepius; a temple of the gods called Epidotae (Liberal Givers, referring to the beneficent gods collectively); a temple dedicated to Hygieia, Asclepius, and Apollo surnamed the Egyptian; and a building beyond the sacred enclosure for the reception of the dying and of women in labor because it was unlawful for anyone to die or be born within the sanctuary. A festival was celebrated in the sacred grove in honor of Asclepius with music and gymnastic games.

The site of the sacred enclosure is still covered with ruins, a long period of excavation notwithstanding. Only the foundations of the temple of Asclepius are preserved, but enough of the fragments have been recovered to afford a good description and selected models of parts of the temple. The west pediment featured the war with the Amazons and the east one the sack of Troy, rather curious choices for a sanctuary of healing. There are some ruined columns of a temple of Artemis. The tholos, already mentioned, was behind the temple of the god, and its concentric foundations are clearly defined. The Epidoteion (temple of the Epidotae) and an Anaceion (dedicated to the Dioscuri) are known only by inscriptions. There are several other buildings, including a temple of Aphrodite, which can be traced. The curative powers attributed to this sanctuary attracted shrines of healing gods of foreign countries, and among these was a sanctuary of the Egyptian gods. The theater, which is the best preserved in Greece, dates from the fourth century B.C. It is still in use for annual summer drama festivals and is famous for its acoustics. It seats fourteen thousand. Above the theater are the remains of the temple of Apollo Maleates, the worship of whom preceded that of Asclepius at Epidaurus.

EPIDAURUS LIMERA (PALEA MONEMVASIA) was a town on the east coast of Laconia, situated at the head of a wide bay formed by the promontory Kremidi on the north and the promontory of Monemvasia on the south. It was a colony from Epidaurus in Argolis and is said to have been built as a result of a command from Asclepius when an Epidaurian ship touched here on its way to Cos (Paus. 3.23.6). It was more than likely founded when the whole east coast of Laconia was subject to Argos (Herod. 1.82). The epithet Limera was probably conferred as a tribute to its excellent harbor. Pausanias (3.23.10) describes the town as situated on a height not far from the sea. He mentions temples of Asclepius and Aphrodite, a temple of Athena on the acropolis, and a temple of Zeus Soter facing the harbor. The ruins of Epidaurus Limera are situated at the spot now called Palea Monemvasia.

The walls, both of the acropolis and town, can be traced completely. Two parts of the town were separated by a cross wall. On the acropolis there is a level space, which was probably the site of the temple of Athena. Toward the sea there are two terrace walls, and upon the terraces may have stood the temples of Aphrodite and Asclepius.

About half a kilometer south of the ruins of Epidaurus near the sea was a deep pool of fresh water about 91 meters long and 27 wide. It was probably the lake of Ino mentioned by Pausanias (3.23.8) as one-third of a kilometer from the altars of Asclepius, which were erected to commemorate the spot where the sacred serpent disappeared into the ground after landing from the Epidaurian ship on its way to Cos.

EPIDELIUM shortened to Delium by Strabo, was a small place on the east coast of Laconia, situated within the territories of Boea about 18.5 km from Cape Malea and 36 from Epidaurus Limera. Epidelium, however, appears to have been little more than a sanctuary of Apollo. The sanctuary was erected at the time of the Mithridatic War when a wooden statue of the god floated to this spot from Delos after the devastation of the island by Metrophanes (Paus. 3.23.2; Strab. 8.6.1). Epidelium probably stood on Cape Kamili, where there are a few ancient remains (Paus. 3.23.2; Strab. 8.6.1).

EPITALIUM (EPITALI) was a town of Triphylia near the coast a little south of the river Alpheius. It was identified with the Homeric Thryon or Thryoessa, a town in the dominions of Nestor, which is described as a place upon a hill near the ford of the river Alpheius (Hom. *Il.* 2.592, 11.710; *Hymn Hom. ad Apoll.* 423). Epitalium was an important military post because it commanded the ford of the Alpheius and the road leading along the coast.

ERASINUS (KEFALARI) is the only river in the plain of Argos that flows during the whole year. Its actual course in the plain of Argos is very short; but the ancients believed that the stream travelled underground from Stymphalus, reappearing among the rocks at the foot of Mount Chaon to the southwest of Argos. The spring comes from among these rocks in several streams and forms a river of considerable size, which flows directly across the plain into the Argolic Gulf. At the spot where the Erasinus issues from Mt. Chaon there are two lofty caverns, dedicated to Pan and Dionysus. The larger one has a sharp, Gothic-like arch and extends 59 meters into the mountain. The only tributary of the Erasinus is the Phrixus.

Pelasgus was a son of Phoroneus and brother of Agenor and Iasus. After their father's death, Iasus received the country around Elis; Pelasgus received the county around the river Erasinus and built Larissa, the citadel of Argos.

ERENEIA was a town in Megaris in which was a monument of Autonoe, daughter of Cadmus. She had left Thebes because of the many misfortunes that overtook her family, notably the death of her son Actaeon and her own participation in the murder of her brother-in-law Pentheus (Paus. 1.44.8). The town probably stood inland on the northern part of the isthmus (Paus. 1.44.5).

ERESUS or ERESSUS (SKALA ERESSOU) so called from Eresus the son of Macar, was a city of Lesbos situated on a hill and reaching down to the sea. From Eresus to Cape Sigrium is 5 km. The city was on the west side of the island, and its ruins are some little distance from a place now called Skala Eressou, which is situated on a hill. According to the poet Archestratus, in his *Gastronomia,* quoted by Athenaeus (3.111), if ever the gods eat flour, they send Hermes to buy it at Eresus.

ERETRIA (ERETRIA) one of the most ancient and, next to Chalcis, the most powerful city on Euboea, was located on the west coast of the island a little south of Chalcis on the edge of the Lelantine plain. The Eretrians were mainly Ionians who were supposed to have come from Eretria in Attica. There were also colonists from the Triphylian Macistus in Elis. Strabo (10.1.10) relates that it was formerly called Melaneis and Arotria. The story of Demarmenus, the fisherman, further connects the two locations. It was he who found the shoulder bone of Pelops in the sea near Eretria. This bone had been necessary, according to an oracle, for the Greeks to be victorious at Troy, and it had been brought from Elis but lost in a shipwreck off the coast of Eretria. Demarmenus concealed it in the sand and consulted the Delphic oracle, which instructed him to return it to the Eleans to avert a plague (Paus. 5.13.5).

Eretria was one of the chief maritime cities of Greece and was prosperous and powerful. Andros, Tenos, and Ceos, as well as other islands, were at one time subject to Eretria (Strab. 10.1.10). According to some accounts, the Eretrians founded colonies on the peninsula of Chalcidice. Eretria is mentioned by Homer (*Il.* 2.537). Its men, along with those from other Euboean cities, were led to Troy in forty ships by Elephenor.

The territory of Eretria extended from sea to sea. It included Amarynthus, Tamynae, Porthmus, Dystus, and Oechalia. Excavations have been carried on since the late nineteenth century. These have revealed a theater, a gymnasium, a Thesmophorion, and several temples and shrines. The temple of Apollo Daphnephorus has only foundations, but the museum at Chalkis has the pediment, which shows Theseus and Antiope. Near the theater are the remains of a small temple and altar of Dionysus.

ERINEUS was a town on the Cephissus River near Eleusis. Some place the rape of Persephone at this spot (Paus. 1.38.5).

ERYMANTHUS (ERIMANTHOS) is a lofty range of mountains on the borders of Arcadia, Achaia, and Elis. From Erymanthus four rivers rise—the Eleian Peneius, the Arcadian Erymanthus, the Achaian Peirus, and the Achaian Selinus. In Arcadia Artemis hunted with her nymphs on Erymanthus. The mountain range is also celebrated in mythology as the haunt of the fierce boar destroyed by Heracles. His fourth labor was bringing back alive the Erymanthian boar. This animal had descended from Mount Erymanthus into Psophis. Heracles chased him through the deep snow and, having worn him out, caught him in a net and carried him to Mycenae (Apollod. 2.5.4).

ERYMANTHUS (ERIMANTHOS) is a river, rising in Mount Erymanthus in Arcadia. It is a tributary of the Alpheius. Philonome was a daughter of Nyctimus and Arcadia and a companion of Artemis. She became by Ares the mother of Lycastus and Parrhasius; but from fear of her father, she threw her twin babes into the river Erymanthus. They were carried by the river-god into a hollow oak tree where they were suckled by a she-wolf until the shepherd Tyliphus found them and took them home. Erymanthus had a temple and a statue at Psophis (Paus. 8.24.6; Aelian. *V.H.* 2.33).

ERYMANTHUS was the original name of PSOPHIS.

ERYTHRAE (ERITHRES) was an ancient town in Boeotia mentioned by Homer (*Il.* 2.499) and said to have been the mother-city of Erythrae in Ionia (Strab. 9.2.12). It lay a little south of the Asopus, at the foot of Mount Cithaeron. Erythras was a son of Leucon and grandson of

Athamas. He was one of the suitors of Hippodameia (Paus. 6.21.11). The town was in ruins in the time of Pausanias. The modern town of Erithres is part of Attica.

ETEONUS a town of Boeotia, lay to the right of the Asopus. Homer (*Il.* 2.497) gives it the epithet "many-ridged." Strabo (9.2.24) says that it was afterward called Scarphe. It probably lay between Scolus and the frontier of the territory of Tanagra. Eteonus, a descendant of Boetus and father of Eleon, was the one from whom Eteonus derived its name.

ETHOPIA (ARGITHEA) was a town or fortress of Athamania situated on a hill commanding Argithea, the capital of the country. It contained a temple of Zeus Acraeus (Liv. 38.2). The site is near the modern village of Argithea in the nome of Karditsa.

ETIS was a town in the south of Laconia, the inhabitants of which were removed to Boeae (Paus. 3.22.11). Boeus was a son of Heracles and founder of Boeae, to which he led colonists from Etis, Aphrodisias, and Side (Paus. 3.22.11).

EUA was the largest of three villages in the territory of Thyreatis, a district of Cynuria. It possessed a sanctuary of Polemocrates, son of Machaon, who was worshipped here as a god or hero of healing. The location of the town is not known.

EUANTHEIA (See OEANTHEIA)

EUBOEA (EVIA) next to Crete, is the largest Greek island. It lies along the coasts of Attica, Boeotia, Locris, and the southern part of Thessaly, from which countries it is separated by the Euboean Sea. Midway along the west coast the strait becomes a narrow channel called Evripos. Euboea is a long and narrow island. The length of the island from north to south is about 150 km; its extreme width is 50 km, but in one part it is not more than 6 km across.

Throughout the whole length of Euboea there runs a range of mountains. They form the backbone of the island and may be regarded as a continuation of the range of Ossa and Pelion and of that of Othrys. In several parts of the island these mountains rise to a great height. The highest one is Mount Dirfis (1,745 meters). The island's northwest extremity is a small peninsula, terminating in the promontory Cenaeum. On this north coast is the promontory Artemisium. The eastern side of the island is much more rocky than the western coast. Rocks rise perpendicularly. The winds are very strong and are called *meltemi*. The Dardanelles current adds additional maritime hazard. Along the whole extent of this coast, which is roughly 167 kilometers in length, there are only five or six villages near the shore. The only port is Kimi.

Euboea is deficient in water. There is not one stream on the whole island into which the smallest boat can enter. There were two streams mentioned by ancient writers, the Cereus and Neleus. It was recorded that sheep drinking the water of the Cereus became black, while those drinking the water of the Neleus became white; if they drank of both they became mottled (Strab. 10.1.14; Plin. 31.9.2).

Euboea, like many of the other Greek islands, is said to have borne other names in the most ancient times. Thus it was called Macris, from its great length in comparison to its width. It was also named: Ellopia from a district in the north part of the island named for Ellops, the son of Ion; Oche from the mountain of this name in the south of the island; and Abantis from the most ancient inhabitants of the island (Strab. 10.1.3; Plin. 4.12.21). Homer (*Il.* 2.536) calls the inhabitants of the island Abantes, though he gives to the island itself the name of Euboea. It was related that the name Abantis was changed into Euboea because of the cow Io, who was even said to have given birth to Epaphus on the island. In Euboea both the spot on which Io was believed to have been killed and the cave in which she had given birth to Epaphus were shown (Strab. 10.1.3). Other writers state that the island was named for Euboea, a daughter of Asopus. The Abantes were Thracians who passed over to Euboea from the Thracian town of Abae; some derived their name from an eponymous hero, Abas. Herodotus (1.146) relates that the Abantes assisted in colonizing the Ionic cities of Asia Minor. The south part of the island was inhabited by Dryopes, who are said to have founded Styra and Carystus (Herod. 8.46; Thuc. 7.57).

In the mythological period it is reported that Canethus, a son of Atlas, gave his name to Mount Canethus in Euboea near Chalcis. Canethus was also one of the sons of Lycaon. Canthus is called a son of Canethus and grandson of Abas, or a son of Abas of Euboea (Apollon. Rhod. 1.78). One of the Argonauts, he is said to have been killed in Libya by Cephalion or Caphaurus. We find also that Pandoros, a son of Erechtheus and Praxithea and grandson of Pandion, founded a colony in Euboea. Another story involves Rhoeo, a daughter of Staphylus. She was beloved by Apollo. When her father discovered that she was pregnant, he put her in a chest and put her adrift in the sea. The chest floated from Naxos to the coast of Euboea, where Rhoeo gave birth to Anius (Diod. 5.62). Subsequently she was married to Zarex. We read also of Tityus, a son of Gaea or of Zeus and Elara, the daughter of Orchomenus. Tityas was a giant in Euboea and the father of Europa (Hom. *Od.* 7.324; Apollod. 1.4.1). Instigated by Hera, he made an assault upon Leto or Artemis when she passed through

Panopaeus to Pytho but was killed by the arrows of Artemis or Apollo, or, according to others, Zeus killed him with a flash of lightning (Paus. 3.18.9; Pind. *Pyth.* 4.160). We also find Euboea among the several places in Greece that claimed the honor of having been the scene of the marriage of Hera and Zeus.

Euboea had a somewhat prominent role in the Trojan War. Elephenor, a son of Chalcodon and prince of the Abantes in Euboea, led the Abantes against Troy in thirty or forty ships. Without being aware of it, he had earlier killed his grandfather Abas, in consequence of which he was obliged to flee Euboea. When the expedition against Troy was undertaken, Elephenor did not return to Euboea but assembled the Abantes on a rock on the Euripus opposite the island. After the fall of Troy, which according to some accounts he survived, he went to the island of Othronos near Sicily and then, driven from there by a dragon, he went to Amantia in Illyria (Lycoph. 1029).

While the Greeks were engaged in the siege of Troy, they were informed by an oracle that the city could not be taken unless one of the bones of Pelops was brought from Elis to Troas. Accordingly, a shoulder bone was fetched from Pisa but was lost off the coast of Euboea together with the ship carrying it. Many years afterward it was dragged up from the bottom of the sea by a fisherman, Demarmenus of Eretria, who concealed it in the sand. Demarmenus then consulted the Delphic oracle about it and was instructed to return the valuable relic to the Eleans to avert a plague (Paus. 5.13.5).

Then we read of Nauplius, who was a king of Euboea and father of Palamedes, Oeax, and Nausimedon. His son Palamedes had been executed for treason by the Greeks during the siege of Troy. Nauplius considered his condemnation totally unjust, and he waited to avenge his son's death. He watched for the return of the Greeks from Troy; as they approached the coast of Euboea, he lighted torches on the most dangerous part of the coast. The sailors thus misdirected crashed their ships on the rocks and perished in the waves or by the sword of Nauplius. He is further said to have gained revenge by sending false messages to the wives of the heroes fighting at Troy. The messages accused the heroes of infidelity. Some of the wives engaged in retaliatory faithlessness, while others committed suicide (Apollod. *Epit.* 6.7–11).

In historical times most of the cities of Euboea were inhabited by Ionic Greeks; and the Athenians are said to have taken the chief role in their colonization. Euboea was divided among six or seven independent cities, of which Chalcis and Eretria on the west coast were the most important. Also there existed on the north end Histiaea, opposite Thessaly; Dium, Aedepeus, Athenae Diades, Orobiae, and Aegae on the west coast opposite Locris; Cerinthus on the east coast; and on the south end of the island Dyslus, Styra, and Carystus. All these cities except Athenae Diades are mentioned in the *Iliad*.

Modern day Evia is an agricultural area rich in minerals. It has also become in recent years a vacation place for Athenians, many of whom own summer homes there.

EUBOEA   was the name of a small mountain in Argolis about 10 km from Mycenae on the road to Argos. At its foot lay the Heraion, the most celebrated temple of Hera. Pausanias (2.17.1) says that the river Asterion had three daughters—Euboea, Prosymna, and Acraea. Euboea was the mountain on the lower part of which the Heraion stood; Acraea the height rising opposite it; and Prosymna the region below it.

EUENUS (EVINOS)   originally called Lycormas, is an important river of Aetolia, rising in the highest summit of Mount Oeta. Its direction is westerly and thereafter southwesterly. It is fed by numerous torrents from the mountains through which it flows, and in winter it becomes swollen and rapid. In ancient times it was difficult to cross in winter because of the great stones that were carried down by the stream. The Euenus is celebrated in mythology as the river at which Heracles slew the Centaur Nessus. Heracles had been married to Deianeira for nearly three years, when, at a repast in the house of Oeneus at Calydon, he killed by accident the boy Eunomus, the son of Architeles. The father of the boy pardoned the murder, as it had not been intentionally committed; but Heracles, in accordance with the law, went into exile with Deianeira. On their way they came to the river Euenus, across which Nessus the Centaur used to carry travellers for a small sum of money. Heracles himself forded the river and gave Deianeira to Nessus to carry. Nessus attempted to rape her; Heracles heard her screams and, as the Centaur brought her to the other side, Heracles shot an arrow into his heart. The dying Centaur called out to Deianeira to take his blood with her, as it was a sure means for preserving the love of her husband (Apollod. 2.7.6; Diod. 4.36; Ov. *Met.* 9.201). This blood was poisonous and later became the cause of Heracles' own death.

The river is said to have derived its name from Euenus, the son of Ares and the father of Marpessa. When his daughter was carried off by Idas, the son of Aphareus, he pursued them; but being unable to overtake them, he threw himself into the Lycormas, which was after that time called by his name (Apollod. 1.7.8; Ov. *Ib.* 515). Some mention the Euenus as the river in which Jason lost the sandal that caused him to be recognized by Pelias.

EUOENUS   was the former name of the island of PEPARETHUS.

EURIPUS (EVRIPOS)   is a very narrow strait separating Euboea from the mainland. Chalcis, the chief city of Euboea, is located on this strait, which is at this point only 37 m across. The Euripus is here divided into two channels by a rock in the middle of the strait. In antiquity a wooden bridge connected Chalcis with the Boeotian coast. Today a kind of rolling drawbridge crosses the channel. In the channel are extraordinary tides, which were frequently mentioned by the ancient writers. This phenomenon still takes place, with the direction of the tide changing as many as seven times a day. Livy (28.6) ascribes it to sudden squalls of wind from the mountains. He might have been right: at least no one so far has proven otherwise.

Elephenor was a son of Chalcodon and prince of the Abantes in Euboea, whom he led against Troy in thirty or forty ships. According to some, Elephenor unknowingly killed his grandfather Abas, in consequence of which he was obliged to quit Euboea. When therefore the expedition against Troy was undertaken, Elephenor did not return to Euboea but assembled the Abantes on a rock on the Euripus opposite the island. (See EUBOEA.)

EUROPUS   was a town of Emathia between Idomene (Idomeni on the Yugoslavian border) and the river plain of Pella. It was probably situated on the right bank of the Axius below Idomene. Europus, from whom this Macedonian town received its name, was a son of Macedon and Oreithyia, the daughter of Cecrops.

EUROTAS (EVROTAS)   is a river that flows throughout the entire length of the Laconian valley between the ranges of Taygetus and Parnon. Its more ancient names were Bomycas and Himerus. In its course three districts may be distinguished: the vale of the upper Eurotas; the vale of the middle Eurotas, or the plain of Sparta; and the vale of the lower Eurotas, or the maritime plain. Eurotas was a son of Myles and grandson of Lelex. He was the father of Sparta, the wife of Lacedaemon. Eurotas is said to have carried the waters stagnating in the plain of Lacedaemon into the sea by means of a canal and to have called the river that arose therefrom Eurotas after himself.

The river rises in the mountains that form the southern boundary of the Arcadian plains of Asea and Megalopolis. It was believed by both Pausanias and Strabo that the Alpheius and the Eurotas had a common origin and that after flowing together for a short distance, they sank underground, the Alpheius reappearing in Arcadia, and the Eurotas in Laconia. All that we know for certain is that the Eurotas is formed by the union of several mountain springs. A little over 2 km from Sparta the Eurotas receives the Oenus and together they enter the Spartan plain. This plain is particularly adapted for the growth of olives. The banks of the Eurotas and the dry parts of its bed are overgrown with a profusion of reeds.

Hera Hypercheiria (One Who Holds Out Her Protecting Hand) was a name under which Hera had a sanctuary at Sparta. The sanctuary had been erected to her at the command of an oracle when the country was inundated by the river Eurotas (Paus. 3.13.8).

EUTRESIS (LEFKTRA)   was an ancient town of Boeotia mentioned by Homer (*Il.* 2.502) and said to have been the residence of Zethus and Amphion before they ruled over Thebes. They had been reared by shepherds in this area. They were here when Antiope escaped from prison, revealed herself as their mother, and told of the suffering to which she had been submitted. They went immediately to Thebes, where they took vengeance on Lycus and Dirce. They then took control of Thebes, which they fortified as they had done with Eutresis.

We are told that Eutresis possessed a celebrated temple and oracle of Apollo, who was there called Apollo Eutresites. About 2 km northeast of Lefktra are foundations of polygonal walls forming an enclosure of about 503 square meters. Nearby is the Arkopodi Fountain, which marked the junction of roads leading variously to Thebes, Thisbe, Thespiae, and Plataea.

GALAXIUS   was a stream in Boeotia from which Apollo derived the surname Galaxius.

GARGAPHIA   was the name of a valley and fountain next to Plataea. Actaeon was the hunter who was torn to pieces by his own fifty hounds. Some say this happened to him because he had seen Artemis bathing in the vale of Gargaphia. When the goddess realized she had been seen naked, she changed Actaeon into a stag, in which form he was dismembered by his dogs (Ov. *Met.* 3.155; Callim. *Lav. Pall.* 110).

GARGETTUS   (See Attican PALLENE)

GENETHLIUM   was a place near Troezen where Theseus is said to have been born (Paus. 2.32.9). The great hero of Attica was the son of Aegeus, king of Athens, and Aethra, the daughter of Pittheus, king of Troezen.

GERAESTUS (MANDELI)   was a promontory of Euboea forming the southwest extremity of the island, now called Mandeli. There was a town on this cape, with a celebrated temple of Poseidon, and at its foot was a small but busy port. The modern port is Potamion, and modern Platanistos is more than likely the site of the ancient temple. Myrtilus was a son of Hermes and charioteer of Oenomaus, king of Elis. He assisted Pelops in winning the chariot race with Oenomaus, a fatal contest in which all suitors of Hippodameia had to compete. Pelops promised

him rewards but treacherously threw him into the sea near Geraestus. That part of the Aegean was subsequently called the Myrtoan Sea. At the moment he expired, Myrtilus pronounced a curse upon the house of Pelops, which was thereafter harassed by the Erinyes. His father placed him among the stars as Auriga (Soph. *Elect.* 509; Eurip. *Orest.* 993). Another famous person connected with Geraestus was Palamedes, son of Nauplius of Euboea. He was falsely accused of treason by Agamemnon, Diomedes, and Odysseus, who caused him to be stoned to death or drowned. Some place his death site at Geraestus.

GERANEIA (GERANIA)   was the name of the mountains that continue Cithaeron across Megaris. They were named Gerancia because during the deluge in the time of Deucalion, Megarus, the son of Zeus, was led by the cries of cranes (*geranai*) to take refuge upon their summit. The Geraneian Mountains form the true boundary of northern Greece and rise above the Isthmus of Corinth like a vast wall from sea to sea. These mountains were the location of the Scironian Rocks and the Molurian Rock. On the summit of the mountain was a temple of Zeus Aphesius. On the plain at the foot of the mountain was the temple of Apollo Latous, near which were the boundaries of Megaris and Corinthia (Paus. 1.44.10).

GERANTHRAE   (See GERONTHRAE)

GERENIA (KITRIES)   was a town of Messenia where Nestor was said to have been brought up after the destruction of Pylos, and where he derived the Homeric surname Gerenian. There is, however, no town of this name in Homer, and many of the ancient critics identified the later Gerenia with the Homeric Enope (*Il.* 1.150; Paus. 3.26.8). It possessed a celebrated sanctuary of Machaon, which bore the name Rhodon. Asclepius also had a temple at Gerenia (Strab. 8.4.4). The ancient town was located at modern Kitries on the east coast of the Bay of Messenia.

GERONTHRAE or GERANTHRAE (GERAKI)   an ancient town of Laconia, was situated in a strategic position on the southwest side of the mountain above the plain of the Eurotas River. Geraki, a ruined town of the middle ages, occupies the same site. Geronthrae possessed a temple and grove of Ares, in whose honor a yearly festival was celebrated and from which women were excluded. On the acropolis stood a temple of Apollo (Paus. 3.22.7). On the north side of the summit of the citadel are the remains of a very ancient Cyclopean wall. The position of the agora is indicated by fountains farther down the hill. Geronthrae was one of the ancient Achaean cities which resisted the Dorian conquerors for a long time. It was at length taken along with Amyclae and Pharis, and colonized by the Spartans.

GLAPHYRAE (GLAFIRA)   was a town of Thessaly mentioned along with Boebe and Iolcus by Homer (*Il.* 2.712), after which the name does not occur. Along with Pherae, Boebe, and Iolcus, Glaphyrae sent men in eleven ships to the Trojan War under the leadership of Eumelus, a son of Admetus and Alcestis. Glaphyrae was near the south shore of Lake Boebeis. The modern village of Glafira is near the remains of the ancient town. The entire circumference of the citadel on the summit of the hill may be traced, and, on its lower side, part of the wall is still standing.

GLAUCIA   was a stream in Boeotia. Glaucia was a daughter of the river-god Scamander in the Troad. When Heracles went to war against Troy, Deimachus, a Boeotian, one of the companions of Heracles, fell in love with Glaucia. But Deimachus was slain in battle before Glaucia had given birth to his child. She fled for refuge to Heracles, who took her with him to Greece and entrusted her to the care of Cleon, the father of Deimachus. She there gave birth to a son, whom she called Scamander and who afterward obtained land in Boeotia. He named the two streams that crossed his territory Scamander and Glaucia.

GLISAS (IPATO)   an ancient town of Boeotia, was mentioned along with Plataea by Homer (*Il.* 2.504). It is celebrated in mythology as the place where the Epigoni fought against the Thebans and where the Argive chiefs who fell in battle were buried (Paus. 1.44.4, 9.5.13). Laodamas was a son of Eteocles and king of Thebes. It was in his reign that the Epigoni marched against Thebes. Laodamas offered them a battle on the river Glisas and slew their leader Aegialeus, but he himself was killed by Alcmaeon (Apollod. 3.7.3). Glisas was about 14 km northeast of Thebes. There are ruins on a hillside near modern Ipato about 1 km north of the National Highway. There is an acropolis, and some of the stones that circled the gravestones of the fallen heroes are still visible. Zeus Hypatus (Most High), sharing the name of neighboring Mount Hypatus, was worshipped at Glisas (Paus. 9.19.3).

GNOSSIS   (See CNOSSUS)

GONNUS (GONI)   was an ancient town of the Perrhaebi in Thessaly, deriving its name from Gouneus, who led the Perrhaebians and Enienes to the Trojan War (Hom. *Il.* 2.748). Its strategic position at the west of the valley of Tempe made it one of the most important places in the northern part of Thessaly. Apart from its military importance, it shared in the religious atmosphere of the Vale of Tempe, which was a center for the worship of Apollo. In Goni, the modern site, have been found remnants of a temple of Athena Polias and foundations of another temple thought to be one of Asclepius. Dedica-

tions to Artemis have been found in the area along with foundations of still another temple so far unidentified. Goni is located 3 km north of the National Highway about 9 km before it crosses the Pinios River proceeding northward.

GONUSA (GONOUSSA)   was a town near Sicyon. Melas was a son of Antassus from Gonusa. He joined the Dorians on their march against Corinth. His services were at first declined, but he was afterwards allowed to fight with the Dorians. He was the ancestor of the family of Cypselus (Paus. 2.4.4, 5.18.7). The modern village of Gonoussa is about 10 km south of the site of ancient Sicyon on the road to Nemea.

GORTYNA (GORTIS)   was a town of Crete that Homer (*Il.* 2.646, *Od.* 3.294) calls Gortyn. According to some it was originally called Larissa and Cremnia. Gortys was a son of Tegeates and Maera, who, according to an Arcadian tradition, built the town of Gortyn. The Cretans regarded him as a son of Rhadamanthys (Paus. 8.53.4). After Homer's time the town was usually called Gortyna.

On Crete this city was second only to Cnossus in importance and splendor. In early times these two great towns formed an alliance that enabled them to hold all of Crete under their power, but later they were engaged in continual hostilities (Strab. 10.4.11).

Gortyna was quite large with a circuit of about 9 km. It stood on a plain of the Lethaeus River about 17 km from the Libyan Sea, on which were situated its two harbors, Lebena and Metallum. Gortyna was among the places in Crete especially sacred to Zeus. It was here where the god in the form of a bull came when he had carried off Europa from Phoenicia and where he was worshipped under the name Zeus Hecatombaeus. Near Gortyna was a famous spring shaded by a plane tree that retained its leaves throughout the winter; people believed that the plane tree spread over the spot where the mating of Europa and the metamorphosed Zeus occurred (Varr. *De Re Rus.* 1.7). Atymnius, a son of Zeus and Cassiopeia, was a beautiful boy who was beloved by Sarpedon (Apollod. 3.1.2). He seems to have been worshipped at Gortyna together with Europa.

There are substantial remains of the city since its importance extended into Roman times and since it was restored as late as the time of Trajan. On the east bank of the river are ruins of the agora, an odeion, and a theater. There is a temple of Asclepius, a temple of Apollo Pythius, and one of Isis. Near the temple of Apollo was a small nymphaion. Most of the finds from here are on display in the museum at Iraklio.

GORTYS or GORTYNA (ATSIHOLOS)   was a town of Arcadia in the district of Cynuria, situated near the Gortynius River, a tributary of the Alpheius. The town is said to have been founded by Gortys, a son of Stymphalus. It was only a village at the time of Pausanias since it had to give up most of its population for the founding of Megalopolis. It contained a celebrated temple of Asclepius built of Pentelic marble. The temple possessed statues of Asclepius and Hygieia by Scopas (Paus. 5.7.1). Columns and foundations remain. There was also a second temple to Asclepius. Hydrotherapy seems to have been a feature of this place, judging from remains of pools. Ruins of the acropolis, located near Atsiholos a few kilometers north of Karitena, show remains of a wall with three gates and five towers.

GRAEA was a name by which OROPUS was also known.

GRAEA was a town Homer often identified with TANAGRA.

GRAECIA was the name the Romans gave to HELLAS.

GYRTON or GYRTONA a town of Perrhaebia in Thessaly, was situated in a fertile plain between the rivers Titaresius and Peneius. Strabo (9.5.18,20) put Gyrton near the mouth of the Peneius, and others placed it in the plains with Phalanna, Atrax, and Larissa. It was an ancient town mentioned by Homer (*Il.* 2.738), and it continued to be a place of importance till later times, when it was called "opulent" by Apollonius Rhodius (1.57). Polypoetes, a son of Peirithous, was one of the Lapiths who joined the Greeks in the Trojan War, commanding the men of Argissa, Gyrton, Ortho, Elone, and Oloosson (Hom. *Il.* 2.738). It was said to have been the original abode of the Phlegyae and to have been founded by Gyrton, the brother of Phlegyas (Strab. 9.5.21). Others derived the name from Gyrtone, who is called a daughter of Phlegyas. Still others say it was founded by Phalerus, a son of Alcon and grandson of Erechtheus or Eurysthenes, who was mentioned among the Argonauts.

GYTHIUM (GITHIO) an ancient Achaean town in Laconia, was situated near the head of the Laconian Gulf, southwest of the mouth of the Eurotas. Gythium stood upon the small stream Gythius in a fertile and well-cultivated plain. After the Dorian conquest it became the chief maritime town in Laconia, and it was therefore regarded as the port of Sparta.

Pausanias observed in the marketplace of Gythium statues of Apollo and Heracles, who were reputed to be the founders of the city. Near them was a statue of Dionysus and on the other side of the marketplace a statue of Apollo Carneius, a temple of Ammon, a bronze statue of Asclepius in a roofless temple with fountain sacred to the god, a sanctuary of Demeter, and a statue of

Poseidon Gaeaochus. On the acropolis was a temple of Athena; and the gates of Castor mentioned by Pausanias appear to have led from the lower city to the citadel (Paus. 3.21.8,9). Opposite Gythium was the island Cranae, to which Paris was said to have carried off Helen from Sparta.

The coast on the mainland side of Gythium was called Migonium, a name derived from the union of Paris and Helen on the opposite island. On this coast was a temple of Aphrodite Migonitis and above it a mountain sacred to Dionysus called Larysium, where a festival was celebrated to this god in the beginning of spring (Paus. 3.22.2). Praxidice was the goddess who carried out the objectives of justice or watched that justice was done to men. When Menelaus arrived in Laconia on his return from Troy, he set up a statue of Praxidice near Gythium, not far from the spot where Paris had founded the sanctuary of Aphrodite Migonitis (Paus. 3.22.2).

Pausanias further describes at the distance of one-quarter kilometer from Gythium a stone on which Orestes is said to have been relieved from his madness. This stone was called Zeus Cappotas (Reliever).

Zeus derived the surname Croceatas from Croceae, a place near Gythium (Paus. 3.21.4). Nereus was worshipped under the name of Geron (Old Man) at Gythium (Paus. 1.21.9). And Poseidon Gaeaochus (Holder of the Earth) had a statue at Gythium, although that epithet was commonly used of Poseidon elsewhere.

Most of the ancient city still lies under modern Githio or has disappeared with the growth of the present city. Only the theater and its surroundings have been excavated.

HAEMONIA was a town in Arcadia founded by Haemon, a son of Lycaon (Paus. 8.44.1; Apollod. 3.8.1).

HAEMONIA or AEMONIA was an earlier name of THESSALY.

HAEMUS or AEMUS is a large range of mountains in the north of Thrace. The mountains were so called because of their cold and snowy climate. Their average height is between 915 and 1,220 meters. The province of Haemimontus in Thrace derived its name from this mountain. Aristaeus, the divine benefactor of man, travelled extensively throughout Greece and at last went to Thrace, where he became initiated into the mysteries of Dionysus. After dwelling for sometime near Mount Haemus, where he founded the town of Aristaeon, he disappeared.

HAGNO was a well on Mount Lycaeus in Arcadia. It was sacred to and named for Hagno, an Arcadian nymph, who is said to have brought up Zeus. When the country was suffering from drought, the priest of Zeus Lycaeus, after having offered up prayers and sacrifices, touched the surface of the well with the branch of an oak tree. Clouds formed immediately and rain fell shortly thereafter. The nymph Hagno was represented at Megalopolis carrying in one hand a pitcher and in the other a bowl (Paus. 8.31.3).

HALAE (THEOLOGOS)   was a town located on the Opuntian Gulf. It belonged to Boeotia in the time of Pausanias and Strabo. It probably got its name from the salt springs that are still found in the vicinity. The fortified area of the city was roughly 325 by 160 meters. A series of three temples of Athena Poliuchos were built on the same site, the final one in the late fifth century B.C. The modern site of Halae is Theologos, which is 5 km off the National Highway, about 20 km before the Atalanti exit.

HALAE ARAPHENIDES (LOUTSA)   was a deme of Attica, so called to distinguish it from Halae Aexonides. It lay on the east coast between Brauron and Araphen and was the harbor of Brauron. From here persons crossed over to Marmarium in Euboea, where the marble quarries of Carystus were located (Strab. 10.1.6). Halae Araphenides was famous for a sanctuary dedicated to Artemis Tauropolis and for its preservation of her statue. Only as late as 1956 were remains of a temple uncovered here and identified as those of the Taurian Artemis. A recently discovered inscription referring to the celebration of a Dionysia suggests that Dionysus was worshipped here as well.

HALIACMON (ALIAKMON)   is a river of Macedonia rising in the Tymphaean mountains. Haliacmon, a son of Oceanus and Tethys, was a river-god of Macedonia. The river flows first southeast through Elimaea, then northeast, forming the boundary between Emathia and Pieria, and finally falls into the Thermaic Gulf. According to the Romans, it formed the line of demarcation between Macedonia and Thessaly, and this is certainly the case today.

HALIACMON   was the earlier name of the INACHUS River in Argolis.

HALIARTUS (ALIARTOS)   a town of Boeotia and one of the cities of the confederation, was situated on the south side of Lake Copais in a pass between the mountain and the lake (Strab. 9.2.27). Haliartus, a son of Thersander and grandson of Sisyphus, was believed to have founded the town of Haliartus. He is further said to have been adopted along with Coronus by Athamas, a brother of Sisyphus (Paus. 9.34.7). Haliartus is mentioned by Homer (*Il.* 2.503), who refers to its well-watered meadows. The territory of Haliartus reached west to

Mount Tilphossium. The Haliartians had a sanctuary of the goddesses called Praxidicae situated near this mountain (Paus. 9.33.3). The Praxidicae were the goddesses who carried out the objectives of justice or watched that justice was done to men. They were called daughters of Ogygus, and their names were Alalcomenia, Thelxinoea, and Aulis. Their sculptured representations consisted merely of heads; and only the heads of animals were sacrificed to them. East of Haliartus was a very ancient temple of Poseidon Onchestius.

The towns of Peteon, Medeon, Ocalea, and Onchestus were situated in the territory of Haliartus. The remains of Haliartus are situated on a hill about 1.5 km west of modern Aliartos between the railroad and the road from Thebes to Livadia. Some parts of the walls of the acropolis remain, but the walls of the exterior town are scarcely traceable anywhere. A temple of Athena has been uncovered on the very top of the acropolis.

The town has connections with several mythological figures. According to Plutarch (*De Gen. Socr.* 578), Alcmena's tomb and that of Rhadamanthys were at Haliartus. Alcmena had married Rhadamanthys, a son of Zeus, after the death of Amphitryon. Cecrops, one of the earliest kings of Athens, had a shrine at Haliartus. He is said to have founded the ancient Boeotian towns of Athenae and Eleusis on the river Triton. Dionysus Lysius (Deliverer) had a sanctuary at Thebes near one of the gates. The god received the surname Lysius when he delivered Theban prisoners from the hands of the Thracians in the vicinity of Haliartus (Paus. 9.16.6).

HALIEIS (PORTOHELI)   was a harbor on the southern tip of the Argolid peninsula. It was settled by refugees from Tiryns. It lies across the bay from the modern village of Portoheli. It had a small acropolis with an unidentified shrine on top. About 500 meters from the town a sanctuary of Apollo has been found beneath the sea. Part of a statue of the god was recovered.

HALIMUS (ALIMOS)   a deme of Attica, was situated on the coast between Phalerum and Aexone (Strab. 9.1.20) at a distance of 11.5 km from Athens. It possessed temples of Demeter and Kore (Paus. 1.31.1) and of Heracles.

HALMONES   (See OLMONES)

HALMONIA   was an earlier name of MINYA.

HALUS or ALUS (ALOS)   was a town of Phthiotis in Thessaly, mentioned by Homer (*Il.* 2.682) as one of the towns whose men followed Achilles to Troy in fifty ships. Strabo (9.5.8) describes it as situated near the sea at the end of Mount Othrys, overlooking the plain called Crocium. The country around Halus was called Athamantium from Athamas, the reputed founder of Halus (Strab. 9.5.8). Strabo also says that the river Amphrysus, on the banks of which Apollo is said to have tended the herds of Admetus, flowed near the walls of Halus. The modern town of Alos is just off the National Highway near the Almiros exit, situated at a short distance from the sea. Remains of the walls may still be seen.

HARMA   was an ancient town of Boeotia mentioned by Homer (*Il.* 2.499), which is said to have been so called either because the chariot of Adrastus broke down here, or because the chariot of Amphiaraus disappeared into the earth at this place (Strab. 9.2.11; Paus. 9.19.4). Strabo describes Harma as a deserted village in the territory of Tanagra near Mycalessus, and Pausanias speaks of the ruins of Harma and Mycalessus as situated on the road from Thebes to Chalcis. Aelianus (*V.H.* 3.45) speaks of a lake called Harma, which is possibly the one now called Paralimni. The exact site of Harma is uncertain. A modern village Arma, 6 km northwest of Tanagra, is most likely another example of renaming places to recall ancient and still undiscovered towns. Eleo actually is a more likely location.

HARPINA or HARPINNA (MIRAKA)   was a town of Pisatis in Elis situated on the right bank of the Alpheius River on the road to Heraea about 4 km from the hippodrome of Olympia (Lucian *De Mort. Per.* 35). Harpina is said to have been founded by Oenomaus, who gave it the name of his mother. Harpinna was a daughter of Asopus and became by Ares the mother of Oenomaus (Paus. 5.22.6). Pausanias saw the ruins of the town, which today stand upon a ridge a little north of the village of Miraka.

HEBRUS (EVROS)   the principal river of Thrace, rises in the mountains of Scomius and Rhodope, flows first southeast and then southwest, becomes navigable for smaller vessels at Philippopolis and falls into the Aegean Sea near Aenos. The Hebrus was celebrated in Greek legends. On its banks Orpheus was torn to pieces by the Thracian women, and it is frequently mentioned in connection with the worship of Dionysus.

HECALE   was a deme of Attica, probably near Marathon since this deme is said to have obtained its name from a woman who hospitably received Theseus into her house when he had set out to attack the Marathonian bull. It contained a sanctuary of Zeus Hecaleius. The modern town of Ekali is 3 km north of Kifissia on the road to Marathon, but its name is another case of modern adoption. The ancient deme lay farther to the northeast.

HELENA (MAKRONISI)   is a long, narrow island, extending along the east coast of Attica from Thoricus to Sunium and five to seven kilometers from the shore. It was called also Macris because of its length. It was uninhabited in antiquity, and remains so today. Both Strabo (9.1.22) and Pausanias (1.35.1) derive its name from Helen, the wife of Menelaus. Pausanias supposes that it was so called because Helen landed here after the capture of Troy.

HELICE   a town in Achaia and one of the twelve Achaian cities, was situated on the coast between the rivers Selinus and Cerynites and 7.5 km east of Aegium. It seems to have been the most ancient of all the cities in Achaia. Its foundation is ascribed to Ion. Xuthus, his father, was expelled from Thessaly and went to Aegialus (Achaia). After the death of Xuthus, Ion was on the point of marching against the Aegialeans, when their king Selinus gave him his daughter Helice in marriage. After the death of Selinus, Ion succeeded to the throne, and in that way the Aegialeans received the name Ionians, and the town of Helice was built in honor of Ion's wife (Paus. 7.1.4; Apollod. 1.7.2).

Helice possessed a celebrated temple of Poseidon, who was there called Poseidon Heliconius. In the city the Ionians held periodical meetings that were continued in Ionic Asia Minor under the name of Panionia. After the conquest of the country by the Achaians, Helice was made the place of meeting of their League, and it continued to be the Achaian capital till the total destruction of the city by an earthquake in 373 B.C. This catastrophe was attributed to the vengeance of Poseidon, who was angry because the inhabitants of Helice had refused to give their statue of Poseidon to the Ionian colonists in Asia, or even supply them with a model.

Tisamenus, a son of Orestes and Hermione, was king of Argos, but was deprived of his kingdom when the Heracleidae invaded Peloponnesus (Apollod. 2.8.2; Paus. 2.18.7). He was slain in a battle against the Heracleidae (Apollod. 2.8.3), and his tomb was afterward pointed out at Helice, from where at one time his remains were removed to Sparta by command of an oracle (Paus. 7.1.8). Eliki, just off the National Highway and about 8 km east of Egio, recalls the classical Helice but is not the site, which is still unknown.

HELICON (ELIKONAS)   is a mountain of Boeotia lying between Lake Copais and the Corinthian Gulf and can be regarded as a continuation of the range of Parnassus. It is celebrated as the favorite haunt of the Muses, to whom the epithet Heliconian is frequently given.

Helicon is really a range of mountains with several summits. It was the east or Boeotian side of Helicon that was especially sacred to the Muses and contained many objects connected with their worship. The Muses, inspiring goddesses, were daughters of Zeus and Mnemosyne.

Since they liked to dwell on Mount Helicon, they were naturally associated with Dionysus and dramatic poetry, and they are described as the companions, playmates, or nurses of Dionysus. On Helicon was a sacred grove of the Muses, to which Pausanias ascended from Ascra. On the left side of the road before reaching the grove of the Muses was the celebrated fountain of Aganippe, which was believed to inspire those who drank of it, and from which the Muses were called Aganippides. Aganippe, the nymph of the well, is called a daughter of the river-god Termessus (Paus. 9.29.5; Virg. *Eclog.* 10.12).

The position of the Grove of the Muses is fixed at Agios Nikolaos by an inscription discovered there relating to the Museia, or games of the Muses, which were celebrated there under the presidency of the Thespians (Paus. 9.31.3). In the time of Pausanias, the grove of the Muses contained a larger number of statues than any other place in Boeotia, and Pausanias (9.29.5) has given an account of many of them, including one of Eupheme, the nurse of the Muses. The statues of the Muses were removed by Constantine to his new capital, where they were destroyed by fire in A.D. 404.

Four kilometers above the Grove of the Muses was the fountain Hippocrene. Another part of Helicon, also sacred to the Muses, bore the name of Mount Leibethrium. On Mount Leibethrium there was a sacred grotto of the Muses. Pierus, a Macedonian, is said to have been the first who introduced the worship of the nine Muses from Thrace to Thespiae.

The Aloeidae, the giant twin sons of Poseidon by Iphimedeia, were believed to have been the first of all men to worship the Muses on Mount Helicon and to have consecrated the mountain to them. They worshipped only three Muses—Melete, Mneme, and Aoide—and founded the town of Ascra at the foot of Helicon.

Linus, the personification of dirge or lamentation, was the son of Apollo by Calliope. According to a Boeotian tradition, Linus was killed by Apollo because he had ventured upon a musical contest with the god (Paus. 9.29.6). Near Mount Helicon an image of Linus stood in a hollow rock, formed in the shape of a grotto; and every year before sacrifices were offered to the Muses, a funeral sacrifice was offered to him, and dirges (*linae*) were sung in his honor.

Finally, though it seems in sharp contrast to the creative inspiration emanating from Mount Helicon, the orgiastic worship of Dionysus seems to have spread southward to Mounts Helicon and Parnassus from Thrace, where it was first established.

The directions for locating the sanctuary of the Muses, which has been excavated, the fountains of Aganippe and Hippocrene, and other sites in this area are complicated. These places do not appear on most maps, and guides are advisable.

HELLAS or GRAECIA (ELLADA) was a country in Europe, the inhabitants of which were called Graeci or Hellenes. Among the Greeks themselves Hellas did not refer to any particular country bounded by certain geographical limits but was used in general to signify the totality of places where Hellenes had settled. In the most ancient times Hellas was a small district of Phthiotis in Thessaly, in which was situated a town of the same name. Hellen was a son of Deucalion and Pyrrha or, according to others, a son of Zeus and Dorippe, or of Prometheus and Clymene and a brother of Deucalion. By the nymph Orseis he became the father of Aeolus, Dorus, and Xuthus, to whom some add Amphictyon. Hellen, according to tradition, was king of Phthia in Thessaly, i.e., the country between the rivers Peneius and Asopus. This kingdom he left to Aeolus. Hellen is the mythical ancestor of all the Hellenes or Greeks, as opposed to the more ancient Pelasgians. The name Hellenes was at first confined to a tribe inhabiting a part of Thessaly, but subsequently it was extended to the whole Greek nation (Hom. *Il.* 2.684; Herod. 1.56; Thuc. 1.3; Paus. 3.20.6).

As the inhabitants of this district, the Hellenes, gradually spread over the surrounding country, their name was adopted by other tribes. These tribes became integrated in language, manners, and customs with the original Hellenes until eventually the whole of the north of Greece from the Ceraunian and Cambunian Mountains to the Corinthian Isthmus was designated by the name Hellas. Peloponnesus was generally spoken of during this time of assimilation as distinct from Hellas Proper. But subsequently Peloponnesus and the Greek islands were also included under the general name of Hellas, in opposition to the land of the barbarians. Still later, even Macedonia and the southern part of Illyria were sometimes considered part of Hellas. The Romans called the land of the Hellenes Graecia, from which we have derived the name Greece. They probably gave this name to the country because they first became acquainted with the tribe of the Graeci, who inhabited the west coast of Epeirus. This tribe claimed descent from Graecus, a son of Thessalus.

The greatest length of Hellas from Mount Olympus to Cape Taenarum was about 417 km; its greatest width from the west coast of Acarnania to Marathon in Attica was about 300 km. Its area was somewhat less than that of Portugal. (Today the total area of Greece is close to that of the state of New York.) On the north it was separated by the Cambunian and Ceraunian Mountains from Macedonia and Illyria; and on the other three sides it was bounded by seas, namely by the Ionian Sea on the west, and by the Aegean on the east and south. It is one of the most mountainous countries of Europe and possesses few extensive plains and few continuous valleys. The inhabitants were thus separated from one another by barriers not easy to cross and were naturally led to form separate political communities. At a later time the north of Greece was generally divided into ten districts: Epeirus, Thessalia, Acarnania, Aetolia, Doris, Locris, Phocis, Boeotia, Attica, and Megaris. The south of Greece, or Peloponnesus, was usually divided into ten districts as well: Corinthia, Sicyonia, Phliasia, Achaia, Elis, Messenia, Laconia, Cynuria, Argolis, and Arcadia.

Before the Hellenes had spread over the country that came to be called Graecia, it was inhabited by various tribes whom the Greeks called by the collective name of barbarians (*barbaroi*). Of these the best known and most widely distributed were the Pelasgians. From them a considerable part of the Greek population was descended. They traced their ancestry to Pelasgus, a descendant of Phoroneus, king of Argos, and it was generally believed by the Hellenes that the Pelasgi spread from Argos to the other parts of Greece.

HELOS (ELOS)   a town of Laconia, situated east of the mouth of the Eurotas close to the sea in a plain that, though marshy near the coast, was described as the most fertile part of Laconia. In the earliest times it appears to have been the leading town on the coast, as Amyclae was in the interior; these two places are mentioned together by Homer (*Il.* 2.584; *Hymn Hom. ad Apoll.* 410). Helos is said to have been founded by Heleius, the youngest son of Perseus and Andromeda. He had earlier joined Amphitryon in the war against the Teleboans and had received from him the islands of the Taphians (Apollod. 2.4.5,7; Strab. 10.2.14). The Dorians conquered the inhabitants of Helos and reduced them to slavery; and, according to some, their name became the general designation of the Spartan bondsmen, or Helots. The modern town of Elos is the site of Helos. The name of Helos is still given to the plain of the lower Eurotas.

HELUS   a town belonging to Nestor, mentioned by Homer (*Il.* 2.594), was placed by some on the Alpheius River and by others on the Alorian marsh, where a sanctuary was dedicated by the Arcadians to Artemis. Its position is unknown (Strab. 8.3.24).

HEPHAESTIDAE   (See IPHISTIADAE)

HERACLEIA (IRAKLIA)   an ancient place of Pisatis in Elis, but a village in the time of Pausanias, was 8 or 9 km from Olympia. It contained medicinal waters issuing from a fountain sacred to the Ionic nymphs and flowing into the neighboring stream called Cytherus or Cytherius, which is possibly the brook near the modern village of Iraklia (Strab. 8.3.32; Paus. 6.22.7).

HERACLEIA TRACHINIA   (See TRACHIS)

HERAEA   the most important Arcadian town on the lower Alpheius, was situated near the border of Elis and on the road from Arcadia to Olympia. It is said to have been founded by Heraeeus, a son of Lycaon and originally to have been called Sologorgus. Heraea was at one time the chief village among eight others that lay scattered upon the banks of the Alpheius and its tributaries, the Ladon and Erymanthus. When it was visited by Pausanias, it was still a place of some importance. He describes its temples, baths, plantations of myrtles, and other trees along the banks of the Alpheius. Among its temples he mentions two sacred to Dionysus, one to Pan, and another to Hera, whose worship was very ancient at Heraca (Paus. 8.26.1,2). Of Hera's temple only some ruins were left. It is further recalled that a wine made here was celebrated in antiquity and was said to make women fruitful.

The site of Heraea seems rather certain. It is on the Alpheius River about 1.5 km upstream from the confluence of the Alpheius and Ladon. There was at one time an excavation here, but no monuments are visible. Heraea was separated from Pisatis by the river Erymanthus and from the territory of Megalopolis by the river Buphagus.

HERAION or **HERAEUM**   (See ARGOS)

HERCYNA   was a small stream rising near Lebadeia at the foot of Mount Laphystius and emptying into Probatia, which flowed into Lake Copais. Hercyna was a divinity of the lower world. She was a daughter of Trophonius, and once while she was playing with Kore, the daughter of Demeter, in the grove of Trophonius near Lebadeia, she let a goose fly away, which she had carried in her hand. The bird flew into a cave and concealed itself under a block of stone. When Kore pulled the bird from its hiding place, a well gushed forth from under the stone. The well was called Hercyna. On the bank of the rivulet a temple was afterward erected with the statue of a maiden carrying a goose in her hand; and in the cave there were two statues of Trophonius and Hercyna with staffs entwined by serpents. These statues resembled the statues of Asclepius and Hygieia (Paus. 9.39.2). Hercyna founded the worship of Demeter at Lebadeia, who thereby received the surname Hercyna. Hercyna herself was worshipped at Lebadeia in common with Zeus, and sacrifices were offered in common to both (Liv. 45.27).

HERMIONE (ERMIONI)   was a town at the southern end of the Argolid peninsula possessing a territory named Hermionis. The sea between the south coast of Argolis and the island of Hydrea was called after the peninsula

Hermionicus Sinus. That part of the sea was regarded as distinct from the Argolic and Saronic gulfs.

Hermione was founded by the Dryopes, who are said to have been driven out of their homes on Mount Oeta and its adjacent valleys by Heracles, and to have settled in Peloponnesus, where their three chief towns were Hermione, Asine, and Eion (Herod. 8.43,47). Hermion, a son of Europs and grandson of Phoroneus, was, according to a tradition of Hermione, the founder of the city (Paus. 2.34.4). Hermione is mentioned by Homer (*Il.* 2.560) along with its kindred city Asine. Asine and Eion were conquered at an early period by the Dorians.

When Hermione became a Dorian city, the inhabitants still retained some of the ancient Dryopian customs. It continued to be the chief seat of the worship of Demeter Chthonia, who appears to have been the principal deity of the Dryopians; the Asinaeans, who had settled in Messenia after their expulsion from Argolis, continued to send offerings to Demeter Chthonia at Hermione.

The city stood upon a promontory, on either side of which was a harbor. There were still several temples standing on this promontory in the time of Pausanias (2.34.11–35.11), of which the most remarkable was the one sacred to Poseidon. Of the numerous temples mentioned by Pausanias the most important was the ancient Dryopian sanctuary of Demeter Chthonia, situated on Mount Pron. It was said to have been founded by Chthonia, daughter of Phoroneus, and Clymenus her brother (Eurip. *Herc. Fur.* 615). Chthonia meant either "Subterranean" or "Goddess of the Earth," that is, "Protectress of the Fields." According to an Argive legend, Demeter in her wandering search for Kore came to Argolis, where she was ill-received by Colontas. Chthonia, his daughter, was unhappy with her father's conduct and, when Colontas and his house were burnt by the goddess, Chthonia was carried off by her to Hermione, where Chthonia built a sanctuary to Demeter Chthonia and instituted the festival of the Chthonia in the goddess' honor (Paus. 2.35.4). Opposite this temple was one sacred to Clymenus; and to the right was the Stoa of Echo, which repeated the voice three times.

In the same vicinity there were three sacred places surrounded with stone fences; one was named the sanctuary of Clymenus, the second that of Pluto, and the third that of the Acherusian lake. This lake near Hermione was believed to be connected with the underworld (Paus. 2.35.10). In the sanctuary of Clymenus there was an opening in the earth that the Hermionians believed to be the shortest road to Hades, and consequently they put no money in the mouths of their dead to pay the ferryman of the lower world (Paus. 2.35.10; Strab. 8.6.12). The twelfth labor of Heracles was fetching Cerberus from the underworld. It is not surprising that Hermione is one of

the places mentioned as the place where he appeared with Cerberus.

In the time of Pausanias, Mases served as the harbor of Hermione. Toward the east the frontier of the Hermionis and Troezenia was marked by a temple of Demeter Thermasia, close to the sea, 15 km west of Cape Scyllaeum (Spathi). Demeter's name has been preserved in that of modern Thermisia.

Artemis was worshipped in Hermione under the name of Iphigeneia (Paus. 2.35.1). Statues of the Charites are mentioned in Hermione. Eileithyia had a sanctuary here (Paus. 2.35.8). And the worship of Helios was established in later times (Paus. 2.34.10). There was a separate temple of Hestia at Hermione. This temple contained no image of the god- dess, only an altar (Paus. 2.35.2). Athena Promachorma (Protectress of the Bay) had a sanctuary on Mount Buporthmos near Hermione (Paus. 2.34.9).

HIERAPYTNA (IERAPETRA)   was a town on the south coast of Crete that stood in the narrowest part of the island opposite Minoa on the north coast. It was a town of great antiquity, and its foundation was ascribed to the Corybantes. It bore the successive names of Cyrba, Pytna, Camirus, and Hierapytna (Strab. 10.3.19,20). Its main deities were Zeus, Hera, Athena (with surnames Polias and Oleria) and Apollo. It was, like other towns around Mount Dicte, especially sacred to Zeus. The founding Corybantes were, of course, among the nurses of Zeus and are credited with making noises with drums and cymbals to muffle the crying of the infant from discovery by Cronus, who would have devoured him. Remains of a theater and an amphitheater can be seen, but the city has not been excavated.

HIMERUS   was an earlier name of the EUROTAS River.

HIPPOCRENE   was the famous fountain located on Mount Helicon in Boeotia. It was 3.5 km above the Grove of the Muses. The two fountains of Aganippe and Hippocrene supplied the streams called Olmeius and Permessus, which, after uniting their waters, flowed by Haliartus into Lake Copais.

When the nine daughters of Pierus engaged the Muses in a contest on Mount Helicon, it became dark when the daughters of Pierus began to sing. During the song of the Muses however, the heaven, the sea, and all rivers stood still to listen, and Helicon rose heavenward with delight, until the winged horse Pegasus, on the advice of Poseidon, stopped its rising by kicking it with his hoof; and from this kick there arose Hippocrene, the inspiring fountain of the Muses. Others say that Pegasus caused the spring to gush forth because he was thirsty (Paus. 9.31.9).

HIPPOCRENE   was a sacred fountain at Troezen. Orestes came here to be purified for the murders of Clytemnestra and Aegisthus. This fountain, like Hippocrene on Mount Helicon, was supposed to have been created by Pegasus striking his hoof on the ground (Paus. 2.31.12).

HIPPOLA (ANO BOULA)   was a town of Laconia, a little northwest of the promontory of Taenarum, in ruins in the time of Pausanias. It contained a temple of Athena Hippolaitis (Paus. 3.25.9). It probably stood at Ano Boulá, about 4 km north of Gerolimena, where inscriptions have been found.

HISTIAEA   (See OREUS)

HOLMONES   (See OLMONES)

HOMOLE or HOMOLIUM (OMOLIO)   was a town of Thessaly situated at the foot of Mount Homole, where the Peneius emerges from the Tempe gorge. It was on a route to Thessaly from Dium and controlled the east end of the pass. Mount Homole was a part of the chain of Ossa and is sometimes used as a synonym for Ossa. It was celebrated as a favorite haunt of Pan, who had a sanctuary here (Theocrit. 7.103), and as the abode of the Centaurs and the Lapiths. Pausanias (9.8.6) describes it as the most fertile mountain in Thessaly and well supplied with fountains. The site of the town is near Omolio, which is 5 km east of where the National Highway crosses the Pinios River. Some of the walls remain, and there are foundations of an unidentified temple.

HYAMPOLIS (EXARHOS)   was an ancient town of Phocis mentioned by Homer (*Il.* 2.521), and said to have been founded by the Hyantes after they had been expelled from Boeotia by the Cadmeians (Paus. 10.35.5). It was situated on the road leading from Orchomenus to Opus, at the entrance of a valley that formed a pass from Locris into Phocis and Boeotia. Pausanias (10.35.7) mentions a temple of Artemis, who was the deity chiefly worshipped in the city as Apollo was in neighboring Abae.

The ruins of Hyampolis may be seen near the village of Exarhos, which is south of the highway running between Heronia and Atalanti. The direct distance to this ruin from the summit of Abae is not more than 2.5 km in a northwestern direction. Here may be seen the circuit wall, part of a stoa, and foundations (probably of a theater).

HYDRUSSA   was the original name of CEOS.

HYDRUSSA   was the original name of IULIS.

HYDRUSSA   was another name of TENOS.

HYETTUS (LOUTSI)   a village of Boeotia, was said to have been founded by the Argive Hyettus. This Hyettus is famous because he was the first man known to have exacted punishment from an adulterer. He was exiled from Argos for slaying Molurus, son of Arisbas, whom he caught in bed with his wife. He came to King Orchomenus, who gave him property on which he built Hyettus. The village possessed in the time of Pausanias a temple of Heracles frequented by the sick for the cure of their diseases, where the hero was worshipped in the form of a rude stone (Paus. 9.23.4). The site of Hyettus is near Loutsi, which is about 10 km north of Kastro (ancient Copae).

HYLE (ILIKI)   was an ancient town in Boeotia situated upon Lake Hylica, which derived its name from this place (Hom. *Il.* 2.500, 5.708, 7.221; Strab. 9.2.20). Hyle, for whom the town was named, was a daughter of Thespius. Tychius of Hyle was a mythical artisan mentioned by Homer (*Il.* 7.219–223) as the maker of Ajax's shield of seven ox hides covered with a plate of brass.

When Lake Kopais was drained, the waters rose in Lake Iliki and Lake Paralimni, submerging what was thought to be the remains of Hyle on the west shore of Iliki. However, in 1965–1966 the whole level of Paralimni sank low enough to expose the remains of two ancient towns, the one at its southwest end identified as Hyle and renamed Iliki.

HYLE   was a town in Crete, from which Apollo derived the surname Hylatus, since Hyle was sacred to him.

HYLEESA   was another name by which the island of CALAUREIA was known.

HYMETTUS (IMITOS)   is a mountain in Attica renowned in ancient times for its honey and marble. The plain of Athens is bounded on the southeast by this lofty range, which is separated from that of Pentelicus by a valley about 3.5 km in length. Hymettus, the highest point of which is 1,027 meters, is separated by the Pirnari Glen into two parts—the northern or greater Hymettus and the southern or lesser Hymettus, which formerly bore the name Anhydrus (Waterless). The latter terminates in the promontory of Zoster. Zeus Ombrius (Rain-Giver) had an altar on Mount Hymettus (Paus. 1.32.2). A statue of Zeus Hymettus and an altar of Zeus Epacrius were also supposed to have been on Hymettus. There is some evidence that there was also an altar of Heracles. On the hill of Moni Kessariani on the side of the mountain is a famous fountain, known in ancient times as Kyllou Pera; its waters were supposed to cure sterility. The spring supplied Athens with drinking water before the construction of the Marathon Dam. A temple of Aphrodite was adjacent, and the spot was made famous by Ovid (7.670–861) describing the sad legend of Cephalus and Procris. Eos, goddess of dawn, carried away the handsome youth Cephalus from the summit of Mount Hymettus to Syria, but she afterward restored him to his wife Procris.

HYPEREIA   was a town in Argolis. It was named for Hyperes, a son of Poseidon and Alcyone, and a king of Troezen (Paus. 2.30.7).

HYPEREIA   was an earlier name of the island of CALAUREIA.

HYPEREIA   was a spring near Pherae that was said to have derived its name from Hyperes, a son of Melas and Eurycleia.

HYPERESIA   was the Homeric town in Achaia, the name of which was later changed to AEGEIRA.

HYPERTELEATUM (FINIKI)   was a place about 8 or 9 km east of Asopus in Laconia. It was said to have possessed a temple of Asclepius. No evidence has been discovered of such a temple at the modern site of Finiki, but a sanctuary of Apollo Hyperteleates has been identified there from inscriptions. It was the sanctuary for the Eleuthero-Laconian federation.

HYPSI   a place in Laconia containing temples of Asclepius and Artemis Daphnaea, was situated 5.5 km from the temple of Apollo Carneius on Mount Cnacadium (Paus. 3.24.8). These temples have never been found, and the site of Hypsi remains unknown.

HYPSUS   was a town of Arcadia in the district Cynuria, situated upon a mountain of the same name. It was said to have been founded by Hypsus, a son of Lycaon. Pausanias (8.35.7) calls it a ruined city.

HYRIA (PARALIA AVLIDOS)   was a Boeotian town mentioned by Homer (*Il.* 2.496) along with the other Boeotian cities led by Peneleos and others to the Trojan War. It had been placed by some near Aulis, but its position was quite uncertain. The late Carl Blegen placed it at Paralia Avlidos, which is 6 km north of the National Highway exit for Skimatari.

Hyrieus, a son of Poseidon and Alcyone, was king of Hyria. He retained the brother architects, Agamedes and Trophonius, to build a treasury for him. In building it, they schemed to place one stone in such a manner that it could be removed and allow them entry to the treasury. In this way they constantly robbed the treasury. The king set traps to catch the thieves, and Agamedes was finally caught in one of these traps. Trophonius cut off his

brother's head to prevent identification. Hyrieus was married to the nymph Clonia, by whom he became the father of Nycteus, Lycus, and Orion. Nycteus and Lycus, according to some, were obliged to quit their country on account of of their murder of Phlegyas. They then settled at Hyria. Lycus usurped the government of Thebes. Nycteus killed himself in despair because his daughter Antiope, who was pregnant by Zeus, fled to Epopeus at Sicyon. Before he died he exacted a promise from Lycus to take revenge on Epopeus. Lycus accordingly slew Epopeus and kept Antiope as his prisoner, but was later killed by Antiope's sons, Amphion and Zethus. Orion, the last son of Hyrieus, was a very handsome giant and hunter and said to have been called Candaon by the Boeotians. He is called by some a Theban and by others a Tanagraean, but this may well be because Hyria sometimes belonged to Thebes and sometimes to Tanagra.

Euphemus was a son of Poseidon by Europa. According to one account, he was an inhabitant of Hyria. He was one of the Calydonian hunters and the helmsman of the vessel of the Argonauts. By the power granted him by his father, he could walk on the sea. Eurypylus was another son of Poseidon, by Celaeno. One tradition calls him a hero of Hyria. In the *Iliad* (2.734) he is represented as having led the men of Ormenium and other places to Troy. From Hyria he went to Libya and there became connected with the Argonauts. He is said to have married Sterope, the daughter of Helios, by whom he became the father of Lycaon and Leucippus.

HYRIE   was the original name of the island of ZACYNTHUS.

HYRMINE (LOUTRA IRMINIS?)   was a town of Elis upon the coast, mentioned by Homer (*Il.* 2.616) as one of the towns of the Epeii. It is said to have been founded by Actor, the son of Hyrmine, who was a daughter of Epeius. In the time of Strabo (8.3.10) the town had disappeared, but its site was marked by a rocky promontory near Cyllene called Hormina or Hyrmina (Paus. 5.1.6,11). Some have thought that the town occupied the position of Kastro on the peninsula of Hlemoutsi, but others have placed it farther north at the modern harbor of Loutra Irminis (changed from the earlier, less attractive name of Kounoupeli, or "Mosquitoville"), where, on a projecting point of land, are some ancient ruins.

HYSIAE   was a town of Boeotia at the northern foot of Mount Cithaeron and on the road from Thebes to Athens. It was said to have been a colony from Hyria and to have been founded by Nycteus, father of Antiope (Strab. 9.2.12). Hysiae was in ruins in the time of Pausanias (9.2.1), who noticed there an unfinished temple of Apollo and a sacred spring. Those who drank from the spring were supposed to be able to predict the future.

IALYSUS (IALISO) was one of the three ancient Doric towns on the island of Rhodes. According to Strabo (14.2.6,7), Tlepolemus built the town of Lindus, Ialysus, and Cameirus and named them after three Danaids. Tlepolemus was a son of Heracles by Astyoche. He was king of Argos, but after slaying his uncle Licymnius, he was obliged to take flight. In conformity with the command of an oracle, he settled in Rhodes, from where he joined the Greeks in the Trojan War with nine ships (Hom. *Il.* 2.653; Apollod. 2.8.2). At Troy he was slain by Sarpedon, and his wife Philozoe instituted funeral games in commemoration of his death. Others attribute the name of the town to Ialysus, a son of Cercaphus and Cydippe or Lycippe and a grandson of Helios. He was a brother of Lindus and Cameirus, in conjunction with whom he possessed the island of Rhodes, where he was regarded as the founder of the town of Ialysus.

The Telchines were cultivators of the soil and ministers of the gods and as such they went from Crete to Cyprus and from there to Rhodes. The three towns of Cameirus, Ialysus, and Lindus were their principal seats. Hera was particularly worshipped by them at Ialysus. After they foresaw that the island would be inundated, they migrated to other parts of Greece.

Ialysus was situated about 10 km to the southwest of the city of Rhodes, and it would seem that the rise of the city of Rhodes was the cause of the decay of Ialysus for in the time of Strabo (14.2.12) it existed only as a village. Orychoma, its citadel, had a temple of Athena and Zeus Polieus, the foundations of which can still be seen. In the territory of Ialysia was a place called Castaniae (now Theologos), which had a temple of Apollo Erethimus; the remains are still visible. The site of ancient Ialysus is still occupied by a village Ialiso.

ICARIA (DIONISSOS) was the Attic deme in which Icarius received Dionysus, the god who taught him the art of making wine. Icarius was an Athenian who lived in the reign of Pandion and hospitably received Dionysus upon his arrival in Attica. The god showed him his gratitude by teaching him the cultivation of the vine and giving him bags full of wine. Icarius now rode about in a chariot and distributed the precious gifts of the god; but some shepherds, whom their friends intoxicated with wine and who thought they were poisoned by Icarius, slew him and threw his body into the well Anygrus. Others say that the body was buried under a tree. After a long search, his daughter Erigone found his grave, led there by his faithful dog Maera. In her grief she hanged herself on the tree under which he was buried. Zeus or Dionysus placed her, together with Icarius and his cup, among the stars; Erigone became the Virgin, Icarius Bootes or Arcturus, and Maera the dog star. The god then punished the ungrateful Athenians with a plague or a mania, in which all the Athenian maidens hanged themselves as Erigone

had done (Gell. 15.10). The oracle when consulted answered that Athens should be delivered from the curse as soon as Erigone should be propitiated and the two bodies should be found. The bodies were not discovered, but a festival was initiated in honor of Erigone, and fruits were offered up as a sacrifice to her and her father. The *ascoliasmos,* or dancing on a leather bag filled with air and smeared with oil, at the festivals of Dionysus was likewise traced to Icarius, who was said to have killed a ram for having injured the vines, made a bag of his skin, and then performed a dance.

Icaria has been located on the north side of Mount Pendeli near the village of Dionissos. It has been only partially excavated.

ICARIA or ICARUS (IKARIA) is an island of the Aegean to the west of Samos. The island is in reality a continuation of the range of hills crossing Samos from east to west. The island, which gave its name to the whole of the surrounding Icarian Sea, derived its own name, according to tradition, from Icarus, who was believed to have fallen into the sea near this island (Ov. *Met.* 8.195). The cape forming the easternmost point of the island was called Drepanum or Dracanum (Strab. 14.1.15), and near it was a small town of the same name. According to some traditions, Dionysus was born on Cape Dracanum, and Artemis had a temple, the Tauropolion, near the small town of Isti. It was also told that on a voyage from Icaria to Naxos, the pirates who rented a ship to Dionysus tried to sell him in Asia. But he performed feats of magic, turning parts of the ship into plants and animals and himself into a lion, whereupon the pirates went mad and threw themselves into the sea, where they were changed into dolphins (Apollod. 3.5.3).

In earlier times the island was said to have been called Doliche, Macris, and Ichthyoessa. Metapontus was king of Icaria and married to Theano.

ICARIAN SEA (IKARIO PELAGOS) is the southeastern part of the Aegean along the coasts of Caria and Ionia, which derived its name from the island of Icaria, though, according to legend, it was so called from Icarus, the son of Daedalus. When Daedalus was forced to flee from Crete, he attached wings made of wax to his and his son's bodies. He also advised his son not to fly too high; but Icarus, forgetting the advice of his father, flew so high that the sun melted the wax of his wings, and he fell down into the sea, which was called after him the Icarian Sea (Ov. *Met.* 8.195). His body, which was washed on shore, was said to have been buried by Heracles (Paus. 9.11.5).

ICHNAE was a town in Phthiotis in Thessaly, celebrated for its worship of Themis, who was surnamed Ichnaea, translated by some as "the Tracing Goddess" (*Hymn. Hom. ad Apoll.* 94; Strab. 9.5.14).

ICHTHYOESSA was an earlier name of the island of ASTYPALAEA.

ICHTHYOESSA was an earlier name of the island of ICARIA.

IDA (IDI) is the central and highest point of the mountain range that crosses the island of Crete from west to east. Mount Ida was the locality connected with the legends of Zeus, and there was a cavern on its slopes sacred to him (Diod. 5.70). Crete was the earliest seat of worship of Rhea. The common tradition was that Zeus was born in Crete either on Mount Dicte or Mount Ida, and Rhea concealed his birth from Cronus. She entrusted the baby to the Curetes and the nymphs Adrasteia and Ida, the daughters of Melisseus. They fed him with milk of the goat Amaltheia, and the bees of the mountain provided him with honey (Apollod. 1.1.6). The district around Mount Ida was particularly sacred to Zeus. Apollonius Rhodius (3.132) relates that Adrasteia gave to the infant Zeus a beautiful globe to play with, and on some Cretan coins Zeus is represented sitting upon a globe. Cynosura was another Idaean nymph named as one of the nurses of Zeus; he later placed her among the stars (Arat. 35).

The Cretan Ida, like its Trojan namesake, was connected with the working of iron, and the Idaean Dactyls, the legendary discoverers of metallurgy, are assigned sometimes to the one and sometimes to the other location. The tradition that assigns to them the Cretan Ida describes them as the sons of Zeus by the Idaean nymph Ida and as the earliest inhabitants of Crete. Some say that they went there with Mygdon (or Minos) from Phrygia and discovered the iron in Mount Berecynthus (Diod. 5.64; Cic. *De Nat. Deor.* 3.16).

Other beings associated with Mount Ida were Cres, Olenus, and Onetor. Cres was a son of Zeus by a nymph of Mount Ida, from whom the island of Crete was believed to have derived its name. Olenus was a person living on Mount Ida who wanted to take upon himself the punishment that his wife had deserved through her pride in her own beauty; he was metamorphosed along with her into stone (Ov. *Met.* 10.68). Onetor was a priest of Zeus on Mount Ida (Hom. *Il.* 16.605).

ILISSUS (ILISSOS) a small river in Attica, rises on the north slope of Mount Hymettus, receives the brook Eridanus near the Lyceum outside the walls of Athens, and loses itself in the marshes of the Athenian plain. The Ilissus is usually dry.

The Muses, Oreithyia, Pharmaceia, and Boreas are all connected with the Ilissus River. Musae Ilissiades was a name the Muses acquired from their having an altar on the Ilissus (Paus. 1.19.6). Oreithyia was a daughter of Erechtheus and Praxithea. Once she strayed beyond the river Ilissus and was carried off by Boreas, by whom she became the mother of Cleopatra, Chione, Zetes and Calais (Apollod. 3.15.1; Apollon. Rhod. 1.215). Pharmaceia was the nymph of a fountain with poisonous powers near the Ilissus. She is described as a playmate of Oreithyia (Plat. *Phaedr.* 229). Boreas, the north wind, had a temple on the Ilissus (Herod. 7.189).

IMBRASUS was a small river in the island of Samos. According to a fragment from Callimachus (213), this river, once called Parthenius, flowed in front of the ancient sanctuary of Hera outside the town of Samos, and the goddess derived from it the surname Imbrasia. Some believed Hera to have been born on this river (Apollon. Rhod. 1.187; Paus. 7.4.4).

INACHUS (INAHOS) a river in Argolis, rises in Mount Artemisium on the borders of Arcadia. Near its sources it receives a tributary called the Cephissus, which rises in Mount Lyrceium. It flows in a southeast direction, east of the city of Argos into the Argolic Gulf. This river is often dry in summer. Inachus, a son of Oceanus and Tethys and king of Argos, reproached Zeus for his treatment of Io. Then Zeus sent a Fury to pursue him. Inachus became a river-god when he threw himself into a river to escape the Fury. The river had earlier been called Cormanor or Haliacmon. When Inachus decided in favor of Hera in her dispute with Poseidon for possession of Argos, Poseidon deprived him and two other judges, the river-gods Asterion and Cephissus, of their water, so that they became dry except in rainy seasons (Paus. 2.15.5; Apollod. 2.1.4). Some of the ancients looked upon Inachus as a native of Argos, who after the flood of Deucalion led the Argives from the mountains into the plains and confined the waters within their proper channels; at other times they regarded him as an immigrant who had come across the sea as the leader of an Egyptian or Libyan colony and had united the Pelasgians whom he found scattered on the banks of the Inachus.

INATUS (TSOUTSOUROS) was a city of Crete situated on a mountain and river of the same name. It was about 50 km west of Hierapytna. The present site is thought to be Tsoutsouros, a town on the coast south of Kastelliana. Eileithyia, goddess of childbirth, was worshipped here and from the town received her surname Inatia (Callim. *Frag.* 168).

INTERNUM MARE was one Latin name for the MEDITERRANEAN SEA.

IOLCUS (VOLOS) was an ancient city of Magnesia in Thessaly situated at the head of the Pagasaean Gulf and at the foot of Mount Pelion. It was celebrated in the heroic age as the residence of Jason and the place where the

Argonauts assembled. It is given the epithets "well-built" and "spacious" (*Il.* 2.712, *Od.* 11.256). It is said to have been founded by Cretheus (Apollod. 1.9.11) and to have been colonized by Minyans from Orchomenus (Strab. 9.2.40).

Cretheus was one of the many sons of Aeolus and Enarete. His brother Salmoneus had a daughter Tyro, who as a maiden fell in love with the river-god Enipeus. Poseidon lusted for her and assumed the appearance of Enipeus, impregnated her, and became by her the father of Pelias and Neleus. The twin babies were exposed by their mother. One of them was kicked by a mare that passed by so that his face became black, and a shepherd who found the children called him Pelias. During this time Tyro suffered abuse from Sidero, her father's second wife. A marriage was then arranged for her with her uncle Cretheus, and she became by him the mother of Aeson, Pheres, and Amythaon.

When the twins grew up, they discovered who their mother was, and Pelias killed Sidero at the altar of Hera for all her injustices toward Tyro. After the death of Cretheus, Pelias did not allow his step-brother, the rightful heir, to rule the country, and after expelling even his own brother Neleus he ruled at Iolcus. He married Anaxibia, by whom he became the father of Acastus, Peisidice, Pelopia, Hippothoe, and Alcestis. By other women he had daughters Medusa, Amphinome, Euadne, Asteropaea, and Antinoe.

Meanwhile Aeson had two sons, Jason and Promachus. Pelias had been told by an oracle that he should be killed by a descendant of Aeolus, so he put to death all the Aeolidae. Promachus was killed, but Jason was saved by his relatives. They pretended that he had died of natural causes but spirited him away to Mount Pelion and entrusted him to Cheiron the Centaur to be educated (Pind. *Nem.* 3.94). Pelias was then advised by the same oracle to be on guard against a man with only one shoe. Once when Pelias offered up a sacrifice to Poseidon, he invited people from all over the countryside, and Jason arrived with only one sandal. He had lost the other in crossing the Anaurus River, on the banks of which he had lived as a peasant. On the arrival of Jason at Iolcus, Pelias remembered the oracle about the man with one shoe but concealed his fear, hoping to destroy him in some way. When Jason claimed the throne of his ancestors, Pelias declared himself ready to yield; but as Jason was blooming in youthful vigor, Pelias entreated him to propitiate the ghost of Phrixus by going to Colchis and fetching the Golden Fleece. Others say that Pelias asked Jason what he would do if he were told by an oracle that he should be killed by one of his subjects. Jason, on the suggestion of Hera, who hated Pelias, answered that he would send him out to fetch the Golden Fleece, which was in the possession of King Aeetes in Colchis and was guarded by an ever-watchful dragon. Knowing the suicidal nature of the enterprise, several members of the family of the Aeolidae went to Iolcus to intercede with Pelias on behalf of Jason. Among these was Amythaon, a son of Cretheus and Tyro and brother of Aeson and Pheres. He was also father of Bias and Melampus. In any case, Jason accepted the proposal, and heralds were sent to all parts of Greece to invite heroes to join him in the expedition. At the request of Jason, Argus, a son of Phrixus or Arestor, built the ship Argo. When all were assembled at Iolcus, they set out on their voyage. Most of the Argonauts were descended from the Minyans, who were an ancient race of heroes at Orchomenus, Iolcus, and other places. The Argonauts are therefore often called Minyae.

After acquiring the Golden Fleece and many other adventures, Jason returned to Iolcus with Medea, the daughter of Aeetes. According to Ovid (*Met.* 7.162), Jason found his aged father Aeson still alive, and Medea made him young again, but according to the common tradition, Pelias had been responsible for killing him. Jason's mother had also killed herself. After these crimes had been committed, Jason arrived and delivered the fleece to Pelias. He then dedicated the ship Argo to Poseidon on the Isthmus and called upon Medea to take vengeance on Pelias. Medea restored a ram to youth by boiling the dissected parts of its body in a cauldron in the presence of the daughters of Pelias. She then persuaded the daughters of Pelias to cut their father to pieces and boil them, pretending that in this way they would restore him to youth and vigor, as she had before changed the ram into a lamb. But Pelias remained dead, and his son Acastus expelled Jason and Medea from Iolcus. After the murder of their father, the daughters are said to have fled from Iolcus. Jason later gave Alcestis in marriage to Admetus, Amphinome to Andraemon, and Euadne to Canes. Other legends do not mention Jason's expulsion from Iolcus but simply relate that Jason returned and became by Medea the father of Medeius, who was educated by Cheiron as Jason had been. Jason is mentioned among the Calydonian hunters.

Acastus, the son of Pelias, had been one of the Argonauts and also took part in the Calydonian hunt. When his sisters had dismembered their father through Medea's persuasion, Acastus, as stated, expelled Jason and Medea and instituted funeral games for his father. Glaucus, a son of Sisyphus, took part in these games. He lived at Potniae and fed his horses with human flesh to make them spirited and warlike. The gods punished him for this. During the games, the four horses which Glaucus drove became frightened and upset the chariot (Paus. 3.18.9, 5.17.4). According to others, they tore Glaucus to pieces. Also during these games it happened that Astydameia, the wife of Acastus, fell in love with young Peleus, who had come to Acastus to be purified of the murder of Euryrion. When Peleus refused to be seduced by her, she accused him to her husband of having attempted to rape her (Apollod. 3.13.2). Acastus, however, did not take immediate revenge for the alleged crime. Later, when he and Peleus hunted on Mount Pelion and Peleus had fallen asleep, Acastus took his sword from him and left him alone and exposed. Peleus was nearly destroyed by the Centaurs, but he was saved by Cheiron or Hermes. He returned to Iolcus and killed Acastus and Astydameia. Apollodorus does not mention the death of Acastus but he says that Peleus, assisted by Jason and the Dioscuri, merely conquered and destroyed Iolcus (Apollod. 3.13.7).

Thessalus succeeded Acastus on the throne of Iolcus. A son of Jason and Medea who was educated at Corinth, he was the eponymous ancestor of the Thessalian race.

The inhabitants of Iolcus worshipped Hera under the name Pelasga. Zeus Hetaereius (Protector of Companies or Associations of Friends) was believed to have been offered the first sacrifices by Jason when the Argonauts were assembled for their expedition (Athen. 13.572).

The site of the ancient city has been very little excavated, mainly because of the growth of the modern city of Volos. Excavations since 1958 have revealed the existence of two Mycenaean palaces, and attempts are being made to identify one of them with the residence of Pelias.

IONIAN ISLANDS (IONIA NISSIA)   derived their name from the Ionian Sea. This name is now given to a group of seven principal islands (Eptanisos). The islands are Kerkira, Paxi, Lefkada, Ithaki, Kefalonia, Zakinthos, and Kithira (which is now administered by Pireas). Some of these islands figured prominently in Homeric poems. (See CORCYRA, ITHACA, DULICHIUM, etc.)

Aristaeus was an ancient divinity worshipped in various parts of Greece, such as Thessaly, Ceos, and Boeotia, but especially in the islands of the Aegean, Ionian, and Adriatic Seas, which had once been inhabited by Pelasgians.

IONIAN SEA (IONIO PELAGOS)   is the name given to the sea that separates Greece from Sicily and southern Italy. The name would seem to come from a very early time when the Ionians still inhabited the shores of the Corinthian Gulf and the part of Peloponnesus later known as Achaia. Early writers derived the name from a hero Ionius or Ion or from the wanderings of Io. No trace of the name is found in the Homeric poems; and it occurs for the first time in Aeschylus (*Prom.* 840).

IPHISTIADAE or HEPHAESTIADAE (IRAKLIO)   is the name of a deme of Attica. Iphistiadae appears to have

been the correct form of the name. It was most likely derived from an obscure hero Iphistus. This deme contained a Heracleion, or temple of Heracles, which has probably given its name to the modern village of Iraklio. The modern village is about 4 or 5 km southwest of Kifissia and Maroussio.

IRA   was an earlier name of ABIA in Messenia.

ISMARUS (ISMAROS)   is a mountain rising on the east of Lake Ismaris on the south coast of Thrace (Virg. *Ecl.* 6.30, *Georg.* 2.37). Homer (*Od.* 9.40,198) speaks of Ismarus as a town of the Cicones, on or at the foot of the mountain. The district about Ismarus produced wine that was highly esteemed (Athen. 1.30; Ov. *Met.* 9.641). After the taking of Troy, Odysseus sailed for home but was thrown by a storm upon the coast of Ismarus. He there ravaged and plundered the town, and as he was not able to induce his men to depart in time, the Cicones hastened toward the coast from the interior and slew seventy-two of his companions. Mount Ismaros is a short distance from modern Alexandroupolis.

ISMENUS (ISMENOS)   is the eastern stream flowing around Thebes. It rises from a fountain, which was called Melia in antiquity. Melia was represented as the mother of Ismenus and Tenerus, the hero of the plain into which the Ismenus flows. It was sacred to Ares, who was said to have stationed a dragon to guard it (Callim. *Hymn. in Del.* 80; Pind. *Pyth.* 11.6). Some say it derived its name from Ismenus, a son of Asopus and Metope. It had previously been called the Ladon. The little brooks Dirce and Strophie are called daughters of Ismenus (Callim. *Hymn. in Del.* 77). According to other traditions, Ismenus was a son of Amphion and Niobe, who was struck by the arrow of Apollo and leaped into the river, which was called Ismenus after him (Apollod. 3.5.6). Others say it was named from Ismenius, a son of Apollo and Melia. The river was earlier known as the Cadmus or the Ladon.

Others connected with this river were Caanthus, Apollo, and Amphiaraus. Apollo Ismenius had a temple on the river. The sanctuary of the god, at which the Daphnephoria was celebrated, bore the name Ismenion and was situated outside the city of Thebes. Caanthus was a son of Oceanus and brother of Melia. He was sent out by his father in search of his sister who had been abducted, and when he found that she was in the possession of Apollo and that it was impossible to rescue her from him, he threw fire into the Ismenion. The god then killed Caanthus with an arrow. His tomb was shown by the Thebans on the spot where he had been killed, near the river Ismenus (Paus. 9.10.5). Adrastus and Amphiaraus were the only heroes who survived the battle of the Seven against Thebes. Amphiaraus was pursued by Periclymenus and fled toward the river Ismenus. Here the earth opened before his chariot, but Zeus made him immortal (Pind. *Nem.* 9.57; *Ol.* 6.21).

ISSA   was said to have been an earlier name of the island of LESBOS.

ISTHMUS OF CORINTH   (See CORINTHIAN ISTHMUS)

ITANUS (ERIMOUPOLIS)   was a town on the east coast of Crete near the modern port of Erimoupolis, which is located on Finikodasos Bay and the promontory of Sideros. Its founder was Itanus. He was either a son of Phoenix, the brother of Europa, or he was a bastard son of one of the Curetes. In effect, this suggests that Itanus was a Phoenician colony. Historically, Itanus was founded by Theran colonists of Cyrene and was one of the first Cretan cities to mint coins, some of which depicted a marine deity.

ITHACA (ITHAKI)   so celebrated as the scene of a large portion of the Homeric poems, lies off the coast of Akarnania and is separated from Kefalonia by a channel about 6 or 7 km wide. Its name is said to have been derived from the hero Ithacus, mentioned in the *Odyssey* (17.207). He was a son of Pterelaus, from a line that started when Poseidon carried Hippothoe, daughter of Mestor, to the Echinades Islands. Hippothoe then bore Taphius, who colonized Taphos, a group of islands neighboring Ithaca (Hom. *Od.* 17.207). Polyctor, the brother of Ithacus, also gave his name to Polyctorium, a place in Ithaca.

The royal line of Ithaca is obscure. Arcisius, of unknown ancestry, was the father of Laertes, who was the father of Odysseus. Laertes in his youth had enjoyed the ideal hero's life by participating in both the Argo's voyage and the Calydonian boar hunt. He had also conquered the town of Nericum on the coast of Cephallenia. He had married Anticleia, the daughter of the famous thief Autolycus, a son of Hermes. Autolycus lived on Mount Parnassus and was renowned for his cunning. Once when he came to Ithaca as a guest, the nurse placed his newly-born grandson on his knees, and he gave the child the name of Odysseus. In his youth, Odysseus once visited Autolycus on Parnassus; while hunting there, he was wounded by a wild boar and consequently carried the scar on his thigh. At an early age he was distinguished for his courage, his knowledge of navigation, and his eloquence and skill as a negotiator. On one occasion when the Messenians had carried off some sheep from Ithaca, Laertes sent him to Messene to demand reparation. He there met with Iphitus, who was seeking the horses stolen from him, and who gave him the famous bow of Eurytus. This bow Odysseus used only in Ithaca, regarding it as too valuable to be employed in the field. He was one of the suitors of Helen, and it is said that he was the one who proposed that the suitors swear to defend the chosen bridegroom against anyone who should insult him on Helen's account. Tyndareus, to show him his gratitude, persuaded his brother Icarius to give Penelope in marriage to Odysseus. By Odysseus she had an only child, Telemachus, who was yet an infant at the time when her husband went with the Greeks to Troy. Some traditions state that Odysseus later tried to back down on this oath regarding Helen and that Agamemnon and Menelaus visited him and persuaded him, with the help of Palamedes, to join the Greeks against Troy. When Palamedes came, Odysseus pretended to be mad; he yoked an ass and an ox to a plough and began to sow salt. Palamedes, to try him, placed the infant Telemachus before the plough, and thus Odysseus was obliged to honor the promise he made as one of Helen's suitors. This occurrence is said to have been the cause of his hatred of Palamedes. In any case, he joined the Greeks and distinguished himself on the plains of Troy. But no part of his adventures is so celebrated as his wanderings after the destruction of Troy and his ultimate return to Ithaca. After many adventures he came to the Phaeacians. When they heard his story, they gave him presents and sent him home in a ship.

One night after Odysseus had fallen asleep, his ship reached the coast of Ithaca; the Phaeacians who had accompanied him carried him and his presents on shore and left him. He had now been away from Ithaca for twenty years, and when he awoke he did not recognize his native land. Athena, in order that he would not be recognized, had enveloped him in a cloud. As he was lamenting his fate, the goddess told him where he was, concealed his presents from the Phaeacians, and advised him about how to take vengeance upon the enemies of his house. During his absence his father Laertes, bowed down by grief and old age, had withdrawn into the country, his mother Anticleia had died of sorrow, his son Telemachus had grown into manhood, and his wife Penelope had rejected all the offers that had been made to her by importunate suitors from the neighboring islands (Hom. *Od.* 11.180, 13.336, 15.355, 16.108). During the last three years of Odysseus' absence more than one hundred nobles of Ithaca, Same, Dulichium, and Zacynthus had been suing for the hand of Penelope, and in their visits to her house had treated all that it contained as if it had been their own (Hom. *Od.* 1.246, 13.377, 14.90, 16.247). She deceived them by stating that she must finish a shroud that she was weaving for Laertes, her aged father-in-law, before she should choose one of them to marry. During the day she accordingly worked at the shroud, and at night she unravelled the work (Hom. *Od.* 19.149; Propert. 29.5). By this means she succeeded in putting off the suitors. But at length her stratagem was betrayed by her servants, and, in consequence, the faithful Penelope, who was pining and longing for her husband's return, was importuned more and more by the impatient suitors.

Meanwhile, Telemachus, who was still an infant at the time when his father went to Troy, had in his absence of nearly twenty years grown to manhood. After the gods in council had determined that Odysseus should return home, Athena, assuming the appearance of Mentes, king of the Taphians, went to Ithaca and advised Telemachus to eject the troublesome suitors from the house and to go to Pylos and Sparta to gather information concerning his father. Telemachus followed the advice, but the suitors refused to leave his house; and Athena, in the form of Mentor, accompanied Telemachus to Pylos. Mentor, a son of Alcimus and a friend of Odysseus, had been entrusted with the care of Odysseus' house in his absence. On Odysseus' return, Mentor assisted him against the suitors and brought about a reconciliation between him and the people (Hom. *Il.* 22.206, 24.445). After Telemachus had also visited Sparta, he returned home where he found his father with the swineherd Eumaeus. Odysseus was disguised as a beggar, but Telemachus would not have recognized him in any case since he had not seen him for so long. Odysseus told him who he was and father and son now agreed to punish the suitors. Still in the disguise of a beggar, he accompanied Telemachus and Eumaeus to the town. On his arrival he was abused and insulted by the goatherd Melanthius and the suitors, who even tried to kill Telemachus; but his old dog recognized him, as did his nurse Eurycleia (by the scar from his youth). Penelope, who still did not recognize him in his disguise, received him kindly.

The plan of revenge was now put into motion. Penelope reluctantly agreed to promise her hand to the one who should conquer the others in shooting with the bow of Odysseus. As none of the suitors was able to handle it, Odysseus himself took it up and, having ordered all the doors to be shut and all arms to be removed, he began his contest with the suitors. Supported by Athena, his son, and some faithful servants, he killed all the suitors and the servants who had collaborated with them. The minstrel and the herald Medon alone were spared. Odysseus now revealed himself to Penelope and went to see his aged father. Almost at once the report of the death of the suitors was spread abroad, and their relatives rose in arms against Odysseus; but Athena, who assumed the appearance of Mentor, brought about a reconciliation between the people and the king.

As for the last period of his life, some say that Telegonus, the son of Odysseus by Circe, was sent out by his mother to seek his father. A storm cast him upon Ithaca, where he began to plunder in order to obtain provisions. Odysseus and Telemachus attacked him, but

he slew Odysseus, and his body was afterward carried to Aeaea (Hor. *Carm.* 3.29.8).

While the Homeric tradition describes Penelope as a most chaste and faithful wife, some later writers relate that by Hermes or by all the suitors together she became the mother of Pan (Lycoph. 772; Cic. *De Nat. Deor.* 3.22). Odysseus for this reason cast her out, and she went to Sparta and then to Mantineia, where her tomb was shown in later years (Paus. 8.12.3). According to another tradition, Penelope, with Telemachus and Telegonus, who had killed his father, went to Aeaea where they buried the body of Odysseus. Telegonus then married Penelope, by whom he became the father of Italus (Hes. *Theog.* 1014).

In the post–Homeric traditions we read that Telemachus became the father of Perseptolis either by Polycaste, the daughter of Nestor, or by Nausicaa, the daughter of Alcinous. Others relate that he was induced by Athena to marry Circe and became by her the father of Latinus, or that he married Cassiphone, a daughter of Circe. In a quarrel with his mother-in-law he killed her, for which act he was killed by Cassiphone. He is also said to have had a daughter called Roma, who married Aeneas. One account states that Odysseus, because of a prophecy that his son was dangerous to him, sent him away from Ithaca.

Others connected with these events can be separated into two groups: friends or foes of Odysseus and family. The friends, many of whom predated Odysseus' departure for the war, included Achaemenides, a son of Adamastus of Ithaca and a companion of Odysseus. Odysseus left him behind in Sicily when he fled from the Cyclops. Here he was found by Aeneas, who took him with him (Virg. *Aen.* 3.613; Ov. *Ep. ex Pont.* 2.2.25). Dolius was an aged slave of Penelope, whom she had received from her father on her marrying Odysseus and who took care of her garden. When Odysseus returned from his wanderings, Dolius and his six sons welcomed him and was ready to join his master against the relatives of the suitors (Hom. *Od.* 4.735, 24.498). Eumaeus the swineherd, already mentioned, was a son of Ctesius, king of the island of Syrie; he had been carried away from his father's house by a Phoenician slave, and Phoenician sailors sold him to Laertes (Hom. *Od.* 15.403). Eurycleia the nurse, already mentioned, was a daughter of Ops and had been purchased by Laertes and retained by Telemachus. When Odysseus returned, she recognized him, though he was in the disguise of a beggar, by a scar, and afterward she faithfully assisted him against the suitors (Hom. *Od.* 1.429, 4.742, 19.385). Halitherses, a son of Mastor of Ithaca, was a soothsayer; during the absence of Odysseus he remained behind in Ithaca and assisted Telemachus against the suitors (Hom. *Od.* 2.15, 7.253, 24.451). Medon was a herald in the house of Odysseus (Hom. *Od.* 4.677, 22.357). Mentes, already mentioned, was a son of Anchialus, king of the Taphians north of Ithaca. He was connected by ties of hospitality with the house of Odysseus. Mentor, also mentioned previously, was a son of Alcimus and a friend of Odysseus, who entrusted to him the care of his house while he was away (Hom. *Od.* 2.226, 22.235). On Odysseus' return, Mentor assisted him in the contest with the suitors and, with the assistance of Athena, brought about a reconciliation between him and the people (Hom. *Od.* 22.206, 24.445). Peisenor of Ithaca was a herald of Telemachus (Hom. *Od.* 2.38). Philoetius, the celebrated cowherd of Odysseus, was frequently mentioned in the *Odyssey.*

Ancient writers have listed the suitors of Penelope, but it is only necessary to point out a few of the principals. Antinous, a son of Eupeithes of Ithaca, even attempted to make himself master of the kingdom and threatened the life of Telemachus (Hom. *Od.* 4.630, 16.371). When Odysseus appeared in the disguise of a beggar, Antinous insulted him and threw a footstool at him (Hom. *Od.* 18.42). On this account he was the first of the suitors to fall by the hands of Odysseus (Hom. *Od.* 22.8). Eupeithes of Ithaca actually owed Odysseus a debt since once Eupeithes had attacked the Thesprotians, the allies of the Ithacans, and Odysseus had protected him from the indignation of the people of Ithaca. Eupeithes, however, wanted to avenge the death of his son Antinous, who was slain by Odysseus, and he accordingly led a band of Ithacans against Odysseus but fell in the struggle (Hom. *Od.* 16.436, 24.469,523). Amphimedon was a son of Melaneus of Ithaca, and Agamemnon had stayed with his family when he came to call upon Odysseus to join the Greeks against Troy. Odysseus subsequently recognized Melaneus in Hades (Hom. *Od.* 24.103). Amphimedon was slain by Telemachus (Hom. *Od.* 22.284). Melanthius, a son of Dolius, was a goatherd of Odysseus. He sided with the suitors and was killed by Odysseus (Hom. *Od.* 17.212, 21.176, 22.474). Phemius, the famous minstrel, was a son of Terpius and with his songs entertained the suitors in the house of Odysseus (Hom. *Od.* 1.154, 17.263). Polybus of Ithaca, father of the suitor Eurymachus, was slain by the swineherd Eumaeus (Hom. *Od.* 1.339, 22.284).

The island of Ithaca is divided by the Gulf of Molo into two nearly equal parts, connected by a narrow isthmus not more than 1.5 km across and on which stands the citadel of ancient Alalcomenae, traditionally known as the Castle of Odysseus. Ithaca everywhere rises into rugged hills, of which the chief is the mountain Anoge in the northern division, which is identified with the Neritos of Virgil (*Aen.* 3.271) and the "bough-swaying" Neriton of Homer (*Od.* 9.21). Its forests have now disappeared.

The Homeric Fountain of Arethusa is identified with a spring that rises at the foot of a cliff, still called Korax, fronting the sea near the southeast end of Ithaca. This is said to be the stream at which the swine of Eumaeus were watered. On the plateau of Marathia to the south is the possible location of the pigsties of Eumaeus. From there a path leads down to the bay of Agios Andreas, where Telemachus probably landed on his return from Pylos to avoid ambush by the suitors.

The Homeric port of Phorcys (*Od.* 13.345) is supposed to be represented by a small bay now called Dexia on the southern side of the Gulf of Molo. This inlet is adjacent to Vathi, the capital and site of ancient Ithaca. At a cave on the side of the small mountain above this gulf and at a short distance from the sea is placed the Grotto of the Nymphs, in which the sleeping Odysseus was deposited by the Phaeacians who brought him from Scheria (Hom. *Od.* 13.116). The port was dedicated to Phorcys, the old man of the sea.

ITHOME (FANARI)   a town of Histiaeotis in Thessaly, described as "Ithome of the crags" by Homer (*Il.* 2.729), is placed by Strabo (9.5.17) within a quadrangle formed by the four cities of Tricca, Metropolis, Pelinnaeum, and Gomphi. Podaleirius, a son of Asclepius, with his brother Machaon led the Thessalians of Tricca, Ithome, and Oechalia against Troy in thirty ships. Ithome probably occupied the site of the castle that stands on the summit above the village of Fanari.

ITHOME (ITHOMI)   is a mountain in Messenia. This mountain derived its name from the nymph Ithome. According to Messenian tradition, Ithome and Neda, from whom a river of the country derived its name, were said to have nursed Zeus and to have bathed the infant god in the well Clepsydra (Paus. 4.33.2). Ithomatas was a surname of Zeus derived from this same hill, where the god had a sanctuary and where an annual festival, the Ithomaea, was celebrated in his honor (Paus. 4.33.2). A convent occupies the site of this sanctuary, where there is some evidence of early human sacrifice.

ITON or **ITONUS** (ALMIROS)   a town of Phthiotis in Thessaly, called "mother of flocks" by Homer (*Il.* 2.696), was situated 11 km from Halus on the river Cuarius or Coralius and above the Crocian plain (Strab. 9.5.14). The site has been placed a few kilometers southwest of modern Almiros. Iton had a celebrated temple of Athena, whose worship, under the name Athena Itonia, was carried by the Boeotians, when they were expelled from Thessaly into the country named after them (Strab. 9.5.14; Apollod. 2.7.7). Her worship spread into the country about Lake Copais, where the Pamboeotia was celebrated in the neighborhood of a temple and grove of Athena (Paus. 9.34.1; Plut. *Amat. Narr.* 4). No temple of Athena Itonia so far has been found at Iton, but a pan–Thessalian sanctuary of Athena Itonia was located in

1963 near modern Filia, which is in the area in which the Boeotians first settled when they left Thessaly.

After his labors Heracles had many additional adventures, among which was his campaign against the Dryopes. Later he assisted Aegimius, king of the Dorians, against the Lapiths. As Heracles proceeded to Iton in Thessaly he was challenged to single combat by Cycnus, a son of Ares and Pelopia (Hes. *Scut. Herc.* 58), but Cycnus was slain.

IULIS (KEA) was the most important town on Ceos. Iulis was situated on a hill about 4.5 km from the sea and on the same site as the modern Kea in the northern part of the island. There are several remains of Iulis; the most important is a colossal lion about 9 meters in length, which lies a short walk east of the town. According to a legend, Ceos was originally called Hydrussa and was inhabited by nymphs, who afterward crossed over to Carystus, having been frightened away from the island by a lion. Aphrodite Hecaerge (Hitting at a Distance) was worshipped at Iulis.

The laws of Iulis were very celebrated in antiquity, and hence "Cean Laws" were used proverbially to indicate any excellent institutions. These laws related to the morals of the citizens and their mode of life. It is said that every citizen above sixty years of age was obliged to put an end to his life by poison (Aelian. *V.H.* 3.37).

IXIAE or **IXIA** was a district on the island of Rhodes. Apollo derived his surname Ixius from this area (Strab. 4.2.12). The modern city of Rhodes has a nearby resort area Ixia, but the place referred to as a "stronghold" by Strabo (4.2.12) lay between Lindus and Mount Atabyris.

LACEDAEMON was the alternate name of SPARTA. (See also LACONIA.)

LACIADAE was a deme of Attica on the Sacred Way between Sciron and the Cephissus and near the sacred fig tree. Lacius was an Attic hero, to whom a sanctuary was erected at this site (Paus. 1.37.2).

LACONIA, LACONICA, or LACEDAEMON (LAKONIA) is the southeast district of Peloponnesus. Its most ancient name was Lacedaemon, which is the only form found in Homer (*Il.* 2.581, 3.239,244) who applies this name both to the country and to its capital. The name was derived from Lacedaemon. The later name Laconia was derived from a mythical hero Lacon.

The topography of Laconia exercised a strong influence upon the history of the people. It is a long valley surrounded on three sides by mountains and open only on the fourth to the sea. On the north it is bounded by the southern barrier of the Arcadian Mountains. Running south from these are the parallel ranges of Taygetus and Parnon. Taygetus divides Laconia and Messenia and terminates in the promontory Taenarum, now Cape Tenaro, the southern most tip of Greece and Europe. Parnon stretches along the east coast and terminates in the promontory of Maleas. The river Eurotas flows through the entire length of the valley lying between these mountain masses; it eventually empties into the Gulf of Lakonia. On the north side there are only two natural passes by which the plain of Sparta could be invaded. On the west side was the formidable height of Taygetus, and on the east side the rocky coastline.

Taygetus is the highest mountain in Peloponnesus, with its greatest height being immediately above Sparta. The principal summit of the mountain was called Taletum in antiquity and was sacred to the Sun; horses and other victims were here sacrificed to this god (Paus. 3.20.4). Heavily forested Taygetus was one of the favorite haunts of the huntress Artemis (Hom. *Od.* 6.103), and the excellence of Laconian dogs was proverbial in antiquity (Aristot. *H.A.* 6.20; Virg. *Georg.* 3.405).

The Eurotas flows through the entire length of the valley between the ranges of Taygetus and Parnon. In its course three districts may be distinguished: the valleys of the upper Eurotas, the middle Eurotas, and the lower.

Laconia was originally inhabited by the Leleges. According to tradition, Lelex was the first king. He was married to the Naiad Cleochareia, by whom he became the father of Myles and Polycaon. He had a shrine at Sparta (Apollod. 3.10.3; Paus. 3.1.1, 4.1.1). Lelex was succeeded by his son Myles, who was regarded as the inventor of mills (Paus. 3.1.1, 20.2). Myles was succeeded by his son Eurotas, who channelled the waters that were spread over the plain and gave his own name to the river he had thus formed. He died without male offspring and was succeeded by Lacedaemon, the son of Zeus and Taygete, who married Sparta, the daughter of his predecessor, and became by her the father of Amyclas, Eurydice, and Asine. Lacedaemon gave to the people and the country his own name; he gave to the city that he founded the name of his wife. He was believed to have built the sanctuary of the Charites, which stood between Sparta and Amyclae, and to have given to those divinities the names of Cleta and Phaenna (Paus. 3.18.6). A shrine was erected to him in the neighborhood of Therapne (Paus. 3.20.2).

Amyclas, the son of Lacedaemon, founded the city called after him Amyclae. He was married to Diomede, the daughter of Lapithus, by whom he became the father of Argalus, Cynortas, and Hyacinthus. Hyacinthus, the youngest and most beautiful of his sons, was accidentally killed by Apollo and was buried below the statue of Apollo at Amyclae. On the death of Amyclas the empire came to Argalus and afterward to Cynortas. Cynortas had a son Oebalus, who married Gorgophone, the daughter of

Perseus, and became by her the father of Tyndareus. When Tyndareus came to the throne, the kingship was disputed by Hippocoon, who was the elder, although bastard son of Oebalus. Hippocoon was aided by Icarius, another brother. Tyndareus was forced to flee, but was later restored by Heracles, who killed the usurpers. The throne next passed to Menelaus, the son-in-law of Tyndareus. Menelaus was succeeded by Orestes, the son of Agamemnon, who married Hermione, the daughter of Menelaus. Orestes was succeeded by his son Tisamenus, who was reigning when the Dorians invaded the country under the guidance of the Heracleidae. In the threefold division of Peloponnesus among the descendants of Heracles, Lacedaemon fell to the share of Eurysthenes and Procles, the twin sons of Aristodemus. According to the common legend, the Dorians conquered Peloponnesus at once; but in Laconia, at least, it was some time before they obtained possession even of all the places in the plain of Sparta. According to some, the Dorian conquerors divided Laconia into six districts: Sparta they kept for themselves; Amyclae was given to the Achaian Philonomus, who betrayed the country to them; Las, Pharis, Aegys, and an unidentified sixth town were governed by viceroys and were allowed to receive new citizens.

In the Spartan plain the three chief towns were Sparta, Amyclae, and Pharis, all near each other and close to the Eurotas. Therapne may be regarded as almost a part of Sparta. In the plain was a sanctuary of Zeus Messapeus, belonging to a village called Messapeae. Beyond it at the entrance into the mountains was the Homeric city of Bryseae. In the mountains was a sanctuary of Demeter Eleusinia, and 3 km farther was Lapithaeum, near which was Derrhium. Four kilometers from Derrhium was Harpleia, which bordered upon the plain (Paus. 3.20.7). Some identify Harpleia with the present site of Mistra, but others believe that Mistra represents the Homeric Messe.

The road from Sparta to Megalopolis followed the valley of the Eurotas. Pausanias mentions several monuments on this road. One was the tomb of Ladas. This tomb is described as 9 km from Sparta. Later on was the town of Pellana, the frontier fortress of Sparta. Eighteen kilometers from Pellana was Belemina (Paus. 3.21.3). Near Belemina were Aegys and Tripolis. After crossing the bridge over the Eurotas, the traveller saw on his right hand Mount Thornax, upon which stood a colossal statue of Apollo Pythaeus, guarding the city of Sparta, which lay at his feet. A little farther on was Sellasia, which was the main security of Sparta in the valley of the Oenus, as Pellana was in the valley of the Eurotas. The road to Argos followed the Oenus, and to the west of the road lay Caryae. From this place to the territory of the Threatis in Argolis was a forest of oaks called Scotitas, which derived

its name from a temple of Zeus Scotitas, about 2 km west of the road (Paus. 3.10.6). On the ridge of Mount Parnon the boundaries of Argolis and Laconia were marked by stone pillars called hermae. There was also a town Oenus, from which the river derived its name.

The road to Tegea passed over a high and mountainous district called Sciritis in antiquity. The two towns in Sciritis were Scirus and Oeum.

On the road from Sparta to Gythium, the chief port of the country, was Croceae. It was about 25 km from Sparta and celebrated for its quarries. Gythium was 20 km beyond Croceae. Above Gythium in the interior was Aegiae. Opposite Gythium was the island Cranae.

To the east of Gythium was Trinasus, situated upon a promontory, which formed the northeast end of the peninsula terminating in Cape Taenarum. Fifteen kilometers beyond Trinasus was Helos, also upon the coast. South of Helos 5.5 km along the coast was Acriae, and 11 km south of Acriae, Asopus. Nine kilometers south of Asopus was a temple of Asclepius in a spot called Hyperteleatum. Thirty-seven kilometers south of Asopus was the promontory and peninsula Onugnathus, connected with the mainland by a narrow isthmus. Between Onugnathus and Malea was a considerable bay called Boeaticus Sinus from the town of Boeae, situated at its head. In this vicinity were three ancient towns called Etis, Aphrodisias, and Side, which were founded by the Dorians. Between Boeae and Malea was Nymphacum, with a cave near the sea in which was a fountain of fresh water. The promontory Malea is the most southerly point in Greece with the exception of Taenarum. It was much dreaded by ancient sailors on account of the winds and waves of the two seas, which here meet together. On the promontory was a statue of Apollo. South of Malea was the island Cythera. Going up the east coast were Side, Epidelium, Epidaurus Limera, Zarax, Cyphanta, and Prasiae, the last of which was near the border of Argolis. In the interior between the Eurotas and Mount Parnon were Geronthrae, Marius, Glyppia, and Selinus.

Seven and a half kilometers south of Gythium was Las upon the coast, which some writers call Asine. Five and a half kilometers from Las was Hypsi in the interior, and a little below Las was the river Smenus. Immediately south of this river was the temple of Artemis Dictynna on a promontory now called Ageranos. In the same area was a village called Araenus or Araenum, where Las, the eponymous founder of the city of Las, was said to have been buried. South of the promontory of Ageranos was a stream, the Scyras, beyond which were an altar and temple of Zeus (Paus. 3.25.1). The Taenarian peninsula is connected with that of Taygetus by an isthmus three-quarters of a kilometer across. In ancient times there were two harbors on the peninsula named Psamathus and Achilleius Portus; the extremity of the peninsula was

Cape Matapan. Rounding the point one came to the town of Taenarum. North of Taenarum was the promontory Thyrides. On this promontory were the towns of Hippola and Messa. North of Messa was Oetylus. Fifteen kilometers north of Oetylus was Thalamae, situated inland, and 4 km from Thalamae was Pephnus upon the coast. Four kilometers north of Pephnus upon the coast was Leuctra or Leuctrum; and 12 km north was Cardamyle, 1.5 km from the sea. North of Cardamyle was Gerenia, the northernmost of the Eleuthero-Laconian towns. Alagonia was in the interior 5.5 km from Gerenia.

Worship in Laconia centered on six or eight of the principal gods. Zeus was worshipped here under the surname of Agetor (Leader and Ruler of Men) and Soter (Savior). Artemis Soteira (Saving Goddess) was the name of the goddess in Laconia, as was Artemis Limnaea (Inhabiting or Born in a Lake or Marsh). She was worshipped under this latter name on the frontier between Laconia and Messenia (Paus. 3.2.6). She also had the surname Cnagia, derived from Cnageus, a Laconian, who accompanied the Dioscuri in their war against Aphidna, where he was made a prisoner. He was sold as a slave and carried to Crete where he served in the temple of Artemis: but he escaped from there with a priestess of the goddess, who carried her statue to Sparta (Paus. 3.18.4).

Ares had been a principal god in Colchis, where the Golden Fleece was suspended on an oak tree in a grove sacred to him. From there the Dioscuri were believed to have brought to Laconia the ancient statue of Ares that was preserved in the temple of Ares Theritas on the road from Sparta to Therapne (Paus. 3.19.7,8). He also had temples at Geronthrae and at Sparta.

Athena Pareia had a statue in Laconia, perhaps so called only from its being made of Parian marble (Paus. 3.20.8). Asclepius Philolaus (Friend of the People) had a temple in Laconia (Paus. 3.22.9). Demeter Epipole was a name of the goddess at Lacedaemon. Traces of the worship of Rhea were found in Laconia (Paus. 3.22.4).

Dion was a king in Laconia and husband of Iphitea, the daughter of Prognaus. Apollo, who had been kindly received by Iphitea, rewarded her by conferring upon her three daughters, Orphe, Lyco, and Carya, the gift of prophecy, on condition, however, that they should not betray the gods nor search after forbidden things. Afterwards, Dionysus also came to the house of Dion; he was not only well received, like Apollo, but also won the love of Carya. Therefore Dionysus soon paid Dion a second visit under the pretext of consecrating a temple, which the king had erected to him. Orphe and Lyco, however, guarded their sister, and when Dionysus had reminded them, in vain, of the command of Apollo, they were seized with raging madness; they went to the heights of Taygetus where they were metamorphosed into rocks.

Carya, the beloved of Dionysus, was changed into a nut tree. When the Lacedaemonians were informed of it by Artemis, they dedicated a temple to Artemis Caryatis.

The Dioscuri were important in Laconia. They were sons of Leda and Tyndareus. They were born, according to different traditions, at different places, such as Amyclae, Mount Taygetus, Thalamae, or the island of Pephnos. The Dioscuri were engaged in an expedition against Athens when Theseus carried off Helen and hid her at Aphidna. They participated in the expedition of the Argonauts. They also had a famous and fatal battle with the sons of Aphareus. Once, in conjunction with Idas and Lynceus, they had carried off a herd of cattle from Arcadia, and it was left to Idas to divide the booty. He cut up a bull into four parts and declared that whichever of them should first succeed in eating his share should receive half the oxen and that the second should have the other half. Idas thereupon not only ate his own quarter but also devoured that of his brother's in addition. Then he drove the whole herd home to Messene. The Dioscuri invaded Messene and drove away the cattle of which they had been deprived and many more in addition. This became the occasion of a war between the Dioscuri and the sons of Aphareus, which was carried on in Messene or Laconia. In this war Castor, the mortal twin, fell by the hands of Idas. Zeus thereafter allowed Polydeuces to live and die on alternate days since Polydeuces had vowed to die with his brother.

LADON (LADON)   is a river in Arcadia. Below Heraea the Alpheius River receives the Ladon, which rises near Cleitor. Ladon, the river-god, was described as a son of Oceanus and Tethys and as the husband of Stymphalis, by whom he became the father of Daphne and Metope. Metope was married to Asopus and was the mother of Thebe. Daphne was loved and pursued by Apollo. When Daphne was on the point of being overtaken by him, she prayed to Gaea, who opened the earth and received her; and in order to console Apollo, Gaea created the laurel tree, from the boughs of which Apollo made himself a wreath. Ladon was also said to be the father of Thelpusa, from whom the town of Thelpusa in Arcadia derived its name.

LADON   was an earlier name of the Theban stream ISMENUS.

LAGIA   was an earlier name of the island of DELOS.

LAMIA (LAMIA)   was a town in the district Phthiotis in Thessaly. The modern city occupies the site of ancient Lamia. The only remains of the ancient city are pieces of the walls of the acropolis and some remains of the town walls at the foot of the hill. Foundations of a fourth-century shrine have also been reported. On the opposite side of the town was a small river which, we learn from Strabo (9.5.10), was called Achelous. The port of Lamia was named Phalara, now Stilis. Lamius or Lamus was a son of Heracles and Omphale, from whom Lamia was believed to have derived its name (Diod. 4.31; Ov. *Her.* 9.54).

LAMPA   (See LAPPA)

LAMPEIA (LAMPIA)   is a part of the lofty range of Erymanthus on the boundaries of Arcadia, Achaia, and Elis. Lampeia extends southward from the main range. The fourth labor of Heracles was to capture alive the Erymanthian boar. This animal had descended from Mount Erymanthus (according to others, from Mount Lampeia) into Psophis.

LAMPTRA (LAMBRIKA and AGIA MARINA)   was the name of two Attic demes—Upper Lamptra and Lower or Maritime Lamptra. These places were between Anagyrus, Thorae, and Aegilia. Upper Lamptra was probably situated at Lambrika, a village a few kilometers from the sea, at the southeast end of Mount Hymettus; and Lower Lamptra was probably on the coast at Agia Marina. Cranaus, an autochthon and king of Attica, reigned at the time of the flood of Deucalion. He was married to Pedias, by whom he became the father of Cranae, Cranaechme, and Atthis (believed to be the eponym of Attica). Cranaus was deprived of his kingdom by Amphictyon, his son-in-law, and after his death he was buried in the deme of Lamptra, where his tomb was shown as late as the time of Pausanias (1.31.2).

LAPHYSTIUM (LAFISTIO)   is an extension of Mount Helicon, running towards Lake Copais and separating the plains of Coroneia and Lebadeia. It is of volcanic origin. It possessed a sanctuary of Zeus Laphystius. When the second wife of Athamas, Ino, contrived to have Phrixus and Helle, the children of Nephele, Athamas' first wife, put to death, she convinced Athamas that a plague in Boeotia could be averted only by their sacrifice. According to Pausanias (9.34.4), Athamas wished to sacrifice Phrixus at the foot of Mount Laphystium on the altar dedicated to Zeus Laphystius. Dionysus Laphystius also acquired a surname from Mount Laphystium. From him the female Bacchants were called Laphystiae in the Macedonian dialect.

Heracles Charops (Bright-Eyed or Joyful Looking) was a name under which the hero had a statue near Mount Laphystium. On that particular spot he was believed to have brought Cerberus from the underworld (Paus. 9.34.4).

LAPPA or LAMPA (ARGIROUPOLI)   was an inland town of Crete, with a district extending from sea to sea

and possessing the port Phoenix. It was founded by Agamemnon and was named after one Lampos, a Tarrhaean; it might have been a colony of Tarrha. Modern Argiroupoli is located on the site of Lappa.

LARISSA (LARISSA)   was the citadel of Argos. Larissa, the Pelasgic name for citadel, was an impressive sight. It was built on a solitary, conical mountain 274 meters in height with steep, rocky sides. Larissa was a daughter of Pelasgus, from whom this citadel and two Thessalian towns are believed to have derived their names (Paus. 2.23.9). Strabo (13.3.4) on the other hand, calls her a daughter of Piasus, a Pelasgian prince. Pelasgus was a son of Phoroneus and brother of Iasus and Agenor. After their father's death, the two elder brothers divided his dominions between themselves in such a manner that Pelasgus received the country about the river Erasinus and built Larissa.

Zeus Larissaeus derived his surname from Larissa (Paus. 2.24.4). The same held true for Apollo Larissaeus.

LARISSA (LARISSA)   an important town of Thessaly, the capital of the district Pelasgiotis, was situated in a plain on the right, or south, bank of the Peneius. Larissa was a daughter of Pelasgus from whom this and another Thessalian town are believed to have derived their names (Paus. 2.23.9). Strabo (13.3.4), on the other hand, calls her a daughter of Piasus, a Pelasgian prince. Larissa had a strongly fortified citadel (Diod. 15.61). The city is not mentioned by Homer, but some commentators identify it with Homer's Argissa (*Il.* 2.738). Its foundation was ascribed to Acrisius. The plain of Larissa was formerly inhabited by the Perrhaebi, who were partly expelled by the Larissaeans and partly subjugated.

The history of Larissa is interwoven with the history of the Lapiths, and it is difficult ot say at which point Larissa can be said to have emerged as a kingdom with its own royal line. The ancient contest of the Lapiths and Centaurs was one of the major subjects of classical artists, and the story eventually involves the city of Larissa. To begin with, Peneius, the river-god, begot by Creusa, the daughter of the river Asopus, two children, Hypseus and Stilbe. Hypseus became king of the Lapiths and by Chlidanope had four children, Cyrene, Alcaea, Themisto, and Astyageia. Stilbe, his sister, was the mother by Apollo of two sons, Centaurus and Lapithes. Nothing can be learned of Centaurus, although his name anticipates the race of Centaurs, who were created a few generations later. Lapithes, on the other hand, is regarded as the ancestor of the Lapiths (Hom. *Il.* 12.128; Diod. 4.69, 5.61). He made his home near the Peneius River and ruled over the region. He married Orsinome, the daughter of Eurynomus, and had two sons, Phorbas and Periphas (some say also Triopas). Phorbas migrated to Elis, where he had a share in the government. Earlier the

Rhodians in pursuance of an oracle are said to have invited him to their island to deliver it from snakes. He was the father of Augeas, Actor, and Diogeneia.

Periphas, the other son of Lapithes, married Astyageia, the daughter of his great-uncle Hypseus, and had by her eight sons, the oldest of whom was Antion. Antion married Perimela, the daughter of Amythaon, and became by her the father of Ixion. When he was grown, Ixion promised that he would give many gifts to Deioneus for the hand of his daughter Dia. But later Ixion refused to honor his promise, and Deioneus took as security his mares. Ixion thereupon summoned Deioneus to visit him to receive the promised gifts but instead pushed him into a burning pit. Then he could find no one willing to purify him of the heartless murder, except Zeus himself. During the rites Ixion lusted after Hera and tried to seduce her. Zeus made a figure of Hera from a cloud and sent it to Ixion, who immediately embraced it and produced the Centaurs. For this and other impious crimes he was bound by Zeus upon a wheel and after death had to suffer punishment for all eternity. Meanwhile, by Perimela he had produced Peirithous, who eventually succeeded his father on the throne at Larissa. The Centaurs demanded of Peirithous their share of their father's kingdom, and when he would not yield it they made war on him and the Lapiths. At a later time they made up their differences, and Peirithous announced his plan to marry Hippo-dameia, the daughter of Butes. He invited many guests, including his best friend Theseus, and he also invited the Centaurs. The Centaurs did not have a head for wine and soon became drunk and assaulted the female guests (as well as a few boys). Theseus and the Lapiths, outraged, slew many of the Centaurs and drove the rest out of the city. Among the slain or wounded Centaurs were Rhoetus, Asbolus, Cyllarus, and Erigdysus. Cheiron, the wisest and most just of the Centaurs and instructor of Achilles and other heroes, was not involved in the fray but was exiled nevertheless. Likewise was Astylus, a seer among the Centaurs, who tried to dissuade the Centaurs from fighting against the Lapiths. The rowdy Centaurs took up residence in Cape Malea, where they plundered travellers and slew their neighbors. Peirithous, after several adven-tures, died in Hades where he had attempted to abduct Persephone. He was worshipped at Athens, along with Theseus, as a hero.

Peirithous and Hippodameia had a son, Polypoetes, who joined the Greeks in the Trojan War, commanding the men of Argissa, Gyrton, Orthe, Elone, and Oloosson (Hom. *Il.* 2.738). At the funeral games of Patroclus he gained the victory in throwing the iron ball (Hom. *Il.* 23.836). After the fall of Troy, Polypoetes and Leonteus are said to have founded the town of Aspendus in Pamphylia.

Also taking part in the Trojan War from Larissa were Leonteus, Hippothous, and Pylaeus. Leonteus was a son of Coronus and a prince of the Lapiths. Coronus had made war on Aegimius, king of the Dorians, over a border dispute; Heracles, who was offered a share in the country, assisted the outnumbered Dorians. Coronus was killed (Apollod. 2.7.7). In conjunction with Polypoetes, Leonteus led the Lapiths in forty ships against Troy (Hom. *Il.* 2.745). He was the grandson of Caenus and great-grandson of Elatus. Caenus and his brother Polyphemus had taken part in the expedition of the Argonauts. Polyphemus was married to Laonome, a sister of Hera-cles. Of Elatus nothing is known, except that he married Hippeia and started the aforementioned line of heroes. Hippothous and Pylaeus were Trojan allies. They led a band of Pelasgian auxiliaries from Larissa to the assis-tance of the Trojans. While engaged in dragging away the body of Patroclus, Hippothous was slain by Telamonian Ajax (Hom. *Il.* 2.840, 17.288). The father of both Hippothous and Pylaeus was Lethus, a son of Teutamas. Teutamas will be remembered as the Larissan king who entertained Acrisius, the grandfather of Perseus. Acrisius, remembering the oracle that said he would die at the hands of his grandson, fled to Larissa when Perseus returned to Argos. Perseus followed him to assure him there was no cause for concern and to persuade him to return to Argos. Teutamas celebrated games in honor of his guests, and Perseus, who took part in them, acciden-tally struck Acrisius and killed him. Acrisius was buried outside the city of Larissa. Both Elatus and Teutamas present a certain puzzle in the line of kings and nobles of Larissa. For neither is there parentage recorded. In view, however, of their status and chronological placement, it is not unlikely that they were both sons of Periphas and consequently younger brothers of Antion. Periphas had eight sons, and only Antion is named by any mythogra-pher or historian.

There are very few remains of the ancient city of Larissa. The acropolis was in the northwest part of the city, but no walls remain. The agora was south of the citadel. A foundation there can possibly be identified with the temple of Apollo, which is known to have been located in the city. Sculptures relevant to Poseidon, Dionysus, and Athena have also been found at Larissa.

LARISSA was an earlier name of GORTYNA.

LARISSUS or LARISUS (RIOLITIKO or MANA) was a river in Achaia forming the boundary between Achaia and Elis. It rose in Mount Scollis and emptied into the sea 5.5 km from Dyme (Paus. 7.17.3; Strab. 8.7.5). Athena Larissaea derived her surname from this river, where the goddess had a sanctuary (Paus. 7.17.3).

LARYMNA (LARIMNA) was the name of two towns in Boeotia on the river Cephissus, distinguished as Upper and Lower Larymna (Strab. 9.2.13). Larymna, the daughter of Cynus, gave her name to these towns (Paus. 9.23.4). Strabo relates that the Cephissus emerged from its subterranean channel at the Upper Larymna and joined the sea at the Lower Larymna; and that Upper Larymna had belonged to Phocis until it was annexed to the Lower or Boeotian Larymna by the Romans. Upper Larymna belonged originally to the Opuntian Locrians, and Lycophron (1146) mentions it as one of the towns of Ajax Oileus. The ruins are situated on the shore of the Bay of Larmes, a short distance from the old mouth of the Cephissus. The circuit of the walls is less than 1.5 km. Dionysus Larymna had a temple there with a statue (Paus. 9.23.4).

LAS (PASSAVA)   one of the most ancient towns of Laconia, was situated upon the west coast of the Laconian Gulf. According to Pausanias (3.24.6), the town was ten stadia (about 2 km) from the sea and forty stadia (about 7.5 km) from Gythium. The most ancient town was on the summit of Mount Asia, but the later town was situated in a hollow lower down. It is mentioned by Homer (*Il.* 2.585) and is said to have been destroyed by the Dioscuri, who hence derived the surname Lapersae (Strab. 8.5.3). Outside the walls Pausanias (3.24.6,7) saw a statue of Heracles, and among the ruins he noticed a statue of Athena Asia. The modern town was near a fountain called Galaco from the milky color of its water, and near it was a gymnasium, in which stood an ancient statue of Hermes. In addition to the ruins of the old town on Mount Asia there were also buildings on the two other mountains mentioned above: on Mount Ilium was a temple of Dionysus, and on the summit a temple of Asclepius; on Mount Cnacadium was a temple of Apollo Carneius.

Las is spoken of by Polybius (5.19) and Strabo (8.5.2) under the name of Asine; and thus it has been supposed that some of the fugitives from Asine in Argolis may have settled at Las and given their names to the town. Las stood upon the hill of Passava. The fountain Galaco rises between the hill of Passava and the village of Karvelas, which is 2.5 km west of Passava.

LEBADEIA (LIVADIA)   was a town near the western boundary of Boeotia, described by Strabo (9.2.38) as lying between Mount Helicon and Chaeroneia. It was situated at the foot of a high cliff. Pausanias (9.39.1) relates that this height was originally occupied by the Homeric city of Mideia (*Il.* 2.507), from where the inhabitants under the conduct of Lebadus, an Athenian, migrated into the plain and founded there the city named after him. Arcesilaus, a son of Lycus and Theobule, was the leader of the Boeotians in the Trojan War. He led his people to Troy in ten ships and was slain by Hector (Hom. *Il.* 2.495, 15.329). According to Pausanias (9.39.2), his

remains were brought back to Boeotia, where a monument was erected to his memory in the neighborhood of Lebadeia.

Lebadeia was originally an insignificant place, but it rose into importance in consequence of its possessing the celebrated oracle of Trophonius. Trophonius and Agamedes were sons of Erginus, king of Orchomenus, and had distinguished themselves as architects, especially in building temples and palaces. Among others, they built a temple of Apollo at Delphi and a treasury of Hyrieus, king of Hyria in Boeotia (Paus. 9.37.3; Strab. 9.3.9). In the construction of the treasury of Hyrieus, Agamedes and Trophonius contrived to place one stone in such a manner that it could be removed and allow them anonymous entrance to the treasury. Agamedes and Trophonius now constantly robbed the treasury; and the king, seeing that locks and seals were unbroken while his treasures were constantly decreasing, set traps to catch the thief. Agamedes was caught in one of these traps, and Trophonius cut off his head to prevent identification. After this, Trophonius was immediately swallowed up by the earth. On this spot there was afterward in the grove of Lebadeia the so-called cave of Agamedes with a column by the side of it. Here also was the oracle of Trophonius, and those who consulted it first offered a ram to Agamedes and invoked him (Paus. 9.39.4). The oracle was consulted both by Croesus and by Mardonius (Herod. 8.134), and it continued to be consulted even in the time of Plutarch, when all the other oracles in Boeotia had become silent (Plut. *De Def. Or.* 5). Pausanias himself consulted the oracle, and he speaks of the town in terms that describe it as the most flourishing place in Boeotia in his time. The city continues to be inhabited under the slightly altered name of Livadia and is a thriving agricultural center.

The modern town is situated on two opposite hills, rising on either bank of a small stream called Hercyna by Pausanias. Pausanias (9.39.2–7) says that the Hercyna rose in a cavern from two fountains close to one another, one called the fountain of Lethe and the other the fountain of Mnemosyne. Persons who were going to consult the oracle were obliged to drink from the latter fountain. Hercyna was a divinity of the lower world. She was a daughter of Trophonius, and once while she was playing with Kore, the daughter of Demeter, in the grove of Trophonius, she let a goose fly away, which she had carried in her hand. The bird flew into a cave and concealed itself under a block of stone. When Kore pulled the bird from its hiding place, a well gushed forth from under the stone. The well was called Hercyna. On the bank of the rivulet a temple was afterward erected with the statue of a maiden carrying a goose in her hand; and in the cave there were two statues of Trophonius and Hercyna with staffs entwined by serpents. The statues resembled the statues of Asclepius and Hygieia (Paus.

9.39.2). Hercyna herself founded the worship of Demeter at Lebadeia. Hercyna was worshipped at Lebadeia in common with Zeus, and sacrifices were offered in common to both (Liv. 45.27).

The sacred grove probably was located on the west side of the stream, on which the greater part of the modern town stands. The most remarkable objects in the grove of Trophonius were: the temple of the hero containing his statue by Praxiteles, resembling a statue of Asclepius; a wooden statue of Trophonius at Lebadeia that was attributed to Daedalus; a temple of Demeter surnamed Europa; a statue of Zeus Hyetius (Sender of Rain); and higher up, upon the mountain, the oracle. Still higher up was the hunting place of Persephone; a large unfinished temple of Zeus Basileus, a temple of Apollo, and another temple containing statues of Cronus, Zeus, and Hera. Pausanias likewise mentions a chapel of the Agathos Daimon (Good Daemon) and of Tyche (Good Fortune). Here those who were going to consult the oracle first passed a certain number of days. Pausanias (9.39.4) also mentions a sacred well and a throne of Mnemosyne near the oracle. Mnemosyne was the goddess of memory and the mother of the Muses.

Near the Turkish mosque, now converted into a chapel of the Panagia, on the west side of the river was discovered the temple of Zeus Basileus. A festival, the Basileia, was celebrated in this area in the month of Panamos (August-September) and included athletic contests and horse races. Southwest of the temple was recently discovered the site of the oracle. It consists of a well about 4 m deep, at the bottom of which is a cavity the width of a person's body. A person who consulted the oracle descended the well, which was constructed of masonry, at the bottom of which was a small opening on the side of the wall. Upon reaching the bottom, he lay upon his back and put his legs into the hole and followed with the rest of his body. The oracle was revealed in different ways to different people, to some by sight, to others by sound. When a person emerged, he was taken by the priests to the throne of Mnemosyne and asked what he discovered. Everyone was obliged to write on wooden tablets the nature of the revelation.

LEBEN (LENTAS)   a coastal town of Crete, was a harbor of Gortyna, which was 20 km inland. It possessed a celebrated temple of Asclepius (Philostr. *Vit Apoll.* 9.11) and also a temple of the nymphs. The modern hamlet of Lentas is adjacent to the ruins, which include substantial remains of the temple of Asclepius.

LECHAEUM (LEHEO)   was the port on the Corinthian Gulf, connected with Corinth by means of the Long Walls, which were 2.25 km in length (Strab. 8.6.22; Xenoph. *Hellen.* 4.4.17). The Long Walls ran nearly due north, and the space between them was sufficient for an army to draw up for battle. The port must have been artificial, originally created by dredging. Its site is now indicated by a lagoon surrounded by sand dunes. Lechaeum was the chief station of the Corinthian ships of war. It was also the commercial port that handled traffic from Greece, Italy, and Sicily. The proximity of Lechaeum to Corinth prevented it from becoming an important town like Peiraeus. The only public building in the place mentioned by Pausanias (2.2.3) was a temple of Poseidon, who was called Lechaeus by Callimachus (*Hymn. in Del.* 271). The temple of the Olympian Zeus was probably situated upon the low ground between Corinth and the shore of Lechaeum (Paus. 3.9.2). Lechaeum was named for Leches, a son of Poseidon and Peirene, just as Cenchreae, the other port of Corinth, was named for his brother Cenchrias.

LECYTHUS (TORONI)   was a town with a temple to Athena in the peninsula of Sithonia in Chalcidice, not far from Torone. During the Peloponnesian War (431–404 B.C.) the town was attacked by Brasidas, who took it by storm and consecrated the entire cape to the goddess. Everything was demolished except Athena's temple and the buildings connected with it (Thuc. 4.115,116). At the site, adjacent to Toroni, the walls of the citadel may still be seen.

LEIMONE   according to Strabo (9.5.19) was the later name of the Homeric ELONE.

LEMNOS (LIMNOS)   one of the larger islands in the Aegean Sea, is situated nearly midway between Mount Athos and the Hellespont. It is nearly bisected by two deep bays. On the east side of the island is a rock projecting into the sea mentioned by Aeschylus (*Agam.* 283) in his description of the beacon fires between Mount Ida and Mycenae announcing the capture of Troy. Low hills cover two-thirds of the island, their rocky barrenness showing evidence of the effects of volcanic fire. It is easy to account for its connection with Hephaestus, who when hurled from heaven by Zeus is said to have fallen upon Lemnos (Hom. *Il.* 1.594). The island was therefore sacred to Hephaestus (Ov. *Fast.* 3.82), who was frequently called the Lemnian god (Ov. *Met.* 4.185; Virg. *Aen.* 8.454). From its volcanic appearance it derived the name Aethalëia. It was also related that fire was seen to blaze forth from one of its mountains, called Moschylus (Lycoph. 227). The name Lemnos is said to have been derived from the name of the Great Goddess, who was called Lemnos by the original inhabitants of the island.

The earliest inhabitants of Lemnos, according to Homer (*Il.* 1.594, *Od.* 8.284), were the Sinties, a Thracian tribe. When the Argonauts landed at Lemnos they found it inhabited only by women, who had murdered all their husbands and had chosen as their queen Hypsipyle, the daughter of Thoas, the former king of the island. Thoas was a son of Dionysus and Ariadne. He was king of Lemnos and married to Myrina, by whom he became the father of Hypsipyle and Sicinus. When the Lemnian women killed all the men on the island, Hypsipyle saved Thoas and concealed him. Afterward he was discovered by the other women and killed (Apollod. 3.6.4), or he escaped to Tauris or to the island of Oenoe near Euboea, which was afterward called Sicinus. In the version of the story in which he is killed, Hypsipyle celebrates funeral games for him during the visit of the Argonauts. One of the contestants was Erginus, who succeeded Tiphys as helmsman of the Argo. He was ridiculed by the Lemnian women because, although still young, he had gray hair; but in the foot race he still managed to conquer Zetes and Calais, the sons of Boreas, the north wind (Pind. *Ol.* 4.29).

Some of the Argonauts settled here and became by the Lemnian women the fathers of the Minyae, the later inhabitants of the island. The Minyae were driven out of the island by the Tyrrhenian Pelasgians, who had been expelled from Attica. Meanwhile, though, the Argonauts who continued on the journey left progeny on the island. Hypsipyle bore to Jason two sons, Euneus and Nebrophonus. Euneus later supplied wine to the Greeks during their war against Troy. He purchased Lycaon, a Trojan prisoner, from Patroclus for a silver urn (Hom. *Il.* 7.468, 23.741). The Euneidae, a famous family of cithara players in Lemnos, traced their origin to Euneus. From Lemnos the Minyae spread out to Thera and Elis Triphylia (Herod. 1.146, 4.145; Pind. *Ol.* 14.4, *Pyth.* 4.69; Apollon. Rhod. 1.229).

It is also related that these Pelasgians out of revenge for their Attican exile raided the coast of Attica during the festival of Artemis at Brauron and carried off some Athenian women, whom they made their concubines. During this raid the Tyrrhenians are said to have taken away the statue of Artemis Brauronia to Lemnos, which might explain a Lemnian Artemis. Aristophanes in his lost play *Lemnian Women* had mentioned Bendis along with the Brauronian Artemis and the Great Goddess, so it seems evident that the Lemnians worshipped a goddess akin to Hecate, Artemis, Bendis, or Persephone. The children of the kidnapped Athenian women hated their half-brothers born of Pelasgian women and consequently were murdered along with their mothers by the Pelasgians. Because of this atrocity and because of the earlier murder of the Lemnian husbands by their wives, "Lemnian deeds" became proverbial throughout Greece for all atrocious acts (Herod. 6.128).

Lemnos, although sending no men to the Trojan War, did have an important role. Philoctetes, a son of Poeas and Demonassa, was the most celebrated archer in the Trojan War (Hom. *Od.* 3.190, 8.219). He led the warriors from Methone, Thaumacia, Meliboea, and Olizon against Troy in seven ships. But on the way he was left behind by his men on the island of Lemnos because he was ill from a wound received from a snakebite. The ulcerated wound produced such agony and such stench that Odysseus and the Atreidae decided to leave him on the solitary coast of Lemnos (Ov. *Met.* 13.315). According to some he was left behind there because the priests of Hephaestus on Lemnos knew how to heal the wound, and Pylius, a son of Hephaestus, is said to have actually cured him. The usual story is that Philoctetes remained in Lemnos during the whole period of the Trojan War until in the tenth year Odysseus and Diomedes came to tell him that an oracle had declared that Troy could not be taken without the arrows of Heracles (which he had given to Philoctetes). Another tradition says that he was cured and that while the war against Troy was going on he and Euneus conquered the small islands off the Trojan coast and drove out their Carian inhabitants. As a reward for these exploits he received part of Lemnos, which he called Acesa.

In the earliest times Lemnos appears to have contained only one town, which had the same name as the island (Hom. *Il.* 14.230); but at a later period we find two towns, Myrina and Hephaestias. According to Pliny (36.13.19), Lemnos had a celebrated labyrinth supported by 150 columns and with gates so well balanced that a child could open them. Such an structure has not been found.

The religion of the Lemnians has already been mentioned. Hephaestus was a principal god there. The story goes that he once took his mother's part in an argument and thus offended Zeus so much that he was seized by the leg and hurled down from Olympus. Hephaestus was a whole day in falling, but in the evening he came to earth on the island of Lemnos, where he was kindly received by the Sintians (Hom. *Il.* 1.590; Val. Flacc. 2.85; Apollod. 1.3.5). Later writers describe his lameness as a result of this fall. His favorite place on earth was Lemnos. He was believed to have great healing powers, and Lemnian earth from the spot where he fell was believed to cure madness, the bites of snakes, and hemorrhage.

The Cabeiri were mystic divinities who occurred in various parts of the ancient world. The earliest mention of them was in a last drama of Aeschylus entitled *Cabeiri*, in which the poet brought them into contact with the Argonauts on Lemnos, when they provided the Argonauts with Lemnian wine (Plut. *Quaest. Conviv.* 2.1). It appears that Aeschylus regarded the Cabeiri as original Lemnian divinities, who had power over everything that contributed to the good of the inhabitants and especially over the vineyards. Sacrifices were offered to the Cabeiri on Lemnos.

Artemis Orthia, who was also called Iphigeneia or
Lygodesma, was regarded in these manifestations as the
goddess of the moon. Her worship was probably brought
to Sparta from Lemnos. Polyxo, the nurse of Queen
Hypsipyle, was celebrated as a prophetess in Lemnos
(Apollon. Rhod. 1.668; Val. Flacc. 2.316). The Thracians
conceived the chief divinity of the Samothracian and
Lemnian mysteries as Rhea-Hecate.

Finally, the story of the great hero Orion takes place
partially on Lemnos. Orion was a son of Hyrieus of Hyria
in Boeotia, and he was a very handsome giant and hunter.
Once he came to Chios and fell in love with Merope, the
daughter of King Oenopion. Oenopion constantly
deferred the marriage until one day Orion, being intoxicated, raped the maiden. Oenopion blinded him for the
act. Being informed by an oracle that he should recover
his sight if he would go towards the east and expose his
eyes to the rays of the rising sun, Orion followed the
sound of a Cyclops' hammer to Lemnos, where
Hephaestus gave to him Cedalion as his guide.

LEPETYMNUS, LEPETHYMNUS, or LEPETHYMUS (LEPE-
DIMNOS)   is a mountain in the northern part of
Lesbos near Methymna. The sepulcher and tomb of the
hero Palamedes are said to have been here (Philostr. *Vit.
Apoll.* 4.13.150). There also is a story concerning a temple
of Apollo and a shrine of the hero Lepetymnus connected
with the same mountain.

LEPREUM (LEPREO)   the chief town of Triphylia in
Elis, was situated in the southern part of the district
18.5 km from Samicum and 7.5 km from the sea. Triphylia is said to have been originally inhabited by the
Cauconians. Caucon was a son of Celaenus, who was
believed to have carried the worship of Demeter from
Eleusis to Messene, where he was revered as a hero. His
tomb was shown in Lepreum (Paus. 5.5.5). The Caucones
were later expelled by the Minyae, who took possession
of Lepreum (Herod. 4.148). One tradition derived the
name of the town from Lepreus, a son of Caucon,
Glaucon, or Pyrgeus (Aelian. *V.H.* 1.24; Paus. 5.5.4) by
Astydameia. He was a grandson of Poseidon and a rival of
Heracles both in his strength and his powers of eating;
but he was conquered and slain by Heracles. Another
tradition says that Lepreum received its name from
Leprea, a daughter of Pyrgeus. Still another derivation of
the name claims that dwellers in the land were afflicted
with a disease called leprosy. This leprosy was probably a
skin disease akin to psoriasis.

Eventually, Lepreum and the other cities of Triphylia were conquered by the Eleians, who governed
them as subject places. The ruins of Lepreum are situated
upon a hill near the modern village of Lepreo. These
ruins show that Lepreum was a town of some size. Zeus
Leucaeus was worshipped here (Paus. 5.5.5). The grave

of Lycurgus, son of Aleus, was said to be here. Also there
was a sanctuary of Demeter. Not far from the city was a
spring called Arene, deriving its name from the wife of
Aphareus.

LEPSIA (LIPSI)   is a tiny island north of Leros and
east of Patmos. It is not mentioned by any ancient writer
except Pliny (5.36.134), and he indeed only mentions it
in a list with other islands of the Aegean. It is only 15 sq.
km. There are fewer than one thousand inhabitants,
mostly living in the village of Lipsi. Remains of a
sanctuary, probably of Apollo (Lepsius?) have been
found. A little inland an altar to Zeus Genethlius has been
found.

LERNA (LERNI)   is the name of a marshy district at
the southeast extremity of the Argive plain near the sea
and celebrated as the spot where Heracles as his second
labor slew the many-headed Hydra. This monster was the
offspring of Typhon and Echidna and was raised by Hera.
It ravaged the country of Lerna and dwelt in a swamp
near the well of Amymone. It had nine heads, the middle
of which was immortal. Heracles hunted the monster with
burning arrows, and then with his club or a sickle he cut
off its heads; but in the place of each head he cut off, two
new ones grew. A gigantic crab also came to the assistance
of the Hydra and wounded Heracles. However, with the
assistance of his faithful companion Iolaus he burned
away the heads of the Hydra and buried the ninth or
immortal one under a huge rock. Having thus conquered
the monster, he poisoned his arrows with its bile so the
wounds inflicted by them became incurable.

In this part of the plain there are many springs that
flood the area and turn it into a marsh. The name of
Lerna is usually given to the whole district, but some
writers apply it more particularly to the river and the
lake. The district was thoroughly drained in antiquity and
covered with sacred buildings. A road led from Argos to
Lerna, and the distance from the gate of the city to the
seacoast of Lerna was 7.5 km. Above Lerna is Mount
Pontinus, on whose summit Pausanias saw the remains of
a temple of Athena Saitis. The grove of Lerna reached
from Mount Pontinus to the sea and was bounded on one
side by the river Pontinus and on the other by the river
Amymone. Amymone was one of the daughters of Danaus
and Elephantis. When Danaus arrived in Argos, the
country was suffering from a drought, and Danaus sent
out Amymone to fetch water. Meeting a stag, she shot at it
but hit a sleeping satyr, who rose and pursued her.
Poseidon appeared and rescued her from the satyr but
then enjoyed her himself. After that he showed her the
springs at Lerna (Apollod. 2.1.4).

The grove of Lerna contained two temples. Demeter
Prosymna and Dionysus were worshipped in one,
Dionysus Saotes in the other. In this grove a festival called

the Lernaea was celebrated in honor of Demeter and Dionysus. Pausanias (2.37.5,6) also mentions the fountain of Amphiaraus and the Alcyonian pool, through which the Argives say that Dionysus descended into Hades in order to recover Semele. The Alcyonian pool was said to be unfathomable. The circumference of the pool is estimated by Pausanias as only one-third of a stadium (61.5 meters); its shore was covered with grass and rushes. Pausanias was told that even though the lake appeared placid, anyone attempting to swim across it was dragged down to the bottom. Here Prosymnus is said to have pointed out to Dionysus the entrance to the lower world. A nocturnal ceremony was connected with this legend and expiatory rites were performed by the side of the pool. In keeping with the infernal aspect of Lerna, some accounts place the rape of Persephone here (Paus. 2.36.7).

LEROS (LEROS)   is one of the Notii Sporades in the Aegean. It is situated northwest of Calymna (Kalimnos), and the two islands are believed to have been the Calydnian Islands mentioned by Homer (*Il.* 2.677). It was colonized by Milesians (Strab. 14.1.6). Before its occupation by the Milesians it was probably inhabited by Dorians. The ancient town of Leros was situated in the west of the modern town. Leros contained a sanctuary of Artemis Parthenos, in which the sisters of Meleager were transformed into guinea fowls (Meleagrides). Thereafter, these birds were always kept in the sanctuary of the goddess (Athen. 14.655). The temple has not been located but very likely was in the vicinity of the modern Parthenio.

LESBOS (LESVOS)   is situated off the coast of that part of Turkey once known as Mysia, exactly opposite the opening of the Gulf of Adramyttium (Edremit). The island is 312 km from Athens. Its northern part is separated from the mainland by a channel about 11.5 km wide. In shape Lesbos may be roughly described as a triangle. The northern point was called the promontory of Argennum, the eastern Sigrium, and the southeastern Malea. The surface of the island is mountainous. The principal mountains were called Ordymnus in the west, Olympus in the south, and Lepethymnus in the north.

Tradition says that the first inhabitants of Lesbos were Pelasgians, and Xanthus was their legendary ruler. He was a son of Triopas and Oreasis and king of the Pelasgians at Argos. Afterward he settled in Lesbos (Diod. 5.81; Callim. *Hymn. in Del.* 41). Next came Ionians and others under Macareus, who is said by Diodorus Siculus (5.80) to have introduced written laws two generations before the Trojan War. Macareus, or Macar, was a son of Helios and Rhodos, or, according to others, a son of Crinacus, who after the murder of Tenages fled from Rhodes to Lesbos (Hom. *Il.* 24.544; Diod. 5.56; Plat. *Leg.*

8.838). Macareus was responsible for colonizing the neighboring islands of Chios, Samos, and Cos. He even sent a colony back to Rhodes (Diod. 5.81).

The last settlers were Aeolians under the leadership of Lesbus, who appears in Strabo (13.1.3) under the name Gras and who is said to have married Methymna, the daughter of Macareus. The city of Methymna was named for her (Diod. 5.81). Mitylene was the elder daughter of Macareus. By Poseidon she became the mother of Myton. The city of Mitylene was named for her. Still another daughter was Issa, who was beloved by Apollo. She gave her name to the island, which was called at first Issa, and also to a city on the island (Ov. *Met.* 6.124; Strab. 1.3.19). Six Aeolian cities, each of which originally had separate possessions and an independent government, made up territories into which Lesbos was divided. These six were Methymna, Arisba, Antissa, Eressus, Pyrrha, and Mytilene.

Lesbos is mentioned both in the *Iliad* (24.544) and *Odyssey* (4.342), and it is evident that its cities were flourishing at a very early period. Odysseus on his voyage to Troy wrestled in Lesbos with Philomeleides, the king of the island, and conquered him (Hom. *Od.* 4.342). According to others, Odysseus and Diomedes slew him by a stratagem.

Another Greek hero, Achilles, also had associations with the island. Diomede, a daughter of Phorbas of Lesbos, was beloved by Achilles (Hom. *Il.* 9.665). Trambelus was a son of Telamon and Theaneira and king of the Leleges, who according to some was killed in Lesbos by Achilles. The hero regretted his action when he learned that Trambelus was a son of Telamon.

Lesbos was celebrated for poetry and especially poetry in combination with music. The head and lyre of Orpheus were supposed to have been carried by the waves of the sea to Lesbos. Orpheus, it will be remembered, was torn to pieces by the Thracian women. His head was thrown into the Herbrus River, down which it floated to the sea and was carried to Lesbos, where it was buried at Antissa. His lyre was also said to have been carried to Lesbos. The astronomers taught that the lyre was then placed by Zeus among the stars at the request of Apollo and the Muses. Apollo Malloeis had a sanctuary in Lesbos; the sanctuary was believed to have derived its name from Melus, a son of Manto.

Two stories connected with Lesbos are frequently told. Nyctimene was a daughter of Epopeus, king of Lesbos. Pursued and raped by her father, she concealed herself in the shade of forests where she was metamorphosed into an owl (Ov. *Met.* 2.590). The other story is about Enalus. The Penthelides, the first settlers in Lesbos, had received an oracle from Amphitrite commanding them to sacrifice a bull to Poseidon and a virgin to Amphitrite and the Nereids as soon as they should, on their journey to Lesbos, come to the rock Mesogeion. Accordingly, the leaders of the colonists caused their daughters to draw lots, the result of which was that the daughter of Smintheus or Phineus was to be sacrificed. When she was on the point of being thrown into the sea, her lover Enalus embraced her and leaped with her into the water. But both were saved by dolphins. In another story, he swam into a stormy sea and came back followed by octopi, one of which was carrying a stone, which Enalus took and dedicated in a temple (Plut. *Sept. Sapient. Conviv.* 163).

LESSA (LIGOURIO?) was a village of Epidauria on the boundaries of the territory of Argos and at the foot of Mount Arachnaeum. Pausanias (2.25.10) saw there a temple of Athena. The ruins of Lessa have not been identified, but the most probable site is a hill near Ligourio. On the outside of the walls near the foot of the mountain are the remains of an ancient pyramid near a church that contains some Ionic columns. Another possibility is a hilltop 5 km north of Nauplia near Agios Adriano, where there are Cyclopean walls and a chapel built on temple foundations.

LETE (LITI) was a town of Macedonia located at the only usable pass between the Thermaic Gulf and the region of Mygdonia. Near this pass and the modern site at Liti, 12 km northwest of Thessaloniki have been found ancient ruins, notably remains from a temple of Demeter and Kore. The town of Lete received its name from the temple of Leto, which was erected in the vicinity.

LETRINI (AGIOS IOANNIS) was a town in Elis situated near the sea upon the Sacred Way leading from Elis to Olympia, at the distance of 33 km from Elis and 22 from Olympia. It was said to have been founded by Letreus, a son of Pelops (Paus. 6.22.8). While the Greeks were engaged in the siege of Troy, they learned from an oracle that the city could not be taken unless one of the bones of Pelops were brought from Elis to Troy. Accordingly, the shoulder bone was fetched from Letrini (some say Pisa), lost before reaching Troy, but later recovered and forwarded to accomplish its purpose.

In the time of Pausanias nothing remained of Letrini except a few houses and a temple of Artemis Alphaea. Artemis was thought by some to have been the object of the affection of the river-god Alpheius. Once as he pursued her, she fled to Letrini and here covered her face and the faces of her companion nymphs with mud so that Alpheius could not discover or distinguish her (Paus. 6.22.9). This resulted in the building of a temple of Artemis Alphaea at Letrini. Letrini may be placed at the village and monastery of Agios Ioannis between Pirgos and the coastal village of Katakolo, where a part of a large statue was found in the mid–nineteenth century.

LEUCAE ISLANDS (See APTERA)

LEUCAS or LEUCADIA (LEFKADA) is an island in the Ionian Sea separated by a narrow channel from the coast of Acarnania. It was named for Leucadius, a son of Icarius and Polycaste and a brother of Penelope and Alyzeus. Leucas was originally a part of the mainland and as such is described by Homer (*Od.* 24.377), who calls it a peninsula of the mainland. After the fall of Troy, Aeneas wandered widely, often founding temples to his mother, Aphrodite. Among other places he stopped in Leucas. Homer (*Od.* 24.377) also mentions Nericus, its well-fortified town. Its earliest inhabitants were Leleges and Teleboans (Strab. 7.7.2), but it was afterward populated by Acarnanians. In the seventh century B.C. the Corinthians under Cypselus founded a new town near the isthmus, which they called Leucas, and here they settled their own citizens and the inhabitants of the old town of Nericus.

Leucas is about 33 km in length and from 10 to 12 km wide. The name of the island is derived from its white cliffs, the mythological derivation notwithstanding. The interior is rugged and there is little cultivation except where terraces have been planted in the mountainside and covered with vineyards. The highest ridge of the mountains rises about 1,082 meters above sea level. The ruins of the ancient town of Leucas are situated 2.5 km to the southeast of the modern city of Lefkada. The ancient enclosure is almost entirely traceable. These and walls lower down are remains of Nericus, which continued to be the ancient acropolis, while the Corinthians gave the name Leucas to the town they built on the shore below.

In addition to Leucas, other important towns were Phara and Hellomenum. The celebrated promontory Leucatas, forming the southwest end of the island is a broken, white cliff rising on the west side perpendicularly from the sea to a height of at least 600 meters. On its summit stood the temple of Apollo surnamed Leucatas and Leucadius (Ov. *Trist.* 3.1.42, 5.2.76). Cephalus was a son of Deion and husband of Procris. He is said to have put an end to his life by leaping into the sea from Cape Leucas, on which he had built a temple of Apollo in order to atone for having killed his wife Procris (Strab. 10.2.9; Paus. 1.37.4).

Among Greek mariners of the present day this cape retains the evil reputation it bore in ancient times because of its dark water, strong currents, and fierce gales. Of the temple of Apollo nothing but the foundations now exist. At the annual festival of the god that was celebrated here, it was the custom to throw a criminal from the cape into the sea. He was given a small measure of hope, for to help break his fall birds of all kinds were attached to him, and if he reached the sea uninjured, boats were ready to pick him up (Strab. 10.2.9; Ov. *Her.* 15.165, *Trist.* 5.2.76). This rite and the story of Cephalus must have given rise to the well-known story of Sappho's leap from this rock in order to seek relief from the pangs of love.

LEUCOSIA was an earlier name of the island of SAMOTHRACE.

LEUCTRA (LEFKTRA) was a village situated on the road from Thespiae to Plataea. Leucippus was a son of Perieres and Gorgophone and brother of Aphareus. He was the father of Arsinoe, Phoebe, and Hilaeira and prince of the Messenians. He is mentioned among the Calydonian hunters, and the town of Leuctra is said to have derived its name from him (Paus. 3.26.4). The site of Leuctra is marked by a mound on the summit of the ridge on the south side of the valley of Thespiae. In ancient times Leuctra was described as "shady," but today its surrounding territory is quite barren. It is placed near the modern village of Lefktra.

LEUCTRA (LEFKTRO) was a town of Laconia situated on the east side of the Messenian Gulf, 4 km north of Pephnus and 11 km south of Cardamyle. The ruins of Leuctra are still called Lefktro, but it is the name of a promontory instead of a town. Leuctra was said to have been founded by Pelops and was claimed by the Messenians as originally one of their towns. Pausanias (3.26.5) saw in Leuctra a temple and statue of Athena on the acropolis, a temple and a statue of Cassandra (there called Alexandra), a marble statue of Asclepius, another of Ino, and wooden figures of Apollo Carneius.

LIBETHRA or LIBETHHRIUM was a town in Macedonia near Dium. When Orpheus was dismembered by the Thracian women, the Muses collected the fragments of his body and buried them at Libethra at the foot of Olympus. The subsequent transfer of his bones to Dium is evidently a local legend. Pausanias (9.30.5) reports a tradition that the town was once destroyed. He says that an oracle had declared that when the sun fell on the bones of the poet, the city should be destroyed by a boar. The inhabitants of Libethra ridiculed this. Then the column of Orpheus' monument was accidentally broken so that a gap was made by which light broke in upon the tomb. That same night the flooded mountain stream named Sus (Swine) rushed down from Mount Olympus upon Libethra, destroying its buildings and the entire population. After this calamity the remains of Orpheus were moved to Dium, 4 km from Libethra towards Olympus, where the inhabitants erected a monument to him. In the time of Alexander the Great there was a statue of Orpheus made of cypress at Libethra (Plut. *Alex.* 14).

Strabo (9.2.25) mentions this place when speaking of Helicon and suggests that along with the worship of the Muses the names of mountains, caves, and springs were transferred from Mount Olympus to Helicon. Therefore the Muses were called Libethrides as well as Pierides.

LIBETHRIAS or LIBETHRIUS was a part of Mount Helicon sacred to the Muses. It is described by Pausanias (9.34.3) as 7.5 km from Coroneia and is therefore probably the mountain of Zagara, which is completely separated from the great heights of Helicon by an elevated valley. On Mount Libethrias there were statues of the Muses and of the Libethrian nymphs and two fountains called Libethrias and Petra, which resembled the breasts of a woman pouring forth water like milk (Paus. 9.34.3). There was a grotto of the Libethrian nymphs (Strab. 9.2.25). Nymphae Libethrides was a name sometimes applied also to the Muses that they derived from the Libethrias spring on Helicon; or, according to others, from the Macedonian town Libethrium.

LICHADES (MONOLIA?) are a group of three small islands between the promontory of Cenaeum (Lihada) in Euboea and that of Cnemides (Knimis) in Locris. They are said to have derived their name from Lichas, who was here thrown into the sea by Heracles when he was suffering from the poisoned garment sent to him by Deianeira (Strab. 1.3.30). It will be recalled that the dying Centaur Nessus had given Deianeira the garment dipped in his blood and told her that if she should give it to Heracles when she doubted him, the garment would restore his love. Instead it drove him insane and brought about his death.

LILAEA (LILAIA) was a town of Phocis situated at the foot of Mount Parnassus and at the sources of the Cephissus (Hom. *Il.* 2.522, *Hymn Hom. ad Apoll.* 240; Strab. 9.2.19). It was named for Lilaea, a Naiad and daughter of Cephissus. It was 33.5 km from Delphi by the road over Parnassus. Pausanias (10.33.2) saw at Lilaea a theater, an agora, and baths, with temples of Apollo and Artemis. The ruins of Lilaea are situated about three-quarters of a kilometer from the sources of the Cephissus. The entire outline of the walls remains. Some of the towers on the walls are still intact. East of Lilaea was a sanctuary of Demeter, remains of which have been unearthed.

LIMNAE (ARTEMISSIA) was the location on the boundary of Messenia and Laconia that had a temple of Artemis Limnatis. The temple was used jointly by the Messenians and Lacedaemonians. An outrage offered by the Messenians to some Lacedaemonian virgins at the festival of this goddess is said to have been the cause of the First Messenian War (Strab. 6.1.6; Paus. 3.2.6). The possession of this temple was a frequent subject of dispute between the Lacedaemonians and Messenians. The ruins of the temple of Artemis Limnatis have been discovered in the village of Volimos about 5 km northwest of Artemissia.

LINDUS (LINDOS)   one of the most important and most ancient towns on the island of Rhodes, was situated on the east coast, a little to the north of a promontory of the same name. In the Homeric catalog Lindus, together with the two other Rhodian cities, Ialysus and Cameirus, was said to have taken part in the war against Troy (Hom. *Il.* 2.656). Their inhabitants were Dorians and formed the three Dorian tribes of the island. Previous to the year 408 B.C., when the city of Rhodes was built, Lindus, like the other cities, formed a little state unto itself. However, when Rhodes was founded, a great part of the population and the common government were transferred to the new city. Lindus, though it lost its political prestige, still remained an important place from a religious point of view because it contained two ancient and much revered sanctuaries—one of Athena, called the Lindian, and the other of Heracles. The sanctuary of Athena was believed to have been built by Danaus (Diod. 5.58) or, according to others, by his daughters on their flight from Egypt (Herod. 2.182; Strab. 14.2.11). Danaus on his way from Egypt first landed at Rhodes, where he set up an image of Athena Lindia. According to Herodotus (2.182), a temple of Athena was built at Lindus by the daughters of Danaus, and according to Strabo (14.2.6), Tlepolemus built the towns of Lindus, Ialysus, and Cameirus and gave them the names of three Danaids. Tlepolemus was a son of Heracles by Astyoche. He was king of Argos but, after slaying his uncle Licymnius, he was obliged to take flight and, in conformity with the command of an oracle, settled in Rhodes. From here he led the men from the three cities of Rhodes to the Trojan War with nine ships (Hom. *Il.* 2.653; Apollod. 2.8.2).

The sanctuary of Athena Lindia occupies most of the acropolis. The temple stands at the edge of the cliff at the south point of the acropolis and overlooks one of the most impressive views in Greece. The temple of Heracles was remarkable on account of the vituperative and abusive language with which the worship was conducted. This temple contained a painting of Heracles by Parrhasius; and Lindus appears to have possessed several other paintings by the same artist (Athen. 12.543, 15.687).

The site of Lindus, described by Strabo (14.2.11) as on the side of a hill looking toward Alexandria and the south, cannot be mistaken; and the modern, neat, little town of Lindos is exactly the spot occupied by the ancient Dorian city. The remains of the theater are at the foot of the hill, and on the acropolis are seen the ruins of two Greek temples, which most probably belonged to the Lindian Athena and Zeus Polieus.

It must be remarked, too, that Rhodes was the seat of the worship of the Telchines. These were a family, a class of people, or a tribe, said to have been descended from Thalassa or Poseidon. Some accounts have them coming from Crete to Cyprus and then to Rhodes. Rhodes was their principal seat of worship and was named after them Telchinis. But the Telchines abandoned Rhodes because they foresaw that the island would be inundated. One of them, Lycus, went to Lycia where he built a temple of the Lycian Apollo. This god had been worshipped by the Telchines at Lindus. Apollo Loemius (Deliverer from Plague) was a name of the god at Lindus. Apollo Smintheus was a name derived from the word for mouse. The mouse was regarded by the ancients as inspired by the vapors rising from the earth and as a symbol of prophetic power. A temple of Apollo Smintheus existed at Lindus.

LISSUS (LISSOS)   was a town on the south coast of Crete. Its present site is near Agios Kirkos. The place occupies a small hollow of hills facing the sea, like an amphitheater. The main divinity here was Dictynna, but excavation has uncovered an important sanctuary of Asclepius. The sanctuary probably grew up because of a spring of curative water. The site has produced more sculpture than any site in Crete except Gortyna. Most of these sculptures represent Asclepius or Hygieia.

Of all the towns on this part of the coast, Lissus alone seems to have struck coins. The types of the coins are either maritime or indicative of the worship of Dictynna, as might have been expected on this part of the island. Other coins refer to the Dioscuri and Artemis.

LOCRIS   was the country inhabited by the Locri. These were an ancient people in Greece and were said to have been descended from the Leleges. Many supposed the name of the Locrians to be derived from Locrus, an ancient king of the Leleges. The Locrians, however, at a very early period became integrated with the Hellenes. In the Homeric poems they always appear as Hellenes; and, according to some traditions, even Deucalion, the founder of the Hellenic race, is said to have lived in the Locrian town of Opus (Pind. *Ol.* 9.63; Strab. 9.4.2). In historical times the Locrians were divided into two distinct tribes, differing from each other in customs and habits. The eastern Locrians, called the Opuntii and Epicnemidii, inhabited the east coast of Greece opposite the island of Euboea; the western Locrians lived on the Corinthian Gulf and were separated from the eastern Locrians by Mount Parnassus and all of Doris and Phocis (Strab. 9.4.2). The eastern Locrians are the ones referred to by Homer (*Il.* 2.527–535). The western Locrians, most probably a colony of the eastern Locrians, were represented as a semibarbarous people (Thuc. 1.5).

The Locri Epicnemidii and Opuntii inhabited a narrow area on the east coast of Greece, from the pass of Thermopylae to the mouth of the Cephissus River. This territory was bisected by a narrow strip of Phocis, which extended to the Euboean Sea and contained the Phocian seaport town of Daphnus. The Locrians north of Daphnus were called Epicnemidii from Mount Cnemis; and those south of this town were named Opuntii from Opus, their principal city. On the west the Locrians were separated from Phocis and Boeotia by a range of mountains extending from Mount Oeta and running parallel to the coast. The fertility of the whole of the Locrian coast was praised by ancient writers.

One pass across the Locrian Mountains led into Phocis to Tithronum, another to Elateia, and a third to Hyampolis, Abae, and Orchomenus.

The eastern Locrians followed Ajax, the son of Oileus, to the Trojan War in forty ships. They came from the towns of Cynus, Opus, Calliarus, Besa, Scarphe, Augeiae, Tarphe, and Thronium (Hom. *Il.* 2.527–535). Oileus was a son of Hodoecus and Laonome, grandson of Cynus, and great-grandson of Opus. He was king of the Locrians and married to Eriopis, by whom he became the father of Ajax. He was also the father of Medon by Rhene. He is mentioned among the Argonauts. Neither Homer, Herodotus, Thucydides, nor Polybius makes any distinction between the Opuntii and Epicnemidii, and Opus was regarded as the chief town of all the eastern Locrians.

Eucleia was a divinity, the personification of glory, and was worshipped in Boeotia and Locris, where she had an altar and a statue in every marketplace. Persons on the point of marrying used to offer sacrifices to her. It will be remembered, too, that Abderus was a Locrian. He was a favorite of Heracles, torn to pieces by the mares of Diomedes. He was a son of Thromius, according to some. Heracles built the town of Abdera to honor him.

The Locri Ozolae inhabited a district upon the Corinthian Gulf, bounded on the north by Doris and Aetolia, on the east by Phocis, and on the west by Aetolia. This district is mountainous, and for the most part unproductive. The only river mentioned by name is the Hylaethus, now the Morno, which runs in a southwest direction and empties into the Corinthian Gulf near Naupactus. The frontier of the Locri Ozolae on the west was close to the promontory of Antirrhium. The eastern frontier on the coast was close to the Phocian town of Crissa. Locris was on the west side of the Crissaean Gulf, and Phocis was on the east. The origin of the name of Ozolae is uncertain. Some derived it from the verb *ozein* (to smell), either from the stench arising from a spring at the foot of Mount Taphiassus, beneath which Nessus the Centaur is said to have been buried, or from the abundance of asphodel that scented the air. Others derived it from the odorous, undressed skins worn by the ancient inhabitants. The Locrians themselves derived the name from the branches (*ozoi*) of a vine produced in their country. They were said to have been a colony from the Opuntian Locrians. The chief and only important town

of the Ozolae was Amphissa, situated on the borders of Phocis.

LONGAS   was said to be a district in Boeotia. Athena Longatis was worshipped there. The location of the place is unknown.

LUSI (KATO LOUSSI)   was a town in the north of Arcadia. Lusi was situated in the upper valley of the Aroanius on the site of Kato Loussi, which stands in the northeast corner of the valley at the foot of Mount Helmos, about 8 km from Kalavrita.

The territory of Lusi was laid waste by the Aetolians in the Social War (Polyb. 4.18), but in the time of Pausanias (8.18.8) there were no longer even any ruins of the town. Its name, however, was preserved because of its temple of Artemis Lusia or Hemerasia (Soother). The goddess was so called because it was here that the daughters of Proetus were cured of their madness. These maidens, Iphinoe, Lysippe, and Iphianassa, were seized with madness, and Melampus promised to cure them if the king would give him and his brother Bias part of his kingdom. Proetus eventually did so. Melampus and Bias with a band of youths pursued the women as far as Sicyon and eventually discovered them hidden in a cave. Iphinoe died in the pursuit, but the surviving sisters were cured by purifications in the temple of Artemis near Lusi, and Melampus and Bias married them (Paus. 8.18.3). Proetus founded this temple of Artemis Hemerasia, which was regarded throughout the whole Peloponnesus as an inviolable asylum. It was situated near Lusi, 7.5 km from Cynaetha (Callim. *Hymn. in Dian.* 233). Some ruins were discovered above Lusi toward the end of the plain and on the road to Cynaetha (Kalavrita), and, further, some ancient foundations were discovered at the middle of three springs in the more westerly of the two plains of Loussi (formerly Soudena). Austrian archaeologists excavated here in 1901 and found remains of the temple of Artemis. A large cave can be seen on the western side of the Aroanian mountains, in which the inhabitants of Soudena were accustomed to take refuge during war and which is probably the cave referred to in the legend of the daughters of Proetus.

LYCAEUS or LYCEUS (LIKEO)   is a mountain of Arcadia in the district of Parrhasia, from which there is a view of the greater part of Peloponnesus. Its height is about 1,420 meters. It was one of the chief seats of the worship of Zeus in Arcadia where Hagno, an Arcadian nymph, brought up Zeus. On Mount Lycaeus there was a spring sacred to and named after her. When the country was suffering from drought, the priest of Zeus Lycaeus offered up prayers and sacrifices and then touched the surface of the spring with the branch of an oak tree. This was supposed to produce clouds followed by rain. On the summit of Lycaeus called Olympus were the sacred grove and altar of Zeus Lycaeus. Human sacrifices are said to have been practiced here down to classical times. There was also a hippodrome and a stadium where games called Lycaea were celebrated in honor of Zeus. No one was allowed to enter the temple of Zeus Lycaeus, and if anyone forced his way in, he was believed to die within one year and to lose his shadow (Paus. 8.38.6; Pind. *Ol.* 13.154). According to others, those who entered it were stoned to death by the Arcadians or were called stags and obliged to take flight to save their lives (Plut. *Quaest. Gr.* 39). Near the hippodrome was a temple of Pan, surnamed Lycaeus. There are still remains of the hippodrome extending from south to north; and near its north end there are considerable remains of a cistern about 15 meters in length from east to west. A little further west is a ruin called Hellenikon, apparently part of a temple; and near the church of Agios Elias is the summit where the altar of Zeus formerly stood. In the eastern part of the mountain stood the sanctuary and grove of Apollo Parrhasius or Pythius and left of it the place called Cretea (Paus. 8.38.2; Pind. *Ol.* 9.145, 13.154). The river Neda rose in Mount Cerausium, which was a part of Mount Lycaeus.

LYCASTUS   was a town of Crete mentioned in the Homeric catalog (Hom. *Il.* 2.647). Strabo (10.4.14) says that it had entirely disappeared, having been conquered and destroyed by the Cnossians. The site is not known. Lycastus was a son of Minos and Itone and king of Crete. He was married to Ida, the daughter of Corybas (Diod. 4.60). The town of Lycastus received its name from him or from an autochthon of the same name.

LYCOA   was a town of Arcadia in the district Maenalia, at the foot of Mount Naenalus, with a temple of Artemis Lycoatis. It was in ruins in the time of Pausanias (8.36.7), and its location is uncertain.

LYCOREIA (LIKERI)   was the name given to the highest summit of Parnassus. Lycorus was a son of Apollo and the nymph Corycia, and this summit was believed to have been named for him (Paus. 10.6.2). One writer mentioned a Lycoreion, which appears to have been a sanctuary of the Lycorian Zeus. The altar of Zeus was on this highest summit of Parnassus where Deucalion is said to have landed after the deluge (Lucian, *Tim.* 3; Apollod. 1.7.2). The inhabitants of Delphi were said to have been saved from the flood by following the howling of wolves, which led them to the summit, where they founded Lycoreia (Paus. 10.6.2). Apollo Lycoreus is a name of Apollo, perhaps in the same sense as Lyceius; but he is usually so called with reference to Lycoreia of Parnassus (Apollon. Rhod. 4.1490; Callim. *Hymn. in Apoll.* 19).

LYCORMAS   was the original name of the EUENUS River.

LYCOSURA (LIKOSSOURA)   was a town of Arcadia in the district Parrhasia at the foot of Mount Lycaeus and near the river Plataniston on the road from Megalopolis to Phigalia. It is called by Pausanias (8.38.1) the most ancient town in Greece and is said to have been founded by Lycaon, the son of Pelasgus. Lycaon was king of Arcadia. According to some he was a barbarian who even defied the gods (Ov. *Met.* 1.198); others describe him as the first civilizer of Arcadia, who built the town of Lycosura and introduced the worship of Zeus Lycaeus. He built a temple to the god and instituted the festival of Lycaea in his honor of him; he further offered to him bloody sacrifices and, among others, his own son, in consequence of which he was metamorphosed into a wolf. By several wives he became the father of a large number of sons, some say fifty (Apollod. 3.8.1). The sons of Lycaon are said to have been notorious for their insolence and impiety, and Zeus visited them in the disguise of a poor man to test them. They invited him to a repast, and on the suggestion of one of them, Maenalus, they mixed into one of the dishes set before him the entrails of a boy whom they had murdered. However, Zeus pushed away the table that bore the horrible food, and the place where this happened was afterward called Trapezus. Lycaon and all his sons, with the exception of Nyctimus, were killed by Zeus with a flash of lightning, or, according to others, were changed into wolves. Some say that the flood of Deucalion occurred in the reign of Nyctimus as a punishment for the crimes of the Lycaonids.

Lycosura was in ruins in the time of Pausanias (8.38.1), since its inhabitants had been removed to Megalopolis upon the founding of the latter city. The ruins are 11.5 km west of Megalopoli. They include ruins of a temple of Despoena. The cult statues in marble were found in fragments, reconstructed, and sent to the National Museum in Athens. Despoena was a chthonic deity identified with Demeter and Persephone. Pausanias also saw a sanctuary of Pan.

LYCTOS, LYCTUS, or LYTTUS (XIDAS)   was one of the most important cities of Crete. It was founded by Lyctus, a son of Lycaon. According to the Hesiod's *Theogony* (477), Rhea fled here to give birth to Zeus in a cave of Mount Aegaeon near Lyctus. She had, the story goes, previously given Cronus a stone wrapped in a cloth which he swallowed, thinking it the child. The inhabitants of this ancient Doric city called themselves colonists of Sparta (Aristot. *Polit.* 2.7), and the worship of Apollo appears to have prevailed there (Callim. *Hymn. in Apoll.* 33). Lyctos appears in the Homeric catalog (Hom. *Il.* 2.647). Idomeneus, the son of Deucalion and grandson of Minos, was a man of great beauty and a hero in the Trojan

War. He is sometimes called Lyctius or Cnosius from the towns of Lyctus and Cnossus. The walls of the ancient city with circular bastions and other fortifications exist upon a mountain nearly in the center of the island. The town of Arsinoe and the harbor of Chersonesus are assigned to Lyctus. The present site is adjacent to modern Xidas, about 25 km southeast of Iraklio.

LYRCEIA or **LYRCEIUM (SHINOHORI)**   was a town in Argolis about 12 km from Argos and the same distance from Orneae. It lay on the road Climax, which ran from Argos northwesterly along the bed of the Inachus. The town is said to have been originally called Lynceia and to have obtained this name from Lynceus, who fled here when all of his brothers, the sons of Aegyptus, were murdered by the daughters of Danaus on their wedding night. He gave intelligence of his safe arrival in this place to his faithful wife Hypermnestra by holding up a torch; and she in like manner informed him of her safety by raising a torch from Larissa, the citadel of Argos. The name of the town was afterward changed to Lyrceia from Lyrcus, a son of Abas. It was in ruins in the time of Pausanias (2.25.4,5). Its remains may still be seen on a small elevation called Skala between the village of Shinohori and the Inahos River.

LYTTUS   (See LYCTOS)

MACAREAE   was a town of Arcadia in the district of Parrhasia, 4 km from Megalopolis on the road to Phigalia and one-third of a kilometer from the Alpheius. It was in ruins in the time of Pausanias, as its inhabitants had been relocated to Megalopolis when it was founded (Paus. 8.3.2,27.4,36.9). The town derived its name from Macar, a son of Lycaon (Paus. 8.3.1; Apollod. 3.8.1). Its site was probably engulfed in the settlement that attended the expansion of Megalopolis.

MACARIA   was an earlier name of RHODES.

MACEDONIA (MAKEDONIA)   was the name applied to the country occupied by the tribes dwelling north of Thessaly and Mount Olympus, east of the mountain chain northeast of the Pindus range and west of the Axius River.

The Macedonians owed their name to an eponymous ancestor; according to some, this was Macedonus, son of Lycaon, from whom the Arcadians were descended (Apollod. 3.8.1) or Macedon, son of Zeus and brother of Magnes, or a son of Aeolus.

Macedonia was distinguished in two parts—Upper Macedonia and Lower Macedonia. While Upper Macedonia never became important, Lower Macedonia has long been famous in the history of the western world. This was because of the royal dynasty of Edessa, the original center of government. These kings called themselves Her-

acleidae and traced their descent to the Temenidae of Argos. Respecting this family there were two legends. According to one of them, the kings were descended from Caranus, and according to the other from Perdiccas. Temenus was a son of Aristomachus, one of the Heracleidae. He was one of the leaders of the Heraclediae into Peloponnesus and, after the conquest of the peninsula, he received Argos as his share. His descendants, the Temenidae, were expelled from Argos and founded the kingdom of Macedonia. Thereafter, the kings of Macedonia called themselves Temenidae (Herod. 8.138; Thuc. 2.99). After the legend of the foundation of the Macedonian kingdom, there is nothing but a long blank until the reign of King Amyntas (about 520–500 B.C.) and his son Alexander (about 480 B.C.). Herodotus (8.137–139) gives a list of five successive kings between the founder Perdiccas and Alexander—Perdiccas, Argaeus, Philippus, Aeropas, Alcestas, Amyntas, Alexander.

A military dispostion, personal valor, and a certain freedom of spirit were the national characteristics of this people. They were not considered Greeks by the genuine Hellenes, but they were not regarded as barbarians in the same sense as their neighbors the Thracians.

Upper Macedonia was divided into Elimeia, Eordaea, Orestis, and Lyncestis. This subdivision, extending as far as Illyricum to the west and Thrace to the east, constituted Paeonia. Lower Macedonia contained the maritime and central provinces, which were the earliest acquisitions of the kings, namely Pieria, Bottiaeis, Emathia, and Mygdonia.

As to the religion of the Macedonians, Athena Alcis (Strong) was worshipped there (Liv. 42.51). So was Artemis Tauropolis, whose head appeared on Macedonian coins. They paid particular reverence to the Cabeiri. Philip and Olympias were initiated in the Samothracian mysteries, and Alexander erected altars to the Cabeiri at the close of his eastern expedition (Plut. *Alex.* 2; Philostr. *De Vit. Apoll.* 2.43).

Linus, the personification of a dirge or lamentation, was a son of Apollo, who met a tragic death at an early age. After the battle of Chaeroneia, Philip of Macedon was said to have carried away the remains of Linus from Thebes to Macedonia. Later he was persuaded by a dream to send the remains back to Thebes.

Sithon, king of the Hadomantes in Macedonia, was a son of Poseidon and Assa. He was married to the nymph Mendeis, by whom he became the father of Pallene and Rhoeteia. Pallene, because of her beauty, had many suitors, and Sithon promised her to the one who could conquer him in single combat. However, since he killed all of them, Pallene was threatened with spinsterhood. Finally he allowed Dryas and Cleitus to fight for her, promising to give her to the conqueror. Pallene, who loved Cleitus, persuaded her servant to bribe the charioteer of Dryas to remove the axle pins from the wheels of his master's chariot. During the fight, Dryas' chariot broke down and he was killed by Cleitus. Sithon, who learned of the trick, built a funeral pyre for Dryas and was going to burn Pallene along with the corpse. After the fire was lit, Aphrodite appeared and a shower of rain extinguished the pyre. Sithon was thus obliged to change his mind and gave his daughter to Cleitus.

MACISTUS or MACISTUM   a town of Triphylia in Elis, was said to have been called also Platanistus. The town got its name from Macistus, a son of Athamas and brother of Phrixus. It was originally inhabited by the Paroreatae and Caucones, who were driven out by the Minyae. Macistus was situated upon a hill in the north of Triphylia and appears to have been the chief town in the north of the district, as Lepreum was in the south. It was near Samicum on the coast and had the superintendence of the celebrated temple of the Samian Poseidon (Strab. 8.3.13). From these circumstances there can be little doubt that Macistus was situated upon the heights of Mount Kaiafa.

Some ancient historians mentioned only Samicum, and others only Macistus. It is likely that the Minyans built Macistus on the heights overlooking Samicum when that city declined and that the more ancient name was later revived for the newer city. The Macistians had a temple of Heracles situated upon the coast near Acidon (Strab. 8.3.21), and from this temple the hero derived the surname Macistus.

MACRIS   was an earlier name of the island of CHIOS.

MACRIS   was another name for the island of EUBOEA.

MACRIS   was another name for the island of HELENA.

MACRIS   was an earlier name of the island of ICARIA.

MAENALUS (DAVIA)   was a town of Arcadia and the capital of the district Maenalia, which later formed part of the territory of Megalopolis. The town was founded by Maenalus, a son of Lycaon. The town was in ruins in the time of Pausanias (8.3.4,36.8), who mentions a temple of Athena, a stadium, and a hippodrome as belonging to the town. The remains of polygonal walls on the hill on the right bank of the river Helisson and opposite the village Davia probably represent the ancient town. Agathodaemon (Good God), a divinity in honor of whom the Greeks drank a cup of unmixed wine at the end of every repast had a temple here. It was situated on the road from Megalopolis to Maenalus (Paus. 8.36.5).

MAENALUS (MENALO)   is a lofty mountain in Arcadia forming the western boundary of the territories of Mantineia and Tegea. It was especially sacred to the god Pan, who was called Maenalius Deus (Ov. *Fast.* 4.650). The inhabitants of the mountain fancied that they had frequently heard the god playing on his pipes. The chief pass through Maenalus is near the modern town of Tripoli. The Roman poets frequently used the adjectives Maenalius and Maenalis as synonyms for Arcadian. Therefore, the constellation of the bear was called sometimes Maenalia Arctos. Arcas was the ancestor and eponymous hero of the Arcadians. His mother was Callisto, whom Zeus changed into a bear. Once Arcas pursued her in the chase, and Zeus placed both Arcas and Callisto among the stars (Ov. *Met.* 2.410). The tomb of Arcas was shown at Mantineia, where his remains had been carried from Mount Maenalus at the command of the Delphic oracle (Paus. 8.9.2).

Others connected with this mountain were Artemis and Protogeneia. The Arcadian Artemis was the goddess of the nymphs and the chase and often hunted on Maenalus. Protogeneia was a daughter of Deucalion and Pyrrha. She was married to Locrus but had no children. Zeus, however, carried her off and became by her, on Mount Maenalus, the father of Opus. Endymion is also called by some a son of Protogeneia.

MAGNESIA (MAGNISIA)   inhabited by the Magnetes, was the long and narrow strip of country between Mounts Ossa and Pelion on the west and the sea on the east, extending from the mouth of the Peneius on the north to the Pagasaean Gulf on the south. This portion of Thessaly derived its name from Magnes, a son of Argos and Perimele and father of Hymenaeus. The Magnetes were members of the Amphictyonic League and were settled in this district in Homeric times (Hom. *Il.* 2.756). The chief city of Magnesia was Iolcus.

Dolops was a son of Hermes who had a sepulchral monument in the neighborhood of Peiresiae and the coast of Magnesia, which was visible at a great distance. The Argonauts landed there and offered up sacrifices (Apollon. Rhod. 1.584).

MALEA   was a town in the district of Aegytis in Arcadia. Its territory was called the Maleatis. Leuctra was described as a fortress situated above the territory of Malea; and since Leuctra was probably at or near modern Leontari, Malea must have been in the same vicinity. Heracles was connected by friendship with Cheiron, the wisest and most just of the Centaurs, but one of his poisoned arrows was the cause of Cheiron's death. During his struggle with the Erymanthian boar, Heracles became involved in a fight with the Centaurs, who fled to Cheiron in the neighborhood of Malea. Heracles shot at them, and one of his arrows struck Cheiron, who, although immortal, did not want to live any longer and gave up his immortality to Prometheus.

MALEA (MALEAS) is a promontory of Laconia and the most southerly point in Greece with the exception of Taenarum. It was much dreaded by the ancient sailors on account of the winds and currents of the two seas, which meet here. When Menelaus on his return from Troy reached Malea, Zeus sent a storm that tossed part of Menelaus' fleet onto the coast of Crete. Also, Odysseus on his return from Troy was driven by a north wind toward Cape Malea and past it to the coast of Libya. On the promontory Apollo Maleates had a statue.

MALIS was a small district at the head of the Maliac Gulf, surrounded on all sides by mountains and open only to the sea. The river Spercheius flowed through it. It extended a little north of the valley of the Spercheius to the narrowest part of the straits of Thermopylae. Anticyra was the northernmost town and Anthela was the southernmost. According to one writer, the Malians derived their name from a town Malieus. No other mention can be found of this town except that it, in turn, was said to have derived its name from Malus, a son of Amphictyon. The Malians were probably Dorians. Heracles, the great Doric hero, is represented as the friend of Ceyx of Trachis, and Mount Oeta was the scene of the hero's death. There were three divisions of the Malians: Paralii, Priests, and Trachinii. Some supposed that the Priests were possessors of the sacred spot on which the Amphictyonic meetings were held; others thought they might be the inhabitants of the Sacred City, to which, according to Callimachus (*Hymn. in Del.* 287), the Hyperborean offerings were sent from Dodona on their way to Delos and that this sacred city was the city of Oeta.

MANTINEIA (MANDINIA) was one of the most ancient and powerful towns in Arcadia, located on the borders of Argolis, south of Orchomenus and north of Tegea. Its territory was called Mantinice. The city is mentioned in the Homeric catalog, and, according to tradition, it derived its name from Mantineus, a son of Lycaon (Hom. *Il.* 2.607; Paus. 8.8.4). Following the Trojan War Aepytus, son of Hippothous, was king in Arcadia. He was reigning at Mantineia when Orestes left Mycenae and settled in Arcadia. There was at Mantineia a sanctuary, which no mortal was ever allowed to enter. Aepytus disregarded the sacred custom, crossed the threshold, was immediately struck with blindness, and died soon after (Paus. 8.5.5).

Mantineia originally consisted of four or five distinct villages, the inhabitants of which were collected into one city (Xenoph. *Hellen.* 5.2.6; Strab. 8.3.2; Diod. 15.5). The territory of Mantineia was bounded on the west by Mount Maenalus and on the east by Mount Artemisium, which separated it from Argolis. Its northern frontier was a low range of hills, separating it from Orchomenus. Its southern frontier, which divided it from Tegeatis, was formed by a ridge from Mount Maenalus on one side and by a ridge from Mount Artemisium on the other. The territory of Mantineia formed part of the plain now called the Plain of Tripoli from the modern town of this name, located between the ancient Mantineia and Tegea. The city stood upon the Ophis River nearly in the center of the plain of Tripoli.

The circuit of the walls (3,942 meters and of oval shape) is almost complete. It had nine or ten gates, and there were many towers built at regular intervals. Of the buildings in the interior of the city described by Pausanias, few remains are left. Nearly in the center of the city are the ruins of a theater, and west of the theater have been observed the foundations of the temple of Aphrodite Symmachia, which the Mantineians erected to commemorate the share they had taken in the battle of Actium (Paus. 8.9.6).

There were several roads leading from Mantineia. Two led north of the city to Orchomenus, one passing by the fountain of Alalcomeneia and the other over Mount Anchisia and its temple of Artemis Hymnia, which formed the boundary between Mantineia and Orchomenia. Another road led from Mantineia on the west to Methydrium. Two roads led southward, one southeast to Tegea and the other southwest to Pallantium. On the southeast road about 1.5 km from the city was the temple of Poseidon Hippius, and 1 km beyond it were the tombs of the daughters of Pelias. Three and one-half kilometers farther on was the tomb of Areithous, who was said to have been slain in a narrow pass by Lycurgus (Hom. *Il.* 7.143). On the road from Mantineia to Pallantium was the temple of Zeus Charmon (Paus. 8.12.1).

Two roads led east to Argos, called Prinus and Climax. The Prinus ascended Mount Artemisium, passing the fountain of Arne about 2 km from the city and reaching the sources of the Inachus near the temple of Artemis, which set the boundary between Mantineia and Argolis. Climax ran from Argos along the Inachus to Lyrceia and Orneae. Across the mountain it descended into Mantinice by steps cut out of the rock. About 1 km from the city it reached the fountain of the Meliastae where were temples of Dionysus and Aphrodite Melaenis (Paus. 8.6.5).

Tombs and monuments abounded at Mantineia. Apart from those already mentioned were the tombs or monuments of Antinoe, Arcas, Diomeneia, Maera, the Peliades, and Penelope. Antinoe was a daughter of Cepheus. At the command of an oracle she led the inhabitants of Mantineia from the location of the old town to a place where the new town was to be founded. She had a monument at Mantineia commemorating this event (Paus. 8.8.4). Arcas was the ancestor and eponymous hero of the Arcadians. His tomb was shown at Mantineia, where his remains had been carried from Mount Maenalus at the command of the Delphic oracle (Paus. 8.9.3). Diomeneia was a daughter of Arcas, and a bronze statue of her stood in the marketplace at Mantineia (Paus. 8.9.9). Maera was a daughter of Atlas and married to Tegeates, the son of Lycaon. Her tomb was shown both at Tegea and Mantineia, and Pausanias (8.12.7) thinks she was the same whom Odysseus saw in Hades. The Peliades fled to Mantineia from Iolcus after they had participated in the murder of their father. Their tombs were shown here (Paus. 8.11.3). Penelope, represented by some writers as unchaste during Odysseus' absence and cast out by him, went to Sparta and from there to Mantineia, where her tomb was shown in later times (Paus. 8.12.6).

The Mantineians worshipped Athena Alea, Zeus Epidotes (Liberal Giver), Zeus Soter (Savior), Artemis Hymnia, and Poseidon. Artemis Hymnia, as stated, had a temple between Orchomenus and Mantineia; her priestess was at first always a virgin until after the time of Artistocrates when it was decreed that she should be a married woman (Paus. 8.5.12). As for Poseidon, some writers contended that like Zeus he was concealed by Rhea to prevent his being devoured by Cronus. She hid him among a flock of lambs and pretended to have given birth to a young horse, which Cronus devoured. A spring in the vicinity of Mantineia, where this is said to have happened, was believed to have derived from this event the name of the Lamb's Well or Arne (Paus. 8.8.2).

The ruins of Mantineia are not located adjacent to a town but are easily reached about 12 km north of Tripoli off the highway that leads to Levidi.

MARATHON (MARATHONAS) was a small plain in the northeast of Attica containing four cities: Marathon, Probalinthus, Tricorythus, and Oenoe. These four originally formed the Tetrapolis, one of the twelve districts into which Attica was divided before the time of Theseus. Here Xuthus, who married the daughter of Erechtheus, is said to have reigned; and here the Heracleidae, when driven out of Peloponnesus, took refuge and defeated Eurystheus (Strab. 8.7.1). The people of Marathon claimed to be the first in Greece who paid divine honors to Heracles, and they possessed a sanctuary in the plain. Marathon is also celebrated in the legends of Theseus, who conquered the ferocious bull that terrorized the plain (Plut. *Thes.* 14; Strab. 9.1.22). It will be remembered that Androgeus, son of Minos, was sent out by Aegeus, king of Athens, to conquer the Marathonian bull, but he was killed by the beast. Androgeus had conquered all his opponents in the Panathenaic games, and Aegeus feared him. According to Diodorus Siculus (4.60), Aegeus had him murdered near Oenoe. Theseus, son of Aegeus,

captured the Marathonian bull, which had proved the undoing of Androgeus. Theseus, after his own death, was said to have appeared to aid the Athenians in the battle of Marathon (490 B.C.).

Marathon appeared to be a place of importance (Hom. *Od.* 7.80). Its name was derived from an eponymous hero Marathon, who is described by Pausanias (1.15.3, 2.1.1), as a son of Epopeus, king of Sicyon, who fled into Attica in consequence of the cruelty of his father. Plutarch (*Thes.* 32) calls him an Arcadian, who accompanied the Dioscuri in their expedition into Attica and voluntarily sacrificed himself before the battle.

After Theseus united the twelve independent districts of Attica into one state, the name Tetrapolis gradually fell into disuse; and the four places of which it consisted became Attic demes—Marathon, Tricorythus, Oenoe (belonging to the tribe Aeantis), and Probalinthus (belonging to the tribe Pandionis). But Marathon was superior to the other three, and its name was applied to the whole district.

The plain of Marathon is open to a bay of the sea on the east, and it is shut in on the opposite side by the heights of Pendeli. A long, rocky promontory to the north, anciently called Cynosura and now Marathonas, affords shelter to the bay. The plain is about 10 km long and 5 wide. A river called the Marathona flows through the center of the plain.

The modern town of Marathonas is on the road from Lake Marathona to the battle site, where may be seen the tombs of the Athenians and Plataeans. Near the former tomb are the remains of the celebrated temple of Heracles, in whose sacred enclosure the Athenians were encamped before the battle of Marathon (Herod. 6.108). In connection with the battle there was current an interesting story. Echetlus was a mysterious being who appeared among the Greeks during the battle. He resembled a rustic, and he slew many of the Persians with his plow. After the battle, when he was sought, he was not to be found anywhere; when the Athenians consulted the oracle, they were commanded to worship the hero Echetlaeus, that is, the hero with the *echetli* (plowshare). Echetlus was to be seen in the painting in the Stoa Poikile at Athens, which represented the battle of Marathon (Paus. 1.15.4,32.5).

Close to the sea, on a hillock in the southern marsh there are some ancient remains, which may be those of the temple of Athena Hellotia, which surname the goddess is said to have derived from the location of the temple in the marsh of Marathon. There was also a temple of the Pythian Apollo in this area.

At a little distance from the plain is a mountain of Pan with a cavern. Inside are formations of rocks resembling goats. At Athens the worship of Pan was not introduced till the time of the battle of Marathon, after which time he had this sanctuary.

On the road to Rhamnous near Kato Souli several springs issue from the foot of the rocks on the left side of the road. These springs are the fountain of Macaria, which Pausanias (1.32.6) mentions. It is still called the Macarian Spring. It derived its name from Macaria, a daughter of Heracles, who sacrificed herself in behalf of the Heracleidae before the victory that they gained over the Argives in this plain.

MARGANA or MARGALAE   a town in the Pisatis in Elis, was supposed by some to be the Homeric Aepy (Strab. 8.3.24). Its site is unknown, but it was probably east of Letrini, the modern Agios Ioannis.

MARIUS (MARIO)   a town of Laconia belonging in the time of Pausanias to the Eleuthero-Lacones, was situated 18.5 km east of Geronthrae. It contained a sanctuary of all the gods and one of Artemis, and at each there were abundant springs (Paus. 3.22.8). It is represented by Mario, which stands on the road from Geraki (ancient Geronthrae) over the mountains to Kremasti. There are ruins of the ancient town about 2.5 km to the south of the modern village, and the place is still characterized by its copious fountains.

MARONEIA (MARONIA)   was a rich and powerful city of the Cicones in Thrace, situated on the Aegean Sea not far from Lake Ismaris (Herod. 7.109). It was said to have been founded by Maron, a son of Dionysus (Eurip. *Cycl.* 5.100,141). He was a priest of Apollo at Maroneia, where he himself had a sanctuary. He was the hero of sweet wine and is mentioned among the companions of Dionysus (Hom. *Od.* 9.197; Athen. 1.33; Diod. 1.18). It is reported that the city's ancient name was Ortagurea. The people of Maroneia especially venerated Dionysus probably because of the superior character of their wine, which was celebrated as early as the days of Homer (*Od.* 9.196). This wine was universally esteemed and was said to possess the odor of the nectar consumed by the gods (Nonn. *Dionys.* 1.12, 17.6, 19.11). The modern town of Maronia is about 2 km from the sea on the west slope of Mount Ismaros.

MASES   an ancient city in the district Hermionis in the Argolid peninsula, was mentioned along with Aegina by Homer (*Il.* 2.562). In the time of Pausanias (2.36.3) it was used as a harbor by Hermione. It ws probably situated on the west coast of Hermione at the head of the deep bay of Kiladia, which is protected by a small island.

MECONE   was the sacerdotal name for SICYON.

MEDEON   was a town of Phocis, destroyed along with the other Phocian towns at the termination of the Sacred War (348 B.C.), and never again rebuilt (Paus. 10.3.2). Strabo (9.2.26) places it on the Crissaean Gulf about 30 km from Boeotia, and Pausanias (10.36.6) says that it was near Anticyra. Medeon was a son of Pylades and Electra, from whom the town received its name.

MEDITERRANEAN SEA or INTERNUM MARE   is the name of the great inland sea touching the coasts of southern Europe, north Africa, and Asia Minor. It extends on the west from the Straits of Heracles, which separate it from the Atlantic, to the coasts of Syria and Asia Minor on the east. In the northeast it terminates at the Hellespont. It is about 3,333 km in length. Most of the ancients believed that the Mediterranean received its waters from the Atlantic and poured them through the Hellespont and the Propontis into the Euxine, but others, on the contrary, maintained that the waters came from the Euxine into the Mediterranean. The different parts of the Mediterranean are called by different names, which may be consulted separately. (See ADRIATIC SEA, AEGEAN SEA, TYRRHENIAN SEA, etc.)

Thalassa was the earliest personification of the Mediterranean and was described as a daughter of Aether and Hemera (Lucian *Dei Marin.* 11). Nereus was a son of Pontus and Gaea and husband of Doris, by whom he became father of the fifty Nereids. He is described as the wise and unerring old man of the sea, at the bottom of which he dwelt. His empire was the Mediterranean or more particularly the Aegean. He was believed to have the power of prophesying the future. The trident was one of his attributes. The Nereids were marine nymphs of the Mediterranean. They are described as lovely divinities, dwelling with their father at the bottom of the sea, and they were believed to be propitious to all sailors and especially to the Argonauts. They were worshipped in several parts of Greece but especially in seaport towns and on the Isthmus of Corinth.

Poseidon was the great god of the Mediterranean Sea. His palace was in the depths near Aegae in Euboea, where he kept his horses with bronze hoofs and golden manes. With these horses he rode in a chariot over the waves of the sea, which became smooth as he approached. Usually he hitched the horses himself, but sometimes he was helped by Amphitrite. Poseidon's symbol was the trident. Being the ruler of the sea, he was described as gathering the clouds and calling forth storms, but at the same time he had the power to grant a successful voyage and save those who were in danger. All other marine divinities were subject to him. He used these powers both destructively and benignly in connection with the Trojan War. He sided with the Greeks, but he hated Odysseus and tried to destroy him as he attempted to reach home after the war.

Amphitrite was wife of Poseidon and goddess of the Mediterranean Sea. When Poseidon sued for her hand, she fled to Atlas, but her lover sent spies after her, among them Delphinus, who thus made the marriage possible and was rewarded by the grateful god by being placed among the stars. She became by Poseidon the mother of Triton, Rhode, and Benthesicyme. She was frequently represented in works of art, sometimes riding on marine animals. The temple of Poseidon on the Corinthian Isthmus contained a statue of her. She also appeared on the temple of Apollo at Amyclae and on the throne of the Olympian Zeus.

MEGALOPOLIS (MEGALOPOLI)   one of the most recent of the Grecian cities and the later capital of Arcadia, was founded in 370 B.C., a few months after the battle of Leuctra, and was finished three years later. The city was more than 9 km in circumference, while the territory assigned to it was more extensive than that of any other Arcadian state, extending north about 38 km from the city. It was bounded on the east by the territories of Tegea, Mantineia, Orchomenus, and Caphyae, and on the west by those of Messene, Phigalia, and Heraea.

Megalopolis was located in the middle of a plain and, unlike most Greek cities, possessed no height that might be converted into an acropolis. The city lay upon both banks of the Helisson, which flowed through it from east to west and divided it into two nearly equal parts. The Helisson flows into the Alpheius about 4 km from the city. Almost all traces of the walls of Megalopolis have disappeared. The two most important buildings were the theater, on the left or south side of the river, and the agora on the north. The colossal remains of the theater are conspicuous in the whole plain. On the east side of the theater was the stadium. Here is a fountain sacred to Dionysus; and below the stadium towards the river were a sanctuary of Aphrodite and an altar of Ares. East of the temple of Dionysus there is another source of water, by which we can fix the position of the temple of Asclepius Paidos; above which on a hill was a temple of Artemis Agrotera. Nearby was a house built for Alexander the Great. In this same locality there were a few foundations of a temple sacred to Apollo, Hermes, and the Muses.

In the center of the agora was an enclosure sacred to Zeus Lycaeus, who was the guardian deity of all Arcadia. It had no entrance, but its interior was exposed to public view. Here could be seen two altars of the god, two tables, two eagles, and a statue in stone of Pan. In front of this sacred enclosure was a statue of Apollo in brass, 3.5 meters high, which was brought from Bassae by the Phigalians to adorn the new capital. This colossal statue probably stood on the west side of the sanctuary of Zeus. To the right of the statue was the temple of the Mother of the Gods, of which only the columns were standing in the time of Pausanias (8.30.4). On the north side of the agora lay the stoa of Philip, the son of

Amyntas. Near it were the remains of the temple of Hermes Acacesius. A smaller adjacent stoa contained the archives. Beyond the stoa of the archives was a temple of Tyche.

The stoa Myropolis was more than likely on the east side of the agora. At its east end was a temple of Zeus Soter, containing a statue of the god seated between the goddesses Megalopolis and Artemis Soteira. At the west end was the sanctuary of the Great Goddesses Demeter and Kore; the sanctuary contained several temples. To the north of the agora behind the stoa of Philip there were two low hills, on one of which stood the temple of Athena Polias and on the other the temple of Hera Teleia, both in ruins by the time of Pausanias. The foundations of these temples are still visible.

There were eight principal roads leading from Megalopolis. The road to Messene passed at the distance of 1.33 km from the city a temple of the goddesses called Maniae, a name of the Eumenides; on this spot Orestes became insane on account of the murder of his mother. A little farther on was a small earthen mound called the Monument of the Finger because here Orestes in his madness bit off one of his fingers. Still farther was a place called Ace, the spot where Orestes was healed of his madness; it contained another temple of the Eumenides. Finally, there was a sanctuary named Cureion because here Orestes cut off his hair. The road to Carnasium in Messenia ran north of the former road but parallel to it. It led eventually to the Hermaion, named Despoena, a boundary between the territories of Megalopolis and Messenia. The road to Sparta crossed the Alpheius at about 5.5 km and followed the intersecting Theius for 7.5 km. The road to Methydrium ran north from Megalopolis. Two and one-half kilometers from the city was a place called Scias, with a temple of Artemis Sciatis, founded by the tyrant Aristodemus. The other road branched off to the right to Methydrium, ascending to the fountain Cruni and from there descending 5.5 km to the tomb of Callisto, a high earthen mound, upon which was a temple of Artemis Calliste. The road to Maenalus led along the Helisson to the foot of Mount Maenalus. Near it was a temple of Pan. The road to Phigalia crossed the Alpheius at 3.5 km and passed the ruins of Daseae and Acacesium. At two-thirds of a kilometer from Acacesium was the temple of Despoena, one of the most celebrated sanctuaries in Peloponnesus. Adjoining was a temple of Pan, above which stood the ancient city of Lycosura. The road to Pallantium and Tegea passed through Ladoceia, the ruins of Haemoniae and Oresthasium, the villages of Aphrodisium and Athenaeum, and the ruins of Asea, near which were the sources of the Alpheius and the Eurotas. The road to Heraea crossed through several towns, including the ruins of Trapezus.

In addition to the divinities already mentioned, Megalopolitans paid tribute to several other beings. One of these was Agathodaemon (Good God). In honor of this divinity the Greeks drank a cup of unmixed wine at the end of every repast. A temple dedicated to him was situated on the road from Megalopolis to Maenalus. Pausanias (8.36.5) suggests that the name was an epithet of Zeus. Hermes Agetor had a statue at Megalopolis (Paus. 8.32.1). This surname described him as the leader and ruler of men. Ammon, a Libyan divinity, was worshipped in Greece at an early time. At Megalopolis he was represented with the head of a ram (Paus. 8.32.1). Poseidon Epopsius (Superintendent) was known at Megalopolis (Paus. 8.30.1).

Hagno was an Arcadian nymph who is said to have brought up Zeus. She was represented at Megalopolis carrying in one hand a pitcher and in the other a bowl. Myrtoessa was a nymph of a spring of the same name in Arcadia; she was represented in Megalopolis along with Archiroe, Hagno, Anthracia, and Nais (Paus. 8.31.2). In later times, the worship of Helios was established in Megalopolis (Paus. 8.9.2).

Finally, Aphrodite Mechanitis (Skilled in Inventing) was worshipped at Megalopolis (Paus. 8.31.3,36.3). Aphrodite Pandemos (Common to All People) was also worshipped here (Paus. 8.31.3). Sacrifices offered to her consisted of white goats.

MEGARA (MEGARA)   was a city in Greece Proper situated about 1.5 km from the Saronic Gulf in a plain about 10 or 11 km in length and the same in width. It was bounded on the west by the Geraneian Mountains, on the east and north by the Kerata Mountains, and on the south by the sea. The city stood on a low hill with a double summit, on each of which there was an acropolis, one named Caria and the other Alcathoe. Below the city was a port town named Nisaea, the port being formed by an island called Minoa. The city was connected with its port town by long walls as in Athens and Corinth.

Phoroneus, son of the river Inachus and king of Peloponnesus, had a son Car, who built the citadel of Megara and called it Caria. He also built the temple of Demeter called Megara, from which the place derived its name (Paus. 1.39.5,40.6). The tomb of Car was shown as late as the time of Pausanias (1.44.6) on the road from Megara to Corinth. Twelve generations later, Lelex came from Egypt and gave the inhabitants the name Leleges. He was a son of Poseidon and Libya and became king of Megara. His tomb was later shown below Nisaea, the acropolis of Megara (Paus. 1.39.6). Cleson was the son of Lelex and had three children, Tauropolis, Cleso, and Pylas. Tauropolis and Cleso were believed to have found and buried the body of Ino, which had been washed up on the coast of Megara (Paus. 1.42.7). Pylas next succeeded to the throne, but shortly afterward killed Bias, his

father's brother, and had to flee to Peloponnesus, where he founded Pylos. He gave Megara to Pandion, who had married his daughter Pylia (Apollod. 3.15.5; Paus. 1.39.6). Pandion, son of Cecrops and Metiadusa, was a king of Athens. Being expelled from Athens by the Metionidae, he had fled to Megara and there married Pylia. He became by her the father of Aegeus, Pallas, Nisus, and Lycus. He also had an illegitimate son, Oeneus. His only daughter was married to his brother-in-law Sciron. Pandion's tomb was shown in the territory of Megara near the rock of Athena Aethyia on the seacoast (Paus. 1.5.3), and at Megara he was honored with a shrine (1.41.6).

The Pandionidae returned from Megara to Athens and overthrew the Metionidae. Aegeus, the eldest among them, obtained Athens; Lycus the east coast of Attica; Nisus, Megaris, and Pallas the south coast (Apollod. 3.15.6; Paus. 1.5.4). Sciron, the son of Pylas, was married to the daughter of Pandion and disputed with Nisus the government of Megara; but Aeacus, king of Aegina, who was chosen arbitrator, decided that Nisus should have the rule of Megara and Sciron the command in war (Paus. 1.39.5).

Nisus married Abrota, by whom he became the father of Scylla. When Minos, on his expedition against Athens, took Megara, Nisus died because his daughter Scylla, who had fallen in love with Minos, pulled out the purple or gold hair that grew on top of her father's head and on which his life depended (Apollod. 3.15.5,6,8). Minos, who was horrified at the conduct of this unnatural daughter, ordered Scylla to be fastened to the poop of his ship and afterward drowned her in the Saronic Gulf. According to others, Minos left Megara in disgust, but Scylla leapt into the sea and swam after his ship; but her father, who had been changed into an eagle, perceived her and shot down upon her, whereupon she was metamorphosed into either a fish or a bird (Ov. Met. 8.6; Virg. Georg. 1.405). The promontory of Scyllaeum was also named for her (Paus. 2.34.7). The tradition at Megara itself knew nothing of this expedition of Minos, giving Iphinoe as the name of the daughter of Nisus and representing her as married to Megareus. Nisa was said to have been an earlier name of Megara, and Nisaea, the port town of Megara, derived its name from Nisus. The tomb of Nisus was shown at Athens behind the Lyceum (Paus. 1.19.4). Abrota, the wife of Nisus, deserves further mention. She was a daughter of Onchestus of Boeotia. On her death Nisus commanded all the Megarian women to wear a garment of the same kind as Abrota had worn, which was called *aphabroma* and was still in use in the time of Plutarch (*Quaest. Gr.* 295).

Megareus, son of Onchestus and thus brother of Abrota, was also called a son of Poseidon. He was married to Iphinoe, the daughter of Nisus, by whom he became father of Euippus, Timalcus, and Euaechme, to whom Ovid (10.575) adds Hippomenes. According to a Boeotian tradition, Megareus with his army went to the assistance of Nisus against Minos but fell in the battle and was buried at Megara, which was called after him. According to a Megarian tradition, which discarded the account of an expedition of Minos against Megara, Megareus, both as brother-in-law and son-in-law to Nisus, succeeded him in the government of Megara.

Megareus left the government to Alcathous, his son-in-law, because his own sons had died before him (Paus. 1.39.5). Alcathous was a son of Pelops and Hippodameia and brother of Atreus and Thyestes. He first married Pyrgo and afterward Euaechme, daughter of Megareus, and was the father of Echepolis, Callipolis, Iphinoe, Periboea, and Automedusa. Pausanias (1.41.3) relates that after Euippus, the son of King Megareus, was destroyed by the Cithaeronian lion, Megareus, whose elder son Timalcus had been killed by Theseus, offered his daughter Euaechme and his kingdom to him who should slay the lion. Alcathous undertook the task, conquered the lion, and thus obtained Euaechme for his wife and afterward became the successor of Megareus. In gratitude for this success he built at Megara a temple of Artemis Agrotera and Apollo Agraeus. He also restored the walls of Megara, which had been destroyed by the Cretans (Paus. 1.41.6). In this work he was said to have been assisted by Apollo; and the stone upon which the god placed his lyre while he was at work was even in late times believed, when struck, to give forth a sound similar to that of a lyre (Paus. 1.42.2; Ov. *Met.* 8.15). Echepolis, one of the sons of Alcathous, was killed during the Calydonian hunt in Aetolia, and when his brother Callipolis hastened to carry the sad news to his father, he found him busy offering a sacrifice to Apollo. Thinking it unfit to offer sacrifices at such a moment, Echepolis snatched away the wood from the altar. Alcathous misinterpreted this as an act of sacrilege and killed his son on the spot with a piece of wood (Paus. 1.42.7). The acropolis of Megara was called by a name derived from that of Alcathous (Paus. 1.42.1). Iphinoe was the only remaining child of Alcathous about whom anything is known. She died a virgin. The women of Megara previous to their marriage offered to her a funeral sacrifice and dedicated a lock of hair to her (Paus. 1.43.4). So ended the line of kings established by Lelex. It was related that Hyperion, the son of Agamemnon, was the last king of Megara and that after his death a democratic form of government was established (Paus. 1.43.3).

Other persons having connections with Megara were: Polyidus, Adrastus, Alcmena, Alope, Hippolyte, Iphigeneia, Sciron, and Tereus. Polyidus was a son of Coeranus, a grandson of Abas, and a great-grandson of Melampus. He was a celebrated soothsayer at Corinth.

When Alcathous had murdered his own son Callipolis at Megara, he was purified by Polyidus, who erected at Megara a sanctuary of Dionysus and a statue of the god, which was covered all over except the face (Paus. 1.43.5; Apollod. 3.3.1). Manto was a daughter of Polyidus and sister of Astycrateia. The tombs of these two sisters were shown at Megara near the entrance of the sanctuary of Dionysus (Paus. 1.43.5). Euchenor was a son of Coeranus and a grandson of Polyidus. He died in the Trojan War (Paus. 1.43.6).

Adrastus was the Argive hero who participated in the battles of the Seven against Thebes, of which he was the only survivor, and the expedition of the Epigoni. On his return from that battle, Adrastus, weighed down by grief at the death of his son Aegialeus, died at Megara and was buried there (Paus. 1.43.1). After his death he was worshipped at Megara and other places. Alcmena, the mother of Heracles, died in Megaris, according to Pausanias (1.41.1), on her way from Argos to Thebes; she was buried in the place she died, at the command of an oracle. Alope was a daughter of Cercyon of Eleusis and was beloved by Poseidon, by whom she became the mother of a son, whom she exposed immediately at his birth. The child was suckled by a mare and rescued by shepherds, who brought him to the attention of Cercyon, who recognized him and had him exposed a second time. The child was fed and found as before, and the shepherds called him Hippothous. Alope was killed, and her body was changed by Poseidon into a fountain, which bore her name. There was a monument of Alope on the road from Eleusis to Megara on the spot where she was believed to have been killed by her father (Paus. 1.39.3).

Hippolyte was the queen of the Amazons, who marched with her army into Attica, where she was defeated by Theseus. She fled to Megara, where she died in grief and was buried. Her tomb, which was shown in later times, had the form of an Amazon's shield (Paus. 1.41.7; Plut. *Thes.* 27). Iphigeneia also had a tomb and shrine at Megara, according to Pausanias (1.43.1).

Sciron was a famous robber who haunted the frontier between Attica and Megaris. He not only robbed travellers who passed through the country but also compelled them to wash his feet on the Scironian Rocks, during which operation he kicked them with his foot into the sea. At the foot of the rock there was a tortoise that devoured the bodies of the robber's victims. Sciron was slain by Theseus in the same manner in which he had killed others (Plut. *Thes.* 10; Paus. 1.44.8). He is not to be confused with the son of Pylas mentioned previously.

Tereus was a son of Ares in Daulis and afterwards Phocis. Some traditions place him at Pegae in Megaris (Paus. 1.41.8). Pandion, king of Athens, called in Tereus for assistance against an enemy, and gave him his daughter Procne in marriage. They had a son Itys. Tereus concealed Procne and said she was dead so that he might marry Philomela, the sister of Procne, and he cut out Philomena's tongue so she could not talk. Philomela learned the truth and wove the story of the deed into a garment. Procne thereupon killed Itys and served his flesh to Tereus, who suspected his brother of the deed and killed him. Tereus learned what had happened and pursued the sisters with an ax. All three were changed into birds. According to the Megarian tradition, Tereus, being unable to overtake the women, killed himself. The Megarians showed the tomb of Tereus in their own country, and an ancient sacrifice was offered to him. Procne and Philomela were believed to have escaped to Attica and to have wept themselves to death (Paus. 1.41.9).

The religion of Megara observed particularly the worship of the Olympian gods Athena, Apollo, Aphrodite, Zeus, Demeter and Persephone, Artemis, and Dionysus. Athena Aethyia was a name of the goddess at Megara signifying a diver and figuratively a ship, so that the name must have had reference to the goddess teaching the art of shipbuilding or navigation. Athena also had a sanctuary on the acropolis under the surname Nike (Paus. 1.42.4; Eurip. *Ion* 1529). Apollo Agraeus (Hunter) was worshipped at Megara. After he had killed the lion of Cithaeron, Alcathous erected a temple to Apollo under this name (Paus. 1.41.4). Apollo also had the surname Archegetes at Megara (Paus. 1.42.5). The name has reference to Apollo as leader and protector of colonies or as the founder of towns in general. Apollo Decatephorus (God to Whom the Tenth Part of the Booty is Dedicated) was also known at Megara. Pausanias (1.42.5) remarks that the statues of Apollo Pythius and Apollo Decatephorus at Megara resembled Egyptian sculptures. Aphrodite was worshipped here. So was Zeus under the surname Conius (Dust-maker), who had a temple in the citadel of the city (Paus. 1.40.5). Demeter Thesmophoros (Lawgiver) was the goddess, in honor of whom the Thesmophoria were celebrated at Athens in the month of Pyanepsion and to whom a sanctuary was erected at Megara (Paus. 1.42.6). The worship of Demeter was introduced into Sicily by colonists from Megara and Corinth. A temple of Persephone was mentioned at Megara.

A rather large number of lesser divinities were also worshipped here. Eileithyia, the goddess of birth, had a sanctuary here (Paus. 1.44.3). At Megara a statue of Eros, god of love, together with those of Himerus and Pothos, stood in the temple of Aphrodite. Pothos was the personification of desire and Himerus of longing love. This group of statues was the work of Scopas (Paus. 1.43.6). The Moirae (Fates) were represented along with their father at Megara (Paus. 1.40.4). Hesiod calls them the daughters of Nyx; later writers called them daughters

of Erebus (Darkness) and Nyx (Night), Cronus and Nyx, Gaea and Oceanus, and Ananke (Necessity). Finally, the Sithnid nymphs were worshipped at Megara (Paus. 1.40.1).

Megara certainly was in early times regarded as part of Attica; and in this way Strabo (9.1.5) accounts for the omission of its name in the *Iliad*; Megarians were included along with the Athenians under the general name of Ionians. The most certain event in the history of Megara is its conquest by the Dorians. This event is connected in tradition with the expedition of the Peloponnesians against Athens. The Dorian invaders were defeated by the voluntary sacrifice of Codrus; but Megaris was nevertheless conquered and a Corinthian and Messenian colony founded at Megara. After Megara had become an independent city, its prosperity rapidly increased, and in the seventh century B.C. it was one of the most flourishing commercial cities of Greece.

The Megarians had a reputation for decadence and self-indulgence. Of the Megarian games we have three kinds mentioned: the Dioclean, celebrated in honor of the hero Diocles; the Alcathoan, celebrated in honor of Alcathous; and the Smaller Pythian, in honor of the Pythian Apollo, whose worship was very ancient in Megara.

Pausanias (1.40–44) gives a description of the sacred buildings of Megara. He begins with the aqueduct of Theagenes, which was supplied with water from the fountain of the nymphs called Sithnides. Near it was an ancient temple containing a statue of Artemis Soteira and statues of the twelve gods said to be by Praxiteles. Beyond, in the sacred enclosure of Zeus Olympius, was a magnificent temple containing an unfinished statue of the god. From there Pausanias ascended to the citadel named Caria, passing by a temple of Dionysus Nyctelius, a sanctuary of Aphrodite Apostrophia, an oracle of Nyx, and a roofless temple of Zeus Conius. Here also was the Megaron, or temple of Demeter, said to have been founded by Car during his reign.

Below the north side of the Carian acropolis was the tomb of Alcmena near the Olympieion. From here Pausanias was conducted to a place called Rhus, because the waters from the neighboring mountains were collected there, until they were turned off by Theagenes, who erected on the spot an altar to Achelous. It was probably this water that supplied the fountains of the Sithnides. Near this place was the monument of Hyllas, and not far from it were temples of Isis, Apollo Agraeus, and Artemis Agrotera (said to have been dedicated by Alcathous after he had slain the Cithaeronian lion). Below these were the shrine of Pandion and the monuments of Hippolyte and Tereus.

On the ascent to the citadel Alcathoe, Pausanias saw on the right the sepulcher of Megareus and near it the hearth of the gods called Prodromeis, to whom Alcathous sacrificed before building the walls. Here was the stone upon which Apollo laid his lyre when he was assisting Alcathous. Beyond was the council house of the Megarians, formerly the sepulcher of Timalcus, son of Megareus, who was killed in the expedition of the Dioscuri against Aphidna. And on the summit of the acropolis was a temple of Athena, containing a statue of the goddess, entirely gilded except for the face, hands, and feet, which were of ivory. Here also were temples of Athena Nike and Aeantis. The temple of Apollo was originally of brick but had been rebuilt of white marble by Hadrian. Here also was a temple of Demeter Thesmophoros and below it the tomb of Callipolis.

On the road leading to the Prytaneion was the shrine of Ino, the shrine of Iphigeneia, and a temple of Artemis said to have been erected by Agamemnon. In the Prytaneion were tombs of Menippus, son of Megareus, and Echepolis, son of Alcathous; nearby was a stone called Anaclethra, because here Demeter sat down and called her daughter. After many sepulchers for military heroes came the Dionysion or temple of Dionysus, near which was the temple of Aphrodite with several statues by Praxieteles. Nearby was a temple of Tyche with an image of the goddess by Praxieteles. A neighboring temple contained statues of the Muses and a Zeus in bronze.

On the descent from the agora there stood a little to the right the temple of Apollo Prostaterius (Protector), with a statue of the god by Praxiteles. In the ancient gymnasium near the Nymphades gates was a pyramidal stone worshipped as Apollo Carinus. Near it was a temple of the Eileithyiae, or goddesses of childbirth.

On the road to the port of Nisaea was a temple of Demeter Malophoros. The acropolis of Nisaea still existed in the time of Pausanias. On the descent from the acropolis facing the sea there was the tomb of Lelex. Near Nisaea was a small island called Minoa, where the fleet of the Cretans was moored during the war against Nisus (Paus. 1.44.3).

Megara still retains its ancient name, but it is a vastly unattractive modern city. There are hardly any remains of antiquity. On the east acropolis there are a few remains of the ancient walls. None of the numerous temples mentioned by Pausanias can be identified with certainty. A large fountain on the north side of the town is all that remains of the celebrated fountain of the Sithnid nymphs. A cave below the acropolis of Caria is thought to have been a Roman sanctuary of Demeter.

MEGARIS the territory of Megara, occupied the greater part of the large isthmus that extends from the foot of Mount Cithaeron to the Acrocorinthus and which connects northern Greece with Peloponnesus. The border between Megaris and Corinth differed over the years, but eventually the territory of Corinth reached as far as the

Scironian Rocks. On the north Megaris was separated from Boeotia by Mount Cithaeron and to the east and northeast it was separated from Attica by two summits called Kerata (Horns). The river Iapis, which flowed into the sea a little to the west of the Horns, was the boundary of Megaris and Attica.

Megaris is a mountainous country and has no plain except the one in which its capital, Megara, was located. The main range of Mount Cithaeron runs from west to east, and another chain stretches across Megaris, running into the peninsula. The mountains were called Geraneia and are said to have received this name because, in the deluge of Deucalion, Megareus, the son of Zeus and a Sithonian nymph, was led by the cries of cranes to take refuge upon their summit. Further south rises the Oneian range.

Three roads ran across the Geraneian Mountains into Peloponnesus. One ran from the west coast of Megaris across the rocky peninsula of Perachora down to the Corinthian Gulf. The second road passed through the center of the Geraneia. The third road led along the east coast, the shortest way between Megara and Corinth. Part of this road is a pass cut from rock above sheer cliffs, and this pass was the celebrated Scironian Rocks, from which Sciron used to throw strangers into the sea and from which he was himself hurled by Theseus (Paus. 1.44.8). The tortoise at the foot of the rock, which was said to devour the victims, was probably a rock called by this name from its shape and which gave rise to the tale. Near the south end of the pass, where the road begins to descend, is the Molurian Rock, from which Ino (or Leucothea) threw herself with her son Melicertes (Palaemon) into the sea. On the summit of the mountain was a temple of Zeus Aphesius. On the descent into the plain was the temple of Apollo Latous, near which were the boundaries of Megaris and the Corinthia (Paus. 1.44.9,10).

Megaris contained only one town of importance, Megara, with its harbor Nisaea. The other towns in the country were Aegosthena and Pegae (Pagae) on the Corinthian Gulf, Tripodiscus and Rhus in the interior, Phibalus on the boundaries of Attica, and Phalycon and Polichne, of which the sites are uncertain. There was also a fortress, Geraneia, situated on one of the mountains of the same name, but its position is also unknown.

The mythological and religious history of Megaris is identical with that of Megara. (See MEGARA.)

MEILICHUS is a river of Achaia, emptying into the sea between the promontory Rhium and Patrae. Eurypylus, a Thessalian, directed by the Delphic oracle, came to Aroe to be cured of a madness incurred by looking at an image of Dionysus concealed in a chest, which had been brought from Troy. At Aroe the inhabitants offered each year to Artemis Triclaria a human sacrifice consisting of the fairest youth and the fairest maid of the town. An oracle had told them they would be released from this sacrifice if a foreign divinity should be brought to them by a foreign king. When the sacrifice was about to start, Eurypylus produced the chest and the sacrifice was stopped. Instead, the festival of Dionysus Aesymnetes was instituted. During the night of this festival a priest carried the chest outside the town and all the children of the place, adorned with garlands of wheat ears, as the sacrificial victims once had been, went down to the banks of the river Meilichus, which had before been called Ameilichus. There they hung up their garlands, purified themselves, and then put on other garlands of ivy, after which they returned to the sanctuary of Dionysus Aesymnetes.

MELAENAE or MELAENEAE (KOKKORAS)   a town of Arcadia in the territory of Heraea and on the road from Heraea to Megalopolis, was founded by Melaeneus, the son of Lycaon (Paus. 8.26.8); but it was deserted in the time of Pausanias and overflowed with water. The ruins are near the village of Kokkoras north of the Alpheius, where are the remains of a Roman bath. The town was said to be frequently inundated.

MELAENAE   was, according to some, a fortified deme on the frontier of Attica and Boeotia, celebrated in Attic mythology as the place for which Melanthus and Xanthus fought. It was sometimes called Celaenae. Melanthus was one of the Neleidae and king of Messenia, from where he was driven out by the Heracleidae on their conquest of Peloponnesus. On the advice of a oracle Melanthus sought refuge in Attica. In a war between Attica and Boeotia, Xanthus, the Boeotian king, challenged Thymoetes, the king of Athens and the last of the Thesiadae, to single combat. Thymoetes declined the challenge because he was old and ailing. Melanthus agreed to stand in his place if he could be assured of winning the throne as a reward for victory. This was accomplished, and the reign of the Thesiadae ended. During the reign of Melanthus, the Ionians were expelled from Aegialus by the Achaeans and came to Athens as a place of refuge (Herod. 1.147, 5.65).

MELAMPHYLUS   was an earlier name of the island of SAMOS.

MELANEIS   was an earlier name of ERETRIA in Euboea.

MELANTII SCOPULI   some rocks in the Aegean Sea where Apollo appeared to the Argonauts, probably lay between Icaria and Myconos (Apollod. Rhod. 4.1707).

MELAS (MELAS)   is a river of Malis, which in the time of Herodotus (7.198) flowed into the Maliac Gulf

1 km from Trachis. It now empties into the Sperhios River after uniting its waters with the Gorgo. The Meliades, or Maliades, were nymphs of the district of Malis near Trachis (Soph. *Phil.* 715).

MELIBOEA (MELIVIA)   was an ancient town of Magnesia in Thessaly, mentioned by Homer (*Il.* 2.717) as one of the places subject to Philoctetes. Philoctetes, son of Pheas and Demonassa, was the most celebrated archer in the Trojan War. He led the warriors from Methone, Thaumacia, Meliboea, and Olizon against Troy in seven ships. On the voyage he was left behind by his men on the island of Lemnos because he was ill of a wound received from the bite of a snake. Medon, the son of Oileus and Rhene, undertook the command of his men (Hom. *Il.* 2.716).

Magnes was a son of Aeolus and Enarete. Some called his wife Meliboea and say that he named the town of Meliboea for her, just as he called the region of Magnesia after himself. Meliboea was situated upon the seacoast and is described by Livy (44.13) as situated at the roots of Mount Ossa and by Strabo (9.5.22) as lying between Ossa and Pelion. It has been placed at the village of Melivia.

MELINE   was a town in Argolis from which Aphrodite Melinaea derived her name (Lycoph. 403).

MELITAEA or MELITEIA (MELITEA)   was an ancient town of Phthiotis in Thessaly, located near the Enipeus River about 2 km from the town of Hellas (Strab. 9.5.6). The inhabitants of Melitaea affirmed that their town was anciently called Pyrrha, and they showed in the marketplace the tomb of Hellen, the son of Deucalion and Pyrrha. Others say Melitaea was built by Meliteus, son of Zeus by an Othreian nymph. He was exposed in a wood by his mother, fearing that Hera should discover the affair. But Zeus watched over him. He was reared by bees and survived. At length he was found by his step-brother Phagous, who took the boy and gave him the name of Meliteus, from his having been reared by bees. Some have identified Melitaea with ruins of an ancient fortress situated upon a hill on the left bank of the Enipeus, at the foot of which stands the small village of Melitea.

MELITE   was an Athenian deme of the tribe Cecropis located west of the Inner Cerameicus. The exact limits of this deme cannot be determined, but it appears to have given its name to the whole hilly district in the west of the Asty, comprising the Hill of the Nymphs, of the Pnyx, and of the Museion, and including within it the separate demes of Scambonidae and Collytus. Melite is said to have been named after a wife of Heracles and daughter of Myrmex. It was one of the most populous parts of the city and contained several temples as well as houses of distinguished men. In Melite were the Hephaesteion, the Eurysaceion, the Colonus Agoraeus, the temple of Heracles Alexicacus, the Melanippeion (in which Melanippus, the son of Theseus, was buried), and the temple of Athena Aristobula (built by Themistocles near his own house). Eurysaces, a son of Telamonian Ajax and Tecmessa, according to an Attic tradition, settled at Melite after he and his brother Philaeus had given up to the Athenians the island of Salamis. Eurysaces was honored like his father with an altar at Athens (Paus. 1.35.3).

MELITE was an earlier name of the island of SAMOTHRACE.

MELOS (MILOS) is the most southwesterly of the Cyclades and for this reason was sometimes called Zephyris. Other names were Memblis, Mimallis, Siphis, Acyton, and Byblis. Along with the other Cycladic islands it once was absorbed by the Cretan empire associated with Minos. Not far off Peloponnesus, it later became part of the Mycenaean civilization. Then after the Doric invasion it was colonized by Dorian Lacedaemonians. The island is roughly 21.5 km long by 13 wide and, apart from Mount Profitis Ilias (751 meters), is made up of low hills. Its welfare depends more on mining than agriculture.

The famous Venus de Milo came from here. So did the celebrated statue of Poseidon now in the National Museum of Athens. This was uncovered on the site of the sanctuary of Poseidon near the port. A sanctuary of Asclepius has been found, which yielded a head of the god now in the British Museum. In view of these world-famous discoveries, it is strange that no mythological stories are related in which Melos serves as a locale.

MELPEIA (KATO MELPIA) was a village in Arcadia, situated upon Mount Nomia, which is a portion of Mount Lycaeus, so called because Pan was said to have here discovered the melody (*melos*) of the syrinx (Paus. 8.38.11). The modern town Kato Melpia on the site of ancient Melpeia is in Messinia.

MEMBLIARUS was the original name of the island of ANAPHE.

MEMBLIS was another name for the island of MELOS.

MENDE (KALANDRA) was a town of Pallene situated on the southwest side of the cape (modern Kassandra). It was a colony of Eretria in Euboea, which became subject to Athens with the other cities of Pallene and Chalcidice. Together with Scione, Mende was located on the broadest part of the peninsula and its site is at Kalandra. Its coins depicted Silenus with a wine jar riding

upon an ass. These no doubt advertised the wine for which Mende was famous (Athen. 1.23,29, 4.129, 8.364, 9.784).

Protesilaus, according to some traditions, was not killed in the Trojan War but returned home, bringing with him Aethylla, a sister of Priam, who was his prisoner. When he landed on the peninsula of Pallene between Mende and Scione and had gone some distance from shore to fetch water, Aethylla persuaded the other women to set fire to the ships. Protesilaus, accordingly, was obliged to remain there and built the town of Scione.

MEROPE was an earlier name of the island of SIPHNOS.

MEROPIS was an earlier name of the island of COS.

MESATIS was a town between Antheia and Aroe in Achaia. When the Achaians had driven out the Ionians, Patreus, the son of Preugenes, the son of Agenor, forced the Achaians to leave Antheia and Mesatis and to settle in Aroe, which he later named Patrae. Dionysus derived his surname, Mesateus, from this town, where, according to a tradition at Patrae, the god had been reared (Paus. 7.18.4). Mesatis was apparently very close to Patrae.

MESEMBRIA (MESIMVRIA) was a Greek city of Thrace on the Aegean Sea and not far from the mouth of the Lissus River (Herod. 7.108). It has been excavated since 1966. A sanctuary of Cybele was discovered that has yielded all manner of artifacts illustrating the worship of the goddess, which was prominent in this area.

MESSA (MEZAPOS) was one of the nine cities of Laconia enumerated by Homer (*Il.* 2.502), who described it as "abounding in pigeons." Strabo (8.5.3) says that the position of Messa was unknown; but Pausanias (3.25.9) mentions a town and harbor named Messa, which is identified by most modern scholars with the Homeric town. This Messa, now Mezapos, is situated on the west coast of Mani, and the cliffs in the neighborhood are said to abound in wild pigeons.

MESSAPIUM is a mountain of Boeotia. It lies between Mount Hypatus and the Euripus River. It is connected with Mount Ptoum on the north by a ridge of hills. At its foot was the town Anthedon (Aeschyl. *Agam.* 293; Paus. 9.22.5). It was named for Messapus, who, when he came into Iapygia in Italy, called the country Messapia (Strab. 9.2.13).

MESSENE (ITHOMI) was the later capital of Messenia. Earlier the name had been applied to the country inhabited by the Messenians, but there was no city of this name before the one founded by Epaminondas. The foundation of the city was attended with great ceremony and the celebration of solemn sacrifices. First, sacrifices were offered to Epaminondas as founder, to Dionysus and Apollo Ismenius, by the Argives to the Argive Hera and Zeus Nemeius, by the Messenians to Zeus Ithomatas and the Dioscuri. Next, prayer was offered to the ancient heroes and heroines of the Messenian nation that their protecting spirits would dwell in the new city.

Messene was situated upon a rugged mountain, which rises between the two great Messenian plains and thus overlooks the whole country. This mountain has two summits—Ithome, the northern, and Eua, the southern. Mount Ithome is one of the most striking features in all Peloponnesus. Upon this summit the acropolis of Messene was built, but the lower city was located in a hollow on the west side of the ridge. The city was connected by a wall with its acropolis. There are considerable remains of the ancient city, and the walls may still be largely traced. Their circumference is about 10 km. Near the ancient town is the modern village of Mavromati. This village should not be confused with one of the same name near the city of Messini farther south, although newer maps appear to have changed the name of the Mavromati near Ithomi to Arsino.

In describing Messene, Pausanias first mentions the agora, which contained a fountain called Arsinoe. In the agora, probably in the center, was a statue of Zeus Soter. Structures surrounding the agora or nearby included: temples of Poseidon and Aphrodite; a marble statue of the mother of the gods, the work of Damophon, who also made the statue of Artemis Laphria; a temple of Eileithyia; a sacred building of the Curetes; and a sanctuary of Demeter, containing statues of the Dioscuri. But the temple of Asclepius contained the greatest number of statues, all of which were made by Damophon. The temple of Messene contained her statue in gold and Parian marble, while the back part was adorned with pictures representing the Messenian heroes and kings. A building called Hierosythion contained statues of all the gods worshipped by the Greeks. There was a gymnasium with monuments to historical heroes. On the summit was a temple of Zeus Ithomatas; and an annual festival called Ithomaea was celebrated in honor of the god (Paus. 4.31.6–4.33.2).

The walls of Messene are the best preserved in Greece. The sanctuary of Zeus Ithomatas is now covered by a monastery. On the slopes of Ithomi are the remains of the temple of Artemis Limnatis and a spring. Some identify the spring with the Clepsydra, but others make the claim for the spring in Arsino, which most likely accounts for its name change from Mavromati. Below Arsino is a sanctuary of Asclepius, long thought to be the agora, which still remains to be located. Connected to the sanctuary on the west side is a structure thought to be a small temple of Artemis Orthia.

MESSENIA (MESSINIA)   the southwest district of Peloponnesus, is bounded on the east by Laconia, on the north by Elis and Arcadia, and on the south and west by the sea. It is separated from Laconia by Mount Taygetus. Its southern frontier is made up of mountains that form the watershed of the rivers Neda, Pamisus, and Alpheius. On its south is the Messenian Gulf.

Messenia for the most part resembles Laconia. The Pamisus in Messenia, like the Eurotas in Laconia, flows through the entire length of the country from north to south. Of the smaller rivers the most important is the Nedon, flowing into the Messenian Gulf at Pherae (Kalamata). On it was a town of the same name and a temple of Athena Nedusia (Strab. 8.4.4). The most outstanding feature on the west coast is the bay of Pylos, now called Navarino, which is the best harbor in Peloponnesus.

The mountains include Ithome and Eira, which were natural fortresses in the upper plain, Elaeum, Aegaleum, Buphras, Tomeus, and Temathia. Four promontories are mentioned by name by ancient writers: Acritas, Coryphasium, Platamodes, and Cyparissium.

The earliest inhabitants of Messenia are said to have been Leleges. Polycaon, the younger son of Lelex, the king of Laconia, married the Argive Messene and took possession of the country, which he named after his wife. Messene was a daughter of Triopas, the son of Phorbas, the son of Lapithes, the son of Apollo and Stilbe. She induced Polycaon to take possession of the country. She also introduced there the worship of Zeus and the mysteries of the Great Goddess of Eleusis. In the town of Messene she was honored with a temple and heroic worship (Paus. 4.1.6). Polycaon built several towns, among them Andania, where he took up his residence as the first king of Messenia.

Five generations later, Aeolians came into the country under Perieres, a son of Aeolus. Perieres was the father of Aphareus and Leucippus by Gorgophone, the daughter of Perseus. Aphareus was married to Arene and had three sons, Idas, Lynceus, and Peisus. He was believed to have founded the town of Arene in Messenia, which he called after his wife. He received Neleus, son of Cretheus (or Poseidon), and Lycus, the son of Pandion, who had fled from their countries into his dominions. To Neleus he assigned a tract of land in Messenia, and from Lycus he and his family learned the orgies of the great gods (Paus. 4.2.6). Leucippus was prince of the Messenians and the father of Arsinoe, Phoebe, and Hilaeira. Two of these Leucippides, Phoebe and Hilaeira, were priestesses of Athena and Artemis and betrothed to their cousins, Idas and Lynceus. But the Dioscuri carried them off and married them (Apollod. 3.12.8,10.3). According to some, this was the occasion for the fatal battle between the Dioscuri and the Aphareidae (Ov. *Her.* 16.327, *Fast.* 5.709). The brothers also took part in the Calydonian hunt and in the expedition of the Argonauts.

Idas was married to Marpessa. Their daughter was called Alcyone. Idas had carried off Marpessa, the daughter of Euenus, with whom Apollo was also in love. Idas was assisted by Poseidon, who gave him a winged chariot. Euenus, who pursued him, could not overtake him, but Apollo found him in Messene and took the maiden from him. The two lovers fought for her possession, but Zeus intervened and left the decision with Marpessa. She chose Idas, realizing that Apollo would desert her when she grew old.

The usual story about the battle of Idas and Lynceus with the Dioscuri is as follows. Once they and the Dioscuri carried away a herd of oxen from Arcadia, and Idas was given the task of allotting the booty. He cut up a bull into four parts and declared that whichever of them should first succeed in eating his share should receive half the oxen, and the second should have the other half. This agreed upon, Idas proceeded to eat not only his own quarter but also that of his brother. Idas then drove the whole herd to his home in Messene (Pind. *Nem.* 10.60; Apollod. 3.11.2). The Dioscuri then invaded Messene, driving away the cattle of which they had been deprived and many more in addition. This became the occasion of a war between the Dioscuri and the Aphareidae, which was carried out in Messenia. In this war Castor, the mortal one of the twins, was killed by Idas, but Pollux slew Lynceus, and Zeus killed Idas with a flash of lightning. Idas and Lynceus were thought to be buried in Messenia. They were represented in a painting, together with their father Aphareus, in a temple in Messene. Idas alone was represented on the chest of Cypselus, in the act of leading Marpessa out of the temple of Apollo, who had abducted her (Paus. 5.18.2).

On the extinction of the family of Aphareus, the eastern half of Messenia was united with Laconia and came under the sovereignty of the Atreidae; the western half continued to belong to the kings of Pylos (Paus. 4.3.2). Of the seven cities that Agamemnon offered to Achilles in the *Iliad* (9.149), some were undoubtedly in Messenia; but as only two, Pherae and Cardamyle, retained their Homeric names in the historical age, the identity of the other five is uncertain.

The kings of Pylos sprang from Cretheus, the brother of Perieres. He married Tyro, the daughter of another brother, Salmoneus. Tyro by Poseidon bore twin sons, Pelias and Neleus. As stated above, Neleus had fled to Messenia and been assigned by Aphareus a tract of land in the western half. He founded Pylos. One account says that he became one of Heracles' lovers and received Messene from him. In any case, the Neleidae were well

established in Messenia at the time of the Trojan War. One remembers the story of Odysseus and his mission to Messenia to recover sheep stolen from Ithaca. On this trip he met with Iphitus, who gave him the famous bow of Eurytus. Machaon, a son of Asclepius, with his brother Podaleirius, led the men of Tricca, Ithome, and Oechalia to Troy in thirty ships, and he was killed there. His remains were carried to Messenia by Nestor. His tomb was believed to be at Gerenia, where a sanctuary was dedicated to him; in Machaon's sanctuary sick persons sought relief from their sufferings. It was there that Glaucus, son of Aepytus and king of Messenia, was believed to have first paid him heroic honors (Paus. 4.3.9). Nestor, of course, was prominent in the Trojan War, as was his son Antilochus, who upon reaching maturity joined his father at Troy and was killed there. The Neleidae continued through Perseptolis and Sillus, grandsons of Nestor.

With the conquest of Peloponnesus by the Dorians, a new epoch commenced in the history of Messenia. This country fell to the lot of Cresphontes, who is represented as driving the Neleidae out of Pylos and making himself master of the whole country. Cresphontes was the great-great grandson of Heracles. According to some, he divided Messenia into five parts, of which he made Stenyclarus the royal residence. In the other four towns he appointed viceroys and gave to the former inhabitants the same rights and privileges as the Dorian conquerors. The Dorians were not happy with this arrangement, and Cresphontes tried various means of resolving the difficulties inherent in dual populations. In spite of these concessions, the Dorians put Cresphontes and all his children to death, with the exception of Aepytus, who was then very young and was living with his grandfather Cypselus in Arcadia. The throne of Cresphontes was in the meantime occupied by the Heraclid Polyphontes, who also forced Merope, the wife of Cresphontes and mother of Aepytus, to become his wife (Apollod. 2.8.5). When Aepytus had grown to manhood, he returned to his kingdom, killed his father's murderers, and put Polyphontes to death with the help of Holca, his father-in-law. He left a son, Glaucus, and because of him the subsequent kings of Messenia were called Aepytidae instead of the more general name Heraclids (Paus. 4.3.8). Glaucus distinguished himself by his piety toward the gods and was, as already observed, the first who offered sacrifices to Machaon. The Aepytidae continued to reign in Stenyclarus till the sixth generation—their names after Glaucus being Isthmius, Dotadas, Sybotas, Phintas—when the first Messenian war with Sparta began.

A few gods and heroes are associated with Messenia: Caucon, Dryops, Thetis, and Zeus. Caucon was a son of Celaenus, who was believed to have carried the orgies of the Great Goddess from Eleusis to Messene, where he was worshipped as a hero. The Asinaeans in

Messenia worshipped Dryops as their ancestral hero and as a son of Apollo, and they celebrated a festival in honor of him every other year. His shrine was adorned with a very archaic statue of the hero (Paus. 4.34.6). Thetis, the mother of Achilles, was worshipped in Messenia (Paus. 3.22.2). And finally, the Messenians claimed that Zeus was born in their land (Paus. 4.33.1).

The principal towns of Messenia were: Andania, the capital of the Messenian kings before the Dorians; Oechalia, the reputed residence of Eurytus; Ampheia; Stenyclarus, the capital of the Dorian conquerors; Ira or Eira; Messene, with its citadel Ithome; Polichne; Dorium; Pherae on the left bank of the Nedon, the chief town in the plain; Abia, said to be the Homeric Ira; Calamae; Limnae; Corone and Asine, both on the Messenian Gulf; Methone, supposed to be the Homeric Pedasus; Erana; Cyparissia; and Pylos.

METAPONTIS   was an earlier name of the island of SYME.

METHANA (MEGALOHORI)   is a rocky peninsula connected by a narrow isthmus to the territory of Troezen in Argolis and containing a city of the same name. The highest mountain of the peninsula is volcanic Helona (743 meters), and there are hot sulfurous springs that were used in antiquity for medicinal purposes.

The Athenians took possession of the peninsula during the Peloponnesian War and fortified the isthmus. There are still traces of an ancient fortification. The capital lay on the west coast, and the ruins are near a small village called Megalohori, although a town about 5 km to the east is called Methana. Part of the walls of the acropolis and an ancient town on the north side still remain. Within the citadel stands a chapel containing stones that probably belonged to a temple of Isis. Pausanias (2.34.1) also speaks of statues of Hermes and Heracles in the agora.

METHONE (METHONI)   an ancient town in the southwest corner of Messenia, has always been an important place, both in ancient and in modern times, because of its excellent harbor. It is located at the extreme point of a rocky ridge that runs into the sea opposite the island of Sapienza. It is now occupied by a tower and lighthouse, which is connected by a bridge with the fortification of Methoni. According to most ancient writers (Strab. 8.4.1; Paus. 4.35.1), Methone was the Homeric Pedasus, one of the seven cities that Agamemnon offered to Achilles (Hom. *Il.* 9.294). Homer (*Il.* 9.152) gives to Pedasus the epithet "vine-clad," and Methone seems to have been celebrated in antiquity for the cultivation of the grape. The eponymous heroine Methone is called the daughter of Oeneus (Wine-Man),

and the same reference applies to the Oenussae Islands lying opposite the city.

Pausanias found at Methone a temple of Athena Anemotis (Storm-Stiller) and one of Artemis. Neither has been located. Like other places in Greece that have been continuously inhabited, Methone contains few ancient remains.

METHONE (PALEO ELEFTHEROHORIO/METHONI)   was a town of Pieria in Macedonia on the Thermaic Gulf, one of the earliest Greek colonies on this coast. It was named for Methon, a kinsman of Orpheus (Plut. *Quaest. Gr.* 11). Philoctetes, the celebrated archer of the Trojan War, led the warriors from Methone, Thaumacia, Meliboea, and Olizon against Troy in seven ships. Methone was also the name of Philoctetes' mother. The ruins of Methone are located between Paleo Eleftherohorio on the National Highway and Methoni on the coast.

METHYDRIUM (PIRGAKIO)   a town in central Arcadia, situated 31.5 km north of Megalopolis (Paus. 8.35.5), obtained its name, "a place between waters," from being situated on a height between the two rivers Maloctas and Mylaon. It was founded by Orchomenus, a son of Lycaon, who also founded the Arcadian Orchomenus (Apollod. 3.8.1; Paus. 8.3.3), but its inhabitants were relocated to Megalopolis when it was built. It never recovered its former population and is mentioned by Strabo (8.8.2) among the places of Arcadia that had almost entirely disappeared. It did exist as a village in the time of Pausanias, who saw there a temple of Poseidon Hippius upon the river Mylaon. He also mentions above the river Maloetas a mountain called Thaumasium, on the side of which was a cave where Rhea took refuge when pregnant with Zeus. At the distance of 5.5 km from Methydrium was a fountain called Nymphasia (Paus. 8.36.3).

The location of Methydrium is near Pirgakio, a small village just south of the Tripoli-Olympia highway, where the two rivers Nemnitza and Vourvoulistra meet. The Nymphasia fountain is likely the spring at Vitina, about 5.5 km from Pirgakio.

METHYMNA (MITHIMNA)   was the most important town in Lesbos after Mytilene. It was situated on the north shore of the island. The town derived its name from Methymna, a daughter of Macar, who was married to Lesbus (Diod. 5.81). The city of Methymna was a rival of Mytilene, but after the Peloponnesian War and its capture by the Lacedaemonians, it fell into decline. On the same spot at present stands the town of Mithimna (alternately called Molivos).

We have no information concerning the buildings of ancient Methymna. It evidently possessed a good harbor.

Its chief fame was connected with its excellent wine. Pausanias (10.19.3) tells a story of some fishermen of Methymna dragging in with their nets a rude image of Bacchus, which was afterward worshipped there. Dionysus Methymnaeus was a name derived from Methymna (Rich in Vines).

Methymna was the birthplace of Arion, the semilegendary poet and musician, who was rescued by dolphins when he was robbed by pirates and leapt overboard. Methymna was also the home of Peisidice, the daughter of a king, who out of love for Achilles opened to him the gates of her native city but was stoned to death at the command of Achilles by his soldiers.

METOPE   was another name for the STYMPHALUS River.

METROPOLIS (MITROPOLI)   was a town of the region Histeaeotis in Thessaly. Strabo (9.5.17) says that Metropolis was made up of three insignificant towns but that a larger number was afterward added, among which was Ithome. Metropolis was seldom mentioned in very early times. Its remains are placed at the village of Mitropoli about 9 km southwest of Karditsa. The poorly preserved city wall is about 5 km in circuit. Among sculptures found, there is one in low relief representing a draped figure seated upon a rock in the company of worshippers, one of whom holds a hog. It has been conjectured that the seated figure represents Aphrodite Castnietis, the chief goddess of the city, to whom, Strabo (9.5.17) says, hogs were offered in sacrifice.

MICRA SILILIA   was another name for the island of NAXOS.

MIDEA or MIDEIA (MIDEA)   an ancient city of Argolis, was originally called Persepolis and is mentioned by Apollodorus (2.4.4) in connection with Perseus, who is said to have founded the towns of Midea and Mycenae. It was said to have derived its name from the wife of Electryon and was celebrated as the home of Electryon and the birthplace of his daughter Alcmena (Paus. 2.25.9). Alcmena had ten brothers, who, with the exception of Licymnius, fell in a battle against the sons of Pterelaus, who had carried off the cattle of Electryon. Electryon, on setting out to avenge the deaths of his sons, left his kingdom and his daughter to Amphitryon, who unintentionally killed him. Sthenelus, the king of Mycenae, consequently expelled Amphitryon, who together with Alcmena and Licymnius went to Thebes. Alcmena derived the surname Mideatis from the town.

Midea is mentioned in the earliest division of the country, along with the Heraion and Tiryns, as belonging to Proetus (Paus. 2.16.2). It was the residence of Hippodameia in her banishment (Paus. 6.20.7). When

Atreus and Thyestes were persuaded by their mother, Hippodameia, to kill Chrysippus, their stepbrother, they had to flee, dreading the consequences of their deed. Sthenelus, king of Mycenae and husband of their sister Nicippe, invited them to come to Midea, which he assigned to them (Apollod. 2.4.6). When afterward Eurystheus, the son of Sthenelus, marched out against the Heracleidae, he entrusted the government of Mycenae to his uncle Atreus. It was from Midea that Pelops had the remains of Hippodameia conveyed, at the command of an oracle, to Olympia.

The ruins were long thought to be the same as those at Dendra, but the site is a few kilometers farther east, located atop a hill above the modern village of Midea.

MIEZA (LEFKADIA)   was a Macedonian city, which has been located near Lefkadia between Veria and Edessa. Some also make the claim for nearby Naoussa. Its founder was thought to be Mieza, a sister of Beroea and granddaughter of Macedon. Alexander the Great established an Aristotelian school at Mieza. The town was also famous for a stalactitic cavern (Plin. 31.2.20).

MIGONIUM   in or near the island of Cranae in Laconia, gave the surname Migonitis to Aphrodite, since she had a temple there (Paus. 3.2.1). (See GYTHIUM.)

MILETUS (MILATOS)   a town in Crete, was mentioned in the Homeric catalog (Hom. *Il.* 2.647). Idomeneus led the men from here, Cnossus, Gortys, Lyctus, Lycastus, Rhytium, and Phaestus to the Trojan War in eighty ships. The town was also the site of the story of the theft of the golden dog by Pandareos. He was a son of Merops of Miletus. He stole a golden dog, which Hephaestus had made, from the temple of Zeus and carried it to Tantalus. Zeus sent Hermes to Tantalus to recover the dog, but Tantalus said the dog was not in his possession. Zeus therefore took the animal by force and buried Tantalus under Mount Sipylus. Pandareos fled to Athens and then to Sicily, where he died with his wife Harmothoe. He had three daughters, Aedon, Merope, and Cleodora. Aedon married Zethus, brother of Amphion, but Merope and Cleodora were left orphans when their parents perished. They were adopted by the gods and cared for, until, once unattended, they were carried off by the Harpies (Hom. *Od.* 19.518, 20.67). Polygnotus painted them in the Lesche of Delphi (Paus. 10.30.1).

Miletus, which no longer existed in the time of Strabo (10.4.14), was looked upon by some writers as the mother-city of the Ionian colony of the same name (Apollod. 3.1.2,3). The site of the Homeric city has been explored. Its present site is Milatos, at which considerable remains of walls both of the acropolis and city are still to be seen.

MIMALLIS   was another name for the island of MELOS.

MINOA   was another name by which the island of PAROS was known.

MINTHA (MINTHI)   is a mountain in the Triphylian division of Elis. It rises to a height of 1,222 meters and is the highest mountain in Elis. It was one of the seats of the worship of Hades. It was named for Mintha or Mentha, the Cocythian nymph, beloved by Hades and changed by Persephone into a mint plant (Ov. *Met.* 10.729). According to others, she was changed into dust, from which Hades caused the mint plant to grow. The plant was sacred to Persephone. The mountain had at its foot a temple of Hades and a grove of Demeter.

MINYA   was a city of Thessaly said to have been formerly called Halmonia and to have derived its name from Minyas. It is mentioned by Pliny (4.8.15) under the name Almon and in conjunction with the Minyan Orchomenus in Thessaly.

    The Minyae were an ancient race in Greece, said to have been descended from Minyas, the son of Orchomenus, who originally lived in Thessaly and afterward migrated into Boeotia and founded Orchomenus. Most of the Argonautic heroes were Minyae; and some of them, having settled on the island of Lemnos, continued to be called Minyae. These Lemnian Minyae were driven out of the island by the Tyrrhenian Pelasgians and took refuge in Lacedaemon, from where some of them migrated to Thera and others to Triphylia in Elis (Herod. 4.145–48).

MINYEIUS   was the Homeric name for the ANIGRUS River in Triphylian Elis.

MOGLENA   was a later name of ALMOPIA.

MOLORCHIA   was a place near Nemea said to have been founded by Molorchus, a poor man of Cleonae, who hospitably received Heracles when he went out to slay the Nemean lion (Apollod. 2.5.1).

MOLOSSIA   was a part of EPEIRUS.

MOLYCREIUM, MOLYCREIA, or MOLYCRIA (VELVINA)   was a town of Aetolia situated near the seacoast and at a short distance from the promontory Antirrhium. It is identified by most scholars with the modern Velvina, which is about 10 km northwest of Nafpaktos. It is said by Strabo (10.2.6) to have been built after the return of the Heracleidae into Peloponnesus. It was considered sacred to Poseidon, and a temple uncovered there in 1924 may be a temple of the god, although inscriptions refer to Athena.

MYCALESSUS (RITSONA)   was an ancient town of Boeotia mentioned by Homer (*Il.* 2.498; *Hymn. Hom. ad Apoll.* 224). It was said to have been so called because the cow which was guiding Cadmus and his comrades to Thebes lowed (*emykesato*) in this place (Paus. 9.19.4). Strabo (9.2.11) calls Mycalessus a village in the territory of Tanagra and locates it upon the road from Thebes to Chalcis. In the time of Pausanias it had ceased to exist, but he saw its ruins on his way to Chalcis (Paus. 9.19.4). He also mentions a temple of Demeter Mycalessia standing in the territory of the city upon the seacoast and situated to the south of the Euripus. There are a few remains of walls at Ritsona. The temple of Demeter was probably a little north of Aulis.

MYCENAE (MIKINES)   is one of the most ancient towns in Greece and celebrated as the home of Agamemnon. It is situated at the northeast end of the plain of Argos on a rugged height, which is closed in on the east by two summits of a mountain range. It is described by Homer (*Od.* 3.263) as situated in a recess (*mycho*) overlooking the Argeian plain. Some later writers suggested that the origin of the name was the word *myces* (mushroom) since Perseus, during the founding of Mycenae, became thirsty and drank water that had collected in a mushroom cap. The ancients, however, derived the name from an eponymous heroine, Mycene, daughter of Inachus and wife of Arestor (Hom. *Od.* 2.120; Paus. 2.16.4). The position of Mycenae commanded the upper part of the great Argeian plain. The most important roads from the Corinthian Gulf, the roads from Phlius, Nemea, Cleonae, and those from Corinth united above Mycenae and passed by the city. It was said to have been built by Perseus (Strab. 8.6.19; Paus. 2.15.4,16.3), and its massive walls were believed to have been the work of the Cyclopes. It was the favorite residence of the Pelopidae, and under Agamemnon was regarded as the first city in Greece. Its greatness belongs only to the heroic age, and it ceased to be a place of importance after the return of the Heracleidae and the settlement of the Dorians in Argos, which then became the leading city in the plain.

    The mythological history of Mycenae was perhaps the most frequent subject of Greek drama, merging two famous lineages into the climax of the Trojan War and its vengeful aftermath. Perseus was the first king of Mycenae, having founded it and Midea after the death of Acrisius. At Argos he had successfully opposed the introduction of the Bacchic orgies (Paus. 2.20.3,22.1). As already stated, the walls of Mycenae were supposed to have been built by the Cyclopes.

    By Andromeda, Perseus became the father of Alcaeus, Sthenelus, Heleius, Mestor, Electryon, Gorgophone, and Autochthe. He was worshipped as a hero in Argos and Mycenae, as well as in Seriphos and Athens. He was succeeded by Electryon, who was married to Anaxo, the daughter of Alcaeus. By her Electryon had ten sons and a daughter, Alcmena, the mother of Heracles. While Electryon was reigning at Mycenae, the sons of Pterelaus, together with the Taphians, invaded his territory, demanded the surrender of the kingdom, and drove away his oxen. The sons of Electryon entered upon a battle with the sons of Pterelaus, but the combatants on both sides fell, so that Electryon had only one son, Licymnius, left, and Pterelaus likewise only one, Eueres. The Taphians, however, escaped with the oxen, which they entrusted to Polyxenus, king of the Eleans. From there they were afterward brought back to Mycenae by Amphitryon, the son of King Alcaeus of Troezen, after he had paid a ransom. Electryon now resolved upon avenging the death of his sons and to make war upon the Taphians. During his absence he entrusted his kingdom and his daughter Alcmena to Amphitryon on condition that he should not marry her till after his return from the war. Amphitryon now restored to Electryon the oxen he had brought back to Mycenae. One of the oxen turned wild, and as Amphitryon attempted to strike it with his club, he accidentally struck the head of Electryon and killed him on the spot. Sthenelus, the brother of Electryon, found this a great opportunity to dispose of Amphitryon, so he exiled him. Taking with him Alcmena and Licymnius, Amphitryon went to Thebes.

Sthenelus was married to Nicippe, the daughter of Pelops and therefore the sister of Atreus and Thyestes. Their son was Eurystheus, who imposed the labors on Heracles, notably those of bringing wild creatures like the Ceryneian stag, the Erymanthian boar, and the flesh-eating mares of Diomedes alive to Mycenae. Eurystheus employed Copreus to inform Heracles of the labors he had to perform (Hom. *Il.* 15.639); Apollod. 1.5.1). Copreus was a son of Pelops and father of Periphetes. After having murdered Iphitus, he fled from Elis to Mycenae. He is also called the herald of Eurystheus.

The curse that Myrtilus placed on the race of Pelops (see PISA) reached its culmination in the house of Atreus. Atreus was a son of Pelops and Hippodameia, a grandson of Tantalus, and a brother of Thyestes and Nicippe. He was first married to Cleola, by whom he became the father of Pleisthenes; then to Aerope, who was the mother of Agamemnon, Menelaus, and Anaxibia, either by Pleisthenes or by Atreus; and lastly to Pelopia, the daughter of his brother Thyestes. The story of Atreus begins with a crime, for he and his brother Thyestes were persuaded by their mother, Hippodameia, to kill their stepbrother Chrysippus, the son of Pelops and the nymph Axioche or Danais. Atreus and Thyestes then took to flight, dreading the consequences of their deed. Sthenelus, king of Mycenae, and husband of their sister Nicippe, invited them to come to Midea, which he assigned to them (Apollod. 2.4.6). Sthenelus died, and

his son Eurystheus became king. When he marched out against the Heracleidae, he left the government of Mycenae in the hands of his uncle Atreus. Eurystheus was killed in Attica, and Atreus became his successor in the kingdom of Mycenae.

From this moment, crimes and calamities followed one another in rapid succession in the house of Tantalus. Thyestes seduced Aerope, the wife of Atreus. For this crime Thyestes was driven from Mycenae by his brother; but from his place of exile he sent Pleisthenes, the son of Atreus, whom he had brought up as his own child, commanding him to kill Atreus. Atreus, however, killed the would-be assassin without knowing that it was his own son. When he learned the truth, he sought ways to take revenge. He feigned to be reconciled to Thyestes and invited him to Mycenae. When Thyestes accepted, Atreus killed the two sons of Thyestes, Tantalus and Pleisthenes, and had their flesh prepared and placed as a meal before Thyestes. After Thyestes had begun to eat, Atreus ordered the arms and bones of the children to be brought in, and Thyestes, struck with horror at the sight, cursed the house of Tantalus and fled. Even Helios, the sun, turned away his face from the grisly scene (Aeschyl. *Agam.* 1598). The kingdom of Atreus was now cursed with a famine, and an oracle advised Atreus to call back Thyestes. Atreus went in search of him and came to King Thesprotus. There he married his third wife, Pelopia, the daughter of Thyestes, whom Atreus believed to be the daughter of Thesprotus. Pelopia was at the time pregnant by her own father, and after having given birth to a boy, Aegisthus, she exposed him. The child, however, was found by shepherds and suckled by a goat, which caused him to be called Aegisthus. Later Atreus learned from Pelopia about the exposed child and looked for him in case he had survived. He found the boy and brought him up as his own son. In the night in which Pelopia had shared the bed of her father, she had taken from him his sword, which she afterward gave to Aegisthus. This sword became the means by which Pelopia discovered the incestuous intercourse between herself and her father, and she immediately killed herself. Atreus meanwhile sent Aegisthus to kill Thyestes, whom Agamemnon and Menelaus had fetched from Delphi and who was promptly imprisoned by Atreus. The sword that Aegisthus carried revealed, however, the father and son to each other. Aegisthus immediately became loyal to his real father and returned and slew his uncle Atreus, while he was offering a sacrifice on the seacoast. Aegisthus and his father now took over the kingdom as their due inheritance. They also exiled Agamemnon and Menelaus.

The two brothers wandered about for a time and at last came to Sparta, where Agamemnon married Clytemnestra, the daughter of Tyndareus. Some say she was married to Tantalus, son of Thyestes, whom Agamemnon killed to gain Clytemnestra (Paus. 2.22.3). By her he became the father of Iphigeneia, Chrysothemis, Electra, and Orestes. The manner in which Agamemnon came to the kingdom of Mycenae is differently related. From Homer (*Il.* 2.108), it appears as if he had peaceably succeeded Thyestes, while according to others (Aeschyl. *Agam.* 1605), he expelled Thyestes and usurped his throne. After he had become king of Mycenae, he rendered Sicyon and its king subject to himself (Paus. 2.7.1) and became the most powerful prince in Greece. When Homer (*Il.* 2.108) attributes to Agamemnon the sovereignty over all Argos, the name Argos here signifies Peloponnesus, or the greater part of it, for the city of Argos was governed by Diomedes.

When Helen, the wife of Menelaus, was carried off by Paris, the son of Priam, Agamemnon and Menelaus called upon all the Greek chiefs for assistance against Troy. The chiefs met at Argos in the palace of Diomedes, where Agamemnon was chosen their chief commander. After two years of preparation the Greeks assembled at Aulis. Here Agamemnon killed a stag sacred to Artemis and caused her to send a plague on the Greeks and further to hold their ships in port by producing a perfect calm. Seers said that Artemis could not be appeased unless Iphigeneia, Agamemnon's daughter, was sacrificed. When Agamemnon refused to sacrifice her, Odysseus went secretly to Mycenae and persuaded Clytemnestra to send Iphigeneia to Aulis by pretending that she was to be married to Achilles. She was sacrificed (or rescued by Artemis), and the Greeks were able to sail. Agamemnon alone had one hundred ships in addition to the sixty that he had lent to the Arcadians. Among Mycenaeans going to Troy were: Calchas, a son of Thestor of Mycenae, who was the wisest soothsayer among the Greeks at Troy; Eurymedon, a son of Ptolemaeus and charioteer of Agamemnon, whose tomb was shown at Mycenae in later years (Hom. *Il.* 4.228; Paus. 2.16.6); Ptolemaeus, his father, son of Peiraeas, who went along also as charioteer to Agamemnon; Periphetes, son of Copreus; and Demodocus, the famous bard of the *Odyssey.* Although Demodocus was described as a Laconian, he had followed Agamemnon to Mycenae after winning the prize at the Pythian games. Euphorbus was also connected with Mycenae. A son of Panthous, he was one of the bravest among the Trojans. He was slain by Menelaus, who subsequently dedicated the shield of Euphorbus in the temple of Hera near Mycenae (Paus. 2.17.3). It is a well-known story that Pythagoras asserted that he had once been the Trojan Euphorbus, that from a Trojan he had become an Ionian, and from a warrior a philosopher (Philostr. *Vit. Apoll.* 1.1).

The story of Telephus can also be repeated here. He was a son of Heracles and married to Astyoche, daughter of Priam of Troy. At the beginning of the Trojan War he was discovered to be a Greek and his aid was enlisted to become allied against Troy. He refused because of his wife and was wounded in a scuffle with Achilles. The wound would not heal, and an oracle said that only the one who wounded him could heal him. Telephus sought Agamemnon's help but had to threaten to kill the infant Orestes before he received help. The Greeks meanwhile received an oracle that without the aid of Telephus they could not reach Troy, so it was not difficult to persuade them to do as he asked. Achilles cured Telephus by means of the rust of the spear by which the wound had been inflicted. Telephus in return pointed out to the Greeks the road which they had to take (Ov. *Met.* 12.112, *Trist.* 5.2,15).

At the taking of Troy Agamemnon received Cassandra, the daughter of Priam, as his prize, by whom, according to some, he had two sons, Teledamas and Pelops. He came back and landed in Argolis, the dominion of Aegisthus, who had seduced Clytemnestra during the absence of her husband. In order not to be surprised by the return of Agamemnon, he sent out spies, and when Agamemnon came, Aegisthus invited him to a repast and had him and his companions treacherously murdered during the feast (Hom. *Od.* 4.524). Clytemnestra at the same time murdered Cassandra. The tragic poets have variously modified the story of the murder of Agamemnon. Aeschylus (*Agam.* 1492) makes Clytemnestra alone murder Agamemnon; she threw a net over him while he was in the bath and stabbed him with three strokes. Her motive is partly her jealousy of Cassandra and partly her adulterous life with Aegisthus. According to some, Aegisthus committed the murder with the assistance of Clytemnestra. Euripides (*Orest.* 26) mentions a garment that Clytemnestra threw over him instead of a net, and both Sophocles (*Elect.* 530) and Euripides represent the sacrifice of Iphigeneia as the cause for which Clytemnestra murdered him. After the deaths of Agamemnon and Cassandra, their two sons were murdered upon their tomb by Aegisthus (Paus. 2.16.7). Agamemnon was represented on the pedestal of the Rhamnusian Nemesis (Paus. 1.33.8), on the chest of Cypselus, and he was painted in the Lesche of Delphi by Polygnotus (Paus. 10.25.2). Menelaus erected a monument in honor of his brother on the Aegyptus River (Hom. *Od.* 4.584). Pausanias (2.16.6) states that in his time a monument of Agamemnon was still extant at Mycenae. Cassandra's tomb was either at Amyclae or Mycenae (Paus. 2.16.5), for the two towns disputed the possession of it. After the murder of Agamemnon, Aegisthus reigned seven years longer over Mycenae until in the eighth year Orestes, the son of Agamemnon, returned home and avenged the death of his father by putting the adulterers to death (Hom. *Od.* 1.28). Aletes, the son of Aegisthus, assumed the government of Mycenae after the false report that Orestes and Pylades had been sacrificed to Artemis at

Tauris. When Orestes, Iphigeneia, and Electra were reunited at Delphi, they returned to Mycenae, where Orestes killed Aletes and Electra married Pylades (Apollod. 3.10.6).

According to the Homeric account, Agamemnon on his return from Troy was murdered by Aegisthus and Clytemnestra before he had a chance to see Orestes (Hom. *Od.* 11.542). It is said that Orestes was supposed to have been killed along with Agamemnon. But Electra secretly entrusted her brother to the slave who was responsible for him. This slave carried him to Strophius, king in Phocis, who was married to Anaxibia, the sister of Agamemnon. According to some, Orestes was saved by his nurse Geilissa (Aeschyl. *Choeph.* 732) or by Arsinoe or Laodameia (Pind. *Pyth.* 11.25), who allowed Aegisthus to kill her own child in the belief that it was Orestes. In the house of Strophius, Orestes grew up together with the king's son Pylades, with whom he formed a close and intimate friendship (Eurip. *Orest.* 804). While in Phocis he received messages from the vengeful Electra, urging him to avenge his father's death. He consulted the oracle of Delphi and was instructed to carry out the plan for revenge. He therefore went to Argos. He pretended to be a messenger of Strophius, who had come to announce the death of Orestes and brought the ashes of the "deceased." After having visited his father's tomb, upon which he sacrificed a lock of his hair, he revealed himself to Electra, who had been abused by Aegisthus and Clytemnestra. Thus, in the eighth year after his father's murder, Orestes killed the murderers and attended their burial ceremonies. For the revenge he took he gained great fame.

Orestes also gained the wrath of the Erinyes for his act of matricide. Immediately after the murder of his mother he was seized with madness and took to flight. According to Euripides, Orestes not only became mad, but since the Argives in their anger wanted to stone him and Electra to death and since Menelaus refused to save them, Pylades and Orestes murdered Helen, and her body was removed by the gods. Orestes also threatened to kill Hermione, the daughter of Menelaus and his own intended bride. But Apollo intervened, and Orestes betrothed himself to Hermione and Pylades to Electra. But according to the common account, Orestes fled from land to land, pursued by the Erinyes. On the advice of Apollo, he took refuge with Athena at Athens. The goddess offered him protection and appointed the court of the Areiopagus to decide his fate. The Erinyes brought forward their accusation, and Orestes made the command of the Delphic oracle his excuse. When the court voted and was equally divided, Orestes was acquitted by the command of Athena. He therefore dedicated an altar to Athena Areia (Paus. 1.28.5). According to another version of the legend, Orestes begged Apollo to deliver him from

his madness and incessant wandering. The god advised him to go to Tauris in Scythia in order to bring back to Athens the image of Artemis believed to have fallen there from heaven. Orestes and Pylades accordingly went to Tauris where Thoas was king, and on their arrival they were seized by the natives in order to be sacrificed to Artemis, according to the custom of the country. But Iphigeneia, the priestess of Artemis, was the sister of Orestes, and, after having recognized each other, all three escaped with the statue of the goddess (Eurip. *Iphig. Taur.* 800,1327). According to some writers, she had been rescued by Artemis from being sacrificed at Aulis and carried to Tauris, where she became a priestess of the goddess. She is said to have died at Brauron in Attica where she was still a priestess.

After his return, Orestes took possession of his father's kingdom at Mycenae, which had been usurped by Aletes; and when Cylarabes of Argos died without leaving any heir, Orestes also became king of Argos. The Lacedaemonians of their own accord made him their king because they preferred him, the grandson of Tyndareus, to Nicostratus and Megapenthes, the sons of Menelaus by a slave. The Arcadians and Phocians increased his power by allying themselves with him (Paus. 2.18.5, 3.1.4). He married Hermione and became by her the father of Tisamenus (Paus. 2.18.6). In his reign the Dorians under Hyllus are said to have invaded Peloponnesus (Paus. 8.5.1). He died of the bite of a snake in Arcadia, and his body, in accordance with an oracle, was afterward carried from Tegea to Sparta. Electra married Pylades and became by him the mother of Medon, Hellanicus, and Strophius. Her tomb was shown in later times at Mycenae (Paus. 2.16.7).

The religion of Mycenae was much the same as that at Argos and Tiryns. Mycenae was one of Hera's favorite places on earth. Her most celebrated sanctuary was situated between Argos and Mycenae at the foot of Mount Euboea. The vestibule of the temple contained ancient statues of the Charites, the bed of Hera, and the shield of Euphorbus. The sitting colossal chryselephantine statue of Hera in this temple was the work of Polycletus. She wore a crown on her head adorned with the Charites and Horae; in one hand she had a pomegranate, and in the other a scepter headed with a cuckoo (Paus. 2.17,22). Acraea was a daughter of the river-god Asterion near Mycenae, who together with her sisters Euboea and Prosymna acted as nurses to Hera. Acraea, a hill opposite the temple of Hera, derived its name from her (Paus. 2.17.2). Hera Acraea thus received her surname from this hill. Of the statues of Hera that Pausanias saw in the Heraion the most ancient was one made of the wild pear tree, which Peirasus, the son of Argus, was said to have dedicated at Tiryns and which the Argives, when they took that city, transferred to the Heraion (Paus. 2.17.5).

Apollo Agyieus, protector of the streets and public places, was worshipped at Mycenae (Paus. 2.19.8). So was Demeter Mysia, who had a temple between Argos and Mycenae. Demeter's surname is said to have been derived from an Argive Mysius, who received her kindly during her wanderings and built a sanctuary to her (Paus. 2.18.3).

Pausanias visited the ruins and mentioned the Lion Gate, the fountain Perseia, and "subterranean buildings" of Atreus and his sons, which he called treasuries. He mentioned tombs of Atreus, of his charioteer Eurymedon, of Electra, and a sepulcher in common of Teledamas and Pelops, who are said to have been twin sons of Cassandra. But, he said, Clytemnestra and Aegisthus were buried outside the walls, being thought unworthy of burial where Agamemnon lay (Paus. 2.16.5–7).

From the village of Mikines the road to the acropolis of Mycenae runs 2 km, overlooking the ravine of Havos, or Chaos. It passes the Treasury of Atreus, or Tomb of Agamemnon, the largest and best preserved of the tholos tombs, dating to about 1300 B.C. "A connection with Atreus (if the Atreids are indeed historical) is less impossible than has previously been thought: a date of 1300 is only two generations before the most likely date of the Trojan War, and Atreus is said to have been Agamemnon's father. If the tomb was a family vault, there is at least a chance that it was the veritable tomb of Agamemnon" (Rossiter, Stuart. *Greece*. London: Benn, 1977, p. 264). The tholos is a circular, domed chamber 13 meters high and 14.5 meters in diameter, formed by blocks in thirty-three concentric courses without mortar and gradually diminishing in height. The single block, the keystone, which constituted the final course could be removed, and this is how these so-called "beehive" tombs were entered by grave robbers.

Beyond Grave Circle B are two other tholos tombs. One is known as the Tomb of Clytemnestra and was partially excavated by Sophie Schliemann in 1876. The so-called Tomb of Aegisthus, which lay east of that of Clytemnestra, was excavated by the British School in 1922.

The road now reaches the acropolis built on a triangular hill. The walls are thick and mostly Cyclopean. The famous Lion Gate was overlooked by a tower, which faced the unshielded side of anyone who approached. Inside the gate to the right is Grave Circle A, the Royal Cemetery. This is probably the location pointed out to Pausanias as the graves of Agamemnon and his companions. It was Schliemann's sincere belief that what he had found was in fact the grave of all those who on their return from Troy were murdered by Aegisthus. The belief was fortified by the contents of Grave III, in which were found skeletons of two infants wrapped in sheets of gold together with the remains of three women. Schliemann

decided that these were Cassandra with her two servants and the twins that she had borne to Agamemnon.

The palace itself contains no mythological allusions except for a small room with a red stucco bath, which is pointed out as the place of Agamemnon's murder. Of special interest to the modern visitor is the secret cistern approached by a passage through the wall and descending stairs. As at Tiryns, it was the source of water in case of siege.

MYCENAE   was a town in Crete, the foundation of which was attributed to Agamemnon. Some have taken this name to be a misreading of Myrina, which was mentioned as a city in Pliny (4.12.59).

MYCHUS   was the port of ancient BULIS.

MYCONOS (MIKONOS)   is a small island, one of the Cyclades, in the Aegean Sea, lying east of Delos and north of Naxos. Myconos is about 16.5 km in length and 10 in its greatest width. It is in most parts a barren rock. The rocks of Myconos are granite, and the landscape is strewn with immense blocks of this stone. This probably gave rise to the fable that the giants subdued by Heracles lay under Myconos. The tomb of the Locrian Ajax was also shown at Myconos.

Myconos was colonized from Athens by the Neleid Hippocles. Ancient writers said that the inhabitants lost their hair at an early age. The inhabitants also had a bad reputation because of their avarice and meanness (Athen. 1.8).

Two cities were mentioned by ancient writers. One was Myconos, which occupied the site of the modern town, where scarcely any ancient ruins remain. Although a second city was referred to, it was never named, and its location is unknown. Very few remains of antiquity have been found in any part of the island.

MYONIA or MYON (AGIA EVTHIMIA)   a town of the Locri Ozolae, was situated on a pass leading from Aetolia into Locris. Pausanias (10.38.8) describes it as a small town situated on a hill about 5.5 km from Amphissa, containing a grove and an altar of the gods called Meilichii and above the town a temple of Poseidon. The Meilichii were certain divinities who were placated with nocturnal sacrifices. The site of Myonia is Agia Evthimia, a small village between Amfissa and Galaxidi containing remains of walls and towers.

MYRINA (MIRINA)   a town on Lemnos, stood on the west side of the island. On its peninsula stands the modern Mirina, which is still the chief town of the island. It contains about 3,700 inhabitants and has a good port. Myrina was a daughter of Cretheus and the wife of Thoas, and the town is said to have received its name from her.

Others say the name came from Myrina, an Amazon (Strab. 12.8.6).

MYRRHINUS (MERENDA)   a deme of Attica, lay to the east of Prasiae, now Porto Rafti, at Merenda, as it appears from inscriptions found at this place. Merenda is about 3 km southeast of Markopoulo. Artemis Colaenis was worshipped at Myrrhinus (Paus. 1.31.4). Her surname was derived from a mythical king, Colaenus, who was believed to have reigned even before the time of Cecrops (Paus. 1.31.5).

MYRSINUS   was the Homeric name for MYRTUNTIUM.

MYRTOAN SEA (MIRTOO PELAGOS)   is the part of the Aegean south of Euboea, Attica, and Argolis, which derived its name from the small island Myrtus, though others suppose it to come from Myrtilus, whom Pelops threw into this sea or from the maiden Myrto (Paus. 8.14.11; Apollon. Rhod. 1.752). Myrtilus, son of Hermes, was the charioteer of Oenomaus of Elis, and, having betrayed his master, he expected to be rewarded by Pelops, whom he helped in winning Hippodameia. Instead he was thrown into the sea by Pelops near Geraestus in Euboea. At the moment he expired he pronounced a curse upon the house of Pelops. Hermes placed him among the stars as Auriga. His tomb was shown at Pheneus behind the temple of Hermes, where the waves were believed to have washed his body on the coast. There he was also worshipped as a hero and honored with nocturnal sacrifices (Paus. 8.14.11). (See PISA.)

Pliny (4.11.18) makes the Myrtoan Sea a part of the Aegean; but others distinguish between the two, representing the Aegean as terminating at the promontory Sunium in Attica.

MYRTUNTIUM   was called Myrsinus by Homer (*Il.* 2.615), who mentions it among the towns of the Epeii. The men of Myrsinus, along with those of Hyrmine, Olen, Alesium, Elis, and Buprasium followed four leaders to the Trojan War in ten ships. Myrtuntium is described as situated on the road from the city of Elis to Dyme in Achaia at the distance of 13 km from Elis and near the sea. Its location is not known.

MYTILENE (MITILINI)   was—and remains—the most important city on the island of Lesbos. One reason for the continued preeminence of Mytilene is to be found in its location. Its harbors appear to have been excellent. Originally it was built upon a small island, and thus two harbors were formed, one on the north and the other on the south. The former was a harbor for ships of war, and the latter was the mercantile harbor.

The ancient city was quite beautiful, and its fortifications were strong. It is one of the few cities of the Aegean that have continued without lapse in importance up to the present day. In ancient times it was especially famous as a center for exporting wine. In view of the fame of Lesbian wine, an interesting law was in effect at Mytilene. It held that offenses committed by the drunk should be more severely punished than those committed by the sober (Arist. *Pol.* 2.9.9).

Mytilene was believed to have received its name from Mytilene, a daughter of Macar or Pelops, who became by Poseidon the mother of Myton. Others think it might have been named for her son. Still others derive it from an individual named Mytilus.

An interesting story comes from Mytilene. Phaon was the celebrated favorite of the poetess Sappho. He was a boatman at Mytilene and already old and of ugly appearance; but on one occasion he very willingly, and without accepting payment, carried Aphrodite across the sea, for which the goddess gave him youth and beauty. After this Sappho is said to have fallen in love with him (Aelian. *V.H.* 12.18; Lucian *Dial. Mort.* 9).

NARYCUS, NARYX, or NARYCIUM (RENGINIO)   a town of the Locri Opuntii, was the reputed birthplace of Ajax. Ajax, the son of Oileus, king of the Locrians, and Eriopis, is also called the Lesser Ajax (Hom. *Il.* 2.527). He led his Locrians in forty ships against Troy. He is described as one of the great heroes among the Greeks and acts frequently in conjunction with Telamonian Ajax. He is small of stature and wears a linen cuirass, but is brave and intrepid, especially skilled in throwing the spear, and, next to Achilles, the most swift-footed among all the Greeks. The Locri Opuntii worshipped Ajax as their national hero, and so great was their faith in him that when they drew up their army in battle array, they always left one place open for him, believing that, although invisible to them, he was fighting for and among them.

Narycus was near the border of Phocis (Diod. 14.82) with an outlet to the sea at Thronium. It commanded the route from the north to central Greece. There are remains of Hellenic walls at the town of Renginio, where Narycus was located.

NAUBOLEIS   was a more ancient name of DRYMAEA.

NAUPACTUS (NAFPAKTOS)   an important town of the Locri Ozolae and the best harbor on the north coast of the Corinthian Gulf, was situated just within the entrance of this gulf, a little east of the promontory of Antirrhium. It is said to have derived its name from the Heracleidae having here built the fleet with which they crossed over to Peloponnesus (Strab. 9.4.7; Paus. 10.38.10; Apollod. 2.8.2).

Hippotes was a son of Phylas and a great-grandson of Heracles. When the Heracleidae, during their invasion of Peloponnesus, were encamped near Naupactus, Hippotes killed the seer Carnus. In consequence of this the army of the Heracleidae began to suffer very severely, and Hippotes by the command of an oracle was banished for a period of ten years (Apollod. 2.8.3; Paus. 3.13.4).

Aristodemus, a son of Aristomachus and a descendant of Heracles, was married to Argeia, by whom he became the father of Eurysthenes and Procles. According to some traditions he was killed at Naupactus by a flash of lightning, just as he was setting out on his expedition into Peloponnesus (Apollod. 2.8.2), or by an arrow of Apollo because he had consulted Heracles instead of the Delphic oracle about the return of the Heracleidae (Paus. 3.1.6).

Although Naupactus owed its historical importance to its harbor at the entrance of the Corinthian Gulf, it was probably originally chosen as a site for a city because of its protecting hill, fertile plain, and abundant supply of water. Pausanias (10.38.12,13) saw at Naupactus a temple of Artemis, a cave sacred to Aphrodite, a temple of Poseidon, and the ruins of a temple of Asclepius. At the Kefalovrisi Spring about 1 km east of Nafpaktos is a terrace that was the site of a sanctuary of Asclepius. A number of inscriptions have been found, but no remains of an actual temple. Artemis Aetole was worshipped at Naupactus. In her temple was a statue of white marble representing her in the act of throwing a javelin (Paus. 10.38.12). There is modern evidence that Dionysus also had a cult here. The classical remains were unfortunately incorporated into later buildings and fortifications.

NAUPLIA (NAFPLIO)   the port of Argos, was situated upon a rocky peninsula, connected with the mainland by a narrow isthmus. It was a very ancient place and is said to have derived its name from Nauplius, the son of Poseidon and Amymone. He was a famous navigator and father of Proetus and Damastor. He is the reputed founder of the town of Nauplia. He is also said to have discovered the constellation of the Great Bear. Pausanias (4.35.2) tells us that the Nauplians were Egyptians belonging to the colony that Danaus brought to Argos. At the time of Pausanias, Nauplia was deserted. He noticed the ruins of the walls of a temple of Poseidon, certain forts, and a fountain named Canathus, by washing in which Hera was said to have renewed her virginity every year (Paus. 2.38.2). Palamedes, for whom the citadel was probably named, was a son of Nauplius but not the one described above. The ancient acropolis was most likely on the Kale rock, which faces the Palamedi.

NAXOS (NAXOS)   the largest and most fertile of the Cyclades, is situated in the middle of the Aegean Sea about halfway between mainland Greece and Asia Minor. It lies east of Paros, from which it is separated by a channel about 10 km wide. It is about 31.5 km in length and 25 in breadth at its widest part. It had several other names in ancient times. It was called Strongyle from its round shape, Dionysias from its excellent wine and its consequent connection with the worship of Dionysus, and Micra Sililia from the fertility of its soil (Plin. 4.12.22; Diod. 5.50–52); but the poets often gave it the name Dia. It is said to have been originally inhabited by Thracians and then by Carians, and to have derived its name from Naxus, the Carian chieftain, son of Polemo and father of Leucippus (Diod. 5.50,51). Leucippus became king of Naxos and was the father of Smerdius.

In historical times Naxos was colonized by Ionians from Attica (Herod. 8.46) and eventually became the most powerful of the Cyclades. The ancient capital of the island, also called Naxos, was situated upon the northwest coast. Its site is occupied by the modern capital. On a small, detached rock, called Palati, about 45.5 meters in front of the harbor, are the ruins of a temple, which tradition calls a temple of Dionysus but which probably was dedicated to Apollo. It consists of three huge marble slabs, two perpendicular and one laid across.

In the center of the island a mountain, now called Zia, rises to the height of 914 meters. From its summit twenty-two islands may be counted; and in the distance may be seen the outline of the mountains of Asia Minor. This mountain appears to have been called Drius in antiquity (Diod. 5.51); its modern name is probably derived from the ancient name of the island—Dia. Another mountain is called Korono, which reminds one of the Naxian nymph Coronis, who brought up the young Dionysus (Diod. 5.52).

The fertility of Naxos has been equally celebrated in ancient and modern times. Herodotus (5.28) says that it excelled all other islands in prosperity. In keeping with the excellence of its wine, Naxos was celebrated in the legends of Dionysus, particularly those relating to Ariadne.

One of the most remarkable curiosities in the island is an unfinished colossal figure, still lying in an ancient marble quarry near the north end of the island. It is about ten meters in length and has always been called by the inhabitants a figure of Apollo. It is more likely to represent Dionysus. On the side of the hill, at a short distance from the statue we still find the inscription "Boundary of Apollo's sacred territory." It has been conjectured that the statue may have been intended as a dedicatory offering to Delos.

Naxos, among other places, was mentioned as the birthplace of Dionysus. The nymphs Philia, Coronis, and Cleis in Naxos are said to have been his nurses. The orgiastic worship of the god seems to have been first established in Thrace and to have from there spread southward to Mounts Helicon and Parnassus, to Thebes,

Naxos, and throughout Greece. Dionysus Meilichius (God Who Can Be Propitiated, or the Gracious) was known here (Athen. 3.78). One of the stories concerning Dionysus tells of his abduction from Naxos. Acoetes was the son of a poor fisherman in Maeonia, who served as a pilot in a ship. After landing at Naxos, some of the sailors brought with them on board a beautiful sleeping boy, whom they found on the island and whom they wished to take with them. But Acoetes, who recognized the boy as the god Dionysus, tried in vain to dissuade them. When the ship had reached the open sea, the boy awoke and wanted to be carried back to Naxos. The sailors refused. At that moment vines began to twine around the vessel, tigers appeared, and the sailors, seized with madness, jumped into the sea and were changed into dolphins. Acoetes alone was saved and conveyed back to Naxos, where he was initiated in the Bacchic mysteries and became a priest of the god. Some writers called the crew of the ship Tyrrhenian pirates.

Poseidon is said to have disputed possession of Naxos with Dionysus (Plut. *Quaest. Conviv.* 9.6). But the sovereignty of the younger god is manifest in another story. Butes was a son of Boreas, a Thracian, who was hostile toward his stepbrother Lycurgus, and therefore compelled his father to emigrate. He accordingly went with a band of colonists to the island of Strongyle, afterward called Naxos. But as he and his companions had no women, they made predatory excursions and came to Thessaly, where they carried off the women who were just celebrating a festival of Dionysus. Butes himself took Coronis; but she invoked Dionysus, who struck Butes with madness so that he threw himself into a well (Diod. 5.50). Earlier, these pirates had made another raid into Phthiotian Achaia. They carried off from Mount Drius the women who were solemnizing a festival of Dionysus. Among them was Iphimedeia and her daughter Pancratis by Aloeus. They were carried to Naxos. Here King Agassamenus made Pancratis his wife after the two chiefs of the pirates, Sicelus and Hecetorus (or Scellis and Cassamenes), who were likewise in love with her, had killed each other. Otus and Ephialtes, the brothers of Pancratis, in the meantime came to Naxos to liberate their mother and sister. They gained the victory, but Pancratis died (Diod. 5.50). The Aloeidae also died here. Ephialtes had sued for the hand of Hera and Otus for that of Artemis. In Naxos Artemis appeared to them in the form of a stag and ran between the two brothers, who, both aiming at the animal at the same time, shot each other dead. Another story has them fetching back their mother and sister from Naxos and then returning to settle there and rule over the Thracians. However, they killed each other in a dispute that had arisen between them. They were worshipped as heroes by the Naxians.

The most well-known connection of Dionysus with Naxos comes, however, with the story of Ariadne. She was the daughter of Minos who fell in love with Theseus and helped him destroy the Minotaur and escape from the labyrinth. Theseus, in turn, promised to marry her, and she accordingly left Crete with him; but when they arrived on the island of Naxos, she was killed there by Artemis (Hom. *Od.* 11.324) at the instigation of Dionysus because he was indignant at the profanation of his grotto by the lovemaking of Theseus and Ariadne. In this case Ariadne was probably killed by Artemis at the moment she gave birth to her twin children, for she is said to have had two sons by Theseus, Oenopion and Staphylus. The more common tradition, however, was that Theseus left Ariadne on Naxos alive. But here the statements again differ, for some relate that he was forced by Dionysus to leave her (Diod. 4.61, 5.51; Paus. 10.29.3), and that in his grief he forgot to taken down the black sail that occasioned the death of his father. According to others, Theseus faithlessly forsook her on the island, and different motives are given for this act of faithlessness (Plut. *Thes.* 20; Ov. *Met.* 175, *Her.* 10). According to this tradition, Ariadne put an end to her own life in despair, or was saved by Dionysus, who in amazement at her beauty made her his wife, raised her among the immortals, and placed the crown he gave her as a marriage gift among the stars. According to some writers she became by Dionysus the mother of Oenopion, Thoas, Staphylus, Latromis, Euanthes, and Tauropolis.

NEAE (AGIOS EFSTRATIOS)   was a small island near Lemnos, on which Philoctetes, according to some writers, was bitten by a water snake. Pliny (2.87.89) places it between Lemnos and the Hellespont, but it is probably Agios Efstratios, which lies south of Lemnos.

NEAPOLIS (KAVALA)   was a coastal city, a colony of Thasos, on the same site as modern Kavala. It commanded a strategic position, through which led the coastal pass that joined Asia and Europe. The remains of Neapolis are few. The walls of the ancient city were built of granite blocks and are still visible on the north side of the Kavala peninsula. There was a sanctuary of the patron goddess, probably Artemis Tauropolis or Bendis, the Thracian version of Artemis. Some remains from it have been uncovered. Some columns of a later temple built on the site are in the Kavala Museum.

NECROMANTEION (See EPHYRA)

NEDA (NEDAS)   a river of Peloponnesus, rises in Mount Cerausium, a branch of Mount Lycaeus in Arcadia, and flows in a westerly direction past Phigalia, first forming the boundary between Arcadia and Messenia and afterward between Elis and Messenia. It empties into the

Ionian Sea and near its mouth is navigable for small boats. Neda was an Arcadian nymph, from whom the river Neda and also a town derived their name. She was believed, together with Theisoa and Hagno, to have nursed the infant Zeus (Callim. *Hymn. in Jov.* 38; Paus. 8.38.3). In a Messenian tradition Neda and Ithome were called nurses of Zeus (Paus. 4.33.1). She was represented at Tegea in the temple of Athena Alea (Paus. 8.47.2).

NEDON (KALAMATA)   is a river of Messenia, not to be confused with the Neda River. It flows into the Messenian Gulf east of the Pamisus at Pherae. It rises in the mountains on the boundary of Laconia and Messenia and is now called the river of Kalamata. On it there was a town of the same name and also a temple of Athena Nedusia (Strab. 8.4.4), who derived her surname from this river.

NEMEA (NEMEA)   is the name of a valley in the territory of Cleonae, where Heracles slew the Nemean lion and where the Nemean games were celebrated every other year. It is described by Strabo (8.6.19) as situated between Cleonae and Phlius. Nemea was a daughter of Asopus and gave her name to this region (Paus. 2.15.3). The valley lies in a direction nearly north and south and is about 4 or 5 km long and about 1.25 km wide. It is encircled by mountains. There is a remarkable mountain on the northeast, called in ancient times Apesas, now Fokas, nearly 914 meters high, with a flat summit visible from both Argos and Corinth. On this mountain Perseus is said to have first sacrificed to Zeus Apesantius (Paus. 2.15.4). The Nemea River, fed by several tributaries, earned for the plain the epithet "well-watered" (Theocrit. 25.182). One of the natural caverns on the road to Tretus and about 2.5 km from the sacred grove of Nemea was pointed out as the cave of the Nemean lion (Paus. 2.15.2).

The first labor of Heracles was the fight with the Nemean lion. The mountain valley between Cleonae and Phlius was inhabited by a lion, the offspring of Typhon and Echidna. Eurystheus ordered Heracles to bring him the skin of this monster. Heracles, after having unsuccessfully used his club and arrows against the lion, blocked up one of the entrances to the den and entered by the other. He strangled the animal with his bare hands and lost a finger in the process. He returned to Eurystheus carrying the dead lion on his shoulders, and the terrified Eurythesus fled, ordering Heracles to make future deliveries outside the gates of the city (Diod. 4.11; Apollod. 2.5.1).

The name of Nemea was applied exclusively to the sacred grove in which the games were celebrated. Like Olympia and the sanctuary on the Corinthian Isthmus, it was not a town. The sacred grove consisted only of the temple, theater, stadium, and other monuments. There was a village in the neighborhood called Bembina, of which, however, the exact site is not known (Strab. 8.6.19). The haunts of the Nemean lion are said to have been near Bembina (Theocrit. 25.202). Some said that the Nemean games were instituted in honor of Pronax (Aelian. *V.H.* 4.5). He was a son of Talaus and Lysimache and a brother of Adrastus and Eriphyle. He was the father of Lycurgus and Amphithea (Apollod. 1.7.13). It was also in this sacred grove that Hermes is supposed to have killed Argus. Zeus, it will be remembered, loved Io, the daughter of Inachus, who founded the worship of Hera at Argos. Io was a priestess of Hera, and Zeus metamorphosed her into a cow so that Hera would not know of the adultery. Hera asked for the cow and placed it under the care of Argus Panoptes, who tied her to a tree. Hermes was commissioned by Zeus to deliver Io, so Hermes slew Argus and Io escaped.

The chief building in the sacred grove was the temple of Zeus Nemeius, the patron god of Nemea, in whose honor games were celebrated (Paus. 2.20.3). This temple had a bronze statue, the work of Lysippus. When Pausanias (2.15.2) came here, the roof had fallen, and the statue no longer remained. Three columns of the temple are still standing amidst a heap of ruins. The foundations of an altar forty-one meters long may also be seen. Among the other monuments in the sacred grove were the tombs of Opheltes and of his father Lycurgus. The former was surrounded with a stone enclosure and contained certain altars; the latter was a mound of earth (Paus. 2.15.3). Lycurgus was a son of Pheres and Periclymene, a brother of Admetus, and king of the country around Nemea. He was married to Eurydice or Amphithea, by whom he became the father of Opheltes, whose name was said to have been changed to Archemorus (Forerunner of Death) on the following occasion. When the seven heroes on their expedition against Thebes stopped at Nemea for a supply of water, Hypsipyle, the nurse of the child Opheltes, left the child alone while showing the way to the Seven. In this brief interval the child was killed by a serpent. He was buried by the Seven. But as Amphiaraus saw in this accident an omen boding destruction to him and his companions, they called the child Archemorus and instituted the Nemean games in honor of him (Apollod. 3.6.4). In this first Nemean game, Amphiaraus won the victory in the chariot race and in throwing the discus (Apollod. 3.6.4). Pausanias also mentions a fountain called Adrasteia. At the foot of the mountain are the remains of the stadium. Today it is still in the process of being excavated. Between the stadium and the temple of Zeus are some Hellenic foundations and two fragments of Doric columns.

NEON (TITHOREA)   an ancient town of Phocis, said to have been built after the Trojan War (Strab. 9.5.18), was situated at the foot of Mount Tithorea, one of the peaks of Mount Parnassus. Tithorea was a nymph of Mount Parnassus, whose name was given to the mountain peak and the town of Tithorea (Paus. 10.32.9). It was 15 km from Delphi across the mountains. It was destroyed twice in historical times but was subsequently rebuilt and named Tithorea after the mountain on which it was situated. The new town, however, was not on the same site as the ancient one.

The city existed in the time of Pausanias but had begun to decline before he came there. He mentions, however, a theater, the enclosure of an ancient agora, a temple of Athena, and the tomb of Antiope and Phocus. Phocus, a son of Ornytion of Corinth, is said to have been the leader of a colony from Corinth into the territory of Tithorea and Mount Parnassus, which derived from him the name of Phocis (Paus. 2.4.3,29.3). He is said to have cured Antiope of her madness and to have made her his wife (Paus. 9.17.7). Antiope was a daughter of Nycteus and Polyxo or of the river-god Asopus in Boeotia. She became by Zeus the mother of Amphion and Zethus. Dionysus threw her into a state of madness on account of the vengeance her sons had taken on Dirce. She was buried with Phocus in one common tomb (Paus. 9.17.7).

The ruins of Neon are situated at the modern town of Tithorea. A considerable part of the modern town is located within the ruined walls of the ancient city. Much of the wall and many of the towers remain.

NERICUS was a well-fortified town on the island of Leucas, mentioned by Homer (*Od.* 24.377). Its earliest inhabitants were Leleges and Teleboans (Strab. 7.7.2), but it was afterward inhabited by Acarnanians until they were displaced by Corinthians in the seventh century B.C. The Corinthians founded a new town near the isthmus, which they called Leucas. Here they settled one thousand of their citizens and moved the inhabitants of the old town of Nericus to join them (Strab. 2.7.2).

Laertes was a son of Arceisius and father of Odysseus. In his youth he had conquered Nericus and is also said to have taken part in the Calydonian hunt and in the expedition of the Argonauts (Apollod. 1.9.16).

NERITUS or NERITON (NIRITO) was the name of a mountain in Ithaca. Neritus was a son of Pterelaus in Ithaca, from whom the mountain was named (Hom. *Od.* 9.22, 17.207). Ithaca everywhere rises into rugged hills of which the chief is the mountain of Anoge in the northern part, which is identified with the Neritus of Virgil (*Aen.* 3.271) and the Neriton of Homer (*Od.* 9.21). The "waving forests" of Homer have now disappeared, and the mountain slopes are gray and barren.

NESTUS (NESTOS) was the river that constituted the boundary of Thrace and Macedonia in the time of Philip and Alexander. Thucydides (2.96) states that it

rose in Mount Scomius, from which the Hebrus also descended. It emptied into the sea near Abdera (Herod. 7.109). Nessus, the god of the river Nestus (also called Nessus or Nesus) in Thrace, was a son of Oceanus and Tethys.

NICOPOLIS (NIKOPOLI) was a city of Epeirus erected by Augustus in commemoration of the victory of Actium (31 B.C.). It was situated north of the entrance of the Ambracian Gulf. The end of the promontory is now occupied by the city of Preveza; and Nikopoli, the present city, lies 5 km to the north of this town. After the battle of Actium, Augustus built a sanctuary of Neptune here but dedicated it to Mars as well (Suet, *Div. Aug.* 18). The city was populated by inhabitants taken from Ambracia, Anactorium, Thyrium, Argos Amphilochicum, and Calydon. Augustus also instituted at Nicopolis a quinquennial festival called Actia in commemoration of his victory. This festival was sacred to Apollo Actius and was celebrated with music and gymnastic games, horse racing, and sea fights. It was probably the revival of an old festival since there was an ancient temple of Apollo on the promontory of Actium, which was enlarged by Augustus. The festival was declared by Augustus to be a sacred contest, by which it was made equal to the four great Grecian games; it was placed under the superintendence of the Spartans.

The ruins of Nicopolis are still very considerable. They stretch across the narrowest part of the isthmus and include a theater, a stadium, baths, and considerable remains of walls.

NISA was an earlier name of MEGARA.

NISYRUS (NISSIROS) is a rocky island opposite Cnidus between Cos and Telos. It also bore the name of Porphyris on account of its rocks of porphyry. The island is almost circular and is only 15 km in circumference. It is said to have been formed by Poseidon knocking off a portion of Cos with his trident and throwing it on the giant Polybotes (Strab. 10.5.16; Apollod. 1.6.2; Paus. 1.2.4). It is mountainous and volcanically formed. The hot springs of Nisyrus were known to the ancients, as well as its quarries of millstones and its excellent wine. Near its northwest end on a small bay was situated the town of Nisyrus. The same spot is still occupied by Mandraki, near which are considerable remnants of the ancient acropolis, consisting of walls with square towers and gates. Of the town itself, which possessed a temple of Poseidon, very little now remains. Another town was Argos, which still exists under its ancient name and in the neighborhood of which hot vapors are constantly issuing from a chasm in the rock.

As regards the history of Nisyrus, it is said originally to have been inhabited by Carians, until Thessalus, a son of Heracles, occupied the island with his Dorians, who were governed by the kings of Cos (Diod. 5.54). Along with Carpathus, Casus, Cos, and the Calydnian Islands, it sent men to the Trojan War led by Pheidippus and Antiphus, sons of Thessalus (Hom. *Il.* 2.676). It is possible that, after Agamemnon's return from Troy, Argives settled on the island. Herodotus (7.99) calls the inhabitants of Nisyrus Epidaurians.

NOMIA was the name of a mountain near Lycosura. Nomia was an Arcadian nymph, from whom the mountain was named. Pan had a sanctuary on Mount Nomia, and in this vicinity he was supposed to have learned to play the pipes (Paus. 8.38.11).

NONACRIS was a town of Arcadia in the district of Pheneatis and northwest of Pheneus, which is said to have derived its name from Nonacris, the wife of Lycaon. Beneath a rock above the town was the source of the river Styx. Styx was a daughter of Oceanus and wife of Pallas. The place was in ruins in the time of Pausanias (8.17.6), and there is no trace of it today. From this place Hermes is called Nonacriates, meaning Arcadian in the general sense.

NYCTIMUS was the original name of the ALPHEIUS river.

NYMPHAEA was one of the earlier names of the island of COS.

NYSA was a village in Boeotia on Mount Helicon (Strab. 9.2.14). Persephone was said by the Eleusinians to have been carried off by Hades from the Nysaean plain.

NYSA was a town in Thrace in the district between the rivers Strymon and Nestus, which subsequently formed part of Macedonia. It is called Nyssos by Pliny (4.10.17). Nysaeus, Nysius, Nyseus, or Nysigena was a surname of Dionysus, derived from Mount Nysa. The nymphs of Nysa were called Nyseides or Nysiades and are said to have brought up Dionysus. Their names are Cisseis, Nysa, Erato, Eriphia, Bromia, and Polyhymno (Apollod. 3.4.3). There is a tradition in which Dionysus was a son of Ammon and Amalthcia and in which Ammon, from fear of Rhea, carried the child to a cave in the neighborhood of Mt. Nysa, on a lonely island formed by the river Triton. Ammon there entrusted the child to Nysa, the daughter of Aristaeus, and Athena likewise undertook to protect the boy. Another story, with Zeus and Semele as parents, has the child brought to Ino and Athamas for rearing. But Hera threw them into madness and Zeus changed the child into a ram and carried him to the nymphs of Nysa, who brought him up in a cave and were afterward rewarded by Zeus by being placed as the

Hyades among the stars. Silenus, being a constant companion of Dionysus, is said also to have been born at Nysa, and Diodorus Siculus (3.72) even represents him as king of Nysa.

Lycurgus was a son of Dryas and king of the Edones in Thrace. He is famous for his persecution of Dionysus and his worship on the sacred mountain of Nyseion in Thrace. The god himself leaped into the sea, where he was kindly received by Thetis. Zeus thereupon blinded the impious king, who died soon after, for he was hated by the immortal gods (Hom. *Il.* 6.130). Some say that Lycurgus expelled Dionysus from his kingdom and denied his divine power; but being intoxicated with wine he first attempted to rape his own mother and to destroy all the vines of his country. Dionysus then made him go mad, and Lycurgus killed his wife and son and cut off his legs or killed himself. Another story is that he became mad and killed his son Dryas in the belief that he was cutting down a vine. When this was done, he recovered his mind; but his country produced no fruit, and the oracle declared that fertility should not be restored unless Lycurgus was killed. The Edonians therefore tied him and led him to Mount Pangaeum, where he was torn to pieces by horses (Apollod. 3.5.1).

OAXUS (See AXUS)

OCALEA or **OCALEIA** an ancient city of Boeotia, mentioned by Homer (*Il.* 2.501), was situated upon a small stream of the same name somewhere between Haliartus and Alalcomenae. It lay in the middle of a plain in the territory of Haliartus, upon which it was dependent.

Rhadamanthys was a son of Zeus and Europa and brother of King Minos of Crete. From fear of his brother he fled to Ocalea and there married Alcmena, the mother of Heracles, who had been widowed by the death of Amphitryon. In consequence of his justice throughout life, Rhadamanthys became, after his death, one of the judges of the lower world and took up his abode in Elysium (Apollod. 2.4.11, 3.1.2; Hom. *Od.* 4.564, 7.323).

OCHE was an earlier name given to the island of EUBOEA.

ODRYSIA was the territory of the Odrysians, a people from the banks of the Artiscus River of Thrace, which empties into the Hebrus. The Odrysians appear to have been among the barbarians who invaded Thrace after the Trojan War. They were addicted to intoxication, and their long drinking bouts were enlivened by warlike dances performed to a wild and barbarous music (Xenoph. *Anab.* 7.3.32). Among such people it is not surprising to find that Dionysus was the deity most worshipped.

Argiope was a nymph by whom Philammon begot the celebrated bard, Thamyris. She lived at first on Mount Parnassus, but when Philammon refused to take her into his house as his wife, she left Parnassus and went to the country of the Odrysians (Apollod. 1.3.3; Paus. 4.33.3).

OEA (See AEGINA)

OEANTHEIA or OEANTHE (TOLOPHONAS) was an important town of the Locri Ozolae, situated at the west entrance of the Crissaean Gulf. Strabo (6.1.7) says that Locri Epizephyrii in Italy was founded by the Locri Ozolae under a leader named Euanthes; it has been thought that Oeantheia or Euantheia was their place of embarkation. Oeantheia appears to have been the only maritime city in Locris remaining in the time of Pausanias, with the exception of Naupactus. The only ruins at Oeantheia mentioned by Pausanias (10.38.9) were a temple of Aphrodite and one of Artemis, situated in a grove above the town. The remains of the town can be seen on the seashore south of the village of Tolophonas (not to be confused with the modern site of ancient Tolophon, which is near Agii Pandes).

OECHALIA (IHALIA) was a town in Messenia in the plain of Stenyclerus. It was in ruins in the time of Epaminondas (Paus. 4.26.6). Strabo (8.3.6) identified it with Andania, the ancient residence of the Messenian kings, and Pausanias (4.2.2) with Carnasium, which was only 1.5 km from Andania and on the Charadrus River. Carnasium was not a town but a name given to a grove of cypress trees, in which were statues of Apollo Carneius, of Hermes Criophorus, and of Persephone. It was here that the mystic rites of the Great Goddesses were celebrated.

The Messenians claimed that Oechalia was the site of the story of Heracles and Iole, and the remains of Eurytus, the father of Iole, were believed to be buried in the Carnasian grove. Sacrifices to him were offered at Oechalia each year (Paus. 4.3.6,27.6,33.5).

OECHALIA (NEOHORIO) was a town in Thessaly on the Peneius between Pelinna and Tricca, not far from Ithome (Strab. 9.5.17). Mopsus was a son of Ampyx or Ampycus by the nymph Chloris; and because he was a seer, he is also called a son of Apollo by Himantis. He was one of the Lapiths of Oechalia and one of the Calydonian hunters. He is also mentioned among the combatants at the wedding of Peirithous and was a famous prophet among the Argonauts. He is said to have died in Libya from the bite of a snake and to have been buried there by the Argonauts. He was afterward worshipped as an oracular hero (Apollon. Rhod. 1.80, 4.1518). He was represented on the chest of Cypselus at Olympia.

Melaneus was a son of Apollo and king of the Dryopes. He was the father of Eurytus and a famous archer. According to Messenian legend, Melaneus came to Perieres, who assigned to him a town as his property, which he called Oechalia from his wife's name (Paus. 4.2.2). Eurytus, the son of Melaneus and Stratonice, succeeded his father as king of Oechalia. He was a skillful archer and married to Antioche, by whom he became the father of Iole, Iphitus, Molion or Deion, Clytius, and Toxeus. He was proud of his skill in using the bow, and is even said to have instructed Heracles in this art. He offered his daughter Iole as prize to him who should conquer him and his sons in using the bow. Heracles won the prize, but Eurytus and his sons, except for Iphitus, refused to give up Iole, because they feared he might kill his children by her as he had done in the case of Megara, his first wife (Apollod. 2.6.1).

When Eurytus refused to keep his promise about Iole, his son Iphitus tried to persuade him but could not. Soon after this, the oxen of Eurytus were carried off, and Heracles was suspected of being the thief. Iphitus again defended Heracles and went to him and requested his help in finding the oxen. Heracles agreed, but when the two arrived at Tiryns, Heracles, in a fit of madness, threw his friend down from the wall and killed him. He was purified of the murder but his illness persisted, and eventually he sought the help of the Delphic oracle. The oracle told him that he would be restored to health if he would sell himself, serve three years for wages, and surrender his wages to Eurytus as an atonement for the murder of Iphitus (Apollod. 2.6.1,2; Diod. 4.31; Hom. *Il.* 2.730). He accomplished these requirements and had many other adventures. Eventually he returned to Trachis to collect an army to take vengeance on Eurytus. With the assistance of his allies, Heracles took the town of Oechalia and slew Eurytus and his sons but carried his daughter Iole with him as a prisoner. According to Athenaeus (11.461), he put Eurytus and his sons to death because they demanded a tribute from the Euboeans. According to Homer, Eurytus was killed by Apollo, whom he presumed to rival in using the bow (*Od.* 8.226). The urn containing the bones of Eurytus was believed to be preserved in the Carnasian grove; and in Messenian Oechalia sacrifices were offered to him every year (Paus. 4.3.6,27.6,33.5). Clytius, the son of Eurytus, was one of the Argonauts. He was killed during the expedition of Heracles to punish Eurytus, or, according to others by Aeetes (Apollon. Rhod. 1.86). Deioneus was another son. Theseus married him to Perigune, the daughter of Sinis (Plut. *Thes.* 8).

OECHALIA was a town in Euboea in the district of Eretria (Strab. 10.1.10). The Cercopes were droll and thievish gnomes who played a part in the story of Heracles. Their number is commonly stated to have been two, but their names are not the same in all accounts— Olus and Eurybatus, Sillus and Triballus, Passalus and Aclemon, Andulus and Atlantus, or Candulus and Atlas.

Diodorus Siculus (4.31), however, speaks of a greater number of Cercopes. They are called sons of Theia, the daughter of Oceanus; they annoyed and robbed Heracles in his sleep, but they were taken prisoners by him and either given to Omphale or killed or set free again. The place in which they seem to have made their first appearance was Thermopylae, but the comic poem *Kerkopes,* spuriously said to be authored by Homer, probably placed them at Oechalia in Euboea. Others transferred them to Lydia, or the islands called Pithecusae, which derived their name from the Cercopes, who were changed into monkeys by Zeus for having cunningly deceived him (Ov. *Met.* 14.90).

OENEON (GLIFADA?) was a town of the Locri Ozolae east of Naupactus, possessing a port and an enclosure sacred to the Nemean Zeus, where Hesiod was said to have been killed. The territory of Oeneon was separated from that of Naupactus by the river Morno, and Oeneon perhaps stood near the modern village of Glifada (Thuc. 3.95).

OENIADAE (KATOHI) was a town in Acarnania on the west bank of the Achelous about 16 km from its mouth. It was one of the most important of the Acarnanian towns. Its location was naturally fortified, and it overlooked the whole of the south of Acarnania. Oeniadae was surrounded by marshes and its territory extended on both sides of the Achelous. It seems to have derived its name from the mythical Oeneus, the great Aetolian hero.

The ruins of Oeniadae are found near the modern Katohi on the west bank of the Achelous and are surrounded by marshes on every side. To the north these swamps deepened into Lake Melite, now called Lessini. The city occupied an extensive isolated hill, from the southern extremity of which there stretches out a long slope in the direction of the Achelous, connecting the hill with the plain. The entire circuit of the fortifications still exists and cannot be much less than 5 km. The ruins include baths, a theater, and a necropolis but no temples.

OENOE or **OENE** was a small town in Argolis west of Argos, on the left bank of the Charadrus River and on one of the two roads leading from Argos to Mantineia. Above the town was the mountain Artemisium, with a temple of Artemis on the summit. The goddess was worshipped by the inhabitants of Oenoe under the surname Oenoatis. The town was named by Diomedes after his grandfather Oeneus, who died there. After Diomedes slew the usurper Agrius and his sons, he restored Pleuron to Oeneus. But he was too old to rule and the kingdom was assigned to Andraemon, Oeneus' son-in-law. Diomedes took his grandfather with him to Peloponnesus, but some of the sons of Agrius who lay in ambush slew the old man near the altar of Telephus in Arcadia. Diomedes buried the body at Argos and named the town of Oenoe after him (Apollod. 1.8.5).

Heracles in his third labor chased the stag of Ceryneia from Oenoe to Mount Artemisium, where he finally caught it. The location of Oenoe has not yet been determined.

OENOE (INOI) was an Attic deme situated upon the border of Boeotia near Eleutherae and on the road to Plataea and Thebes (Strab. 8.6.16). The deme derived its name from Oenoe, a sister of Epochus (Paus. 1.33.8). Oenoe was situated on the Pythian Way, so called because it led from Athens to Delphi; this road apparently branched off from the Sacred Way to Eleusis. Near Oenoe was a Pythion, or temple of Apollo Pythius, which is said to have formed the northern boundary of the kingdom of Nisus when Attica and the Megaris were divided between the four sons of Pandion (Strab. 9.1.6).

Androgeus, the son of Minos of Crete, was killed in Attica. Most reported that he was killed by the Marathonian bull, but Diodorus Siculus (4.60) claims that King Aegeus himself had him murdered near Oenoe on the road to Thebes because he feared that Androgeus would support the sons of Pallas against him.

OENOE was the original name of the island of SICINUS.

OENONE was an earlier name of the island of AEGINA.

OENOPIA was an earlier name of the island of AEGINA.

OETA was a city at the foot of Mount Oeta (modern Mount Iti) in Thessaly, thought by some to have been the Sacred City mentioned by Callimachus (*Hymn. in Del.* 287), to which the Hyperborean offerings were sent from Dodona on their way to Delos. This site was also the meeting place for the Amphictyony. It was said to have been founded by Amphissus, son of Apollo and Dryope, who was said to have extraordinary strength. Here Amphissus also founded two temples, one of Apollo and the other of the nymphs. At the latter, games were celebrated down to a late time. Dryope was a daughter of King Dryops. She was married to Andraemon but became by Apollo the mother of Amphissus. Once when Dryope was in the temple of Apollo built by her son, the Hamadryades carried her off and concealed her in a forest; in her stead there was seen in the temple a fountain and a poplar. Dryope now became a nymph, and Amphissus built his temple to the nymphs, which no woman was allowed to approach (Ov. *Met.* 9.325). There is a modern village named Iti at the foot of Mount Iti, but it is unlikely that this is the site of ancient Oeta.

OETA (ITI)   a mountain in the south of Thessaly, which branches off from Mount Pindus, runs in a southeast direction and forms the north boundary of central Greece. The only entrance into central Greece from the north is through the narrow opening between Mount Oeta and the sea, celebrated as the pass of Thermopylae. The highest summit of Mount Iti is 2,155 meters. It is noted in mythology as the scene of the death of Heracles. From this mountain the southern district of Thessaly was called Oetaea.

Heracles, poisoned by the garment that Deianeira had soaked in the blood of Nessus the Centaur, prepared for death. He ascended Mount Oeta, raised a pile of wood, mounted the pyre, and ordered it to be set on fire. No one ventured to obey him until at length Poeas, a shepherd who passed by, took pity and lit the pyre. While the pyre burned, a cloud came down from heaven. Amid peals of thunder Heracles was carried to Olympus, where he was honored with immortality. Philoctetes, son of Poeas, was a disciple, friend, and armor bearer of Heracles, who taught him to use the bow and who bequeathed to him his bow with the never-erring poisoned arrows. The site of the pyre was discovered in 1919. It is hexagonal in shape. A small Doric temple is near the pyre, as well as a small monument, thought to be dedicated by Philoctetes after the sack of Troy.

OETYLUS (ITILO)   was a town of Laconia on the east side of the Messenian Gulf, represented by the modern town of Itilo, which has borrowed its name from the ancient town. Oetylus is mentioned by Homer (*Il.* 2.585) and was at a later time one of the Eleuthero-Laconian towns. Pausanias (3.25.10) saw at Oetylus a wooden statue of Apollo Carneius in the agora. Some of the remains here are thought to be from the temple of Serapis. Oetylus was a son of Amphianax and a grandson of Antimachus of Argos. The town of Oetylus was named for him, and there he enjoyed heroic honors. There was a sanctuary of Ino between Oetylus and Thalamus (Paus. 3.26.1).

OLENUS (TSOUKALAIIKA)   a town of Achaia and originally one of the twelve Achaian cities, was situated on the coast and on the left bank of the Peirus River, 7.5 km from Dyme and 15 from Patrae. Olenus was a son of Zeus and the Danaid Anaxithea. On the revival of the Achaian League in 280 B.C., Olenus was still in existence. The inhabitants subsequently left the town and moved to the neighboring villages of Peirae and Euryteiae, and to Dyme. In the time of Strabo (8.7.4) it was in ruins. Some have placed the remains at Kato Ahaia, but since Kato Ahaia is the site of ancient Dyme, and since Olenus was reported to be 7.5 km from Dyme, the ruins located at Tsoukalaiika are a more likely site.

Phorbas, son of Lapithes, according to one tradition, went from Thessaly to Olenus, where Alector, king of Elis, made use of his assistance against Pelops and shared his kingdom with him. (Some represent Pelops as a native of Olenus.) Phorbas then gave his daughter Diogeneia in marriage to Alector, and he himself married Hyrmine, a sister of Alector, by whom he became the father of Augeas and Actor (Diod. 4.69; Apollod. 2.5.5).

Dexamenus, according to some, was a king of Olenus and the father of Deianeira. Heracles seduced Deianeira during his stay with Dexamenus, who had hospitably received him. The hero left, promising to return and marry her. But in his absence the Centaur Eurytion sued for Deianeira's hand, and her father out of fear promised her to him. On the wedding day Heracles returned and killed Eurytion.

OLENUS   an ancient town in the south of Aetolia between the Achelous and the Euenus, was named after a son of Zeus or Hephaestus and is mentioned in the Homeric catalog. The men of Olenus, along with those of Pleuron, Pylene, Chalcis, and Calydon, followed Thoas, son of Andraemon, to the Trojan War in forty ships (Hom. *Il.* 2.639). It was situated near New Pleuron, at the foot of Mount Aracynthus; but its exact site is uncertain. It is said to have been destroyed by the Aeolians, and there were few traces of it in the time of Strabo (10.2.6).

OLIZON   was a town of Magnesia in Thessaly, mentioned by Homer (*Il.* 2.717), who gives it the epithet of "rugged." Its men with those of Methone, Thaumacia, and Meliboea were led by Philoctetes to the Trojan War in seven ships. It possessed a harbor; and as it was opposite Artemesium in Euboea (Plut. *Them.* 8), it has been placed on the isthmus connecting the peninsula of Trikeri with the rest of Magnesia (Strab. 9.5.15).

OLMONES, ALMONES, HOLMONES or HAL-MONES   was a village of Boeotia situated 2 km from Copae and 1 km from Hyettus. It derived its name from Olmus, the son of Sisyphus. Olmus, or Almus, was the father of Minyas, Chryse, and Chrysogeneia. He founded the town of Olmones in the territory of Orchomenus (Paus. 9.34.10). He had come to Eteocles, king of the region and his cousin, and Eteocles had given him this parcel of land. It contained nothing worthy of notice in the time of Pausanias. Its present site is not known.

OLOESSA   was an earlier name of the island of RHODES.

OLOOSSON (ELASSONA)   was a town of Perrhaebia in Thessaly mentioned by Homer (*Il.* 2.738), who gives it the epithet of "white" from its white soil. Polypoetes, a son of Peirithous and Hippodameia, was one of the

Lapiths, who joined the Greeks in the Trojan War, commanding the men of Argissa, Gyrtone, Orthe, Elone, and Oloosson. It is now called Elassona and is a place of some importance. It is situated on the edge of a plain near Tempe and at the foot of a hill, on which there is a large, old monastery, cut off on either side by a deep ravine. The citadel of the ancient town stood upon this hill; and there are a few fragments of ancient walls and some foundations behind and around the monastery.

OLURIS or OLURA   was a place identified with DORIUM.

OLUS (EPANO ELOUNDA)   was a town of Crete. There was a temple to Britomartis in the city, a wooden statue to whom was erected by Daedalus, the mythical ancestor of the Daedalids and father of Cretan art (Paus. 9.40.3). Her image was represented on the coins of Olus. The site is located at Epano Elounda near Spinalonga, where there are ruins.

OLYMPIA (OLIMBIA)   was the temple and Sacred Grove of Zeus Olympius, situated at a small distance west of Pisa in Peloponnesus. It originally belonged to Pisa. In addition to the temple of Zeus Olympius there were several other sacred edifices and public buildings in and around the grove and its immediate neighborhood, but there was no distinct town of Olympia.

The plain of Olympia is open toward the sea on the west but is surrounded on every other side by hills. The most prominent part of the landscape is a nearly isolated hill east of the plain. This is Mount Cronius, or the Hill of Cronus, which is frequently mentioned by ancient writers. Another summit about 1 km from the Alpheius was known anciently as Typaeus and from here women who crossed the river on forbidden days were condemned to be hurled headlong (Paus. 5.6.7). On the west the valley is bounded by the Cladeus, which flows from north to south along the side of the Sacred Grove and empties into the Alpheius. The Alpheius, which flows along the south edge of the plain, has constantly changed its course and has buried beneath the alluvial plain remains of buildings and monuments that stood in the southern part of the Sacred Grove.

The most important of all the festivals at Olympia was the Festival of Zeus, accompanied by the Olympic Games. It took place at the time of the first or second full moon following the summer solstice, i.e., August or September. A sacred truce backed up by severe penalties universally suspended hostilities during the week of the festival. The truce forbade armed forces to enter the territory of Elis and proclaimed absolute sanctuary for visitors. The special representatives of the various cities and states were publicly entertained and housed in special buildings adjoining the Altis (sacred precinct).

Special ambassadors from foreign states were sent at government expense. The ordinary pilgrims were accommodated in tents, or, like the competitors, slept in blankets on the ground. The administration of the Olympic Games was in the hands of the Eleians. Only men and boys whose native tongue was Greek were originally allowed to compete. Non-Greeks, or barbarians, could attend the games as spectators, but slaves were excluded.

Ten months before the date of the games, ten Hellanodicae, or umpires, were chosen, and they supervised training as well as the actual contests. Competitors were required to train for ten entire months. The oath they took on the Altar of Zeus Horceius, swearing strict adherence to regulations, held them, their families, and their native towns accountable for any infraction. The footrace was the oldest event, but other competitive events were added from time to time, eventually even poetry readings and musical contests. Events for boys were begun in 632 B.C.

After each event the victor's name was announced and he was handed a palm. On the final day the victorious competitors were each given a garland of wild olive and entertained in the Prytaneion. A victor had the privilege of erecting a statue in the Altis. It is estimated that by Roman times there were three thousand of these statues.

There were also many statues of heroes. In the ancient gymnasium there was a cenotaph of Achilles at which solemnities were performed before the Olympic games commenced (Paus. 6.23.2). Deiphobus was a son of Priam and was killed defending Troy. Pausanias saw a statue of him, a work of Lycius, which the inhabitants of Apollonia had dedicated there. Euthymus, a hero of Locri in Italy, was a son of the river-god Caecinus. He was famous for his strength and skill in boxing and delivered the town of Temessa from the evil spirit Polites, to whom a fair maiden was sacrificed every year. Euthymus himself disappeared at an advanced age in the river Caecinus (Strab. 6.1.5). He gained several victories at Olympia (Pind. Ol. 74, 76, 77); and a statue of him at Olympia was the work of Pythagoras (Paus. 6.6.6). Idomeneus, the hero of the Trojan War from Crete, had a statue at Olympia, the work of Onatas. This statue stood in a group of images of those who drew lots for the privilege of fighting with Hector. On his shield was a cock (Paus. 5.25.9). The fight at Troy between Achilles and Memnon was often represented by Greek artists; it was depicted in a large group at Olympia, the work of Lycius, which had been dedicated there by the inhabitants of Apollonia (Paus. 5.22.2).

There were many claimants for the establishment and later restoration of the Olympia games. There were also many individuals connected in one way or another with the games. The national Hellenic Zeus had the supernal temple at Olympia. There, too, Zeus was regarded as the father and king of gods and men and as the supreme god of the Hellenic nation. His statue there was made by Pheidias a few years before the outbreak of the Peloponnesian War. According to the tradition of Elis, Cronus was the first ruler of the country, and in the golden age there was a temple dedicated to him at Olympia. Rhea, it is further said, entrusted the infant Zeus to the Idaean Dactyls, who were also called Curetes, and had come from Mount Ida in Crete to Elis. Heracles, one of them, contended with his brother Dactyls in a footrace and adorned the victor with a wreath of olive. In this manner he is said to have founded the Olympic games, and Zeus to have contended with Cronus for the kingdom of Elis (Paus. 5.7.4).

Iamus, a son of Apollo and Euadne, was initiated in the art of prophecy by his father, and was regarded as the ancestor of the famous family of seers, the Iamidae at Olympia (Paus. 6.2.3; Pind. *Ol.* 6.43). At Phaesana, Euadne became by Apollo the mother of the boy, who, when his mother for shame deserted him, was fed with honey by two serpents. When Iamus had grown up, he descended by night into the waters of the river Alpheius and invoked Poseidon and Apollo, beseeching them to reveal to him his destiny. Apollo commanded him to follow his voice and led him to Olympia where he gave him the power to understand and explain the voices of birds and to foretell the future from the sacrifices burning on the altars of Zeus. His powers of prophecy were to begin as soon as Heracles should found the Olympic games (Pind. *Ol.* 6.28).

When Augeas did not pay the reward promised for the cleaning of his stables, Heracles marched with an army of Argives and Tirynthians against Augeas in Elis. He killed him and his sons. After this victory, Heracles marked out the sacred ground on which the Olympic games were to be celebrated, built altars, and instituted the Olympian festival and games (Apollod. 2.7.2; Pind. *Ol.* 11,25).

Aetolus was a son of Endymion. His father compelled him and his two brothers Paeon and Epeius to decide by a contest at Olympia which of them was to succeed him in his kindgom of Elis. Epeius gained the victory and occupied the throne. Aetolus followed him but later was expelled and migrated to the region he called Aetolia.

Amythaon was a son of Cretheus and Tyro and father of Bias and Melampus. Pausanias (5.8.1) mentions him among those to whom the restoration of the Olympic games was ascribed. Clymenus, a son of Cardis in Crete, was said to have come to Elis in the fiftieth year after the flood of Deucalion, restored the Olympic games, and erected altars to Heracles, from whom he was descended (Paus. 5.8.1, 6.21.6). At the command of the Delphic oracle, Iphitus, a son of Haemon, restored the Olympic

games and instituted the cessation of all war during their celebration (Paus. 5.4.5).

When Pelops had gained possession of Hippodameia through his contest with Oenomaus, her father, he went with her to Pisa in Elis and soon made himself master of Olympia also. There he restored the Olympian games with greater spendor than they had ever had before (Pind. *Ol.* 9.16; Paus. 5.8.2). Pelops was honored at Olympia above all other heroes (Paus. 5.13.1). His tomb with an iron sarcophagus existed on the banks of the Alpheius, not far from the temple of Artemis near Pisa. Every year the ephebi there scourged themselves, shedding their blood as a funeral sacrifice to the hero. The spot on which his sanctuary, the Pelopion, stood in the grove Altis was said to have been dedicated by Heracles, who also offered to him the first sacrifices (Apollod. 2.7.2). His sword was shown in the treasury of the Sicyonians at Olympia (Paus. 6.19.6).

Chrysippus, the son of Pelops by a nymph, was the favorite of his father, and this roused the envy of his brothers, who in concert with Hippodameia, prevailed upon the two eldest among them, Atreus and Thyestes, to kill Chrysippus. Hippodameia, dreading the anger of her husband, fled to Midea in Argolis, from where her remains were afterward conveyed by Pelops, at the command of an oracle, to Olympia (Paus. 6.20.7). Some state that Hippodameia killed herself. She had a sanctuary at Olympia in the grove Altis, to which women alone had access, and in the race course at Olympia there was a bronze statue of her (Paus. 6.20.19). Taraxippus was the name of a particular spot in the race course, where horses often became shy and frightened. Superstition was not at a loss to account for this phenomenon, for some said that on that spot Olenius or Dameon had been slain by Cteatus, or because it was the burial place of Myrtilus, Alcathous, or Pelops. Pausanias, however, considers Taraxippus to be a surname of Poseidon Hippius.

Finally, we learn that Chloris, the daughter of Amphion and Niobe who was spared by Artemis, once gained the prize in a footrace during the festival of Hera at Olympia (Paus. 5.16.4). Coroebus, an Eleian, gained a victory in the stadium in the first games in 776 B.C. According to tradition, he slew the daemon Poene, whom Apollo had sent into the country of the Argives. Hē was represented on his tomb in the act of killing Poene, and his statue, which was made of stone, was one of the most ancient that Pausanias saw in the whole of Greece (Paus. 1.43.8, 5.8.3, 8.26.4). The Sacred Grove and its vicinity are crowded with references to the mythological and religious past. South of the gymnasium and wrestling school can be seen remains of the Theocoleon, which was the residence of the priests. The Altis was bounded on the north by the Hill of Cronus and on the remaining sides by walls. Within this enclosure was the Temple of Zeus, the

Heraion, the small Metroon, the Pelopion, and many altars to Zeus and other deities. The Bouleterion (Council House) housed the already mentioned statue of Zeus Horceius, beside which the competitors swore oaths of ethical conduct.

The Temple of Zeus is one of the largest temples in Greece. It was built between 470 and 456 B.C. from remains of Pisa after it was sacked by the Eleians. An earthquake severely damaged it in 175 B.C., but it was rebuilt. Early in the sixth century A.D. it was completely thrown down by earthquakes.

On the east pediment was the preparation for the chariot race between Pelops and Oenomaus; on the west was the battle of the Lapiths and Centaurs. The surviving sculptures are in the Museum. At the top of the east pediment was a gold shield dedicated by the Spartans, and later a bronze Nike was mounted above it. In the interior twelve marble metopes were decorated with scenes from the labors of Heracles. Some of them are in the Museum.

On the floor of the temple are the remains of a mosaic of a boy riding on a Triton. A colonnade supported the wooden ceiling and elevated galleries for the viewing of the statue of Zeus. The statue of Zeus was one of the Seven Wonders of the Ancient World. It was about seven times life-size or about twelve meters high. The base was one meter high and decorated with reliefs of various divinities. Zeus was seated on a throne made of ebony and ivory and decorated with gold and precious gems. The footstool of the throne had a relief of Theseus fighting the Amazons. In the right hand of the statue was a chryselephantine statue of Nike and in the left a scepter with an eagle. Represented nearby were a variety of beings. Among these was Amphitrite, the wife of Poseidon. Amazons were represented in the pediment of the Temple (Paus. 5.10.2). Helios was shown on the pedestal of the Olympian Zeus in the act of ascending his chariot (Paus. 5.11.3). At the entrance to the temple there was a group of nine heroes of the Trojan War, represented as drawing lots for the honor of the single combat with Hector. Opposite stood Nestor shaking the lots in his helmet. Close by on a triangular base was the Nike of the sculptor Paionios. There was a statue of Zeus, dedicated by the Lacedaemonians in the sixth century. Most of the other statues were of victorious Olympic athletes.

At the entrance to the stadium is a row of twelve pedestals that supported the Zanes, bronze statues of Zeus. These were erected from fines imposed on contestants for cheating. Also near the entrance is the supposed site of the Hippodameion, the tomb of Hippodameia, the wife of Pelops. The embankments surrounding the stadium never had seats but could accommodate about forty thousand people. The starting and finishing lines are 182

meters apart, giving origin to the measurement called a stadium.

The treasuries overlook the Altis at the foot of the Hill of Cronus. These small, temple-like structures were dedicated by various cities. Among these is an altar of Gaea. Immediately beyond is an altar to Heracles. At the foot of the terrace steps leading to the treasuries is the Metroon, a small Doric temple, dedicated to the Mother of the Gods. Beyond was a reservoir built by Herodes Atticus and dedicated to Zeus in the name of his wife, who was a priestess of Demeter.

The oldest building in the Sacred Grove is the Heraion, and it is also the best preserved building at Olympia. Originally it was jointly dedicated to Zeus and Hera, but after the temple of Zeus Olympius was built, this temple was sacred to Hera alone. The pedestals of the ancient statues of Zeus and Hera still stand at the west end. The head of Hera has been recovered. The beautiful statue of Hermes by Praxiteles was also found in this temple. Here was housed also the famous cedar chest of Cypselus. This chest had figures carved into the wood, some inlaid with ivory and gold. In this chest Cypselus, the tyrant of Corinth, was hidden by his mother when the Bacchidae sought to kill him after his birth. In gratitude for the saving of Cypselus, the Cypselids, his descendants, dedicated the chest at Olympia. The figures of the chest were of such quantity and depicted so many mythological events that the effect must have been astonishing. A total description can be found in Pausanias (5.17.6–19.10), and it will have to suffice here to point out some of the principal scenes: the race of Pelops and Oenomaus; the fatal necklace of Harmonia; athletic contests between Pisus and Asterion, between Admetus and Mopsus, and between Jason and Peleus; Heracles and the Hydra; personifications, such as Death, Sleep, Night, Justice, and Injustice; Zeus and Alcmena; Menelaus and Helen; Perseus and the Gorgons; Jason and Medea; military scenes; Meilanion and Atalanta; Boreas and Oreithyia; Heracles and Geryones; Theseus and Ariadne; the fight between Achilles and Memnon; a duel between Ajax the Greater and Hector; the Dioscuri rescuing Helen from Aphidna; Priam and Paris; Ajax the Lesser and Cassandra; Polyneices and Eteocles, the sons of Oedipus; Odysseus and Circe; and the death of Patroclus. Altogether there were perhaps 150 identifiable individuals, including some with their livestock; additionally, the chest showed spectators, soldiers, and other individuals not enumerated. Pausanias was unable to identify the maker of the chest, but he consigned the inscriptions to Eumelus of Corinth, an epic poet of the eighth century B.C.

To the south of the Heraion was the Pelopion. This was an enclosure surrounding a small mound and an altar to Pelops, the leading Olympian hero. Nearby was the altar of Zeus Olympius, the most sacred spot in the Altis, where a daily bloody sacrifice was made. The supposed site is marked by a heap of stones. From this spot the Olympic torch is lighted to be carried to modern sites of the games.

Outside the entrance to the Altis was the Prytaneion, where the magistrates lived. Here Olympic victors were feasted, and here was also the altar of Hestia with a perpetual flame.

In the new museum, which opened in 1972, there are many exhibits of mythological significance. The left gallery contains tripods and cauldrons adorned with figures of the Telchines. The adjoining gallery has the great head of Hera from the Heraion. In gallery 4 is the statue of Zeus carrying off Ganymede. In gallery 5 is the celebrated Nike of Paionios. The only piece in the sixth gallery is the Hermes of Praxiteles found in the Heraion in 1877. In the seventh and eighth galleries are other items from the Altis and objects directly concerned with the Olympic games. The huge central hall contains the two sculptures from the pediment of the Temple of Zeus, along with the metopes illustrating the twelve labors of Heracles.

It is not surprising that in this widely visited holy place many gods and heroes were worshipped; even minor divinities enjoyed renown here. In the treasury of the Megarians, for example, there was a statue of Achelous made by Dontas of cedar and gold (Paus. 6.19.12). Agamemnon was worshipped here as a hero. Agon, the personification of solemn contests, was represented in a statue. One could expect, of course, that the river-god Alpheius would be worshipped here. It will be recalled that he loved Artemis and pursued her. Here the two divinities had an altar in common (Paus. 5.14.6). Zeus Apomyius (Driving Away the Flies) was worshipped at Olympia. On one occasion, when Heracles was offering a sacrifice to Zeus at Olympia, he was annoyed by hosts of flies, and in order to get rid of them, he offered a sacrifice to Zeus Apomyius, and the flies withdrew across the river Alpheius (Paus. 5.14.1). Zeus Catharsius (Purifier or Atoner) was a name under which Zeus in conjunction with Nike had a temple here (Paus. 5.14.8).

Ares was worshipped at Olympia. Ececheiria (Armistice or Truce) was personified and represented as a divine being at the entrance of the Temple of Zeus; there was a statue of Iphitus, which Ececheiria was in the act of crowning (Paus. 5.10.10). Eos was represented in the act of praying to Zeus for Memnon. Gaea, as mentioned, had a temple here. So did Hades. Hestia and Poseidon were worshipped in common at Olympia (Paus. 5.26.2). Some legends say that Poseidon sued for her hand but that she swore by the head of Zeus to remain a virgin forever. Athena Hippia was a surname here. Thallo and Carpo, the Horae (Seasons), were also worshipped (Paus. 5.15.3).

The Moirae (Fates) had a sanctuary here (Paus. 5.15.5). The nymphs, as was customary, had a sanctuary near a spring at Olympia (5.15.3). Heracles, on account of his victory over the Moliones, dedicated six altars here.

Themis, the personification of the order of things established by law, custom, and equity, had a temple in common with the Horae (Paus. 5.14.8,17.1).

OLYMPUS (OLIMBOS)   is one of the highest mountains in Greece, the south side of which forms the boundary with Thessaly. Its northern base reaches around the plains of Macedonia, and sometimes it is called a mountain of Macedonia. It forms the eastern end of the Cambunian range and reaches to the sea as far as the mouth of the Peneius River, being separated by the vale of Tempe from Mount Ossa. Its height is 2,973 meters. The lower sides of Olympus are well wooded, but the summit shows wide areas of bare rock. It has a few minor summits; its chief summit is covered with perpetual snow.

In mythology, Olympus was the chief seat of the third dynasty of gods, of which Zeus was the head. With respect to the concept of heaven and Olympus, heaven was a metaphor for the summit of the mountain rather than the reverse. Even the fable of the giants scaling heaven must be understood in this sense; not that they placed Pelion and Ossa upon the top of Olympus to reach the still higher heaven, but that they piled Pelion on the top of Ossa and both on the lower slopes of Olympus to scale the summit of Olympus itself, the abode of the gods. The Titans were the gigantic offspring of Uranus and Ge. One of them, Cronus, fathered by Rhea the Olympian gods, chief of whom was Zeus, the youngest. His older brothers and sisters were swallowed by their father, but Zeus was saved and caused his brothers and sisters to be disgorged. United with them he began a contest against Cronus and the ruling Titans. This contest, usually called the Titanomachia, was carried on in Thessaly, the Titans occupying Mount Othrys, and the sons of Cronus Mount Olympus. It lasted for ten years, and the Titans were overcome and hurled down below Tartarus (Hom. *Il.* 14.279; Hes. *Theog.* 697, 851). The victorious gods continued to occupy Olympus. Olympus was threatened again by the Aloeidae, Otus and Ephialtes. They were the giant sons of Poseidon by Iphimedeia. They were renowned for their extraordinary strength and daring spirit. At a very young age they threatened the Olympian gods with war and attempted to pile Pelion upon Ossa and Ossa upon the slopes of Olympus. They would have accomplished their object had they been allowed to grow up to the age of manhood; but Apollo destroyed them before their beards began to appear (Hom. *Od.* 11.305).

Homer describes the gods as having their several palaces on the summit of Olympus, as spending their days in the palace of Zeus, around whom they sat in solemn assembly, while the younger gods danced before them, and the Muses entertained them with lyre and song. They were hidden from the view of men upon the earth by a wall of clouds, the gates of which were kept by the Horae. These were the divinities of the weather and the ministers of Zeus. The same concepts are found in Hesiod, and to a great extent in the later poets, with whom, however, even as early as the lyric poets and the tragedians, the idea became less material, and the real abode of the gods is gradually transferred from the summit of Olympus to the sky itself.

Zeus was the greatest of the Olympian gods. He ruled the upper regions and dwelt on Olympus, which was believed to penetrate with its lofty summit into heaven itself. The great gods of Olympus were: Zeus himself; Poseidon, his brother; Hera, his sister and wife; Demeter, his sister; Ares, Hephaestus, and Hestia, his children by Hera; Apollo and Artemis, his children by Leto; Hermes, his son by Maia; Athena, his daughter by Metis; and Aphrodite, his daughter by Dione. Olympius was a surname not only of Zeus but of all the gods who were believed to live in Olympus, as distinct from the gods of the lower world.

Although Poseidon generally dwelt in the sea, he still also appeared in Olympus in the assembly of the gods (Hom. *Il.* 8.440).

When Persephone disappeared, Demeter learned that Hades had been her abductor with the consent of Zeus. In her anger she avoided Olympus and dwelt upon earth among men. She produced famine by not allowing the fields to produce. Zeus, anxious that the race of mortals should not become extinct, sent Iris, the messenger goddess, to induce Demeter to return to Olympus. But she would not. At length he sent all the gods of Olympus to conciliate her by entreaties and presents; but she vowed neither to return to Olympus nor to restore the fertility of the earth until she had seen her daughter again. Eventually, Persephone was allowed to leave Hades, but only for part of the year since she had eaten part of a pomegranate while in the underworld. Rhea persuaded Demeter to return to Olympus and to restore fertility to the earth.

Hephaestus Amphigyeeis (Lame or Limping on Both Feet) was a name given to Hephaestus because Zeus threw him from Olympus for having sided with Hera in a dispute (Hom. *Il.* 1.599; Apollod. 1.3.5).

Apollo, though one of the great gods of Olympus, is yet represented in some sort of dependence on Zeus, who is regarded as the source of the powers exercised by his son. Some say Hermes was born on Olympus. He was the herald of the Olympian gods.

During the Trojan War Aphrodite understandably sided with the Trojans. When she endeavored to rescue her son Aeneas in battle, she was pursued by Diomedes, who wounded her in the hand. In her fright she abandoned her son and was carried by Iris in the chariot of Ares to Olympus, where she complained of her misfortune to her mother Dione but was laughed at by Hera and Athena. Aphrodite's dalliance with Ares took place on Olympus.

There were those who came later to Olympus. Dionysus was not considered one of the great Olympian gods, but he was later installed among them. After he had gradually established his divine nature throughout the world, he led his mother, Semele, out of Hades, called her Thyone, and rose with her into Olympus. Hermes is said to have carried the newborn Heracles to Olympus and put him to the breast of Hera while she was asleep. As she awoke, she pushed him away, and the milk thus spilled produced the Milky Way. Heracles immolated himself, became immortal, and was carried up to Olympus.

Besides these, other beings dwelt on Olympus, like Dione. When Aphrodite was wounded, Dione pronounced the threat respecting the punishment of Diomedes, who had wounded her. Themis, the personification of the order of things, dwelt on Olympus and was on friendly terms with Hera. The Muses, as mentioned, seemed to come and go on Olympus as they chose.

Others had dwelt there for varying periods of time. Asteria, sister of Leto, was an inhabitant of Olympus and beloved by Zeus. In order to escape from his embraces, she was metamorphosed first into a quail, threw herself into the sea, and was then metamorphosed into the island Asteria, or Ortygia, afterward called Delos. Ate, a daughter of Eris, goddess of discord, was an ancient divinity who led both gods and men to rash and inconsiderate actions and to suffering. She induced Zeus at the birth of Heracles to take an oath by which Hera was enabled to give to Eurystheus the power that had been destined for Heracles. When Zeus discovered his rashness, he hurled Ate from Olympus and banished her forever from the abode of the gods (Hom. *Il.* 19.126). Pan, son of Hermes, had horns, beard, pug nose, tail, goats' feet, and a hirsute body so that his mother ran away with fear when she saw him; but Hermes carried him into Olympus where all the gods were delighted with him, especially Dionysus. He was brought up by nymphs. Poseidon was in love with the beautiful young Pelops and carried him off, whereupon Pelops, like Ganymede, for a time dwelt with the gods (Pind. *Ol.* 1.46). There was Ganymede, and Hebe before him, who served as cupbearer to the gods. Pegasus, the famous winged horse, originally rose up to the seats of the immortals and afterward lived in the palace of Zeus, for whom he carried thunder and lightning. He was the thundering horse of Zeus; but later writers describe him as the horse of Eos and place him among the stars as the heavenly horse (Arat. 205). The Palladium was an image of Pallas Athena. Athena was brought up by Triton. His daughter, Pallas, and Athena once were exercising together, and Pallas was wounded by Athena and died. Athena caused an image of the maiden to be made, round which she hung the aegis of Zeus, and which she placed by the side of the image of Zeus. Subsequently, when Electra, after being dishonored, fled to this image, Zeus threw it down from Olympus upon the earth. It came down at Troy and remained there, revered as a pledge of the safety of the city.

Finally, others still had connections with Olympus only as a mountain, not necessarily as home of the gods. When Heracles killed Diomedes, king of the Bistones in Thrace, he delivered his man-eating mares to Mycenae. They had become tame after eating the flesh of their master. They were set free and roamed afar. Eventually they were destroyed on Mount Olympus by wild beasts (Apollod. 2.5.8). Euripides connects Orpheus with the Bacchanalian orgies (*Hippol.* 953), ascribes to him the origin of sacred mysteries (*Rhes.* 943), and places the scene of his activities among the forests of Olympus (*Bacch.* 561). After his violent death at the hands of the maddened Maenads, the Muses collected the fragments of his body and buried them at Leibethra at the foot of Olympus.

OLYNTHUS (OLINTHOS)   was a town in Macedonia that stood at the head of the Toronaic Gulf between the peninsulas of Pallene and Sithonia and was surrounded by a fertile plain. Olynthus was a son of Heracles and Bolbe, from whom the Thracian town of Olynthus and the Olynthus River were believed to have received their names (Athen. 8.334). Others have the town named for another Olynthus. Brangas was a son of the Thracian king Strymon and brother of Rhesus and Olynthus. When the last of these three brothers had been killed during a chase by a lion, Brangas buried him on the spot where he had fallen and called the town that he subsequently built there Olynthus.

Olynthus was the most important of the Greek cities on the coast of Macedonia. One extant type of coin from Olynthus—a head of Heracles with the lion's skin—has been described, but there was another with the head of Apollo on one side and his lyre on the other. The remains of Olynthus are at modern Olinthos, about 64 km southeast of Thessaloniki. Many streets and houses have been uncovered, and one of the houses was adorned with mosaics with mythological subjects. The public buildings so far discovered have been few and unimportant.

OMPHALIUM   a plain in Crete, was named from the legend of the birth of the infant Zeus from Rhea. The scene of the event is laid near Thenae, Cnossus, and the river Triton (Callim. *Hymn. in Jov.* 45; Diod. 5.70).

ONCAE   was a village in Boeotia. At Thebes there was an altar and statue of Athena bearing the Phoenician surname Onca. We know from Aeschylus (*Sept.* 166, 489) that there was originally a temple of Athena Onca in this locality, which stood outside the city near one of the gates. This surname was thought by some to be derived from the town of Oncae.

ONCEIUM (KALLIANIO?)   was a place in Arcadia upon the river Ladon near Thelpusa and containing a temple of Demeter Erinys (Paus. 8.25.4). The Ladon, after leaving this temple, passed the temple of Apollo Oncaeates on the left and that of Asclepius Paidos (Boy) on the right (Paus. 8.25.11). The name is derived by Pausanias from Oncus, a son of Apollo, who reigned at this place that he also founded. Demeter, after being metamorphosed into a horse, mixed among his herds and gave him the horse Arion, of which she was the mother by Poseidon (Paus. 8.25.5–7). Some have placed the site of Onceium at Kallianio, which though a few kilometers from the Ladon is on one of its tributaries. Also, the town could still have administered the temple of Demeter, which was directly on the Ladon.

ONCHESTUS   was an ancient town of Boeotia in the territory of Haliartus, said to have been founded by Onchestus, a son of Poseidon (Paus. 9.26.5). Here the Onchestian Poseidon had a temple and a statue (Hom. *Il.* 2.506). Another tradition called this Onchestus a son of Boeotus. Here an Amphictyonic Council of the Boeotians used to assemble (Strab. 9.2.33). Pausanias (9.26.3) says that Onchestus was 15 stadia (3 km) from the mountain of the Sphinx (modern Fagas). Strabo (9.2.33) said that the grove of Poseidon existed only in the imagination of the poets; but Pausanias, who visited the place, mentions the grove as still existing. The site of Onchestus has been identified, and remains of the sanctuary of Poseidon reported. The scanty ruins are between Thebes and Aliartos on a ridge south of the highway.

Atalanta, according to some traditions, was a daughter of Schoeneus and was married to Hippomenes. Her footrace took place in Onchestus, and the sanctuary that the newly married couple profaned by their lovemaking was a temple of Cybele, who metamorphosed them into lions and yoked them to her chariot (Ov. *Met.* 8.318, 10.565). In all traditions the main cause of the metamorphosis is that Hippomanes neglected to thank Aphrodite for the gift of the golden apples. According to Apollodorus (3.15.8), the couple had a son, Megareus. Another person connected with Onchestus was Idas, a native hero, who distinguished himself in the war against Thebes (Stat. *Theb.* 6.553, 7.588).

ONUGNATHUS (ELAFONISSI)   (Jaw of an Ass) was the name of a peninsula and promontory in the south of

Laconia, about 37 km south of Asopus. It is now entirely surrounded with water and is called Elafonissi; but it is in reality a peninsula, for the isthmus by which it is connected with the mainland is only barely covered with water. It contains a harbor, which Strabo (8.5.1) mentions; and Pausanias (3.22.10,23.1) saw a temple of Athena in ruins, and the sepulcher of Cinadus, the steersman of Menelaus.

OPHITEIA   (See AMPHICLEIA)

OPHIUSSA   was an earlier name of the island of RHODUS.

OPHIUSSA   was another name for the island of TENOS.

OPUS (KIPARISSI)   was the chief town of a tribe of the Locri Opuntii, whose name was derived from this place. It stood at the head of the Opuntian Gulf, a little inland, being about 3 km from the shore according to Strabo (9.4.2) or only 1.5 km, according to Livy (28.6). Opus was believed to be one of the most ancient towns in Greece. It was said to have been founded by Opus, a son of Locrus and Protogeneia; and in its neighborhood Deucalion and Pyrrha were reported to have lived after the flood (Pind. *Ol.* 9.62,87). It was the native city of Patroclus (Hom. *Il.* 18.326). Menoetius, son of Actor and Aegina, was the father of Patroclus. He resided at Opus and was an Argonaut. He was also a friend of Heracles. Immediately after the apotheosis of Heracles, his friends who were present at the termination of his earthly career offered sacrifices to him as a hero; and Menoetius established at Opus the worship of Heracles as a hero. This example was followed by the Thebans, until at length Heracles was worshipped throughout Greece as a divinity (Diod. 4.39; Eurip. *Herc. Fur.* 1331). Menoetius was married to Sthenele. Patroclus as a boy involuntarily slew Clysonymus, son of Amphidamas, during a game of dice. In consequence of the accident, Patroclus was taken by his father to Peleus at Phthia, where he was educated together with Achilles, his cousin. Opus is mentioned in the Homeric catalog (Hom. *Il.* 2.531) as one of the Locrian towns subject to Ajax, son of Oileus.

The position of Opus is uncertain, but it has been placed by many at Kiparissi, a village situated southeast of Atalanti. Kiparissi is as far from the sea as Strabo said Opus was, and remains of an ancient city have been found there.

ORCHOMENUS (ORHOMENOS)   was an ancient city of Arcadia. It was situated on a plain surrounded on all sides by mountains. This plain was bounded on the south by a low range of hills, called Anchisia, which separated it from the territory of Mantineia. Passes across the Oligyrtus range led to Pheneus and Stymphalus. The acropolis of Orchomenus stood on the summit of a hill to the west called Trachy. It was one of the most powerful cities of Arcadia in early times. It was founded by an eponymous hero, the son of Lycaon (Paus. 8.3.3). On the death of Arcas, the ancestor of the Arcadians, his dominions were divided among his three sons, of whom Elatus obtained Orchomenus as his portion. The kings of Orchomenus are said to have ruled over nearly all Arcadia. Pausanias (8.5.10–13) gives a list of the kings of Orchomenus, whom he represents at the same time as kings of Arcadia. One of these kings, Aristocrates, the son of Aechmis, was stoned to death by his people for violating the virgin priestess of Artemis Hymnia.

Orchomenus is mentioned by Homer (*Il.* 2.605) who gives it the epithet "rich in flocks." Pausanias mentions (8.13.2), as the most remarkable edifices in the city, temples of Poseidon and Aphrodite, both of which had statues of stone. Close to the city was a wooden statue of Artemis enclosed in a great cedar tree and therefore called Cedreatis.

Walls still remain for part of the acropolis. There were two gates, one opening toward the Charadra, the principal spring of the city. Inside the walls was the agora, south of which can be seen the remains of the temple of Artemis Mesopolitis. Remains of the theater can also be seen. In the lower city were found remains of a temple, which was dedicated either to Aphrodite or Poseidon.

On the slope of Mount Anchisia in the territory of Orchomenus but adjoining that of Mantineia was the temple of Artemis Hymnia, which was held in veneration by all the Arcadians in the most ancient times (Paus. 8.5.11). The priestess of the goddess was always at first a virgin; after the time of Aristocrates, however, it was decreed that she should be a married woman (Paus. 8.5.12). The site of the temple is probably indicated by a chapel of the Virgin Mary, which stands east of Levidi.

According to some, Aeneas proceeded from Thrace, where he spent the winter after the Trojan War, to the Arcadian Orchomenus and settled there. Anchises was supposed to have accompanied him, and he died there. He was buried by Aeneas at the foot of a hill, which received from him the name Anchisia.

ORCHOMENUS (ORHOMENOS)   was a city in the north of Boeotia and in early times the capital of the powerful kingdom of the Minyae. These people, according to tradition, seem to have come originally from Thessaly. We read of a town Minya in Thessaly and also of a Thessalian Orchomenus Minyeus (Plin. 4.8.15). Their ancestral hero, Minyas, is said to have migrated from Thessaly into the northern parts of Boeotia and there to have established the powerful race of the Minyans, whose capital was Orchomenus. As most of the Argonauts were descendants of the Minyans, they are themselves called

Minyae; and the descendants of the Argonauts founded a colony on Lemnos, which was called Minyae. They then colonized Elis Triphylia and the island of Thera (Herod. 1.146, 4.145; Apollon. Rhod. 1.229).

The first king of the Boeotian Orchomenus is said to have been Andreus, a son of the Thessalian river Peneius, from whom the country was called Andreis (Paus. 9.34.6). Andreus assigned part of his territory to the Aetolian Athamas, who adopted two of the grandchildren of his brother Sisyphus; they gave their names to Haliartus and Coroneia. Andreus was succeeded in the other part of his territory by his son Eteocles, who was the first to worship the Charites in Greece (Paus. 9.35.1). Upon the death of Eteocles the sovereignty went to the family of Halmus or Almus, a son of Sisyphus (Paus. 9.36.1). Halmus had two daughters, Chryse and Chrysogeneia. Chryse by the god Ares became the mother of Phlegyas, who succeeded the childless Eteocles and called the country Phlegyantis after himself. Phlegyas died without male heirs, but was the father of Coronis, who became by Apollo the mother of Asclepius. Enraged at this, Phlegyas set fire to the Delphian temple of the god, who killed him with his arrows and condemned him to severe punishment in the lower world. Phlegyas was succeeded by Chryses, the son of Chrysogenia by the god Poseidon. Chryses was the father of the wealthy Minyas, who built the treasury at Orchomenus and gave his name to the Minyan race. Some call him a son of Orchomenus or Eteocles, others of Poseidon, Aleus, Ares, Sisyphus, or Halmus. He is called the husband of Tritogeneia, Clytodora, or Phanosyra and the father of several children, including Orchomenus. Minyas was succeeded by his son Orchomenus, after whom the city was named (Paus. 9.36.6).

There is general agreement that Orchomenus was in the earliest times not only the chief city of Boeotia but also one of the most powerful and wealthy cities of Greece. It has been observed that the genealogy of the city of Orchomenus glitters with names that express wealth, e.g., Chryses and Chrysogeneia. Homer (*Il.* 9.381) even compares the treasures that flowed into the city to those of the Egyptian Thebes. It would seem that at an early period the city of Orchomenus ruled over the whole of northern Boeotia and that even Thebes was for a time compelled to pay tribute to Erginus, king of Orchomenus.

Clymenus was a son of Presbon and king of Orchomenus; he was married to Minya (Paus. 9.37.1; Apollod. 2.4.11). Erginus, a son of Clymenus and Buzyge, became king next. Clymenus was killed by Perieres at the festival of the Onchestian Poseidon. Onchestus was subject to Thebes, and Erginus, the eldest son, undertook to avenge the death of his father. He marched against Thebes and, being victorious, compelled the Thebans to a treaty, in which they had to pay him for twenty years an annual tribute of one hundred oxen. Heracles once met the heralds of Erginus on their way to collect the tribute. He cut off their ears and noses, tied their hands behind their backs, and sent them to Erginus. Erginus then undertook a second expedition against Thebes but was defeated and slain by Heracles, whom Athena had provided with arms. Some say that Erginus made peace with Heracles and devoted all his energy to the promotion of prosperity in his kingdom. He thus arrived at an advanced age without having wife or children. He was advised by the Delphic oracle to take a youthful wife. This he did and became by her the father of Trophonius and Agamedes. According to others, he became the father of Azeus. He is mentioned among the Argonauts and is said to have succeeded Tiphys as helmsman. In funeral games for Thoas on Lemnos he conquered in a footrace in spite of the ridicule of the Lemnian women because, though still young, he had gray hair. Agamedes and Trophonius were distinguished as architects, especially in building temples and palaces. They also built the treasury of Hyrieus in Boeotia, and their attempt to rob it resulted in their deaths. (See LEBADEIA.)

In the Homeric catalog (Hom. *Il.* 2.50) Orchomenus is mentioned along with Aspledon, but distinct from the other Boeotian towns; it alone sent thirty ships to the Trojan War. Ascalaphus was a son of Ares and Astyoche and brother of Ialmenus, together with whom he led the Minyans of Orchomenus in these thirty ships. He was also one of the Argonauts and one of the suitors of Helen. After the destruction of Troy, Ialmenus wandered about with the Orchomenians on the Pontus and founded colonies on the coast of Colchis (Strab. 9.2.42). Sixty years after the Trojan War, the sovereignty of the Minyae seems to have been overthrown by Boeotian immigrants from Thessaly; and Orchomenus became a member of the Boeotian confederacy (Strab. 9.2.3).

Orchomenus was famous for the worship of the Charites and for the festival in their honor celebrated with musical contests. Poets and musicians from all parts of Greece took part in it. Their worship was believed to have been first introduced into Boeotia by Eteocles, the son of Cephissus, in the valley of that river (Paus. 9.35.1). The festival at Orchomenus was called the Charisia or Charitesia. Here the Charites were worshipped from early times in the form of rude stones, which were believed to have fallen from heaven in the time of Eteocles (Paus. 9.38.1; Strab. 9.2.40). They were often represented as the companions of other gods, such as Hera, Hermes, Eros, Dionysus, Aphrodite, the Horae, and the Muses. Pindar (*Pyth.* 12.45) calls Orchomenus the city of the Charites, and Theocritus (16.104) describes them as the goddesses who love the Minyeian

Orchomenus. It was in the marshes in the neighborhood of Orchomenus that the auletic or flute reeds, which influenced the development of Greek music, grew.

The ruins of Orchomenus are to be seen at the town of Orhomenos (formerly Skripou). The Mycenaean tholos tomb described as the Treasury of Minyas is on the road through the town. So is the theater, above which are remains of a temple of Asclepius. At the foot of the terrace of the Asclepieion is the spring of the Charites called Acidalius. The temple of the Charites probably stood on the site of the church of the town's convent.

The monuments noticed by Pausanias (9.38.1) at Orchomenus were temples of Dionysus and the Charites. After the birth of Dionysus, Zeus entrusted him to Hermes, or, according to others, to Persephone or Rhea, who took the child to Ino and Athamas at Orchomenus. They were persuaded to bring him up as a girl to disguise him from the wrath of Hera. She discovered the ruse and threw Ino and Athamas into a state of madness. Zeus, in order to save his child, changed him into a ram and carried him to the nymphs of Mount Nysa. Dionysus Agrionius was a name under which the god was worshipped at Orchomenus and from which his festival in that place, the Agrionia, derived its name. Pausanias also saw the treasury and tomb of Minyas; and he saw a brazen figure bound to a rock by a chain of iron, which was said to be the ghost of Actaeon. Actaeon, son of Aristaeus and Autonoe, was killed by his own hunting dogs when Artemis changed him into a stag after he saw her bathing. Near Orchomenus there was a rock on which Actaeon was said to rest when he was tired from hunting and from which he watched the nude Artemis. According to Orchomenian tradition, the rock of Actaeon was haunted by his specter, and the oracle of Delphi commanded the Orchomenians to bury the remains of the hero, which they might happen to find, and to fix an iron image of him upon the rock. This image is the one referred to by Pausanias (9.38.5), and the Orchomenians offered annual sacrifices to Actaeon at this rock. About 1.5 km from the town, at the sources of the Melas, was a temple of Heracles.

Several individuals of importance were connected with Orchomenus. Amphion was a son of Iasus and husband of Persephone, by whom he became the father of Chloris. In Homer (Od. 11.283) this Amphion, king of Orchomenus, is distinct from Amphion, the husband of Niobe. Chloris became the wife of Neleus, king of Pylos, and by him the mother of Nestor.

Athamas was a son of Aeolus and Enarete. He married the immortal Nephele, by whom he became the father of Phrixus and Helle. But he was secretly in love with the mortal Ino, the daughter of Cadmus, by whom he begot Learchus and Melicertes. Ino tried to get rid of Nephele's children and contrived to have Phrixus sacri-

ficed. Nephele was able to rescue Phrixus, along with Helle, at the last moment by having the ram with the golden fleece fly with them to Colchis. Helle fell off into the sea, but Phrixus arrived in Cochis, where he sacrificed the ram and gave its skin to King Aeetes, who fastened it to a sacred oak in the grove of Ares. He married Chalciope, the daughter of Aeetes, and had several children. According to some traditions, he returned in old age to Orchomenus (Paus. 9.34.7). Hera, for reasons stated earlier, caused Athamas to go mad, and in this state he killed Learchus, and Ino threw herself and her son Melicertes into the sea. Athamas was obliged to flee from Boeotia, and he founded Athamania, married Themisto, and had several sons. Athamas, one of his grandsons, led a colony of Minyans to Teos (Paus. 7.3.6).

Menippe was a daughter of Orion and sister of Metioche. Athena taught them the art of weaving. Once the whole of Aonia was visited by a plague, and the oracle of Apollo Gortynius, when consulted, ordered the inhabitants to propitiate the Erinyes by the sacrifice of two maidens, who were to offer themselves to death of their own accord. Menippe and Metioche offered themselves; they thrice invoked the infernal gods and killed themselves with their shuttles. Persephone and Hades metamorphosed them into comets. The Aonians erected to them a sanctuary near Orchomenus where a propitiatory sacrifice was offered to them every year by youths and maidens. The Aeolians called these maidens Coronides (Ov. Met. 13.685).

Other deities were also identified with the town. Aphrodite was surnamed Acidalia from the spring Acidalius near Orchomenus, in which Aphrodite bathed with the Charites. Enyo was the goddess of war who accompanied Ares in battles. At Orchomenus, a festival called Homoloia was celebrated in honor of Zeus, Demeter, Athena, and Enyo, and Zeus was said to have received the surname Homoloius from Homolois, a priestess of Enyo.

ORESTHASIUM (ATHINE?)   was a town in the south of Arcadia in the district of Maenalia, on the road from Sparta to Tegea. Orestheus was a son of Lycaon and the reputed founder of Oresthasium, which is said afterward to have been called Oresteium, from Orestes (Paus. 8.3.2; Eurip. Orest. 1642). Orestes was doomed to wander in this territory, called "Orestes' land" until he was purified of his mother's murder.

Its inhabitants were removed to Megalopolis when that city was founded. The location of Oresthasium is thought to be at or near the modern village of Athine, southwest of Tripoli and north of the Megalopoli/Tripoli highway, where some ancient remains have been found. Others think it was near Paparis, which is south of Athine.

OREUS (OREI)   formerly called Histiaea (from Histiaea, daughter of Hyrieus) was a town in the north of

Euboea, situated upon the Callas River at the foot of Mount Telethrium and opposite Antron on the Thessalian coast. From this town the whole northern part of Euboea was named Histiaeotis. According to some it was a colony from the Attic deme of Histiaea (Strab. 10.1.3). It was one of the most ancient and most important of the Euboean cities. It occurs in Homer (*Il.* 2.537), who describes it as "rich in vines." Elephenor, son of Ares, led the Abantes from Euboea, Chalcis, Eretria, Cerinthus, Dios, Carystus, Styra, and Histiaea in forty ships against the Trojans. Strabo (10.1.3) says that Oreus was situated upon a lofty hill named Drymus. Livy (28.6) describes it as having two citadels, one overhanging the sea and the other in the middle of the city. There are still some remains of the ancient walls at the west end of the bay, which is still called Diavlos Oreon, or the Strait of Orei.

ORMENIUM (GORITSA) was a town of Thessaly, mentioned in the catalog of ships (Hom. *Il.* 2.734) along with Hypereia and Asterium as belonging to Eurypylus. Eurypylus was a son of Euaemon and Ops. Accordong to others, he was a son of Hyperochis and the father of Ormenus. In the *Iliad* he is represented as having led the men of Ormenium and other places to Troy with forty ships. Ormenium was said to have been founded by Ormenus, a son of Cercaphus, grandson of Aeolus, and father of Amyntor. From him Amyntor is sometimes called Ormenides, and Astydameia, his granddaughter, Ormenis (Hom. *Il.* 2.734, 9.448, *Od.* 15.413; Ov. *Her.* 9.50). This was also the birthplace of Phoenix, the son of Amyntor. According to Apollodorus (2.7.7, 3.13.7), Amyntor, a Calydonian hunter, was king of Ormenium and was slain by Heracles, to whom he refused both passage through his dominions and the hand of his daughter Astydameia.

Phoenix was the son of Amyntor by Cleobule. He was king of the Dolopes and took part not only in the Calydonian hunt but, being a friend of Peleus, accompanied Achilles on his expedition against Troy. His father Amyntor neglected his legitimate wife and attached himself to a mistress, but his mother Cleobule begged Phoenix to seduce her rival. Phoenix yielded to the request of his mother, and Amyntor, who discovered it, cursed him and prayed that he might never be blessed with any offspring. Phoenix left his father's house and he went to Peleus, who received him kindly, made him the ruler of the country of the Dolopes on the frontiers of Phthia, and entrusted to him his son Achilles, whom he was to educate (Hom. *Il.* 9.447). According to another tradition, Phoenix did not dishonor his father's mistress (Phthia or Clytia), but she merely accused him of having made improper advances to her, in consequence of which his father put out his eyes. But Peleus took him to Cheiron the Centaur, who restored to him his sight (Apollod. 3.13.8). Phoenix, moreover, is said to have

called the son of Achilles Neoptolemus after the boy had been called Pyrrhus by Lycomedes, his maternal grandfather (Paus. 10.26.4). Neoptolemus was believed to have buried Phoenix at Eion in Macedonia or at Trachis in Thessaly (Strab. 9.4.14). It must further be observed that Phoenix is one of the mythical beings to whom the ancients ascribed the invention of the alphabet.

Strabo identifies Ormenium with a place in Magnesia named Orminium that was situated at the foot of Mount Pelion. It was 5 km from Demetrias, on the road passing through Iolcus, which was 1 km from Demetrias and 3.5 km from Ormenium. Modern evidence has shown that this location was fairly accurate and that the ancient site lay just southeast of the modern Volos at Goritsa. This position and that of Demetrias across the bay controlled shipping into the harbor of Iolcus. Much of the wall remains on the hill, and there were towers projecting from it.

ORNEAE was a town in the Argeïa, mentioned in the *Iliad* (2.571), which is said to have derived its name from Orneus, the son of Erechtheus (Paus. 2.25.5, 10.35.5). Orneus was father of Peteus and grandfather of Menestheus. Orneas kept its ancient Cynurian inhabitants after the Dorian invasion. It continued independent of Argos for a long time; but it was finally conquered by the Argives, who removed the inhabitants of Orneae to Argos (Paus. 2.25.6).

Orneae was situated on the border of Phliasia and Sicyonia at the distance of 22 km from Argos. Strabo (8.6.24) says that Orneae was situated on a river of the same name above the plain of the Sicyonians. The town stood on the more northern of the two roads that led from Argos to Mantineia. This northern road was called Climax and followed the course of the Inachus. There was at Orneae a sanctuary of Artemis with a standing wooden statue, and there was a second temple dedicated to all the gods. A sanctuary of Priapus had been abandoned by the time of Strabo (8.6.24). The site of Orneae is not known, but it is probably in the vicinity of Gimno and Leondio.

OROBIAE (ROVIES) was a town on the west coast of Euboea between Aedepsus and Aegae. It possessed an oracle of Apollo Selinuntius (Strab. 10.1.3). The town was partly destroyed by an earthquake and a tidal wave in 426 B.C. (Thuc. 3.89). Orobiae seems to be the town called Orope by Stephanus of Byzantium, who describes it as "a city of Euboea, having a very renowned temple of Apollo." There are some remains of the walls of Orobiae at Rovies, which must be a corruption of the ancient name.

OROPUS (SKALA OROPOU) was a town on the borders of Attica and Boeotia and the capital of a district called Oropia after it. The Asopus flows through this plain into the sea. Oropus was originally a town of Boeotia; and, from its position in the maritime plain of the Asopus, it naturally belonged to that country (Paus. 1.34.1). It was, however, a frequent subject of dispute between the Athenians and Boeotians, and the Athenians obtained possession of it long before the Peloponnesian War. From 412 B.C. the town was alternately in the hands of the Athenians and Boeotians until Philip gave it to the Athenians after the battle of Chaeroneia. In 318 B.C. the Oropians recovered their independence.

The position of Oropus was defined by Strabo (9.2.6). He placed it with its harbor Delphinium opposite Eretria in Euboea. The modern village of Oropos stands nearly 3 km from the sea on the right bank of the Asopos. It contains some fragments of ancient buildings and sepulchral stones. However, the site is at the village of Skala Oropou, which is on the coast.

In the territory of Oropus was the celebrated temple of the hero Amphiaraus. He was first worshipped as a hero here and later in all Greece. Cephissus, the divinity of the river Cephissus, had an altar in common with Pan, the nymphs, and Achelous in the temple of Amphiaraus (Paus. 1.34.2). Athena Paeonia (Healing Goddess) also had an altar in the temple of Amphiaraus (Paus. 1.2.4,34.2). She shared the altar with Aphrodite Panaceia and the two daughters of Asclepius, Hygieia and Iaso (Paus. 1.34.3; Aristoph. *Plut.* 701). Iaso was worshipped as the goddess of recovery. Excavations have revealed the temple, altar, spring, and other buildings that might have housed the priests and those caring for the ill. A small theater has also been uncovered.

ORTAGUREA   was an earlier name of MARONEIA.

ORTHE   a town of Perrhaebia in Thessaly, mentioned by Homer (*Il.* 2.739), was said by Strabo (9.5.19) to have become the acropolis of Phalanna. It occurs, however, in the lists of Pliny (4.9.16) as a distinct town from Phalanna. Polypoetes, son of Peirithous and Hippodameia, was one of the Lapiths who joined the Greeks in the Trojan War, commanding the men of Argissa, Gyrtone, Orthe, Elone, and Oloosson (Hom. *Il.* 2.738).

ORTHOSIUM or ORTHIUM   was a mountain in Arcadia from which Artemis is supposed to have derived the surname Orthia. It was at the altar of Artemis Orthia that Spartan boys had to undergo the *diamastigosis,* or ritual flogging.

ORTYGIA   was an earlier name of the island of DELOS.

OSSA (OSSA)   is a high mountain in Thessaly on the coast of Magnesia, separated from Olympus only by the narrow vale of Tempe. Hence it was supposed by the ancients that these mountains were once united and had been separated by an earthquake (Herod. 7.129; Strab. 9.5.2). Ossa is conical in form and has only one summit. It is about 1,525 meters high. To the south of Ossa rises Mount Pelion, and the lowest slopes of the two mountains are united by a low ridge. The length of Ossa along the coast is about 15 km.

The Aloeidae, Otus and Ephialtes, were the twin sons of Poseidon by Iphimedeia. They were renowned in the earliest stories of Greece for their extraordinary strength and daring spirit. When they were nine years old, each of their bodies measured about five meters in breadth and twelve in height. At this early age they threatened the Olympian gods with war and attempted to pile Mount Ossa upon Olympus and Pelion upon Ossa. They would have accomplished their object, says Homer (*Od.* 11.305), had they been allowed to grow to manhood; but Apollo destroyed them before their beards began to appear.

OTHRYS (OTHRIS)   is a lofty chain of mountains that shuts in the plain of Thessaly from the south. It branches off from the range of Pindus and runs nearly due east through Phthiotis to the seacoast. It is 1,728 meters high and heavily forested.

When Zeus waged war on his father Cronus and the Titans, the contest was carried on in Thessaly. This so-called Titanomachia took place between Mount Othrys, which the Titans occupied, and Olympus, which the offspring of Cronus occupied. It lasted for ten years, when at length Gaea promised victory to Zeus if he would deliver the Cyclopes and Hecatoncheires from Tartarus. Zeus accordingly slew Campe, who guarded the Cyclopes, and the latter furnished him with thunder and lightning. Hades gave him a helmet, and Poseidon a trident. The Titans then were overcome and hurled down into a cavity below Tartarus. (Hom. *Il.* 14.279; Hes. *Theog.* 697, 851), and the Hecatoncheires were set to guard them. It must be observed that the fight with the Titans is sometimes confounded by ancient writers with the fight with the Gigantes, the Gigantomachia.

Deucalion, the son of Prometheus, built a ship to escape the flood sent by Zeus to destroy the degenerate race of men. Only Deucalion and Pyrrha, his wife, escaped. They floated for nine days and landed, according to some, on Mount Othrys.

Terambus, son of Euseirus and Eidothea, once was tending his flocks on Mount Othrys. He was under the protection of the nymphs whom he delighted with his songs for he was an accomplished musician and played both the syrinx and lyre. Pan advised him to leave Mount Othrys because a very severe winter was coming on. Terambus, however, did not follow the advice and went so far in his arrogance as to insult even the nymphs, saying that they were not daughters of Zeus. The predicted cold came at length, and, while all his flocks perished, Terambus himself was metamorphosed by the nymphs into a beetle called *cerambyx*. Ovid (*Met.* 7.353) mentions one Cerambus on Mount Othrys, who escaped from the Deucalionian flood by means of wings that he had received from the nymphs.

Melampus, son of Amythaon, possessed prophetic powers and was first to practice the medical arts. He resided for a time in the neighborhood of Mount Othrys.

OXEIAE   was another name for the ECHINADES Islands.

PACTIA   was an earlier name of the island of PAROS.

PAEONIA   was a district adjacent to Macedonia. The district derived its name from Paeon, a son of Endymion and brother of Epeius, Aetolus, and Eurycyde. Paeon failed in a race against his brothers to win the throne in Elis so he went into the farthest exile possible by going to the region drained by the Axius River (Paus. 5.1.5). The Paeones were divided into many tribes, who appear to have occupied the entire country afterward called Macedonia, except for the part that was considered Thrace. As the Macedonian kingdom increased, the district called Paeonia decreased in dimension on every side, though the name continued to be used for the interior country to the north and northeast. Part of this country was a monarchy more or less independent of Macedonia until fifty years after the death of Alexander the Great. The banks of the Axius seem to have been the center of the Paeonian power from the time when Pyraechmes and Asteropaeus led the Paeonians to the assistance of Priam, down to the latest existence of the monarchy. Asteropaeus, a son of Pelegon and grandson of the river Axius, was commander of the Paeonians. He was the tallest among all the men and fought against Achilles, whom he at first wounded, but was afterward killed by him (Hom. *Il.* 21.139). Pyraechmes, the other commander, was slain by Patroclus (Hom. *Il.* 16.287). The Paeonians did not claim kinship with Macedonians, Thracians, or Illyrians but professed to be descended from the Teucri of Troy.

PAGAE   (See PEGAE)

PAGASAE (DIMITRIAS)   was a town of Magnesian Thessaly, situated at the north end of the bay named for it. Pagasae is celebrated in mythology as the port where Jason built the ship Argo and from where he sailed upon his adventurous voyage. In fact, the hero was called Jason Pagasaeus because of the town (Ov. *Met.* 7.1, *Her.* 16.345). Some of the ancients derived the name Pagasae from the numerous springs found at this spot (Strab. 9.5.15). In the time of Strabo, Pagasae was the port of Pherae, which was the principal city in this part of

Thessaly. Pagasae was 16.5 km from Pherae and 3.5 from Iolcos. The ruins of the ancient city may be seen near Volos. The gulf is still called Pagassitikos. The acropolis occupied the summit of some rocky heights above the promontory of modern Pefkakia, and at the foot of the rocks are the springs of which Strabo speaks. The walls of Pagasae were near those of Demetrias, which later virtually absorbed the older city. There are remains of the many towers that guarded the walls. Nees Pagasses is a modern resort town adjacent to the ruins, but the site of modern Dimitrias is closer. Apollo Pagasaeus had a sanctuary there said to have been built by Trophonius (Hes. *Scut. Herc.* 70).

PALAESTINUS   (See STRYMON)

PALEIA   was an earlier name of DYME in Achaia.

PALLANTIUM (PALLANTI)   one of the most ancient towns of Arcadia, in the district of Maenalia, was said to have been founded by Pallas, a son of Lycaon. Some call him a son of Aegeus and state that, being expelled by his brother Theseus, he emigrated into Arcadia. He was the grandfather of Euander. Pallantium was situated west of Tegea in a small plain called the Pallantic Plain (Paus. 8.44.5). It was from this town that Euander was said to have led colonists to Italy. Euander was a son of Hermes and an Arcadian nymph, daughter of Ladon. About sixty years prior to the Trojan War, Euander is said to have led a Pelasgian colony from Pallantium in Arcadia into Italy. The cause of this migration was a feud, in which the allies of Euander was defeated. Others relate that Euander had killed his father, Echemus, at the instigation of his mother and that he was obliged to flee Arcadia. In Italy he built the town Pallantium on the Tiber, which was subsequently incorporated with Rome. From it the Palatium or Palatine Hill at Rome was said to have derived its name.

Pallantium took part in the foundation of Megalopolis, but it continued to exist as an independent state. Later it declined to the status of a village but was restored by Antoninus Pius, who exempted it from taxation because of its reputed connection with Rome. The town was visited by Pausanias (8.44.5), who found here a shrine containing statues of Pallas and Euander, a temple of Persephone, and on the hill above the town, which was anciently used as an acropolis, a temple of the Pure (*Katharoi*) Gods, at whose sanctuary the most solemn oaths were taken. Pausanias hints that these gods were called pure because Pallas did not use human sacrifices in their worship (Paus. 8.44.6). The remains of the town were discovered east of the road from Tripoli to Megalopoli near Pallanti. Very few traces remain of the ancient town, but the foundation of the temple of the Pure Gods is thought to be located in the foundations of the chapel of Agios Ioannis.

PALLENE (KASSANDRA)   is the westernmost of the three promontories of Chalcidice, which run out into the Aegean. It was said to have been called Phlegra earlier and to have been the scene of the conflict between the gods and the earthborn Gigantes (Pind. *Nem.* 1.100, *Isth.* 6.48; Apollod. 1.6.1). This cosmic upheaval could realistically perhaps be traced to earthquakes and volcanic action. The modern name of the peninsula is Kassandra. It produces a variety of crops and is notable for its grain and pasturage.

According to some, Ares begot by Achiroe a son, Sithon, and according to others also two daughters, Pallene and Rhoeteia, from whom two towns derived their names. Sithon was also called a son of Poseidon. He married the nymph Mendeis, by whom he became the father of Pallene and Rhoeteia. He was king of the Hadomantes in Macedonia. Pallene, on account of her beauty, had numerous suitors, and Sithon, who promised her to the one who should conquer him in single combat, killed many who came forward. At length he allowed Dryas and Cleitus to fight for her, promising to give her to the conqueror. Pallene, who loved Cleitus, caused her own tutor Persyntes to persuade the charioteer of Dryas to draw out the nails from the wheels of his master's chariot, so that during the fight his chariot broke and he was killed by Cleitus. Sithon, who learned of the trick, erected a funeral pyre to burn the corpse of Dryas, and he intended also to burn Pallene alive. But Aphrodite appeared, a shower of rain extinguished the fire, and Sithon changed his mind and gave his daughter to Cleitus.

Pallene is associated with Proteus, Aeneas, and Protesilaus. Proteus was described as a son of Poseidon and king of Egypt. For one or another reason he went to Thrace and there married Torone. But as his sons by her robbed and killed strangers, he prayed to his father to carry him back to Egypt. Poseidon accordingly opened a chasm in the earth in Pallene and by means of a passage through the earth under the sea Proteus returned to Egypt. Aeneas stayed in Pallene the winter after the taking of Troy and from there founded the town of Aeneia on the Thermaic Gulf. Then he sailed with his companions to Delos, Cythera and on around Greece to Epeirus. Protesilaus, after the Trojan War, took with him as prisoner, Aethylla, a sister of Priam. On his homeward voyage he landed on the peninsula of Pallene between Mende and Scione. When he had gone some distance from the coast to fetch water, Aethylla persuaded the other women to set fire to the ships. Accordingly, Protesilaus was obliged to remain there and he built the town of Scione.

PALLENE (PALINI)   was a celebrated deme of Attica frequently mentioned by ancient writers. It derived its name from Pallas, son of Pandion and uncle of Theseus. It lay on one of the roads from Athens to Marathon (Herod. 1.62) and in this strategic position was involved in three important military operations in the mythological and early history of Athens: the battle between Theseus and the Pallantidae, the war between Eurystheus and the Heracleidae, and the defeat of the Alcmaeonidae by Peisistratus.

Palini, formerly Karvati, is the site of ancient Pallene. It lies 13 km from Rafina on the road to Athens. The noted temple of Athena Pallenis has so far not been discovered.

PAMISUS (PAMISOS)   is a river in Messenia. Springs near Agios Floros, 8 km east of Messene, were considered by the ancients as the source of the Pamisus before it joined the combined waters of the Amphitus and Leucasia (now called the Pamisos over the entire length of the river system). Near here was a temple to Pamisus, the god of the river, and Pausanias (4.3.10,31.3) mentions annual sacrifices to the river and to the springs, where children were cured of various ailments.

PANAEMA   was a place on the island of Samos. Dionysus with the assistance of his companions drove the Amazons from Ephesus to Samos and there killed a great number of them on a spot named, from the occurrence, Panaema (Plut. *Quaest. Gr.* 56). Its location is not known.

PANGAEUM or PANAGAEUS (PANGEO)   is the great mountain of Macedonia, which, under the modern name of Pangeo, stretches to the east from the left bank of the Strymon at the pass of Amphipolis. Pangaeum produced gold as well as silver. Cadmus was said to have been the first to work the mines of Mount Pangaeum, which later were chiefly in the hands of the Thasians.

Lycurgus, a son of Dryas, was king of the Edones in Thrace. He is famous for his persecution of Dionysus and his worship. Dionysus, on his expeditions, came to the kingdom of Lycurgus but was expelled. He punished the king with madness, so that he killed his son Dryas in the belief that he was cutting down a vine. When this was done, Lycurgus recovered his mind; but his country produced no fruit, and the oracle declared that fertility should not be restored unless Lycurgus were killed. The Edonians therefore tied him and led him to Mount Pangaeum where he was torn to pieces by horses.

PANHELLENIUM (OROS)   is a mountain in the south of Aegina. Aeacus, while he reigned in Aegina, was renowned in all Greece for his justice and piety; he was frequently called upon to settle disputes not only among men but even among the gods themselves (Pind. *Isth.* 8.48; Paus. 1.39.6). He was such a favorite with the gods that when Greece suffered from a severe drought, the oracle of Delphi declared that the calamity would not cease unless Aeacus prayed to the gods that it might. Aeacus himself showed his gratitude by erecting a temple to Zeus Panhellenius on Mount Panhellenium (Paus. 2.30.4), and the Aeginetans afterward built a sanctuary called Aeacion on their island. The modern name of the mountain is Oros; it is visible from all over the Saronic Gulf. Clouds gathering on its peak are a sign of rain, and Zeus Panhellenius was probably worshipped partially as a rain god.

PANOPEUS or PHANOTEUS (AGIOS VLASIOS) was an ancient town of Phocis near the boundary of Boeotia and on the road from Daulis to Chaeroneia. Its ruins at the modern village of Agios Vlasios are about 3.5 km from Heronia. Panopeus was a very ancient town, originally inhabited by the Phlegyae. Panopeus, son of Phocus, was the founder. He was an ally of Amphitryon in the raid on the Taphians, during which he broke an oath to Athena. He paid for this by producing a cowardly son, Epeius. Panopeus was also a member of the Calydonian boar hunt. The town of Panopeus was represented in the Trojan War. Schedius, the king of Panopeus, and his brother Epistrophus were the leaders of the Phocians in the Trojan War (Paus. 10.4.2). Epeius, while he was lacking in valor, did build the wooden horse, which proved the downfall of the Trojans.

Panopeus was also celebrated as the home of Tityus, who was slain by Apollo there because he attempted to assault Leto on her way to Delphi (Hom. *Od.* 10.576; Paus. 10.4.4). Tityus was a son of Gaea or of Zeus and Elara and father of Europa. Instigated by Hera, he made an assault upon Leto or Artemis when she passed through Panopeus to Delphi, but was killed by the arrows of Artemis or Apollo, or, according to others, Zeus killed him with a flash of lightning. He was then cast into Tartarus and there he lay outstretched on the ground, covering 360 ares (nine acres), while two vultures devoured his liver. His gigantic tomb was shown in later times near Panopeus (Paus. 10.4.4), and his fall by the arrows of Artemis and Apollo was represented on the throne of Apollo at Amyclae (Paus. 3.18.15).

Euphemus was a son of Poseidon by Europa, the daughter of Tityus. According to one account he was an inhabitant of Panopeus. He was married to Laonome, the sister of Heracles, and was one of the Calydonian hunters. He also was the helmsman of the Argo and had the power, granted by his father, to walk on the sea just as on firm ground (Apollon. Rhod. 1.182).

There are still considerable remains of the ancient walls of Panopeus upon the rocky heights above Agios Vlasios. There are no longer any remains of the tomb of Tityus, which Pausanias (10.4.4) claimed to have seen, but he mentioned a building of unbaked bricks, containing a statue of Pentelic marble, which was supposed to be intended either for Asclepius or Prometheus. It was believed by some that Prometheus made the human race

out of the sandy-colored rocks in the neighborhood and that they still smelled like human flesh.

PARNASSUS (PARNASSOS) in its widest sense is a range of mountains extending across Phocis and terminating at the Corinthian Gulf between Cirrha and Anticyra. In the narrower sense, Parnassus indicates the highest part of the range a few miles north of Delphi. Deucalion was a son of Prometheus and husband of Pyrrha. When Zeus resolved to destroy the degenerate human race inhabiting the earth, Deucalion on the advice of his father built a ship and carried into it stores of provisions. When Zeus sent a flood all over Hellas, which destroyed all its inhabitants, Deucalion and Pyrrha alone were saved. After their ship had been floating for about nine days, it landed on Mount Parnassus, where they made sacrifices and prayed for the means to restore the human race. They then descended Parnassus and settled at Opus. Hellen was one of their sons. Dorus, the mythical ancestor of the Dorians, was a son of Hellen and brother of Xuthus and Aeolus. He is said to have founded the Doric race in the vicinity of Parnassus (Strab. 8.7.1; Herod. 1.56).

The two highest summits of Parnassus were called Tithorea and Lycoreia. Tithorea was a nymph of the mountain, and the town Tithorea, previously called Neon, was also named for her (Paus. 10.32.6). The summit of Tithorea is northwest of, that of Lycoreia northeast of Delphi. Immediately above Delphi the mountain forms a semicircular range of lofty rocks, at the foot of which the town was built. Icadius, a Cretan and brother of Iapys, came to Parnassus led by Apollo in the guise of a dolphin and there gave Delphi and Crissa their names. Parnassus, a son of Cleopompus or Poseidon and the nymph Cleodora, is said to have been the founder of Delphi and the inventor of the art of foretelling the future from the flight of birds. He is also said to have given his name to Mount Parnassus (Paus. 10.6.1). The overtowering rocks were called Phaedriades (Resplendent), from their facing south and thus receiving the full rays of the sun during the most brilliant part of the day. The sides of Parnassus are well forested, and its summit is covered with snow during the greater part of the year. It contains numerous caves, glens, and ravines.

Parnassus is celebrated as one of the chief seāts of Apollo and the Muses and an inspiring source of poetry and song. It is related that four days after his birth, Apollo went to Mount Parnassus and there killed the dragon Python, who had pursued his mother during her wanderings before she reached Delos. Thriae was the name given to the three prophetic nymphs on Mount Parnassus, by whom Apollo was reared and who were believed to have invented the art of prophecy by means of little stones (*thriae*), which were thrown into an urn (*Hymn. Hom. ad Mer.* 552). Python, the famous dragon who guarded the oracle of Delphi, is described as a son of Gaea. He lived in the caves of Mount Parnassus until he was killed by Apollo, who then took possession of the oracle.

Chione, a daughter of Daedalion, was beloved by Apollo and Hermes on account of her beauty. She gave birth to twins, Autolycus, a son of Hermes, and Philammon, a son of Apollo. She was killed by Artemis for having criticized the goddess' beauty. Her father in his grief threw himself from a rock of Parnassus, but in falling he was changed by Apollo into a hawk. Chione is also called Philonis. Argiope was a nymph by whom Philammon begot the celebrated bard Thamyris. Argiope lived at first on Mount Parnassus, but when Philammon refused to take her into his house as his wife, she left Parnassus and went to the country of the Odrysians in Thrace (Apollod. 1.3.3; Paus. 4.33.3).

Autolycus married Nearea, by whom he was father of Anticleia, the mother of Odysseus. He had his residence on Parnassus and was renowned among men for his cunning and oaths. Once when Odysseus was staying with him, the hero was wounded by a boar during the chase on the mountain; it was by this wound that Odysseus was subsequently recognized by his aged nurse when he returned from Troy. Autolycus is very famous in ancient story as a successful robber, who had even the power of metamorphosing both the stolen goods and himself (Hom. *Il.* 10.267; Apollod. 2.6.2).

Parnassus is often associated with nymphs. On the summit Lycorea is the Corycian cave, from which the Muses are sometimes called the Corycian nymphs. Corycia was the nymph who became by Apollo the mother of Lycorus or Lycoreus and from whom the Corycian cave derived its name. Just above Delphi was the far-famed Castalian spring, which issued from between two cliffs called Nauplia and Hyamplia. Cassotis was a Parnassian nymph, from whom was derived the name of the well Cassotis at Delphi, the water of which gave the priestess the power of prophecy (Paus. 10.24.7). Mount Parnassus was sacred to the Muses as was the Castalian spring, near which they had a temple.

The mountain also was sacred to Dionysus, and on one of its summits the Thyiades held their Bacchic revels. Dionysus compelled the women to quit their houses and celebrate Bacchic festivals on Parnassus. The orgiastic worship of Dionysus seems to have been first established in Thrace and to have spread first southward to Mounts Helicon and Parnassus and from there throughout Greece. Pentheus, the king of Thebes, was opposed to the worship of Dionysus in his kingdom, and he was torn to pieces by his own mother and other Maenads, who believed him to be a wild beast. The place where this occurred was said by some to be Mount Parnassus.

Between Parnassus and Mount Cirphis is the valley of the Pleistus, through which the sacred road ran from Delphi to Daulis and Stiris; and at the point (called Schiste) where the road branched off to these two places, Oedipus slew his father Laius.

PARNES (PARNITHA)   a mountain in the northeast of Attica, in some parts as high as 1,220 meters, was a continuation of Mount Cithaeron. From Mount Cithaeron it stretched eastward as far as the coast at Rhamnus. It had forests abounding in game and on its lower slopes produced excellent wine. It formed part of the boundary between Boeotia and Attica, and its pass, which connected these two countries, was strongly fortified by the Athenians. On the summit of the mountain there was a bronze statue of Zeus Parnethius (Paus. 1.32.2), and there were likewise altars of Zeus Semaleos and Zeus Ombrius or Apemius, where sacrifices were offered to him.

PARORIA   was a village about 2 km from Methydrium. It was founded by Tricolonus, a son of Lycaon. Some say that it was founded and named for Paroreus, the son of Tricolonus (Paus. 8.35.6). Its inhabitants took part in the building of Megalopolis. The site of Paroria has not been established, but it must lie within a very short distance of Pirgakio, the modern vicinity of ancient Methydrium.

PAROS (PAROS)   an island in the Aegean Sea and one of the largest of the Cyclades, lies west of Naxos, from which it is separated by a channel about 10 km wide. It was said to have been originally inhabited by Cretans and Arcadians and to have received its name from Parus, a son of Arcadian Parrhasius. Others say that Iasion, the brother of Dardanus, inspired by Demeter and Kore, went to Sicily and many other places and established the mysteries of these goddesses; for this Demeter rewarded him by yielding to his embraces and she became the mother of Parius, the founder of Paros. The island was also reported to have borne the names Pactia, Demetrias, Zacynthus, Hyleesa, Minoa, and Cabarnis. Cabarnus, a man of Paros, revealed to Demeter the fact that her daughter had been carried off. Some writers have said that on Paros, Cabarnus was the name for any priest of Demeter. The island was colonized by the Ionians. It became prosperous at an early period and sent colonies to Thasus (Thuc. 4.104; Strab. 10.5.7), to Parium on the Propontis, and to Pharus on the Illyrian coast. Paros became subject to Athens after the Peloponnesian War.

Paros was celebrated in antiquity for its white marble, which was widely used in architecture and sculpture. The quarries were chiefly in Mount Marpessa. Parian figs were also celebrated (Athen. 3.76). Paros possessed two harbors. Its chief city, which bore the same name as the island, was on the west coast.

The island is still called Paros and contains several ancient remains. The acropolis overlooks the harbor, and a temple of Athena has been partially preserved. A mosaic depicting the labors of Heracles has been uncovered from one of the houses. In the southwest of the city remains have been found of a temple of Apollo Pythius and one of Asclepius. North of Paros remains of a Delion were found. The sanctuary was dedicated to the main gods of Delos— Apollo, Artemis, Zeus Cynthius, and Athena Cynthia. A small hill southeast of the city was probably the site of the sanctuary of Demeter mentioned by Herodotus (6.134), from whom we learn that the temple was outside the city and stood on a hill.

On Paros a festival, the Charisia or Charitisia, was celebrated in honor of the Charites. Paros is also the location of one of the stories relating to Heracles. Heracles, on his expedition to bring back the girdle of Ares from the Amazons, stopped at Paros. Chryses was a son of Minos and the nymph Pareia. He lived with his three brothers on Paros and murdered two of the companions of Heracles. Heracles, in his anger, slew the descendants of Minos except for two of the nephews of Chryses, Alcaeus and Sthenelus, the sons of Androgeus. Heracles took these two with him and he afterward assigned the island of Thasus to them as their habitation.

PARRHASIA   was a district in the south of Arcadia, to which, according to Pausanias, the towns of Lycosura, Thocnia, Trapezus, Proseis, Acacesium, Acontium, Macaria, and Dasea belonged. The Parrhasii are said to have been one of the most ancient of the Arcadian tribes. At the time of the Peloponnesian War these towns were under the supremacy of Mantineia but were rendered independent by the Lacedaemonians. Homer (*Il.* 2.608) mentions a town of Parrhasia, said to have been founded by Parrhasius, a son of Lycaon, or by Pelasgus, son of Arestor. Zeus was born, according to the legends of the country, in Arcadia in the district of Parrhasia. Rhea bore him where there was a hill sheltered with thick brush. Thereafter the place was so holy that no four-footed animal suffering birthpangs nor any woman could approach it.

PARTHENIA   was an earlier name of the island of SAMOS.

PARTHENIUM (PARTHENI)   is a mountain on the boundary of Arcadia and Argolis, across which there was an important pass leading from Argos to Tegea. It was sacred to Pan. Upon this mountain the courier Pheidippides said that he had encountered Pan on returning from Sparta, where he had gone to ask assistance for the Athenians shortly before the battle of Marathon (Herod. 6.105; Paus. 8.54.6). Pan had a sanctuary on Mount Parthenium (Paus. 8.26.2).

Auge, a daughter of Aleus and Neaera, was a priestess of Athena and, having become by Heracles the mother of a son, she concealed him in the temple of the goddess. In consequence of this profanation of the sanctuary, the country was visited by a famine. When Aleus was informed by an oracle that the temple of Athena was profaned by something unholy, he searched, found the child, and ordered him to be exposed on Mount Parthenium. There he was suckled by a hind and thus gained the name Telephus. He grew up in Arcadia and later went to Mysia. He married a daughter of Priam and had a significant role in the Trojan War. He was later worshipped on Mount Parthenium (Paus. 8.34.6; Apollod. 1.8.6).

PARTHENIUS   was an earlier name of the IMBRASUS River.

PATRAE (PATRA)   a town of Achaia and one of the twelve Achaian cities, was situated on the coast west of the promontory Rhium, near the opening of the Corinthian Gulf (Herod. 1.145). Mount Panachaicus rises immediately behind it to the height of 1,927 meters. Patrae is said to have been formed by a union of three small places, Aroe, Antheia, and Mesatis, which had been founded by the Ionians when they had occupied the country. After the expulsion of the Ionians, the Achaean hero Patreus withdrew the inhabitants from Antheia and Mesatis to Aroe, which he enlarged and called Patrae after himself. Patreus was the son of Preugenes, the son of Agenor. His grave was at Patras in the marketplace in front of an image of Athena. There was also a gilt statue of him along with ones of Preugenes and Atherion. Every year the Patrians sacrificed to Preugenes and Patreus when the festival of the Limnatia (Lady of the Lake) was held. The acropolis of Patrae probably continued to bear the name of Aroe, which was often used as synonymous with Patrae (Paus. 7.20.6–9).

Of the public buildings, the most important appears to have been a temple of Artemis Laphria on the acropolis, with an ancient statue of the goddess. This statue had been removed from Calydon to Patrae by order of Augustus, and an annual festival was celebrated in its honor. There were an Odeion and a theater. On the seaside was a temple of Demeter, which was remarkable because a spring in front of it foretold the fate of sick persons. A mirror was suspended on the water, and on this mirror would appear certain images indicating whether the person would live or die. Opposite the marketplace was a temple of Artemis Limnatis which housed a wooden image of the goddess. Preugenes, in obedience to a dream, stole this wooden image from Sparta. Dionysus Aesymnetes (Lord or Ruler) had a temple at Patrae. The introduction of the worship of Dionysus Aesymnetes ended the practice of human sacrifice in Achaia. Dionysus Calydonius was here also; the god's image was carried from Calydon to Patrae (Paus. 7.21.1). Dionysus Mesateus, Dionysus Antheus, and Dionysus Aroeus were names of the god derived from the three cities that united to make up Patrae. Dionysus was also said to have been educated at Mesatis. At the festival of the god, images of these other manifestations of Dionysus were brought into the sanctuary of Dionysus Aesymnetes. Eurypylus introduced the worship of Dionysus Aesymnetes into Achaia. He also dedicated a sanctuary to Soteria, the goddess of recovery, at Patrae, after he had been cured of his madness. He himself had a monument at Patrae and sacrifices were offered to him each year after the festival of Dionysus. His tomb was near the temple of Artemis Laphria.

Many other gods were honored in and around the city. There was a temple to Asclepius between Dyme and Patrae. There was also a statue of him at Patrae. Athena Panachaea had a temple at Patrae, as did Zeus Olympius. Hera had a statue there, and Apollo a sanctuary. The image of the god was of bronze and naked; on his feet were sandals, and one foot stood upon the skull of an ox. He also had a temple in a grove by the sea with an image of stone. There were temples to Nemesis and to Aphrodite. At the harbor there were two sanctuaries to Aphrodite, one with an image drawn up by fishermen in a net a generation before Pausanias. The other image had face, hands, and feet of stone with the rest of wood. She also had a temple in a grove by the sea with an image of stone. At the harbor was a temple of Poseidon with a standing stone statue. Another Poseidon of bronze was also in the harbor. Ares had a statue of bronze at the harbor. Next to the grove with the temples of Apollo and Aphrodite was a sanctuary of Demeter; she and Kore were standing, but the statue of Gaea there was seated. By the grove were also two sanctuaries of Serapis. In one was a tomb of Aegyptus, the son of Belus. He was said by the people of Patrae to have fled to Aroe because of the misfortunes of his sons and because he shuddered at the mere name of Argos and even more through dread of Danaus.

Melanippus was a youth of Patrae, who was in love with Comaetho, a priestess of Artemis Triclaria. As the parents on both sides would not consent to their marriage, Melanippus profaned the temple of the goddess by his intercourse with Comaetho. The goddess punished the two offenders with instant death and brought plague and famine on the whole country. The oracle of Delphi revealed the reason for these calamities and ordered the inhabitants to sacrifice the handsomest youth and the loveliest maiden to Artemis every year (Paus 7.19.5). As earlier stated, the introduction of the worship of Dionysus Aesymnetes terminated this practice of human sacrifice.

Patrae has continued down to the present day to be one of the most important cities in Peloponnesus. It is perfectly situated for communicating with Italy, the Adriatic, and eastern Greece by means of the Gulf of Corinth and the Corinthian Canal. The modern town occupies the same site as the ancient city. There are very few remains of antiquity at Patrae. The modern citadel contains some pieces of the walls of the ancient acropolis. The seaside temple of Demeter has been located along with its oracular spring, which is near the church of Agios Andreas.

PEDASUS   was the Homeric name of ancient METHONE, or according to others of CORONE.

PEGAE or PAGAE (PSATHA)   was a town of Megaris on the Corinthian Gulf. It was the harbor of Megaris on the west coast and the most important place in the country next to Megara. Strabo (8.1.3) says it was situated on the narrowest part of the Megaric isthmus, the distance from Pegae to Nisaea, the port of Megara, being 22 km. The site of Pegae is said to be the small port of modern Psatha.

Pausanias (1.44.4) saw there a chapel and grave of the hero Aegialeus, the son of Adrastus and the only one of the Epigoni killed in the battle against Thebes. Pausanias saw near the road to Pegae a rock covered with arrow marks that were supposed to have been made by a body of the Persian cavalry of Mardonius, who in the night had discharged their arrows at the rock under the influence of Artemis, mistaking it for the enemy. In commemoration of this event, there was a bronze statue of Artemis Soteira at Pegae.

The scene of the tragedy of Tereus and the sisters Procne and Philomela has by some been placed at Pegae instead of Daulis. According to the Megarian tradition, Tereus, being unable to overtake the women, killed himself. The Megarians showed the tomb of Tereus in their own country, and an annual sacrifice was offered to him. Procne and Philomela, moreover, were there believed to have escaped to Attica and wept themselves to death (Paus. 1.41.9).

PEIRAEUS (PIREAS)   was a deme about 8 km from Athens and one of its seaports. It included Munychia, which was its acropolis. It was fortified with a wall 11 km in circumference (Thuc. 2.13), and long walls connected it with Athens. Peiraeus had three harbors—Munychia (Fanari), Zea (Stratiotiki) and Peiraeus (Drako). The harbor of Zea was probably named for Artemis Zea. The harbor of Peiraeus was divided into two parts: Cantharus for ships of war and Emporium for commercial vessels. Ashore were stoas and colonnaded areas used for mercantile purposes. Between the stoas of Emporium and

Cantharus stood the Aphrodision, or temple of Aphrodite.

Within the fortress of Munychia was a temple of Artemis Munychia, the guardian deity of this citadel. The temple was famous as a place of asylum for state criminals (Xenoph. *Hellen.* 4.11). Near this temple was the Bendideion, or temple of the Thracian Artemis known as Bendis, whose festival was called the Bendideia. At the southwest foot of the acropolis remains of a shrine of Asclepius were found. The agora of Peiraeus was called the Hippodameian Agora and was situated where the long walls from Athens joined the walls of the port city. Behind the Macra Stoa was the sacred enclosure of Zeus Soter. There was, as well, a sacred precinct of Athena Soteira with a bronze statue holding a spear.

In 1959 in the north area of the harbor several bronzes were found, including an archaic Apollo. At the north end of the neck of land called the Eetioneia remains of a shrine attributed to Aphrodite Euploea were found.

PEIRENE (See CORINTH)

PELASGIA   was the earlier name of ARCADIA.

PELASGIA   was an alternate early name of the island of DELOS.

PELION or PELIUM (PILIO)   is a high mountain in Thessaly, extending along the coast of Magnesia. It rises to the south of Ossa, and the lower slopes of the two mountains are connected by a low ridge. It forms a chain of some extent, stretching from Mount Ossa to the end of the Magnesian promontory. It attains its greatest height above Iolcos (Volos). On its east side, Mount Pelion rises almost straight from the sea. Homer (*Il.* 2.757) describes it as covered with waving forests.

Mount Pelion is celebrated in mythology. It plays an important part in the war of the giants and the gods since the giants are said to have piled Ossa upon Pelion in order to scale Olympus. At a very early age the Aloeidae, Otus and Ephialtes, the giant sons of Poseidon, threatened the Olympian gods with war and attempted to pile Mount Ossa upon Olympus and Pelion upon Ossa. They never were able to carry this out, since the gods dispatched them before they reached maturity.

Mount Pelion was said to be the residence of the Centaurs, who were, according to the earliest accounts, a race of men who inhabited the mountains and forests of Thessaly. They are described as leading a rude and savage life, occasionally carrying off the women of their neighbors, as covered with hair and ranging over their mountains like animals. Later writers described them as partly human and partly horse. Ixion begot by a cloud a son Centaurus, who mated with Magnesian mares and begot

the hippocentaurs. These creatures were brought up by the nymphs on Mount Pelion.

Cheiron was the wisest and most just of all the Centaurs. He was the son of Cronus and Philyra. He lived on Mount Pelion, from which he, like the other Centaurs, was expelled by the Lapiths. Sacrifices were offered to him there by the Magnesians until a late time, and the family of the Cheironidae in that area, distinguished for their knowledge of medicine, were regarded as his descendants. Cheiron himself had been instructed by Apollo and Artemis and was renowned for his skill in hunting, medicine, music, gymnastics, and the art of prophecy. All the most distinguished heroes, like Achilles, are described as pupils of Cheiron in these arts. His friendship with Peleus, who was his grandson, is particularly celebrated. Cheiron saved him from the hands of the other Centaurs, who were on the point of killing him, and he also restored to him the sword that Acastus had concealed (Apollod. 3.13.3). Cheiron further informed him in what manner he might gain possession of Thetis, who was doomed to marry a mortal. He is also connected with the story of the Argonauts, whom he received hospitably when they came to his home on their voyage, for many of the heroes were his friends and pupils (Apollon. Rhod. 1.554). He and Heracles were friends, but during a struggle with the other Centaurs, Heracles accidentally shot Cheiron with a poisoned arrow. Cheiron, though immortal, chose to die and gave his immortality to Prometheus. He had been married to Nais, and his daughter Endeis was the mother of Peleus.

Acastus was a son of Pelias and one of the Argonauts. He became king of Iolcus when Medea successfully instigated the murder of Pelias. The funeral games he instituted for his father were attended by Peleus, and Astydameia, the wife of Acastus, fell in love with him. Peleus resisted her advances so she accused him of attempted seduction to Acastus. Acastus took Peleus hunting on Mount Pelion, and, while they were resting, Peleus fell asleep. Acastus took his sword from him and left him alone and exposed so that Peleus was nearly killed by the Centaurs. He was saved by Cheiron, returned to Acastus, and killed him and his wife. After the unpleasant business with Acastus, Peleus married the Nereid Thetis, by whom he became the father of Achilles. Thetis had been wooed by Poseidon and Zeus, but when they learned that the son of Thetis would be more illustrious than his father, both suitors withdrew. Zeus, however, decreed that she should marry a mortal. Cheiron informed Peleus of this and told him how he might get possession of her, even if she should metamorphose herself. She did try assuming various forms, but she gave up and assumed her proper form when Peleus refused to let go his grasp of her. Their wedding was attended by all the gods. The upbringing of Achilles was entrusted to Cheiron, who educated and instructed him in the arts of riding, hunting, and playing the phorminx, and also changed his original name, Ligyron (Whining), to Achilles. Cheiron fed his pupil with the hearts of lions and the marrow of bears. Cheiron also instructed him in the healing art, using the medicinal herbs with which Mount Pelion abounds.

Saved from assassination by his relatives, who pretended he was dead, Jason was entrusted to Cheiron to be educated. According to some, he came from Mount Pelion to Iolcus, found his aged father Aeson still alive, and demanded the throne from Pelias, who had usurped it. Pelias consented to surrender the throne but on the condition that Jason fetch the Golden Fleece from Colchis. Hesiod relates that Jason and Medea settled happily in Iolcus and that their son Medeius was educated by Cheiron on nearby Pelion. Actaeon, the hunter who later was torn to pieces by his own hounds, was also instructed by Cheiron, especially in the art of hunting.

Three other mortals who were associated with Mount Pelion are Melanippe, Cyrene, and Prothous. Melanippe was a daughter of Cheiron. Being with child by Aeolus, she fled to Mount Pelion. Cheiron searched for her, and in order that her condition might not become known, she prayed to be metamorphosed into a mare. Artemis granted the prayer, and in the form of a mare she was placed among the stars. Cyrene, a daughter of Hyseus, was beloved by Apollo, who abducted her from Mount Pelion and took her to Libya, where Cyrene derived its name from her. Prothous was a son of Tenthredon and commander of the Magnetes who lived near Mount Pelion. He was one of the Greek heroes at Troy (Hom. *Il.* 2.758).

It was believed that the cave of Cheiron and a temple of Zeus Actaeus occupied the summit of the mountain. Customarily the sons of the principal citizens of Demetrias, selected by the priest, ascended every year to this temple, clothed with thick skins because of the cold. Between the two summits of Mount Pelion there is a cavern, now commonly known by the name of the Cave of Achilles. Two rivers of Pelion are mentioned, Crausindon and Brychon. Lastly, Pelion was connected with the tale of the Argonauts, since the timber from which the Argo was built was cut down in the forests of the mountain.

PELLA (PELA)   was the capital of Macedonia and the birthplace of Alexander the Great. Its site is located a few kilometers northwest of Thessaloniki. It was a city of considerable size and stood on a height, bounded by marshes caused by the overflowing of a lake. Its remains are all historical. The temple of Athena Alcidemos is the only public building mentioned in history (Liv. 42.51), but the location of the temple is at present not known. However, several objects have been uncovered that have mythological interest. Mosaics show a naked Dionysus seated on a panther, a male and a female Centaur, the rape of Helen by Theseus, and a battle with Amazons. A statue of Poseidon has been found, as well as inscriptions to Asclepius, Zeus Meilichius, Heracles, and the Muses.

PELLANA (PELANA?)   was a town of Laconia on the Eurotas and on the road from Sparta to Arcadia. It was said to have been the residence of Tyndareus when he was expelled from Sparta. Tyndareus, son of Perieres and Gorgophone, was father of Clytemnestra, Castor, and other children by Leda. Early on, he was expelled from Sparta by his stepbrother Hippocoon, and, according to some, he went to Pellana until his kingdom was restored to him by Heracles. Pellana was subsequently the frontier fortress of Sparta on the Eurotas, as Sellasia was on the Oenus. It was one of the cities of the Laconian Tripolis, the other two probably being Carystus and Belemina. It had ceased to be a town in the time of Pausanias (3.21.2), but he noticed there a temple of Asclepius and two fountains, named Pellanis and Lanceia.

Pausanias (8.35.3) says that Pellana was one hundred stadia (18.5 km) from Belemina; but he does not specify its distance from Sparta, nor on which bank of the river it stood. The site has been placed at Pelana west of the river, but some think this was really the site of Carystus, and that Pellana was on the east bank of the river, due west of Sellasia. This second place meets the description because of springs that are found there.

PELLENE (PELLINI)   was a town in Achaia, the most easterly of the twelve Achaian cities. Its territory bordered upon that of Sicyon onto the east and upon that of Aegeira on the west. Pellene was located 11 km from the sea on a strongly fortified hill, the summit of which rose into a peak, dividing the city into two parts. Its name was derived by the inhabitants themselves from the giant Pallas and by the Argives from the Argive Pellen, a son of Phorbas and grandson of Triopas (Paus. 7.26.5). Pellene was a city of great antiquity. It is mentioned in the Homeric catalog (Hom. *Il.* 2.574). According to one tradition the inhabitants of Scione in the peninsula of Pallene in Macedonia professed to be descended from the Achaian Pellenians, who were driven onto the Macedonian coast on their return from Troy (Thuc. 4.120).

The buildings of Pellene are described by Pausanias (7.27.1–4). Of these, the most important were a temple of Athena, with a chryselephantine statue of the goddess, said to have been one of the earlier works of Pheidias; a temple of Dionysus Lampter (Shining or Torchbearer), in whose honor a festival, Lampteria, was celebrated; a temple of Apollo Theoxenus, to whom a festival, Theoxenia, was celebrated; a gymnasium, etc. There were also sanctuaries of Eileithyia, Poseidon, and Artemis. Eleven kilometers from the city was the Mysaion, a temple of the Mysian Demeter. Demeter Mysia was said to have derived her surname from an Argive Mysius, who received her kindly during her wanderings and built a sanctuary to her (Paus. 7.27.4). Near this temple was a temple of Asclepius, called Cyrus. Near Pellene Artemis Soteira was worshipped (Paus. 7.27.5). At both these places there were copious springs. The ruins of Pellene are situated at Pellini. Remains of a sanctuary of Demeter, the Mysaion, and another of Asclepius Cyrus have been placed at the modern village Ano Trikala, southeast of ancient Pellene, to which they belonged.

The harbor of Pellene was called Aristonautae; it was 11 km from Pellene and 22 from Aegeira. It is said to have been so called from the Argonauts having landed there in the course of their voyage (Paus. 7.26.7). It was probably on the site of the modern Xilokastro. A little to the west near the coast was the fortress Olurus, dependent upon Pellene. It has been placed at Kamari.

PELOPIS INSULAE   are nine small islands lying off Methana on the Argolis coast. They must be the islands lying between Epidaurus and Aegina, of which Pityonnesus (modern Angistri) is the largest (Plin. 4.12.20). Pelops was king of Pisa in Elis and from him the great southern peninsula of Greece derived the name Peloponnesus. The nine islands are also said to have been called after him the Pelopian Islands (Paus. 2.34.4).

PELOPONNESUS (PELOPONISSOS)   is the southern part of Greece or the peninsula, which was connected with Hellas proper by the Isthmus of Corinth. It is said to have derived its name, Peloponnesus (Island of Pelops), from the mythical Pelops. This name does not occur in Homer, in whose time the peninsula was sometimes called Apia, from Apis, son of Phoroneus, king of Argos, and sometimes Argos. These names were due to the fact that Argos was the chief power in Peloponnesus at that period. Peloponnesus is bounded on the north by the Corinthian Gulf, on the west by the Ionian or Sicilian Sea, on the south by the Libyan Sea, and on the west by the Cretan and Myrtoan Seas. On the east and south there are three great gulfs, Argolic, Laconian, and Messenian. The ancients compared the shape of the country to the leaf of the plane tree; and its alternate modern name, the Morea, was given to it because of its resemblance to a mulberry leaf. Peloponnesus was divided into various provinces, all of which, with the exception of Arcadia, were bounded on one side by the sea. Arcadia was the center of the country. The other provinces were Achaia in the north, Elis in the west, Messenia in the west and south, Laconia in the south and east and Corinthia in the east and north. An account of the geography of the peninsula is given under these individual names.

Peloponnesus was originally inhabited by Pelasgians. Oceanus and Tethys had a son Inachus, after whom a river in Argos is called Inachus. He and Melia, daughter of Oceanus, had two sons, Phoroneus and Aegialeus. Aegialeus, who died childless, named the whole country Aegialia. Phoroneus then reigned and fathered Apis, Car, and Niobe by a nymph Teledice. Phoroneus is said to have discovered the use of fire. Apis, succeeding him, converted his power into a tyranny and named the land Apia after himself. He was assassinated by Thelxion and Telchis and left no children. But Niobe had by Zeus (and she was the first mortal woman with whom Zeus cohabited) a son Argus, and also, some say, a son Pelasgus, after whom the inhabitants of the Peloponnesus were called Pelasgians. However, Hesiod, quoted by Apollodorus (2.1.1), says that Pelasgus was an autochthon. Argus was the third king of Argos. It is from this Argus that the country afterward was called Argolis and all Peloponnesus derived the name of Argos (Paus. 2.16.1).

Subsequently the Achaians, who belonged to the Aeolic race, settled in the eastern and southern parts of the peninsula, in Argolis, Laconia, and Messenia; the Ionians in the northern part in Achaia; and the Pelasgians chiefly in the central part in Arcadia. Eighty years after the Trojan War, according to mythological chronology, the Dorians, led by the Heracleidae, invaded and conquered Peloponnesus. Pityreus, a descendant of Ion and father of Procles, was the last king in Peloponnesus before the invasion of the Dorians (Paus. 2.26.2, 7.4.3). Heracleidae was a patronymic given to all the sons and descendants of the Greek Heracles; but the name is also applied in a narrow sense to those descendants of the hero who, allied with the Dorians, invaded and took possession of Peloponnesus. The Heracleidae, allied with the Dorians, invaded Peloponnesus to take possession of those countries and rights that their ancestor had duly acquired. This expedition is called the return of the Heracleidae. They did not, however, succeed in their first attempt; the legend mentions five different expeditions. Hyllus, the son of Heracles, eventually fell in single combat with Echemus, king of Tegea, and according to the terms of the contest, the Heracleidae were not to make any further attempt upon the peninsula within the next fifty years.

Thirty years after the Trojan War, Cleodaeus, son of Hyllus, again invaded Peloponnesus; and about twenty years later Aristomachus, the son of Cleodaeus, undertook the fourth expedition. But both heroes fell. About thirty years after Aristomachus (eighty years after Troy) the Heracleidae prepared for a great and final attack. Temenus, Cresphontes, and Aristodemus were the three sons of Aristomachus. On the advice of an oracle, they built a fleet on the Corinthian Gulf; but this fleet was destroyed because Hippotes, one of the Heracleidae, had killed Carnus, an Acarnanian soothsayer, and Aristodemus was killed by a flash of lightning (Apollod. 2.8.2; Paus. 3.1.5). An oracle now ordered the Heracleidae to take a three-eyed man for their commander. He was found in the person of Oxylus, the son of Andraemon, who was seated upon a one-eyed horse (Apollod. 2.8.3). The expedition now successfully sailed from Naupactus toward Rhion in Peloponnesus (Paus. 8.5.6). Their campaign was widely supported, and they conquered Tisamenus, the son of Orestes, who ruled over Argos, Mycenae, and Sparta. The conquerors now succeeded without difficulty, for many of the inhabitants of Peloponnesus spontaneously opened their gates to them, and other places were delivered up to them by treachery (Paus. 2.4.3, 4.3.3). They then distributed the newly acquired possessions among themselves by lot. Such are the traditions about the Heracleidae and their conquest of Peloponnesus.

The Heracleidae established Doric states in Argolis, Laconia, and Messenia, from where they extended their power over Corinth, Sicyon, and Megara. Part of the Achaean population remained in these provinces as tributary subjects to the Dorians under the name of Perioeci; others of the Achaeans passed over to the north of Peloponnesus, expelled the Ionians, and settled in this part of the country, which was called after them Achaia. The Aetolians, who had invaded Peloponnesus along with the Dorians, settled in Elis and became intermingled with the original inhabitants. The peninsula remained under Doric influence during the most important period of Greek history, and opposed to the great Ionic city of Athens. After the conquest of Messenia by the Spartans, it was under their control until their overthrow by the Thebans at the battle of Leuctra in 371 B.C..

We might mention five prominent gods in Peloponnesus. First, the conquest by the Dorians raised Apollo to the rank of the principal divinity in the peninsula. Apollo Nomius was originally a local divinity of the shepherds of Arcadia, who was transformed into and identified with the Dorian Apollo during the process in which the latter became the national divinity of the Peloponnesians. The worship of Artemis was universal in all Greece, but more especially in Arcadia and the whole of Peloponnesus. The worship of Poseidon extended over all Greece and south Italy, but he was more especially revered in Peloponnesus. And finally, the worship of the Dioscuri spread from there over Greece, Sicily, and Italy; their statues were numerous in Greece but particularly in Peloponnesus.

PENEIUS (PINIOS)   a river of Elis, rises on the border of Arcadia, flows by the town of Elis, and empties into the sea between the promontories of Chelonatas and Ichthys. Augeas was a son of Phorbas and king of the Epeians in Elis. One of the labors imposed on Heracles by Eurystheus was to clear in one day the stables of Augeas, who kept in them a large number of oxen. Heracles accomplished this by diverting the rivers Alpheus and Peneius through the stables. Payment in oxen had been promised; when Augeas refused to pay, Heracles made war on him and killed him and his sons.

PENEIUS (PINIOS)   the chief river of Thessaly and one of the most important in all of Greece, rises near Alalcomenae in Mount Lacmon. Its most important tributaries were named the Enipeus, the Lethaeus, and the Titaresius. The Peneius ultimately flows through the vale of Tempe between Mounts Ossa and Olympus into the sea. Poseidon Petraeus was worshipped among Thessalians because the god was believed to have separated the rocks between which the river Peneius flows into the sea (Pind. *Pyth.* 4.246). As a god Peneius is called a son of Oceanus and Tethys. By the Naiad Creusa he became the father of Hypseus, Stilbe, and Daphne. Stilbe became by Apollo the mother of Lapithes and Centaurus (Diod. 4.69). Daphne was extremely beautiful and was pursued by Apollo. When on the point of being overtaken by him, she prayed to Gaea, Mother Earth, who opened the earth and received her. In order to console Apollo, Gaea created the evergreen laurel tree (*daphne*), and from its boughs Apollo made himself a wreath. According to Ovid (*Met.* 1.452), Daphne in her flight from Apollo metamorphosed herself into a laurel tree. Cyrene also is called by some the wife of Peneius and by others his daughter, and thus Peneius is described as the ancestor of Aristaeus.

PENTELICUS (PENDELI)   is the mountain in Attica between Parnes and Hymettus. It was famous for its fine-grained white marble, which was used for the buildings on the Athenian Acropolis. The ancient quarries can still be seen. The most conspicuous is Spilia, near which is a cavern that was used as a sanctuary to the nymphs. Pausanias (1.32.2) also mentions a statue of Athena on the summit.

PEPARETHUS (SKOPELOS)   is an island in the Aegean Sea lying off the coast of Thessaly to the east of Halonnesus. Pliny (4.12.23) describes it as 15 km in circuit and says that it was formerly called Euoenus. It was said to have been colonized by some Cretans under the command of Staphylus (*Hymn. Hom. ad Apoll.* 32). Staphylus was a son of Dionysus and Ariadne. Peparethus was an island of some importance; it possessed three towns, one of which bore the same name as the island (Strab. 9.5.16). Peparethus was celebrated in antiquity for its wine (Athen. 1.29), and Skopelos, which it is now called, still produces wine that has a good market on the mainland.

PEPHNUS (AGIOS NIKOLAOS?)   was a town of Laconia on the east coast of the Messenian Gulf 3.5 km from Thalamae. In front of it was an island of the same name, which Pausanias (3.26.2,3) describes as not larger than a great rock, on which stood, in the open air, bronze statues one foot high of the Dioscuri. There was a tradition that the Dioscuri were born on this island. The island is at the mouth of the river Milea, which is the minor Pamisus of Strabo (8.4.6). On the island are two ancient tombs, which are called those of the Dioscuri. The Messenians said that their territories originally extended as far as Pephnus. Pephnus must have been near Agios Nikolaos, which is about halfway between the known sites of ancient Thalamae and Leuctra.

PERACHORA (See CORINTHUS ISTHMUS)

PERAETHEIS (ARAHAMITES)   was a town in Arcadia named for Peraethus, a son of Lycaon (Paus. 8.3.4). The road from Megalopolis to Maenalus led along the Helisson River to the foot of Mount Maenalus. A side road ran along the left bank of the Elaphus for 3.5 km to Peraetheis, where there was a temple of Pan. South of Arahamites, where the Elafos River rises, are remains of a Doric temple, which is most likely this temple.

PERGAMUS (PLATANIAS?)   was a town in Crete to which a mythical origin was ascribed. According to Virgil (*Aen.* 3.133), it was founded by Aeneas; according to another writer, by Agamemnon; and according to still another, by the Trojan prisoners belonging to the fleet of Agamemnon. It was said to be near Cydonia (Hania) and is mentioned by Pliny (4.12.20) in connection with Cydonia. Consequently, it must have been situated in the western part of the island and has been placed at Platanias. It was thought that the Dictynnaion stood in the territory of Pergamus.

PERSEPOLIS   was an earlier name of MIDEA.

PHAESANA   was a place in Arcadia on the Alpheius River. Aepytus was the son of Elatus and originally ruled over Phaesana. When Cleitor, the son of Azan, died without any issue, Aepytus succeeded him and became king of the Arcadians. Pitana, the mother of Euadne, sent her newly born child to Aepytus at Phaesana. There in later years Euadne became by Apollo the mother of a boy, who, when his mother for shame deserted him, was fed with honey by two serpents. He was found by servants of Aepytus and was named Iamus. Aepytus, who consulted the Delphic oracle about the child, was told that the boy would be a celebrated prophet and the ancestor of a great family of prophets. When Iamus had grown up, he descended by night into the waters of the river Alpheius and invoked Poseidon and Apollo that they might reveal to him his destiny. Apollo commanded him to follow his voice. It led him to Olympia, where he was given the power to understand and explain the voices of birds and to foretell the future from the sacrifices burning on the altars of Zeus. Pindar is the only writer to mention this otherwise unknown place (*Ol.* 6.54).

PHAESTUS (FESTOS)   was a town in the south of Crete, 11 km from Gortyna and 3.5 from the sea. It was said to have derived its name from an eponymous hero Phaestus, a son of Rhopalus and grandson of Heracles, who migrated from Sicyon to Crete and became king in this town (Paus. 2.6.3). According to others, it was founded by Minos (Diod. 5.78; Strab. 10.4.14). It is mentioned by Homer (*Il.* 2.648) and was evidently one of the most ancient places on the island. It was destroyed by the Gortynians, who took possession of its territory. Its port was Matalum, 7.5 km away. Phaestus is one of the best preserved and most impressive ruins in Greece. Its palace, houses, and courts have provided a wealth of information about the town. There are almost no mythological references. One structure at the southwest corner of the palace is thought to be a temple of Rhea.

Galateia was a daughter of Eurytius and the wife of Lamprus, the son of Pandion, at Phaestus. Her husband, who very much wanted a son, gave orders to kill any daughter born to her. Galateia gave birth to a daughter but could not bring herself to comply with her husband's cruel command. She was induced by dreams and soothsayers to bring up the child in the guise of a boy and under the name of Leucippus. When the maiden had thus grown up, Galateia, dreading the discovery of the secret and the anger of her husband, took refuge with her daughter in a temple of Leto and prayed for the goddess to change the girl into a youth. Leto granted the request so in after years the Phaestians offered up sacrifices to Leto Phytia (Creator) and celebrated a festival called Ecdysia in commemoration of the maiden having put off her female attire. A similar story is told of Iphis, a daughter of Ligdus and Telethusa of Phaestus. Iphis was also brought up as a boy and for the same reason. When Iphis had grown up and was betrothed to Ianthe, Isis, who had before advised the mother to treat Iphis as a boy, now metamorphosed her into a youth (Ov. *Met.* 9.665).

PHAESTUS   was a later name of ancient PHRIXA.

PHALANNA (TIRNAVOS?)   was a town of the Perrhaebi in Thessaly, situated on the left bank of the Peneius southwest of Gonnus. Strabo (9.5.19) says that the Homeric Orthe became the acropolis of Phalanna, but Pliny (4.9.16) makes Orthe and Phalanna two distinct towns. Phalanna was said to have derived its name from a daughter of Tyro. Phalanna probably stood near Tirnavos, where are the remains of an ancient city upon a hill

3 km east of the village. Inscriptions indicate a temple of Athena Polias in the area. There was also a sanctuary of Hades and Persephone in Phalanna. A village called Falana is about 10 km east of Tirnavos, but there seems to be no connection with the ancient place.

PHALANTHUM (ALONISTENA?)   was a town and mountain of Arcadia in the district Orchomenia near Methydrium. Phalanthus was a son of Agelaus and grandson of Stymphalus and the reputed founder of Phalanthum (Paus. 8.35.9). The site of Phalanthum is not known, but Alonistena is the modern village closest to it. It apparently lay west of there.

PHALASARNA (FALASARNA)   a town of Crete, located on the northwest side of the island a little south of the promontory Cimarus, was described as having an enclosed port and a temple of Artemis Dictynna. Phalasarna was 11 km from Polyrrhenia (Polirinia), of which it was the port town.

There are considerable remains of the walls of Phalasarna. There are other remains, the most curious of which is an enormous throne cut out of the solid rock on the southwest side of the city. The height of the arms above the seat is about one meter, and its other dimensions are in proportion. It was no doubt dedicated to some deity, probably to Artemis. Near this throne there are two others plus a number of tombs hewn in the solid rock.

PHALERUM (NEA FALIRO)   was a harbor of Athens, named for Phalerus, a son of Alcon and grandson of Erechtheus. He had an altar there dedicated to him (Paus. 1.1.4). The only spot that the ancient Athenians could use as a harbor was the southeast corner of the Phaleric bay. This was accordingly the site of Phalerum, a deme belonging to the tribe Aeantis. For the inhabitants of Athens this location had two advantages not possessed by the harbors of the Peiraic peninsula. First, it was much nearer to the most ancient part of the city, which was built mostly south of the Acropolis, and, secondly, it was accessible at every season of the year by a dry road.

The port of Phalerum was little used after the foundation of Peiraeus; but the place continued to exist down to the time of Pausanias (1.1.4). He mentioned among its monuments temples of Demeter, Zeus, and Athena Sciras and altars of the Unknown Gods, the Sons of Theseus, and of Phalerus. About 4 km away, at the present Cape of Agios Kosmas, there are some ancient remains, probably those of the temple of Aphrodite Colias mentioned by Pausanias (1.1.5). Androgeus, the son of Minos, died, somewhat mysteriously, in Athens, and in consequence Minos made war on the Athenians. Androgeus was worshipped as a hero in Attica, an altar was erected to him in the port of Phalerum (Paus. 1.1.4),

and games, the Androgeonia, were celebrated in his honor every year in the Cerameicus.

PHALYCUM or ALYCUM   a town of Megaris mentioned by Theophrastus (*Hist. Pl.* 2.8), is almost certain to have been the same place as the Alycum of Plutarch, who relates that it derived its name from a son of Sciron, who was buried there (Thes. 32). It perhaps stood at the entrance of the Scironian pass, where there are a few ancient remains.

PHANOTEUS (See PANOPEUS)

PHARAE (FARES?)   a town of Achaia and one of the twelve Achaian cities, was situated on the river Pierus, 13 km from the sea and 28 km from Patrae. It was annexed to Patrae when the latter city was made a Roman colony after the battle of Actium. Pharae contained a large agora, with a curious statue of Hermes. The modern town of Fares, about 28 km south of Patra, is a possible location of the ancient town.

PHARAE or PHERAE (KALAMATA)   was an ancient town of Messenia, situated upon a hill rising from the left bank of the river Nedon and about 1.5 km from the Messenian Gulf. Pharae occupied the site of Kalamata, the modern capital of Messenia; and in antiquity also it seems to have been the chief town in the southern Messenian plain. It was said to have been founded by Pharis, the son of Hermes (Paus. 4.30.2). In the *Iliad* (5.543) it is mentioned as the well-built city of the wealthy Diocles, a vassal of the Atreidae. Diocles was the son of Orsilochus, who was a son of the river-god Alpheius and Telegone. The sons of Diocles were Crethon and Orsilochus. Both sons were slain by Aeneas in the Trojan War (Hom. *Il.* 5.542; Paus. 4.30.2). Pharae was also one of the places offered by Agamemnon to Achilles (Hom. *Il.* 9.151); in the *Odyssey* (3.490), Telemachus rests here on his journey from Pylus to Sparta. Pausanias found at Pharae temples of Tyche, goddess of chance or luck, and of Nicomachus and Gorgasus, grandsons of Asclepius. Gorgasus was one of the sons of Machaon, the son of Asclepius by Anticleia, the daughter of Diocles. After the death of his grandfather, Gorgasus succeeded to the kingdom. He also followed the example of his father by practicing the art of healing, for which he received divine tribute after his death (Paus. 4.30.3). Nicomachus ruled jointly with his brother. Their sanctuary was founded by Isthmius, the son of Glaucus (Paus. 4.3.10). Outside the city there was a grove of Apollo Carneius and in it a fountain.

There are no ancient remains at Kalamata, not surprisingly, because the site has been constantly occupied since ancient times.

PHARE or PHARIS (VAFIO?)   afterward called Pharae, was a town in Laconia in the lower Spartan plain of the Eurotas River, situated upon the road from Amyclae to the sea (Paus. 3.20.3). It was mentioned in the *Iliad* (2.582). With Sparta, Messe, Bryseiae, Amyclae, Helus, Las, and Oetylus it sent men to Troy under Menelaus in sixty ships. It maintained its independence till the reign of Teleclus, king of Sparta; and, after its conquest, continued to be a Lacedaemonian town under the name of Pharae (Paus. 3.2.6).

Phare has been placed at the deserted village of Vafio, which lies south of the site of Amyclae. It contains an ancient treasury, like those of Mycenae and Orchomenus, which is in accordance with Phare having been one of the old Achaian cities before the Dorian conquest. It has been suggested that Menelaus might have been buried here. Most accounts say he was buried at Therapne.

PHARSALUS (FARSALA)   was one of the most important cities of Thessaly, located in the district of Thessaliotis close to the borders of Phthiotis, on the left bank of the Enipeus and at the foot of Mount Narthacium (Kassidiaris). Most likely the city was called Phthia at an earlier time and was the capital of Phthiotis. On one side of the north gateway of the acropolis are the remains of Cyclopean walls; and in the middle of the acropolis is a subterranean construction built in the same manner, just like the Treasury of Atreus at Mycenae. In terms of military security the city had all the best advantages. It was on a hill rising to the height of about 215 meters above the adjacent plain, defended on three sides by precipices. It was well watered, and it overlooked one of the most fertile plains in Greece. Pharsalus reached the highest importance among the cities of Thessaly and became one of the largest cities of Greece. The city was nearly 6.5 km in circumference. Its walls, which were strengthened at intervals with towers, are its most conspicuous remains. There was here a temple of Zeus Thaulius, but it has not been found. Thetis, the Nereid and mother of Achilles, had a temple, the Thetideion, here (Strab. 9.5.6), probably north of the Enipeus on the way to the modern village of Dasolofos. The name of the modern town is Farsala, and it lies at the foot of the ancient acropolis.

PHARYGAE (MENDENITSA)   was a town of the Locri Epicnemidii. It was located on a hill in a fertile and forested area. It was originally called Tarphe because of the thickets in which it stood, and was mentioned under that name by Homer (*Il.* 2.533). In the time of Strabo (9.4.6) it was called Pharygae and was said to have received a colony from Argos. It contained a temple of Hera Pharygaea. It is probably the modern Mendenitsa, which is a dozen or so kilometers from the site of ancient Thermopylae.

PHEIA or PHEA (FIA)   was a city of Elis in the Pisatis, situated on the isthmus connecting the promontory Ichthys (modern Katakolo) with the mainland. Pheia is mentioned by Homer (*Il.* 7.135, *Od.* 15.297) near the Iardanus, which is apparently the mountain stream north of Ichthys and which empties into the sea on the north side of Mount Skafidi. The site is adjacent to the modern hamlet of Fia on the bay of Agios Andreas.

PHENEUS (FENEOS)   was a town in the northeast of Arcadia. Its territory was bounded on the north by the Achaian towns of Aegeira and Pellene, on the east by the region of Stymphalus, on the west by that of Cleitor, and on the south by that of Caphyae and Orchomenus. This territory was enclosed by mountains, part of Mount Cyllene and the Aroanian chain. Two streams unite about the middle of the valley; the united river in ancient times had the name of Olbius or Aroanius (Paus. 8.14.3). The united rivers are carried off by *katavothra,* or subterranean channels in the limestone rocks, and, after flowing underground, reappear as the sources of the river Ladon. In order to direct this river into a single channel to the *katavothra* the inhabitants constructed a canal 9 km in length and 9 meters in width. This great work, which was attributed to Heracles, had become useless by the time of Pausanias (8.14.3), and the river had resumed its original course; but traces of the canal of Heracles are still visible.

Pheneus is mentioned by Homer (*Il.* 2.605) and was more celebrated in mythical than in historical times. It was said to have been founded by Pheneus, an Arcadian autochthon (Paus. 8.14.4). Virgil (*Aen.* 8.165) represents it as the residence of Euander; and its fame in mythical times is indicated by its connection with Heracles. The acropolis contained a ruined temple of Athena Tritonia, with a bronze statue of Poseidon Hippius. On the descent from the acropolis was the stadium, and, on a neighboring hill, the tomb of Iphicles, the brother of Heracles. After he was wounded in the battle with Heracles against the Moliones (see CLEONE), he was carried to Pheneus, where he was nursed by Buphagus and Promne, but died there and was honored with a hero's shrine. There was also a temple of Hermes, the principal deity of the city (Paus. 8.14.10). Myrtilus was a son of Hermes, who assisted Pelops in winning Hippodameia but was betrayed and slain by him and was thrown into the sea in Euboea. His tomb was shown at Pheneus behind the temple of Hermes. There he was also worshipped as a hero and honored with nocturnal sacrifices (Paus. 8.14.11).

There were several roads from Pheneus to the surrounding towns. Of these the north road to Achaia ran through the Pheneatic plain. On this road, about 2.5 km from the city, was a temple of Apollo Pythius, which was in ruins in the time of Pausanias (8.15.5). A little above the temple the road divided; the one on the left led across Mount Crathis to Aegeira, and the other on the right went to Pellene. The boundaries of Aegeira and Pheneus were marked by a temple of Artemis Pyronia.

The western roads led to Nonacris and Cleitor. The south road went to Orchomenus, and the east one to Stymphalus across Mount Geroneium. To the left of Mount Geroneium were two other mountains, Tricrena (Three Fountains), where Hermes was washed after birth by the nymphs of this mountain, and Sepia, where Aepytus is said to have perished from the bite of a snake.

In addition to Hermes, the Cabeiri, Demeter and Persephone, and Artemis found special worship in Pheneus. The Cabeiri were the mystic divinities whose worship was spread throughout Greece. Even the Roman Penates were sometimes considered identical with the Cabeiri (Dionys. 1.67). Some thought that the Penates were carried by Dardanus from Pheneus to Samothrace, and that Aeneas brought them from there to Italy. Demeter Cidaria was a name of the Eleusinian Demeter at Pheneus, derived either from an Arcadian dance called *cidaris* or from a royal headdress of the same name (Paus. 8.15.1). The rape of Persephone was placed by some at Pheneus. Demeter Thesmia and Persephone Thesmia (Law-giver) were honored when the Thesmophoria was celebrated in Athens. Sanctuaries were also erected at Megara, Troezen, Pheneus, and other places to these two goddesses. Odysseus was said to have built a temple to Artemis Heurippe (Finder of Horses) at Pheneus in common with Poseidon Hippius. He built the temple when at length he found his lost horses there (Paus. 8.14.5).

Pausanias does not mention a sanctuary of Asclepius, but archaeologists have found one on the southeast slope of the hill on which Pheneus was located. One of the two buildings has a statue of Asclepius. A huge head of Hygieia in excellent condition was also found in this same building. The site is adjacent to the modern hamlet of Feneos, which is about halfway between Kalivia and Steno.

PHERAE (VELESTINO)   one of the most ancient cities of Thessaly, was located in the southeast corner of Pelasgiotis, west of Lake Boebeis, and 16.5 km from Pagasae, which served as its harbor (Strab. 9.5.15). Pheres was a son of Cretheus and Tyro and brother of Aeson and Amythaon. He was married to Periclymene, by whom he became the father of Admetus, Lycurgus, Eidomene, and Periapis. He was believed to have founded Pherae (Hom. *Od.* 11.259; Apollod. 1.9.11,14). Pherae was most celebrated in mythology as the home of Admetus. He took part in the Calydonian boar hunt and the expedition of the Argonauts. When he had succeeded his father Pheres as king of Pherae, he sought to marry Alcestis, the daughter of Pelias, who had promised her to him on condition that he should come to her in a chariot drawn by boars. Admetus managed to accomplish this

task with the assistance of Apollo, who served him, according to some, because of being in love with him. According to most, however, he was obliged to serve a mortal for one year for having slain the Cyclopes (Apollod. 3.10.4). On the day of his marriage to Alcestis, Admetus neglected to offer a sacrifice to Artemis, and when in the evening he entered the bridal chamber he found there a number of snakes rolled up in a lump. Apollo, however, reconciled Artemis to him and at the same time induced the Moirae to grant to Admetus deliverance from death, if at the hour of his death his father, mother, or wife would die for him. Alcestis offered to die for him, but Persephone, or Heracles, brought her back to the upper world (Apollod. 1.9.15). Eumelus, the son of Admetus, led from Pherae and the neighboring towns eleven ships to the Trojan War (Hom. *Il.* 2.711–15). He was distinguished for his excellent horses, which had once been under the care of Apollo. He was married to Iphthima, the daughter of Icarius.

Situated at the end of the Pelasgian plain, Pherae was surrounded with plantations, gardens, and walled enclosures (Polyb. 18.3). An old and new Pherae are referred to as being about 1.5 km from each other. In the middle of Pherae was a celebrated fountain called Hypereia (Strab. 9.5.18; Pind. *Pyth.* 4.221). Hyperes was a son of Melas and Eurycleia, who lived near the well of Hypereia. The fountain Messeis was probably also in Pherae. Artemis Pheraea had a temple there. Hecate had the surname Pheraea, either because she had been brought up by the shepherds of Pheres or because she was worshipped at Pherae.

The remains of Pherae are situated at Velestino, where the ancient walls may be traced on three sides. On the north side are two flat summits. Below the one on the east, on its southern side, is the fountain Hypereia, which pours from openings in the rock and immediately forms a stream. Dedications to Heracles have been found here and remains of his temple. There are also remains of a temple possibly dedicated to Zeus Thaulius but more likely to Artemis Ennodia.

PHERAE (See PHARAE in Messenia)

PHIGALIA or **PHIALIA** (FIGALIA)   was an ancient town situated in the southwest corner of Arcadia close to the border of Messenia on the right bank of the Neda, about halfway between its sources and its mouth. The city was said to have derived its name from Phigalus, a son of Lycaon, its original founder (Paus. 8.3.1), though in another passage Phigalus is called an autochthon (Paus. 8.39.2). Others derived the name from Phigalia, a Dryad. The town received its later name from Phialus, a son of Bucolion and father of Simus, who is said to have changed the name to Phialia (Paus. 8.5.7). The Phigalians were given to excess both in eating and drinking, to which their cold and forbidding climate may perhaps have contributed (Athen. 4.149, 10.442). Acratophorus was a surname by which Dionysus was worshipped here as the giver of unmixed wine (Paus. 8.39.6).

Phigalia was still a place of importance when visited by Pausanias. He describes it as situated upon a precipitous hill, the greater part of the walls being built upon the rocks (8.39.5). There are still considerable remains of the ancient walls above the modern village of Figalia. The city was nearly 3 km in circumference. The rock upon which it stood slopes down toward the Neda; on the west side is a ravine and on the east side a stream that flows into the Neda. In ancient times a temple of Artemis Soteira stood on the summit of the acropolis. On the slope of the mountain lay the gymnasium and the temple of Dionysus Acratophorus. On a rock near the union of the mountain stream and the Neda, was a temple of Eurynome, supposedly a surname of Artemis. The temple was opened only once a year. In her sanctuary, which was surrounded by cypress trees, she was represented as half woman and half fish (Paus. 8.41.5). Eurynome was an Oceanid who along with Thetis cared for Hephaestus when he was cast down from Olympus. A sanctuary of Asclepius and Hygieia at this location has been attested by ancient writers, but no remains have been found.

Phigalia was surrounded by mountains, of which Pausanias (8.41.7) mentions two by name, Cotilius and Elaius, the former to the left of the city and the latter to the right. Mount Elaius contained a cavern sacred to Demeter Melaenis (Black), a surname acquired because she dressed in mourning and shut herself up in isolation here. The cavern was situated in a grove of oaks. On Mount Cotilius, about 30 km away, was situated the temple of Apollo Epicurius, which was built in the Peloponnesian War by Ictinus, the architect of the Parthenon at Athens. It was erected by the Phigalians in consequence of the relief afforded by Apollo during the plague in the Peloponnesian War, as a result of which he received the surname Epicurius.

The temple stands in a place called Bassae (Vasses), and according to Pausanias (8.41.8) excelled all the temples of Peloponnesus, except that of Athena Alea at Tegea, in the beauty of the stone and the excellence of its structure. Pausanias (8.41.7) particularly mentions that the roof was of stone as well as the rest of the building. This temple still remains almost intact and is, next to the Hephaestion at Athens, the best preserved of the temples of Greece. The frieze of the cella, representing contests between the Centaurs and the Lapiths and between the Amazons and the Greeks, is now in the British Museum. The temple stands in a shallow valley near the summit of Mount Cotilius in the midst of a wilderness of rocks and ancient oaks. A spring rises southwest of the temple and soon afterward disappears into the ground, as Pausanias

has described. North of the temple is the highest summit of the mountain. This summit, and later the whole mountain, was called Cotilius. Here was also a sanctuary of Aphrodite, of which there are still some traces. The grandeur of the ruins of the temple of Apollo have given to the whole of the surrounding district the name of the Columns. The site of Bassae is best reached by the road up the mountain from Andritsena.

PHILAIDAE   a deme of Attica of the tribe Aegeis, appears to have been near Brauron since it is said to have derived its name from Philaeus, the son of Telamonian Ajax, who lived in Brauron. Pausanias (1.35.2) calls Philaeus a son of Eurysaces. Modern findings locate this deme to the west of Vraona.

PHILIA (FILIA)   was a town in Thessaliotis on the right bank of the Curalius (Sophaditikos) River. It had a sanctuary of Athena Itonia (Strab. 9.5.17). This temple probably belonged to Cierium. Recent excavations at Filia have uncovered remains of a sanctuary of Athena, but so far few artifacts have been found. This sanctuary could have been an open-air shrine.

PHILIPPI (FILIPI)   was a city of Macedonia that took its name from its founder, Philip, father of Alexander the Great. Strabo (7. *Frag.* 42) says that originally it was called Crenides (Place of the Fountains) from the numerous springs in which the Angites River had its source. Near Crenides were the principal mines of gold in a hill called Dionysi Collis, probably the same mountain as that where the Satrae had an oracle of Dionysus (Herod. 7.111).

PHLEGRA   was an earlier name of the promontory of PALLENE in Macedonia.

PHLEGYANTIS   was an earlier name of ORCHOMENUS in Boeotia.

PHLIUS (KOUTSI)   was an independent city in the northeast part of Peloponnesus, whose territory was bounded on the north by Sicyonia, on the west by Arcadia, on the east by Cleonae, and on the south by Argolis. This territory is a small valley about 275 meters above sea level, surrounded by mountains from which streams flow down on all sides into the Asopus River. The territory of Phlius was celebrated in antiquity for its wine (Athen. 1.27). According to Strabo (8.6.24), the ancient capital of the country was Araethyrea on Mount Celosse, a city mentioned by Homer (*Il.* 2.571); but the inhabitants subsequently deserted it and built Phlius 5.5 km away. Pausanias (2.12.4,5), however, does not speak of any migration, but says that the ancient capital was named Arantia from its founder Aras, an autochthon, and that it was afterward called Araethyrea from a daughter of Aras. She had a brother Aoris and, like him, was fond of the chase and warlike pursuits. When she died, her brother changed the name of the country from Phliasia to Araethyrea after her. She was the mother of Phlias. The monuments of Araethyrea and her brother, consisting of round pillars, were still extant in the time of Pausanias; and before the mysteries of Demeter were commenced at Phlius, the people always invoked Aras and his two children with their faces turned toward their monuments (Paus. 2.12.4–6). Pausanias says that the town finally received the name of Phlius from Phlias. Some say he was a son of Dionysus and Chthonophyle and a native of Araethyrea. He was one of the Argonauts (Apollon. Rhod. 1.115). According to Pausanias (2.12.5–6), he was a son of Ceisus and Araethyrea and the husband of Chthonophyle, by whom he became the father of Androdamas. Others called him a son of Dionysus and Ariadne. The name Arantia was retained in the time of Pausanias in the hill Arantinus, on which the city stood. Phlius was subsequently conquered by Dorians under Rhegnidas. Some of the inhabitants migrated to Samos, others to Clazomenae.

Pausanias (2.13.3) says that on the acropolis of Phlius was a temple of Hebe in a cypress grove. Here Hebe was surnamed Dia. The earliest Phliasians named the goddess Ganymeda. The greatest honor the Phliasians paid this goddess was the pardoning of suppliants. All those who sought sanctuary here received full forgiveness, and prisoners, when set free, dedicated their shackles on the trees in the grove. There was also a temple of Demeter on the acropolis. On the descent from the citadel there stood on the right a temple of Asclepius (Paus. 2.13.3) and below it the theater and another temple of Demeter. The ruins of Phlius are situated on one of the ridges of Tricaranum, above the right bank of the Asopus. They are of considerable extent, but at present little more than foundations. One kilometer from the town on the Asopus are some ruins that have been considered to be those of Celeae, where Demeter was worshipped (Paus. 2.14.1). In the southern part of the area is the Dioscurion, which is mentioned only by Polybius (4.67,68,73) and which lay on the road from Corinth over Mount Apelauron into the territory of Stymphalus.

Besides those already mentioned, other individuals connected with Phlius included Amphiaraus, Cyathus, Dysaules, and Pelops. Amphiaraus, a descendant of the famous seer, also possessed prophetic powers, which, according to a tradition at Phlius, came to him when he spent a night in the prophetic house of Phlius (Paus. 2.13.6). Cyathus, the youthful cupbearer of Oeneus, was killed by Heracles on account of a fault committed in the discharge of his duty. He was honored at Phlius with a

sanctuary close by the temple of Apollo (Paus. 2.13.8). In other traditions Cyathus is called Eurynomus (Diod. 4.36). Dysaules was a brother of Eleus of Eleusis. According to a tradition at Phlius, he had been expelled from Eleusis by Ion and had come to Phlius, where he introduced the Eleusinian mysteries. His tomb was shown at Celeae, which he is said to have named after his brother Celeus (Paus. 2.14.2). Finally, Pelops, the famous hero for whom Peloponnesus was named, while buried near Pisa, was honored at Phlius by having his chariot displayed in the temple of Demeter (Paus. 2.14.3).

PHLYA (HALANDRI)   was a deme of Attica of the tribe Cecropis. Its site has been placed at Halandri on the avenue from Athens to Pendeli and adjacent to Maroussio. It must have been a place of importance from the number of temples it contained and from its frequent mention in inscriptions (Paus. 1.31.3; Plut. *Them.* 1; Athen. 10.424). Its mystic rites are said to have been older than those of Eleusis. Gaea had an altar here, where she was called the Great Goddess (Paus. 1.31.2). Demeter Anesidora (Sender-up of Gifts) had a temple here. Zeus Ctesius (Protector of Property) was named here, as were Apollo Dionysodotus, Artemis Selasphora, Dionysus Antheus, the Nymphae Ismenides, Athena Tithrone, and Persephone Protogonis.

PHOCIS (FOKIS)   is a small territory in central Greece, bounded—in ancient times—on the west by Doris, on the northeast and east by the Locri Epicnemidii and Locri Opuntii, on the southeast by Boeotia, on the west by the Locri Ozolae, and on the south by the Corinthian Gulf. The Phocians at one time possessed a seaport, Daphnus, on the Euboean Sea, which stood between the Locri Epicnemidii and Opuntii (Strab. 9.3.7). Phocis is quite mountainous. The greater part of it is occupied by the lofty range of Parnassus. On the northeast and east are the Locrian Mountains. Between Mount Parnassus and the Locrian Mountains flows the Cephissus River, which empties eventually into the Euboean Gulf.

Among the earliest inhabitants of Phocis were the Leleges, Thracians, and Hyantes. The aboriginal inhabitants were conquered by the Phlegyae from Orchomenus (Paus. 8.4.4, 10.4.1). The country around Tithorea and Delphi is said to have been first called Phocis from Phocus, a son of Ornytion, and grandson of Sisyphus of Corinth; and the name is said to have been afterward extended to the whole country from Phocus, a son of Aeacus, who arrived there not long afterward (Paus. 2.29.3, 10.1.1). This statement would seem to show that the Phocians were believed to be a mixed Aeolic and Achaian race, as Sisyphus was an Aeolic hero, and Aeacus an Achaian one. Deion, son of Aeolus and Enarete, was king in Phocis and husband of Diomede, by whom he became the father of Asteropeia, Aenetus, Actor, Phylacus, and Cephalus. After the death of his brother Salmoneus, Dion took his brother's daughter, Tyro, into his house and gave her in marriage to Cretheus. Cephalus was married to Procris, by whom he became the father of Archius, the father of Laertes. He is described as beloved by Eos, the goddess of the dawn, because of his extraordinary good looks. But he and Procris were sincerely attached and promised to remain faithful to each other. Once when the handsome Cephalus was amusing himself with the chase, Eos approached him with loving entreaties but was rejected. The goddess then instructed him not to break his vow of fidelity until Procris had broken hers, but advised him to test her. Eos then metamorphosed him into a stranger and gave him rich presents, which he used to tempt Procris. Procris was induced by the brilliant presents to break the vow she had made to Cephalus. When she recognized her husband, she fled to Crete and took refuge with Artemis. The goddess made her a present of a dog and a spear, which were never to miss their object, and then sent her back to Cephalus. Procris returned home in the disguise of a youth and went out with Cephalus to the hunt. When he perceived the excellence of her dog and spear, he proposed to buy them of her; but she refused to part with them for any price except sexual intercourse. When he accordingly agreed to make love to what appeared to be a young man, Procris made herself known to him, and he became reconciled to her. As, however, she still feared the love of Eos, she always jealously watched him when he went out hunting. On one such occasion he killed her by accident with the never-erring spear.

In the Trojan War the inhabitants of Phocis appear under the name Phocians and were led against Troy by Schedius and Epistrophus, the sons of Iphitus (Hom. *Il.* 2.517). Iphitus was a son of Naubolus, who was a son of Ornytus. Like many other fathers of Greek heroes at Troy, Iphitus had been one of the Argonauts (Apollod. 1.9.6; Apollon. Rhod. 1.207). Schedius was killed by Hector, and his remains were carried from Troy to Anticyra in Phocis. He was represented in the Lesche at Delphi (Paus. 10.30.2). Some say that Epistrophus was not his brother but his father. There was another Phocian named Schedius, a son of Perimedes, who was also killed by Hector (Hom. *Il.* 15.515).

When Agamemnon was murdered, it was planned that Orestes would die, too, but Electra secretly entrusted him to the slave who took care of him. This slave carried the boy to Strophius, king of Phocis, who was married to Anaxibia, the sister of Agamemnon. In the house of Strophius Orestes grew up together with the king's son Pylades, with whom he formed a close and intimate friendship, one that has almost become proverbial. Pylades afterward married Electra and became by her the

father of Hellanicus, Medon, and Strophius (Paus. 2.16.5).

Coronis was a daughter of Phoroneus, king of Phocis. She was metamorphosed by Athena into a crow for when she was pursued by Poseidon, she implored the protection of Athena (Ov. *Met.* 2.550). In Phocis Heracles had a temple under the name Misogynis (Woman-Hating), and, as at Rome, women were not allowed to take part in his worship, probably because he had been poisoned by Deianeira.

Phocis owed its chief importance in history to the celebrated oracle at Delphi, which originally belonged to the Phocians. But after the Dorians had obtained possession of the temple, they disowned their connection with the Phocians; and in historical times a hostile climate existed between the Phocians and Delphians.

The Phocians formed an ancient confederation, which assembled near Daulis in a building named Phocicon (Paus. 10.5.1). The chief town, excepting Delphi, was Elateia, situated upon the left bank of the Cephissus, on the road from Locris to Boeotia. Next in importance was Abae, also to the left of the Cephissus, celebrated for its ancient oracle of Apollo.

PHOLEGANDROS (FOLEGANDROS) is an island in the Aegean and one of the smaller of the Cyclades, lying between Melos and Sicinos. It was said to have derived its name from a son of Minos. The modern town of Folegandros stands on the north side of the island on the site of the ancient city, of which there are only a few remains.

PHOLOE (FOLOI) is a mountain in Elis in the Pisatis, or lower valley of the Alpheius. North of the Alpheius, Mount Pholoe, which is an extension of Mount Erymanthus, reaches across the Pisatis from east to west. It terminates in the promontory, running southward far into the sea and opposite the island of Zacynthus. This promontory was called in ancient times Ichthys on account of its shape; it now bears the name Katakolo. Pholus, a Centaur, was a son of Seilenus and the nymph Melia, and the mountain is named for him (Apollod. 2.5.4; Theocrit. 6.149).

PHRIXA (FRIXA) was a town of Triphylia in Elis, situated upon the left bank of the Alpheius about 5.5 km from Olympia (Strab. 8.3.12). It was founded by the Minyae. Phrixa is rarely mentioned in history. Pausanias (6.21.6) said it was situated upon a pointed hill opposite the Leucanias, a tributary of the Alpheius and at a ford of the latter river. This pointed hill is now called Paleofanaro and is conspicuous from both sides of the river. The city thus received the name Phaestus in later times. The city was in ruins in the time of Pausanias (6.21.6), who mentions there a temple of Athena Cydonia, said to have been built by Clymenus of Cydonia and a sanctuary of Artemis Cordaca. He also saw nearby the burial mound of the suitors of Hippodameia, who were killed by Oenomaus.

PHTHIOTIS (FTHIOTIS) was inhabited by the Achaian Phthiotae, under which name they are usually mentioned as members of the Amphictyonic League. This district, according to Strabo (9.5.3), included the southern part of Thessaly. It reached from the Maliac Gulf on the east to Dolopia and Mount Pindus on the west; it stretched as far north as Pharsalus and the Thessalian plains. Phthiotis derived its name from the Homeric Phthia (Hom. *Il.* 1.155, 2.683), which appears to have included in heroic times not only Hellas and Dolopia but also the southern portion of the Thessalian plain. It is probable that Phthia was also the ancient name of Pharsalus. Phthia itself was named for Phthius, a son of Poseidon by Larissa. Hellen, his son by Chrysippe, was the mythical founder of the Thessalian town of Hellas (Strab. 9.5.6).

Deucalion was a son of Prometheus and Clymene. He was king in Phthia and married to Pyrrha. When Zeus, after the treatment he had received from Lycaon, had resolved to destroy the degenerate human race who inhabited the earth, Deucalion, on the advice of his father, built a ship and carried into it stores of provisions. When Zeus did send a flood all over Hellas, which destroyed all its inhabitants, Deucalion and Pyrrha alone were saved. They restored the human race by sowing stones in accordance with an oracle of Themis. They contributed their part by becoming parents of Hellen, Amphictyon, Protogeneia, and others. Strabo (9.5.14) states that near the coast of Phthiotis there were two small islands of the name of Deucalion and Pyrrha. Hellen, their son, became by the nymph Orseis the father of Aeolus, Dorus, and Xuthus. He was king of Phthia, and this country he left to Aeolus. Hellen is the mythical ancestor of all the Hellenes, or Greeks, as distinguished from the more ancient Pelasgians. The name Hellenes was at first confined to a tribe inhabiting a part of Thessaly, but subsequently it was extended to the whole Greek nation (Hom. *Il.* 2.684; Herod. 1.56; Thuc. 1.3; Paus. 3.20.6).

Achaeus was a son of Xuthus and Creusa and consequently a half brother of Ion and grandson of Hellen. The Achaeans regarded him as the author of their race and derived from him their own name as well as that of Achaia, which was formerly called Aegialus. When his uncle Aeolus died in Thessaly, from where he himself had come to Peloponnesus, he went there and made himself master of Phthiotis, which now also received from him the name Achaia. Achaeus had two sons, Architeles and Archander, who migrated from Phthiotis to Argos and married two of the daughters of Danaus, Automate and Scaea.

Meanwhile the Phthiotian line had been continued through Aeolus via his son Deion, who married Diomede, daughter of his brother Xuthus. One of their sons was Actor, who by Aegina was the father of Menoetius, who in turn was the father of Patroclus.

By the same Aegina, who was a daughter of the river Asopus, Zeus became the father of Aeacus. His famous son was Peleus, king of the Myrmidons at Phthia. He had been born and grew up on Aegina, where he helped kill his stepbrother and was exiled. He went to Phthia, where he was purified of the murder by Eurytion, the other son of Actor, who was king. Peleus married Antigone, Eurytion's daughter, and received with her one-third of Eurytion's kingdom (Hom. *Il.* 16.175; Apollod. 3.13.1). By Antigone he became the father of Polydora. As he had come to Thessaly with no companions, he prayed to Zeus for an army, and the god metamorphosed the ants into men, who were accordingly called Myrmidons. Peleus accompanied Eurytion to the Calydonian hunt and involuntarily killed him with his spear. In consequence of this deed he fled from Phthia to Iolcus, where he was again purified by Acastus. He incurred the disfavor of Acastus' wife by rejecting her advances. In consequence of this, she sent a message to Antigone, stating that Peleus was on the point of marrying Sterope, a daughter of Acastus. Antigone promptly hanged herself in despair (Apollod. 3.13.1–3). For the alleged seduction of his wife Acastus made an unsuccessful attempt to destroy Peleus. Later on, Peleus was able to avenge himself on the couple by killing both of them. After that he married Thetis and became the father of Achilles.

Thus Patroclus and Achilles were related by blood in more than one way. When yet a boy, during a game of dice, Patroclus involuntarily killed Clysonymus, a son of Amphidamas, and in consequence of this accident he was taken by his father to Peleus at Phthia, where he was educated together with Achilles. They were educated by Phoenix, who taught them eloquence and the arts of war. This Phoenix was a son of Amyntor. He had encountered problems at home in his youth and was forced to flee to Peleus, who received him kindly, made him ruler of the country of the Dolopes on the frontiers of Phthia, and entrusted to him his son Achilles, whom he was to educate. Achilles also received tutoring in the medical arts from Cheiron the Centaur. The mother of Achilles, Thetis, foretold him that his fate was either to gain glory and die early or to live a long but inglorious life. The hero chose the former. In fifty ships he led his hosts of Myrmidons, Hellenes, and Achaians against Troy (Hom. *Il.* 2.686), where he met his foretold glory and concomitant early death. He was accompanied both by Phoenix and

Patroclus. Patroclus took part in the war on account of his great attachment to Achilles.

Neoptolemus, a son of Achilles and Deidameia, was hero in the Trojan War in his own right. Respecting his return from Troy and subsequent events of his life, accounts vary. According to Homer (*Od.* 3.188, 4.5), he lived in Phthia, the kingdom of his father. Menelaus sent Hermione from Sparta to Phthia because she had been promised to Neoptolemus at Troy. Others say that he first went to Molossia, where he was married to Andromache, becoming by her the father of Molossus, Pielus, Pergamus and Amphialus. From there he returned to Phthia, where he recovered the throne that had in the meantime been taken from Peleus by Acastus. Others say he went to Epeirus because he could not or would not return to Phthia. In any case, the royal line seems to end with him.

One other individual deserves to be mentioned in connection with Phthiotis. This is Pancratis, a daughter of Aloeus and Iphimedeia. Once when Thracian pirates under Butes invaded that district, they carried off from Mount Drius the women who were celebrating a festival of Dionysus. Among them were Iphimedeia and her daughter Pancratis. They were carried to Naxos where King Agassamenus made Pancratis his wife. Otus and Ephialtes, the brothers of Pancratis, came to Naxos to liberate their mother and sister, but even though they were victorious, Pancratis died (Diod. 5.50).

PHYLACE (FILAKI)   was a town in Phthiotis in Thessaly, one of the places subject to Protesilaus and frequently mentioned in Homer (*Il.* 2.695, 13.696, 15.335, *Od.* 11.290). It contained a temple of Protesilaus (Pind. *Isth.* 1.84). The rulers of Phylace sprang from Aeolus and through his son Deion. Phylacus, who founded the city, was a son of Deion; Phylacus married Periclymene, the daughter of Minyas, by whom he became the father of Iphiclus and Alcimede. His daughter is sometimes called by the patronymic Phylaceis; his descendants Podarces, Iphiclus, and Protesilaus are called Phylacides (Hom. *Il.* 2.705; Propert. 1.19). He was the father of Iphiclus, who in turn was the father of Phylacus, Podarces, and Protesilaus. Podarces, with Protesilaus, led the Thessalians of Phylace against Troy. He was the first to leap from the ships onto the Trojan coast (Hom. *Il.* 2.695, 13.681, 15.705). He is also celebrated for the strong affection and fidelity existing between him and his wife Laodameia, the daughter of Acastus. When she heard of his death, she prayed to the infernal gods to be allowed to converse with him for only three hours. The prayer being granted, Hermes conducted Protesilaus to the upper world, and when Protesilaus died a second time, Laodameia died with him. A sanctuary, at which funeral games were celebrated, existed in Phylace (Herod. 7.33,116,120; Paus. 3.4.5; Pind. *Isth.* 1.83). Protesilaus was represented in the Lesche at Delphi.

Two other persons connected with Phylace were Medon and Melampus. Medon was a son of Oileus and a brother of Ajax the Lesser. Having slain Eriopis, one of his mother's kinsmen, he left his father's house and fled to Phylace. Melampus, a son of Amythaon, was looked on by the ancients as the first mortal endowed with prophetic powers, as the person who first practiced the medical arts, and as the one who established the worship of Dionysus in Greece. He first dwelt with Neleus at Pylos; afterward he resided for a time at Phylace near Mount Othrys with Phylacus and Iphiclus, and at last ruled over a third of the territory of Argos (Hom. *Od.* 15.225).

Strabo (9.5.8) describes Phylace as standing between Pharsalus and Phthiotic Thebes, about 18.5 km from the latter. Others have placed it near Filaki in the descent from a pass where there are remains of an ancient town. The situation near the entrance of a pass is well suited to the name of Phylace (Guard or Garrison).

PHYSADEIA   was a fountain near Argos named for Physadeia, a daughter of Danaus (Callim. *Lav. Pall.* 47).

PHYSCEIUS (MALANDRINO)   does not appear to have been mentioned by any ancient writer, but ruins at Malandrino have produced inscriptions designating it as a capital of a state of the Locri Ozolae. There are remains of a wall here and structures connected with it, including an area with a dedication to Zeus. There is written evidence of a cult of Athena Ilias here. This referred to the Locrian tribute of young maidens paid to Athena for the desecration of her altar in Troy by Ajax the Lesser. Malandrino is just off the highway between Amfissa and Naupaktos and roughly 40 km from Amfissa.

PIERIA (PIERIA)   was a narrow strip of land between the mouths of the rivers Peneius and Haliacmon at the foot of Olympus. This district, mentioned by Homer (*Il.* 14.225), was the birthplace of the Muses (Hes. *Theog.* 53) and of Orpheus (Apollon. Rhod. 1.23). Musae Pierides was a name derived from Pieria where they were first worshipped among the Thracians. Others derived the name from an ancient king, Pierus, who is said to have emigrated from Thrace to Boeotia and established their worship at Thespiae (Paus. 9.29.2; Eurip. *Med.* 831; Pind. *Ol.* 11.100).

Pieria was bounded on the west by the great chain of Olympus. Its chief cities were Dium and Pydna. The road between Pella to Larissa passed through Pieria. Homer (*Il.* 2.766) says that Apollo reared the swift steeds of Eumelus Pheretiades in Pieria and, according to the Homeric *Hymn to Hermes* (22,70), the herds of the gods fed in Pieria under the care of Apollo. Hermes was born, some say, on Olympus. A few hours after his birth, he escaped from his cradle, went to Pieria, and carried off some of the oxen of Apollo (*Hymn. Hom. ad Mer.* 17).

Other accounts refer the theft to a later time in the god's life.

PIMPLEIA (LITOHORO)   was a place in Pieria where Orpheus was said to have been born and from which the Muses obtained their epithets of Pimpleides, Pimpleis, and Pimpleiades (Hor. *Carm.* 1.26.9; Stat. *Silv.* 1.4.26). Its site has been identified with Litohoro, which stands 305 meters up the east flank of Olympus and is the principal point of departure for those climbing the mountain.

PINDUS (PINDOS)   is a long and lofty range of mountains in northern Greece, running from north to south about midway between the Ionian and Aegean Seas and forming the backbone of the country. Pindos forms the boundary between Thessaly and Ipiros. In its northern part it is called Lakmos, and here the five principal rivers of northern Greece rise—the Aliakmon, Pinios, Aheloos, Arahthos, and Aoos. To that part of the range south of Lakmos the name Cercetium was given, and one of the principal passes from Epeirus to Thessaly lay across this mountain. Still farther south, a point in the range of Pindus was called Tymphrestus (Timfristos), and from it branch off the two chains of Othrys (Othris) and Oeta (Iti), the first running nearly due east and the second more toward the southeast. A little south of Timfristos the range of Pindos divides into two branches and no longer bears the same name.

   Pamphylus, a son of Aegimius and brother of Dymas, was king of the Dorians at the foot of Mount Pindus. Along with the Heracleidae he invaded Peloponnesus (Apollod. 2.8.3; Pind. *Pyth.* 1.62). The celebrated story of the fight between the Lapiths and Centaurs is usually placed in Thessaly. At its end the Centaurs were expelled from their country and took refuge in the Pindus range on the frontiers of Epeirus.

PIRATES   was the Homeric name for the TAPHIAE Islands.

PISA   a town in Peloponnesus, was in the most ancient times the capital of an independent district called Pisatis, which later became part of the territory of Elis. It was celebrated in mythology as the home of Oenomaus and Pelops and was the head of a confederacy of eight states. Beside Pisa, names for five of the eight are recorded: Salmone, Heracleia, Harpinna, Cycesium, and Dyspontium (Strab. 8.3.31).

   Oenomaus, a son of Ares and Harpinna, was king of Pisa and husband of the Pleiad Sterope, by whom he became the father of Hippodameia. An oracle had declared that he should die if his daughter should marry, and he therefore made it a condition that those who came forward as suitors for Hippodameia's hand should contend with him in the chariot race. The suitor who conquered should receive her, but those who were conquered should suffer death. The race course extended from Pisa to the altar of Poseidon on the Corinthian Isthmus. At the moment when a suitor started the race for Hippodameia, Oenomaus sacrificed a ram to Zeus Areius at Pisa. Areius was a surname that could mean either "Warlike" or "Propitiating and Atoning." After the sacrifice, Oenomaus then armed himself and hastened after the suitor with his swift chariot and four horses, guided by the charioteer Myrtilus. He thus overtook many a lover, whom he put to death, until Pelops, the son of Tantalus, came to Pisa. Pelops bribed Myrtilus, and using the horses that he had received from Poseidon, he succeeded in reaching the goal before Oenomaus. The king then killed himself in despair. Thus Pelops obtained Hippodameia and the kingdom of Pisa (Diod. 4.73). There are some variations of this story. Some say that Oenomaus himself was in love with his daughter and for this reason slew her lovers. Myrtilus also is said to have loved her, and as she wished to marry Pelops, she persuaded Myrtilus to take the nails out of the wheels of her father's chariot. As Oenomaus was dying he pronounced a curse upon Myrtilus, and this curse had its desired effect: as Pelops refused to give to Myrtilus the reward he had promised, or as Myrtilus attempted to embrace Hippodameia, Pelops thrust him down from Cape Geraestus. But Myrtilus, while dying, likewise pronounced a curse upon the house of Pelops, which was afterward the cause of the fatal occurrences in the life of Atreus and Thyestes. According to Pindar (*Ol.* 1.109), Pelops did not gain the victory by any stratagem, but called for assistance from Poseidon, who gave him a chariot and horses by which he overcame Oenomaus. On the chest of Cypselus where the race was represented, the horses of Pelops had wings (Paus. 5.17.7). In order to atone for the murder of Myrtilus, Pelops founded the first temple of Hermes in Peloponnesus (Paus. 5.1.7; he also erected a monument to the unsuccessful suitors, at which an annual sacrifice was offered to them (6.21.7). When Pelops had gained possession of Hippodameia, he went with her to Pisa and soon also made himself master of Olympia, where he restored the Olympic games with greater splendor than they had ever had before (Pind. *Ol.* 9.16; Paus 5.8.2). The tomb of Oenomaus himself was shown on the river Cladeus in Elis (Paus. 6.21.3). His house was destroyed by lightning, and only one pillar of it remained standing (Paus. 5.20.6). Oenomaus had a son, Leucippus. He was in love with Daphne, the extremely beautiful daughter of the river-god Ladon in Arcadia. He approached her in the disguise of a maiden and thus hunted with her. He was discovered during the bath and killed by the nymphs (Paus. 8.20.2,3). It is to be noted, too, that the rape of Persephone was placed by some in the neighborhood of Pisa (Paus. 6.21.1).

Pisa originally held the presidency of the Olympic festival but was deprived of this privilege by the Eleians. The Pisatans, however, made many attempts to recover it; and the history of their wars with the Eleians, which were at last terminated by the destruction of Pisa in 572 B.C., is narrated elsewhere (See ELIS). Although Pisa ceased to exist as a city from this time, the Pisatans, in conjunction with the Arcadians, celebrated the 104th Olympic festival in 364 B.C. Pisa was said to have been founded by an eponymous hero, Pisus, the son of Perieres, and grandson of Aeolus (Paus. 6.22.2); but others derived its name from a fountain Pisa (Strab. 8.3.31). So completely was Pisa destroyed by the Eleians that the fact of its having existed was a disputed point in the time of Strabo, and Pausanias (6.22.1) found its site converted into a vineyard. Its situation, however, was perfectly well known to Pindar and Herodotus. Pindar (e.g., *Ol.* 2.3) frequently identifies it with Olympia, and Herodotus (2.7) refers to Pisa and Olympia as the same point in computing distance from the altar of the twelve gods at Athens. Pisa appears from Pausanias to have occupied a position between Harpinna and Olympia, which were only 3.5 km apart. Another ancient commentator says that Pisa was only six stadia (1 km) from Olympia. It must therefore be placed a little east of Olympia, and its acropolis probably occupied a height on the west side of the rivulet of Miraka, near its junction with the Alpheius. Strabo says that it lay between the mountains Olympus and Ossa, which can only have been heights on different sides of the river.

PITANE   was a hamlet of Sparta. Sparta was formed out of several earlier settlements, which existed before the Dorian conquest and were subsequently combined with the later city, which was founded in their midst. These earlier places were Pitane, Limnae or Limnaeum, Mesoa, and Cynosura, which had been united by a common sacrifice to Artemis (Paus. 3.16.9). The surname of Artemis Pitanatis was derived from Pitane, where she had a temple (Callim. *Hymn. in Dian.* 172; Paus. 3.16.9). The settlements are frequently called *phylae* (tribes) and were regarded as divisions of the Spartans, but it is clear that they are names of places. We are best informed about Pitane, which is called a *polis* by Euripides (*Troad.* 1112) and which is also mentioned as a place by Pindar (*Ol.* 6.46). Herodotus (3.55), who had been there, calls it a deme. It appears from the passage of Pindar that Pitane was at the ford of the Eurotas and consequently in the northern part of the city. Pitane was named for Pitane, a daughter of the river Eurotas, who became by Poseidon the mother of Euadne (Pind. *Ol.* 6.46). It was the favorite and fashionable place of residence at Sparta, like Collytus at Athens and Craneion at Corinth.

PITYUSSA   was an earlier name of the island of CHIOS.

PITYUSSA   was an earlier name of the island of SALAMIS.

PLATAEA or PLATAEAE (PLATEE)   an ancient city of Boeotia, was situated upon the boundaries of Attica at the foot of Mount Cithaeron and between that mountain and the Asopus River, which divided its territory from that of Thebes (Strab. 9.2.31). Plataea and Thebes were about 10 km apart. The Thebans said that Plataea was founded by them (Thuc. 3.61); but Pausanias (9.1.2) represents the Plataeans as autochthonous. They claimed to have derived their name from Plataea, a daughter of Asopus, who had a sanctuary there. Plataea is mentioned in Homer (*Il.* 2.494, 17.602) among the other Boeotian cities. Leitus was a son of Alector and father of Peneleus. He was an Argonaut and commanded the Boeotians in the Trojan War. His tomb was shown in later times at Plataea (Paus. 9.4.2).

The Plataeans received special honor because the battle of Plataea (479 B.C.) was fought and won on their soil. They used the grant of eighty talents from the confederate Greeks to erect a temple to Athena. They were further charged with the chief responsibility of paying annual religious honors to the tombs of the warriors who had fallen in the battle and of celebrating every five years the festival of the Eleutheria in commemoration of the deliverance of the Greeks from the Persian yoke. The festival was sacred to Zeus Eleutherius, to whom a temple was now erected at Plataea.

Hera also had an important temple here. During the Peloponnesian War, the Thebans laid seige to Plataea and eventually took the city. They used the temple of Hera as a sort of barracks but later erected a new temple in her honor (Thuc. 2.71, 3.20,52,68).

After its restoration by Philip, the city continued to be inhabited for many more years. It was visited by Pausanias (9.4.3), who mentions three temples: one of Hera, one of Athena Areia, and a third of Demeter Eleusinia. Pausanias speaks of the temple of Hera, which he describes as situated within the city. This was apparently the temple built by the Thebans after the destruction of Plataea (Thuc. 3.68). The temple of Athena Areia was adorned with pictures by Polygnotus and Onatus and with a statue of the goddess by Pheidias. Of the temple of Demeter Eleusinia Pausanias gives no details. The temple of Zeus Eleutherius (Strab. 9.2.31) seems to have been reduced in the time of Pausanias to an altar and a statue. A legend stated that Rhea gave birth to Zeus at Chaeroneia in Boeotia (Paus. 9.41.3), and in a temple of Zeus at Plataea, Rhea was represented in the act of handing the stone covered in cloth to Cronus (Paus. 9.2.5). This was the stone he swallowed in the mistaken belief that it was Zeus. The altar and statue of Zeus Eleutherius were situated outside the city (Paus. 9.2.5).

The ruins of Plataea are situated near the small village of Platee. The circuit of the walls may still be traced in great part. They are about 4 km in circumference. This, however, was the size of the city restored by Philip. The older city was confined to only a portion of the later one. The temple of Hera was found in 1891, but the temple of Athena Areia has not been identified.

PLATANISTUS   was another name by which MAC-ISTUS was called.

PLEURON (AGRILIA)   was the name of two cities in Aetolia, the territory of which was called Pleuronia (Strab. 10.3.6).

Old Pleuron was situated in the plain between the Achelous and the Euenus rivers, west of Calydon at the foot of Mount Curium, from which the Curetes are said to have derived their name. Pleuron and Calydon were the two chief towns of Aetolia in the heroic age. Pleuron was originally a town of the Curetes, and its inhabitants were engaged in frequent wars with the Aetolians of the neighboring town of Calydon. The history of Pleuron and Calydon in relation to the Curetes is confusing since both towns are represented as being founded by Pleuron and Calydon, the sons of Aetolus. Aetolus, the son of Endymion, had migrated from Elis to the Greek mainland and had given his name to this country and its people. He is reported to have subdued the Curetes six generations before the Trojan War. Yet the Curetes keep appearing in the history of the two cities. It is probably safe to say that Pleuron was an Aetolian stronghold built on the site of the older Curetean town, located on the borders of the territory of Curetis, and that it was joined with Calydon in suppressing frequent forays by the hostile neighbors.

In any case, Pleuron, the son of Aetolus, married Xanthippe and became by her the father of Agenor, Sterope, Stratonice, and Laophonte. Nothing further is known of Pleuron except that he had a hero shrine at Sparta, erected by his great-granddaughter Leda (Apollod. 1.7.7; Paus. 3.13.5). Agenor, his son, married Epicaste, the daughter of Calydon, and by her he became the father of Porthaon, Thestius, and Demonice. King Calydon did not have a son, but apparently he lived long enough to pass his kingdom to Thestius, his grandson, who had meanwhile become king of Pleuron through his father. Thestius married his aunt Laophonte and had by her several children, including Althaea and Leda. During his reign, Icarius and Tyndareus, sons of Perieres, were expelled from Lacedaemon and fled to Thestius at Pleuron. Tyndareus returned eventually to Sparta, taking Leda with him. Icarius remained in Aetolia and Acarnania, where he became the father of Penelope, Alyzeus, and Leucadius.

Meanwhile, Porthaon, the other son of Agenor, married Euryte and by her became the father of Oeneus, Agrius, Alcathous, Melas, Leucopeus, and Sterope (Hom. *Il.* 14.115; Apollod. 1.7.7). When Thestius died, Porthaon became king of Pleuron and Calydon. Then the kingdom passed to his eldest son Oeneus. Oeneus was married to his cousin Althaea, daughter of Thestius, and became by her the father of Meleager, Gorge, and several other daughters. By Melanippe he became the father of Tydeus. Homer (*Il.* 9.532) relates that Oeneus once neglected to sacrifice to Artemis, in consequence of which she sent a monstrous boar into the territory of Calydon, which was hunted and killed by Meleager on the occasion of the celebrated boar hunt. (See CALYDON.)

The hero Bellerophon was hospitably received by Oeneus and received a costly girdle as a present from him (Hom. *Il.* 6.216). After a long reign, Oeneus was deprived of his kingdom by the sons of his brother Agrius, who imprisoned him. But he was subsequently avenged by Diomedes, the son of Tydeus, who killed Agrius and his sons and restored the kingdom either to Oeneus himself or to Andraemon, who had married Gorge, the daughter of Oeneus. By this time Oeneus was quite old and probably incapable of ruling the two cities. Afterward, Diomedes took his grandfather with him to Peloponnesus, but some of the sons of Agrius who lay in ambush slew the old man in Arcadia. Diomedes buried his body at Argos and named the town of Oenoe after him (Apollod. 1.8.5).

In the Trojan War, Thoas, the son of Andraemon, led the Aetolians against Troy in forty ships (Hom. *Il.* 2.638). By the time of his reign the Curetes had finally been expelled and had migrated to Acarnania. Sixty years after the Trojan War, a group of Aeolians, who had been driven out of Thessaly along with the Boeotians, migrated into Aetolia and settled in the country adjacent to Pleuron and Calydon, which was afterward called Aeolis (Strab. 10.3.4; Thuc. 3.102).

Pleuron is rarely mentioned in the historical period. It was abandoned by its inhabitants, says Strabo (10.2.4), in consequence of the ravages of Macedonians in the historical period.

The inhabitants subsequently built the town of New Pleuron, which was situated at the foot of Mount Aracynthus south of the older city. The site of New Pleuron was probably represented by the ruins called the Kastro Irinio, a few minutes ride from Messolongi. The walls are 1.5 km in circumference with seven gates and thirty-one towers. The remains of a temple of Athena have been found under a Byzantine chapel. The outstanding remains within the walls are a small theater and a cistern. The two Pleurons are adjacent and near the highway north of Messolongi. The nearest town is Agrilia, which may be used as a direction to the vicinity.

The story of Cycnus is associated with Pleuron. Cycnus was a son of Apollo by Hyria. He was a handsome hunter living in the district between Pleuron and Calydon and though beloved by many, he repulsed all lovers. Only one, Phyllius, persisted in his love. Cycnus at last gave him three seemingly impossible tasks to accomplish, but Phyllius managed to do them. Finally, Phyllius received a bull as a prize, and Cycnus wanted it. When Phyllius refused to give it up, Cycnus in exasperation leaped into Lake Canope, which was called after him the Cycnean lake. His mother followed him, and both were metamorphosed by Apollo into swans.

PLOTAE   was the original name of the STROPHADES Islands.

POEEESSA (PISSES)   was situated on the southwest side of the island of Ceos on a steep promontory. Its ruins are inconsiderable and still preserve their ancient name. Athena Nedusia had a sanctuary on the Neda River in Messenia (from which she derived the name) and another at Poeeessa (Strab. 10.5.6). The sanctuary on Ceos was said to have been founded by Nestor on his return from Troy and to have derived its name from Nedon, a place in Laconia (Strab. 8.4.4).

POEMANDRIA   was an earlier name of TANAGRA.

POIEESSA   was an earlier name of the island of RHODES.

POLYCTORIUM   was a place in Ithaca, which received its name from Polyctor, a son of Pterelaus, prince of Ithaca (Hom. *Od.* 17.207).

POLYRRHENIA (POLIRINIA)   was a town in the northwest of Crete, whose territory occupied the whole west end of the island, extending from north to south. Strabo (10.4.13) describes it as lying west of Cydonia about 5.5 km from the sea and 11 from Phalasarna; he also says that it contained a temple of Dictynna. The ruins of Polyrrhenia, near Polirinia, show the remains of ancient walls from three to five meters high. Agamemnon is said to have visited here on his journey home from Troy.

PONTINUS (PONTINOS)   is a mountain in Argolis over which the road led from Argos to Tegea. Athena Saitis had a sanctuary on this mountain near Lerna (Paus. 2.36.8). The surname of the goddess was traced by the Greeks to the Egyptians, among whom Athena was said to have been called Sais.

PORPHRUSA or PORPHYRIA   was an earlier name of the island of CYTHERA.

PORPHYRIS   was another name of the island of NISYRUS.

POSEIDIUM (POSEIDONIO)   was the easternmost promontory of Samos. It was sacred to Poseidon (Strab. 14.1.13). Today it is still called Poseidonio.

POSEIDONIUM (AKRA POSIDI)   was the southwest cape of Pallene, probably so called from a temple of Poseidon. The cape still retains the name Posidi.

POSIDIUM or POSEIDIUM (AKRA STAVROS)   was a promontory in Thessaly in Phthiotis, described by Strabo (7. *Frag.* 32) as lying between the Maliac and Pagasaean gulfs. It was sacred to Poseidon. It is now called Akra Stavros.

POTACHIDAE   (See BOTACHIDAE)

POTAMUS (DASKALIO?)   a deme of Attica, lay on the east coast north of Thoricus. It was celebrated as containing the sepulcher of Ion (Paus. 1.31.3). Ion was the ancestor of the Ionians. He was, according to some traditions, king of Athens between the reigns of Erechtheus and Cecrops. He there became the father of four sons: Geleon, Aegicores, Argades, and Hoples. According to these four, he divided the Athenians into four classes, which derived their names from his sons. The harbor of Potamus was probably the modern Daskalio; and the deme itself is placed at the ruins situated on a height 3 km to the southwest of Daskalio. However, it should be pointed out that there were more than one deme named Potamus. Also, recent investigation has separated Upper and Lower Potamus from Potamus Deiradiotes, a coastal deme, and placed them in the Illisos valley.

POTHEREUS   was a river of Crete mentioned by Vitruvius (1.4). Zeus Dictaeus had a temple at Prasus on the banks of the river Pothereus (Strab. 10.4.6).

POTNIAE (TAKI?)   was a village of Boeotia on the road from Thebes to Plataea. It was in ruins in the time of Pausanias and contained a grove sacred to Demeter and Kore. Potniae is celebrated in mythology as the home of Glaucus, a son of Sisyphus and father of Bellerophon. He despised the power of Aphrodite and did not allow his mares to breed, that they might be stronger for racing. According to others, he fed them on human flesh for the purpose of making them spirited and warlike. This angered Aphrodite and the other gods, who punished him in this way. When Acastus celebrated the funeral games of his father Pelias at Iolcus, Glaucus took part in them with a chariot and four horses; but the animals were frightened and upset the chariot (Apollod. 1.9.28). According to others, they tore Glaucus to pieces, having drunk water from a sacred well, which caused them to go mad. Others said the madness was caused by a herb called *hippomanes*. The Corinthian Isthmus was said to be haunted by the shade of Glaucus, who frightened horses during races. The spot at which this happened was called Taraxippus (Paus. 6.20.19).

According to Strabo (9.2.32), some authorities regarded Potniae as the Hypothebae of Homer (*Il.* 2.505). Human sacrifices might have been offered to Dionysus in earliest times, but this custom was softened into symbolic scourging, or animals were substituted for men, as at Potniae (Paus. 9.8.1,2). The animal most commonly sacrificed was a ram. Potniae has been placed by some in the vicinity of the modern village of Taki, 3 km from Thebes on the road to Lefktra.

PRAESUS or PRASUS (PRESSOS)   was a town in Crete belonging to the Eteocretes and containing the temple of the Dictaean Zeus. Mount Dicte was in the territory of Praesus (Strab. 10.4.6). The territory of Praesus extended across the island to either sea. It is said to have been the only place on Crete, with the exception of Polichna, that did not take part in the expedition against Camicus in Sicily, which was to avenge the death of Minos. Minos pursued Daedalus after his winged escape from Crete. He eventually tracked him down at Camicus, the realm of King Cocalus of Sicily. Here Minos was killed by Cocalus and his daughters. It is related that the Praesii were accustomed to sacrifice swine before marriage (Athen. 9.376). The ruins of Praesus are still called by the slightly altered name of Pressos.

PRASIAE or BRASIAE (PARALIA TIROU)   was a town on the east coast of Laconia, described by Pausanias (3.24.3) as the farthest of the Eleuthero-Laconian places on this part of the coast. The name of the town was derived by the inhabitants from the noise of the waves (*brazein*). Among the curiosities of Prasiae, Pausanias (3.24.5) mentions a cave where Ino nursed Dionysus, a temple of Asclepius and another of Achilles, and a small promontory upon which stood four bronze figures not more than one foot in height. Its site has been placed at Paralia Tirou.

PRASIAE (PORTO RAFTI)   was a deme of Attica on the east coast between Potamus and Steiria. It had an excellent harbor, from which the Theoria, or sacred procession, used to sail. This was a commemoration of the successful return of Theseus from Crete. Here was a temple of Apollo and also the tomb of Erysichthon. Erysichthon, a son of Cecrops and Agraulos, died without issue in his father's lifetime on his return from Delos, from where he brought to Athens the ancient image of Eileithyia (Paus. 1.18.5). The ruins of the deme are seen on the northeast side of the bay. The harbor, now called

Porto Rafti, is the best on the east coast of Attica and is both deep and wide. The entrance of the harbor is more than 1.5 km in breadth; and in the center of the entrance there is a rocky islet, upon which is a colossal statue of white marble. The harbor has derived its modern name from the statue, since it is commonly supposed to bear some resemblance to a tailor (*rhaphtis*) at work. It is thought that the statue belongs to the Roman period and probably to the first or second century after the Christian era.

PRASUS   (See PRAESUS)

PROERNA (NEON MONASTIRI)   was a town of Phthiotis in Thessaly on the road from Thaumacia to Pharsalus. Very little is known of its history, and it did not play a part in any mythological event. However, in 1965 a foundation was excavated that was identified by objects located in conjunction with the building as a shrine of Demeter. This appears to be the first shrine of Demeter discovered in Thessaly.

PROSCHIUM (AGIOS GEORGIOS)   a town of Aetolis, between the rivers Achelous and the Euenus, is said to have been founded by the Aetolians when they moved from the Homeric Pylene higher up into the country. Proschium possessed a shrine said to have been dedicated by Heracles to his cupbearer Cyathus, whom he had unintentionally killed. Proschium lay west of Calydon and Pleuron and fairly near the Achelous. It has been placed on the west part of Mount Zigos (the ancient Aracynthus) near the monastery of Agios Georgios near Kalivia.

PROSYMNA (PROSIMNA)   was an ancient town in Argolis, in whose territory the celebrated Heraion, or temple of Hera, stood (Strab. 8.6.11). Statius (*Theb.* 4.44) gives it the epithet "lofty." Pausanias (2.17.2) mentions only a district of this name. The modern village of Prosimna (formerly Vervati) is about 7 km northeast of the Heraion. In 1935 excavations were conducted 2 km west of the village, and Greek and Roman remains were found. About 1 km northwest was found a tholos tomb.

PSOPHIS (TRIPOTAMO)   was a city in the northwest of Arcadia. A very ancient place, it is said to have been originally called Erymanthus and its territory to have been ravaged by the Erymanthian boar (Paus. 8.24.4). One of the labors of Heracles was the capture of this monster. The Erymanthian boar descended from Mount Erymanthus into Psophis, where Heracles caught him with a net after chasing him in deep snow. The town afterward received the name of Phegia or Phegeia from the founder, Phegeus. He was a brother of Phoroneus, the king of Psophis, and the father of Arsinoe, Pronous, and

Agenor. The city was called Psophis by Echephron and Promachus, sons of Heracles, who are said to have come from Sicily and named the town after their mother Psophis, daughter of Eryx (Paus. 8.24.2). Echephron and Promachus each had a shrine at Psophis. Others derived the name from Psophis, a son of Arrhon.

Psophis, while still called Phegia, was celebrated as the home of Alcmaeon, who fled here from Argos, after slaying his mother. It will be remembered that Alcmaeon slew his mother for her part in the death of his father. Because of this deed he became demented and was haunted by the Erinyes. He came to Phegeus in Psophis, who purified him and gave him his daughter Arsinoe in marriage. To her he gave the necklace of Harmonia, which he had taken when he murdered his mother. But Psophis was stricken by famine because of harboring a matricide, and the oracle advised Alcmaeon to go to Achelous. Achelous gave him his daughter Callirrhoe, who soon expressed a desire to have the necklace. Alcmaeon returned to Psophis to get it from Phegeus. He was slain for this outrage by Agenor and Pronous, the brothers of Arsinoe, at the instigation of Phegeus. But when the two brothers came to Delphi, where they intended to dedicate the necklace, they were killed by Amphoterus and Acarnan, the sons of Alcmaeon and Callirrhoe (Apollod. 3.7.5). In consequence, however, of their connection with Alcmaeon, the Psophidii took part in the second expedition against Thebes and refused to join the other Greeks in the Trojan War (Paus. 8.24.10).

On the west side of the town there is a rapid stream, the Aroanus, which was impassable during winter. This inaccessibility made the city strong. On the east side flows the Erymanthus. Since the western torrent joins the Erymanthus on the south side of the city, its three sides are surrounded by rivers and thus it was rendered secure in ancient times. On the remaining side toward the north, a hill and a wall completed the security of the city. About 914 meters below the junction of the two rivers the united stream is joined by a third, smaller river. From these three rivers the place is now called Tripotama.

Pausanias (8.24.6) saw at Psophis a ruined temple of Aphrodite Erycina. This surname was derived from Mount Eryx in Sicily, where Aphrodite had a famous temple, which was said to have been built by Eryx, her son by the Sicilian king, Butes (Diod. 4.83). Psophis, a daughter of Eryx, was believed to have founded this temple (Paus. 8.24.2). Besides the already mentioned shrines of Promachus and Echephron, there was the tomb of Alcmaeon; and near the Erymanthus was a temple sacred to that stream (Paus. 8.24.6).

Psophis was about 3 km in circumference. On the road from Psophis to Thelpusa lay Tropaea, upon the left bank of the Ladon, near which was the grove of Aphrodision, after which came a column with an ancient inscription upon it marking the boundaries of Psophis and Thelpusa.

PSYTTALEIA (PSITALIA)   is a small island off the Attic coast between Peiraeus and Salamis. The island is now called Psitalia and is about 1.5 km long and from 180 to 275 meters wide. The god Pan had a sanctuary on this island (Paus. 1.36.2; Aeschyl. *Pers.* 448).

PTELEUM (PTELEOS)   was a town of Thessaly on the southwest side of Phthiotis and near the entrance of the Pagasaean Gulf. It stood between Antron and Halos about 20 km from Halos. It is mentioned by Homer (*Il.* 2.697) as governed by Protesilaus, to whom the neighboring town of Antron also belonged. Pteleum stood near the modern village of Pteleos upon a hill now bearing the remains of a town and castle of the Middle Ages. On its side is a large marsh, which perhaps earned for it the Homeric epithet "couched in grass."

PTELEUM   a town of Triphylia in Elis belonging to Nestor (Hom. *Il.* 2.594), is said by Strabo (8.3.25) to have been a colony from the Thessalian Pteleum. This town had disappeared in Strabo's time, but its uninhabited site was still called Pteleasimum. There is a town a few kilometers northwest of Andritsena named Ptelea, but any connection with the ancient town is unlikely.

PTOUM (PTOIO)   is a mountainous ridge in Boeotia. It extends from the Evian Sea inland as far as Lake Iliki, lying a little east of the village of Akrefnio. On this mountain was a celebrated sanctuary of Apollo Ptous (Paus. 9.23.6; Herod. 8.135), which has been excavated since 1885. Ptous was a son of Athamas and Themisto, from whom both the mountain and the sanctuary were believed to have derived their name (Apollod. 1.9.2). Apollo also had a sanctuary on the mountain. A sacred spring rose near these two sanctuaries. An altar of another deity stood before Apollo's temple, and its foundations may be seen. From the area several objects have been taken, such as archaic *kouroi* now in the museums at Athens and Thebes. Finally, this was the site of the Ptoia, or festivals celebrating Apollo Ptous, which featured musical contests. The Ptoia were held till the end of the second century A.D.

PYLENE   an ancient town of Aetolia between the Achelous and the Euenus, was mentioned in the Homeric catalog (Hom. *Il.* 2.639). Strabo (10.2.6) says that the Aeolians, having removed Pylene higher up, changed its name to Proschium. The site of Pylene is not known.

PYLUS (AGRAPIDOHORI)   was a town in Elis, described by Pausanias (6.22.5) as located on the mountain road from Elis to Olympia and at the place where the Ladon flows into the Peneius. Pausanias says that it was eighty stadia (15 km) from Elis. The ruins at Agrapidohori probably mark the site. The Eleian Pylus is said to have been built by Pylas, son of Cteson of Megara, who founded the Messenian Pylus and who, upon being expelled from there by Peleus, settled at the Eleian Pylus (Paus. 4.36.1). Pylus was said to have been destroyed by Heracles and to have been afterward restored by the Eleians; but the story of its destruction by Heracles more properly belongs to the Messenian Pylus. The inhabitants of Messenian Pylus claimed that it was their town that Homer had in view when he asserted that the Alpheius flowed through their territory (*Il.* 5.545). Pausanias (6.22.5) saw only the ruins of Pylus.

PYLUS (KAKOVATOS)   was a town in Triphylia mentioned only by Strabo (8.3.14), who surnamed it Triphyliacos, Arcadicos, and Lepreaticos. He described it as situated about 5.5 km from the sea on the rivers Mamathus and Arcadicus, west of the mountain Minthe and north of Lepreum. When the Eleians conquered the Triphylian towns, they annexed Pylus to Lepreum (Strab. 8.3.30). The village Kakovatos on the west side of Mount Minthe and between two rivers seems to fit Strabo's directions. In fact, on older maps the town is called Pilos-Kakovatos. Mintha, a Cocythian nymph beloved by Hades, was metamorphosed by Demeter or Persephone into a plant called after her *minthe* (mint), or, according to others, she was changed into dust from which Hades caused the mint plant to grow forth. At the foot of Mount Minthe there was a temple of Hades and a grove of Demeter (Strab. 8.3.14; Ov. *Met.* 10.729).

PYLUS (KASTRO)   was a town in Messenia, located on the promontory Coryphasium (Korifassi), which forms the northern end of the bay of Navarino. Below the ruined fortress at the north end there is a cavern called the Grotto of Nestor. This cavern is eighteen meters long, twelve wide, and twelve high, having an arched roof. This cave was, according to the Peloponnesian tradition, the one into which the infant Hermes drove the cattle he had stolen from Apollo. Soon after his birth he stole the cattle. In order not to be discovered by the traces of his footsteps, he put on sandals and drove the oxen to Pylos, where he killed two and concealed the rest in a cave. The skins of the slaughtered animals were nailed to a rock, and part of their flesh was prepared and consumed, and the rest burnt; at the same time, he offered sacrifices to the twelve gods, whence he is called the inventor of divine worship and sacrifices (*Hymn. Hom. ad Mer.* 125). Apollo pursued the boy, and Hermes denied he had stolen the cattle. But he finally admitted the theft and conducted Apollo to Pylus and restored his oxen. Hermes had meanwhile invented the lyre from a tortoise shell and strings, and Apollo was so charmed with the sound that

he allowed Hermes to keep the cattle. The cavern has stalactites shaped like animals and hanging hides.

The fortress of Pylus was visited by Pausanias (4.36.2), who saw there a temple of Athena Coryphasia, the so-named house of Nestor (containing a picture of him), Nestor's tomb, and the cavern described above (also said to have been the stable of the oxen of Neleus and Nestor).

The Pylian dynasty started with Cretheus, son of Aeolus, and Tyro. Their sons were Amythaon, Aeson, Pheres, and the twins, Pelias and Neleus. Amythaon dwelt at Pylus and by Idomene became the father of Bias, Melampus, Aeolia, and, according to some, Cteson. According to Pindar (*Pyth.* 4.220), he and several other members of his family went to Iolcus to intercede with Pelias on behalf of Jason. Pausanias (5.8.2) mentions him among those to whom the restoration of the Olympian games was ascribed. Pylas was a son of Cteson and king of Megara, but after having slain Bias, his own father's brother, he founded the town of Pylus and gave Megara to Pandion, who had married his daughter Pylia. Melampus was regarded by the ancients as the first mortal to be endowed with prophetic powers, as the person who first practiced the medical art, and as the one who established the worship of Dionysus in Greece. He married Iphianassa, by whom he became the father of Mantius and Antiphates. Melampus at first dwelt with Neleus at Pylus.

Meanwhile, Tyro prior to her marriage to Cretheus is said to have loved the river-god Enipeus; and in the form of Enipeus, Poseidon once appeared to her and became by her the father of Pelias and Neleus. Tyro exposed the two boys, but they were found and reared by horsemen or shepherds. After the death of Cretheus, the two brothers quarreled about the succession to the throne of Iolcus. Neleus, who was expelled, went with Melampus and Bias to Pylus, which his uncle Aphareus had given to him (Apollod. 1.9.9). Neleus thus became king of Pylus, a town he found in existence when he arrived there; but some state that he himself built Pylus, or at least that he erected the royal palace there (Paus. 4.2.3, 36.1). Neleus was married to Chloris, a daughter of Amphion, and by her was the father of Nestor and eleven other sons. When Heracles had killed Iphitus, he went to Neleus to be purified; but Neleus was a friend of Eurytus, the father of Iphitus, and refused to purify Heracles (Diod. 4.3). In order to take vengeance, Heracles afterward marched against Pylus and slew the sons of Neleus with the exception of Nestor. Neleus was thus reduced to a state of defenselessness, and Augeas, king of the Epeians, used this opportunity to make forays on Pylus. Among other things, Augeas intercepted and retained for himself a team of four horses that Neleus had sent to the Olympic games (Hom. *Il.* 11.699). Neleus took vengeance for this by carrying away the flocks of the Epeians (Hom. *Il.* 11.670), causing them to retaliate by invading the territory of Pylus. Pausanias (2.2.2) says that Neleus died at Corinth and that he, in conjunction with Nestor, restored the Olympic games. The descendants of Neleus, the Neleidae, were expelled from their kingdom by the Heracleidae and migrated for the most part to Athens (Paus. 2.18.9).

Two other sons of Neleus besides Nestor deserve mention. One was Periclymenus, who was one of the Argonauts. Poseidon gave him the power to change himself into different forms and conferred upon him great strength, but he was nevertheless slain by Heracles at the taking of Pylus (Apollod. 1.9.9, 2.7.3; Apollon. Rhod. 1.156). According to some, Periclymenus escaped Heracles in the shape of an eagle. Alastor, another son, was also slain by Heracles. According to one story, he was to be married to Harpalyce, who, however, was taken from him by her own father, who practiced incest with her.

It was Nestor, though, who was the most famous of this dynasty. He was the husband of Eurydice, by whom he became the father of Peisidice, Polycaste, Perseus, Stratius, Aretus, Echephron, Peisistratus, Antilochus, and Thrasymedes. After the death of Eurydice, he married Anaxibia, the daughter of Atreus and sister of Agamemnon. Others, probably more correctly, call her a daughter of Cratieus. When Heracles invaded the country of Neleus and slew his sons, Nestor alone was spared because at the time he was not at Pylus but among the Gerenians, where he had taken refuge (Hom. *Il.* 11.692; Apollod. 2.7.3; Paus. 3.26.8). This story is connected with another about the friendship between Heracles and Nestor. Nestor is said to have taken no part in the carrying off from Heracles the oxen of Geryones, and Heracles rewarded him by giving Messene to him. Heracles became more attached to Nestor even than to Hylas and Abderus. Nestor, in return, is said to have introduced the custom of swearing by Heracles. Pausanias (4.3.1) states that Nestor lived at Messenia after the death of the sons of Aphareus. When a young man, Nestor was distinguished as a warrior, and in a war with the Arcadians he slew Ereuthalion (Hom. *Il.* 4.319, 7.133, 23.630). In the war with the Eleians he killed Itymoneus and took from them large flocks of cattle (Hom. *Il.* 11.670). When, after this, the Eleians laid siege to Thryoessa, Nestor went out on foot without the war steeds of his father, and gained a glorious victory (Hom. *Il.* 11.706). He also took part in the fight of the Lapiths against the Centaurs (Hom. *Il.* 1.260) and is mentioned among the Calydonian hunters and the Argonauts; but he owes his fame chiefly to the Homeric epics, in which his share in the Trojan War is immortalized. After he helped Odysseus persuade Achilles and Patroclus to join the Greeks against Troy, he sailed with

his Pylians in sixty ships (Hom. *Il.* 2.591). At Troy he took part both in the council and in the field of battle. His most striking features were his wisdom, justice, bravery, knowledge of war, his eloquence, and his old age. He is said to have ruled over three generations of men, and his advice and authority were regarded as almost divine. Notwithstanding his advanced age, he was brave and bold in battle and distinguished above all others for drawing up horses and men in battle array. After the fall of Troy he, together with Menelaus and Diomedes, returned home safely to Pylus (Hom. *Od.* 3.165), where Zeus granted him the full enjoyment of old age, surrounded by intelligent and brave sons (Hom. *Od.* 4.209). He was found here by Telemachus, who visited him to inquire about Odysseus. In addition to his hospitality, Nestor sent his own son to conduct Telemachus to Sparta.

Antilochus was the son of Nestor by Anaxibia. For some unexplained reason he was exposed as an infant on Mount Ida and suckled by a dog. He is named among the suitors of Helen. According to the Homeric account, he accompanied his father to Troy. He appears in the Homeric epics as one of the youngest, handsomest, and bravest of the Greeks, and is beloved by Achilles. He fell at Troy by the hand of Memnon. He was painted by Polygnotus in the Lesche at Delphi. Thrasymedes, another son, accompanied Nestor to Troy and returned with him to Pylus. He was the father of Sillus, and his tomb was shown at Pylus (Paus. 2.18.7). With Alcmaeon, the son of Sillus, the royal line disappeared when the Neleidae were expelled by the Heracleidae.

The Neleid kingdom extended west as far as that of the Atreidae and north as far as the Alpheius, or even beyond. Upon the invasion of Peloponnesus by the Dorians, three generations after Nestor, the Neleidae left Pylus and moved to Athens where they obtained the throne. The situation of this Pylus was a subject of much dispute among the Grecian geographers. Pausanias (4.36.1) unhesitatingly placed the city of Nestor on the promontory of Coryphasium.

The Palace of Nestor lies about 10 km farther north on the highway to Hora. It has been excavated since 1952. It was here that Nestor ruled for three generations and sent ninety ships to Troy. Near the palace are tholos tombs like the ones at Mycenae. In the palace was found a store of Linear B tablets. It seems evident that the whole area embracing the palace and the city of Pylus was meant when Homer referred to "sandy" Pylus. The kingdom, of course, was far vaster, as described above.

PYRASUS (NEA ANHIALOS)   was a town of Phthiotis in Thessaly, mentioned by Homer (*Il.* 2.695) along with Phylace and Iton. Pyrasus was located on the Pagasaean Gulf 3.5 km from Phthiotic Thebes, for which it was the harbor (Strab. 9.5.14). It had disappeared in the time of Strabo. It was known in later times as Demetrium from the temple of Demeter, spoken of by Homer and described by Strabo as two stadia from Pyrasus. The modern site of Pyrasus is Nea Anhialos, about 15 km southwest along the coast from Volos.

PYRGUS (ELIA?)   was the most southerly town of Triphylia in Elis, at the mouth of the river Neda, upon the Messenian frontier (Strab. 8.3.22). It was one of the settlements of the Minyae. Its site is placed at some ancient remains upon the right bank of the Neda not far from its mouth. This would place it very near the modern village of Elis.

PYRPILE   was an early name of the island of DELOS.

PYRRHA   was an earlier name of ancient MELITAEA.

PYRRHA   was an earlier name of THESSALY.

PYRRHICHUS (PIRRIHOS)   was a town of Laconia located about the center of the promontory ending in Cape Taenarum and about 2 km from the Scyras River. According to some, it derived its name from Pyrrhus, the son of Achilles; according to others the name was from Pyrrhicus, one of the Curetes. The Curetes were the priests entrusted with guarding Zeus when he was born on Crete. Silenus was also said to have been brought up here. He was a son of Pan and constant companion of Dionysus. He was described as a jovial old man with a bald head and pug nose; he was fat and round like his wine bag, which he always carried, and generally as intoxicated. Pyrrhichus contained temples of Artemis Astrateia and of Apollo Amazonius, the two surnames referring to the tradition that the Amazons did not proceed further than this place. It was said that Artemis stopped their progress here. There was also a fountain, said to be a gift of Silenus, in the agora (Paus. 3.25.3). The ruins of the town were discovered near the village of Pirrihos, where were found the fountain of which Pausanias speaks, the torso of a female statue, and the remains of baths.

PYTHIUM (PITHIO)   was a town of Perrhaebia in Thessaly located at the foot of Mount Olympus and forming a tripolis with the two adjacent towns of Doliche and Azorus. Pythium derived its name from a temple of Apollo Pythius situated on one of the summits of Olympus. Games were also celebrated here in honor of Apollo. Pythium commanded an important pass across Mount Olympus. This pass and that of Tempe are the only two leading from Macedonia to the northeast of Thessaly. Its site is placed at modern Pithio, which is 5 km off the road leading from Elassona to Kokkinopolos and Livadi, though no remains of the ancient town have been discovered there.

PYTHO (See DELPHI)

PYTNA   was an earlier name of HIERAPYTNA.

RHAMNUS (RAMNOUS)   was a deme of Attica, belonging to the tribe Aeantis. It derived its name from a thick, prickly shrub that still grows there. The town stood on the east coast of Attica about 11 km from Marathon and on the road leading from Marathon to Oropus (Paus. 1.33.2.). It was one of the main fortresses in Attica. The deme was chiefly celebrated in antiquity because of its worship of Nemesis. Nemesis was the personification of moral reverence for law, dispenser of happiness or unhappiness according to the deserts of men, avenger of culpable action especially based on hubris or pride. There was a tradition that Zeus begot by Nemesis at Rhamnus an egg, which Leda found and from which Helen and the Dioscuri sprang, whence Helen herself is called Rhamnusia (Callim. *Hymn. in Dian.* 232; Paus. 1.33.7). On the pedestal of the Rhamnusian Nemesis, Leda was represented leading Helen to Nemesis. The temple of the goddess was at a short distance from the town. It contained a celebrated statue of Nemesis, which, according to Pausanias (1.33.4), was the work of Pheidias and was made by him out of a block of Parian marble that the Persians had brought with them for the construction of a trophy. The statue was 4.5 meters high, and on its base were several figures in relief.

Rhamnus stood in a small plain, 5 km in length, which, like that of Marathon, was shut out from the rest of Attica by surrounding mountains. The town itself was situated upon a rocky peninsula, surrounded by the sea for two-thirds of its circumference and by a mountain ridge on the other. It was about three-quarters of a kilometer in circumference, and its remains are considerable. At the head of a narrow and shallow valley that leads to the principal gate stand the ruins of the temple of Nemesis. They are upon a large, artificial platform, supported by a wall of pure white marble. Actually, remains of two temples are on the platform, and it is thought that the smaller is an earlier temple destroyed by the Persians. The larger was the rebuilt temple honoring the goddess for vengeance on the barbarians. Some have supposed that the smaller temple was dedicated to Themis. But it is more probable that both temples were dedicated to Nemesis and that the smaller temple was in ruins before the larger one was erected and dedicated to Nemesis alone. On the slope of the hill overlooking the main gate of the fortress a small sanctuary was also dedicated to Aristomachus, a local hero and physician said to have been buried at Marathon.

RHARIAN PLAIN   was a plain adjacent to Eleusis. Pausanias (1.38.6) said that the Eleusinians had a temple of Triptolemus, another of Artemis Propylaea, and a third of Poseidon Patros (Father). They also had a fountain called Callichorum, where the Eleusinian women first instituted a dance and sang in honor of Demeter.

Triptolemus was the son of Celeus and Metaneira. Demeter, on her arrival at Eleusis, undertook the care of newly born Demophon, a brother of Triptolemus. In order to make the child immortal, Demeter at night put him into a fire. But his mother Metaneira discovered the proceeding, screamed out, and the child was consumed by the flames. As a compensation for this bereavement, the goddess gave to Triptolemus a chariot with winged dragons and seeds of wheat. Triptolemus first sowed barley in the Rharian Plain, and from there spread the cultivation of grain all over the earth. In later times an altar and threshing floor of Triptolemus were shown there (Paus. 1.38.6). Some writers called him a son of Rharus, of whom no other mention is to be found and who, apparently, gave his name to the Rharian Plain.

RHENEIA (See DELOS)

RHOCCA (ROKKA)   was a town of Crete where there was a temple to Artemis Rhoccaea (Aelian. *De Nat. Anim.* 12.22). Remains have been found at Rokka, which is 8 or 9 km southeast of the port of Kissamos.

RHODES (RODOS)   is one of the chief islands of the Aegean about 12 km from the coast of what was ancient Caria. In the earliest times it is said to have borne the names of Ophiussa, Stadia, Telchinia, Asteria, Aethraea, Trinacria, Corymbia, Poeeessa, Atabyria, Macaria, and Oloessa. It extends from south to north and is about 171 km in circumference. A chain of mountains runs the length of the island with Atabyris as its highest point. The towns were mostly situated on the coast. Mount Atabyris is 1,390 meters above sea level, and on top of it stood a temple of Zeus Atabyrius. Rhodes was believed to have at one time risen out of the sea. Helios, the sun, is described as the son of Hyperion and Theia and the brother of Selene and Eos. He was worshipped in various places but especially at Rhodes. Sacrifices to Helios consisted of white rams, boars, bulls, goats, lambs, especially white horses, and honey. The cock was also especially sacred to him.

The Telchines, the most ancient inhabitants of Rhodes, are said to have immigrated from Crete (Pind. *Ol.* 7.23). The Telchines were a family, a class of people, or a tribe, said to have been descended from Thalassa or Poseidon (Diod. 5.55). It is probably owing to this story about their origin that they were described as marine beings without feet and with fins in place of hands. They have also been said to have originally been the dogs of Actaeon, who were changed into men. The following are mentioned as the individual Telchines—Mylas, Atabyrius, Antaeus, Megalesius, Hormenus, Lycus, Nicon, Simon, Chryson, Argyron, Chalcon.

The accounts of the Telchines are few and scanty. In them the Telchines appear in three different manifestations. As cultivators of the soil and ministers of the gods they came from Crete to Cyprus and from there to Rhodes, Crete, and Boeotia. Rhodes was their principal seat and was named Telchinia after them. On the island they inhabited the three towns of Cameirus, Lindus, and Ialysus. From Ialysus the Telchines are called Ialysii (Ov. *Met.* 7.365). However, the island was abandoned by them because they foresaw that it would be flooded, and therefore they scattered in different directions. Lycus went to Lycia, where he built the temple of the Lycian Apollo, a god who had been worshipped by them at Lindus. Hera had been worshipped at Ialysus and Cameirus. Athena at Teumessus in Boeotia bore the surname Telchinia. Nymphs also were called after them Telchiniae. Rhea entrusted Poseidon to them, and they in conjunction with Capheira, a daughter of Oceanus, brought him up. Rhea, Apollo and Zeus, however, are described as hostile to the Telchines for Apollo is said to have assumed the shape of a wolf and to have thus destroyed the Telchines, and Zeus is said to have caused their destruction by a flood (Ov. *Met.* 7.367). Secondly, as sorcerers, the Telchines had eyes and appearance said to be destructive. They had power to induce hail, rain, and snow, and to assume any form they pleased; they further mixed Stygian water with sulphur in order to destroy animals and plants (Strab. 14.2.7). And finally as artists, the Telchines are said to have invented useful arts and institutions and to have made images of the gods. They worked in brass and iron, making the sickle of Cronus and the trident of Poseidon. This last feature of the Telchines seems to have been the reason for their being identified with the Idaean Dactyls, and Strabo (10.3.19) even states that those of the nine Rhodian Telchines who accompanied Rhea to Crete and there brought up the infant Zeus were called Curetes. The Telchines, about whom many fabulous stories are related, are said to have been nine in number, and their sister Halia became by Poseidon the mother of six sons and one daughter, Rhodos, from whom the island ultimately received the name it still bears. Halia, after leaping into the sea, received the name of Leucothea and was worshipped as a divine being by the Rhodians (Diod. 5.55). Some said that the sea nymph Rhodos, or Rhode, was a daughter of Helios and Amphitrite.

When the gods distributed among themselves the various countries of the earth, the island of Rhodes was yet covered by the waves of the sea. Helios was absent at the time of the distribution; and as no one drew a lot for him, he was not to have any share of the earth. But at that moment the island of Rhodes rose out of the sea and, with the consent of Zeus, Helios took possesion of it. By the nymph of the island he then became the father of seven sons (Pind. *Ol.* 7.100; Ov. *Met.* 4.204). Some writers derive the name Rhodes from *rodon* (rose) for the rose appears as a symbol on coins of the island, so that Rhodes would be "the Island of the Roses." After the Telchines had disappeared, Helios created a new race of inhabitants, who were called after him Heliadae; they were seven in number and became ancestors of seven tribes, which partly peopled Rhodes itself and partly emigrated to Lesbos, Cos, Caria and Egypt. Macar, or Macareus, was a son of Helios and Rhodos, who after the murder of his brother Tenages fled from Rhodes to Lesbos (Hom. *Il.* 24.544; Diod. 5.56). Leucippus was the leader of this colony that Macareus conducted. Armenius, one of the Argonauts, was believed to have been a native of Rhodes and to have settled in the country called Armenia after him (Strab. 11.14.12). The Heliadae are said to have greatly distinguished themselves by the progress they made in the sciences of astronomy and navigation. After this, various immigrations from foreign places are mentioned: Egyptians under Danaus, Phoenicians under Cadmus, Thessalians and Carians, each of these are said to have left some of their numbers on Rhodes.

Danaus was a son of Belus and a grandson of Poseidon. He was brother of Aegyptus and father of fifty daughters and the mythical ancestor of the Danai. According to the common story, he was a native of Chemnis in upper Egypt and migrated from there to Greece. Belus had given Danaus Libya, while Aegyptus had obtained Arabia. Danaus had reason to believe that the sons of his brother were plotting against him, and fear or the advice of an oracle instructed him to build a very large ship and to set sail with his daughters. On his flight he first landed at Rhodes, where he set up an image of Athena Lindia. According to the story in Herodotus (2.181), a temple of Athena was built at Lindus by the daughters of Danaus, and according to Strabo (14.2.8), Tlepolemus built the towns of Lindus, Ialysus, and Cameirus and called them thus after the names of three Danaids. From Rhodes Danaus and his daughters sailed to Peloponnesus.

The Rhodians, upon the advice of an oracle, are said to have invited Phorbas, a son of Lapithes, onto their island to deliver it from snakes. Afterward they honored him with heroic worship (Diod. 5.58). From this circumstance he was called Ophiuchus and was placed among the stars.

Some Dorians or Heracleidae appear to have been settled on Rhodes as early as the Trojan War, for the Heraclid Tlepolemus is described as having sailed to Troy with nine ships (Hom. *Il.* 2.653). Tlepolemus was a son of Heracles by Astyoche. He was king of Argos but after slaying his uncle Licymnius, he was obliged to take to flight. At the command of an oracle, he settled on Rhodes,

where he built the towns of Lindus, Ialysus, and Cameirus, and from where he joined the Greeks in the Trojan War. He was slain at Troy by Sarpedon. His wife Philozoe instituted funeral games in commemoration of his death.

Helen Dendrites (Goddess of the Trees) occurs as a name of Helen at Rhodes. The following story is related to account for her surname. After the death of Menelaus, Helen was driven from Sparta by two illegitimate sons of her husband. She fled to Rhodes and sought the protection of her friend Polyxo, the widow of Tlepolemus. But unknown to Helen, Polyxo hated her because her own husband had been killed in the war. Therefore, once while Helen was bathing, Polyxo sent out her servants in the disguise of the Erinyes with the command to hang Helen on a tree. For this reason the Rhodians afterward built a sanctuary to Helen Dendrites (Paus. 3.19.10).

After the Trojan War Althaemenes, a Heraclid from Argos, led other settlers to Rhodes (Strab. 14.2.6; Diod. 15.59; Apollod. 3.2.1). He was a son of Catreus, king of Crete. In consequence of an oracle that Catreus would lose his life by one of his children, Althaemenes left Crete together with his sister Anemosyne in order to avoid becoming the instrument of his father's death. He landed on Rhodes at a place he called Cretenia, and in commemoration of the god of his own native island, he erected on Mount Atabyris an altar to Zeus Atabyrius. His sister was seduced there by Hermes, but Althaemenes, disbelieving the account, kicked her to death. When Catreus grew old, he wanted to see his only son once more in order to place his crown in his hands. Accordingly, he sailed to Rhodes. Upon landing there, he and his companions were attacked by shepherds, who thought they were pirates. During the struggle, Althaemenes came to the protection of his subjects and killed his father. When he became aware of what he had done, he prayed to the gods and was swallowed up by the earth. The Rhodians afterward worshipped him as a hero. After this time the Rhodians quietly developed the resources of their island and rose to great prosperity and affluence.

The three most ancient towns of the island were Lindus, Ialysus, and Cameirus, which were believed by some to have been founded by three grandsons of the Heliad Ochimus bearing the same names. Ochimus was a Rhodian king, a son of Helios and Rhodos. He was married to the nymph Hegetoria and was the father of Cydippe, who married Ochimus' brother Cercaphus (Diod. 5.56,57). Ialysus was a son of Cercaphus and grandson of Helios. He was a brother of Lindus and Cameirus, in conjunction with whom he possessed the island of Rhodes, where he was regarded as the founder of the town Ialysus (Diod. 5.57; Pind. *Ol.* 7.74). Cameirus similarly founded the town of Cameirus and Lindus that of Lindus (Diod. 5.57). Athena took the surname Lindia from Lindus. These three towns, together with Cos,

Cnidus, and Halicarnassus, formed what was called the Doric hexapolis, which had its common sanctuary on the Triopian peninsula on the coast of Caria. Apollo was the tutelary deity of the confederation (Herod. 1.144). The rapid progress made by the Rhodian towns at a comparatively early period is sufficiently attested by their colonies in the distant countries of the west. Thus they founded settlements in the Balearic Islands; Rhode on the coast of Spain; Parthenope, Salapia, Siris, and Sybaris in Italy; and Gela in Sicily; meanwhile the countries nearer home were not neglected because Soli in Cilicia, and Gagae and Corydalla in Lycia were likewise Rhodian colonies.

The island of Rhodes, which appears even in the earliest traditions to be extremely wealthy (Hom. *Il.* 2.670; Pind. *Ol.* 7.49), is in many parts indeed rough and rocky, especially on the coast near the city of Rhodes, and the district about Lindus. On the whole, however, it is extremely fertile: its citrus crops, figs, pears, pistachios and olives are much esteemed, and its saffron, oil, marble, sponges, and fish were spoken of in ancient times. The most important products of Rhodian industry were ships, arms, and military engines. Besides the places already mentioned, the ancients noticed Ixia and Mnasyrium, two forts in the south, and a place called Achaia. According to Strabo (14.2.5), Rhodes surpassed all other cities for the beauty and convenience of its ports, streets, walls, and public edifices, all of which were adorned with a profusion of works of art. The principal statues were in the temple of Dionysus and the gymnasium; but the most extraordinary statue, which is described as one of the seven wonders of the ancient world, was the bronze statue of Helios, commonly called the Colossus of Rhodes. It was the work of Chares of Lindus, who employed twelve years upon its execution. It cost three hundred talents and was thirty-two meters in height. The Colossus stood at the entrance of one of the ports. It was overthrown by an earthquake about 224 B.C., only fifty-six years after its erection. The Rhodians were commanded by an oracle not to rebuild it (Pind. *Ol.* 7.54).

The foundations of the temple of Aphrodite are seen in the lower city just west of the harbor. A little west of that are remains of a shrine of Dionysus. But the buildings most worth seeing are across the city in its southwest part. The foundations of the temple of Zeus and Athena can be seen on the north end of the acropolis. Farther south is the temple of Apollo Pythius, adjacent to a theater and stadium. It is difficult to see in these ruins the beauty and harmony that caused Lucian (*Amor.* 8) to compare the city of Rhodes to the beauty of Helios himself.

RHODOPE (RODOPI)   is a mountain chain forming the west continuation of Haemus and the boundary

between Thrace and Macedonia. On its desolate heights lived the fierce Satrae, a Thracian people noted for their love of freedom. The great sanctuary and oracle of the Thracian Dionysus was also found here. The Strymon River had its sources in Rhodope (Strab. 7. *Frag.* 36).

RHODOS (See RHODES)

SALAMIS (SALAMINA)   is an island lying between the west coast of Attica and the east coast of Megaris and forming the southern boundary of the bay of Eleusis. It is separated from the coasts both of Attica and of Megaris by a narrow channel. Its form is that of an irregular semicircle. It measures 16.5 km north and south and slightly more east and west. In ancient times it is said to have been called Pityussa from the pines that grew there and also Sciras and Cychreia from the names of two heroes, Scirus and Cychreus. Scirus was a soothsayer of Dodona who, in the reign of Erechtheus, came to Salamis and was afterward given heroic honor on the island. He perished along with Erechtheus in fighting against Eumolpus (Paus. 1.36.4). Cychreus, a son of Poseidon and Salamis, became king of the island of Salamis, which was called Cychreia after him and which he delivered from a dragon. He was subsequently honored as a hero and had a sanctuary on Salamis (Apollod. 3.12.7; Diod. 4.72). According to other traditions, Cychreus himself was called a dragon on account of his savage nature and was expelled from Salamis by Eurylochus; but he was received by Demeter at Eleusis and appointed a priest to her temple. Others again said that Cychreus had brought up a dragon that was expelled by Eurylochus (Strab. 9.1.9). There was a tradition that while the battle of Salamis was going on, a dragon appeared in one of the Athenian ships and that an oracle declared the dragon to be Cychreus (Paus. 1.36.1).

The island is said to have obtained the name Salamis from the mother of Cychreus, who was also a daughter of Asopus. It was colonized at an early period by the Aeacidae of Aegina. Telamon, the son of Aeacus, fled here after the murder of his half-brother Phocus and became sovereign of the island (Paus. 1.35.1). Glauce was a daughter of Cychreus who married Actaeus and, according to some, became by him the mother of Telamon. Most say, however, that Aeacus was the father of Telamon and Peleus by Endeis. Telamon emigrated from Aegina to Salamis and was married first to Glauce and afterward to Periboea, a daughter of Alcathous, by whom he became the father of Ajax. He was one of the Calydonian hunters and one of the Argonauts. After Telamon and Peleus had killed their stepbrother Phocus, they were expelled by Aeacus from Aegina. Telamon went to Cychreus, who bequeathed to him his kingdom. Telamon is said to have been a great friend, or even lover, of Heracles and to have joined him in his expedition against Laomedon of Troy. By one of Laomedon's daughters, Hesione, he became the father of Teucer. Teucer, the best archer among the Greeks at Troy, was thus the half brother of Ajax the Greater. On his return from the Trojan War, Telamon refused to receive him in Salamis, because he had not avenged the death of Ajax, or because he had brought with him neither the remains of Ajax, nor Tecmessa, nor his son Eurysaces. Teucer, therefore, in consequence of a promise of Apollo, sailed away in search of a new home. This he found on the island of Cyprus, where he founded the town of Salamis.

This Ajax was called by Homer Telamonian Ajax, Ajax the Greater, or simply Ajax, whereas the other Ajax, the son of Oileus, is always distinguished by some epithet, such as "Lesser." According to Homer (*Il.* 2.557), Ajax joined the expedition against Troy with his Salaminians in twelve ships and was, next to Achilles, the most distinguished and the bravest among the Greeks. He is described as tall of stature, his head and broad shoulders rising above those of all the Greeks (Hom. *Il.* 3.226); in beauty he was inferior to none but Achilles (Hom. *Od.* 11.550, 24.17). According to Apollodorus (3.12.7) and Pindar (*Isth.* 6.51), Ajax became invulnerable in consequence of a prayer that Heracles offered to Zeus while he was on a visit to Salamis. The child was called Aias from Aitos, an eagle, which appeared immediately after the prayer as a favorable omen. According to Lycophron (445), Ajax was born before Heracles came to Telamon, and the hero made the child invulnerable by wrapping him up in his lion's skin. Ajax is also mentioned among the suitors of Helen (Apollod. 3.10.8). He was worshipped on Salamis as the guardian hero of the island; he had a temple with a statue there and was honored with a festival, the Aianteia. According to some, the wife of Ajax was Glauca, by whom he had a son Aeantides. By Tecmessa he had Eurysaces, who was named after the broad shield of his father (Soph. *Aj.* 575). An Athenian tradition related that Eurysaces and his brother Philaeus had given up to the Athenians the island of Salamis, which they had inherited from their grandfather and that the two brothers received property in Attica in return (Plut. *Sol.* 10). One of the brothers then settled at Brauron and the other at Melite. Eurysaces was honored like his father, at Athens, with an altar (Paus. 1.35.3).

Salamis continued to be an independent state until about the beginning of the fortieth Olympiad (620 B.C.), when a dispute arose for its possession between the Athenians and Megarians. The Athenians supported their claims by a line in the *Iliad* (2.558), which represents Ajax ranging his ships with those of the Athenians, but the Megarians cited another version of the line. The Athenians, moreover, asserted that the island had been deeded to them by Philaeus and Eurysaces, sons of the Telamonian Ajax, when they took up their own residence in Attica. These arguments were considered sufficient by the Spartan arbitrators, and Salamis was awarded to the Athenians (Plut. *Sol.* 10; Strab. 9.1.10). It then became an Attic deme until the time of Macedonian rule.

The old city of Salamis, the home of Ajax, stood upon the south side of the island toward Aegina (Strab. 9.1.9) and is identified with the remains of some Hellenic walls upon the southwest coast. Some have said that Paris and Helen consummated their elopement on Salamis (Lycoph. 110).

When Salamis became an Athenian deme, a new city was built at the head of a bay on the east side of the island and opposite the Attic coast. In the time of Pausanias this city had fallen into decay. There remained, however, a ruined agora and a temple of Ajax, containing a statue of the hero in ebony; also a temple of Artemis, which had been erected in honor of the victory over the Persians, and a temple of Cychreus (Paus. 1.36.1). There are still some remains of the city close to the village of Ambelakia.

In Salamis there was a promontory, Sciradium, containing a temple of Ares, erected by Solon because he there defeated the Megarians (Plut. *Sol.* 9). This site has been identified with the temple of Athena Sciras.

SALGANEUS (DROSSIA)   was a town on the east coast of Boeotia between Chalcis and Anthedon. It was considered an important place because it commanded the north entrance to the channel of the Euripus (Diod. 19.77; Liv. 35.37,46,51). The remains of the town stand directly under the highest summit of Mount Messapium where the plain ends. The citadel occupied a hill rising from the shore. There are remains of walls on the crest of the summit and on the southeast side of the height. Apollo Salganeus was a name of the god derived from the town (Strab. 9.2.9). The site is between the modern towns of Drossia and Loukissia.

SALMONE   an ancient town of Pisatis in Elis, said to have been founded by Salmoneus, stood near Heracleia at the sources of the Enipeus River, a branch of the Alpheius. Its site is uncertain. Salmoneus was a son of Aeolus and a brother of Sisyphus. He was first married to Alcidice and afterward to Sidero; by the former wife he was the father of Tyro. He originally lived in Thessaly, but emigrated to Elis where he built the town of Salmone (Strab. 8.3.31). He then went so far in his arrogance that he claimed to be equal to Zeus and ordered sacrifices to be offered to himself; he even imitated the thunder and lightning of Zeus, but the father of the gods killed the presumptuous man with his thunderbolt, destroyed his town, and punished him in the lower world (Apollod. 1.9.7; Lucian *Tim.* 2; Virg. *Aen.* 6.585; Claud. *In Rufin.* 514). Modern Salmona is a tiny place near the confluence of the Enipeas and Alfios Rivers but not at the source, as the ancient town was reported to be. Its name is either a coincidence or an example of the affectation of naming towns from ancient and unlocated places in an area.

SAME (SAMI)   was the most ancient city in Cephallenia. The men from Same joined those from Cephallenia, Ithaca, Neritus, Crocyleia, Zacynthus, and the coast of Epeirus in twelve ships under Odysseus (Hom. *Il.* 2.303,631). In the *Odyssey* (20.288, 22.285) we read that Ctesippus, a son of Polytherses of Same, one of the suitors of Penelope, was killed by Philoetius, the cowherd.

The city stood upon the east coast and upon the channel separating Cephallenia from Ithaca (Strab. 10.2.13). It appears that the city had two citadels, the smaller called Cyatis and the larger unnamed (Liv. 38.28,29).

Sami is the name of the modern town and also that of the bay upon which it stands. It stands at the north end of a wide valley, which borders the bay. There are considerable remains of the town walls. The circuit of the city was roughly 3 km. A grotto sacred to Pan has been excavated near the town.

SAMICUM (SAMIKO)   was a town of Triphylia in Elis, situated near the coast about halfway between the mouths of the Alpheius and the Neda and a little north of the Anigrus. It stood upon a spur of Mount Kaiafaa, which here comes so close to the coast that only a narrow pass is left. Because of the position commanding this pass, a city probably existed here from the earliest times. Samicum was therefore identified with the Arene of Homer (*Il.* 2.591, 11.723), which is placed near the mouth of the Minyeius, a river supposed to be the same as the Anigrus (Strab. 8.3.19; Paus. 5.6.2). Arene belonged to the dominions of Nestor. According to Pausanias (4.2.4,3.7), it was built by Aphareus, who named it for Arene, both his wife and half-sister. Samicum was at first the name of the fortress and the same name was also given to the surrounding plain (Strab. 8.3.18; Paus. 5.5.3). The original name of ancient Samicum was Samos. The ruins of Samicum are found at Samiko. The ruined walls are 1.8 meters thick and about 2.5 km in circumference.

Near Samicum on the coast was a celebrated temple of the Samian Poseidon (Paus. 6.25.6). It was the center of the religious worship of the six Triphylian cities, all of which contributed to its support. In the vicinity of Samicum there were celebrated medicinal springs, which were said to cure cutaneous diseases. Lagoons stretch along the coast, and the river Anigrus flows into the one of them and then into the sea. The lagoon is deep, being fed by springs; in summer it was said to be very fetid and the air extremely unwholesome, which Strabo (8.3.19) attributed to the Centaurs washing their wounds in the Anigrus. There were two caves, one sacred to the Nymphae Anigrides, and the other to the Atlantides. It

was in the cave of the Anigrides that persons who were going to use the waters first offered up their prayers to the nymphs (Strab. 8.3.19; Paus. 5.5.11).

SAMOS (SAMOS)   is a large island in that part of the Aegean called the Icarian Sea. The word denotes a height, especially by the coast. The following earlier names of Samos are also mentioned: Parthenia, Anthemus, Melamphylus, Dryusa, and Cyparissia. Some of these probably had to do with physical characteristics of the island. Samos was, and is, well forested.

Ancaeus was a son of Poseidon and Astypalaea and king of the Leleges on Samos. He was the husband of Samia, a daughter of the river-god Maeander, and by her the father of Perilaus, Enudus, Samus, Alitherses and Parthenope (Paus. 7.4.1). Parthenia the wife of Samus gave her name to the island in this early period. This Ancaeus is frequently confused with Ancaeus, the son of Lycurgus, who was both an Argonaut and Calydonian hunter. This Ancaeus is famous for the proverb that originated at the time of his death. Ancaeus planted many vines. A seer said to him that he would not live to taste the wine of his vineyard. When Ancaeus afterward was on the point of drinking some of his own wine, he scorned the seer, who, however, answered: "There is many a slip between the cup and the lip." At that moment a disturbance arose outside, and Ancaeus was told that a wild boar was nearby. He put down his cup, went out to get rid of the animal, and was killed by it.

Samos is crossed from east to west by a chain of mountains. The length of Samos from east to west is about 41.5 km. Its width is very variable. The city of Samos, the capital, is a serviceable harbor on the north. It was formerly called Vathi. The highest mountain (1,433 meters) is Kerketefs. A ridge branches off to the southeast and ends in the promontory of Poseidio. The west end of the island, opposite Icaria, was called Cantharium in ancient times.

The position of Samos was nearly opposite the boundary line of Caria and Ionia, and its early traditions connect it first with Carians and Leleges, and then with Ionians. The first Ionian colony is said to have come from Epidaurus. Procles, the son of Pityreus, was the leader of the Ionians who settled on the island. He was an Epidaurian by birth and led with him a considerable number of Epidaurian exiles. Androclus and the Ephesians attacked Procles and his son Leogorus, who shared the royal power with him, and expelled them (Paus. 7.4.2). We find Samos at an early period in the position of a powerful member of the Ionic confederacy. At this time it was highly distinguished in shipping and navigation. Thucydides (1.13) tells us that the Samians were among the first to make advances in naval construction.

The archaeological interest of Samos is almost entirely concentrated in that plain on the south that contained the sanctuary of Hera at one extremity and the ancient city on the other. This plain is terminated at the southwest by a promontory, which was called by the Genoese Cape Colonna because of a single column of the Heraion that remains standing. Virgil (*Aen.* 1.16) says that Samos was at least second in the affections of Hera; her temple and worship were responsible for much of the fame and prosperity of Samos for many centuries. The temple was never entirely finished and was later burned by the Persians. After its restoration, it was plundered by pirates in the Mithridatic War, then by Verres, and then by Marc Antony. He took to Rome three statues—Athena, Heracles, and Zeus—attributed to Myron. The statue of Athena was made of wood and was supposed to be the work of Smilis, a contemporary of Daedalus. In the time of Tacitus (*Ann.* 4.14), this sanctuary had the rights of asylum. When Pausanias (7.4.4) was there, the Samians pointed out to him a shrub, under the shade of which it was believed that Hera was born on the banks of the Imbrasus River. Thus the river itself was called Parthenias and the goddess Imbrasia. Every year a festival celebrated the divine marriage of Zeus and Hera. In one of the ceremonies the cult statue was wrapped in sacred leaves to restore virginity to the goddess. Admete was a priestess of Hera at Argos but fled with the statue of the goddess to Samos. Pirates were employed by the Argives to recover the statue, but the enterprise did not succeed, for the ship when laden with the statue could not be made to move. The men then took the statue back to the coast of Samos and sailed away. When the Samians found it, they tied it to a tree. Admete purified it and restored it to the temple of Samos. In commemoration of this event, the Samians celebrated an annual festival called Tonea. This story seems to be an invention of the Argives, by which they intended to prove that in Argos the worship of Hera was older than on Samos. In part of the vast temple complex was also a temple of Aphrodite and Hermes.

Poseidon Samius had his temple on Samos. He also had the surname Epactaeus there. Eros was also worshipped. One of the famous prophetic women of antiquity was the Samian Sibyl. Samos is also known as the home of Zalmoxis. Zalmoxis, named from the bear skin (*zalmos*) in which he was clothed as soon as he was born, was a Getan, who had been a slave to Pythagoras on Samos. He was freed and acquired great wealth. He also acquired large stores of knowledge from Pythagoras and from the Egyptians, whom he visited in the course of his travels. He returned to Getae, introducing civilization and religious ideas that he had gained, especially regarding the immortality of the soul. First a priest, he came to be regarded as a deity among the Getae.

SAMOS   was the original name of the ancient town of SAMICUM.

SAMOTHRACE (SAMOTHRAKI)   is an island in the north of the Aegean, opposite the mouth of the Hebrus and lying north of Imbros and northeast of Lemnos. It is of an oval shape, 13 km in length and 10 in width. It is remarkable for its extreme elevation. No island in the entire Aegean is so high except Crete. The elevation of its highest point is 1,597 meters. The ancient city with the same name as the island was on the north; its modern name is Paleopolis. The modern capital, however, is Samothraki. Pausanias (7.4.3) says that Samothrace was colonized by emigrants from Samos. The earlier names of Samothrace were Dardania, Electris, Melite, and Leucosia. Diodorus Siculus (5.47) speaks of its inhabitants as autochthons. The chief mythological interest in this island is connected with the Cabeiri. Pelasgians are said by Herodotus (2.51) to have first inhabited the island and to have introduced the mysteries. The Cabeiri were mystic divinities who occurred in various parts of the ancient world. The meanings of their name, their character, and their nature are obscure. Strabo (10.3.21) speaks of the origin of the Cabeiri, saying that Camillus, a son of Cabeiro and Hephaestus, had three sons and three daughters called Cabeiri, and the three Cabeirian nymphs were the children of Cabeira, the daughter of Proteus, by Hephaestus. Sacrifices were offered to the Corybantes as well as to the Cabeiri on Lemnos (the place with which they are first identified), Imbros, and the towns of the Troad. They were considered inferior in dignity to the Great Gods on account of their origin, but the Samothracian mysteries were considered second in importance only to the Eleusinian mysteries. The Cabeiri shared these rites with the Great Gods. They were most likely fertility spirits whose power to bring protection and good fortune was widely acclaimed. The Argonauts, following the urging of Orpheus their shipmate, stopped at Samothrace in order to be initiated into the mysteries and gain special guidance on their voyage. Axieros was a daughter of Camillus and one of the three Samothracian Cabeiri. According to one commentator, she was the same as Demeter. The two other Cabeiri were Axiocersa (Persephone) and Axiocersus (Hades).

The Dactyli were fabulous beings originally from Phrygia to whom the discovery of iron and the art of metallurgy was ascribed. They are sometimes confounded or identified with the Curetes, Corybantes, Cabeiri and Telchines; or they are described as the fathers of the Cabeiri and Corybantes (Strab. 10.3.7–8). Diodorus Siculus (5.64) states that the Dactyls also gave incantations and followed magical practices and that consequently they developed a following in Samothrace and that Orpheus was their disciple in these things.

Rhea, the mother of the gods, was widely worshipped and thus became identified with a variety of mother goddesses in countries close to Greece. The

Thracians, for example, conceived the chief divinity of the Samothracians and Lemnian mysteries as Rhea-Hecate.

Samothrace appears in the *Iliad* (13.12). Poseidon gazes from the height of the island (Mount Fengari) upon incidents of the war. At least one writer called Samothrace a Trojan island. The tradition was that Dardanus dwelt there before he went to Troy and that he introduced the Cabeiric mysteries from there into Asia. Dardanus, a son of Zeus and Electra, was the mythical ancestor of the Trojans. He was married to Chryse in Arcadia, who bore him two sons, Idaeus and Deimas. These sons ruled for a time over the kingdom of Atlas in Arcadia, but then they separated on account of a great flood and the calamities resulting from it. Deimas remained in Arcadia while Idaeus emigrated with his father. They first arrived in Samothrace, which they called Dardania, and after having established a colony there, they went to Phrygia. Iasion was another son of Zeus and Electra. Some accounts say that being driven from his home by a flood in Arcadia, he also went to Samothrace, carrying the Palladium. There Zeus himself instructed him in the mysteries of Demeter (Diod. 5.48). Saon was a mythical lawgiver of Samothrace, said to have been another son of Zeus. He united the scattered inhabitants of Samothrace into one state, which he regulated by laws (Diod. 5.48).

Harmonia was a daughter of Ares and Aphrodite or of Zeus and Electra in Samothrace. Those who described Harmonia as a Samothracian related that Cadmus on his voyage to Samothrace, after being initiated into the mysteries, saw Harmonia and carried her off with the assistance of Athena.

Philip of Macedon and Olympias were both initiated into the Carbeiric mysteries. Later Germanicus sailed to the island with the view of becoming initiated, but he was deterred by an omen (Tac. *Ann.* 2.54).

The ruins here are impressive. The acropolis at Paleopolis is walled and has two towers overlooking the sea. West of the hill stood the Sanctuary of the Great Gods. Excavations were begun in 1863. To the left of the entrance to the sanctuary was the Anactoron, which served as a hall of initiation. Next to it was the Arsinoeion, the largest circular building known in Greek architecture. It was dedicated to the Great Gods by Queen Arsinoe about 280 B.C.. The altar is the earliest preserved part of the sanctuary. Outside is a sacred rock from which libations were poured. Another sacred altar stands by a spring in a partly artificial recess, perhaps the Cave of Hecate Cerynthia. The sacred enclosure remains in foundations. Within it probably stood a statue of Aphrodite and Pothos (Desire) by Scopas. The remains of the Hieron are in the south part of the sacred area. This was used for the higher initiation ceremonies. A marble ceiling beam is preserved, but the marble floor has disappeared. The spectators' benches on either side are reminiscent of those at Eleusis. On the west of the Hieron were two buildings, one the Hall of Votive Gifts and the other the Altar Court. The outline of the theater can be traced, although only two seats remain. On the ridge above the theater was the stoa, and farther on is the Nike Fountain. It was here that the famous Nike now called Winged Victory stood. It formed the central monument of the fountain. This Nike went to the Louvre in 1863. Across the river to the east was the Ptolemaion, a gateway to the sanctuary dedicated to the Great Gods by Ptolemy II Philadelphus. In the Museum can be seen several mythological references, such as a frieze of dancing maidens possibly depicting the wedding of Harmonia and Cadmus, a bust of Teiresias, a headless statue of Persephone, a statuette of Heracles, and a relief of Centaurs.

SARONIC GULF (SARONIKOS KOLPOS)   is a gulf of the Aegean Sea, extending from the promontories of Sunium in Attica and Scyllaeum in Troezenia up to the Isthmus of Corinth. The length, according to ancient geographers, is 138 km. It touches the coasts of Attica, Megaris, Corinth, Epidaurus and Troezen and contains the islands of Aegina and Salamis. It was said to have derived its name from Saron, a king of Troezen. Saron built a sanctuary of Artemis Saronia on the seacoast. Once while chasing a stag into the sea he was drowned, and his body, which washed ashore in the grove of Artemis, was buried there (Paus. 2.30.7). Near Troezen was a little town called Saron, and Troezen itself is said at one time to have been called Saronia. The lagoon in which Saron drowned had been called Phoebaea but was afterward called Saronia. A Troezenian river Saron is also mentioned. Some derived the name of the gulf from *saronis* (oak) (Plin. 4.5.18). Scylla was a daughter of Nisus of Megara. When Minos of Crete took Megara, Scylla fell in love with him and killed her father in order to assist Minos. Minos was horrified at the act and ordered Scylla to be fastened to the stern of the ship and afterward drowned her in the Saronic Gulf (Apollod. 3.15.5).

SCAMBONIDAE   was one of the demes which made up the city of ATHENS.

SCARPHE (SKARFIA)   was a town of the Locri Epicnemidii mentioned by Homer (*Il.* 2.532) as contributing soldiers, along with Cynus, Opus, Calliarus, Augeiae, Tarphe, and Thronium, for service in the Trojan War. Soldiers from these towns were led by Ajax the Lesser. According to Strabo (9.4.4), it was 2 km from the sea and 5.5 from Thronium. It appears from Pausanias (7.15.3) that it lay on the direct road from Elateia to Thermopylae by Thronium. The town may therefore be placed between the modern villages of Skarfia and Molos.

SCARPHE   was a later name, according to Strabo (9.2.24), of ETEONUS.

SCHERIA was the Homeric island that has been identified with CORCYRA.

SCHISTE the name of the road leading from Delphi into central Greece, was more particularly applied to the spot where the road divided into two and which was called Treis Celeuthai (Three Roads), counting the road to Delphi as one of the three. At the spot where the three roads met was the tomb of Laius and his charioteer, who were here slain by Oedipus. It must have stood at the entrance of the Zemeno, the opening between the mountains Cirphis and Parnassus, which leads to Delphi. The road from this point became very steep and rugged toward Delphi.

SCHOENUS was a town in Boeotia mentioned by Homer (*Il.* 2.497), and placed by Strabo (9.2.22) upon a river of the same name on the road to Anthedon 9 km from Thebes. Schoenus was the birthplace of the celebrated Atalanta, the daughter of Şchoeneus (Paus. 8.35.10). Schoeneus, a son of Athamas and Themisto, was king in Boeotia and father of Atalanta and Clymenus. He wanted only sons and exposed Atalanta when she was born. But she was suckled by a bear and later found by hunters. Growing up, she loved the hunt above all else and wished to remain a virgin so she could continue this pursuit. She became famous for various exploits and was welcomed home by her father. He proposed to find a husband for her. Atalanta was reluctant, so she made marriage contingent upon a suitor winning a footrace with her; a suitor who lost, however, also lost his head. Eventually Hippomenes (or Melanion) won the race by throwing golden apples at intervals in her path, which she stopped to collect. According to the distance given by Strabo (9.2.22), the site of Schoenus would be about 4 km north of the National Highway at the intersection for Thebes.

SCHOENUS (PALEO KALAMAKI) on the Saronic Gulf was the only town on the Corinthian Isthmus in ancient times. Situated at the narrowest part of the Isthmus, it was the port of the Isthmian sanctuary and the place at which goods were transported across the Isthmus by means of the *diolkos,* (causeway). The harbor, which is now called Paleo Kalamaki, is exposed to the east and southeast. The site of the town is indicated by a few fragments of Doric columns. Melicertes was a son of Athamas and Ino. When his mother was driven mad by Hera, she threw herself and her son into the sea. Melicertes was transformed into a sea deity and called Palaemon. His body was washed ashore at Schoenus, where subsequently the altar of Palaemon was erected. There his body was found by his uncle Sisyphus, who, on the command of the Nereids, instituted the Isthmian games and the sacrifice of black bulls in honor of the deified Palaemon (Paus. 2.1.3).

SCIAS was a place 2.5 km from Methydrium in Arcadia. It had a temple of Artemis Sciatis, founded by the tyrant Aristodemus. It has never been located.

SCILLUS a town of Triphylia in Elis, was situated 3.5 km south of Olympia. In its early history it was razed along with Pisa in 572 B.C.. It remained desolated till about 392 B.C., when the Lacedaemonians colonized Scillus and gave it to Xenophon. He left a description of the place, which he says was situated twenty stadia (3.5 km) from the Sacred Grove of Zeus on the road from Olympia to Sparta. Scillus stood upon the Selinus, which was also the name of the river flowing by the temple of Artemis at Ephesus. Here Xenophon, from a part of the spoils acquired in the Asiatic campaign, built a temple to Artemis, modeled on the celebrated temple at Ephesus, and instituted a festival to the goddess. In the area also stood a temple of the Scilluntian Athena (Strab. 8.3.14). When Pausanias (5.6.6) visited Scillus five centuries after Xenophon, the temple of Artemis still stood. Today there are no remains to identify Scillus, and its location is not known. However, from the distance and direction given by Pausanias, it must lie close to modern Makrisia. The remains of the temple of Athena have been tentatively identified in the area of Skillountia (formerly Mazi).

SCIONE (NEA SKIONI) was the leading town on the isthmus of Pallene in Macedonia. Although it called itself Achaian, it traced its origin to warriors returning from Troy. Its site must be sought between the capes of Paliuri and Posidi. Protesilaus, who is generally celebrated for being the first Greek to fall at Troy, has another, quite different, tradition on Scione. He survived the war and after the fall of Troy took with him as prisoner Aethylla, sister of Priam, among other captives. On his homeward voyage he landed on the Macedonian peninsula of Pallene between Mende and Scione. When he had gone some distance from the coast to fetch water, Aethylla persuaded the other women to set fire to the ships. Accordingly, Protesilaus was obliged to remain there and he built the town of Scione.

SCIRAS was an earlier name of the island of SALAMIS.

SCIRONIAN ROCKS (SKIRONIDES PETRAI) is the pass between Megara and Corinth. The old road between the two cities runs along a narrow ledge cut in the rocks halfway up the sides of the cliff. According to a Megarian tradition, these rocks derived their name from Sciron, a military commander of the Megarians, who was the first to make a footpath along the rocks (Paus. 1.44.6); but, according to the more common tradition, they were named after the famous robber Sciron, who haunted the frontier between Attica and Megaris. He not only robbed the travelers who passed through the country but compelled them to wash his feet on the Scironian Rocks, during which operation he kicked them with his foot into the sea. At the foot of the rock there was a tortoise that devoured the bodies of the robber's victims. He was slain by Theseus in the same manner in which he had killed others (Plut. *Thes.* 10; Diod. 4.59). In the pediment of the royal Stoa at Athens there was a group of figures of burnt clay representing Theseus in the act of throwing Sciron into the sea (Paus. 1.3.1).

SCIRUM was a small place, near a stream of the same name, just outside the Athenian walls on the Sacred Way. It was not a deme. It derived its name from Scirus, a prophet of Dodona, who fell in the battle between the Eleusinians and Erechtheus and was buried in this spot (Paus. 1.36.4).

SCOLUS was a town of Boeotia mentioned by Homer (*Il.* 2.497) and described by Strabo (9.2.23) as a village near Mount Cithaeron. Pausanias (9.4.4), in his description of the route from Plataea to Thebes, says that if the traveler were, instead of crossing the Asopus, to follow that river for about forty stadia (7 km), he would arrive at the ruins of Scolus, where there was an unfinished temple of Demeter and Kore. Strabo (9.2.23) says that Scolus was so disagreeable and rugged that it gave rise to the proverb: "Never let us go to Scolus, nor follow any one there." The site of Scolus is uncertain, but it probably stood near the modern village of Dafni, which is about 7 km east of Erithres.

SCOTUSSA (SKOTOUSSA) was a town of Pelasgiotis in Thessaly, lying between Pherae and Pharsalus near the frontiers of Phthiotis. Scotussa is not mentioned in Homer, but according to some accounts the oracle of Dodona in Epeirus originally came from this place (Strab. 7.7.12). The ruins of Scotussa are found at Skotoussa. The city was about 4 or 5 km in circumference, but not very much of the wall has been preserved. The acropolis stood at the southwest end of the site, below which, on the east and north, the ground is covered with foundations of buildings.

SCYLLAEUM (AKRA SKILI) a promontory of Troezenia and the most easterly point of the Peloponnesus, is said to have derived its name from Scylla, the daughter of Nisus; she, after betraying Megara and Nisaea to Minos, was thrown by him into the sea and was washed ashore on this promontory. Scyllaeum formed, along with the opposite promontory of Sunium in Attica, the entrance to the Saronic Gulf. It is now called Akra Skili.

SCYROS (SKIROS) an island in the Aegean Sea and one of the northern Sporades, was so called from its ruggedness. It lies east of Euboea and contains a town of the same name. When Achilles reached the age of nine, the seer Calchas declared that Troy could not be taken without his aid. Thetis, knowing that this war would be fatal to him, disguised him as a girl and placed him among the daughters of Lycomedes, king of the Dolopians of Scyros. There he was called by the name Pyrrha on account of his golden locks. But his real character did not remain concealed for long, because one of his companions, Deidameia, became mother of a son, Pyrrhus or Neoptolemus, by him. The Greeks at last discovered his place of concealment and an embassy was sent to Lycomedes, who, though he denied the presence of Achilles, yet allowed the messengers to search his palace. Odysseus discovered the young hero by a stratagem, and Achilles immediately promised his assistance to the Greeks. The name Pyrrhus was said to have been given to the son of Achilles by Lycomedes because he had fair hair or because Achilles, while disguised as a girl, had borne the name Pyrrha. He was called Neoptolemus (Young Warrior) because either Achilles or Pyrrhus himself had fought in early youth. He was brought up in Scyros in the house of Lycomedes, from where he was fetched by Odysseus to join the Greeks in the war against Troy (Hom. *Od.* 11.508) because it had been prophesied by Helenus that Neoptolemus and Philoctetes, with the arrows of Heracles, were necessary for the taking of Troy. It should be mentioned, too, that Iphis, the beloved of Patroclus, was from the island of Scyros (Hom. *Il.* 9.667).

According to another tradition, Scyros was conquered by Achilles (Hom. *Il.* 1.668; Paus. 1.22.6); and this conquest was connected in Attic legend with the death of Theseus. When Theseus accompanied Peirithous to Hades in an attempt to kidnap Persephone, he was imprisoned there until rescued by Heracles. Menestheus, an Erechthid, took command in his absence and incited the people against Theseus. When he returned, Theseus found himself unable to reestablish his authority and retired to Scyros. At first he was hospitably received by Lycomedes. But eventually Lycomedes, fearing the influence of so powerful a person upon his own subjects, pushed him over a cliff. Some related that the cause of the violence was that Lycomedes would not give up the estates that Theseus owned on Scyros or that Lycomedes wanted to gain the favor of Menestheus (Plut. *Thes.* 35). It was to avenge his death that Peleus sent Achilles to conquer the island (Plut. *Thes.* 35). In 476 B.C. an oracle directed the Athenians to bring home the bones of Theseus; but it was not until 469 B.C. that the island was conquered and the bones carried to Athens, where they were preserved in the Theseion.

Scyros is divided into two parts by a narrow isthmus. The modern town of Skiros on the east side of the island stands upon the site of the ancient city. It covers the north and west sides of a high, rocky peak, which on the east falls steeply to the sea. Therefore Homer (*Il.* 1.664) correctly described the ancient city as the "lofty" Scyros. The walls are still traceable in many parts. The city was barely 3 km in circumference. On the isthmus south of Scyros a deep bay still retains the name Achilli, which is probably the site of the Achilleion, or sanctuary of Achilles, mentioned by one writer. Athena was the divinity chiefly worshipped on Scyros. Her temple stood upon the shore close to the town (Stat. *Achill.* 1.285, 22.21).

SEBRION was a place in Sparta. Dorceus, a son of Hippoccon, had a heroon at Sparta jointly with his brother Sebrus. The well near the sanctuary was called Dorceia, and the place around it Sebrion (Paus. 3.15.2). It is probable that Dorceus is the same person as Corcyleus in Apollodorus (3.10.5), where his brother is called Tebrus.

SELEMNUS is a river of Achaia flowing into the sea between the promontories of Drepanum and Rhium, a little east of Argyra (Paus. 7.23.1). Argyra, the nymph of a well in Achaia, was in love with a beautiful shepherd boy, Selemnus, and visited him frequently. But when his youthful beauty vanished, she forsook him. The boy now pined away with grief, and Aphrodite, moved to pity, changed him into the river Selemnus. There was a popular belief in Achaia that an unhappy lover bathing in the water of this river would forget the grief of love (Paus. 7.23.2).

SELLASIA (AGIOS KONSTANTINOS?) was a town of Laconia, situated in the valley of the Oenus on the road leading from Tegea and Argos; it was one of the main outposts of Sparta. The ruins of Sellasia probably lie adjacent to the hill of Paleogoula about 1.5 km north of Agios Konstantinos. The city was about 2.5 km in circumference. The walls were from 3 to 3.5 meters thick. The town was in ruins in the time of Pausanias (3.10.7). Its name has been connected with Artemis Selasia.

SEPIA was a mountain in Arcadia near the road from Pheneus to Stymphalus. Aepytus was a king of Arcadia, a son of Eilatus, who ruled over Phaesana on the Alpheius. He is said to have been killed during a chase on Mount Sepia by the bite of a venomous snake (Paus. 8.4.7,16.3). His tomb was still shown there in the time of Pausanias, who was anxious to see it because it was mentioned in Homer (*Il.* 2.604).

SEPIAS (AKRA SIPIA) was a promontory of Magnesia, opposite the island of Sciathos and forming the northeast extremity of Thessaly. It is now called Akra Sipia. It is celebrated in mythology as the spot where Peleus lay in wait for Thetis and from where he carried off the goddess (Eurip. *Androm.* 1266).

SERIPHOS (SERIFOS) is an island in the Aegean Sea, one of the Cyclades, lying between Cythnos (Kithnos) and Siphnos (Sifnos). It possesses a town of the same name with a harbor.

Seriphos is celebrated in mythology as the place where Danae and Perseus were driven ashore in the chest in which they had been exposed by Acrisius. Perseus was the son of Zeus and Danae and a grandson of Acrisius, king of Argos. Acrisius, who had no male issue, consulted the Pythian oracle and received the answer that if Danae should give birth to a son, he would kill his grandfather. Acrisius accordingly shut up his daughter in a subterranean room made of brass or stone. But Zeus, having metamorphosed himself into a shower of gold, came down through the roof of the room and became by her the father of Perseus. When Acrisius discovered that Danae had given birth to a son, he threw both mother and son into a chest and cast them into the sea. But Zeus caused the chest to land on Seriphos, where Dictys, a fisherman, found them and carried them to his brother, King Polydectes. Polydectes made Danae his slave and courted her favor, but in vain. In order to obtain the exclusive possession of her, he sent off Perseus, who had in the meantime grown up to manhood, to the Gorgons to fetch the head of Medusa. Another account states that Polydectes married Danae and caused Perseus to be brought up in the temple of Athena. When Acrisius learned this, he went to Polydectes, who, however, intervened on behalf of the boy, and Perseus promised not to kill his grandfather. Acrisius, however, was detained in Seriphos by storms, and during that time Polydectes died. During the funeral games the wind caught a disk thrown by Perseus and hit Acrisius in the head and killed him. Perseus then proceeded to Argos and took possession of the kingdom of his grandfather.

According to the common tradition, Perseus went on the quest for Medusa's head and was able to accomplish his purpose. The deed was done only with the reluctant assistance of the Graeae, sisters of the Gorgons, and the provision by various gods and nymphs of winged sandals, a bag, an invisible helmet, a sickle, and a mirror. He used the mirror to avoid looking at Medusa, an act that would have turned him to stone, and the sickle to sever her head. With the head in the bag, he eluded the pursuing Gorgons and after rescuing and marrying Andromeda, he returned to Seriphos. He found his mother with Dictys in the temple, where she had fled from the embraces of Polydectes. Perseus found the king at a banquet and metamorphosed him and all his guests (and some say, the whole island) into stone; then he presented the kingdom to Dictys. Perseus, accompanied by Danae and Andromeda, went to Argos. He eventually killed Acrisius by accident during games at Larissa, where Acrisius had fled. He was worshipped in several places, including Seriphos.

Seriphos was colonized by Ionians. By subsequent writers it was always mentioned with contempt on account of its poverty and insignificance (Aristoph. *Acharn.* 542; Plat. *De Re Pub.* 1.329), and it was for this reason employed by the Roman emperors as a place of banishment for state criminals (Tac. *Ann.* 2.85, 4.21; Juv. 6.564, 10.170). It is curious that ancient writers made no mention of the iron and copper mines of Seriphos, which evidence shows were worked in antiquity.

The modern town stands upon the site of the ancient city on the east side of the island and contains less than five hundred inhabitants. It is built upon a steep rock about 244 meters above the sea. There are only a few remains of the ancient city.

SICINOS (SIKINOS)   is a small island in the Aegean Sea, lying between Pholegandros and Ios and containing a town of the same name. It is said to have been originally called Oenoe from its cultivation of the vine but later to have been named Sicinos after a son of Thoas and Oenoe. Thoas, a son of Dionysus and Ariadne, was king of Lemnos and the father of Hypsipyle. When the Lemnian women killed all the men on the island, Hypsipyle hid her father, who later escaped to Oenoe, later Sicinus, where he became the father of Sicinus. Wine is still the chief product of the island. It was probably colonized by Ionians. There are some remains of the ancient city situated at the town of Sikinos. There is also still extant an ancient temple of the Pythian Apollo, now converted into a church.

SICYON (SIKIONA)   was an important city of Peloponnesus situated about 3 km from the Corinthian Gulf. It stood on a hill, protected on every side by precipices, which can be ascended only by one or two narrow passages from the plain. A river flows on either side of the hill, the one on the east side being the Asopus and the one on the west the Helisson. When Sicyon was at the height of its power, the city consisted of three parts, the acropolis, the lower town, and the well-fortified port town.

Sicyon was one of the most ancient cities of Greece and is said to have existed under the name of Aegialeia long before the arrival of Pelops in Greece. It was also called Mecone (Strab. 8.6.25), which was apparently its priestly name. As Mecone it is celebrated as the "dwelling place of the blessed" and as the spot where Prometheus instituted the Hellenic sacrifices and deceived Zeus. Once in the reign of Zeus when gods and men were disputing with each other at Mecone (afterwards Sicyon), Prometheus attempted to deceive Zeus and rival him in prudence. He cut up a bull and divided it into two parts. He wrapped the best parts and the intestines in the skin and at the top he placed the stomach, which is one of the worst parts; in a second parcel he wrapped bones covered with fat. When Zeus pointed out to him how badly he had made the division, Prometheus asked him to choose one of the parcels. But Zeus, angry and seeing through the strategem of Prometheus, chose the heap of bones covered with the fat. He avenged himself by withholding fire from mortals, but Prometheus stole it in a hollow tube. Zeus punished him by putting him in chains fastened to a pillar. There every day an eagle consumed his liver, which grew back every night. Thus Prometheus was exposed to perpetual torture.

Sicyon was also called Telchinia, and this name referred to its being one of the earliest seats of metal work. Its name Aegialeia was derived from a mythical autochthon Aegialeus. Its later name Sicyon was said to have been derived from an Athenian of this name, who became king of the city and who is represented as a son either of Marathon or Metion (Paus. 2.6.5).

Aegialeus is said, in some traditions, to have been the son of Inachus, the first king of Argos, and the brother of Phoroneus. Europs, his son, succeeded him and was followed by Telchis and then Apis, the son of Telchis. Apis was said to have been such a powerful prince that prior to the arrival of Pelops, Peloponnesus was called Apia after him (Paus. 2.5.7). According to Apollodorus (2.1.1), Apis was a son of Phoroneus and a tyrant to such a degree that he was assassinated by Telchis and Thelxion. The writer does not make their relationship clear and, in fact, has Apis die childless. In Pausanias (2.5.6), however, Thelxion is the son of Apis and consequently the next king of Apia. He was succeeded by Aegyrus, his son, and Aegyrus was succeeded by Thurimachus, his son. Leucippus, son of Thurimachus, came next to the throne, but did not produce a son. Calchinia, his daughter, by Poseidon became the mother of Peratus, to whom the kingdom passed upon the death of Leucippus. Plemnaeus was the son of Peratus and was cursed with an odd malady that caused the death of his offspring as soon as they were born. Eventually Demeter took pity on him and took his son Orthopolis to rear. Orthopolis thus survived, and Plemnaeus in gratitude built a temple to Demeter (Paus. 2.5.8,11.2). Orthopolis had no sons; however, his daughter Chrysorthe became the mother of Coronus by the god Apollo. Coronus then became the twelfth king of Apia (Sicyon) and produced two sons, Corax and Lamedon, the second being quite a few years the younger. Corax ruled but died childless.

At this time, Epopeus, a son of Poseidon and Canace, came from Thessaly to Sicyon, where he took the kingdom (Paus. 2.6.1). There is no explanation as to how this happened to come about. But Epopeus appeared to be a powerful individual. He is reported to have carried away Antiope, the daughter of Nycteus, from Thebes. Others say that she became pregnant by Zeus and from fear of her father fled to Epopeus at Sicyon, whom she married. Nycteus killed himself in despair but charged his brother Lycus to avenge him on Epopeus and Antiope. Lycus accordingly marched against Sicyon, took the town, slew Epopeus, and carried Antiope with him to Eleutherae in Boeotia. During her imprisonment there, she gave birth to twin sons, Amphion and Zethus. Previous to his death Epopeus dedicated a temple to Athena (Paus. 2.6.3; Apollod. 1.7.4). The temple of Athena was destroyed by lightning, but the tomb of Epopeus was preserved and shown there in later times (Paus. 2.11.1). Although Epopeus had a son, Marathon, the kingdom reverted to its proper line, and Lamedon, the younger son of Coronus, was old enough to take the throne.

Lamedon married Pheno, the daughter of Clytius, by whom he became the father of Zeuxippe. During his reign, war arose between him and the sons of Achaeus, and he brought in as an ally a hero named Sicyon from Attica. The identity of the father of Sicyon was uncertain, and Marathon, Metion, Erechtheus, and Pelops have all been named. It is reasonable to suppose that Marathon was the father since there was an already established connection between the two families. When Lamedon gave Sicyon his daughter Zeuxippe in marriage, this certainly would have legitimized the reign of Epopeus, if Sicyon was indeed his grandson. In any case, Sicyon next became king, and the land was called after him Sicyonia and its capital Sicyon. Chthonophyle was the only off-spring from this union, and she had Hermes for a lover. By him she had Polybus, who became the next king following Sicyon. Chthonophyle went on to marry Phlias, the son of Dionysus; and their son was Androdamas. Polybus was said to have found the infant Oedipus floating in a chest, where he had been placed by Laius to prevent fulfillment of the dire prophecy. He was thus reared by Polybus and his wife. Polybus had no sons but gave his daughter Lysianassa in marriage to Talaus, son of Bias, who reigned in Argos. Talaus' son Adrastus quarrelled with Amphiaraus during their joint rule at Argos, and Adrastus was obliged to flee for his safety to his grandfather Polybus in Sicyon. When Polybus died without heirs, Adrastus succeeded him on the throne of Sicyon, and during his reign he is said to have instituted the Nemean games (Hom. *Il.* 2.572; Pind. *Nem.* 9.30). Later he was reconciled with Amphiaraus and returned to Argos. He participated in both battles against Thebes. After his death he was worshipped at Sicyon, where his memory was celebrated in tragic choruses (Herod. 5.67).

After Adrastus returned to Argos, the throne was occupied by Ianiscus, a descendant of Clytius, the father-in-law of Lamedon. Ianiscus came from Attica, and once more an earlier bloodline was merged in the royal succession. The line was broken upon the death of Ianiscus, when he was succeeded by Phaestus, said to have been one of the sons of Heracles. Phaestus is said to have established at Sicyon the custom of worshipping Heracles as a god since before he had only been honored as a hero (Paus. 2.10.1). In obedience to an oracle Phaestus migrated to Crete, and the next king was Zeuxippus, the son of Apollo and the nymph Sillis. On the death of Zeuxippus, the rule passed back to the Heraclid line to Hippolytus, son of Rhopalus, son of Phaestus. This Hippolytus gave up the kingdom without a struggle to Agamemnon, who led an army against Sicyon, and agreed to become subject to the Mycenaeans. Hippolytus was the father of Lacestades, who became a regent under Agamemnon. When Phalces, the son of Temenus, with the Dorians, invaded Sicyon at night, he did no violence to Lacestades since he, too, was a Heraclid. In consequence of this connection, the inhabitants were not expelled or reduced to subjection. While the Dorian conquerors in other states were divided into three tribes (Hylleis, Pamphyli, and Dymanatae), the original Sicyonians were formed into a fourth tribe under the name Aegialeis, which possessed the same political rights as the other three (Paus. 2.6.7; Herod. 5.68). In fact, Lacestades was made a co-ruler. Phalces also founded the temple of Hera Prodromia (Paus. 2.6.7,11.2). Sicyon was now a Dorian state, and from that time its history in the modern sense began.

Other individuals connected with the city and territory were Echepolus, Marsyas, and Meleager. Echepolus Anchisiades was a patronymic to designate Echepolus, the son of Anchises of Sicyon (Hom. *Il.* 23.296). He had made Agamemnon a present of the mare Aethe, in order not to be obliged to accompany him to Troy (Hom. *Il.* 23.293). Marsyas was an early Phrygian musician who challenged Apollo to a musical contest. When Apollo won, he had the presumptuous Marsyas flayed alive. His flute was cast into the river Marsyas; it was carried then by the Maeander to the Asopus, where it was washed ashore in Sicyon. The flute was dedicated to Apollo in his temple in the agora. The spear with which Meleager slew the Calydonian boar was also dedicated in that temple of Apollo (Paus. 2.7.9).

Pausanias came to Sicyon from Corinth. After crossing the Asopus, he noticed the Olympieion on the right. He entered by the Corinthian gate and proceeded to the acropolis. Here he noticed temples of Tyche and the Dioscuri, of which there are still some traces. Below the acropolis was the theater, the remains of which are well preserved. Near the theater was the temple of Dionysus, from which a road led past the ruined temple of Artemis Limnaea to the agora. Dionysus was worshipped under two surnames, Acoreites and Lysius. Lysius meant "Deliverer," and the Theban Phanes was said to have introduced his worship at Sicyon (Paus. 2.7.6). At the entrance to the agora was the temple of Peitho (Persuasion). In the agora itself was the temple of Apollo, which appears to have been the chief sanctuary in Sicyon. Nearby was an altar to Poseidon Isthmius and statues of Zeus Meilichius and of Artemis Patroa, the former resembling a pyramid, the latter a column. In the agora was a bronze statue of Zeus, a gilded statue of Artemis, remains of a temple of Apollo Lyceius (meaning either "Lycian," "Wolf-Slayer," or "Giver of Light"), and statues of the daughters of Proetus, of Heracles, and of Hermes Agoraeus (Paus. 2.9.6,7). Proetus, it will be remembered, was king of Argos, whose daughters were seized with madness, and Melampus the seer promised to cure them in exchange for partial rule in Argos. Melampus with a band of youths pursued the women as far as Sicyon and there purified them. Proetus then is reported to have founded a sanctuary of Hera between Sicyon and Titane and a sanctuary of Apollo at Sicyon (Paus. 2.7.8,12.2).

Pausanias then proceeded to the gymnasium, which contained a marble statue of Heracles by Scopas and a temple of Heracles in a sacred enclosure. From there the road led to two large enclosures, sacred to Asclepius and Aphrodite. Asclepius, of course, was the god of the medical art. We find that by him Aristodeme, a Sicyonian woman, became the mother of Aratus. Asclepius had appeared to her in the form of a dragon. A painting of her and the dragon existed in the temple of Asclepius. Nicagora of Sicyon was the wife of Echetimus; she was believed to have brought the statue of Asclepius in the form of a dragon from Epidaurus to Sicyon on a car drawn by mules (Paus. 2.10.3). Hypnos Epidotis (Liberal Giver) was a name of the god of sleep at Sicyon; the god had a statue in the temple of Asclepius, which represented him in the act of putting a lion to sleep (Paus. 2.10.2). Hygieia, the goddess of health, was worshipped in the same temple as her father, Asclepius (Paus. 2.11.6). From the Aphrodision, Pausanias went past the temple of Artemis Pheraea to the gymnasium of Cleinias, which was used for the training of the ephebi, and which contained statues of Artemis and Heracles. From here he turned towards the Sacred Gate, near which once stood a celebrated temple of Athena built by Epopeus. This temple had been struck by lightning and nothing remained but the altar; this temple may perhaps have been the one sacred to Athena Colocasia, mentioned by Athenaeus (3.72). There were two adjoining temples, one sacred to Artemis and Apollo, built by Epopeus, and the other sacred to Hera, erected by Adrastus, who himself was worshipped by the people of Sicyon (Herod. 5.68; Pind. *Nem.* 9.20). The worship of Hera at Sicyon was very ancient. This temple was built to Hera Alexandros (Defender of Men).

On the road descending from the Heraion to the plain was a temple of Demeter; and close to the Heraion were the ruins of the temple of Apollo Carneius. The origin of Apollo's surname is uncertain. Some derived it from Carnus, an Acarnanian soothsayer, whose murder by Hippotes provoked Apollo to send a plague on the army of Hippotes while he was on his march to Peloponnesus. Apollo was propitiated by the introduction of the worship of Apollo Carneius (Paus. 3.13.4). It has already been mentioned that the temple of Hera Prodromia was founded by Phalces, the son of Temenus (Paus. 2.11.1,2).

Two roads led from Sicyon to Phlius; between these two roads at the distance of 3.5 km from Sicyon was a sacred grove containing a temple of the Eumenides.

Besides the divinities already mentioned we find references to the worship or deeds of several others. The Apotropaei were certain divinities by whose assistance the Greeks believed that they were able to avert any threatening danger or calamity. Their statues stood at Sicyon near the tomb of Epopeus (Paus. 2.11.1). Hebe Dia, a manifestation of the goddess of youth, had a temple at Sicyon (Paus. 2.13.3). Pan, the great god of flocks and shepherds, had a sanctuary here (Paus. 2.10.2). The Venti (Winds) had an altar between Titana and Sicyon. Upon this altar a priest offered a sacrifice to the winds once every year (Paus. 2.12.1).

SIDE (VELANIDIA?)   was a town on the east coast of Laconia, a little north of the promontory of Malea. It was said to have existed before the Dorian conquest and to have derived its name from a daughter of Danaus (Paus. 3.22.11). The inhabitants were moved by the Dorian conquerors to the neighboring town of Boeae. This town had been founded by Boeus, a son of Heracles, who led colonists there from Etis, Aphrodisias, and Side (Paus. 3.22.11). Side probably occupied the site of Velanidia, where there is a port.

SIPHAE or **TIPHA** (ALIKI)   was a town of Boeotia on the Corinthian Gulf, said to have derived its name from Tiphys, the pilot of the Argonauts. He was a son of Hagnius from the town of Siphae (Apollon. Rhod. 1.105). In the time of Pausanias the inhabitants of Siphae pointed out the spot where the ship Argo anchored on its return from its celebrated voyage. The same writer mentions a temple of Heracles at Siphae, in whose honor an annual festival was celebrated. It has been located on a promontory south of Xironomi, and that places it adjacent to Aliki on the Gulf of Dovrenis. There are substantial remains of walls here and other structures from the fifth century B.C.

SIPHIS   was another name for the island of MELOS.

SIPHNOS (SIFNOS)   is one of the Cyclades lying near Seriphos. It was originally called Merope and also

Acis. Siphnos was colonized by Ionians from Athens. It was said to have derived its name from Siphnos, the son of Sunius. Siphnos was once wealthy from its gold and silver mines, and the treasury of the Siphnians at Delphi, in which they deposited one-tenth of the produce of their mines, was equal in wealth to the treasuries of the most opulent states. Their mines later became less productive, and Pausanias (10.11.2) relates that because the Siphnians neglected to send one-tenth of their treasure to Delphi, the gods destroyed their mines by a tidal wave. So, by the time of Strabo (10.5.1), the poverty of the Siphnians had become proverbial. Siphnos had a city of the same name and also the towns of Apollonia and Minoa. The ancient city occupied the same site as the modern town, now called Kastro, which lies on the east side of the island. There are some remains of ancient walls and a temple dating from the seventh century B.C.

SITHONIA (SITHONIA)   is the central one of three promontories that run out into the Aegean from the great peninsula of Chalcidice. The Sithonian peninsula, which, though not as hilly as that of Acte, is not so inviting as Pallene. It was the first, it appears, to have been occupied by the Chalcidic colonists. Cleitus was king of the Sithones in Thrace, who gave his daughter Chrysonoe or Torone in marriage to Proteus, who had come to Thrace from Egypt.

SOLOGORGUS   was the original name of HERAEA.

SOULIA (AGIA GALINI)   a small ancient city on the south coast of Crete, was the harbor of Sybarita. Remains of a sanctuary of Artemis, the chief deity of the city, were found here in the late nineteenth century. The main part of the town probably lay on a hill about 1 km northeast of Agia Galini.

SPALATHRA   was a town of Magnesia in Thessaly on the Pagasaean Gulf. Prothous, a son of Tenthredon, was commander of the Magnetes who lived in the vicinity of Mount Pelion and the Peneius River. He was one of the Greek heroes at Troy, leading forty ships to the war (Hom. *Il.* 2.758). He was said to be from Spalathra (Lycoph. 899).

SPARTA (SPARTI)   was the capital of Laconia and the chief city of Peloponnesus. It was also called Lacedaemon, which was the original name of the country. Sparta stood at the upper end of the middle valley of the Eurotas and on the right bank of the river. The city was built upon a range of low hills and upon an adjoining plain. These are foothills of Mount Taygetus and rise almost immediately from the bank of the river. The Eurotas River is divided into two arms by a small island opposite the old city. This is the most important point in the topography of the site of Sparta. To the east of it is a hill, on the side of which the theater can be seen. A great part of it remains, but the seats have almost entirely disappeared.

The city lay on two hills and the hollow between and extended in a plain beyond the south hill. A stream called Trypiotiko emptied into the Eurotas here, and two canals also crossed the plain. On the southern one, above its junction with the Trypiotiko, stood the small village of Psychico.

Lelex was one of the original inhabitants of Laconia, which was called after him, its first king, Lelegia. He was married to the Naiad Cleochareia, by whom he became the father of Myles, Polycaon, and Eurotas. He had a shrine at Sparta (Apollod. 3.10.3; Paus. 3.1.1,12.5). Some call his wife Peridia and his children Myles, Polyclon, Bomalchus, and Therapne, while Eurotas is represented as a son of Myles and a grandson of Lelex. In other traditions, again, Lelex is described as a son of Spartus and as the father of Amyclas. By the nymph Clete Eurotas became the father of Sparta. She married Lacedaemon, a son of Zeus by Taygete. By her, Lacedaemon became the father of Amyclas, Eurydice, and Asine. He was king of the country that he named after himself, while he gave to his capital the name of his wife, Sparta (Apollod. 3.10.3; Paus. 3.1.2). He was believed to have built the sanctuary of the Charites, which stood between Sparta and Amyclae and to have given those divinities the names of Cleta and Phaenna (Paus. 3.18.4). A shrine was erected to him in the vicinity of Therapne (Paus. 3.20.2). Sparta, his wife, was represented on a tripod at Amyclae (Paus. 3.18.8).

Amyclas became king of Laconia and was regarded as the founder of the town of Amyclae (Paus. 3.1.3). He had three sons, the most famous of which was Hyacinthus. Hyacinthus was the youngest son and a youth of extraordinary beauty, beloved by Thamyris and Apollo. It was Apollo who unintentionally killed him during a game of discus (Apollod. 1.3.3). Some traditions state that he was beloved also by Zephyrus, the west wind (or Boreas, the north wind), who, from jealousy of Apollo, caused the discus to strike the head of the youth and kill him (Lucian *Dial. Deor.* 14). From the blood of Hyacinthus there sprang the flower of the same name, on the leaves of which there appeared the expression of woe, *"AI, AI"* or the letter *Y,* (upsilon), being the initial of (H)Yacinthus. Hyacinthus was worshipped at Amyclae as a hero, and a great festival, the Hyacinthia, was celebrated in his honor. Argalus, the eldest son of Amyclas, was his successor to the throne of Sparta (Paus. 3.1.3). It was Cynortas, the remaining son, however, who was destined to carry on the royal line. After the death of his brother Argalus, he became king of Sparta and father of Oebalus. His tomb was shown at Sparta not far from the Scias (Paus. 3.1.3,13.11; Apollod. 3.10.3).

Oebalus has always presented a kind of genealogical dilemma. According to some he was a son of Perieres and a grandson of Cynortas. He first married the nymph Bateia, by whom he had several children. Dealing first with the two other families involved with Oebalus or his descendants before continuing with the royal line, we turn first to his son Hippocoon by the nymph Bateia. He was the eldest son of Oebalus and step-brother to Tyndareus, Peirene and Arene. After his father's death, Hippocoon expelled his brother, Tyndareus, in order to take over the kingdom; but Heracles led Tyndareus back and slew Hippocoon and his sons. This act was in retaliation for Hippocoon's assistance to Neleus and for his having slain Oeonus. Oeonus, a son of Licymnius of Midea in Argolis, was the first victor at Olympia in the footrace. He was killed at Sparta by the sons of Hippocoon but was avenged by Heracles, whose kinsman he was, and was honored with a monument near the temple of Heracles (Paus. 3.14.6,15.2; Apollod. 2.7.3; Diod. 4.33). The number and names of Hippocoon's sons are different in the different writers. Apollodorus mentions twelve, Diodorus ten, and Pausanias only six. Ovid (*Met.* 8.314) mentions the sons of Hippocoon among the Calydonian hunters. Alcon was one of these sons mentioned as a Calydonian hunter and as having been slain by Heracles. He had a shrine at Sparta (Apollod. 3.10.5; Paus. 3.14.8). Enarephorus, another son, was a most passionate suitor of Helen when she was quite young. Tyndareus, therefore, entrusted the maiden to the care of Theseus (Apollod. 3.10.5; Plut. *Thes.* 31). Enarephorus had a shrine at Sparta (Paus. 3.15.1). Dorceus and Sebrus, two other sons, also had a common shrine. The fountain near the sanctuary was called Dorceia, and the place around it Sebrion (Paus. 3.15.2).

Gorgophone, the wife of Oebalus, had earlier married Perieres, the son of Aeolus. By him she had Aphareus, Icarius, and Leucippus. Aphareus was father of the famous Idas and Lynceus by Arene. Idas was married to Marpessa and became by her the father of Cleopatra or Alcyone. With Lynceus he took part in the Calydonian hunt and the voyage of the Argo. The most celebrated part of the story of the Aphareidae, Idas and Lynceus, is their fight with the Dioscuri, with whom they had grown up from their childhood. In this battle, which grew out of a contest over cattle the four had stolen, all the principals were killed except Polydeuces, who was immortal. The tomb of the Aphareidae was shown at Sparta as late as the time of Pausanias (3.13.1). Icarius had been expelled, along with his half-brother Tyndareus, by Hippocoon. The brothers fled to Thestius at Pleuron. Subsequently, when Heracles had slain Hippocoon and his sons, Tyndareus returned to Sparta while Icarius remained in Acarnania. According to Apollodorus (3.10.5), Icarius also later returned. While in Acarnania he became the father of

Penelope, Alyzeus, and Leucadius. When Penelope was betrothed to Odysseus, Icarius tried to persuade him to remain in Sparta, but Odysseus declined and departed with Penelope. Leucippus was father of Phoebe, Hilaeira, and Arsinoe. Phoebe and Hilaeira were priestesses who were carried off by the Dioscuri. Phoebe became by Polydeuces the mother of Mnesileus (Apollod. 3.10.3). By Apollo their sister Arsinoe became the mother of Eriopis.

It is, however, the children of Oebalus and Gorgophone who carried on the royal house of Sparta. Gorgophone married Oebalus on the death of her first husband, Perieres, and became by him mother of Peirene, Arene, and Tyndareus. Her two marriages were close enough so that her children by both husbands were fairly close in age. It should be pointed out that the patronymic Oebalides is not necessarily applied only to the descendants of Oebalus but to the Spartans generally, and hence it occurs as an epithet of Hyacinthus, Castor, Pollux, and Helen. As stated, Tyndareus fled from Hippocoon with Icarius to Aetolia. There he married Leda, the daughter of Thestius and, as stated, was afterwards restored to his kingdom. One night Leda was embraced both by Zeus and Tyndareus, and the result was the birth of Polydeuces and Helen, the children of Zeus, and of Castor and Clytemnestra, the children of Tyndareus. According to the common legend, Zeus visited Leda in the disguise of a swan and she produced two eggs, from which Zeus' children were born. She also had two other children, Timandra and Philonoe. Tyndareus was believed to have built the temple of Athena Chalcioecos at Sparta. When Castor and Polydeuces had been received among the immortals, Tyndareus invited Menelaus to come to Sparta and surrendered his kingdom to him. His tomb was shown at Sparta as late as the time of Pausanias (3.17.4).

Castor and his twin brother Polydeuces had many glorious adventures. The Dioscuri, as they were called, were said to have been born at Amyclae or on Mount Taygetus. The first notable event of their lives was their expedition against Athens. Theseus had carried off their sister Helen and kept her in confinement at Aphidna. While Theseus was absent from Attica and Menestheus was endeavoring to usurp the government, the Dioscuri marched into Attica and ravaged the country round the city. Academus revealed to them that Helen was kept at Aphidna, and they rescued her. Menestheus then opened to them the gates of Athens, and Aphidnus adopted them as his sons, so that they might be initiated into the mysteries. The Athenians paid divine honors to them. They took part in both the Calydonian boar hunt and the expedition of the Argonauts. Afterward they married Hilaeira and Phoebe, the daughters of Leucippus, who were priestesses of Artemis and Athena respectively. They engaged in a fatal battle with Idas and Lynceus, and Castor was killed. Polydeuces begged also to die, but being immortal was allowed to live and die on alternate days. These heroic youths, who were also believed to have reigned as kings of Sparta (Paus. 3.1.5), received divine honors at Sparta, though not till forty years after their war with the sons of Aphareus (Paus. 3.13.11). They were regarded as mighty helpers of mankind, but they were worshipped more especially as protectors of travellers by sea. They were also thought of as protectors of travellers in general, and consequently of the law of hospitality, the violation of which they punished severely (Paus. 3.16.2,3). They were regarded as presidents of the public games (Pind. *Ol.* 3.38, *Nem.* 10.53), and at Sparta their statues stood at the entrance to the race course (Paus. 3.14.7). They were believed to have invented the war dance and martial music. Owing to their warlike character, it was customary at Sparta for the two kings, whenever they went out to war, to be accompanied by symbolic representations of the Dioscuri. Sepulchral monuments of Castor existed in the temple of the Dioscuri near Therapne (Pind. *Nem.* 10.56; Paus. 3.20.1) and at Sparta (Paus. 3.13.1). Temples and statues of the Dioscuri were very numerous in Greece, particularly in Peloponnesus.

The royal line of Sparta continued, however, through Helen. She was extraordinarily beautiful and in her youth was carried off by Theseus to Attica, as already related. She was brought back by the Dioscuri, along with Aethra, the mother of Theseus, who became a slave of Helen. After her return to Sparta, princely suitors appeared from all parts of Greece, but after a consultation with Odysseus, who was one of them, Tyndareus gave her in marriage to Menelaus, who became by her the father of Hermione and, some say, Nicostratus. Odysseus had advised Tyndareus to make the suitors swear that they would defend the chosen bridegroom against anyone who should insult him on Helen's account. Tyndareus, to show his gratitude, persuaded his half-brother Icarius to give Penelope in marriage to Odysseus; or, according to others, Odysseus gained her by conquering his competitors in a footrace (Apollod. 3.10.9; Paus. 3.12.4).

Not long after the birth of her last child by Menelaus, Helen was carried away from Sparta by Paris, prince of Troy, the son of Priam and Hecuba, and the favorite of Aphrodite. The most common agreement is that she went willingly, under the influence of Aphrodite, but some accounts say she was taken by force. The marriage between Paris and Helen was consummated on the island of Cranae opposite Gythium. By Helen, Paris became the father of Bunicus, Corythus, Aganus, Idaeus, and Helen. He was represented in art as a beardless young man of almost feminine beauty. Helen was accompanied during her abduction by Clymene, a relative of Menelaus (Hom. *Il.* 3.144). After the taking of Troy, Clymene was given to Acamas. She was represented as a captive by Polygnotus in the Lesche of Delphi (Paus. 10.26.1).

Menelaus was a son of Atreus and younger brother of Agamemnon and Anaxibia. When Helen was carried away by Paris, Menelaus and Odysseus set out to Troy to claim her back. Menelaus was hospitably treated by Antenor (Hom. *Il.* 3.206), but the journey was of no avail. The Trojan Antimachus even advised his fellow citizens to kill Menelaus and Odysseus (Hom. *Il.* 11.139). In order, therefore, to avenge the rape of Helen and to punish the offender, Menelaus and his brother resolved to march against Troy with all the forces that Greece could muster. Odysseus and Menelaus also consulted the Delphic oracle, and at Delphi Menelaus dedicated the necklace of Helen to Athena Pronoea. Menelaus in sixty ships led the inhabitants of Lacedaemon, Pharis, Sparta, Messe, Bryseiae, Amyclae, Helos, Las, and Oetylus against Troy (Hom. *Il.* 2.581). At Troy he was under the special protection of Hera and Athena and one of the most gallant heroes. He was among the first to sail away from Troy, accompanied by his wife, Helen, and Nestor. He met many obstacles to his return and wandered for eight years in the eastern parts of the Mediterranean. He learned of Agamemnon's death before arriving home, and he arrived at Sparta on the very day Orestes was burying Clytemnestra and Aegisthus. Afterward he lived with Helen at Sparta in peace, comfort, and wealth. At the time when Telemachus came to him to inquire after his father, Menelaus was just solemnizing the marriage of his daughter Hermione to Neoptolemus and that of his son Megapenthes with a daughter of Alector (Hom. *Od.* 4.1). According to the Homeric poems, Menelaus was athletic in build; he spoke little, but what he said was always impressive; he was brave and valiant but milder than Agamemnon, intelligent and hospitable. Menelaus was worshipped as a hero at Therapne, where his tomb and that of Helen were shown (Paus. 3.19.9). On the chest of Cypselus he was represented at the moment when, after the taking of Troy, he was on the point of killing Helen (Paus. 5.18.3).

Thus the royal line of Sparta was continued through Hermione. She was married at first, briefly, to Neoptolemus, son of Achilles. According to some, he returned after the war to Phthia, the kingdom of his father. Menelaus sent Hermione there from Sparta because at Troy he had promised her to Neoptolemus. According to others, Neoptolemus came to Sparta to receive Hermione because he had heard that she was betrothed to Orestes, her cousin. Shortly after his marriage to Hermione he went to Delphi, some say to consult the oracle about the means of obtaining children by Hermione, and was murdered there. After Orestes had murdered Clytemnestra and Aegisthus, he fled from land to land pursued by the Erinyes but eventually was delivered from his madness. He returned to Mycenae, where he took possession of his father's kingdom, which had been usurped, and when Cylarabes of Argos died without heirs, Orestes also became king of Argos. The Lacedaemonians made him their king of their own accord because they preferred him, the grandson of Tyndareus, to Nicostratus and Megapenthes, the sons of Menelaus by a slave. The Arcadians and Phocians increased his power by allying themselves with him (Paus. 2.18.5; Pind. *Pyth.* 11.24). He married Hermione and became by her the father of Tisamenus. He is said to have led colonists from Sparta to Aeolis, and the town of Argos Oresticum in Epeirus is said to have been founded by him at the time he wandered about in his madness. In his reign the Dorians under Hyllus invaded Peloponnesus (Paus. 8.5.1). He died of the bite of a snake in Arcadia, and his body, in obedience to an oracle, was afterward carried from Tegea to Sparta and buried there (Paus. 3.11.10).

Tisamenus then was king of Argos but was deprived of his kingdom when the Heracleidae invaded Peloponnesus. He was slain in battle against them and his tomb was shown at Helice, from where his remains were removed to Sparta by command of an oracle (Paus. 7.1.8). With him ended the long line begun by Lelex.

Aristodemus, a son of Aristomachus and a descendant of Heracles, was married to Argeia, by whom he became the father of Eurysthenes and Procles. Argeia was the daughter of Autesion and sister of Theras. Theras was famous for colonizing the island of Thera, where he led Lacedaemonians and Minyans of Lemnos from Sparta. His son Oeolycus and grandson Aegeus were honored at Sparta with a shrine (Herod. 4.149; Paus. 3.15.8). According to some traditions, Aristodemus was killed at Naupactus by a flash of lightning just as he was setting out on his expedition into Peloponnesus (Apollod. 2.8.2) or by an arrow of Apollo at Delphi because he had consulted Heracles instead of the Delphic oracle about the return of the Heracleidae (Paus. 3.1.6). According to this tradition, Eurysthenes and Procles were the first Heraclid kings of Lacedaemon; but a Lacedaemonian tradition stated that Aristodemus himself came to Sparta, was the first king of his race, and died a natural death (Herod. 6.52). Eurysthenes and Procles were twins and were born, according to the common account, before their father's return to Peloponnesus; but, according to the genuine Spartan story, their births occurred after Aristodemus' return and occupation of his allotment in Laconia. He died immediately after the birth of his children and had not even time to decide which of the two should succeed him. Their mother professed to be unable to name the elder, and the Lacedaemonians applied to the oracle at Delphi. They were instructed to make them both kings but give the greater honor to the elder. This remaining difficulty was removed by watching which of the children was first washed and fed by the mother. The first rank was accordingly given to Eurysthenes and retained by his descendants (Herod. 6.51,52). Their uncle Theras was,

during their minority, their joint guardian and regent (Herod. 4.147). They were married to two sisters, twins like themselves, the daughters of Thersander, the Heracleid king of Cleonae, by name Lathria and Anaxandra, whose tombs were to be seen at Sparta in the time of Pausanias (3.16.6). The two brothers are said to have united with the son of Temenus to restore Aepytus, the son of Cresphontes, to Messenia. Otherwise, they were in continual strife. Strabo (8.5.5) states that they maintained themselves by taking foreigners into their service. Procles is reported to have died one year before his brother and was much the more famous for his achievements (Cic. *De. Div.* 2.43). The line of kings descended from Procles was called, after his son or grandson Eurypon, the Eurypontidae (Herod. 6.51, 8.131). At that point the succession of Heraclid kings proceeded into history. It is recorded that in the reign of Teleclus, the eighth of the Agid kings of Sparta, the Spartans subdued the Achaian towns of Amyclae, Pharis, and Geronthrae. Not long after these successes, Teleclus was slain by the Messenians in a temple of Artemis Limnatis on the borders. According to the Spartan account, he had gone there to sacrifice with a company of maidens and fell in an attempt to rescue them from the violence of the Messenians. The Messenian statement, however, was that he had treacherously brought with him a body of Spartan youths disguised as girls and with daggers hidden under their dresses for the purpose of murdering a number of the noblest Messenians at the festival and that the objects of the plot had killed him and his associates in self-defense (Herod. 7.204).

Compared with the Acropolis of Athens, the shapeless heap of ruins occupying the low hills on the Eurotas appear insignificant. They present nothing to remind the spectator of the city that once ruled Peloponnesus and the greater part of Greece. The site of Sparta differs from that of almost all Grecian cities. Protected by high mountains, the Spartans were not obliged, like the other Greeks, to live within the walls of a city but were able to live in the midst of their plantations and gardens.

It must not, however, be supposed that Sparta was destitute of handsome public buildings. Notwithstanding the simplicity of the Spartan habits, their city became, after the Messenian wars, one of the chief seats of poetry and art. The law of Lycurgus dictated stark simplicity in private dwellings. Even the palace of the kings subscribed to this regulation. But the temples of the gods were built with great magnificence, and the spoils of the Persian wars were employed in the erection of a beautiful stoa in the agora. Sparta was not walled until the Macedonian period, and its walls and gates were still standing when Pausanias visited Sparta in the second century A.D. Today not a trace of them remains.

It has been observed that Sparta resembled Rome in its site because of its being built on and around several hills. It also resembled Rome in being formed out of several earlier settlements, which existed before the Dorian conquest and gradually coalesced with the later city, which was founded in their midst. These earlier places, which are the hamlets (*comae*) mentioned by Thucydides (1.10), were four in number: Pitane, Limnae or Limnaeum, Mesoa, and Cynosura. They were united by a common sacrifice to Artemis (Paus. 8.16.9). Pitane, at the ford of the Eurotas in the north of the city, was the favorite and fashionable place of residence at Sparta, like Collytus at Athens and Craneion at Corinth. It was near the temple and stronghold of Issorion (see below). Limnae was situated upon the Eurotas, having derived its name from the marshy ground that adjoined it (Strab. 8.5.1). It is probable that Mesoa was in the southeast part of the city and Cynosura in the southwest.

The acropolis and the agora stood in the middle of this scattering of suburbs. This acropolis, while on the highest point of the city, stood where there was area enough to build the numerous buildings reported to have existed there.

The chief building on the acropolis was the temple of Athena Chalcioecos, the guardian goddess of the city. It was said to have been begun by Tyndareus but not completed until many years later. It was covered with plates of bronze and was therefore called the Bronze House; thus the goddess received the surname Chalcioecos, and the festival in her honor the name Chalcioecia. On the bronze plates there were represented in relief the labors of Heracles, the exploits of the Dioscuri, Hephaestus releasing his mother from her chains, the nymphs arming Perseus for his expedition against Medusa, the birth of Athena, and Amphitrite and Poseidon. There was also a bronze statue of the goddess (Paus. 3.17.2). The Bronze House stood in a sacred enclosure surrounded by a colonnade and containing several sanctuaries. There was a separate temple of Athena Ergane. Near the south stoa was a temple of Zeus Cosmetas, and before it the tomb of Tyndareus. To the left of the Bronze House was a temple of the Muses. Sacrifices were offered to them before engaging in battle (Paus. 3.17.5). Behind this was a temple of Ares Areius with ancient wooden statues, and to its right was a very ancient statue of Zeus Hypatus (Most High). Near the altar of the Bronze House stood statues of Aphrodite Ambologera (Delaying Old Age) and of the brothers Sleep and Death (Paus. 3.18.1).

The agora was a spacious place with colonnades, from which the streets led to the different quarters of the city. There was a place called Chorus, marked off from the rest of the agora, because the Spartan youths here danced in honor of Apollo at the festival of the Gymnopaedia.

This place was adorned with statues of the Pythian deities, Apollo, Artemis, and Leto; and near it were temples of Gaea, of Zeus Agoraeus, of Athena Agoraea, of Apollo, of Poseidon Asphaleius, and of Hera. In the agora was a huge statue representing the people of Sparta and a temple of the Moirae (Fates), near which was the tomb of Orestes, whose bones had been brought from Tegea to Sparta. Here also was a Hermes Agoraeus bearing Dionysus as a child and, inside the old Ephoreia, where the ephors originally administered justice, was the tomb of Aphareus.

The agora was near the acropolis. Descending from the acropolis was the way to the so-called Alpion, beyond which was a temple of Ammon and probably also a temple of Artemis Cnagia (Paus. 3.18.2). This surname was derived from Cnageus, a Laconian who accompanied the Dioscuri in their war against Aphidna and was made prisoner. He was sold as a slave and carried to Crete where he served in the temple of Artemis. He escaped from there with a priestess of the goddess, who carried her statue to Sparta (Paus. 3.18.3). The agora was in the hollow east of the acropolis.

The principal street leading out of the agora was named Aphetais. It ran toward the south wall and was bordered by a succession of monuments. One of these was the temple of Athena Celeutheia, with a statue of the goddess dedicated by Odysseus, who erected three statues of Celeutheia in different places. Lower down the Aphetais were the shrines of Iops, Amphiaraus, and Lelex, the sanctuary of Poseidon Taenarius, a statue of Athena dedicated by the Tarentini, the place called Hellenion, so called because the Greeks are said to have held counsel there either before the Persian or the Trojan wars, the tomb of Talthybius (the herald of Agamemnon at Troy), an altar of Apollo Acreitas, a place sacred to the earth named Gaseptum, a statue of Apollo Maleates, and close to the city walls the temple of Dictynna. In the Hellenion, on the other side of the Aphetais, there was a sanctuary of Arsinoe, the sister of the wives of Castor and Polydeuces. Next came a temple of Artemis and next the tombs of the Iamidae, the Eleian prophets, the temple of Zeus Tropaeus built by the Dorians after conquering the Achaean inhabitants of Laconia, the temple of Rhea, and the shrine of Hippolytus and Aulon. The Aphetais, upon leaving the city, joined the great Hyacinthian road that led to the Amyclaion (Paus. 3.12.1–9).

The next most important street leading from the agora ran in a southeast direction. It is usually called Scias. Near the Scias was a round structure containing statues of the Olympian Zeus and Aphrodite; next came the tombs of Cynortas, Castor, Idas, and Lynceus, and a temple of Kore Soteira. The other buildings along this street were the temple of Apollo Carneius, who was worshipped here before the Dorian invasion, a statue of

Apollo Aphetaeus, and an altar sacred to Zeus, Athena, and the Dioscuri, all surnamed Ambulii. Opposite was the place called Colona and the temple of Dionysus Colonatas. Near Colona was the temple of Zeus Euanemus (Giver of Favorable Wind). On a neighboring hill was the temple of the Argive Hera and the temple of Hera Hypercheiria, containing an ancient wooden statue of Aphrodite Hera. The temple of Hera Hypercheiria had been erected to her at the command of an oracle when the country had been flooded by the Eurotas River (Paus. 3.13.8).

Pitane lay partly inside and partly outside the city. Here was the tomb of Taenarus, the sanctuaries of Poseidon Hippocurius and of the Aeginetan Artemis, and a temple of Artemis Issoria, also called Limnaea. There were also temples of Thetis, of Demeter Chthonia, and of the Olympian Zeus. The Dromos, which was used as a place for running, extended along the stream southward and contained gymnasia. The Roman amphitheater and the stadium were included in the Dromos. There also was a statue of Heracles, near which was the house of Menelaus. After the Dromos came the temples of the Dioscuri, of the Graces, of Eileithyia, or Apollo Carneius, and of Artemis Hegemone. On the right of the Dromos was a statue of Asclepius Agnitas; at the beginning of the Dromos there were statues of the Dioscuri Aphetarii; and a little further the shrine of Alcon and the temple of Poseidon Domatites (Domestic) (Paus. 3.14.8).

South of the Dromos was a broader level called Platanistas because of the plane trees that grew there in abundance. It was a round island formed by streams and was reached by two bridges, on each of which there was a statue of Heracles at one end and of Lycurgus at the other. The Spartan ephebi came to Platanistas to fight weaponless battles with one another. The running streams surrounding the Platanistas were the canals of the Trypiotiko. The ephebi sacrificed the night before the contest at the Phoebaion, which stood outside the city south of the Platanistas. The Platanistas was bordered on one side by a colonnade. Behind this colonnade there were several heroic monuments, among which were those of Alcimus, Enarephorus, of Dorceus, with the fountain Dorceia, and of Sebrus. Near the latter was the sanctuary of Helen and that of Heracles, with the monument of Oeonus, whose death he here avenged by slaying the sons of Hippocoon. The temple of Heracles was close by the city walls (Paus. 3.14.8).

From the Dromos two other streets branched off. One led to a temple of Athena Axiopoenos (Avenger), under which name Heracles built this temple after he had killed Hippocoon and his sons; the other led to another temple of Athena, founded by Theras, near which was an ancient wooden statue of Enyalius in fetters. Enyalius was a son of Ares and Enyo and a god of war; but the god came

to be identified so closely with Ares that the name was considered an epithet. The youth of Sparta sacrificed young dogs to Ares under the name of Enyalius (Paus. 3.14.9).

The painted Lesche, a pavilion, was in the vicinity of the Dromos and was surrounded by shrines of Cadmus, Oeolycus, Aegeus, and Amphilochus, and the temple of Hera Aegophagus. There were also monuments in the area of the theater. Among these were a temple of Poseidon Genethlius, shrines of Cleodaeus (grandson of Heracles) and Oebalus, a temple of Asclepius, the most celebrated of all the temples of this god in Sparta, with the shrine of Teleclus on its left. On a hill not far away was an ancient temple of Aphrodite Areia (Paus. 3.17.5), on an upper story of which was a second temple of Aphrodite Morpho (Fair-shaped); in its vicinity was a temple of Hilaeira and Phoebe containing their statues, and an egg suspended from the roof said to have been that of Leda. In a house called Chiton was woven the robe for the Amyclaean Apollo. Near the Chiton was the house of Phormion, who offered hospitality to the Dioscuri when they entered the city as strangers (Paus. 3.16.2).

In the place known as Limnae was the temple of Artemis Orthia and Leto. This temple of Artemis Orthia was, as already noted, the common place of meeting for the four villages of Pitane, Mesoa, Cynosura, and Limnae. Limnae was partly in the city and partly in the suburbs. Artemis Orthia was another name for the Brauronian Artemis. Here boys were scourged at her altar in such a manner that it became sprinkled with their blood. This cruel ceremony was believed to have been introduced by Lycurgus instead of the human sacrifices that had until then been offered to her. The word *orthia* had reference either to the phallus or to the fact that her statue stood erect.

The east bank of the Eurotas was not occupied by any part of Sparta. On the road to Therapne was a statue of Athena Alea standing between the city and a temple of Zeus Plusius. Therapne stood upon the Menelaion, or Mount Menelaus, which rose immediately after one crossed the river. The Menelaion derived its name from a temple of Menelaus containing the tombs of Menelaus and Helen, where men and women often went, the men imploring Menelaus to grant them bravery and success in war, the women invoking Helen to bestow beauty upon them and their children. The foundations of the temple were discovered in 1834, along with several small figures in clay, which were probably dedicatory offerings to Menelaus and Helen made by the poorer classes. Therapne was said to have derived its name from a daughter of Lelex and was the Achaean citadel of the district. It is described by the poets as the lofty, well-towered Therapne surrounded by thick woods (Pind. *Isth.* 1.31) and guarded by the Dioscuri. Here was the fountain of Messeis, and it was probably upon this height that the temple of Menelaus stood. Consequently, Therapne is said to have been in Sparta, or is mentioned as synonymous with Sparta. The Phoebaion, which has been described as the open space on the right bank of the Eurotas, contained a temple of the Dioscuri. Not far from this place was the temple of Poseidon, surnamed Gaeaochus (Paus. 3.20.2).

Sparta's worship was quite varied and included certain divinities not covered in the above catalog of monuments. One such being was Abaris, a Hyperborean priest of Apollo who came to Greece and enjoyed high esteem. He was said to have ridden through the air on an arrow. He cured diseases, removed plagues, and built at Sparta a temple of Kore Soteira (Paus. 3.13.2).

Zeus Agamemnon was worshipped at Sparta. Zeus Ambulius was also worshipped, supposedly designating the god as a delayer of death. Zeus Epidotes was also revered. Epidotes (Liberal Giver) occurs both as a surname of other divinities, such as Zeus, and as a divinity in his own right.

Athena, the Dioscuri and Ares, Artemis, and Eros were all worshipped in Sparta. Athena Poliuchos described the goddess as protector of the city (Paus. 3.17.2). The Dioscuri were said to have brought from Colchis to Sparta the ancient statue of Ares, which was preserved in the temple of Ares Theritas on the road from Sparta to Therapne (Paus. 3.19.7). Artemis Corythallia had a festival, the Tithenidia, at which the Spartan boys were carried into her sanctuary (Athen. 4.139). Artemis Mysia was worshipped in a sanctuary near Sparta (Paus. 3.20.9). And Sparta was one of the few cities in which worship of Eros, the god of love, took place.

Hero worship naturally flourished in Sparta, and in addition to the aforementioned heroa and shrines, there were a number of others. A sanctuary to Achilles existed on the road from Arcadia to Sparta (Paus. 3.20.8). Astrabacus, a son of Irbus and brother of Alopecus, was a Laconian hero of the royal house of Agis. He and his brother found the statue of Artemis Orthia in a bush and became mad at the sight of it. He is said to have been the father of Damaratus by the wife of Ariston. He had a sanctuary at Sparta and was worshipped there as a hero (Paus. 3.16.9; Herod. 6.69). Pleuron, son of Aetolus and founder of Pleuron in Aetolia, also had a shrine here (Paus. 3.13.8; Apollod. 1.7.7).

On the banks of a small stream, the Tiasa, on the south of the city, stood the sanctuary of Phaena and Cleta, the Spartan Charites. Across this stream was the road to Amyclae.

In view of the multitude of buildings and monuments described by Pausanias, one might expect more extensive ruins at Sparta. The ruins that survive lie north and northeast of the modern town. The theater, the second largest in Greece, lost much of its masonry to Mistra. There are remains of the temple of Athena Chalcioecus, the sanctuary of Artemis Orthia, the altar of Lycurgus, and one or two unidentified shrines. In the Museum one can see a stele representing Helen and Menelaus, a head and statue of Artemis, and sculptures of Heracles, Hermes, Asclepius, and the Dioscuri. A mosaic from a Roman villa portrays Orpheus; another shows Zeus with Europa.

SPERCHEIUS (SPERHIOS) is a river of south Thessaly rising in Mount Tymphrestus and flowing into the Maliac Gulf. In ancient times it joined the sea at Anticyra, but now it falls into the sea about 1.5 km from Thermopylae. The Dryas and Melas unite their streams and flow into the Spercheius, as does the Asopus. Spercheius is celebrated in mythology as a river-god and is mentioned in connection with Achilles (Hom. *Il.* 17.142). Spercheius was the father of Menesthius by Polydora, the daughter of Peleus. Menesthius was one of the commanders of the hosts of Achilles (Hom. *Il.* 16.173). Dryops was also a son of Spercheius by the Danaid Polydora. He was king of the Dryopes, who derived their name from him and were believed to have occupied the country from the valley of the Spercheius and Thermopylae as far as Mount Parnassus. The Maliades were nymphs worshipped in the district of the Malians on the Spercheius (Soph. *Phil.* 725).

SPHETTUS (KOROPI) was one of the twelve ancient cities of Attica and subsequently a deme. Its location has given rise to much dispute over the years, but it has now been established that the deme lay adjacent to the modern rural center of Koropi. Sphettus and Anaphlystus are represented as sons of Troezen, who migrated into Attica (Paus. 2.30.9).

SPLEDON (See ASPLEDON)

SPORADES (SPORADES) or the "Scattered," is a group of islands in the Aegean, Cretan and Carpathian seas, so called because they are scattered throughout these seas, in opposition to the Cyclades, which lie around Delos in a circle. But the distinction is not strictly observed, and we find several islands sometimes ascribed to the Cyclades and sometimes to the Sporades. Today the Sporades refer to three island groups scattered in the Aegean to the east, north, and south of the Cyclades. However, most people and travel guides limit the name to the islands lying off Euboea to the north and northeast—Skiathos, Skopelos, Alonissos, and Skiros. Pheidippus, a son of Thessalus, the Heraclid, and his brother Antiphus led the warriors of the Sporades in thirty ships against Troy. These islands, as named by Homer (*Il.* 2.678) were Nisyrus, Carpathus, Casus, Cos, and the Calydnian Islands.

STADIA   was an earlier name of the island of RHODES.

STENYCLARUS (STENIKLAROS)   was a town in the north of Messenia and the capital of the Dorian conquerors, built by Cresphontes. Stenyclarus was a Messenian hero from whom the town was named. Andania had been the ancient capital of the country (Paus. 4.3.7). The town afterward ceased to exist, but its name was given to the northern of the two Messenian plains (Paus. 4.33.4; Herod. 9.64). The site of the city is not known today, but the plain retains the ancient name in the modern spelling of Steniklaros.

STIRIS   was a town of Phocis situated 22 km by a mountain road from Chaeroneia. The people of Stiris claimed descent from an Athenian colony of the Attic deme of Steiria led by Peteos, when he was driven out of Attica by Aegeus. He was a son of Orneus and father of Menestheus (Hom. *Il.* 2.552, 4.338; Plut. *Thes.* 32). Pausanias (10.35.8) describes the city as situated upon a rocky summit, with only a few springs. In the time of Pausanias the city possessed a temple of Demeter Stiria; the temple was made of crude brick and contained two statues, one of Pentelic marble, the other of ancient workmanship with extensive repairs (Paus. 10.35.10). The ruins of Stiris are situated upon a flat hill about 2 or 3 km east of the monastery of Ossios Loukos. A tiny place named Stiri is in the opposite direction, west of Ossios Loukas.

STRATIA   was another name for NEAE.

STRATUS (STRATOS)   was located between modern Agrinio and Amfilohia in Acarnania on the west bank of the Achelous. Its extensive remains cover three hills and incorporate the modern village of Stratos. Its walls enclose a fourth century temple of Zeus. Stratus was the ancient capital and largest city of Acarnania.

STRATUS   was an earlier name of DYME.

STRONGYLE   was another name for the island of NAXOS.

STROPHADES (STROFADES)   formerly called Plotae, are two small islands in the Ionian Sea about 55 km south of Zacynthus and 75 km from Cyparissia in Messenia, to which city they belonged. Zetes and Calais, the sons of Boreas, the north wind, pursued the Harpies to these islands, which were called the "turning" islands because the Boreadae returned there from the pursuit (Apollon. Rhod. 2.296; Apollod. 1.9.21). The Harpyiae (Snatchers) are personified storm winds, but were in mythology ugly creatures with wings. They were sent to harass the blind Phineus, and whenever a meal was placed before him, they darted down and carried it off. They were described as birds with the heads of maidens with long claws on their hands and with faces pale with hunger. The Argonauts arrived while the Harpies were torturing Phineus and agreed to deliver him in exchange for certain assistance. When the Harpies snatched Phineus' food, they were attacked by the Boreadae, Zetes and Calais. The Harpies fled, but one fell into the river Tigris and the other reached the Strophades, where she fell down in fatigue. The Boreadae exacted a promise that Phineus would not be bothered again and turned back to join their companions.

STRYMON (STRIMONAS)   is the largest river of Macedonia, after the Axius, and the ancient boundary of that country towards the east. Palaestinus was a son of Poseidon and father of Haliacmon. From grief at the death of his son, Palaestinus threw himself into the river, which was called after him Palaestinus, and subsequently Strymon. Strymon, a son of Oceanus and Tethys, was a river-god of Thrace and is called a king of Thrace. By Euterpe or Calliope he became the father of Rhesus (Apollod. 1.3.4; Eurip. *Rhes.* 347) and by Neaera he became the father of Euadne (Apollod. 2.1.2). The Strymon rises in Mount Scomius and flows through the whole of Macedonia. It then enters Lake Kerkinitis and exits from it near the town of Iraklia. Near Amfipoli it empties into the Strymonic Gulf. A legend says that Heracles rendered the upper course of the river shallow by casting stones into it; thereafter it was not possible to navigate as far up the river. The tenth labor of Heracles was stealing the oxen of Geryones. While driving the cattle back, he had many adventures. After he reached Thrace, Hera made his oxen mad. When in their pursuit Heracles came to the river Strymon, he made himself a road through it by means of huge blocks of stone.

STYMPHALUS (STIMFALIA)   is the name of a town, district, mountain, and river in northeast Arcadia (now in Corinthia). The territory of Stymphalus was a plain about 10 km in length, bounded by Achaia on the north, Sicyonia and Phliasia on the east, the territory of Mantineia on the south, and that of Orchomenus and Pheneus on the west. The plain was surrounded by mountains. Mount Stymphalus, which descended to the plain, was the name of an extension of Mount Cyllene. The district was one of military importance since it commanded one of the chief roads from Arcadia to Argolis.

The mountain at the south end of the plain was called Apelaurum, and at its foot was the subterranean outlet of the lake of Stymphalus. This lake is formed both by runoff from Mount Cyllene and by streams that flow from different parts of the plain. This combined stream was called Stymphalus by the ancients; it was regarded as the principal source of the lake. Most people believed that it flowed underground and reappeared as the Erasinus River in Argolis (Paus. 2.24.6). The Stymphalians worshipped the Erasinus and the Metope, which was another name for the Stymphalus River. In the time of Pausanias the subterranean channel became clogged, and the resulting flood was ascribed to the anger of Artemis.

The city derived its name from Stymphalus, a son of Elatus and grandson of Arcas. He was the father of Parthenope, Agamedes, and Gortys. Pelops, unable to conquer him in war, murdered him by stratagem and cut his body into pieces. For this crime Greece experienced a famine, which was, however, averted by the prayer of Aeacus (Apollod. 3.12.6). The ancient city in which Temenus, the son of Pelasgus, dwelt had entirely disappeared in the time of Pausanias (8.22.2), and all that Pausanias could learn respecting it was that Hera was formerly worshipped there in three different sanctuaries as virgin, wife, and widow. Chera was a surname believed to have been given to Hera by Temenus, the son of Pelasgus. He had brought up Hera and erected to her at Stymphalus three sanctuaries under three different names. To Hera as a maiden, he dedicated one in which she was called Pais; to her as the wife of Zeus, he dedicated a second in which she bore the name Telcia; and he also dedicated a third in which she was worshipped as the Chera, the widow, alluding to her separation from Zeus (Paus. 8.22.2).

Stymphalus is mentioned by Homer (*Il.* 2.608) and also by Pindar (*Ol.* 6.169), who calls it the mother of Arcadia. The only building in the city mentioned by Pausanias was a temple of Artemis Stymphalia, under the roof of which were figures of the Stymphalian birds. Behind the temple stood statues in white marble of young women with the legs and thighs of birds, and these creatures were represented on Stymphalian coins. The sixth labor of Heracles was ridding the vicinity of the Stymphalian birds. These were an innumerable swarm of voracious birds, the daughters of Stymphalus and Ornis. They had brazen claws, wings, and beaks; they used their feathers as arrows and ate human flesh. They had been brought up by Ares and were so numerous that with their droppings and feathers they covered whole fields and meadows and killed men and beasts. From fear of wolves these birds had taken refuge in the lake near Stymphalus, from which Heracles was ordered by Eurystheus to expel them. When Heracles undertook the task, Athena provided him with a brazen rattle. He startled the birds with its noise and, as they attempted to fly away, he killed them with arrows. According to some, he did not kill them but merely drove them away. Afterward they appeared again in the island of Aretias, where they had fled and where they were found by the Argonauts (Apollon. Rhod. 2.1037).

The remains of the city of Stymphalus cover the promontory and extend as far as the fountain, which was included in the city. The circuit of the city walls can be traced. Below the acropolis are foundations of a temple and remains of buildings cut out of the rock on the south side of the hill.

STYRA (NEA STIRA)   was a town of Euboea on the west coast, north of Carystus and nearly opposite the promontory of Cynosura in Attica. The town stood near a bay, in the middle of which is the island of Aegileia (now called Stiranisi). Styra is mentioned by Homer (*Il.* 2.539) along with Carystus. Its inhabitants were originally Dryopian, though they claimed to be descended from the deme of Steiria in Attica (Strab. 10.1.6).

STYX (MAVRONERIA or DRAKONERIA)   is a waterfall in the Aroanian mountains above Vounarianika, a village in the west of Ahaia in the district of ancient Pheneus. The torrent falls into the Crathis. It is by far the highest waterfall in Greece. The inaccessibility of the spot and the desolate area invested the Styx with superstitious reverence. The Styx was transferred by the Greek and Roman poets to the invisible world; but the waterfall continued to be regarded with superstitious terror; its water was supposed to be poisonous; and it was believed that it destroyed all kinds of containers in which it was put with the exception of those made of the hoof of a horse or an ass. It is now called Mavroneria (Black Waters) and sometimes Drakoneria (Terrible Waters).

SUIA   was the harbor of ancient ELYRUS.

SUNIUM (SUNIO)   is the name of a promontory and deme on the south coast of Attica. The promontory, which forms the most southerly point in the nome, or prefecture, rises almost perpendicularly from the sea to a great height and is crowned with the temple of Poseidon. This temple was designed by the same architect who built the temples of Hephaestus and Ares in Athens and the temple of Nemesis at Rhamnus. Eleven columns remain standing from the colonnade that surrounded the pronaos and the cella, where the statue of Poseidon was placed. The frieze showed the battle of the Centaurs, the battle of the gods and giants, and the exploits of Theseus. The proximity of Sunium to the silver mines of Laurium probably contributed to its prosperity. It was frequently used as a place of sanctuary by slaves who escaped from the silver mines. The circuit of the walls may still be traced. Sunium was sacred to Athena and Poseidon. North of the main sanctuary there is a small enclosure dedicated to Athena.

SYBRITA (THRONOS AMARIOU)   was a town of Crete near Eleutherna and famous for its numerous and beautiful silver coins. The types are almost always connected with the worship of Dionysus or Hermes, but Zeus and Apollo have appeared as well. The summit of Kephala formed the acropolis of Sybrita. A temple of Dionysus may have been southwest of the acropolis.

SYME (SIMI)   is an island off the coast of Turkey, to the west of Cape Cynossema (Daracya), between the Cnidian (Resadiye) peninsula and Rhodes, at the entrance of the Sinus Schoenus (Sombeki). The island was described as 60 km in circumference and as having eight harbors (Plin. 5.31.133) and a town of the same name as the island. The island itself is high and barren. Syme was formerly called both Metapontis and Aegle and obtained its later name from Syme, a daughter of Ialysus and Dotis, who, together with Chthonius, a son of Poseidon, is said to have first peopled the island. She was carried here by Glaucus (Athen. 7.296). In the story of the Trojan War, the island Syme enjoys a kind of celebrity, for the hero Nireus is said to have gone with three ships to assist Agamemnon (Hom. *Il.* 2.671). He was a son of Chaopus and Aglaia and next to Achilles the handsomest among the Greeks at Troy, but unwarlike. He came from Syme and commanded his three ships with a small number of men. According to Diodorus Siculus (5.53), he also ruled over a part of Cnidus, and he was slain by Eurypylus or Aeneas. His beauty became proverbial (Lucian *Dial. Mort.* 9). The first historical population of the island consisted of Dorians. There are still a few, unimportant remains of the acropolis.

SYROS (SIROS)   is an island in the Aegean Sea, one of the Cyclades, lying between Rheneia and Cythnus. It is about 33 km in circumference and Homer (*Od.* 15.403) described it as producing excellent wine. Syros had two cities even in the time of Homer, one on the east and the other on the west side of the island. The one on the east side, which was called Syros, stood on the same site as the modern capital of the island, Ermoupoli, which is now a flourishing city of nearly fourteen thousand inhabitants and a busy trading center. In consequence of rapid development, all traces of the ancient city have disappeared. There are ruins of the second ancient city of unknown name. In the *Odyssey* (15.414) this was the kingdom of Ctesius, the father of Eumaeus.

TAENARUM (AKRA TENARO)   a promontory at the lower end of Laconia and the southernmost point of Europe, is now called Akra Tenaro. The whole of the Taenarian peninsula was sacred to Poseidon, who appears to have replaced Helios, the more ancient god of the locality (*Hymn. Hom. ad Apoll.* 411). At the tip of this peninsula was the temple of Poseidon, which was also an asylum for fugitives. It seems to have been an ancient Achaian sanctuary before the Dorian conquest and to

have continued to be the chief sacred place of the Perioeci and Helots. The great earthquake that devastated Sparta in 464 B.C. was believed to have been punishment for the Lacedaemonians having violated the asylum of suppliant Helots (Thuc. 1.128,133). The temple was plundered for the first time by the Aetolians (Polyb. 9.34). Near the sanctuary was a cavern through which Heracles is said to have dragged Cerberus to the upper regions. The twelfth labor of Heracles was to fetch Cerberus back from the lower world. Accompanied by Hermes and Athena, he descended into Hades near Cape Taenarum. He managed to bring the monster back and some say he came back the same way via a cave in Taenarum, but others claim he emerged with the dog at Hermione, Coroneia, or Heracleia.

Among the many dedicatory offerings to Poseidon the most celebrated was the brazen statue of Arion seated on a dolphin, which could still be seen in the time of Pausanias (3.25.7). Arion was the ancient Greek bard who, having won a musical contest in Sicily, was robbed of his prizes by sailors on his way home to Corinth. In order to save his life, he played on his cithara, sang a prayer to the gods, and then leapt overboard. Dolphins, attracted by the music, took him on their backs and carried him to Taenarum, from where he made his way back to Corinth.

We also read of Taras, a son of Poseidon. He is said to have crossed the sea from Taenarum to the south of Italy, riding on a dolphin, and to have founded Tarentum in Italy, where he was worshipped as a hero (Paus. 10.10.8).

Three other individuals associated with the island were Taenarus, Idas, and Euphemus. Taenarum is said to have taken its name from Taenarus, a son of either Zeus or Icarius or Elatus and Erimede (Paus. 3.14.2). Idas was a hero distinguished in the war against Thebes (Stat. *Theb.* 6.553, 7.588). Euphemus was a son of Poseidon and lived at Taenarum. He was one of the Calydonian hunters and an Argonaut. He could walk on the sea as if it were land (Apollon. Rhod. 1.182). He is mentioned as an ancestor of Battus, the founder of Cyrene. When the Argonauts carried their ship through Libya to the coast of the Mediterranean, Triton, who would not let them pass without showing them some act of friendship, offered them a clod of Libyan earth. None of the Argonauts would accept it, but Euphemus did. With that clod of earth he received for his descendants the right to rule over Libya. Euphemus was to throw the piece of earth into one of the chasms of Taenarum, and his descendants in the fourth generation were to go to Libya and cultivate it. The clod was deliberately or accidentally dropped near Thera, which gave the descendants of Euphemus the right to colonize the island, but not till the seventeenth generation after the Argonauts. The seventeenth descendant of Euphemus was Battus of Thera (Pind. *Pyth.* 4.1; Apollon.

Rhod. 2.562). Euphemus was represented on the chest of Cypselus as a victor, with a chariot and two horses (Paus. 5.17.9).

Pausanias mentions two harbors called Psamathe and Limen Achilleios. These are most likely the modern towns of Porto Kagio and Ahilio. The remains of the celebrated temple of Poseidon still exist at the Church of the Asomaton close to Cape Tenaro on the east side of the island. They now form part of the church, and the ancient wall may be traced on one side.

At the distance of 7 km north of the isthmus of the Taenarian peninsula was the town Taenarum, subsequently called Caenepolis. It contained a temple of Demeter and another of Aphrodite, the latter near the sea. The modern village of Agios Kiprianos stands on the site of this town.

TALLAEUS or TALAEUS (MELIDONI)   was the station of Talos, the mythical man of brass and the guardian of the island of Crete. This brazen giant was created by Hephaestus. He was given by Zeus to Europa, or by Hephaestus to Minos, to guard Crete. He marched around Crete three times a day and kept off intruders by pelting their ships with huge rocks. He had a single vein and it was his one vulnerable spot. The Argonauts tried to land on Crete, but he prevented them till Medea lulled him with drugs and drew out the nail that let his blood flow out. The stalactitic grotto of Melidoni between Rethimno and Iraklio has been identified with the place where these events occurred. The cave is also reputed to have been the scene of human sacrifices in front of a statue of Talus.

TAMYNAE (ALIVERI)   was a town of Euboea in the territory of Eretria at the foot of Mount Cotylaeum. It had a temple of Apollo, said to have been built by Admetus (Strab. 10.1.10). Its site has been placed at the village of Aliveri, where there are several ancient remains.

TANAGRA (SKIMATARI)   was a town of Boeotia located on the north bank of the Asopus 24 km from Oropus and 37 from Plataea. Several ancient writers identified Tanagra with the Homeric Graea (Hom. *Il.* 2.498; Lycoph. 644). Tanagra, a daughter of Aeolus and wife of Poemander, gave her name to the town (Paus. 9.20.1). Tanagra was also called Poemandria and its territory Poemandria from the fertile meadows that surrounded the city. Mythology says, however, that Poemander, a son of Chaeresilaus and husband of Tanagra and reputed founder of Tanagra, gave the first name to the city. His children were Ephippus and Leucippus. When Poemander inadvertently killed his own son, he was purified by Elephenor (Paus. 9.20.1; Plut. *Quaest. Gr.* 70). The most ancient inhabitants of Tanagra are said to have been Phoenicians, who came with Cadmus and later migrated from there to Athens (Herod. 5.57).

The city was associated with Naubolus, Orion, Eunostus, and the nymph Eunoste. Naubolus, a son of Lernus and father of Clytoneus, was a king of Tanagra (Apollon. Rhod. 1.135,208). Orion, the very handsome giant and hunter, was called by some a Tanagran and by others a Theban, but this was probably because Hyria, his birthplace, sometimes belonged to one and sometimes the other city. Eunostus was a hero of Tanagra. He was a son of Elinus and brought up by the nymph Eunoste. Ochne, the daughter of Colonus, fell in love with him, but he avoided her; when she accused him before her brothers of trying to rape her, they killed him. Afterward Ochne confessed that she had falsely accused him and threw herself from a rock. Eunostus had a sanctuary at Tanagra in a sacred grove, which no woman was allowed to approach (Plut. *Quaest. Gr.* 40).

The public buildings of Tanagra are described by Pausanias (9.20.3,4). The principal temple was that of Dionysus, which contained a celebrated statue of the god in Parian marble and a Triton, the sea deity. Near it were temples of Themis, Aphrodite, and Apollo, and two of Hermes, in one of which he was worshipped as Criophorus and in the other as Promachus. Nearby was the theater and farther on the gymnasium. Tanagra possessed a considerable territory; and Strabo (9.2.12) mentions four villages belonging to it: Eleon, Harma, Mycalessus, and Pharae.

The ruins of Tanagra are situated 5 km south of the village of Skimatari and about the same distance from modern Tanagra. The site is a large hill on the north bank of the Asopus. The walls of the city, about 3.5 km in circumference, may still be traced, but they are a mere heap of ruins. The place owes its fame to the terra-cotta figures found in the necropolis in 1874. Tanagra and other Boeotian towns manufactured these figurines, which were popular votive offerings and were exported in great numbers. A museum at Skimatari features these figurines and other finds from Tanagra.

TAPHIAE (MEGANISSI and KALAMOS)   were a number of small islands off the west coast of Greece between Leucas and Acarnania, also called the Teleboides. The Taphii or Teleboae are frequently mentioned in the Homeric epics (*Od.* 15.427, 16.426) as pirates. Taphius, a son of Poseidon, was the father of Pterelaus. He led a colony to Taphos and called the inhabitants Teleboans (Apollod. 2.4.5). Oebalus was a son of Telon. He was originally a king of the Teleboans and came from the island of Taphos to Capreae in Italy; and Oebalus settled in Campania (Virg. *Aen.* 7.734). Odysseus went to Anchialus of Taphos to obtain poison for his arrows (Hom. *Od.* 1.259). When Athena visited Telemachus at Ithaca, she assumed the form of Mentes, the leader of the Taphians (Hom. *Od.* 1.105), and the son of Anchialus. He was connected by ties of hospitality with the house of

Odysseus so it was appropriate for Athena to assume his shape. The Taphians or Teleboans are celebrated in the legend of Amphitryon and are said to have been subdued by this hero (Herod. 5.59; Apollod. 2.4.6,7).

Amphitryon was a son of Alcaeus, king of Troezen. While Electryon, the brother of Alcaeus, was reigning at Mycenae, the sons of Pterelaus together with the Taphians invaded his territory, demanded the surrender of his kingdom, and drove away his oxen. The sons of Electryon entered battle with the sons of Pterelaus, but the combatants on both sides all fell, so that Electryon had only oné son, Licymnius, left and Pterelaus likewise only one, Eueres. The Taphians, however, escaped with the oxen, which they entrusted to Polyxenus, king of the Eleans. These oxen were ransomed by Amphitryon. Electryon resolved to make war on the Taphians and entrusted his kingdom and daughter Alcmena to Amphitryon. Before Electryon could get away, however, Amphitryon accidentally killed him. For this he was expelled from Mycenae; he took Alcmena and Lycimnius and went to Thebes. In order to win the hand of Alcmena, Amphitryon prepared to avenge the deaths of her brothers on the Taphians. Assisted by Cephalus, Panopeus, Heleius, and Creon, Amphitryon now attacked and ravaged the islands of the Taphians, but he could not subdue them as long as Pterelaus lived. This chief had on his head one golden hair, the gift of Poseidon, which rendered him immortal. His daughter Comaetho, who was in love with Amphitryon, cut off this hair and caused her father's death. Amphitryon then took possession of the island, put the faithless Comaetho to death, and gave the islands to Cephalus and Heleius. Then he returned to Thebes with his spoils. Heleius was a son of Perseus and Andromeda.

The principal island is called Taphos by Homer (*Od.* 1.417) and by later writers Taphius, Taphiussa, or Taphias (now Meganisi). The next largest island of the Taphii was Carnus (now Kalamos).

TARPHE   was the original name of ancient PHARYGAE.

TARRHA (AGIA ROUMELI)   was a town on the southwest coast of Crete, one of the earliest sites of the worship of Apollo. Its position has been placed on the southwest coast of the island at Agia Roumeli at the entrance of the Samaria Gorge. There are considerable remains of a temple, probably that of Apollo Tarrhaeus, and other buildings.

Carmanor was a Cretan of Tarrha, father of Eubulus and Chrysothemis. He was also the priest of Apollo at Tarrha. He was said to have received and purified Apollo and Artemis after they had slain the monster Python, and it was in the house of Carmanor that Apollo met and fell in love with Acacallis (Paus. 2.7.7, 10.16.5). Chrysothemis

was said to have been a poet and to have won the first victory in the Pythian games with a hymn on Apollo (Paus. 10.7.2).

TAYGETUS (TAIGETOS)   is a mountain chain between Laconia and Messenia, named for Taygete. She was a daughter of Atlas and Pleione, one of the Pleiades. By Zeus she became the mother of Lacedaemon and of Eurotas. According to some traditions, Taygete did not want to yield to Zeus, and in order to protect her from him, Artemis metamorphosed her into a cow. Taygete showed her gratitude towards Artemis by dedicating to her the Cerynitian hind with golden antlers. Some also call her the mother by Tantalus of Pelops. Taygetus is the highest mountain in Peloponnesus and it stretches in an almost unbroken line for 115 km from Leondari in Arcadia to Cape Tenaro. Taygetus rises to its greatest height immediately above Sparta. Its principal summit was called Taletum in antiquity; it was sacred to the sun, and horses and other victims were here sacrificed to this god (Paus. 3.20.4). Zeus Messapeus had a sanctuary between Amyclae and Mount Taygetus. It was said to have been derived from a priest of the name of Messapeus (Paus. 3.20.3). The Dioscuri were born, according to some, on Mt. Taygetus. Carya was a daughter of Dion, who was king in Laconia in the vicinity of Taygetus. She and her sisters had had the gift of prophecy conferred on them by Apollo. Dionysus fell in love with Carya, but her sisters prevented him from seeing her. Apollo had made a condition of his gift that they obey the will of the gods, so this refusal of Dionysus caused them to go insane and climb to the top of Taygetus, where they were metamorphosed into rocks. Carya was changed into a nut tree, and the Lacedaemonians, on being informed of this by Artemis, dedicated a temple to Artemis Caryatis.

Taygetus is roughly 2,400 meters high. After reaching its greatest altitude, it diminishes gradually toward the south. It finally runs down as the backbone of the peninsula that forms the southernmost extremity of Greece. This mountainous district between the Laconian and Messenian gulfs is now called the Mani.

On the sides of Taygetus are forests of pine, which abounded in ancient times with game and wild animals. Pausanias (3.20.4) mentions wild goats, wild boars, stags, and bears. For this reason Taygetus was one of the favorite haunts of the huntress Artemis. Nymphs accompanied her during the chase. Her chariot was drawn by four stags with golden antlers (Callim. *Hymn. in Dian.* 13,81,90).

TEGEA (ALEA)   was one of the most ancient and powerful towns of Arcadia, situated in the southeast of the country. Arcas was the ancestor and eponymous hero of Arcadia. He was the father of Elatus, Apheidas, and Azan, among whom he divided his kingdom. Statues of

Arcas and his family were dedicated at Delphi by the inhabitants of Tegea (Paus. 10.9.5). The territory was called Tegeatis, bounded by Cynuria and Argolis on the east, from which it was separated by Mount Parthenium, by Laconia on the south, by the Arcadian district of Maenalia on the west, and by the territory of Mantineia on the north. The Tegeatae are said to have derived their name from Tegeates. He was a son of Lycaon and the reputed founder of Tegea. He was married to Maera, a daughter of Atlas, by whom he had two sons, Leimon and Scephrus (Paus. 8.53.2). According to a tradition of Tegea, Cydon, the founder of the town of Cydonia in Crete, was also a son of Tegeates (Paus. 8.53.4). The tombs of both Tegeates and Maera were shown in Tegea (Paus. 8.48.6). The Tegeatae originally occupied eight demes, or townships. These had developed under the rule of Apheidas, son of Arcas. When Arcas divided his kingdom among his sons, Apheidas obtained Tegea and the surrounding territory. His brother Elatus was famous for having protected the Phocians and the Delphic sanctuary against the Phlegyans. A statue of him stood in the marketplace at Tegea (Paus. 8.48.8). Under Apheidas a ninth deme was added. The inhabitants of these townships were later incorporated by Aleus into the city of Tegea, of which this hero was the reputed founder. Aleus was a son of Apheidas and grandson of Arcas. He was married to Neaera and is said to have founded the first temple of Athena Alea at Tegea (Paus. 8.23.1; Apollod. 3.9.1). Cepheus was a son of Aleus and an Argonaut from Tegea, of which he was king. He had twenty sons and one daughter, Sterope; nearly all his sons perished in an expedition they undertook with Heracles. This expedition was the capture of Lacedaemon, after which time Heracles returned to Tegea and became by Auge the father of Telephus.

Tegea is mentioned in the *Iliad* (2.607) and in the earliest times was probably the most celebrated of all the Arcadian towns. This appears from its heroic renown since its king Echemus is said to have slain Hyllus, the son of Heracles, in single combat. He was a son of Aeropus and grandson of Cepheus, and he succeeded Lycurgus as king of Arcadia (Paus. 8.5.1). He was married to Timandra, a daughter of Tyndareus and Leda (Apollod. 3.10.6). In his reign the Dorians invaded Peloponnesus, and Echemus succeeded in slaying Hyllus (Paus. 8.5.1). After the fall of Hyllus, the Heracleidae were obliged to promise not to repeat their attempts upon Peloponnesus within the next fifty or one hundred years, and the Tegeatans were honored with the privilege of commanding one wing of the Peloponnesian army whenever the inhabitants of the peninsula undertook an expedition against a foreign enemy (Herod. 9.26; Diod. 4.58). The fight of Echemus and Hyllus was represented on the tomb of Echemus at Tegea (Paus. 8.53.10).

The Tegeatae offered a lengthy and successful resistance to the Spartans, when the latter attempted to extend their dominion over Arcadia. In one of these wars, Charilaus or Charillus, king of Sparta, deceived by an oracle that appeared to promise victory to the Spartans, invaded Tegeatis and not only was defeated but also was taken prisoner along with all his men who had survived the battle (Herod. 1.66; Paus. 8.5.9). More than two centuries afterward in the reign of Leon and Agesicles, the Spartans again fought unsuccessfully against the Tegeatae; but in the following generation, in the time of their king Anaxandrides (ca. 560 B.C.), the Spartans, having obtained possession of the bones of Orestes in accordance with an oracle, defeated the Tegeatae and compelled them to acknowledge the supremacy of Sparta (Herod. 1.65,67; Paus. 3.3.5). The reference to the bones of Orestes is based on the story that during a truce, Lichas, a Spartan, found the remains of Orestes and took them to Sparta, which the oracle had said were necessary for the Spartan victory.

In the time of Strabo (8.8.2), Tegea was the only one of the Arcadian towns that continued to be inhabited, and it was still a place of importance in the time of Pausanias (8.45–48). Tegea was entirely destroyed by Alaric towards the end of the fourth century A.D.

The territory of Tegea formed the southern part of the plain of Tripolitza. Tegea was about 17 km south of Mantineia and about 5 km southeast of the modern town of Tripoli. It was about 6.5 km in circumference. At its site the principal remains are those of the temple of Athena Alea. This temple was said to have been originally built by Aleus, the founder of Tegea. It was burned in 394 B.C. and the new building, which was erected by Scopas, is said by Pausanias (8.45.4) to have been the largest and most magnificent temple in Peloponnesus.

Pausanias begins his description with the temple of Athena Alea. On the front frieze was depicted the Calydonian boar hunt. The frieze on the opposite side showed Telephus fighting Achilles. Pausanias says that both the ancient statue of Athena Alea and the tusks of the Calydonian boar were carried away by Augustus Caesar. The statue was replaced by one of Athena Hippia, which was renamed Alea. On one side of the statue of Athena stood a statue of Asclepius, on the other one of Hygieia, both works by Scopas. Among the votive offerings was the hide of the Calydonian boar, rotted and without bristles. In addition there were a sacred couch of Athena, a painting of Auge, and the shield of Marpessa, a woman of Tegea. Atalanta, the famous huntress, appeared on the pediment of the temple among the Calydonian hunters (Paus. 8.45.5). The priest of Athena was always a boy, whose priesthood probably ended before puberty. The altar of the goddess was made by Melampus, the son of Amythaon. Represented on the altar were Rhea and the nymph Oenoe holding the baby Zeus. On either side were four figures; on one side were Glauce, Neda, Theisoa and Anthracia; on the other were Ida, Hagno, Alcinoe, and Phrixa. These were all nurses of the infant Zeus. There were also statues of the Muses and Mnemosyne, their mother.

At Tegea there was also a sanctuary of Athena Poliatis (Keeper of the City). This sanctuary they called Eryma (Defense), saying that Cepheus, the son of Aleus, received from Athena a promise that Tegea should never be captured while time endured, adding that the goddess cut off some of the hair of Medusa and gave it to him as a safeguard to the city. Others say that Athena gave Heracles a lock of Medusa's hair concealed in an urn, for it had the same paralyzing effect as the head itself. When Heracles went out against Lacedaemon he gave the lock of hair to Sterope, the daughter of Cepheus, as security for the town of Tegea because the sight of it would put the enemy to flight (Paus. 8.47.6; Apollod. 2.7.3).

In the marketplace was a temple of Aphrodite Plinthia with a stone statue and also an image of Ares. Carved in relief on a slab, the image of the war god was called Gynaecothoenas (He Who Entertains Women). At the time of the Laconian war, when Charillus made the first invasion, the women of Tegea armed themselves and lay in ambush under the hill they called Phylactris (Sentry). When the armies met and the battle began, the women emerged and put the Lacedaemonians to flight. Marpessa, surnamed Choera, surpassed the other women in daring. The women offered to Ares their own sacrifice of victory and would not share the sacrificial meat with the men. For this reason Ares got the surname Gynaecothoenas. There were also an altar of Zeus Teleius (Full-grown) with a square statue and tombs of Tegeates and Maera, his wife.

There was a temple of Eileithyia with a statue of Auge. Auge, a daughter of Aleus and Neaera, was a priestess of Athena, and having become by Heracles the mother of a son, she concealed the baby in the temple of the goddess. In consequence of this profanation of the sanctuary, the country was visited by a famine; and when Aleus was informed by an oracle that the temple of Athena was profaned by something unholy, he searched and found the child. The baby was exposed on Mount Parthenium, where he was suckled by a deer, from which circumstance the boy derived the name of Telephus. Auge was surrendered to Nauplius, who was to kill her, but he gave her to Teuthras, king of the Mysians, who made her his wife (Paus. 8.4.9). Her tomb was shown at Pergamum in Mysia. Auge was represented by Polygnotus in the Lesche at Delphi (Paus. 10.28.7). Her connection with the temple of Eileithyia presents a somewhat different version of the story. Aleus discovered her pregnancy and handed her over to Nauplius to be drowned. As they

dragged her along, she fell to her knees and gave birth to her son at the place where the sanctuary of Eileithyia was later built. Subsequently, Telephus was educated by King Corythus in Arcadia. He went to Mysia at the instruction of an oracle and found his mother there. He became king of Mysia and was able to render the Greeks a service in the Trojan War in exchange for curing him of an infected wound, which had been inflicted by Achilles when the Greeks invaded Mysia. He was worshipped on Mount Parthenium, and on the temple of Athena Alea in Tegea he was represented fighting with Achilles.

The Tegeans said they set up statues of Apollo Agyieus (Protector of Streets and Public Places) for the following reason. Apollo and Artemis punished all the men who took no heed of Leto in her flight from Python. When they came to Tegea, Scephrus, the son of Tegeates, spoke with Apollo. Leimon, his brother, thought Scephrus was maligning him and attacked and killed him. He, in turn, was instantly shot down by Artemis. Tegeates and Maera made sacrifices to Apollo and Artemis, but a famine came anyway. The oracle of Delphi ordered a mourning for Scephrus, and a priestess of Artemis, pretending to be Artemis, pursued a man designated as Leimon. At Tegea the statues of Apollo Agyieus were four in number, one set up by each of the tribes. The names given to the tribes are Clareotis, Hippothoetis, Apolloniatis, and Athaneatis; they were named after the lots cast by Arcas to divide the land among his sons and after Hippothous, the son of Cercyon.

There was also a temple of Demeter and Kore, who were surnamed Carpophori, and near this was a temple of Aphrodite called Paphia. The latter was built by Laodice, who was descended from Agapenor, who led the Arcadians to Troy. Not far from it were two sanctuaries of Dionysus, an altar of Kore, and a temple of Apollo with a gilded statue. There was also a temple of Gaea.

The Tegeans also had what they called a Common Hearth of the Arcadians. Here there was an image of Heracles, and on his thigh was represented a wound received in the first fight with the sons of Hippocoon. The elevation on which were located most of the altars of the Tegeans was called the place of Zeus Clarius (of Lots), and it appears that the god received his surname from the lots cast by the sons of Arcas for their share of Arcadia. The house of Aleus was shown in Tegea, as well as the tomb of Echemus, and the fight between Echemus and Hyllus was carved in relief upon a slab.

On the left of the road from Tegea to Laconia there was an altar of Pan and also one of Lycaean Zeus. About 1 km farther was a sanctuary of Artemis Limnatides, with a statue in ebony. About 2 km farther still were the ruins of a temple of Artemis Cnaceatis. Artemis Calliste was also a name by which the goddess was known at Tegea (Paus. 8.35.8).

On the road from Tegea to Thyrea was the tomb of Orestes, from which the Spartans stole the bones. Across the river Garates was another sanctuary of Pan, by which stood an oak sacred to the sylvan god.

On the road from Tegea to Argos was a temple and image of Asclepius. Next there was a sanctuary of Apollo Pythius. In a grove of oaks was a temple of Demeter Corytheuses. Nearby was a sanctuary of Dionysus Mystos. Mount Parthenium then began, and on it was shown a sacred enclosure of Telephus, where he was exposed as an infant and suckled by a deer. A little farther was still another sanctuary of Pan, where it was agreed that he appeared to the messenger Pheidippides, or Philippides, and conversed with him (Paus. 1.28.4). The turtles on Parthenium were thought to be sacred to Pan, since their shells were good for making harps.

TEGYRA (PIRGOS)   was a village of Boeotia 5 km northeast of Orchomenus and located above the marshes of the river Melas. It was celebrated for its oracle and temple of Apollo, surnamed Tegyreius, who was even said to have been born there (Plut. *Pelop.* 8). In its neighborhood was a mountain named Delos. Tegyra has been placed at Pirgos, which is between Orhomenos and the National Highway.

TELCHINIA   was another name for SICYON.

TELCHINIS   was an earlier name for the island of RHODES.

TELEBOIDES   was an earlier name of the TAPHIAE Islands.

TELOS (TILOS)   is a rocky island in the Carpathian Sea between Rhodes and Nisyrus, from the latter of which its distance is only 11 km. It is 15 km in circumference. On the island was a town of the same name, a harbor, hot springs, and a temple of Poseidon. The island was celebrated for a species of ointment. Telos the town was situated on the north coast, and remains of it are still seen above the modern village of Megalo Horio.

TEMENIUM (NEA KIOS?)   was a town in Argolis at the upper end of the Argolic Gulf, built by Temenus, the son of Aristomachus. He was a Heraclid and one of their leaders into Peloponnesus. After the conquest of the peninsula he received Argos as his share (Apollod. 2.8.4). His tomb was shown at Temenium near Lerna (Paus. 2.38.1). His descendants, the Temenidae, being expelled from Argos, are said to have founded the kingdom of Macedonia. Consequently, the kings of Macedon called themselves Temenidae (Herod. 8.138; Thuc. 2.99). Temenium was 9 km from Nauplia and 5 from Argos. The river Phrixus flowed into the sea between Temenium and

Lerna (Paus. 2.36.6). Pausanias saw at Temenium temples of Poseidon and Aphrodite and the tomb of Temenus (2.38.1). The site of Temenium must lie close to the seaside village of Nea Kios.

TEMPE (TEMBI)   a celebrated valley in the northeast of Thessaly, is a gorge between Mounts Olympus and Ossa, through which the waters of the Peneius River flow into the sea. It was believed by ancient historians and geographers that the gorge of Tempe had been produced by an earthquake, but the Thessalians maintained that it was the god Poseidon who had split the mountains. Others supposed that this had been the work of Heracles (Diod. 4.58; Lucan 6.345).

The pass of Tempe was connected with the worship of Apollo. This god was believed to have gone there to receive purification from the slaughter of the serpent Python and afterward to have returned to Delphi bearing in his hand a branch of laurel brought from the valley. Every ninth year the Delphians sent to Tempe a procession of well-born youths; their leader plucked a branch of laurel and brought it back to Delphi. On this occasion a solemn festival, in which the inhabitants of the neighboring regions took part, was celebrated at Tempe in honor of Apollo Tempeites. The procession was accompanied by a flute player.

TENEA (KLENIA)   the most important place in Corinthia after the city of Corinth and her port towns, was situated 11 km south of the capital. The south gate of Corinth was called the Teneatic because it led to Tenea. The Teneatae claimed descent from the inhabitants of Tenedos, who were brought over from Troy as prisoners and settled by Agamemnon in this part of Corinthia; and they said it was in consequence of their Trojan origin that they worshipped Apollo above all the other gods (Paus. 2.5.4). Strabo (8.6.22) also mentions here the temple of Apollo Teneates and says that Tenea and Tenedos had a common origin in Tenes, the son of Cycnus. It was at Tenea that Oedipus was said to have passed his childhood.

Tenea lay in the mountain valley through which flows the river that empties into the Corinthian Gulf east of Corinth. In this valley many archaeological finds have been made. Ruins of Tenea extend from the south edge of modern Hiliomodi to the village of Klenia, altogether about 2 km. At the village of Athikia, northeast of these two towns, there was found an ancient statue of Apollo, a so-called Tenean Apollo.

TENOS (TINOS)   is an island in the Aegean, one of the Cyclades lying between Andros and Delos. It stretches from northwest to southeast and is about 25 km long. It was sometimes called Hydrussa from the number of its springs or Ophiussa because it abounded in snakes (Plin.

4.12.22). The sons of Boreas are said to have been slain on this island by Heracles (Apollon. Rhod. 1.1304). Zetes and Calais were the sons of Boreas, the north wind. They are generally described as winged beings and are mentioned among the Argonauts. They were killed by the arrows of Heracles on the island of Tenos. He had learned that it was they who had persuaded the other Argonauts to abandon him in Mysia. One or both of the two columns that he erected over their graves on Tenos moved when the north wind blew upon them.

The ancient city of Tenos stood at the southwest end of the island where the modern city stands. In the vicinity of the city a celebrated temple of Poseidon and Amphitrite stood in a grove where festivals were celebrated that were much frequented by all the neighboring people. The foundations of the temple are still to be seen. Attributes of Poseidon appeared on the coins of Tenos. Among the curiosities of Tenos was mentioned a fountain, the water of which would not mix with wine (Athen. 2.43).

Tinos is one of the most prosperous islands in the Aegean. This prosperity is a result of its being regarded as the Lourdes of Greece. Thousands of sick and afflicted people come here annually to visit the Church of Panagia Evangelistria in hope of a cure.

TEUMESSUS was a village in Boeotia situated in the plain of Thebes on a low hill of the same name. The name of this hill was given as well to the range of mountains that separated the plain of Thebes from the valley of the Asopus River. Teumessus was on the road from Thebes to Chalcis (Paus. 9.19.1). It is called "grassy" in the Homeric *Hymn to Apollo* (228). Teumessus is celebrated in legends, particularly in regard to the Teumessian fox that ravaged the territory of Thebes.

The only building at Teumessus mentioned by Pausanias (9.19.1) was a temple of Athena Telchinia, without any statue. The surname indicates that the worship of the goddess here was joined in some way with that of the mysterious Telchines, who were regarded as cultivators of the soil and ministers of the gods. (See RHODES.) The modern site of Teumessus is about 8 or 9 km from Thebes north of the road to Halkida on a small isolated hill. There is no town nearby.

TEUTHRONE (KOTRONAS) was a town of Laconia situated on the west side of the Laconian Gulf, 28 km from Cape Taenarum. It was said to have been founded by the Athenian Teuthras (Paus. 3.25.4). The chief deity worshipped here was Artemis Issoria. Issoria was a surname derived from Mount Issorium, on which she had a sanctuary (Paus. 3.14.2,25.4). Teuthrone had a fountain called Naia. Its ruins exist at the village of Kotronas, and its citadel occupied a small peninsula now called Skopa.

THALAMAE (THALAMES) was a town of Laconia 15 km north of Oetylus and 3.5 from Pephnus (Paus. 3.26.1,2). Pephnus was on the coast on the east side of the Messenian Gulf, and Thalamae was situated inland, probably at or near Thalames (formerly Koutifari) east of Platsa on the Milea River. Thalamae was said to have been founded by Pelops. In the territory of Thalamae on the road to Oetylus was a temple and oracle of Ino or Pasiphae, in which the future was revealed to those who slept in the temple. Pasiphae, an oracular goddess, was believed to be a daughter of Atlas, or to be the same as Cassandra or Daphne, the daughter of Amyclas. Even the Spartan kings sometimes slept in the temple for the purpose of having the meaning of their dreams revealed. The temple probably stood upon the promontory Trahila, where there are some ancient remains. According to some, the Dioscuri were born at Thalamae.

THASOS (THASSOS) is an island in the north of the Aegean Sea off the coast of Macedonia. It was a short sail from Amphipolis and 53 km from Abdera. It was also called Aeria, Aethra, and Chryse, from its gold mines, which were the chief source of the wealth of the island. The highest mountain is 1,045 meters above sea level and is thickly covered with fir trees. The earliest known inhabitants of Thasos were the Phoenicians, who were doubtless attracted to the island by its valuable mines, but who are said to have come here in search of Europa five generations before the birth of the Grecian Heracles. They were led by Thasos, the son of Agenor, from whom the island derived its name (Herod. 2.44, 6.47; Paus. 5.25.12).

The worship of Heracles appeared in Thasos, where Herodotus (2.44) found a temple said to have been built by the Phoenicians sent out in search of Europa. Heracles had been worshipped in Phoenicia principally in the character of a savior. The later Heracles was also involved with the island. Alcaeus was a son of Androgeus, son of Minos and brother of Sthenelus, living with a colony from Crete on the island of Paros. When Heracles, en route to fetch the girdle of Hippolyte, stopped at Paros, some of his companions were slain by the Minoans. Heracles slew them all except Alcaeus and Sthenelus, whom he took with him and to whom he afterward assigned the island of Thasos as their dominion.

The city of Thasos was situated in the north part of the island and had two ports. It stood on three hills, and several remains of the ancient walls exist. On the acropolis were sanctuaries of Apollo Pythius, Athena Poliouchos, and Pan. Elsewhere in the lower town have been found sanctuaries of Poseidon, Dionysus, Artemis, and Heracles, who was the principal deity of the Thasians. The coins of Thasos are numerous, and one represents the head of Dionysus with a kneeling Heracles on the reverse.

THAUMACIA (DOMOKOS)   was a town of Magnesia in Thessaly, one of the four cities whose ships in the Trojan War were commanded by Philoctetes. He was a son of Poeas and the most celebrated archer in the Trojan War. He led the warriors from Methone, Thaumacia, Meliboea, and Olizon against Troy in seven ships. Thaumacia was said to have been founded by Thaumacus, the father of Poeas. It is probably represented by the paleokastro of Skiti, one of the villages on the Magnesian coast. It was situated on the pass leading from the Spercheius valley to the west plain of Thessaly. The acropolis is still identifiable, but the walls are of a later period. Some remains of the ancient walls can be seen.

THEBES (THIVA)   was the leading city of Boeotia. It was situated in the southern of the two plains of the country, both of which are surrounded by mountains. Orchomenus was the leading city in the northern plain. Thebes is said to have derived its name from Thebe, a daughter of Prometheus, or from Thebe, the wife of Zethus (Apollod. 3.5.6).

Athens and Sparta, which were the centers of Grecian political and cultural life in the historical period, were not as rich as Thebes in mythical renown. Argos and Mycenae, whose mythical periods were full of glorious recollections, did not remain important in historical times. Thebes was preeminent in both times. After the battle of Leuctra it was even for a short period the ruling city of Greece. The most celebrated mythological events have Thebes as their center. The sieges by the seven heroes and the Epigoni and the misfortunes of her royal houses were the favorite subjects of the tragedians. The great seer Teiresias lived there, as did the great musician Amphion. Dionysus and Heracles were born there.

According to the generally accepted tradition, Thebes was founded by Cadmus, the leader of a Phoenician colony, who called the city Cadmeia, a name which was afterward confined to the citadel. Cadmus was a son of Agenor and Telephassa and brother of Europa, Phoenix, and Cilix. When Europa was carried off by Zeus to Crete, Agenor sent out his sons in search of their sister, enjoining them not to return without her. All searches being fruitless, Cadmus and Telephassa settled in Thrace. Here Telephassa died, and Cadmus, after burying her, went to Delphi to consult the oracle respecting his sister. The god commanded him to desist from further seeking, to follow a cow of a certain kind, and to build a town on the spot where the cow should lie down. Cadmus eventually found the cow described by the oracle in Phocis among the herds of Pelagon and followed her into Boeotia, where she sank down. On that spot Cadmus built Thebes, with the acropolis Cadmeia. As he intended to sacrifice the cow here to Athena, he sent some companions to the nearby well of Ares for water. This well was guarded by a dragon, a son of Ares, who killed the men sent by Cadmus. Cadmus promptly slew the dragon, and, on the advice of Athena, sowed the ground with the teeth of the monster. A crop of armed men grew up and fought to the death among themselves until only five were left. These were Echion, Udaeus, Chthonius, Hyperenor, and Pelor, who, according to the Theban legend, were the ancestors of the noblest families in Thebes. They bore the name Spartoi (Sown Men) into historical times. After this, Athena assigned to Cadmus the government of Thebes, and Zeus gave him Harmonia for his wife. The marriage solemnities were honored in the Cadmeia by the presence of all the Olympian gods. Cadmus gave to Harmonia the famous robe and necklace that he had received from Hephaestus, or from Europa, and became by her the father of Autonoe, Ino, Semele, Agave, and Polydorus. Subsequently, Cadmus and Harmonia left Thebes and went to the Illyria. After this, Cadmus had another son, whom he called Illyrius. In the end, Cadmus and Harmonia were changed into dragons and were removed by Zeus to Elysium.

The accounts of why Cadmus left Thebes vary. Some say he was expelled by Amphion and Zethus, or by Dionysus. One tradition says that when he discovered the birth of Dionysus by his daughter Semele, he shut up the mother and her child in a chest and threw them into the sea (Paus. 3.24.3). According to Herodotus (2.49), however, Melampus learned and received the worship of Dionysus from Cadmus, and other traditions, too, represent Cadmus as worshipping Dionysus (Eurip. *Bacch.* 181). According to Euripides, Cadmus resigned the government of Thebes to his grandson Pentheus, after whose death he went to Illyria.

Many view the story of Cadmus as a mythical version of the migration of Phoenicians into Greece, by means of which certain aspects of civilization (the alphabet, the art of mining, and the worship of Dionysus) came into the country.

Cadmus had one son, Polydorus. He later became king of Thebes and married Nycteis, by whom he became the father of Labdacus. Cadmus also had four daughters, Ino, Semele, Agave, and Autonoe. Ino became the wife of Athamas and the mother of Melicertes.

Semele was beloved by Zeus and became the mother of the god Dionysus. While Semele was pregnant, Hera, motivated by jealousy, appeared to her in the form of an aged nurse, Beroe, and persuaded her to ask Zeus to come to her in the same splendor and majesty with which he appeared to Hera. Zeus, who had promised that he would grant her every request, appeared to her as the god of thunder, and Semele was consumed by the fire of lightning; but Zeus saved her child Dionysus (Apollod. 3.4.3). Pausanias (9.2.3) relates that Actaeon was in love with Semele, and that Artemis caused him to be torn to pieces by his dogs to prevent his marrying her. The inhabitants of Brasiae in Laconia related that Semele, after having given birth to Dionysus, was thrown by her father Cadmus into a boat and set adrift and that her body was carried to the coast of Brasiae, where it was buried. Dionysus, whose life was saved, was brought up at Brasiae (Paus. 3.24.3). After Dionysus became an adult, the tradition continues, Semele was brought by her son out of the lower world and carried up to Olympus as Thyone. A statue of her and her tomb were shown at Thebes (Paus. 9.12.3,16.7).

Most accounts of the infant Dionysus say that he was entrusted to the care of Hermes. Others mention the Hyades, the rain nymphs, as his nurses. When the Thracian Lycurgus threatened the safety of Dionysus and his companions, the Hyades fled with the infant god to Thebes, where they entrusted him to Ino, his aunt. Zeus showed the Hyades his gratitude by placing them among the stars. When Dionysus had grown up, Hera caused him to go mad, and in this state he wandered about through many countries of the earth. During this time he introduced the cultivation of the vine in many places. Eventually he returned to Thebes, where he compelled the women to leave their homes and to celebrate Bacchic festivals on Mount Cithaeron or Mount Parnassus. Pentheus, who then ruled at Thebes, endeavored to stop the riotous proceedings and went out to the mountains to seek the Bacchic women; but his own mother, Agave, in her Bacchic frenzy, mistook him for an animal and tore him to pieces (Theocrit. 26; Eurip. *Bacch.* 1142; Ov. *Met.* 3.714). After Dionysus had thus proved to the Thebans that he was a god, he went to Argos.

The orgiastic worship of Dionysus seems to have been first established in Thrace and to have spread southward to Mounts Helicon and Parnassus, to Thebes, Naxos, and throughout Greece. Dionysus Lysius (Deliverer) had a sanctuary at Thebes near one of the gates. There was a story that the god had received that name from once having delivered Theban prisoners from the hands of the Thracians near Haliartus (Paus. 9.16.6).

Agave was the wife of Echion, one of the Spartoi, by whom she became the mother of Pentheus, who succeeded his grandfather Cadmus as king of Thebes. When Semele, during her pregnancy with Dionysus, was destroyed by the sight of the splendor of Zeus, her sisters spread the report that she had only endeavored to conceal her guilt by pretending that Zeus was the father of the child and that her destruction was a just punishment for her falsehood. With the death of her son Pentheus, Agave later paid a bitter price for this malicious report.

Autonoe was the wife of Aristaeus, by whom she became the mother of Actaeon. Autonoe together with her sister Agave tore Pentheus to pieces in their Bacchic fury, as related. At last grief and sadness at the terrible tragedy of her father's house induced her to leave Thebes, and she went to Megara, where her tomb was shown in later years (Paus. 1.44.5). Aristaeus, her husband, was the ancient divinity of flocks and shepherds, of fields and groves. He was born in Cyrene but came to Thebes when he was grown. He learned from Cheiron the Centaur and the Muses the arts of healing and prophecy. He married Autonoe, who bore him several sons, among whom was Actaeon. This young hunter accidentally saw Artemis bathing in a stream and was changed by her into a stag, which was torn to pieces by Actaeon's own dogs. After the death of Actaeon, Aristaeus left Thebes and went to Ceos.

After the death of Pentheus, Cadmus retired to Illyria, as stated, and his son Polydorus became king of Thebes. Polydorus was succeeded by his son Labdacus. Labdacus lost his father at an early age and was placed first under the guardianship of Nycteus and afterward under that of Lycus, a brother of Nycteus. When Labdacus had grown to manhood, Lycus surrendered the government to him. Nycteus was a son of Hyrieus by the nymph Clonia; he was the brother of Lycus and Orion and husband of Polyxo, by whom he became the father of Antiope. Antiope was carried off by Epopeus, king of Aegialeia (Sicyon); and Nycteus, who, as the guardian of Labdacus, was staying at Thebes, took revenge by invading the territory of Sicyon with a Theban army. He was defeated, and being severely wounded, he was carried back to Thebes, where, on his deathbed, he appointed Lycus guardian of Labdacus and at the same time exacted a promise from him to take vengeance on Epopeus. When Labdacus had grown up, Lycus surrendered the government to him; but as Labdacus died soon after, Lycus again became the guardian of Laius, the son of Labdacus, but was expelled by his own great-nephews, Amphion and Zethus (Paus. 9.5.6; Eurip. *Herc. Fur.* 27). A very different account is found in Apollodorus (3.5.5). According to it, Nycteus and Lycus were the sons of Chthonius and were obliged to leave their country on account of the murder of Phlegyas. They then settled at Hyria; but Lycus was chosen commander by the Thebans and usurped the government that belonged to Laius. He maintained himself for twenty years in this unlawful position, until he was slain by Amphion and Zethus. Nycteus killed himself in despair because his daughter, who was with child by Zeus, fled to Epopeus at Sicyon. Before he died, Nycteus commissioned Lycus to take vengeance on Epopeus. Lycus fulfilled his promise for he slew Epopeus and kept Antiope prisoner.

After Nycteus died, Antiope was exposed to the persecutions of her uncle and his cruel wife Dirce. Dirce had her put in chains; but Zeus helped her to escape to Mount Cithaeron, where she gave birth to twin sons, Amphion and Zethus. According to Apollodorus, she remained in captivity for a long time after the birth of her sons, who had been exposed and rescued and brought up by shepherds and did not know their descent. Hermes (according to others, Apollo or the Muses) gave Amphion a lyre, with which he became skilled. His brother, on the other hand, spent his time in hunting and tending the flocks. The two brothers fortified the town of Entresis near Thespiae and settled there. Antiope, who had in the meantime been very ill-treated by Lycus and Dirce, escaped from her prison, her chains having miraculously been loosened; and her sons, on recognizing their mother, went to Thebes, killed Lycus, tied Dirce to a bull and had her dragged to death. The two then threw her body into a well, known thereafter as the Well of Dirce. After having taken possession of Thebes, the two brothers fortified the town by a wall. It is said that when Amphion played his lyre, the stones in the area moved into place to form the wall. Locrus, a son of Zeus and Maera, is said to have come from Argos to assist Zethus and Amphion in the building of Thebes. In order to bring the two accounts together regarding the building of Thebes, later writers said that Cadmus founded the Cadmeia, or citadel, and that Amphion and Zethus built the lower city and gave to the united city the name Thebes (Paus. 9.5.2,6).

Amphion married Niobe, who bore him many sons and daughters, all of whom were killed by Apollo and Artemis. Niobe was a daughter of Tantalus by the Pleiad Taygete or the Hyad Dione and the sister of Pelops. The number of her children by Amphion is usually six sons and six daughters. Being proud of the number of her children, she boasted that she was superior to Leto, who had given birth only to two children. Apollo and Artemis, indignant at such presumption, slew all the children of Niobe. For nine days their bodies lay in their blood without burial for Zeus had changed the people into stones; but on the tenth day the gods themselves buried them. Niobe herself, who had gone to Mount Sipylus, was metamorphosed into stone, and even thus continued to feel the misfortune with which the gods had visited her (Hom. *Il.* 24.603–17; Apollod. 3.5.6). According to Homer (*Il.* 24.605), all the children of Niobe fell by the arrows of Apollo and Artemis; but later writers state that one of her sons, Amphion or Amyclas, and one of her daughters, Meliboea, were saved and that Meliboea, having turned pale with terror at the sight of her dying brothers and sisters, was afterward called Chloris. According to Homer, the youths and maidens perished in their mother's house, but, according to Apollodorus, the sons were killed by Apollo during a chase on Mount Cithaeron, and the daughters by Artemis at Thebes, not far from the royal palace. According to Ovid (*Met.* 6.218–302), the sons were slain while they were engaged in gymnastic exercises in a plain near Thebes, and the daughters during the funeral of their brothers. Others,

again, transfer the scene to Lydia or make Niobe, after the death of her children, go from Thebes to Lydia, to her father Tantalus on Mount Sipylus. There Zeus, at her own request, metamorphosed her into a stone, which during the summer always shed tears (Ov. *Met.* 6.303; Paus. 8.2.5). The tomb of the children of Niobe was shown at Thebes. Ovid. *(Met.* 6.271) relates that Amphion killed himself with a sword from grief at the loss of his children. According to others, he was killed by Apollo because he made an assault on the Pythian temple of the god. Amphion was buried together with his brother at Thebes. Of Zethus not much else was written. According to some, he was married to Aedon and, according to others, to Thebe. Aedon was the mother of Itylus by him. Envious of Niobe, who had six sons and six daughters, she formed the plan of killing the eldest of Niobe's sons but by mistake slew her own son. Zeus relieved her grief by changing her into a nightingale, whose melancholy tunes were thought to be lamentations about her child (Apollod. 3.5.5).

According to a commentator on Homer, Eurymachus, a prince of the Phlegyes, attacked and destroyed Thebes after the deaths of Amphion and Zethus, but there is no other mention of this event. Laius next became king, and with him commences the memorable story of Oedipus and his family. After his father Labdacus died, Laius was, as already stated, placed under the guardianship of Lycus, and on the death of Lycus, Laius was obliged to take refuge with Pelops in Peloponnesus. While there he fell in love with Chrysippus, a son of Pelops, and carried him back to Thebes. When Amphion and Zethus, the murderers of Lycus, who had usurped the throne, had lost their lives, Laius returned to Thebes and ascended the throne of his father. He married Iocasta, a daughter of Menoeceus, a grandson of Pentheus, and sister of Hipponome and Creon (Apollod. 2.4.5, 3.5.7).

As Laius had no issue, he consulted the oracle, which informed him that if a son should be born to him he would lose his life by the hand of his own child. When, therefore, at length Iocasta gave birth to a son, they pierced his feet, bound them together, and then exposed the child on Mount Cithaeron. There he was found by a shepherd of King Polybus of Corinth, and he was called Oedipus because of his swollen feet. When he was brought to the palace at Corinth, the king and his wife Merope brought him up as their own child. Once, however, Oedipus was taunted by a Corinthian with not being the king's son. As a result, he proceeded to Delphi to consult the oracle. The answer he obtained there was that he should slay his father and commit incest with his own mother. Thinking that Polybus was his father, he resolved not to return to Corinth. On his road between Delphi and Daulis, he met his real father, Laius, and as

Polyphontes, the charioteer of Laius, wanted to push him out of the way, a scuffle ensued in which Oedipus slew both Laius and Polyphontes, and one part of the oracle was fulfilled. The two corpses are said to have been buried on the same spot by Damasistratus, king of Plataea.

In the meantime, the celebrated Sphinx had appeared in the neighborhood of Thebes. She was the monstrous offspring of Typhon and Echidna. According to some, she had been sent into Boeotia by Hera, who was angry with the Thebans for not having punished Laius, who had abducted Chrysippus from Pisa. According to others, she was sent by Ares, who wanted to take revenge because Cadmus had slain his son, the dragon. In either case, she is said to have come from the most distant parts of Ethiopia. At Thebes she settled on a rock and put a riddle to every Theban who passed by, and whoever was unable to solve the riddle was killed by the monster. The Thebans decided to offer a reward for her destruction and proclaimed that their deliverer should be made king and receive Iocasta as his wife. Oedipus was one of those who came forward. When he approached the Sphinx, she gave the riddle, which some say she had learned from the Muses, as follows: "A being with four feet has two feet and three feet, and only one voice; but its feet vary, and when it has most it is weakest." Oedipus solved the riddle by saying that the being was man, and the Sphinx in blind anger at once threw herself from the rock.

Creon, the brother of Iocasta, who had been king since the death of Laius, then gave the government of Thebes to Oedipus and also gave to him his sister in marriage. By his own mother, Creon's sister, he became the father of Eteocles, Polyneices, Antigone, and Ismene. In consequence of this incestuous alliance, of which no one was aware, the country of Thebes was visited by a plague, and the oracle ordered that the murderer of Laius must be expelled before the plague could be lifted. Oedipus accordingly pronounced a solemn curse upon the unknown murderer and declared him an exile; but when he endeavored to discover the murderer, he was informed by the seer Teiresias that he himself was both the parricide and the husband of his mother. Iocasta now hanged herself, and Oedipus put out his own eyes. Oedipus in his blindness was expelled from Thebes by his sons and brother-in-law, Creon, who again undertook the government. In his exile, Oedipus was guided and accompanied by Antigone to Attica. He arrived in the grove of the Eumenides near Colonus; he was there honored by Theseus in his misfortune and, according to an oracle, the Eumenides removed him from the earth, and no one was allowed to approach his tomb (Soph. *Oed. Col.* 166). According to Homer (*Od.* 11.270, *Il.* 23.679), Oedipus, tormented by the Erinyes, continued to reign at Thebes

after Iocasta's death; he fell in battle and was honored at Thebes with funeral solemnities.

After their father's flight from Thebes, Eteocles and Polyneices governed the kingdom by turns. But this arrangement did not work out, and in consequence of disputes, Polyneices, fearing assassination, fled to Argos. Adrastus, son of Talaus, was king at Argos, and an oracle had told him that his daughters would marry a boar and a lion, and these turned out to be Tydeus of Calydon and Polyneices of Thebes, one with a boar on his shield and the other with a lion. Having given his daughters to them, Adrastus promised to assist them in returning to their countries, from which they had had to flee. Adrastus therefore prepared for war against Thebes, although Amphiaraus, his brother-in-law, foretold that all who should engage in it should perish, with the exception of Adrastus (Apollod. 3.6.1). Thus arose the celebrated war of the Seven against Thebes, in which Adrastus was joined by six other heroes, Polyneices, Tydeus, Amphiaraus, Capaneus, Hippomedon, and Parthenopaeus.

Amphiaraus was a son of Oicles and Hypermnestra. On his father's side he was descended from the famous seer Melampus. He was one of the Calydonian hunters and one of the Argonauts. For a time he reigned at Argos in common with Adrastus, but when a feud broke out between them, Adrastus took to flight. They later became reconciled, and Adrastus gave his sister Eriphyle in marriage to Amphiaraus. By her he became father of Alcmaeon, Amphilochus, Eurydice and Demonassa. On marrying Eriphyle, Amphiaraus had sworn that he would abide by the decision of Eriphyle on any point in which he should differ in opinion from Adrastus. When, therefore, Adrastus called upon him to join the expedition of the Seven, Amphiaraus, although he foresaw its unfortunate issue and at first refused to take any part in it, was nevertheless persuaded by his wife to join his friends. Eriphyle had her reasons, for she had been enticed to induce her husband by the necklace of Harmonia, which Polyneices had given her. Amphiaraus, upon leaving Argos, enjoined his sons to avenge his death on their heartless mother. On the way to Thebes, the heroes instituted the Nemean games. During the war against Thebes, Amphiaraus fought bravely, but still he could not suppress his anger at the whole undertaking. When Tydeus, whom he regarded as the originator of the expedition, was severely wounded by Melanippus, and as Athena was hastening to render him immortal, Amphiaraus cut off the head of the dead Melanippus and gave Tydeus his brains to drink; Athena, struck with horror at the sight, withdrew. Finally, Adrastus and Amphiaraus were the only heroes who survived. Amphiaraus was pursued by Periclymenus and fled toward the river Ismenius. Here the earth opened before he was overtaken by his enemy and swallowed up Amphiaraus together with his chariot and charioteer, Baton. But Zeus made him immortal, and he was worshipped as a hero all over Greece. His departure to Thebes was represented on the chest of Cypselus. Pausanias (3.18.12) mentions a contest between Amphiaraus and Lycurgus, son of Pronax, depicted on the throne at Amyclae.

Capaneus was a son of Hipponous. In the battle he had his station at the Ogygian or Electrian gate. During the siege he was presumptuous enough to say that even the fire of Zeus should not prevent him from scaling the walls of the city; but when he was ascending the walls with a ladder, Zeus struck him with a flash of lightning. While his body was burning, his wife Euadne leaped into the flames and destroyed herself. According to some, he was resurrected by Asclepius.

Hippomedon was a son of Aristomachus and was slain by Hyperbius or Ismarus (Aeschyl. *Sept.* 490; Soph. *Oed. Col.* 1318; Apollod. 3.6.3).

Parthenopaeus is sometimes called a son of Ares or Meilanion and Atalanta (Apollod. 3.9.2,6.3; Paus. 3.12.9), sometimes of Meleager and Atalanta, and sometimes of Talaus and Lysimache (and consequently a brother of Adrastus). He was killed at Thebes by Asphodicus, Amphidicus or Periclymenus.

Tydeus was a son of Oeneus, and while he was still a prince of Calydon, he had to flee his kingdom because of a murder he committed. He fled to Adrastus, who purified him and gave him his daughter Deipyle in marriage. With Adrastus he then went against Thebes, where he was wounded by Melanippus. The incident has been related above. Tydeus died from his wounds and was buried by Maeon, a Theban, the son of Haemon, whose life Tydeus had earlier spared (Paus. 9.18.2). Melanippus also slew Mecisteus, the brother of Adrastus. The tomb of Melanippus was shown in the neighborhood of Thebes on the road to Chalcis (Apollod. 3.6.8; Paus. 9.18.1).

Each of the Seven attacked one of the celebrated gates of the city, and all except Adrastus were defeated and killed, just as Amphiaraus had prophesied. Polyneices and Eteocles fell by each other's hands, although some say that Leades, son of Astacus, killed Eteocles and others that Megareus killed him (Apollod. 3.6.8; Aeschyl. *Sept.* 474). Adrastus alone escaped by reason of the swiftness of his horse Areion, the gift of Heracles. Creon then resumed control of the government of Thebes. He refused to allow the bodies of the six heroes to be buried.

Antigone had remained with her father in Attica until he died. She returned to Thebes, and Haemon, the son of Creon, fell in love with her. Meanwhile the battle against Thebes took place, and while everyone else submitted to Creon's edict forbidding, under heavy penalty, the burial of the dead Argives, Antigone alone defied the tyrant and buried the body of Polyneices. According to Apollodorus (3.7.1), Creon had her buried

alive in the same tomb with her brother. According to Sophocles, she was just shut up in a subterranean cave, where she killed herself, and Haemon, on hearing of her death, killed himself by her side. Thus Creon, too, received his punishment. In addition to that, Adrastus went to Athens and implored the assistance of the Athenians. Theseus was persuaded to undertake an expedition against Thebes; he took the city and delivered up the bodies of the fallen heroes to their friends for burial (Apollod. 3.7.1). Creon's wife was Eurydice, and he also had two daughters, Henioche and Pyrrha. Statues of the two girls were erected at the temple of the Ismenian Apollo at Thebes (Paus. 9.10.3).

Ten years after the catastrophe of the Seven, the descendants of the seven heroes went against Thebes to avenge their fathers, and this war is called the war of the Epigoni (After-Born). According to some traditions, this war was undertaken at the request of Adrastus, who still thirsted for revenge. The names of the Epigoni are not the same in all accounts, but the common list contains Alcmaeon, Aegialeus, Diomedes, Promachus, Sthenelus, Thersander, and Euryalus.

Alcmaeon, as stated, was the son of Amphiaraus and Eriphyle and brother of Amphilochus, Eurydice, and Demonassa. His mother was induced by the necklace of Harmonia, which she received from Polyneices, to persuade her husband Amphiaraus to take part in the expedition against Thebes. Before he set out, Amphiaraus made his sons promise to kill their mother as soon as they were grown. When the Epigoni prepared for a second expedition against Thebes, the oracle promised them victory if they chose Alcmaeon as their leader. He was at first reluctant to undertake the command, as he had not yet avenged his father. But his mother, who had now received from Thersander, the son of Polyneices, the robe of Harmonia also, persuaded him to join the expedition. Alcmaeon distinguished himself greatly in the war and slew Laodamas, the son of Eteocles. After the fall of Thebes he learned why his mother had urged him on, and killed her on the advice of an oracle of Apollo. According to some traditions, he did so with the assistance of his brother Amphilochus. Euripides in his lost tragedy *Alcmaeon,* according to Apollodorus (3.7.7), stated that after the fall of Thebes, Alcmaeon married Manto, the daughter of Teiresias, and that he had two children by her, Amphilochus and Tisiphone, whom he gave to Creon, king of Corinth, to educate. The wife of Creon, jealous of the extraordinary beauty of Tisiphone, afterward sold her as a slave, and Alcmaeon himself bought her, without knowing she was his daughter (Diod. 4.66). Alcmaeon later married Callirrhoe, a daughter of the river Achelous. Callirrhoe induced him to procure for her the robe and necklace of Harmonia, and in this attempt he lost his life. Alcmaeon after his death was worshipped as a hero, and at Thebes he seems to have had an altar near the house of Pindar (*Pyth.* 8.80), who calls him his neighbor and the guardian of his property and also seems to suggest that prophetic powers were ascribed to him, as to his father Amphiaraus. He was represented with a statue at Delphi and on the chest of Cypselus (Paus. 5.17.7, 10.10.4).

Aegialeus was a son of Adrastus and Amphithea. He was the only one among the Epigoni who fell in the war. He was worshipped as a hero at Pegae in Megaris, and it was believed that his body had been carried there from Thebes and buried (Paus. 1.44.4).

Diomedes, the son of Tydeus, was yet a boy when Tydeus fell in the war against Thebes. He took part in the war of the Epigoni, but real distinction came to him in the greater battle that took place shortly after, the Trojan War.

Promachus was the son of Parthenopaeus. Sthenelus was the son of Capaneus and belonged to the family of the Anaxagoridae in Argos. He was the father of Cylarabes (Hom. *Il.* 5.109; Paus. 2.18.5). Thersander was a son of Polyneices and Argeia. He was married to Demonassa, by whom he became the father of Tisamenus. After having been made king of Thebes, he went with Agamemnon to Troy and was slain by Telephus.

Finally, Euryalus was a son of Mecisteus, whose father, while not one of the Seven, was a brother of Adrastus and had been killed in the earlier battle. Euryalus was a brave warrior, and at the funeral games of Oedipus he conquered all his competitors with the exception of Epeius, who excelled him in wrestling. He accompanied Diomedes to Troy, where he was one of the bravest heroes, and slew many Trojans. In the painting of Polygnotus at Delphi, he was represented as being wounded; and there was also a statue of him at Delphi, which stood between those of Diomedes and Aegialeus (Paus. 10.10.4).

The Epigoni gained a victory over the Cadmeians at the river Glisas and drove them back inside the city. Upon the advice of the seer Teiresias, the Cadmeians abandoned the city and fled to Illyria under the guidance of Laodamas, son of Eteocles.

Teiresias was a son of Eueres and Chariclo. He belonged to the ancient family of Udaeus at Thebes and was one of the most renowned soothsayers in all antiquity. He was blind from his seventh year but lived to a very old age. The cause of his blindness was believed to have been the fact that he had revealed to men things that should be known only to gods; others said that he had seen Athena while she was bathing. Chariclo prayed to Athena to restore his sight to him, but as the goddess was unable to do this, she conferred upon him the power to understand the voices of the birds and gave him a staff, with the help of which he could walk as safely as if he had his eyesight (Apollod. 3.6.7; Calim. *Lav. Pall.* 75).

Another tradition gives a different reason for his blindness. Once, when on Mount Cithaeron, he saw a male and a female serpent coupling; he struck them with his staff, and as he happened to kill the female, he himself was metamorphosed into a woman. Seven years later he again saw two serpents, and, now killing the male, he again became a man. It was for this reason that Zeus and Hera, when they were disputing as to whether a man or a woman enjoyed sexual intercourse more, referred the matter to Teiresias, who could judge of both. He declared in favor of the assertion of Zeus that women got more pleasure from the sex act. Hera, indignant at the answer, blinded him, but Zeus gave him the power of prophecy and granted him a life that was to last for seven or nine generations. In the War of the Seven against Thebes, he declared that Thebes should be victorious if Menoeceus would sacrifice himself; and during the war of the Epigoni, when the Thebans had been defeated, he advised them to initially enter negotiations for peace but to take flight if granted that option by the enemy. He himself fled with them (or, according to others, he was carried to Delphi as a captive), but on his way he drank from the well of Tilphossa and died. His daughter Manto (or Daphne) was sent by the victorious Argives to Delphi as a present to Apollo. Another daughter of his is called Historis.

Even in the lower world Teiresias was believed to retain the powers of perception, while the souls of other mortals were mere shades, and there also he continued to use his golden staff. His tomb was shown in the neighborhood of the Tilphossian fountain near Thebes (Paus. 9.18.4). The oracle connected with his tomb lost its power and became silent at the time of an Orchomenian plague. He was represented by Polygnotus in the Lesche at Delphi (Paus. 10.29.8). Manto, his daughter, was herself a prophetess, first of the Ismenian Apollo at Thebes, where monuments of her existed (Paus. 9.10.3), and subsequently of the Delphian and Clarian Apollo. After the taking of Thebes by the Epigoni, she, with other captives, was dedicated to Apollo at Delphi. The god sent the captives to Asia, where they founded the sanctuary of Apollo near the place where Colophon was later built. Rhacius, a Cretan who had settled there before, married Manto and became by her the father of Mopsus. According to Euripides, she had previously become the mother of Amphilochus and Tisiphone by Alcmaeon. Being a prophetess of Apollo, she is also called Daphne.

Thus the Epigoni became masters of Thebes and placed Thersander, son of Polyneices, on the throne. According to the mythical chronology, the war of the Seven took place twenty years before the Trojan expedition and thirty years before the capture of Troy; and the war of the Epigoni was placed fourteen years after the first expedition against Thebes and consequently only four years before the departure of the Greeks against Troy.

There is another important event in the mythical times of Thebes, that was not interwoven with the series of the legends already related. This is the birth of Heracles at Thebes and the important services he rendered to his native city in his war against Orchomenus.

Alcaeus, king of Troezen, was a son of Perseus and married to Hipponome, the daughter of Menoeceus of Thebes, by whom he became the father of Amphitryon and Anaxo. When Amphitryon's uncle Electryon was going to be away avenging the murder of his sons by the Taphians who had stolen oxen from Electryon, he entrusted his kingdom and his daughter Alcmena to Amphitryon, on condition that he should not marry her till after Electryon's return from the war. Electryon returned, and Amphitryon managed to recover the oxen. One of them turned wild, and as Amphitryon attempted to strike it with his club, he accidentally struck Electryon, killing him on the spot. Sthenelus, the brother of Electryon, took this opportunity to expel Amphitryon, who together with Alcmena and her sole surviving brother, Licymnius, went to Thebes. Here he was purified by Creon, his uncle. In order to win the hand of Alcmena, Amphitryon prepared to avenge the death of Alcmena's brothers on the Taphians and requested Creon's help, which the latter promised on condition that Amphitryon should deliver the Cadmean country from a wild fox that was creating a great problem there. But since this fox could not be overtaken by anyone, Amphitryon went to Cephalus of Athens, who possessed a famous dog, which could overtake every animal it pursued. Cephalus was persuaded to lend Amphitryon his dog on condition that he should receive a part of the spoils of the expedition against the Taphians. This dog was called Laelaps, the storm wind personified. Procris, the wife of Cephalus, had received this extremely swift animal from Artemis. The dilemma of the supernatural animals was resolved by Zeus, who changed them both into stone. This stone was shown in the vicinity of Thebes (Apollod. 2.4.6; Ov. *Met.* 7.771).

Assisted by Cephalus, Panopeus, Heleius, and Creon, Amphitryon now attacked and ravaged the islands of the Taphians. They succeeded in conquering the Taphians and, after giving the islands to Cephalus and Heleius, Amphitryon returned to Thebes with his spoils, out of which he dedicated a tripod to Apollo Ismenius (Apollod. 2.4.6,7; Paus. 9.10.4; Herod. 5.9). During his absence, Zeus, in the disguise of Amphitryon, visited Alcmena and, pretending to be her husband, related to her how he had avenged the death of her brothers. He also caused this night to be given the duration of three nights. When Amphitryon himself returned on the next day and gave an account of his achievements, she was surprised at the repetition, but Teiresias revealed the mystery to her alone. On the day on which Heracles was to be born, Zeus boasted of his becoming the father of a man who was to rule over the heroic race of Perseus. Hera prevailed upon him to confirm by an oath that the descendant of Perseus born on that day should be the ruler. She delayed the birth of Heracles for seven days, so that Eurystheus, the son of Sthenelus, might be born first and thus be entitled to the rights she had requested. She did this with the assistance of the Pharmacides, the sorceresses or witches, who had the power to delay births (Paus. 9.11.3). She also enlisted the help of the Moirae and Eileithyia, the goddess of birth. Alcmena had a friend Galinthias, a daughter of Proetus of Thebes. When Alcmena was finally on the point of giving birth to Heracles and the Moirae and Eileithyia were endeavoring to prevent or delay the birth, Galinthias suddenly rushed in with the false report that Alcmena had given birth to a son. The hostile goddesses were so surprised at this information that the charm was broken, and Alcmena was enabled to give birth to Heracles. The deluded goddesses avenged the deception practiced upon them by Galinthias by metamorphosing her into a weasel or cat. Hecate, however, took pity upon her and made her her attendant, and Heracles afterward erected a sanctuary to her. At Thebes it was customary at the festival of Heracles first to offer sacrifices to Galinthias. Others call this friend Historis, a daughter of Teiresias (Paus. 9.11.3).

Thus Heracles was born. Alcmena brought into the world two boys, Heracles, the son of Zeus, and Iphicles, the son of Amphitryon, who was one night younger than Heracles. Zeus, in his desire not to leave Heracles the victim of Hera's jealousy, made her promise that if Heracles executed twelve great works in the service of Eurystheus, he should become immortal (Diod. 4.9).

It is said that Alcmena, from fear of Hera, exposed her son in a field near Thebes, afterward called the Field of Heracles. Here he was found by Hera and Athena, and Hera was prevailed upon by Athena to put him to her breast, and she then carried him back to his mother. Only a few months after his birth, Hera sent two serpents into the apartment where Heracles and his brother Iphicles were sleeping. Heracles killed the serpents with his own hands. He was brought up at Thebes, where in his youth he grew strong in body and mind, and in the confidence of his own power he defied even the immortal gods. As the hero grew up, he was instructed by Amphitryon in riding in a chariot, by Autolycus in wrestling, by Eurytus in archery, by Castor in fighting with heavy armor, and by Linus in singing and playing the lyre. Linus was killed by his pupil with the lyre because he had scolded him. Being charged with murder, Heracles exonerated himself by saying that the deed was done in self-defense; and Amphitryon, in order to prevent similar occurrences, sent him to attend his cattle. In this manner he spent his life until his eighteenth year. During this time he went out to slay the Cithaeronian lion, which was killing the flocks of Thespius, king of Thespiae.

On his return to Thebes, Heracles met the envoys of King Erginus of Orchomenus, who were going to obtain the annual tribute of one hundred oxen, which they had compelled the Thebans to pay. This subjugation had come about as a result of a war waged by the sons of Clymenus, who had been murdered by the Thebans at a festival of the Onchestian Poseidon. Heracles, in his patriotic indignation, cut off the noses and ears of the envoys and sent them back to Erginus. Erginus thereupon marched against Thebes; but Heracles, who received a suit of armor from Athena, defeated and killed the enemy and compelled the Orchomenians to pay double the tribute that they had formerly received from the Thebans. In this battle Amphitryon was killed. His tomb was shown at Thebes in the time of Pausanias (1.41.1). The glorious manner in which Heracles delivered his country gained for him immortal fame among the Thebans, and Creon rewarded him with the hand of his eldest daughter, Megara, by whom he became the father of several children.

After the battle with the Minyans, Hera caused Heracles to go mad, and in this state he killed his children by Megara and two of Iphicles' children. He consulted the oracle at Delphi; the Pythia ordered him to live at Tiryns and to serve Eurystheus for the space of twelve years, after which he should become immortal. Heracles accordingly went to Tiryns and did as he was bid by Eurystheus. Iphicles his brother had meanwhile married Automedusa, the daughter of Alcathous, by whom he became the father of Iolaus. Later he married the youngest daughter of Creon (Apollod. 2.4.11). He accompanied Heracles on several expeditions and is also mentioned among the Calydonian hunters.

After the accomplishment of the twelve labors and being released from the servitude of Eurystheus, Heracles returned to Thebes. There he gave Megara in marriage to Iolaus because, having lost his children by her during his madness, he felt that the gods frowned on this union. He then left Thebes and during his brief years thereafter he apparently never returned. According to some, Alcmena lived with her sons after the death of Eurystheus at Thebes and died there at an advanced age. When the sons of Heracles wished to bury her, Zeus sent Hermes to take her body away, carry it to the islands of the blessed, and give her in marriage there to Rhadamanthys. Hermes accordingly took her out of her coffin and put into it a stone so heavy that the Heracleidae could not move it from the spot. When, on opening the coffin, they found the stone, they erected it in a grove near Thebes, which in later times contained the sanctuary of Alcmena

(Paus. 9.16.7). She was also represented on the famous carved chest of Cypselus at Olympia.

Thebes is frequently mentioned in Homer (*Il.* 4.406, *Od.* 11.263), who speaks of its celebrated seven gates; but its name does not occur in the catalog of the Greek cities that fought against Troy, as it was probably supposed not to have recovered from its recent devastation by the Epigoni. Later writers, however, related that Thersander, the son of Polyneices, went with Agamemnon to Troy and was slain in Mysia by Telephus before the beginning of the siege. Upon his death the Thebans chose Peneleos as their leader because of the very young age of Tisamenus, the son of Thersander (Paus. 9.5.14,15). In the *Iliad* (2.494) Peneleos is mentioned as one of the leaders of the Boeotians, but is not otherwise connected with Thebes.

According to other accounts, Thebes was taken by the Thracians and Pelasgians during the Trojan War and its inhabitants driven into exile in Thessaly, from where they returned at a later period (Strab. 9.2.3; Diod. 19.53). According to the chronology of Thucydides (1.42), the Cadmeians continued in possession of Thebes until sixty years after the Trojan War, when they were driven out of their city and country by the Aeolic Boeotians from Thessaly. This seems to have been the genuine tradition; but as Homer (*Il.* 2.494) gives the name Boeotians to the inhabitants of the country called Boeotia in later times, Thucydides endeavors to reconcile the authority of Homer with the other tradition on the supposition that a portion of the Aeolic Boeotians had settled in Boeotia previously and that these were the Boeotians who sailed against Troy.

Pausanias (9.5.10–16) gives us a list of the kings of Thebes, the successors of Tisamenus. Autesion was a son of Tismenus and grandson of Thersander. He is called the father of Theras and Argeia. By Argeia Aristodemus became the father of Eurysthenes and Procles. He was a native of Thebes, where he had succeeded his father as king, but at the command of an oracle he went to Peloponnesus and joined the Dorians (Apollod. 2.8.2; Paus. 3.15.6, 9.5.15,16). On his departure, Damasichthon was chosen to be king. He was the son of Opheltes, the son of Peneleos. His son was Ptolemaeus, who was the father of Xanthus, the last king of Thebes. From then on the Thebans decided it was better to have a majority government than have everything depend on one man. (Paus. 10.5.16). But with the exception of one event, we know absolutely nothing of Theban history till the dispute between Thebes and Plataea in the latter part of the sixth century B.C.

Thebes stood on one of the hills of Mount Teumessus, which divides southern Boeotia into two distinct parts, the northern being the plain of Thebes and the southern the valley of the Asopus. On this site water was plentiful, and the topography was well adapted for defense. The hill upon which the town stands rises about 46 meters above the plain. It is bounded on the east and west by two small rivers, the Ismenus and Dirce. The Ismenus rises from a fountain called Melia in antiquity. Melia was the mother of Ismenus and Tenerus, the hero of the plain through which the Ismenus flows. It was sacred to Ares, who was said to have stationed a dragon to guard it. The Dirce rises from several fountains.

As in the case of certain other Greek cities, Thebes has been continuously occupied, and newer cities have been built atop the old. Thebes was also destroyed time after time so the modern city shows few traces of the past. It is built over the Cadmeia, and only partial excavations have been carried out.

The most interesting point in the plan of Thebes was the position of the seven celebrated gates. These gates were differently named by different writers, so it is perhaps well to go with the names upon which Pausanias and Apollodorus concur, and Pausanias makes their location clear in his descriptions. Pausanias (9.8.7) says that the Electra was the gate by which a traveler from Plataea entered Thebes. Electra was said to be a sister of Cadmus (Paus. 9.8.3). There was a hill on the right of the gate sacred to Apollo Ismenius. In this sanctuary, called the Ismenion, the Daphnephoria was celebrated. On the left of the gate were the ruins of a house said to be that of Amphitryon. The gate Proetides was on the northeast side of the city, since it led to Chalcis (Paus. 9.18.1). Proetus was a son of Thersander and father of Maera. The gate Neitae was on the northwest side since it led to Onchestus and Delphi. Neis was a daughter of Zethus, or of Amphion by Niobe. According to Pausanias (9.8.3), Neis was a son of Zethus. The fourth gate was probably situated on the west side of the city and was called Crenaeae because it was near one of the fountains of Dirce. Near the fountain was a hill called Oncos, from which Athena derived the name Onca. The fifth gate was called Ogygian from Ogygus, the most ancient king of Thebes, in whose time the deluge is said to have taken place. This flood refers to the inundation when the waters of Lake Copais rose above its banks and covered the whole valley of Boeotia. This flood is usually called Ogygian after him (Paus. 9.5.1; Apollon. Rhod. 3.1177). He was the father of Alalcomenia, Thelxinoea, and Aulis. This gate was most likely between the gates Neitae and Proetides on the north. The exact positions of the sixth gate, Homoloides, and the seventh, Hypsistae, are doubtful. Homoloeus was a son of Amphion, and some say the gate was named for him. Others derive the name from the hill Homole or from Homolois, a daughter of Niobe (Paus. 9.8.3). Pausanias relates that after the victory of the Epigoni at Glisas, some of the Thebans fled to Homole in Thessaly; and that the gate, through which the exiles reentered the city when they were recalled by Thersander, was named the Homoloides. Little remains of the Cadmeian walls, and the sites of the gates are mainly speculation.

The division of the city and its monuments have been described by Pausanias in Sections 9–18 of Book 9. The city was divided into two parts by the Strophia, a stream that ran about midway between and parallel with the river Dirce on the west and the river Ismenus on the east. Between the Strophia and the Dirce was the Cadmeia, the citadel, while the part between the Strophia and the Ismenus was the lower city, said to have been added by Amphion and Zethus (Paus. 9.5.2,6). The Cadmeia was again divided by a slight depression near the fountain of Dirce and the Crenaean gate into two hills, of which the larger and the higher one to the south was the acropolis proper and called the Cadmeia, while the north hill formed the agora of the acropolis. The east half of the city was also divided between the Strophia and the Ismenus into two parts, of which the southern consisted of the hill Ismenius and the northern of several minor hills known under the general name of Ampheion. Aeschylus (*Sept.* 528) describes the tomb of Amphion as standing near the north gate. This tomb of Amphion (and Zethus) can be seen today. Made of crude bricks, it occupies the summit of a hill at the north end of the city. Thebes consisted of four parts, two belonging to the acropolis and two to the lower city.

Leaving Potniae, Pausanias entered Thebes on the south by the gate Electra and noticed the hill Ismenius sacred to Apollo, named from the river Ismenus flowing by it. Upon the hill was a temple of Apollo. Above the Ismenion, Pausanias noticed the fountain of the Ismenus sacred to Ares. This is the one that had been guarded by the dragon slain by Cadmus. It was, as mentioned, later known as the Melia.

In the Cadmeia were the house of Amphitryon, containing the bedchamber of Alcmena, said to have been the work of Trophonius and Agamedes; a monument of the children of Heracles by Megara; the temple of Heracles; and, near it, a gymnasium and stadium, both bearing the name of Heracles. Nearby was an altar of Apollo Spodius. Between the acropolis and the agora of the Cadmeia was an altar and statue of Athena bearing the Phoenician surname of Onga, or Onca, said to have been dedicated by Cadmus (Paus. 9.12.2). Some derived the name from a village named Onca or Oncae. Sophocles (*Oed. Tyr.* 20) speaks of two temples of Athena at Thebes, in one of which she was surnamed Onca and in the other Ismenia. In the agora of the Cadmeia the house of Cadmus is said to have stood; and in this place also were shown statues of Dionysus; a temple of Ammon; the place where Teiresias observed the flight of birds; a temple of Tyche; three wooden statues of Aphrodite, with the surnames of Urania, Pandemos, and Apostrophia; and a temple of Demeter Thesmophoros (Paus. 9.16.3–5).

Across the Strophia, near the gate Poetides was the theater with the temple of Dionysus (Paus. 9.16.6). In this part of the city, sometimes referred to as the Ampheion, the following monuments are mentioned: ruins of the house of Lycus and a monument of Semele; monuments of the children of Amphion; and a temple of Artemis Eucleia. Eucleia was a daughter of Heracles who died a virgin and had an altar and statue in every marketplace, on which persons about to marry offered sacrifices to her. Eucleia was frequently identified with Artemis, as is seen in the existence of this temple (Paus. 9.17.1). Near the temple were statues of Apollo Boedromius and of Hermes Agoraeus; the funeral pyre of the children of Amphion, distant one-half a stadium from their tombs; two statues of Athena Zosteria; and the monument of Zethus and Amphion, being a mound of earth.

Outside the gate Proetides on the road to Chalcis were monuments of Melanippus, Tydeus, and the sons of Oedipus, and 2.5 km beyond the last was the monument of Teiresias. Pausanias also mentions a tomb of Hector (9.18.5) and of Asphodicus (9.18.6) at the fountain Oedipodeia. In this fountain Oedipus washed off the blood of his murdered father. Asphodicus was the slayer of Parthenopaeus in the war of the Seven. On the same road was the village Teumessus (Paus. 9.19.1). Outside the gate Proetides toward the north were the gymnasium of Iolaus, a stadium, and the shrine of Iolaus. Outside the gate Neitae were the tomb of Menoeceus, the son of Creon, and a monument marking the spot where the two sons of Oedipus slew each other. The whole of this locality was called the Syrma (Dragging) of Antigone, because, being unable to carry the dead body of her brother Polyneices, she dragged it to the funeral pyre of Eteocles. The road that left this gate went to Onchestus. On it were a temple of Themis, then temples of the Moirae, and of Zeus Agoraeus, and, a little farther, a statue of Heracles surnamed Rhinocolustes because he here cut off the noses of the heralds of Orchomenus. The grove of Demeter Cabeiraea and Persephone was 4.5 km beyond, and 1 km farther was a temple of the Cabeiri. These mysterious divinities were also identified at Thebes with three ancient statues of Aphrodite, which Harmonia had taken from the ships of Cadmus (Paus. 9.16.3; Herod. 3.37). These statues have already been mentioned. Aphrodite Apostrophia (Expeller) described her as the goddess who expelled from the hearts of men the desire after sinful pleasure and lust. Her worship under this name was believed to have been instituted by Harmonia together with that of Aphrodite Urania and Pandemos, and the antiquity of her statues confirmed this belief. To the right of the temple of the Cabeiri was the Teneric

plain and to the left a road that at the end of 9 km reached Thespiae (Paus. 26.1,6).

Other religious connections with Thebes included the Dionysiac festivals that were celebrated every third year under the patronage of Dionysus Amphietes. Dionysus Lysius (Deliverer) had a sanctuary near one of the gates and there was a story that the god had received his surname from the fact of his once having delivered Theban prisoners from the hands of the Thracians near Haliartus (Paus. 9.16.6). A Theban named Phanes is said to have introduced the worship of Dionysus Lysius from Thebes to Sicyon (Paus. 2.7.6). There was also a story about the Ismenion. Caanthus was a son of Oceanus and brother of Melia. He was sent out by his father in search of his sister, who had been carried off, and when he found that she was in the possession of Apollo and that it was impossible to rescue her from the god, he threw fire into the sacred grove of Apollo. The god then killed Caanthus with an arrow. His tomb was shown by the Thebans on the spot where he had been killed, near the river Ismenus. A wooden statue of Heracles at Thebes was believed to be the work of the famous Daedalus. Enyo was the goddess of war, who delighted in bloodshed and the destruction of towns. At Thebes and Orchomenus, a festival called Homoloia was celebrated in honor of Zeus, Demeter, Athena, and Enyo, and Zeus was said to have received the surname of Homoloius from Homolois, a priestess of Enyo.

Artemis Gaeeochos (Holder of the Earth) described the goddess as a protector of the city (Soph. *Oed. Tyr.* 160). Linus, the personification of a dirge or lamentation, was described as a son of Apollo by a Muse. He died an early and violent death, and sacrifices to him were accompanied by dirges. His tomb was claimed both by Argos and Thebes. After the battle of Chaeroneia, Philip of Macedonia was said to have carried away the remains of Linus from Thebes to Macedonia. Subsequently, however, the king was induced by a dream to send the remains back to Thebes. The Thebans distinguished between an earlier and a later Linus; the latter was said to have instructed Heracles in music but to have been killed by the hero. Methapus was an Athenian who is said to have introduced at Thebes the worship of the Cabeiri. He was much skilled in all kinds of mysteries and orgies and made several alterations in the mysteries at Andania (Paus. 4.1.7,8). Persephone was worshipped at Thebes, which Zeus is said to have given to her as an acknowledgement for a favor she had bestowed on him. Plutus, the personification of wealth, is described as the son of Iasion and Demeter. At Thebes there was a statue of Tyche (Fortune) with Plutus represented as her child. He was commonly represented as a boy with a cornucopia.

Thebes, like several other places, claimed to be the birthplace of Zeus. A sanctuary to Rhea Dindymene was there (Paus. 9.25.3).

THEBES (MIKROTHIVES)   often called the Phthiotic Thebes, was located at the north end of the ancient Crocean plain. It was also known as the Achaean or Thessalian Thebes. It shared this plain with Halus. To the west were Pherae and Pharsalus, and to the north were Demetrias and Pagasae (Strab. 9.5.8). It was the main harbor on the Pagasaean Gulf until Demetrias was founded. Its acropolis, overlooking the plain, was surrounded by a Cyclopean wall that is still visible. There are forty or so towers along the wall. Athena Polias was worshipped here, and the foundations of a temple excavated here probably belonged to her. A sanctuary of Asclepius was more than likely here as well since a head, identified as his, was recently unearthed. Modern Mikrothives is adjacent to the ancient ruins. It is just slightly east of the National Highway, a dozen kilometers or so above Almiros.

THEISOA (THISOA)   a town of Arcadia (now of Elis) in the district Cynuria or Parrhasia, on the north slope of Mount Lycaeus, was called after the nymph Theisoa, one of the nurses of Zeus, who was worshipped there. The other nymphs were Neda and Hagno (Paus. 8.38.3). Its inhabitants were removed to Megalopolis when it was founded. The modern village of Thisoa is four or so kilometers northeast of Rovia near Andritsena.

THELPUSA (TOUMBITSI)   was a town in the west of Arcadia, situated on the east bank of the Ladon River. Its territory was bounded on the north by that of Psophis, on the south by that of Heraea, on the west by that of Elis and Pisatis, and on the east by that of Cleitor, Tripolis, and Theisoa (not to be confused with the Eleian/Arcadian Theisoa). The town was said to have derived its name from a nymph, the daughter of the Ladon River, probably the nymph of the stream flowing through the lower part of the town into the Ladon.

When Pausanias (8.25.3) visited Thelpusa, the city was nearly deserted, so that the agora, which was formerly in the center of the city, then stood at its end. He saw a temple of Asclepius and another of the twelve gods, the latter of which had fallen into utter ruin. He also mentions two temples of importance in the vicinity of Thelpusa, one above and the other below the city. The one above was the temple of Demeter Eleusinia, containing statues of Demeter, Persephone, and Dionysus made of stone. The temple below the city was also sacred to Demeter, whom the Thelpusians called Erinys (Lycoph. 1038; Callim. *Frag.* 107). It was situated at a place called Onceium, where Oncus, the son of Apollo, is said once to have reigned (Paus. 8.25.4). Below this temple stood the temple of Apollo Oncaeates on the left bank of the Ladon, and on the right that of the boy Asclepius, with the sepulcher of Trygon, said to have been the nurse of Asclepius (8.25.11). It is also related that Autolaus, a son of Arcas, found and brought up the infant Asclepius when he was exposed in Thelpusa (Paus. 8.25.11). The ruins of Thelpusa stand upon the slope of a considerable hill near a village formerly called Vanena. There are only a few traces of the walls of the city. Near the Ladon are some Hellenic foundations and the lower parts of six columns. The village of Toumbitsi is 1.5 km below, at a place where a promontory projects into the river, upon which there is an apparently artificial mound. This mound is probably the tomb of Trygon, the nurse of Asclepius, and Toumbitsi is the site of the temple of Asclepius.

THERA (THIRA or SANTORINI)   is an island in the Aegean about 130 km north of Crete and about 36 km south of Ios. Thera is said to have been formed by a clod of earth thrown from the ship Argo. Euphemus was a son of Poseidon by Mecionice, Oris, or the Oceanid Europa. He was married to Laonome, the sister of Heracles, but had children by other women as well. He was one of the Calydonian hunters and the helmsman of the Argo. By a power that his father granted to him, he could walk on the sea as if it were firm ground (Apollon. Rhod. 1.182). He is mentioned as the ancestor of Battus, the founder of Cyrene. When the Argonauts carried their ship through Libya to the coast of the Mediterranean, Triton offered them a clod of Libyan earth as an act of friendship. None of the other Argonauts would accept it but Euphemus did. With that clod of earth he received for his descendants the right to rule over Libya. Euphemus was to throw the clod of earth into one of the chasms of Taenarum in Peloponnesus, and his descendants four generations later would then go to Libya and possess and cultivate the land. When, however, the Argonauts passed the island of Calliste, or Thera, that clod of earth by accident fell into the sea and was carried by waves to the coast of the island. The colonization of Libya would now start from Thera, but not till the seventeenth generation of descendants of Euphemus. The seventeenth descendant of Euphemus was Battus of Thera (Pind. *Pyth.* 4.1; Apollon. Rhod. 2.562). According to Apollonius Rhodius (4.1755), the island of Thera itself had arisen from the clod of earth that Ephemus purposely threw into the sea. Euphemus was represented on the chest of Cypselus as victor, with a chariot and two horses (Paus. 5.17.9).

The island received the name of Calliste when it first emerged from the sea. It was first inhabited by the Phoenicians, who were left there by Cadmus. Membliarus was a son of Poecilus, a Phoenician, and a relative of Cadmus. Cadmus left him at the head of a colony on the island (Herod. 4.147; Paus. 3.1.8). Eight generations afterward it was colonized by Lacedaemonians and

Minyae of Lemnos (i.e., descendants of the Argonauts by Lemnian women) under the guidance of the Spartan Theras, the son of Autesion, who gave his name to the island (Herod. 4.147; Apollon. Rhod. 4.1762). The Minyae were an ancient race of heroes at Orchomenus, Iolcus, and other places. Their ancestral hero, Minyas, is said to have migrated from Thessaly into the north part of Boeotia and there to have established the powerful race of the Minyans, with the capital of Orchomenus. As the greater part of the Argonauts were descended from the Minyans, they are themselves called Minyae; and the descendants of the Argonauts founded a colony in Lemnos, which was called Minyae. From there they proceeded to Elis Triphylia and to the island of Thera.

Apollo Carneius was worshipped in various parts of Greece, including Thera. Some attempted to explain the surname as derived from Carnus, a son of Zeus and Europa, whom Leto and Apollo brought up. Apollo was especially attached to him. The remains of the temple of Apollo Carneius have been found in the ancient city of Thera. Next to the temple is a terrace where the Carneia, or festival of Apollo, was held. Between this building and the stoa was a temple of Dionysus. Another temple of Apollo and temples of Egyptian gods have been found in the west of the city. In the north end of the city a sanctuary of Demeter and Kore has been discovered.

The only importance of Thera in history is owing to its being the mother-city of Cyrene in Africa, which was founded by Battus of Thera in 631 B.C. (Herod. 4.150). Thera and the surrounding islands have been the scene of volcanic action in ancient as well as modern times. The distance around the inner curve of the island's horseshoe-like area is 20 km and around the outer curve is 30 km. Its width is not over 5 km at any point. Opposite Thera to the west is Thirassia. Southeast of it is Nea Kameni. These three islands enclose an expanse of water nearly 30 km in circumference, which is in reality the crater of a great volcano. The principal modern town of the island is now called Thira and is situated in the center of the curve of the gulf. The island is well cultivated and the chief product is wine.

THERAPNE   (See SPARTA)

THERMOPYLAE (THERMOPILES)   that is, "Hot Gates," is a celebrated narrow pass leading south from Thessaly. Lying between Mount Oeta and a marsh along the Maliac Gulf, it was the only way an enemy could cross into southern Greece. Near the united streams of the Phoenix and the Asopus, Mount Oeta came so close to the marsh that it left space for only three or four persons marching abreast. The area has changed in modern times by alteration in the course of the rivers and by drainage.

In the immediate vicinity of the pass was the town of Anthela, celebrated for the temples of Amphictyon and of the Amphictyonic Demeter, containing seats for the members of the Amphictyonic Council, who held their autumnal meetings here. Amphictyon was a son of Deucalion and Pyrrha. He was regarded as founder of the amphictyony of Thermopylae, and in consequence of this belief a sanctuary of Amphictyon was built in the village of Anthela on the Asopus, which was the most ancient place of meeting of the amphictyony. Demeter Amphictyonis was worshipped at Anthela, and sacrifices were offered to her at the beginning of every meeting (Herod. 7.200; Strab. 9.4.17). At Anthela, Mount Oeta was not so close to the sea and a plain opened up a little more than three-quarters of a kilometer in width. But near Alpeni, the first town of the Locrians, the space contracted again. At this pass were some hot springs, which were consecrated to Heracles (Strab. 9.4.13). Athena, in order to please Heracles, had called forth the hot spring here, and near it was an altar of Heracles surnamed Melampygos. It should be observed that hot springs in general were sacred to Heracles.

The Cercopes were droll and thievish gnomes who played a part in the story of Heracles. Their number is commonly stated as two, but Diodorus Siculus (4.31) speaks of several Cercopes. They are called sons of Theia, the daughter of Oceanus; they annoyed and robbed Heracles in his sleep, but they were taken prisoners by him, and either given to Omphale or killed or set free again. The place in which they seem to have made their first appearance was Thermopylae (Herod. 7.216). The Cercopes were said to have been changed into monkeys by Zeus for having cunningly deceived him (Ov. *Met.* 14.90).

Across this pass the Phocians had in ancient times built a wall against attacks of the Thessalians (Herod. 7.176,200). It appears from this description that the proper Thermopylae was the narrow pass near the Locrian town of Alpeni, but the name was also applied in general to the whole area from the mouth of the Asopus to Alpeni.

THERMUM (THERMO)   was the chief city of Aetolia and the place where the meetings of the Aetolian league were usually held and an annual festival celebrated. It had a renowned temple of Apollo, which was probably used in connection with the festival. It was situated in the very heart of Aetolia, at the northeast end of Lake Trichonis and on a height of Mount Panaetolium. It was deemed inaccessible to any army and regarded as a place of refuge. In a sense, it was the acropolis of all Aetolia. The road to it ran from Metapa on Lake Trichonis through the village of Pamphia. The remains of the wall of Thermum show that the city was about 4 km in circumference. In the northeast part of a large enclosed area are remains of the temple of Apollo Thermius. Metopes from the temple show Perseus with the head of Medusa, Heracles(?) with a

boar, and Chelidon and Aedon dismembering Itys. To the east is a smaller temple with metopes of the Charites, Iris, and a Centaur. Another temple in the same area is thought to be one belonging to Artemis. The modern town is called Thermo (formerly Kefalovriso).

THESPIAE (THESPIES)   was an ancient city of Boeotia situated at the foot of Mount Helicon, looking toward the south and the Crissaean Gulf, where its port town Creusa or Creusis was located (Strab. 9.2.25; Paus. 9.26.6). Thespiae was said to have derived its name from Thespia, a daughter of Asopus, or from Thespius, a son of Erechtheus, who migrated from Athens. His descendants are called Thespiades. The city is mentioned in the catalog of Homer (*Il.* 2.498). In the time of Strabo, Thespiae and Tanagra were the only places in Boeotia that could be considered cities (Strab. 9.2.25).

Eros, or Love, was the deity chiefly worshipped at Thespiae; and the earliest representation of the god in the form of a rude stone still existed in the city in the time of Pausanias (9.27.1). The courtesan Phryne, who was born at Thespiae, presented to her native city the celebrated statue of Eros by Praxiteles. Thespiae greatly profited from this tourist attraction. In the time of Pausanias there was only an imitation of it at Thespiae by Menodorus. Among the other works of art in this city Pausanias (9.27.6) saw a statue of Eros by Lysippus, statues of Aphrodite and Phryne by Praxiteles; the agora, containing a statue of Hesiod; the theater, a temple of Aphrodite Melaenis, a temple of the Muses, containing their statues in stone; and an ancient temple of Heracles. At Thespiae sacrifices to Aphrodite consisted of incense and garlands of flowers. Next to Eros, the Muses were specially honored at Thespiae; and the festivals of the Erotidia and Museia celebrated by the Thespians on Mount Helicon at the end of every four years are mentioned by several ancient writers. The Muses are frequently called Thespiades by the Latin writers. Musae Pierides was one of their names from an ancient king, Pierus, who is said to have emigrated from Thrace into Boeotia and established their worship at Thespiae (Paus. 9.29.3). At Thespiae Plutus, the personification of wealth, was worshipped; he was represented as the child of Athena Ergane.

The remains of Thespiae are situated adjacent to the village of Thespies. A wall surrounding the ancient town enclosed among other buildings a temple of the Muses. A temple of Apollo was uncovered about 2 km to the southwest.

THESPROTIA (THESPROTIA)   was a district of Epeirus inhabited by the Thesproti. It extended along the coast from the Ambracian Gulf to the north as far as the river Thyamis and inland as far as the territory of the Molossians. The southeast part of the country on the coast, from the river Acheron to the Ambracian Gulf, was

called Cassopaea from the town Cassope and was sometimes considered a separate district. Acheron is a river in Thesprotia, a country that appeared to the earliest Greeks as the end of the world to the west, and the locality of the river led them to the belief that it was the entrance into the lower world. When subsequently Epeirus and the countries beyond the sea became better known, the Acheron or the entrance to the lower world was transferred to other more distant parts, and at last the Acheron was placed in the lower world itself. Acherusia was a lake or swamp in Thesprotia, through which the river Acheron flowed. It was considered by some to be actually in the lower world.

The Thesproti were the most ancient inhabitants of Epeirus and are said to have derived their name from Thesprotus, the son of Lycaon. They were Pelasgians, and their country was one of the chief seats of the Pelasgic nation. Here was the oracle of Dodona, the great center of Pelasgic worship. From Thesprotia came the Thessalians, who took possession of the country afterward called Thessaly.

THESSALY (THESSALIA)   at one time the largest political division of Greece, was the whole country lying north of Thermopylae as far as the Cambunian Mountains and bounded upon the west by the Pindus range. But the name Thessaly was more specifically applied to the great plain, by far the widest and largest in all Greece, enclosed by the four great mountain barriers of Pindus, Othrys, Ossa and Pelion, and the Cambunian Mountains. The enclosed plain of Thessaly is interrupted only at the northeast corner by the celebrated vale of Tempe, which separates Ossa from Olympus and is the only way of entering Greece from the north except by a pass across the Cambunian Mountains. This plain is drained by the river Peneius and its tributaries. The valley might once have been a vast lake. The lake of Nessonis at the foot of Mount Ossa and that of Boebeis at the foot of Mount Pelion are possibly remains of this lake. In addition to the plain there were two other districts included under the general name of Thessaly. One was Magnesia, being a long, narrow strip of country extending along the coast of the Aegean Sea from Tempe to the Pagasaean Gulf and bounded on the west by Mounts Ossa and Olympus. The other was a long, narrow valley at the extreme south of the country, lying between Mounts Othrys and Oeta and drained by the river Spercheius.

Thessaly is said to have been originally known by the names of Pyrrha, Aemonia, and Aeolis. The first two names belong to mythology. When Peleus overthrew Acastus and his wife and reestablished himself as ruler of Iolcus, he annexed it to Aemonia. The last name refers to the period when the country was inhabited by Aeolians, who were afterward expelled from the country by the Thessalians about sixty years after the Trojan War. The

Thessalians are said to have come from Thesprotia in Epeirus; but at what period their name became the name of the country cannot be determined. It does not occur in Homer, who mentions only the principalities that made it up and does not give any general name to the country. The name Thessaly was derived either from Thessalus, a son of Haemon, or from Thessalus, a son of Jason and Medea. The latter Thessalus was educated at Corinth and afterward succeeded Acastus on the throne of Iolcus (Diod. 4.55).

Thessaly was divided in very early times into four districts: Histiaeotis, Pelasgiotis, Thessaliotis, and Phthiotis. They made up, however, only the great Thessalian plain. To these were added the four districts of Magnesia, Dolopia, Oetaea, and Malis. Thus there were eight districts altogether. Perrhaebia was, properly speaking, not a district since Perrhaebi was the name of a Pelasgic people settled in both Histiaeotis and Pelasgiotis.

Histiaeotis, inhabited by the Hestiaeotae, was the northwest part of Thessaly, bounded on the north by Macedonia, on the west by Epeirus, on the east by Pelasgiotis, and on the south by Thessatiotis. The Peneius may be said in general to have formed its southern limit.

Pelasgiotis, inhabited by the Pelasgiotae, the east part of the Thessalian plain, was bounded on the north by Macedonia, on the west by Histiaeotis, on the east by Magnesia, and on the south by the Pagasaean Gulf and Phthiotis. The name shows that it was originally inhabited by Pelasgians; and one of the chief towns in the district was Larissa, which was of Pelasgic origin.

Thessaliotis, the southwest part of the Thessalian plain, was so called because it was first occupied by the Thessalians who came from Thesprotia. It was bounded on the north by Histiaeotis, on the west by Epeirus, on the east by Pelasgiotis, and on the south by Dolopia and Phthiotis.

Phthiotis, inhabited by the Phthiotae, was the southeast of Thessaly, bounded on the north by Thessaliotis, on the west by Dolopia, on the south by the Maliac Gulf and on the east by the Pagasaean Gulf. Its inhabitants were Achaeans and are frequently called the Achaian Phthiotae. It is in this district that Homer (2.683) places Phthia and Hellas Proper and the dominions of Achilles.

Magnesia, the most easterly district of Thessaly, was a long, narrow slip of country extending from the Peneius on the north to the Pagasaean Gulf on the south, and bounded on the west by the great Thessalian plain. It was a mountainous country, as it included Mounts Ossa and Pelion. Its inhabitants were the Magnetes.

Dolopia, inhabited by the Dolopes, was a small district bounded on the east by Phthiotis, on the north by Thessaliotis, on the west by Athamania, and on the south by Oetaea. The Dolopes were an ancient people, for they

are not only mentioned by Homer (9.484) but they also sent deputies to the Amphictyonic Assembly.

Oetaea, inhabited by the Oetaei and Aenianes, was a district in the upper valley of the Spercheius, lying between Mounts Othrys and Oeta and bounded on the north by Dolopia, on the south by Phocis, and on the east by Malis.

Malis was a district in the south of Thessaly on the shores of the Maliac Gulf and opposite the northwest point of the island of Euboea. It extended as far as the pass of Thermopylae. Its inhabitants, the Malians, were Dorians and belonged to the Amphictyonic League.

The Thessalians, as stated, were a Thesprotian tribe. Under the guidance of leaders, who are said to have been descendants of Heracles, they invaded the west part of the country, afterward called Thessaliotis, and drove out or enslaved the ancient Aeolian inhabitants. The Thessalians afterward spread over the other parts of the country, forcing the Perrhaebi, Magnetes, Achaean Phthiotae, etc., to submit to their authority and pay them tribute. The population of Thessaly therefore consisted of three distinct classes: The Penestae, who were serfs; the subject people; and the Thessalian conquerors, who participated in the public administration and whose lands were cultivated by the Penestae. For some time after the conquest, Thessaly was governed by kings of the race of Heracles; but the kingly power seems to have been abolished in early times and the government in the separate cities became oligarchical, the power being chiefly in the hands of a few great families descended from the ancient kings.

Many gods and important individuals were associated in one or another way with Thessaly. Athena, for example, was educated, according to some traditions, by Triton, and her name became associated with his, so that afterward various traditions about her birthplace were tied up with a river or well of that name, as in Crete, Thessaly, Boeotia, and Arcadia. Inhabitants of those districts asserted that Athena had been born there. Zeus Carius (Carian) and Zeus Phyxius (God Who Protects Fugitives) were names of Zeus in Thessaly (Paus. 2.21.2, 3.17.9). Hera Pelasga (Pelasgian) was a name of the Thessalian Hera. Poseidon did not create the horse in Attica, according to some, but in Thessaly, where he also gave famous horses to Peleus (Lucan 6.396; Hom. *Il.* 23.277). Aristaeus, an ancient divinity of agriculture and beneficence, was worshipped in Thessaly, where he was regarded as the protector of flocks and bees (Virg. *Georg.* 1.14, 4.283,317). His mother, Cyrene, was carried off from Mount Pelion by Apollo to Libya, where Aristaeus was born. And, finally, the contest between the gods and the Titans took place in Thessaly, the Titans occupying Mount Othrys and the sons of Cronus Mount Olympus.

The war lasted ten years until the Olympians finally overthrew the Titans and cast them into Tartarus.

Aeolus was a son of Hellen and brother of Dorus and Xuthus. He is described as the ruler of Thessaly and regarded as the founder of the Aeolic branch of the Greek nation. He married Enarete, by whom he had several sons and daughters. The most ancient version of the story mentions only four sons: Sisyphus, Athamas, Cretheus, and Salmoneus, representatives of the four main branches of the Aeolic race. According to one writer, he also had a son named Macareus, who, after having committed incest with his sister Canace, killed himself. According to Ovid (*Her.* 11), Aeolus threw the baby to the dogs and sent his daughter a sword with which she killed herself.

The Aloeidae were the giant sons of Iphimedeia by Poseidon. According to Diodorus Siculus, the Aloeidae were Thessalian heroes who rescued their mother and sister from Thracian pirates. They delivered them on the island of Naxos, where they settled as rulers. They were said to have founded the town of Aloium in Thessaly. They were believed to have been the first of all men who worshipped the Muses on Mount Helicon and to have consecrated this mountain to them. Some said their bones were seen in Thessaly, although most accounts have them buried in Boeotia.

Butes was a son of Boreas. He helped colonize Naxos and with his companions made predatory excursions to kidnap women. In Thessaly they carried off the women who were just celebrating the festival of Dionysus. Butes himself took Coronis; but she invoked Dionysus, who struck Butes with madness, so that he threw himself into a well (Diod. 5.50).

Autolycus was a Thessalian, son of Deimachus, who together with his brothers Deileon and Phlogius joined Heracles in his expedition against the Amazons. He got lost from the expedition and founded the town of Sinope, where he was worshipped as a god and had an oracle.

The Centaurs, according to earliest accounts, were a race of men who inhabited the mountains and forests of Thessaly. In these earliest accounts they appeared merely as gigantic, savage, or animal-like beings; in later writers they are described as monsters, whose bodies were partly human and partly those of horses. These creatures were described as the offspring of Centaurus, the son of Ixion by a cloud. Centaurus had sexual intercourse with Magnesian mares and thus produced this mixture of man and horse. Others said that they were the offspring of Ixion himself who coupled with his own mares. Still others claimed that Zeus changed himself into a horse and had intercourse with Dia, the wife of Ixion.

The Centaurs are particularly celebrated in ancient story for their fight with the Lapiths which arose at the marriage feast of Peirithous. This fight is sometimes put in connection with the combat of Heracles with the Centaurs (Apollod. 2.5.4; Diod. 4.12; Eurip. *Herc. Fur.* 181). The scene of this contest is placed by some in Thessaly. It ended with the Centaurs being expelled from their country and taking refuge on Mount Pindus on the frontiers of Epeirus. Cheiron is the most celebrated of the Centaurs. Lapithes was a son of Apollo and Stilbe and father of Phorbas, Triopas, and Periphas. He was regarded as the ancestor of the Lapiths in the mountains of Thessaly. They were governed by Peirithous, who, being a son of Ixion, was a half brother to the Centaurs. The latter, therefore, demanded their share in their father's kingdom, and, as their claims were not satisfied, a war arose between the Lapiths and Centaurs, which, however, was terminated by a peace. But when Peirithous married Hippodameia and invited the Centaurs to the solemnities, a bloody war stirred by Ares broke out between the two groups. The Centauri were defeated.

Phorbas was a son of Lapithes and Orsinome and a brother of Periphas and Triopas. The Rhodians, in pursuance of an oracle, are said to have invited him to their island to deliver it from snakes, and afterward to have honored him with heroic worship. From this circumstance he was called Ophiuchus and is said to have been placed among the stars. According to another tradition, Phorbas went from Thessaly to Olenus, where Alector, king of Elis, made use of his assistance against Pelops and shared his kingdom with him.

Myrmidon was a son of Zeus and Eurymedusa, whom Zeus deceived in the disguise of an ant (*Myrmex*). Her son was for this reason called Myrmidon and was regarded as the ancestor of the Myrmidons in Thessaly. He was married to Peisidice, by whom he became the father of Antiphus and Actor. Another version of the story is that when Zeus made his son Aeacus king of Thessaly there were no inhabitants, so he metamorphosed all the ants of the country into men, who were thence called Myrmidons.

In Thessaly, Pelasgus was described as the father of Chlorus and as the grandfather of Haemon, or as the father of Haemon and as the grandfather of Thessalus, or again as a son of Poseidon and Larissa and as the founder of the Thessalian Argos (Dionys. 1.17). Finally, there was a tradition that in Thessaly Medea entered into a contest with Thetis about her beauty, which was decided by Idomeneus in favor of Thetis.

THESTIA   was a town in Aetolia and was mentioned only by Polybius (5.7.7). The site is unknown, but Polybius said that it was situated in the north part of the upper plain of Aetolia. The name is perhaps connected with Thestius, one of the old Aetolian heroes. He was a son of Ares and father of Leda, Althaea, and Hypermnestra, as well as several sons.

THESTIUS was another name by which the ACHELOUS River was called.

THETIDIUM was a place in Thessaly close to Pharsalis. It derived its name from Thetis, the mother of Achilles, the national hero of the Achaean Phthiotae.

THISBE (THISVI) was a town of Boeotia situated at a short distance from the sea, under the south side of Mount Helicon, bordered by the territories of Thespiae and Coroneia (Strab. 9.2.28). Thisbe, for whom the town was named, was a Boeotian nymph (Paus. 9.32.3). Thisbe was mentioned by Homer (*Il.* 2.502), who says that it abounded in wild pigeons. The only public building at Thisbe mentioned by Pausanias (9.32.3) was a temple of Heracles, to whom a festival was celebrated. The modern village of Thisvi lies in a little hollow surrounded on all sides by low cliffs. The walls of Thisbe were about 1.5 km in circumference. The port of Thisbe is now called Vathi. The shore is very rocky and abounds in wild pigeons.

THOAS was another name by which the ACHELOUS River was called.

THOCNIA (THOKNIA) was a town of Arcadia in the district of Parrhasia, situated on a bluff above the Amnius River, which flows into the Helisson, a tributary of the Alpheius. The town was said to have been founded by Thocnus, the son of Lycaon. It was deserted in the time of Pausanias (8.29.5), as its inhabitants had been moved to Megalopolis. It has been placed at modern Thoknia (formerly Vromosella).

THORICUS (THORIKO) a town of Attica on the southeast coast and about 10 km north of the promontory of Sunium, was originally one of the twelve cities into which Attica is said to have been divided before the time of Theseus and was afterward a deme belonging to the tribe Acamantis. Thoricus is celebrated in mythology as the home of Cephalus, whom Eos carried off to dwell with the gods because of his extraordinary beauty.

The fortifications of Thoricus surrounded a small plain, which stopped at the harbor of the city. The acropolis seems to have stood upon a hill, on the north side of which are the ruins of a theater. In the plain, to the west, are the remains of a quadrangular colonnade with Doric columns. The modern name of the town is Thoriko.

THORNAX was a mountain near the city of Hermione in Argolis. Between it and Mount Pron the road ran from Hermione to Halice. It was subsequently called Coccygium because Zeus was said to have here transformed himself into a cuckoo to gain access to Hera. On its summit was a temple of Zeus Coccygius (Paus. 2.36.1,2). Several places in Greece claimed the honor of having been the scene of Hera's marriage to Zeus, including Mount Thornax (Paus. 2.17.4,36.2).

THORNAX was a town in Laconia on the road from Sparta to Sellasia, upon which stood a colossal statue of Apollo Pythaeus (Herod. 1.69; Paus. 3.10.8). This statue was similar to the one at Amyclae. The Spartans sought to buy gold from Sardis to embellish the statue, but Croesus gave it as an offering to the god. The gold was used for the Amyclaean statue instead of the one at Thornax because the one at Amyclae had more status. Thornax lay somewhere west of the Eurotas and south of Sellasia. The shrine has not been found.

THRACE (THRAKI) the modern political division of Greece, is a relatively medium-sized area, bounded on the north by the Rodopi mountain range, on the west by the Nestos River, on the east by the Evros River, and on the south by the Aegean. But ancient Thrace was of far greater extent, having no definite boundaries but regarded as comprising all that part of Europe lying on the north of Greece. According to legend, Oceanus had four daughters, Asia, Libya, Europa, and Thracia. It appears that Thrace was elevated to the rank of one of the four quarters of the known—or rather unknown—world. But as the Greeks expanded their geographical knowledge, the designation Thrace became more and more restricted in its application.

This region was terra incognita among ancient—and even fairly modern—writers, except for the few Grecian colonies on the coast. The loftiest peaks belonged to Rhodope, and the rivers were the Nestus; the Travus, which falls into Lake Bistonis; the Schoenus; and the Hebrus, the principal river of Thrace. All these empty into the Aegean. Thrace produced wine and grain and various culinary and medicinal herbs. Several varieties of ivy grew in the country and were sacred to Dionysus. Among the animals of Thrace, white horses were repeatedly mentioned. The famous steeds of Rhesus were "whiter than snow" (Hom. *Il.* 10.437; Eurip. *Rhes.* 304). Homer (*Il.* 14.227) called the Thracians Hippopoli (Busied with Horses), and cavalry always formed a large part of their armies. One of the twelve labors of Heracles was to bring to Mycenae the savage mares of Diomedes, king of the Bistones, in Thrace. Diomedes, a son of Ares and Cyrene, fed his mares with human flesh. Heracles took companions with him on this eighth labor, including his lover Abderus. When they seized the animals in a surprise attack, they were followed to the coast by the Bistones. Heracles left Abderus to watch the mares while he engaged the Bistones, and Abderus was eaten by them. Heracles defeated the Bistones, fed Diomedes to the mares, built the town of Abdera, and returned to Mycenae with the then tame mares (Apollod. 2.5.8; Diod. 4.15).

The valleys of Thrace were well adapted for oxen, and the hills for sheep. Swine and asses were raised, and fishing was pursued. The principal mineral productions of Thrace were gold and silver, most of which came from the mountainous district between the Strymon and the Nestus. The Thasians had gold mines near Abdera. According to Pliny (33.21.66), gold was found in the sands of the Hebrus. Cadmus was said to have been the first who worked the mines of Mount Pangaeum in Thrace.

References to the Thracians as a distinct race abound in mythology, but, on closer examination, the Thracians often turn out to be racially diffused with near relatives in lower Greece. Nevertheless, they tended to be characterized as the barbaric fringe to the northeast of the more or less civilized centers. Their manners were crude and they lived by war and plundering. The only gods they worshipped were Ares, Dionysus, and Artemis, but their kings worshipped Hermes, swore by him, and claimed descent from him. They practiced polygamy. Their music was rude and noisy. Their worship of Dionysus and Cotytto was celebrated on mountain tops with loud music, shouting, and noises like the bellowing of cattle (Strab. 10.3.16).

The deity most worshipped by the Thracians was Dionysus, whom they, as well as the Phrygians, called Sabazius. The mythical stories respecting Orpheus and Lycurgus are closely related with the worship of this god, who had an oracle on Rhodope. Herodotus (7.111) states that the mode of delivering the answers of this oracle resembled that which prevailed at Delphi. A Mount Nysa, from which the god was believed to have derived his name, was not only in Thrace and Libya, but mountains of the same name were also found in different parts of the ancient world where he was worshipped and where he was believed to have introduced the cultivation of the vine. On his passage through Thrace in his wanderings to spread this cultivation, he was brutally treated by Lycurgus, the king of the Edones, and leapt into the sea to seek refuge with Thetis. All the host of Bacchantic women and satyrs who had accompanied him were taken prisoner by Lycurgus. The country of the Edones immediately ceased to be fertile, and Lycurgus became mad and killed his own son, whom he mistook for a vine. According to others, he cut off his own legs in the belief that he was cutting down some vines. When this was done, his madness ceased, but the country still remained barren. Dionysus declared that it would remain so till Lycurgus died. The Edones in despair took their king and put him in chains, and Dionysus had him torn to pieces by horses. The god then proceeded through Thrace with no further resistance and eventually returned to Thebes. The orgiastic worship of Dionysus seems to have been first established in Thrace and to have spread southward from

there. Dionysus Bassareus was a name of the god, which, according to the explanation of the Greeks, was derived from *bassara* or *bassaris,* the long robe that the god himself and the Maenads used to wear in Thrace. The Maenads themselves are often called Bassarae or Bassarides.

Oeagrus was a king of Thrace and father of Orpheus and Linus (Apollod. 1.3.2). Hence the sisters of Orpheus are called Oeagrides, in the sense of the Muses (Mosch. 3.37). Orpheus, whose mother was said to be the Muse Calliope, lived in Thrace during the period of the Argonauts, whom he accompanied in their expedition. Presented with the lyre by Apollo and instructed by the Muses in its use, he enchanted with its music not only the wild beasts but the trees and rocks upon Olympus, so that they moved from their places to follow the sound of his lyre. He rendered the Argonauts many services with his music. After his return from the expedition, he took up his abode in a cave in Thrace and employed himself in the civilization of its wild inhabitants. He lost his wife Eurydice by a snake bite, followed her to Hades, and won her back by the power of his lyre; but he lost her again by violating the condition of not looking back at his restored wife till they reached the upper world. His grief for Eurydice led him to treat with contempt the Thracian women, who in revenge tore him to pieces under the excitement of their Bacchanalian orgies. The astronomers taught that the lyre of Orpheus was placed by Zeus among the stars, at the intercession of Apollo and the Muses.

Worship in Thrace was not, however, confined to Dionysus. Artemis was worshipped here but under her Thracian identity with Bendis or Cotytto. Some of the ceremonies had something in common with the worship of Artemis on Delos (Herod. 4.33). The festival of Cotytto, called the Cotyttia, also resembled that of the Phrygian Cybele and was celebrated on hills with riotous proceedings. Dogs were sacrificed to Artemis in Thrace.

Rhea became known to the Thracians, with whom she became a divinity of far greater importance than she had been before in Crete. She was also connected with the Thracian goddess Bendis or Cotys (Hecate) and identified with Demeter. The Thracians conceived the chief divinity of the Samothracian and Lemnian mysteries as Rhea-Hecate.

Aeolus, son of Hippotes or Poseidon and Arne, was ruler of the winds. Some accounts place his residence in Thrace. One remembers the connection of the winds with the Trojan War. When the funeral pyre of Patroclus could not be made to burn, Achilles promised to offer sacrifices to the winds, and Iris, hastening to them, found them feasting in the palace of Zephyrus in Thrace. Boreas and Zephyrus at the invitation of Iris hurried across the Thracian sea into Asia to cause the fire to blaze (Hom. *Il.* 23.185). Zephyrus, the west wind, was a son of Astraeus and Eos. Zephyrus and Boreas are frequently mentioned together and both dwelt in a palace in Thrace. Zephyrus was married to Chloris, whom he had carried off by force, and by whom he had a son Carpus. By the Harpy Podarge he fathered the horses Xanthus and Balius, which belonged to Achilles.

Aristaeus was the ancient god of agriculture and beneficence. Finally, after moving about to many places, he went to Thrace, where he became initiated in the mysteries of Dionysus, and after having dwelled for some time near Mount Haemus, where he founded the town of Aristaeon, he disappeared.

The warlike character of the tribes of Thrace led to the belief that Ares' residence was in that country, and here and in Scythia were the principal seats of his worship. His worship in the countries north of Greece seem to indicate that his worship was introduced into Greece from Thrace.

The first connection of the Greeks with Thrace was mainly through commercial colonies planted upon its various coasts. The foundation of the town of Aristaeon by Aristaeus has already been mentioned. Cleitus, the king of the Sithones in Thrace, had come from Egypt. Proteus, according to some traditions, was a son of Poseidon and king of Egypt. He went to Thrace and there married Torone, the daughter of Cleitus. But as his sons by her used great violence toward strangers, he prayed to his father Poseidon to carry him back to Egypt. Poseidon accordingly opened a chasm in the earth in Pallene, and by means of a passage through the earth under the sea Proetus returned to Egypt. Penthilus, a son of Orestes and Erigone, is said to have led a colony of Aeolians to Thrace. He was the father of Echelas and Damasias (Paus. 3.2.1, 5.4.3).

Colonies were settled from Thrace as well. Butes, son of Boreas, a Thracian, was hostile toward his stepbrother Lycurgus and was therefore compelled by his father to emigrate. Butes and other Thracians colonized Strongyle (Naxos), carrying off women from Thessaly for purposes of propagating the colony. In later accounts, the Cyclopes were regarded as skillful architects and appear much different from the one-eyed shepherds of the Homeric poems or the blacksmith assistants to Hephaestus. They are described as a Thracian tribe that derived its name from a king Cyclops. They were expelled from their homes in Thrace and went to Crete and to Lycia. From there they followed Proetus to protect him by the gigantic walls that they constructed against Acrisius. The grand fortifications of Argos, Tiryns, and Mycenae were in later times regarded as their work (Apollod. 2.1.2; Strab. 8.6.11; Paus. 2.16.6).

Eumolpus (Good Singer) was a Thracian who is described as having come to Attica either as a bard, a warrior, or a priest of Demeter and Dionysus. He was said

to be the son of Poseidon and Chione, the daughter of Boreas. He was exposed at birth in a chest on the sea and it was carried by the sea to Ethiopia, where Eumolpus grew up. After marrying, he tried to seduce his wife's sister, and so he was expelled with his son Ismarus. They went to the Thracian king Tegyrius. Eumolpus was obliged to take flight again when he displeased Tegyrius. He went to Eleusis and formed a friendship with the Eleusinians. Tegyrius persuaded him to return to Thrace and gave him his kingdom, but eventually the Eleusinians, who were at war with Athens, asked him to return to them. He did return with a numerous band of Thracians, but he was slain by Erechtheus. Mythology regards him as the founder of the Eleusinian mysteries and the first priest of Demeter and Dionysus. He was also sometimes described as the inventor of the cultivation of the vine and of fruit trees in general.

Inevitably, Heracles was connected with Thrace. He has already been mentioned in conjunction with his eighth labor of fetching the flesh-eating mares of Diomedes. During his ninth labor, the fetching of Hippolyte's girdle, he rescued Hesione, the Trojan princess, from a sea monster, but Laomedon refused to compensate him as promised. Heracles threatened war on Troy and landed in Thrace, where he slew Sarpedon, a son of Poseidon and a brother of Poltys in Thrace (Apollod. 2.5.9). During his tenth labor, the fetching of the oxen of Geryones, he drove the cattle across Thrace, where Hera made them go mad and Heracles had to pursue them a great distance.

It might be expected that Thrace was involved with the Trojan War. Acamas, a son of Eussorus, was one of the leaders of the Thracians in the war and was slain by the Telamonian Ajax (Hom. *Il.* 2.844, 5.462). Antenor, the wisest among the elders at Troy, aided the Greeks toward the end of the war and was spared by them at the sack of the city. According to some, after the fall of Troy, he went with the Heneti to Thrace and then to the west coast of the Adriatic where the foundation of several towns was ascribed to him. Demophon, the son of Theseus and Phaedra, went with the Greeks to Troy, where he liberated his grandmother Aethra. On his return from Troy, Phyllis, the daughter of the Thracian king Sithon, fell in love with him and he consented to marry her. But before the nuptials were celebrated, he went to Attica to settle his affairs and deliver Aethra, and as he tarried longer than Phyllis had expected, she thought he had forsaken her and killed herself. She was, however, metamorphosed into a tree, and Demophon, when he at last returned and saw what had happened, embraced the tree and pressed it to his bosom, whereupon buds and leaves immediately came forth (Ov. *Ars Am.* 3.38). Some accounts replace Demophon with his brother Acamas. Peiroos was a son of Imbrasus of Aenus and the commander of the Thracians who were allied with Priam in the war (Hom. *Il.* 2.844, 20.484). Rhesus was a son of King Eioneus in Thrace and an ally of the Trojans. He possessed horses white as snow and swift as the wind, which were carried off by night by Odysseus and Diomedes, the latter of whom murdered Rhesus himself in his sleep (Hom. *Il.* 10.435,495).

Others connected with Thrace were the Amazons, Brangas, and Harpalyce. The Amazons were a warlike race of women who raided Thrace and many other places. Brangas was a son of the Thracian king Strymon and brother of Rhesus and Olynthus. When the last of these three brothers had been killed during a chase by a lion, Brangas buried him on the spot where he had fallen and called the town that he subsequently built there Olynthus. Harpalyce was a daughter of Harpalycus, king of the Amymnaeans in Thrace. As she lost her mother in her infancy, she was brought up by her father with the milk of cows and mares and was trained in all manly exercises. After the death of her father, whom she had once delivered from the hands of the Myrmidons, she spent her time in the forests as a robber, being so swift in running that horses were unable to overtake her. Finally, however, she was caught in a snare by shepherds, who killed her.

Sithon, a son of Poseidon and Assa, was married to the nymph Mendeis, by whom he became the father of Pallene and Rhoeteia. He was king of Thrace. Pallene, on account of her beauty, had numerous suitors, and Sithon, who promised her to the one who should conquer him in single combat, slew many. At length he allowed Dryas and Cleitus to fight for her, promising to give her to the conqueror. Pallene, who loved Cleitus, caused her own instructor Perysyntes to induce the charioteer of Dryas to draw out the nails from the wheels of his master's chariot so that during the fight he broke down with his chariot and was killed by Cleitus. Sithon, who was informed of the trick, erected a funeral pyre on which he intended to burn the corpse of Dryas and his own daughter; but when the pyre was ready, Aphrodite appeared, a shower of rain extinguished the fire, and Sithon changed his mind and gave his daughter to Cleitus. The other daughter, Rhoeteia, had named for her the Trojan promontory of Rhoeteium.

THRIA (ASPROPIRGOS)   was an important deme of Attica, from which part of the Eleusinian plain was called the Thriasian Plain. When Attica was invaded from the west, the Thriasian Plain was the first to suffer from the onslaught of the enemy. Thria is placed adjacent to Aspropirgos, which is 2 km north of the Athens-Corinth portion of the National Highway. A temple of Aphrodite Phila is said to have been in Thria (Athen. 6.255). The Thriasian plain extends about 15 km along the Eleusinian Gulf and is usually identified with the Rharian Plain, supposedly the first field to bear crops after Demeter

recovered Persephone. It is now one of the most highly industrialized areas of Greece.

THRONIUM (KENOURGI)   was the chief town of the Locri Epicnemidii, situated 3.5 km from the coast and 5.5 km from Scarpheia on the river Boagrius. It is mentioned by Homer (*Il.* 2.533), who speaks of it as near the river Boagrius. It was at one time partly destroyed by an earthquake. Its site is on a hill adjacent to Kenourgi, about 5 km southeast of Skarfia.

THRYON or THRYOESSA   was a Homeric town identified with EPITALIUM.

THURIA (MIKROMANI)   was a town of Messenia, situated in the east part of the south Messenian plain upon the river Aris and about 15 km from Pharae, which was 1.5 km from the coast (Paus. 4.31.1). It was generally identified with the Homeric Antheia, though others supposed it to be Aepeia (Strab. 8.4.5). It must have been a place of considerable importance since the distant Messenian Gulf was even named Thuriatis Kolpos after it. Its site is thought to be adjacent to Mikromani, which is near the village of Thouria, about 8 km northwest of Kalamata. (See also AEPEIA and ANTHEIA.)

THYIA   a place in Phocis, where the Delphians erected an altar to the winds, derived its name from Thyia, a daughter of Cephissus or Castalius and the mother of Delphus by Apollo (Herod. 7.178).

THYMOETADAE (KERATSINI)   a deme of Attica, derived its name from Thymoetes, a king of Attica, son of Oxyntas. It possessed a port, from which Theseus secretly set sail on his expedition to Crete (Plut. *Thes.* 19). This small, circular port at the entrance to the Bay of Salamis seems to have been the same as the Phoron Limen (Thieves' Port), so called from its being frequented by smugglers. Foundations of a temple are to be seen upon a hill near the beach and additional remains at 1/2 km on the road to Athens. This temple was probably the Heracleion, which was held in common by the demes of Xypete, Peiraeus, and Phalerum. It was situated on the Attic side of the Strait of Salamis. The harbor was probably the point from which the passage boats to Salamis departed, and consequently the Heracleion became the most noted place on this part of the Attic shore. It was on the heights of Aegaleos above this temple that Xerxes watched the battle of Salamis.

THYRAEUM   a town of Arcadia in the district of Cynuria, was said to have been founded by Thyraeus, a son of Lycaon. Its site has not been located, but it was probably due north of Megalopolis.

THYREA   the chief town in Cynuria, the district on the borders of Laconia and Argolis, was situated on a bluff on the bay of the Thyreatean Sea. The territory of Thyrea was called Thyreatis. Its coastal plain included the modern town of Astros. In a war between the Lacedaemonians and Tegeatans, a truce was concluded, and during this truce the Lacedaemonian Lichas found the remains of Orestes at Tegea or Thyrea in the house of a blacksmith. He took them to Sparta, which according to an oracle could not gain the victory unless it possessed the remains of Orestes (Herod. 1.67; Paus. 8.54.4).

TILPHOSSIUM (PETRA)   was the name of a mountain of Boeotia on the south side of Lake Copais between the plains of Haliartus and Coroneia. At the foot of the hill was a small fountain of Tilphossa or Tilphussa, where the seer Teiresias is said to have died. When the Epigoni took Thebes, he advised the Thebans to flee. He himself fled with them, but on his way he drank from the fountain of Tilphossa and died (Apollod. 3.7.3; Paus. 9.33.1). His tomb was shown near the fountain. Tilphusa was the nymph of the fountain, which was sacred to Apollo (*Hymn. Hom. ad Apoll.* 247). The hill bears the form of a letter *T,* with its foot turned toward the north. It is now called Petra. The pass between Tilphossium and the lake was one of great importance in antiquity because the high road from northern Greece to Thebes passed through it. This pass was very narrow and was completely commanded by the fortress Tilphossaeum or Tilphusium, on the summit of the hill (Dem. *De Fals. Leg.* 385,387).

The Praxidicae, the daughters of Ogyges, were regarded as supernatural beings who watched over oaths and saw that they were not taken rashly or thoughtlessly. Their names were Alalcomenia, Thelxionoea, and Aulis, and they had a temple in common at the foot of Mount Tilphossium. The representations of these divinities consisted of mere heads and no parts of animals were sacrificed to them except heads (Paus. 9.33.3).

TIPHA   (See SIPHAE)

TIRYNS (TIRINTHA)   one of the most ancient cities of Greece, lay a short distance southeast of Argos, on the right of the road leading to Epidaurus (Paus. 2.25.8) and about 4 km from Nauplia. Its massive walls belong to the same era as those of Mycenae (Paus. 2.16.5). Homer (*Il.* 2.559) calls it "walled Tiryns." The Cyclopes were described as a Thracian tribe, deriving their name from King Cyclops. They were expelled from their homes in Thrace, and some of them went to Lycia. From there they followed Proetus back to Argos to protect him from Acrisius by the gigantic walls that they constructed. The massive fortifications of Argos, Tiryns, and Mycenae were regarded as their works. The wall at Tiryns is from 6 to

7.5 meters in thickness, and it has two entrances, one on the east and the other on the south side.

The city was said to have derived its name from Tiryns, the son of Argus (Paus. 2.25.8), or from Tiryns, a daughter of Halus and sister of Amphitryon. Proetus was a son of Abas and twin brother to Acrisius. In the dispute between the brothers for the kingdom of Argos, Proetus was defeated and expelled. Proetus fled to Iobates in Lycia and married his daughter. Iobates restored Proetus to his kingdom by armed force. Tiryns was taken and fortified by the Cyclopes, and Acrisius then shared his kingdom with his brother, surrendering to him the territory of Tiryntha, i.e., the Heraion, Midea, and the coast of Argolis (Paus. 2.16.2). Proetus was the father of three daughters, Lysippe, Iphinoe, and Iphianassa. When these daughters came to maturity, they were stricken with madness, probably for resisting the worship of Dionysus. In this state they wandered through Peloponnesus. Melampus the seer eventually cured them but exacted two-thirds of Proetus' kingdom for himself and his brother Bias. Besides these daughters Proetus had a son, Megapenthes. When Bellerophon came to Proetus to be purified of a murder, the wife of Proetus fell in love with him, but Bellerophon rejected her advances. She charged him with trying to seduce her. Proetus sent Bellerophon to Lycia with a letter advising Iobates, his father-in-law, to kill him. Iobates sought to avoid a direct murder and sent him to kill the fearful Chimaera instead. With the help of the winged horse Pegasus, Bellerophon was able to accomplish the perilous task.

Megapenthes, the son of Proetus, ceded Tiryns to Perseus, who passed it down to his descendant Electryon. Perseus, after accidentally killing his grandfather Acrisius, had left the kingdom of Argos to Megapenthes in exchange for Tiryns. Alcmena, the daughter of Electryon, married Amphitryon, who would have succeeded to the throne had he not been expelled by Sthenelus, king of Argos. Their son Heracles afterward regained possession of Tiryns, where he lived for many years. Heracles is usually said to have been born at Thebes, but some say that Amphitryon was not expelled from Tiryns till after the birth of Heracles (Diod. 4.10). When he had killed his children by Megara, he went mad and then consulted the oracle of Delphi as to where he should settle. The Pythia first called him by the name of Heracles—for up until then his name had been Alcides or Alcaeus—and ordered him to live at Tiryns and to serve Eurystheus for twelve years, after which he should become immortal. Heracles accordingly went to Tiryns and did as he was bid by Eurystheus. Once, he killed his friend Iphitus by hurling him from the walls of Tiryns in a fit of madness. Although Tiryns was closely connected with the Heracleidae, the city remained in the hands of the old Achaian population after the return of the Heracleidae and the conquest of Peloponnesus by the Dorians.

When Pausanias (2.25.8) visited the city in the second century, he saw nothing but the remains of the walls of the citadel, and beneath them toward the sea the so-called chambers of the daughters of Proetus. No trace of the lower city appears to have been left. The citadel was named Licymna after Licymnius, son of Electryon, who was slain at Tiryns by Tlepolemus, son of Heracles (Strab. 8.6.11; Pind. *Ol.* 7.47).

Peirasus, a son of Argus, was said to have made and dedicated at Tiryns a statue of Hera made of wild pear wood. When the Argives took Tiryns, they transferred the statue to the Heraion (Paus. 2.17.5). The exiled Tirynthians settled at Halieis at the southern tip of the Argolid peninsula.

TISAEUM (TISSEO)   is a mountain 644 meters in height on the promontory of Aeantium in Magnesia in Thessaly at the entrance of the Pagasaean Gulf, on which stood a temple of Artemis.

TITANE   was a place in Sicyonia, upon the left bank of the Asopus, 11 km from Sicyon and 7.5 from Phlius. It was located on the top of a hill, which had been the home of one of the Titans. It was celebrated for a temple of Asclepius, reported to have been built by Alexanor, the son of Machaon, the son of Asclepius. In this temple the servants of the god attended to patients who came there for the recovery of their health. Within the temple stood statues of Asclepius and Hygieia and of the heroes Alexanor and Euamerion. Alexanor was himself worshipped there, and sacrifices were offered to him only after sunset. Telesphorus (The Completing) is the name of a medical divinity mentioned now and then in connection with Asclepius. Pausanias (2.11.7) says that in the sanctuary of Asclepius at Titane sacrifices were offered to Euamerion, to whom a statue is there erected, and that Euamerion was called Telesphorus at Pergamum and Ausius at Epidaurus.

There was also a temple of Athena at Titane, situated upon a hill and containing an ancient wooden statue of the goddess. On the descent from the hill there was an altar of the winds, in which a priest offered sacrifices once a year (Paus. 2.12.2). Proetus, son of Abas and brother of Acrisius, is said to have founded a sanctuary of Hera between Sicyon and Titane (Paus. 2.12.2).

The ruins are just southeast of Gonoussa. The acropolis stands on a hill and is surrounded by walls rising to 7 to 9 meters and flanked by three or four towers. On this hill stands a chapel of Agios Tryphon, containing fragments of Doric columns. Here stood the temple of Athena mentioned by Pausanias (2.12.1). The other parts of the ridge are covered with ancient founda-

tions; and upon this part of the mountain the temple of Asclepius must have stood.

TITARUS (TITAROS)   is a mountain, a part of the Cambunian range, in Thessaly. The chief tributary of the Peneius on the north is the Titaresius, which rises in Titarus and joins the main stream between Larissa and the vale of Tempe. Mopsus, the celebrated seer, was one of the Lapithae of Titarus and one of the Calydonian hunters. He is also mentioned among the combatants at the wedding of Peirithous and was a famous prophet among the Argonauts. He was represented on the chest of Cypselus. He was worshipped as an oracular hero. Mopsus Titaresius was a name derived from the river Titaresius, near which he was born (Hom. *Il.* 2.751).

TITHOREA   (See NEON)

TITTHIUM (VELANIDIA)   was the highest mountain of those surrounding the sanctuary of Asclepius at Epidaurus. It lies to the north and today is called Velanidia. Titthium, its ancient name, referred to Asclepius' having been suckled (*titthi,* nipple) by a goat when he was exposed by Coronis on this mountain. Before that the mountain was called Myrtion. Here he was fed by a goat and watched by a dog, until at last he was found by Aresthanas, a shepherd, who saw the boy surrounded by a luster like that of lightning.

TITYRUS (ONIHAS)   is a mountain in the northwest part of Crete, about 30 km northwest of Cydonia. Upon it was the sanctuary or temple called Dictynnaeum (Strab. 10.4.12). One of its ridges formed the headland also called Tityrus or Psacum (Akra Spanda).

TOMARUS or TMARUS (TOMAROS)   is a mountain in Epeirus. The temple of Dodona stood at its foot. From Tomarus the priests of Zeus Dodonaeus are said to have been called Tomuri (Strab. 7.7.11; Callim. *Hymn. in Cer.* 52). At Dodona Zeus was mainly a prophetic god, and the oak was sacred to him. He was said to have been reared there by the Dodonaean nymphs. It has been claimed that there were one hundred fountains at the foot of Mount Tomarus (Plin. 4.1.3).

TORONE (TORONI)   was a town of Chalcidice in Macedonia, situated upon the southwest coast of the peninsula of Sithonia. It was said to have derived its name from Torone, a daughter of Proteus or Poseidon and Phoenice. Others called her the wife of Proteus. Polygonus was a son of Proteus, a grandson of Poseidon and brother of Telegonus. The two brothers were killed by Heracles at Torone when they challenged him to a contest in wrestling (Apollod. 2.5.9).

Torone was a Greek colony founded by the Chalcidians of Euboea and was originally the leading settlement of the Chalcidians in this area. The gulf between the peninsulas of Sithonia and Pallene was called until recent times Kolpos Toroneos, now the Kolpos Kassandras. Its port was called Cophos (Deaf) because being separated from the sea by two narrow passages the noise of the waves was never heard there. It is still called Koufos, and Toroni likewise retains its ancient name.

TRACHIS (IRAKLIA)   was a city of Malis in the district called after it Trachinia. It was situated in a plain at the foot of Mount Oeta, a little northwest of Thermopylae. It commanded the approach to Thermopylae from Thessaly and was of great military importance. The city was 1 km from the river Melas, slightly north of the gorge of the Asopus. According to Thucydides (3.92), Trachis was forty stadia (7 km) from Thermopylae and twenty (3.5 km) from the sea. Modern Iraklia is the town nearest to the ruins of Trachis. Trachis is mentioned in Homer (*Il.* 2.682) as one of the cities subject to Achilles.

Trachis is celebrated in the legends of Heracles as the scene of his death. Heracles, after accidentally killing Eunomus at Calydon, where he had lived for three years in the house of his father–in–law, set out in voluntary exile with Deianeira. On the road they came to the river Euenus, and Nessus the Centaur, who made a practice of carrying people across for a small fee, offered to take Deianeira. After Heracles had crossed, Nessus tried to rape Deianeira, but Heracles killed him with an arrow. The dying Centaur urged Deianeira to take his blood with her as a sure means of preserving the love of her husband. From the river Euenus, Heracles now proceeded to Trachis, where he was kindly received by Ceyx, whom he helped in conquering the Dryopes. Later in Trachis he collected an army to take vengeance on Eurytus of Oechalia. In fact, he spent the last years of his life at Trachis. But on one of his trips he abducted Iole, and word got back to Deianeira, who feared that Iole would supplant her in the affection of her husband. Via Lichas, an attendant of Heracles, she sent a garment to him, which she had steeped in the blood of Nessus. Scarcely had the garment become warm on the body of Heracles than the poison in it penetrated all parts of his body. He tried to tear the garment off but it adhered. In agony he was conveyed to Trachis. Deianeira, seeing what she had done, hanged herself. Heracles commanded Hyllus, his eldest son by Deianeira, to marry Iole as soon as he reached manhood. He then ascended Mount Oeta, raised a pile of wood, ascended it, and ordered it to be set on fire. Ceyx, the lord of Trachis, had been a close friend of Heracles. He was the father of Hippasus, who fell in battle fighting as the ally of Heracles (Apollod. 2.7.6). According to others, Ceyx was a nephew of Heracles, who built for him the town of Trachis. Alcmena, the mother of Heracles, after the death of her heroic son, fled with her sons from the Argolis to Trachis because she feared Eurytheus, who still remained in power.

Some relate that Peleus, the father of Achilles, went to Ceyx at Trachis after he was exiled from Aegina; and as he had come to Thessaly without companions, he prayed to Zeus for an army, and the god metamorphosed the ants (*myrmikes*) into men, who were consequently called Myrmidons.

TRAPEZUS (MAVRIA)   was a town of Arcadia in the district of Parrhasia, a little to the south of the river Alpheius. It derived its name from its founder, Trapezus, the son of Lycaon, or from *trapeza* (table) because Zeus here overturned the table on which Lycaon offered him human food (Paus. 8.3.2,3; Apollod. 3.8.1). Lycaon was a son of Pelasgus. According to most accounts, he and his many sons were notorious for their insolence and impiety. Zeus visited them in the disguise of a poor man in order to observe for himself the extent of their evil doing. They invited him to a repast, and on the suggestion of one of them, Maenalus, they mixed into one of the dishes set before him the entrails of a boy whom they had murdered. However, Zeus pushed away the table that bore the horrible food, and the place where this happened was afterward called Trapezus. Lycaon and all his sons, with the exception of the youngest, Nyctimus, were killed by Zeus with a flash of lightning, or, according to others, were changed into wolves (Paus. 8.2.5). There was still another version of the story. Arcas was the ancestor and eponymous hero of the Arcadians, from whom the country and its inhabitants derived their name. According to some, Arcas was a son of Lycaon, whose flesh the father set before Zeus to try his divine character. Zeus upset the table, as described, and destroyed the house of Lycaon by lightning, but restored Arcas to life. When Arcas had grown up, he built on the site of his father's house the town of Trapezus.

It was Hippothous who transferred the seat of government from Tegea to Trapezus. He was a son of Cercyon and father of Aepytus and succeeded Agapenor as king in Arcadia (Paus. 8.5.4; Ov. *Met.* 8.307). When Megalopolis was founded in 371 B.C., the inhabitants of Trapezus refused to remove to the new city; and having thus incurred the wrath of the other Arcadians, they left Peloponnesus and took refuge in Trapezus on the Black Sea, where they were received as a kindred people. The statues of some of their gods were removed to Megalopolis, where they were seen by Pausanias (8.30.4–32.5). Trapezus stood above the modern Mavria.

TRETOS (TRETOS)   is a mountain west of the main highway between Argos and Corinth. The name means "perforated," applied both to the split summit, which the pass Dervenakia crosses, and to the large number of caves in the mountain. This was the area inhabited by the Nemean lion, which was slain by Heracles during his first labor.

TRICCA (TRIKALA)   an ancient city of Thessaly in the district Histiaeotis, stood on the north bank of the Peneius River. This city is said to have derived its name from Tricca, a daughter of Peneius. It is mentioned in Homer (*Il.* 2.729) as subject to Podaleirius and Machaon, the two sons of Asclepius. They led the Thessalians of Tricca against Troy. They both were skilled in the medical art. Podaleirius, on his return from Troy, was cast by a storm on the coast of Syros in Caria, where he settled (Paus. 3.26.11). Asclepius, according to some traditions, was born at Tricca (Strab. 14.1.39) where he had a temple. This temple was regarded as the oldest and most venerable of all the temples of the god (Strab. 9.5.17). It was visited by the sick, whose cures were recorded there, as in the temples of Asclepius at Epidaurus and Cos (Strab. 8.6.15). There were probably physicians attached to the temple.

Trikala is now one of the largest towns in this part of Greece. A castle occupies a hill projecting from the last ridge of the Antihasia Mountains, but there are few traces of the ancient city. Remains of what appears to be an Asclepieion have been partially excavated.

TRICOLONI (TRILOFO?)   was a town north of Megalopolis on the road to Methydrium. It was in ruins at the time of Pausanias (8.35.6). Tricoloni, which was founded by Tricolonus, a son of Lycaon, still possessed a temple of Poseidon, standing upon a hill in a grove of trees. We may place Tricoloni near the modern Trilofo on the edge of the plain of Megalopolis, but so far no evidence of an ancient town has been uncovered.

TRINACRIA   was an earlier name of the island of RHODES.

TRIPHYLIA   was the name of the smallest of the three divisions of Elis. It was founded by Triphylus, a son of Arcas (Polyb. 4.77; Paus. 10.9.3). It has very little level land since the Arcadian Mountains here reach almost to the sea. Along nearly all of the Triphylian coast there is a series of lagoons. At a later time, the Alpheius was the north boundary of Triphylia; but at an earlier period the territory of Pisatis must have extended south of the Alpheius, though all its chief towns lay to the north of the river. The mountain along the south side of the Alpheius immediately opposite Olympia was originally called Ossa but was afterward called Phellon (Strab. 8.3.14,31). Further south are two ranges of mountains, between which the river Anigrus flows into the sea. Of these the more northerly is called Lapithas, as in ancient times, and the more southerly, Minthi, also as in ancient times.

Minthi, which is the loftiest mountain in Elis (1,222 meters), was one of the seats of the worship of Hades; and the herb from which it derived its name, was sacred to Persephone. The river Neda divided Triphylia from Messenia.

TRIPODISCUS   was an ancient town of Megaris. Tripodi allegedly was mentioned by Homer, along with Aegeirussa and Nisaea, as part of the dominions of Telamonian Ajax of Salamis. The verse containing these names was omitted by the Athenians, who substituted for it another to prove that Salamis, in the time of the Trojan War, belonged to Athens (Strab. 9.1.10). Tripodiscus lay at the foot of Gerancia on the road from Delphi to Argos. Pausanias (1.43.8) relates that it derived its name from a tripod, which Coroebus the Argive brought from Delphi, with the injunction that wherever the tripod fell to the ground, he was to settle there and build a temple to Apollo. Remains of an ancient town have been noted at the foot of Mount Geraneia on the road from Plataea to the Isthmus, 7 or 8 km to the north of Megara.

Linus, the personification of a dirge or lamentation, was described as a son of Apollo and Psamathe. When Psamathe gave birth to Linus, she exposed the child out of fear of her father Crotopus. The child was found and brought up by shepherds but was later torn to pieces by dogs. Psamathe's grief revealed to her father the nature of the situation, and he condemned her to death. Apollo consequently brought a plague on Argos that did not cease until Crotopus quitted Argos and settled at Tripodiscus (Paus. 1.43.7).

TRITAEA (KATO VLASSIA)   a town in Achaia and the most inland of the twelve Achaian cities, was 22 km from Pharae. Its site is probably represented by the remains at Kato Vlassia on the Selinus River near the border of Arcadia. Tritaea was the daughter of Triton and a priestess of Athena, by whom Ares became the father of Melanippus, who gave to a town in Achaia the name of his mother (Paus. 7.22.5). Sacrifices were offered there to Ares and Tritaea in the temple of Athena (Paus. 7.22.6).

TRITON   was a river in Boeotia flowing by Alalcomenae into Lake Copais. It was from this stream that Athena derived the surname of Tritogeneia. Athena was said to have been educated with Pallas by the marine god Triton, Pallas' father. The connection of Athena and Triton afterward caused various traditions about her birthplace, so that wherever there was a river or fountain of that name (as in Crete, Thessaly, Boeotia, Arcadia, and Egypt) the inhabitants of those places asserted that Athena was born there. The most ancient seat of her worship in Greece was the banks of this river in Boeotia. On its banks were two ancient Pelasgian towns, Athenae and Eleusis, which were, according to tradition, swallowed up by the lake. From here her worship was carried by the Minyans into Attica, Libya, and other countries. The two towns of Athenae and Eleusis were said by some to have been founded by Cecrops, the first king of Attica, who was described as an autochthon and as having an upper body of a human and the lower body of a serpent.

TRITTA was a name sometimes applied to early CNOSSUS.

TROEZEN (TRIZINA) was a city of Peloponnesus, whose térritory formed the southeast corner of Argolis. It was situated about 2.5 km from the coast in a fertile plain. Few cities of Peloponnesus were as old, and many of the legends of Troezen are closely connected with those of Athens. This fact suggests that its original population was of the Ionic race. According to the Troezenians themselves, their country was first called Oraea from the Egyptian Orus, who migrated there, and was next named Althepia from Althepus, the son of Poseidon and Leis, who was the daughter of Orus. In the reign of this king, Poseidon and Athena contended, as at Athens, for the land of the Troezenians, but, through the mediation of Zeus, they became the joint guardians of the country (Paus. 2.30.6). Because of this, says Pausanias (2.30.6), a trident and the head of Athena are represented on the ancient coins of Troezen. Althepus was succeeded by Saron, who built a temple of Artemis Saronia in a marshy place near the sea, which was therefore called the Phoebaean Marsh. The annual festival of Artemis was called Saronia (Paus. 2.30.7,32.9). Once while chasing a stag into the sea, Saron was drowned; his body, which was washed onto the shore in the grove of Artemis, was buried there, and the gulf between Attica and Argolis was, from this circumstance, called the Saronic Gulf. The Phoebaean Marsh was also renamed Saronis because Saron was buried in the ground belonging to the temple. Near Troezen there was a little town called Saron, and Troezen itself is said at one time to have been called Saronia. Besides the ancient names of Troezen already pointed out, one can also mention Aphrodisias, Apollonias, Anthanis, and Poseidonias.

The next kings after Saron are Hyperes and Anthas, who founded two cities named Hypereia and Antheia. Hyperes was a son of Poseidon and Alcyone. The island of Calaureia off the coast of Troezen was likewise believed to have received the name Hypereia from him (Plut. *Quaest. Gr.* 19). Anthas was his brother. Besides Antheia, he also is said to have founded Anthedon. Aetius, the son of Hyperes, inherited the kingdom of his father and uncle and called one of the cities Poseidonias. In his reign, Troezen and Pittheus, sons of Pelops by Dia, settled in the country and divided the power with Aetius. But the Pelopidae soon supplanted the earlier dynasty, and, on

the death of Troezen, Pittheus united the two Ionic settlements into one city, which he called Troezen after his brother. The close connection between Attica and Troezen, already referred to, is also intimated by the legend that two important demes of Attica, Anaphlystus and Sphettus, derived their names from two sons of King Troezen (Paus. 2.30.8).

Pittheus was father of Aethra and grandfather and instructor of Theseus. When Theseus married Phaedra, Pittheus took Hippolytus into his house (Paus. 1.22.2). His tomb and the chair on which he had sat in judgment were shown at Troezen for many years (Paus. 2.31.3). He is said to have taught the art of speaking and even to have written a book upon it (Paus. 2.31.4). Aethra, his daughter, is called Pittheis (Ov. *Her.* 10.31). Aethra was once directed in a dream by Athena to go to the island of Sphaeria with libations for Sphaerus. While she was there, she was forced into intercourse with Poseidon. For this reason, Aethra dedicated on the island a temple to Athena Apaturia (Deceitful) and called the island Hiera (Sacred) instead of Sphaeria. She also introduced among the young women of Troezen the custom of dedicating their girdles to Athena Apaturia on the day of their marriage (Paus. 2.33.1). At a later time Aethra became the mother of Theseus by Aegeus. In the night in which this took place, Poseidon also was believed to have had intercourse with her. According to Plutarch (*Thes.* 6), her father spread this report so that Theseus might be regarded as the son of Poseidon, who was much revered at Troezen. Later on she lived in Attica and was carried to Lacedaemon by the Dioscuri, where she became a slave of Helen, with whom she was taken to Troy.

According to the common tradition, Theseus was the son of Aegeus, king of Athens, and Aethra. When he reached maturity, Theseus, by his mother's directions, took the sword and sandals, the tokens that had been left beneath a large stone by Aegeus as proof of his paternity, and proceeded to Athens. Eager to emulate Heracles, he went by land, displaying his strength and courage by destroying the robbers and monsters that infested the country. By means of the sword that he carried, Theseus was recognized by Aegeus, acknowledged as his son, and declared his successor. After his Cretan expedition, his slaying of the Minotaur, his marriage to and abandoning of Ariadne, and his inadvertent contribution to the suicide of his father, Theseus became king of Athens. He was said also to have carried off Anaxo, a woman of Troezen, whose sons he slew and whose daughters he raped (Plut. *Thes.* 29). One of his greatest adventures was his invasion of the land of the Amazons and carrying off of their queen, Antiope. Subsequently Amazons made war on Attica. By Antiope Theseus had a son named Hippolytus. After the death of Antiope, Theseus married Phaedra. When Theseus was about to marry Phaedra, he sent his son to Pittheus to be brought up and to be the future king of Troezen. He did this because he wished that neither Hippolytus nor future children by Phaedra would rule the other. Afterward Pallas and his sons rebelled against Theseus. After putting them to death he went to Troezen for purification, and Phaedra first saw Hippolytus there. Falling in love with him, she became the instrument for his death. The Troezenians had a myrtle with pierced leaves. They said it did not grow originally in this fashion but that the holes had been made by Phaedra with a hairpin because of her frustration over her unrequited love of her stepson.

Alcaeus, a son of Perseus and husband of Hipponome, was the father of Amphitryon and Anaxo and king at Troezen, probably next after Pittheus. At the time of the Trojan War, Troezen was subject to Argos (Hom. *Il.* 2.561). The Dorian settlers, who came from Argos after the conquest, appear to have been received on friendly terms by the ancient inhabitants. Even though Troezen became a Doric city, it still retained its Ionic sympathies and traditions. At an early period Troezen was a powerful maritime state, and it founded the cities of Halicarnassus and Myndus in Caria (Paus. 2.30.8; Herod. 7.99). The Troezenians may also have been the chief founders of Poseidonia (Paestum), which has been called a Doric colony.

Troezen was a place of importance in the time of Strabo (8.6.14), and during Pausanias' time it continued to possess a large number of public buildings. Pausanias (2.31.1–32.10) divided these into three classes: those in the agora and its vicinity, those in the sacred enclosure of Hippolytus, and those upon the acropolis. In the center of the agora, surrounded with colonnades, was a temple of Artemis Soteira (Saving Goddess), said to have been dedicated by Theseus. It contained altars of the infernal gods. Behind the temple stood the monument of Pittheus, the founder of the city, surmounted by three chairs of white marble, upon which he and two advisors administered justice. Not far from there was the temple of the Muses, founded by Ardalus, a son of Hephaestus. Ardalus is said to have invented the flute and to have built the temple of the Muses, who derived from him the surname Ardalides or Ardaliotides (Paus. 2.31.3). In this temple, Pittheus himself was said to have learned the art of discourse. Before the temple was an altar where sacrifices were offered to the Muses and to Sleep, the deity whom the Troezenians considered the most friendly to these goddesses.

Near the theater was the temple of Artemis Lyceia, founded by Hippolytus. In front of the temple there was the stone upon which Orestes was purified by nine Troezenians. The so-called tent of Orestes, in which he took refuge before his expiation, stood in front of the temple of Apollo Thearius, which was the most ancient temple that Pausanias knew. The water used in the purification of Orestes was drawn from the sacred fountain Hippocrene by the hoof of Pegasus. In the vicinity was a statue of Hermes Polygius, with a wild olive tree and a temple of Zeus Soter.

The sacred enclosure of Hippolytus was the most prominent sight in the city and took up considerable space. The Troezenians refused to accept the story of his being dragged to death by his horses, but his grave was shown at Troezen. They worshipped him as the constellation Auriga and dedicated to him this spacious sanctuary, which was founded by Diomedes. This hero of the Trojan War also instituted the Pythian games there. He himself was subsequently worshipped as a divine being. Hippolytus was worshipped with the greatest honors, and each virgin before her marriage dedicated a lock of her hair to him (Eurip. *Hippol.* 1424; Paus. 2.32.1). Besides the temple of Hippolytus, the sacred enclosure included a temple of Apollo Epibaterius, also dedicated by Diomedes. On one side of the enclosure was the stadium of Hippolytus, and above it the temple of Aphrodite Catascopia, so called because Phaedra beheld from this spot Hippolytus as he exercised naked in the stadium. In the neighborhood was shown the tomb of Phaedra, the monument of Hippolytus, and the house of the hero, with the fountain called the Herculean in front of it.

On the acropolis was the temple of Athena Polias or Sthenias; and on the slope of the mountain was a sanctuary of Pan Lyterius, so called because he put a stop to a plague. Lower down was the temple of Isis, built by the Halicarnassians, and also one of Aphrodite Acraea.

The ruins of Troezen are adjacent to the village of Trizina. They consist only of pieces of wall of Hellenic masonry or of Roman brickwork, dispersed over the lower slopes of the height, upon which stood the acropolis, and over the plain at its foot. The acropolis occupied a rugged and lofty hill, commanding the plain below and presenting one of the most extensive and striking prospects in Greece. There are in the plain several ruined churches, which probably mark the site of ancient temples. Some have thought to identify a temple overlooking the cavity formerly occupied by the stadium as remains of the temple of Aphrodite Catascopia. The acropolis and lower city have been excavated. On the acropolis are remains of a small temple dedicated possibly to Aphrodite Acraea. The temple of Hippolytus, along with his gymnasium and stadium, have been discovered. Near the temple was an Asclepieion.

The territory of Troezen was bounded on the west by that of Epidaurus, on the southwest by that of Hermione, and was surrounded on every other side by the sea. The fertile plain in which Troezen stood was bounded on the south by a range of mountains, which ended in the promontories Scyllaeum and Bucephala, the most easterly points of Peloponnesus. Above the promontory Scyllaeum and nearly due east of Troezen was a large bay named Pogon. The port town, which was named Celenderis (Paus. 2.32.8), appears to have stood at the west end of the bay of Pogon since ancient remains have been found here.

Among the other beings worshipped at Troezen we find both gods and heroic individuals. We might expect to find Dionysus, the god of wine. After he had established his divine nature throughout the world, he led his mother out of Hades, called her Thyone, and rose with her into Olympus. The place where he had come forth with Semele from Hades was shown by the Troezenians in the temple of Artemis Soteira (Paus. 2.31.2). The maritime importance of Troezen is perhaps hinted at in its worship of the already mentioned Apollo Epibaterius (God Who Conducts Men on Board a Ship). Helios, the sun god, was worshipped here (Paus. 2.31.8). Artemis Lyceia had a temple here said to have been built by Hippolytus (Paus. 2.31.6). The worship of Themis, the personification of the order of things, was established at Troezen, where an altar was dedicated to the Themides (Paus. 2.31.8). Demeter, surnamed Thesmia or Thesmorphoros, was celebrated with a sanctuary here (Paus. 2.32.7).

According to Troezenian legend, there came once during an insurrection at Troezen two Cretan maidens, Auxesia and Damia. During the rioting the two maidens were stoned to death, causing the Troezenians to pay divine honors to them and institute the festival of the Lithobolia (Paus. 2.32.3). Cillas was the charioteer of Pelops. His real name, according to Troezenian tradition, was Sphaerus. His tomb was shown near the town of Cilla in the neighborhood of the temple of Apollo (Paus. 5.10.7). And, last but not least, there was a connection of Troezen with Heracles. His twelfth labor was to bring the monster Cerberus from the underworld. He accomplished this and brought the monster into the upper world in the neighborhood of Troezen.

XYPETE was a deme of Attica belonging to the tribe Cecropis. It was said to have been also called Troia, because Teucrus led from there an Attic colony into Phrygia (Dionys. 1.61; Strab. 13.1.48). It has been located northeast of Peiraeus. Xypete, Peiraeus, Phalerum, and Thymoetadae formed a tetrapolis, with a temple of Heracles in common.

ZACYNTHUS (ZAKINTHOS) is an island lying off the coast of Peloponnesus, opposite the promontory Chelonatas in Elis and 11 km to the south of the island of Cephallenia. The island is said to have been originally called Hyrie and to have been colonized by Zacynthus, the son of Dardanus, from Psophis in Arcadia. The acropolis of the city of Zacynthus was thus named Psophis (Paus. 8.24.3). The Zacynthians were a colony of Achaians

from Peloponnesus (Thuc. 2.66). In Homer (*Il.* 2.634), who gives the island the epithet of "woody," Zacynthus forms part of the dominions of Odysseus. When the Greeks assembled in the port of Aulis, Odysseus joined them with twelve ships and men from Cephallenia, Ithaca, Neriton, Crocyleia, Zacynthus, Same, and the coast of Epeirus (*Il.* 2.303,631). Later, Aeneas on his wanderings after Troy founded a temple of Aphrodite here.

The leading town of the island, also named Zacynthus, was located on the east shore. Its site is occupied by the modern capital Zante, but nothing remains of the ancient city except a few columns and inscriptions. The situation of the town upon the margin of a semicircular bay is very picturesque. The citadel probably occupied the site of the modern castle.

ZACYNTHUS was an earlier name of the island of PAROS.

ZARAX (LIMENAS GERAKAS) was a town with a good harbor on a promontory on the east coast of Laconia. Zarax was a hero who was believed to have been instructed in music by Apollo and had a shrine near Eleusis. Pausanias (1.38.4) takes him to be a Laconian hero and the founder of the town of Zarax. He has also been called a son of Carystus or Carycus, as a grandson of Cheiron, and as the father of Anius by Rhoeo. Like Prasiae and other places on this part of the Laconian coast, Zarax passed into the hands of the Argives in the time of the Macedonian supremacy. Pausanias found in it nothing to mention but a temple of Apollo next to the harbor. It is now called Limenas Gerakas, and there are still ruins of the ancient town. The promontory bears the same name, and there is a port on its north side.

ZEPHYRIA was another name of the island of MELOS.

ZERYNTHUS was a town in Thrace not far from the borders of the Aenianes. It contained a cave of Hecate, a temple of Apollo, and another of Aprhodite. Aphrodite Zerynthia's sanctuary was said to have been built by Phaedra.

ZOETIA (ZONI?) was a town on the road from Megalopolis to Methydrium. It was founded by Zoeteus, a son of Tricolonus, son of Lycaon (Paus. 8.35.6). It was in ruins at the time of Pausanias, but there still remained a temple of Demeter and Artemis. Its modern site is uncertain, but remains at Zoni have been suggested as a good possibility.

ZONE was a town on the south coast of Thrace on a promontory of the same name, a short distance to the west of the entrance of Lake Stentoris. Lake Stentoris was near the mouth of the Hebrus (Evros). According to Apollonius Rhodius (1.29), it was to this place that the woods followed Orpheus when set in motion by his wondrous music.

ZOSTER (VOULIAGMENI)   is a promontory in Attica. Mount Hymettus, which bounded the Athenian plain on the south, terminated in the promontory of Zoster, opposite which was a small island called Phaura. At Zoster, upon the sea, stood four altars, sacred respectively to Athena, Apollo, Artemis, and Leto (Paus. 1.31.1). It was here that Leto loosened her girdle at the onset of labor pains on her way to Delos. Apollo Zosterius also had a sanctuary here. The hill of Zoster terminates in three capes; that in the middle is a low peninsula, which shelters in the west a deep inlet called Vouliagmeni. The island of Phaura is now called Fleves.

Modern Place-Names
Associated with Ancient Locations

This is an alphabetical list of the modern names given in parentheses in many entries directly after the ancient name that begins each entry in the text. Modern names that may be mentioned incidentally elsewhere in the entry are not included, but if two modern names are given in parentheses in a single entry (as they are for STYX, TAPHIAE, and some others), then both appear in this list. The majority of these modern names are modified spellings of ancient ones. Some will be altogether different from the earlier names, particularly when an ancient site is located adjacent to a place that developed in modern times.

Modern transliterations are those used by the Greek National Tourist Organisation so that this list will correspond to GNTO maps and road signs. Each place in the list is also identified in parentheses by its nome, or prefecture, so that it can be more easily located and not confused with another place with an identical name. However, in order to avoid confusion, places on islands are identified by island rather than nome. Islands themselves are identified by island group, e.g., Dodekanissa, Kiklades. Crete (Kriti) is divided into four nomes, and places there are identified by both the island and the nome. In effect, each place in the list is designated by its next largest political division.

MODERN NAME	ANCIENT NAME	MODERN NAME	ANCIENT NAME
Afidnes (Attiki)	Aphidna	Agios Ioannis (Ilia)	Letrini
Afitos (Halkidiki)	Aphytis	Agios Konstantinos (Lakonia)	Sellasia
Ageranos (Lakonia)	Arainus		
Agia Evthimia (Fokis)	Myonia	Agios Nikolaos (Kriti: Lasithio)	Caeno
Agia Galini (Kriti: Rethimno)	Soulia		
		Agios Nikolaos (Messinia)	Pephnus
Agia Kiriaki (Magnisia)	Aphetae	Agios Vlasios (Viotia)	Panopeus
Agia Marina (Attiki)	Lamptra, Lower	Agrapidohori (Ilia)	Pylus
Agia Roumeli (Kriti: Hania)	Tarrha	Agrilia (Etolia-Akarnania)	Pleuron
Agii Theodori (Korinthia)	Crommyon	Ahaia (Peloponissos)	Achaia
Agios Efstratios (Nissia Anatolikou Egeou)	Neae	Aharnes (Attiki)	Acharnae
		Aheloos (Kentriki Ellas)	Achelous
Agios Georgios (Etolia-Akarnania)	Proschium	Aheron (Ipiros)	Acheron
		Aherousia (Preveza)	Acherusia
Agios Georgios (Viotia)	Coroneia	Ahinades (Ionia Nissia)	Echinades

MODERN NAME	ANCIENT NAME	MODERN NAME	ANCIENT NAME
Ahinos (Fthiotis)	Echinus	Arhees Kleones (Korinthia)	Cleonae
Akademia (Attiki)	Academia	Arhia Epidavros (Argolis)	Epidaurus
Akarnania (Kentriki Ellas)	Acarnania	Arisvi (Lesvos)	Arisba
Akra Posidi (Halkidiki)	Poseidonium	Arkadia (Peloponissos)	Arcadia
Akra Sipia (Magnisia)	Sepias	Armenio (Larissa)	Armenium
Akra Skili (Pireas)	Scyllaeum	Arta (Arta)	Ambracia
Akra Stavros (Magnisia)	Posidium	Artemisi (Argolis)	Artemisium
Akra Tenaro (Lakonia)	Taenarum	Artemissia (Messinia)	Limnae
Akrata (Ahaia)	Aegae	Artemissio (Evia)	Artemisium
Akrefnio (Viotia)	Acraephnium	Askra (Viotia)	Ascra
Akrokorínthos (Korinthia)	Acrocorinthus	Asopos (Korinthia)	Asopus
Aktio (Etolia-Akarnania)	Actium	Aspropirgos (Attiki)	Thria
Alalkomenes (Viotia)	Alalcomenae	Astakos (Etolia-Akarnania)	Astacus
Alea (Argolis)	Alea	Astipalea (Dodekanissa)	Astypalaea
Alea (Arkadia)	Tegea	Ataviros (Rodos)	Atabyris
Alfios (Peloponissos)	Alpheius	Athine? (Arkadia)	Oresthasium
Aliakmon	Haliacmon	Athina (Attiki)	Athens
(Makedonia/		Athos (Halkidiki)	Athos
Thessalia)		Atsiholos (Arkadia)	Gortys
Aliartos (Viotia)	Haliartus	Attiki (Kentriki Ellas)	Attica
Alifera (Arkadia)	Aliphera	Avdira (Xanthi)	Abdera
Aliki (Viotia)	Siphae	Avia (Messinia)	Abia
Alimos (Attiki)	Halimus	Axios (Makedonia)	Axius
Aliveri (Evia)	Tamynae	Axos (Kriti: Rethimno)	Axus
Almiros (Magnisia)	Iton	Daskalio? (Attiki)	Potamus
Alonistena? (Arkadia)	Phalanthum	Davia (Arkadia)	Maenalus
Alos (Magnisia)	Halus	Davlia (Viotia)	Daulis
Amarinthos (Evia)	Amarynthus	Dekelia (Attiki)	Deceleia
Ambelokipi (Attiki)	Alopece	Delfi (Fokis)	Delphi
Amfiklia (Fthiotis)	Amphicleia	Didima (Argolis)	Didymi
Amfipoli (Seres)	Amphipolis	Dikti (Kriti: Lasithio)	Dicte
Amfissa (Fokis)	Amphissa	Diktinaio (Kriti: Hania)	Dictamnum
Amikles (Lakonia)	Amyclae	Dilessi (Viotia)	Delium
Amnisos (Kriti: Iraklio)	Amnisus	Dilos (Kiklades)	Delos
Anafi (Kiklades)	Anaphe	Dimitra (Arkadia)	Enispe
Anavissos (Attiki)	Anaphylstus	Dimitrias (Magnisia)	Demetrias
Andikithira (Pireas)	Anticythera	Dimitrias (Magnisia)	Pagasae
Andros (Kiklades)	Andros	Dion (Pieria)	Dium
Ano Boula (Lakonia)	Hippola	Dionissos (Attiki)	Icaria
Ano Vianos (Kriti: Iraklio)	Biennus	Dirkis (Viotia)	Dirce
Anthia (Messinia)	Antheia	Distomo (Viotia)	Ambrysus
Anthili (Fthiotis)	Anthela	Dodoni (Ioanina)	Dodona
Antikira (Viotia)	Anticyra	Domokos (Fthiotis)	Thaumacia
Aptera (Kriti: Hania)	Aptera	Donoussa (Kiklades)	Donusa
Arahamites (Arkadia)	Peraetheis	Doxaras (Larissa)	Crannon
Arakinthos (Etolia-	Aracynthus	Drakoneria (Ahaia)	Styx
Akarnania)		Drimea (Fokis)	Drymaea
Argiroupoli (Kriti:	Lappa	Drossia (Viotia)	Salganeus
Rethimno)		Edessa (Pela)	Aegae
Argithea (Karditsa)	Ethopia	Efira (Ilia)	Ephyra
Argolis (Peloponissos)	Argolis	Egeo Pelagos	Aegean Sea
Argos (Argolis)	Argos	Egies (Lakonia)	Aegiae

MODERN NAME	ANCIENT NAME
Egina (Pireas)	Aegina
Egio (Ahaia)	Aegium
Egira (Ahaia)	Aegeira
Egosthena (Attiki)	Aegosthena
Elafonissi (Lakonia)	Onugnathus
Elassona (Larissa)	Oloosson
Elatia (Fthiotis)	Elateia
Elefsina (Attiki)	Eleusis
Eleftherna (Kriti: Rethimno)	Eleutherna
Elia? (Ilia)	Pyrgus
Elikonas (Viotia)	Helicon
Ellada	Hellas
Elos (Lakonia)	Helos
Enipeas (Ilia)	Enipeus
Enipeas (Thessalia)	Enipeus
Enos (Kefalonia)	Aenos
Epano Elounda (Kriti: Lasithio)	Olus
Epitali (Ilia)	Epitalium
Eretria (Evia)	Eretria
Erimanthos (Arkadia/ Ahaia)	Erymanthus
Erimanthos (Arkadia)	Erymanthus
Erimoupolis (Kriti: Lasithio)	Itanus
Erithres (Attiki)	Erythrae
Ermioni (Argolis)	Hermione
Etolia (Kentriki Ellas)	Aetolia
Evia (Kentriki Ellas)	Euboea
Evinos (Aetolia-Akarnania)	Euenus
Evripos (Evia/Viotia)	Euripus
Evros (Evros)	Hebrus
Evrotas (Lakonia)	Eurotas
Exarhos (Fthiotis)	Abae
Exarhos (Fthiotis)	Hyampolis
Falasarna (Kriti: Hania)	Phalasarna
Fanari (Karditsa)	Ithome
Fares? (Ahaia)	Pharae
Faro (Ikaria)	Dracanum
Farsala (Larissa)	Pharsalus
Feneos (Korinthia)	Pheneus
Festos (Kriti: Iraklio)	Phaestus
Fia (Ilia)	Pheia
Figalia (Arkadia)	Phigalia
Filaki (Magnisia)	Phylace
Filia (Karditsa)	Philia
Filia (Messinia)	Andania
Filiates (Thesprotia)	Cestrine
Filipi (Kavala)	Philippi
Finiki (Lakonia)	Hyperteleatum
Fokas (Korinthia)	Apesas

MODERN NAME	ANCIENT NAME
Fokis (Kentriki Ellas)	Phocis
Folegandros (Kiklades)	Pholegandros
Foloi (Ilia)	Pholoe
Frixa (Ilia)	Phrixa
Fthiotis (Kentriki Ellas)	Phthiotis
Galikos (Makedonia)	Echidorus
Geraki (Lakonia)	Geronthrae
Gerania (Korinthia)	Geraneia
Githio (Lakonia)	Gythium
Glafira (Magnisia)	Glaphyrae
Glifada (Fokis)	Oeneon
Goni (Larissa)	Gonnus
Gonoussa (Korinthia)	Gonusa
Goritsa (Magnisia)	Ormenium
Gortis (Kriti: Iraklio)	Gortyna
Halandri (Attiki)	Phlya
Halki (Dodekanissa)	Chalcia
Halkida (Evia)	Chalcis
Hania (Kriti: Hania)	Cydonia
Heronia (Viotia)	Chaeroncia
Hersonissos (Kriti: Iraklio)	Chersonesus
Hios (Nissia Anatolikou Egeou)	Chios
Hotoussa (Arkadia)	Caphyae
Hriso (Fokis)	Crissa
Ialiso (Rodos)	Ialysus
Idi (Kriti: Iraklio)	Ida
Ierapetra (Kriti: Lasithio)	Hierapytna
Ihalia (Messinia)	Oechalia
Ikaria (Nissia Anatolikou Egeou)	Icaria
Ikario Pelagos	Icarian Sea
Ilia (Peloponissos)	Elis (territory)
Iliki (Viotia)	Hyle
Ilis or Ilida (Ilia)	Elis (city)
Ilissos (Attiki)	Ilissus
Imathia (Makedonia)	Emathia
Imitos (Attiki)	Hymettus
Inahos (Argolis)	Inachus
Inoi (Attiki)	Oenoe
Ionia Nissia (Ionia Nissia)	Ionian Islands
Ionio Pelagos	Ionian Sea
Ipato (Viotia)	Glisas
Ipiros	Epeirus
Iraklia (Fthiotis)	Trachis
Iraklia (Ilia)	Heracleia
Iraklio (Attiki)	Iphistiadae
Ismaros (Evros)	Ismarus
Ismenos (Viotia)	Ismenus
Isthmia (Korinthia)	Corinthian Isthmus
Ithaki (Ionia Nissia)	Ithaca
Ithomi (Messinia)	Ithome

MODERN NAME	ANCIENT NAME	MODERN NAME	ANCIENT NAME
Ithomi (Messinia)	Messene	Kiklades	Cyclades
Iti (Fthiotis)	Oeta	Kilini (Ilia)	Cyllene
Itilo (Lakonia)	Oetylus	Killini (Korinthia)	Cyllene
Kabirio (Viotia)	Cabeiraea	Kinouria (Lakonia)	Cynuria
Kafireus (Evia)	Caphareus	Kinthos (Kiklades)	Cynthus
Kakovatos (Ilia)	Pylus	Kiparissi (Fthiotis)	Opus
Kalamata (Messinia)	Nedon (river)	Kiparissi (Lakonia)	Cyphanta
Kalamata (Messinia)	Pharae or Pherae	Kiparissia (Messinia)	Cyparissia
Kalamos (Ionia Nissia)	Taphiae	Kithero (Viotia)	Cithaeron
Kalandra (Halkidiki)	Mende	Kithira (Pireas)	Cythera
Kalavrita (Ahaia)	Cynaetha	Kitries (Messinia)	Gerenia
Kalidona (Etolia-Akarnania)	Calydon	Kiveri (Argolis)	Apobathmi
Kalimnos (Dodekanissa)	Calymna	Kladeos (Ilia)	Cladeus
Kalivia (Fokis)	Corycium	Klenia (Korinthia)	Tenea
Kallianio? (Arkadia)	Onceium	Knossos (Kriti: Iraklio)	Cnossus
Kambos (Messinia)	Alagonia	Kokkoras (Arkadia)	Melaenae
Kamiros (Rodos)	Cameirus	Koridalos (Attiki)	Corydallus
Kanalia (Magnisia)	Boebe	Korifasio (Messinia)	Coryphasium
Kandila (Etolia-Akarnania)	Alyzia	Korinthos (Peloponissos)	Corinth
Kardamili (Messinia)	Cardamyle	Koropi (Attiki)	Sphettus
Karies? (Lakonia)	Caryae	Koropi (Magnisia)	Corope
Karistos (Evia)	Carystus	Kos (Dodekanissa)	Cos
Karpathos (Dodekanissa)	Carpathus	Kotronas (Lakonia)	Teuthrone
Kassandra (Halkidiki)	Pallene	Koutsi (Korinthia)	Phlius
Kassos (Dodekanissa)	Casus	Kramvonos (Arkadia)	Cretea
Kastelli (Kriti: Hania)	Dreros	Krathis (Ahaia)	Crathis
Kastri? (Larissa)	Amyrus	Krikellos (Etolia-Akarnania)	Argos Amphilochicum
Kastro (Messinia)	Pylus	Kriti	Crete
Kastro (Viotia)	Copae	Krokees (Lakonia)	Croceae
Kato Ahaia (Ahaia)	Dyme	Ladon (Arkadia)	Ladon
Kato Asea (Arkadia)	Asea	Lafistio (Viotia)	Laphystium
Kato Klitoria (Ahaia)	Cleitor	Lakonia (Peloponissos)	Laconia
Kato Ktimeni (Karditsa)	Ctimene	Lambrika (Attiki)	Lamptra, Upper
Kato Loussi (Ahaia)	Lusi	Lamia (Fthiotis)	Lamia
Kato Melpia (Messinia)	Melpeia	Lampia (Arkadia)	Lampeia
Kato Vlassia (Ahaia)	Tritaea	Larimna (Fthiotis)	Larymna
Katohi (Etolia-Akarnania)	Oeniadae	Larissa (Argolis)	Larissa
Kavala (Kavala)	Neapolis	Larissa (Larissa)	Larissa
Kaza (Attiki)	Eleutherae	Lefkada (Ionia Nissia)	Leucas
Kea (Kiklades)	Ceos	Lefkadia (Imathia)	Mieza
Kea (Ceos)	Iulis	Lefktra (Viotia)	Eutresis
Kefalari (Argolis)	Erasinus	Lefktra (Viotia)	Leuctra
Kefalonia (Ionia Nissia)	Cephallenia	Lefktro (Lakonia)	Leuctra
Kehries (Korinthia)	Cenchreae	Leheo (Argolis)	Lechaeum
Kenourgi (Etolia-Akarnania)	Thronium	Lentas (Iraklio)	Leben
		Lepedimnos (Lesvos)	Lepetymnus
Keramikos (Attiki)	Cerameicus	Lepreo (Ilia)	Lepreum
Keratea (Attiki)	Cephale	Lerni (Argolis)	Lerna
Keratsini (Pireas)	Thymoetadae	Leros (Dodekanissa)	Leros
Kerkira (Ionia Nissia)	Corcyra (Corfu)	Lesvos (Nissia Anatolikou Egeou)	Lesbos
Kifissos (Attiki)	Cephissus		
Kifissos (Viotia)	Cephissus	Ligourio? (Argolis)	Lessa

MODERN NAME	ANCIENT NAME	MODERN NAME	ANCIENT NAME
Lihada (Evia)	Cenaeum	Mesimvria (Evros)	Mesembria
Likeo (Arkadia)	Lycaeus	Mesopotamo (Preveza)	Ephyra
Likeri (Fokis)	Lycoreia	Mesopotamo (Preveza)	Necromanteion
Likossoura (Arkadia)	Lycosura	Messinia (Peloponissos)	Messenia
Lilaia (Fokis)	Lilaea	Methoni (Messinia)	Methone
Limenas Amfipolis (Seres)	Eion	Mezapos (Lakonia)	Messa
Limenas Gerakes (Lakonia)	Zarax	Midea (Argolis)	Midea
Limni? (Evia)	Aegae	Mikines (Argolis)	Mycenae
Limnos (Nissia Anatolikou Egeou)	Lemnos	Mikonos (Kiklades)	Myconos
		Mikromani (Messinia)	Thuria
Lindos (Rodos)	Lindus	Mikrothives (Magnisia)	Thebes
Lipsi (Dodekanissa)	Lepsia	Milatos (Kriti: Lasithio)	Miletus
Lissos (Kriti: Hania)	Lissus	Milos (Kiklades)	Melos
Liti (Thessaloniki)	Lete	Minthi (Ilia)	Mintha
Litohoro (Pieria)	Pimpleia	Miraka (Ilia)	Harpina
Livadia (Viotia)	Lebadeia	Mirina (Lesvos)	Myrina
Livanates (Viotia)	Cynus	Mirtoo Pelagos	Myrtoan Sea
Loukissia (Viotia)	Anthedon	Mithimna (Lesvos)	Methymna
Loutra Edipsou (Evia)	Aedepsus	Mitilini (Lesvos)	Mytilene
Loutra Irminis? (Illia)	Hyrmine	Mitropoli (Karditsa)	Metropolis
Loutsa (Attiki)	Halae Araphenides	Molivos (Lesvos)	Methymna
Loutsi (Viotia)	Hyettus	Monolia (Evia)	Lichades
Magnisia (Thessalia)	Magnesia	Nafpaktos (Etolia-Akarnania)	Naupactus
Makedonia	Macedonia		
Makri? (Ionia Nissia)	Dulichium	Nafplio (Argolis)	Nauplia
Makronisi (Attiki)	Helena	Naxos (Kiklades)	Naxos
Malandrino (Fokis)	Physceius	Nea Anhialos (Magnisia)	Pyrasus
Maleas (Lakonia)	Malea	Nea Faliro (Attiki)	Phalerum
Mamousia (Ahaia)	Ceryneia	Nea Kios? (Argolis)	Temenium
Mana (Ahaia)	Larissus	Nea Skioni (Halkidiki)	Scione
Mandeli (Evia)	Geraestus	Nea Stira (Evia)	Styra
Mandinia (Arkadia)	Mantineia	Neapoli (Lakonia)	Boeae
Mandoudi (Evia)	Cerinthus	Nedas (Messinia)	Neda
Marathonas (Attiki)	Marathon	Nemea (Korinthia)	Nemea
Marathonisi (Lakonia)	Cranae	Neohorio (Trikala)	Oechalia
Mario (Lakonia)	Marius	Neon Monastiri (Fthiotis)	Proerna
Maronia (Rodopi)	Maroneia	Nestos (Xanthi)	Nestus
Maroussio (Attiki)	Athmonum	Nikopoli (Preveza)	Nicopolis
Mataranga (Karditsa)	Arne	Nirito (Ithaki)	Neritus
Mavria (Arkadia)	Trapezus	Nissiros (Dodekanissa)	Nisyrus
Mavroneria (Ahaia)	Styx	Ntamouhari (Magnisia)	Casthanaea
Megalohori (Pireas)	Methana	Olimbia (Ilia)	Olympia
Megalopoli (Arkadia)	Megalopolis	Olimbos (Pieria)	Olympus
Meganissi (Ionia Nissia)	Taphiae	Olinthos (Halkidiki)	Olynthus
Megara (Attiki)	Megara	Omolio (Larissa)	Homole
Melas (Fthiotis)	Melas	Onihas (Kriti: Hania)	Tityrus
Melidoni (Kriti: Rethimno)	Tallaeus	Orei (Evia)	Oreus
Melitea (Fthiotis)	Melitaea	Orhomenos (Arkadia)	Orchomenus
Melivia (Larissa)	Meliboea	Orhomenos (Viotia)	Orchomenus
Menalo (Arkadia)	Maenalus	Oros (Egina)	Panhellenium
Mendenitsa (Fthiotis)	Pharygae	Ossa (Magnisia)	Ossa
Merenda (Attiki)	Myrrhinus	Othris (Magnisia)	Othrys

MODERN NAME	ANCIENT NAME	MODERN NAME	ANCIENT NAME
Palea Monemvasia (Lakonia)	Epidaurus Limera	Prosimna (Argolis)	Prosymna
		Psatha (Attiki)	Pegae
Paleo Eleftherohorio/ Methoni (Pireas)	Methone	Psitalia (Pireas)	Psyttaleia
		Pteleos (Magnisia)	Pteleum
Paleo Kalamaki (Korinthia)	Schoenus	Ptoio (Viotia)	Ptoum
Palini (Attiki)	Pallene	Ramnous (Attiki)	Rhamnus
Pallanti (Arkadia)	Pallantium	Renginio (Fthiotis)	Narycus
Pamisus (Messinia)	Pamisus	Riolitiko (Ahaia)	Larissus
Pangeo (Kavala)	Pangaeum	Ritsona (Viotia)	Mycalessus
Paralia Avlidos (Viotia)	Hyria	Rodopi (Rodopi)	Rhodope
Paralia Tirou (Lakonia)	Prasiae	Rodos (Dodekanissa)	Rhodes
Parnassos (Fokis)	Parnassus	Rodovani (Kriti: Hania)	Elyrus
Parnitha (Attiki)	Parnes	Rokka (Kriti: Hania)	Rhocca
Paros (Kiklades)	Paros	Rovies (Evia)	Orobiae
Partheni (Arkadia)	Parthenium	Salamina (Pireas)	Salamis
Passava (Lakonia)	Las	Sami (Kefalonia)	Same
Patra (Ahaia)	Patrae	Samiko (Ilia)	Arene
Pavlos? (Viotia)	Cyrtones	Samiko (Ilia)	Samicum
Pela (Thessaloniki)	Pella	Samos (Nissia Anatolikou Egeou)	Samos
Pelana? (Lakonia)	Pellana		
Pellini (Ahaia)	Pellene	Samothraki (Evros)	Samothrace
Peloponissos	Peloponnesus	Santorini (Kiklades)	Thera
Pendeli (Attiki)	Pentelicus	Saronikos Kolpos	Saronic Gulf
Petalidi (Messinia)	Aepeia	Serifos (Kiklades)	Seriphos
Petalidi (Messinia)	Corone	Sesklo? (Magnissia)	Aeson
Petra (Viotia)	Tilphossium	Shinohori (Argolis)	Lyrceia
Pieria (Makedonia)	Pieria	Sifnos (Kiklades)	Siphnos
Pilio (Magnisia)	Pelion	Sikinos (Kiklades)	Sicinos
Pindos (Ipiros/Macedonia/ Thessalia)	Pindus	Sikiona (Ahaia)	Sicyon
		Simi (Dodekanissa)	Syme
Pinios (Ilia)	Peneius	Siros (Kiklades)	Syros
Pinios (Thessalia)	Peneius	Sithonia (Halkidiki)	Sithonia
Pireas (Pireas)	Peiraeus	Skafidia (Ilia)	Dyspontium
Pirgakio (Arkadia)	Methydrium	Skala Eressou (Lesvos)	Eresus
Pirgos (Karditsa)	Cierium	Skala Oropou (Attiki)	Oropus
Pirgos (Viotia)	Tegyra	Skarfia (Fthiotis)	Scarphe
Pirrihos (Lakonia)	Pyrrhicus	Skimatari (Viotia)	Tanagra
Pisses (Kea)	Poeeessa	Skironides Petrai (Attiki)	Scironian Rocks
Pithio (Larissa)	Pythium	Skiros (Sporades)	Scyros
Platana? (Ilia)	Aepy	Sklavohori (Lakonia)	Bryseae
Platanias? (Kriti: Hania)	Pergamus	Skopelos (Sporades)	Peparethus
Platee (Viotia)	Plataea	Skotoussa (Larissa)	Scotussa
'Plitra (Lakonia)	Asopus	Sparti (Lakonia)	Sparta
Poles (Kea)	Carthaea	Sparto? (Etolia-Akarnania)	Echinus
Polirinia (Kriti: Hania)	Polyrrhenia	Sperhios (Thessalia)	Spercheius
Pontinos (Argolis)	Pontinus	Sporades	Sporades
Poros (Pireas)	Calaureia	Steniklaros (Messinia)	Stenyclarus
Porto Germeno (Attiki)	Aegosthena	Stimfalia (Korinthia)	Stymphalus
Porto Rafti (Attiki)	Prasiae	Stratos (Etolia-Akarnania)	Stratus
Portoheli (Argolis)	Halieis	Strimonas (Makedonia)	Strymon
Poseidonio (Samos)	Poseidium	Strofades (Ionia Nissia)	Strophades
Pressos (Kriti: Lasithio)	Praesus	Sunio (Attiki)	Sunium

MODERN NAME	ANCIENT NAME	MODERN NAME	ANCIENT NAME
Taigetos (Lakonia/ Messinia)	Taygetus	Toroni (Halkidiki)	Torone
Taki? (Viotia)	Potniae	Toumbitsi (Arkadia)	Thelpusa
Tembi (Larissa)	Tempe	Tourkovouni (Attiki)	Anchesmus
Thalames (Lakonia)	Thalamae	Tretos (Korinthia)	Tretos
Thassos (Kavala)	Thasos	Trikala (Trikala)	Tricca
Theologos (Fthiotis)	Halae	Trilofo? (Arkadia)	Tricoloni
Thermo (Etolia-Akarnania)	Thermum	Tripotamo (Ahaia)	Psophis
Thermopiles (Fthiotis)	Thermopylae	Trizina (Pireas)	Troezen
Thespies (Viotia)	Thespiae	Tsoukalaiika (Ahaia)	Olenus
Thesprotia (Ipiros)	Thesprotia	Tsoutsouros (Kriti: Iraklio)	Inatus
Thessalia	Thessaly	Tzia (Kiklades)	Ceos
Thira (Kiklades)	Thera	Vafio? (Lakonia)	Phare
Thisoa (Arkadia)	Theisoa	Vari (Attiki)	Anagyrus
Thisvi (Viotia)	Thisbe	Vasiliko (Messinia)	Dorium
Thiva (Viotia)	Thebes	Vathi (Viotia)	Aulis
Thoknia (Arkadia)	Thocnia	Velanidia (Argolis)	Titthium
Thoriko (Attiki)	Thoricus	Velanidia? (Lakonia)	Side
Thraki	Thrace	Velestino (Magnisia)	Pherae
Thronos Amariou (Kriti: Rethimno)	Sybrita	Velvina (Etolia-Akarnania)	Molycreium
		Veria (Imathia)	Beroea
		Vermio (Imathia)	Bermius
Tilos (Dodekanissa)	Telos	Viotia (Kentriki Ellas)	Boeotia
Tinos (Kiklades)	Tenos	Vlohos (Karditsa)	Asterium
Tirintha (Argolis)	Tiryns	Volos (Magnisia)	Iolcus
Tirnavos? (Larissa)	Phalanna	Vouliagmeni (Attiki)	Zoster
Tisseo (Magnisia)	Tisacum	Vouvala (Larissa)	Azorus
Titaros (Pieria)	Titarus	Vraona (Attiki)	Brauron
Tithorea (Fthiotis)	Neon	Xidas (Kriti: Iraklio)	Lyctos
Tolo (Korinthia)	Asine	Zakinthos (Ionia Nissia)	Zacynthus
Tolophonas (Fokis)	Oeantheia	Zalongo (Preveza)	Cassope
Tomaros (Ioanina)	Tomarus	Zoni? (Arkadia)	Zoetia
Toroni (Halkidiki)	Lecythus		

Guide to Personae

Not every name in the text appears in this list. Exclusions include persons of incidental mention, such as minor family members, and historical figures. Individuals sharing a single name are identified by relationships: son of (s.), daughter of (d.), or other relationships, none of which are abbreviated. Places sharing a single name are also identified, usually by an abbreviated area name: Boeotia (Boeo.), Peloponnesus (Pelop.), etc.

ABARIS
    Sparta
ABAS
    Abae
    Argos
    Argos Pelasgicum
    Euboea
ABDERUS
    Abdera
    Locris
    Thrace
ABIA
    Abia
ABROTA
    Megara
ABSYRTUS
    Corcyra
ACACALLIS
    Crete
    Tarrha
ACACUS
    Acacesium
ACADEMUS
    Academia
    Aphidna
    Athens
    Cephissus (Att.)
ACAMAS (s. Eussorus)
    Thrace

ACAMAS (s. Theseus)
    Athens
    Thrace
ACARNAN
    Acarnania
    Delphi
ACASTUS
    Iolcus
    Pelion
ACHAEMENIDES
    Ithaca
ACHAEUS
    Achaia (Pelop.)
    Achaia (Thess.)
    Athens
    Phthiotis
ACHELOUS
    Achelous
    Cephissus (Boeo.)
    Echinades
    Megara
    Olympia
    Oropus
ACHERON
    Acheron
    Thesprotia
ACHILLES
    Abia
    Achaia (Thess.)

Aepeia
Amyclae
Athens
Aulis
Cardamyle
Corcyra
Halus
Messenia
Methone (Mess.)
Methymna
Olympia
Pelion
Pharae (Mess.)
Phthiotis
Prasiae (Lac.)
Scyros
Sparta
Spercheius
Thessaly
ACIDUSA
    Acidusa
ACOETES
    Naxos
ACONTIUS
    Acontium
    Ceos
ACRAEA
    Acraea
    Asterion

ACRAEA *(cont.)*
    Euboea (Arg.)
    Mycenae
ACRAEPHEUS
    Acraephnium
ACRATOPOTES
    Athens
ACRATUS
    Athens
ACRIAS
    Acriae
ACRISIUS
    Argos
    Larissa (Thess.)
    Seriphos
ACTAEON (s. Aristaeus)
    Boeotia
    Cithaeron
    Gargaphia
    Orchomenus (Boeo.)
    Pelion
    Thebes
ACTAEON (s. Melissus)
    Corinth
ACTAEUS
    Athens
    Attica
ACTOR
    Elis
    Hyrmine
ADMETE
    Argos
    Samos
ADMETUS
    Amphrysus
    Halus
    Pherae
    Tamynae
ADONIS
    Athens
ADRASTEIA
    Crete
    Dicte
    Ida
ADRASTUS
    Argos
    Asopus (Pelop.)
    Attica
    Colonus
    Harma
    Megara
    Sicyon
    Thebes

AEACUS
    Aegina
    Athens
    Panhellenium
    Thessaly
AECHMAGORAS
    Alcimedon
AEDON
    Thebes
AEDOS
    Athens
AEETES
    Corinth
AEGA
    Crete
AEGAEA
    Aegean Sea
AEGAEON (See BRIAREUS)
AEGEUS (s. Oeolycus)
    Sparta
AEGEUS (s. Pandion II)
    Aegean Sea
    Athens
    Delphi
    Troezen
AEGIALEIA
    Argos
AEGIALEUS (s. Adrastus)
    Argos
    Delphi
    Thebes
AEGIALEUS (s. Inachus)
    Achaia (Pelop.)
    Pegae
    Peloponnesus
    Sicyon
AEGICORES
    Athens
AEGINA
    Aegina
    Asopus (Pelop.)
AEGINETES
    Arcadia
AEGISTHUS
    Mycenae
AEGYPTIDES
    Argos
AEGYPTUS
    Patrae
AEGYRUS
    Sicyon
AENEAS
    Actium
    Aeneia

    Ambracia
    Aphrodisias
    Boeae
    Cissus
    Chaonia
    Cythera
    Delos
    Dodona
    Epeirus
    Leucas
    Orchomenus (Arc.)
    Pallene (Mac.)
    Pergamus
    Zacynthus
AEOLIA
    Calydon
AEOLUS (s. Hellen)
    Phthiotis
    Thessaly
AEOLUS (s. Hippotes)
    Thrace
AEPYTUS (s. Cresphontes)
    Messenia
AEPYTUS (s. Elatus)
    Arcadia
    Phaesana
    Sepia
AEPYTUS (s. Hippothous)
    Arcadia
    Mantineia
AEROPE
    Crete
AEROPUS
    Cnesius
AESON
    Aeson
    Iolcus
AETHLIUS
    Elis
AETHRA
    Aphidna
    Athens
    Troezen
AETHYLLA
    Mende
    Pallene (Mac.)
    Scione
AETIUS
    Troezen
AETNAEUS
    Cabeiraea
AETOLUS (s. Endymion)
    Aetolia
    Athens

AETOLUS *(cont.)*
  Calydon
  Elis
  Olympia
AETOLUS (s. Oxylus)
  Elis
AGACLES
  Budeium
AGAMEDE
  Agamede
AGAMEDES
  Arcadia
  Delphi
  Hyria
  Lebadeia
  Orchomenus (Boeo.)
  Thebes
AGAMEMNON
  Abia
  Aegium
  Aepeia
  Amyclae
  Argos
  Aulis
  Cardamyle
  Cephissus (Boeo.)
  Chaeroneia
  Delos
  Delphi
  Ithaca
  Lappa
  Messenia
  Methone (Mess.)
  Mycenae
  Olympia
  Pergamus
  Pharae (Mess.)
  Polyrrhenia
  Sicyon
  Tenea
AGANIPPE
  Aganippe
  Helicon
AGAPENOR
  Arcadia
  Enispe
AGASTHENES
  Elis
AGATHODAEMON
  Maenalus (city)
  Megalopolis
AGAVE
  Cithaeron
  Thebes

AGELAUS
  Calydon
AGENOR (s. Phegeus)
  Delphi
  Psophis
AGENOR (s. Pleuron)
  Calydon
AGENOR (s. Triopas)
  Argos
AGON
  Olympia
AGRAULOS (d. Actaeus)
  Athens
  Attica
AGRAULOS (d. Cecrops)
  Athens
  Attica
AGRIUS
  Calydon
  Pleuron
AICHNIS
  Arcadia
AIDONEUS
  Epeirus
AJAX (THE GREATER)
  Athens
  Salamis
  Tripodiscus
AJAX (THE LESSER)
  Caphareus
  Athens
  Larymna
  Locris
  Myconos
  Naryx
  Scarphe
ALAGONIA
  Alagonia
ALALCOMENES
  Alalcomenae
ALASTOR
  Pylus (Mess.)
ALCAEUS (s. Androgeus)
  Paros
  Thasos
ALCAEUS (s. Perseus)
  Troezen
ALCATHOUS (s. Pelops)
  Cithaeron
  Megara
ALCATHOUS (s. Porthaon)
  Calydon
ALCESTIS
  Pherae

ALCIMEDON
  Alcimedon
ALCIMENES (s. Glaucus)
  Corinth
ALCIMENES (s. Jason)
  Corinth
ALCIMUS
  Sparta
ALCINOUS
  Corcyra
ALCIPPE (d. Ares)
  Athens
ALCIPPE (sister of Astraeus)
  Caicus
ALCMAEON
  Achelous
  Aetolia
  Arcadia
  Argos
  Argos Amphilochicum
  Delphi
  Psophis
  Thebes
ALCMENA
  Athens
  Haliartus
  Megara
  Midea
  Mycenae
  Ocalea
  Thebes
  Trachis
ALCMENA MIDEATIS
  Midea
ALCON (s. Erechtheus)
  Athens
ALCON (s. Hippocoon)
  Sparta
ALCYONEUS
  Corinthian Isthmus
ALECTOR (s. Anaxagoras)
  Argos
ALECTOR (s. Leitus)
  Olenus (Ach.)
ALEGENOR
  Boeotia
ALETES (s. Aegisthus)
  Mycenae
ALETES (s. Hippotes)
  Corinth
ALEUS
  Alea
  Arcadia
  Tegea

ALEXANOR
  Titane
ALIPHERUS
  Aliphera
ALMOPS
  Almopia
ALOEIDAE
  Aganippe
  Aloium
  Anthedon
  Ascra
  Biennus
  Helicon
  Naxos
  Olympus
  Ossa
  Pelion
  Thessaly
ALOEUS
  Asopia
ALOPE
  Alope
  Eleusis
  Megara
ALPHEIUS
  Alpheius
  Arcadia
  Letrini
  Olympia
ALTHAEA
  Calydon
ALTHAEMENES
  Atabyris
  Cretenia
  Rhodes
ALTHEPUS
  Althepia
  Troezen
ALYCUM
  Phalycum
ALYCUS
  Aphidna
ALYZEUS
  Acarnania
  Alyzia
AMALTHEIA
  Aegeira
  Crete
  Dicte
  Ida
AMARYNCEUS
  Elis
AMARYNTHUS
  Amarynthus

AMAZONS
  Aegean Sea
  Athens
  Attica
  Epidaurus
  Olympia
  Panaema
  Phigalia
  Thrace
AMBRACIA
  Ambracia
AMBRAX
  Ambracia
AMBRYSSUS
  Ambrysus
AMMON
  Delphi
  Gythium
  Megalopolis
  Sparta
AMNISIADES
  Amnisus
AMPHIARAUS
  Amyclae
  Argos
  Athens
  Calydon
  Cephissus (Boeo.)
  Harma
  Ismenus
  Lerna
  Nemea
  Oropus
  Phlius
  Sparta
  Thebes
AMPHICLUS
  Chios
AMPHICTYON
  Anthela
  Athens
  Attica
  Thermopylae
AMPHIDAMAS
  Chalcis
  Cythera
AMPHILOCHUS (s. Alcmaeon)
  Argos Amphilochicum
AMPHILOCHUS (s. Amphiaraus)
  Amphilochia
  Argos
  Argos Amphilochicum
  Athens

  Sparta
  Thebes
AMPHIMACHUS (s. Cteatus)
  Elis
AMPHIMACHUS (s. Polyxenus)
  Elis
AMPHIMEDON
  Ithaca
AMPHINOMUS
  Dulichium
AMPHION (s. Iasus)
  Orchomenus (Boeo.)
AMPHION (s. Zeus)
  Aracynthus
  Cithaeron
  Eleutherae
  Eutresis
  Thebes
AMPHISSA
  Amphissa
AMPHISSUS
  Oeta
AMPHITRITE
  Amyclae
  Corinthian Isthmus
  Mediterranean Sea
  Olympia
  Tenos
AMPHITRYON
  Mycenae
  Taphiae
  Thebes
  Tiryns
AMPHOTERUS
  Delphi
AMYCLAS
  Amyclae
  Laconia
  Sparta
AMYMONE
  Amymone
  Argos
  Cydonia
  Lerna
AMYNTOR
  Calydon
  Dolopia
  Eleon
  Ormenium
AMYRUS
  Amyrus
  Iolcus
  Olympia
  Pylus (Mess.)

ANAPHLYSTUS
  Anaphlystus
  Troezen
ANAXAGORUS
  Argos
ANAXANDRA
  Sparta
ANAXIAS
  Amyclae
  Argos
ANAXO
  Troezen
ANCAEUS (s. Lycurgus)
  Arcadia
  Calydon
ANCAEUS (s. Poseidon)
  Astypalaea
  Samos
ANCHIALUS
  Taphiae
ANCHISES
  Anchisia
  Arcadia
  Orchomenus (Arc.)
ANDRAEMON
  Aetolia
  Amphissa
  Calydon
  Elis
  Pleuron
ANDREUS
  Andreis
  Andros
  Orchomenus (Boeo.)
ANDROGEUS
  Athens
  Attica
  Crete
  Marathon
  Oenoe (Att.)
  Phalerum
ANDROMACHE
  Chaonia
  Delphi
  Epeirus
  Ephyra (Epeir.)
ANDROMEDES
  Aegina
ANEMOSYNE
  Rhodes
ANGELOS
  Chios
ANIGRIDES
  Anigrus

ANIUS
  Delos
  Euboea
ANTEIA
  Argos
ANTENOR
  Adriatic Sea
  Thrace
ANTEROS
  Athens
ANTHAS
  Anthane
  Anthedon
  Antheia (Arg.)
  Troezen
ANTHEDON
  Anthcdon
ANTHES
  Calaureia
ANTICLEIA
  Ithaca
ANTIGONE (d. Eurytion)
  Phthiotis
ANTIGONE (d. Oedipus)
  Thebes
ANTILOCHUS
  Messenia
  Pylus (Mess.)
ANTINOE
  Mantineia
ANTINOUS
  Ithaca
ANTION
  Larissa (Thess.)
ANTIOPE (Amazon)
  Athens
  Attica
ANTIOPE (d. Nycteus)
  Cithaeron
  Eleutherae
  Neon
  Sicyon
  Thebes
ANTIPHATEIA
  Cirrha
ANTIPHATES
  Argos
ANTIPHUS
  Carpathus
  Casus
  Cos
  Nisyrus
  Sporades

ANYTUS
  Arcadia
AON
  Aonia
  Boeotia
AONIDES
  Aonia
AORIS
  Araethyrea
  Phlius
APEMOSYNE
  Crete
APHAEA
  Aegina
APHAREUS
  Arene (Mess.)
  Calydon
  Messenia
  Samicum
APHEIDAS
  Arcadia
  Tegea
APHIDNUS
  Aphidna
APHRODITE
  Alopece
  Argos
  Athens
  Attica
  Bura
  Cassope
  Cenchreae
  Cephale
  Corcyra
  Corinth
  Corinthian Isthmus
  Cyllene (Elis)
  Cythera
  Delos
  Dodona
  Epidaurus
  Epidaurus Limera
  Hymettus
  Lechaeum
  Megara
  Messene
  Naupactus
  Oeantheia
  Olympus
  Orchomenus (Arc.)
  Patrae
  Peiraeus
  Phigalia
  Rhodes

APHRODITE *(cont.)*
 Samos
 Samothrace
 Sicyon
 Sparta
 Taenarum
 Tanagra
 Temenium
 Thespiae
 Zacynthus
APHRODITE ACIDALIA
 Acidalius
 Orchomenus (Boeo.)
APHRODITE ACRAEA
 Troezen
APHRODITE AMBOLOGERA
 Sparta
APHRODITE ANADYOMENE
 Cos
APHRODITE ANTHEIA
 Cnossus
APHRODITE APOSTROPHIA
 Megara
 Thebes
APHRODITE ARACYNTHUS
 Aracynthus
APHRODITE AREIA
 Sparta
APHRODITE ARGYNNIS
 Cephissus (Boeo.)
APHRODITE CALASCOPIA
 Troezen
APHRODITE CASTHANITIS
 Casthanaea
APHRODITE CASTNIETIS
 Metropolis
APHRODITE COLIAS
 Anaphlystus
 Phalerum
APHRODITE DELIA
 Delos
APHRODITE ERYCINA
 Psophis
APHRODITE EUPLOEA
 Peiraeus
APHRODITE HECAERGE
 Iulis
APHRODITE HERA
 Sparta
APHRODITE MECHANITIS
 Megalopolis

APHRODITE MELAENIS
 Corinth
 Mantineia
 Thespiae
APHRODITE MELINAEA
 Meline
APHRODITE MIGONITIS
 Gythium
 Migonium
APHRODITE MORPHO
 Sparta
APHRODITE PANACEIA
 Oropus
APHRODITE PANDEMOS
 Athens
 Cos
 Elis
 Megalopolis
 Thebes
APHRODITE PAPHIA
 Tegea
APHRODITE PHILA
 Thria
APHRODITE PLINTHIA
 Tegea
APHRODITE URANIA
 Aegeira
 Athens
 Athmonum
 Elis
 Elis (city)
 Thebes
APHRODITE ZERYNTHIA
 Zerynthus
APIS
 Apia
 Argos
 Peloponnesus
 Sicyon
APOLLO
 Achaia (Pelop.)
 Aegeira
 Aegina
 Aetolia
 Alpheius
 Amarynthus
 Amphrysus
 Amyclae
 Andros
 Aptera
 Arcadia
 Argos
 Astypalaea
 Athens

Attica
Boeae
Boeotia
Calaureia
Calydon
Cameirus
Carthaea
Cassotis
Ceos
Chalcia
Chios
Cirrha
Cithaeron
Corcyra
Corinth
Cos
Crete
Crissa
Cyparissia
Cyrtones
Delium
Delos
Delphi
Didymi
Dotius Campus
Dreros
Epidelium
Larissa (Thess.)
Lebadeia
Lepetymnus
Lepsia
Lilaea
Lyctos
Megalopolis
Megara
Melantii Scopuli
Messenia
Naxos
Oeta (city)
Olympus
Orchomenus (Boeo.)
Parnassus
Paros
Patrae
Peiraeus
Peloponnesus
Peneius (Thess.)
Pherae
Pieria
Phlius
Phocis
Prasiae (Att.)
Rhodes

APOLLO *(cont.)*
- Sicyon
- Sparta
- Tamynae
- Tanagra
- Tarrha
- Tegea
- Tempe
- Tenea
- Thebes
- Thermum
- Thespiae
- Tripodiscus
- Zarax
- Zerynthus
- Zoster

APOLLO ABAEUS
- Abae

APOLLO ACESIUS
- Elis
- Elis (city)

APOLLO ACRAEPHIUS
- Acraephnium

APOLLO ACREITAS
- Sparta

APOLLO ACTIACUS
- Actium

APOLLO ACTIUS
- Actium
- Nicopolis

APOLLO AEGILEUS
- Anticythera

APOLLO AEGLETES
- Anaphe

APOLLO AEGYPTAEUS
- Epidaurus

APOLLO AGRAEUS
- Megara

APOLLO AGYIEUS
- Acharnae
- Mycenae
- Tegea

APOLLO ALEXICACUS
- Athens

APOLLO AMAZONIUS
- Pyrrhichus

APOLLO AMYCLAEUS
- Amyclae
- Sparta

APOLLO APHETAEUS
- Sparta

APOLLO ARCHEGETES
- Megara

APOLLO BOEDROMIUS
- Athens
- Thebes

APOLLO CALYDNEUS
- Calymna

APOLLO CARINUS
- Megara

APOLLO CARNEIUS
- Acarnania
- Cardamyle
- Gythium
- Hypsi
- Las
- Leuctra (Lac.)
- Oechalia (Mess.)
- Oetylus
- Pharac (Mess.)
- Sicyon
- Sparta
- Thera

APOLLO CLARIUS
- Corinth

APOLLO COROPAEUS
- Corope

APOLLO CORYTHUS
- Corone

APOLLO CYNTHIUS
- Cynthus

APOLLO CYPARISSIUS
- Cos

APOLLO DAPHNEPHORUS
- Chaeroneia
- Eretria

APOLLO DECATEPHORUS
- Megara

APOLLO DEIRADIOTES
- Argos

APOLLO DELIUS
- Delos

APOLLO DELPHINIUS
- Athens
- Chalcis
- Cnossus
- Crete
- Crissa
- Delphi
- Didymi
- Dreros

APOLLO DIONYSODOTUS
- Phyla

APOLLO EPIBATERIUS
- Troezen

APOLLO EPICURIUS
- Phigalia

APOLLO ERETHIMUS
- Ialysus

APOLLO EUTRESITES
- Eutresis

APOLLO GALAXIUS
- Galaxius

APOLLO HYPERTELEATES
- Hyperteleatum

APOLLO ISMENIUS
- Ismenus
- Messene
- Thebes

APOLLO IXIUS
- Ixiae

APOLLO LAPHRIUS
- Calydon

APOLLO LARISSAEUS
- Larissa (Arg.)

APOLLO LATOUS
- Corinthian Isthmus
- Geraneia
- Megaris

APOLLO LEUCADIUS
- Leucas

APOLLO LOEMIUS
- Lindus

APOLLO LYCEIUS
- Argos
- Athens
- Delos
- Delphi
- Lindus
- Sicyon

APOLLO LYCOREUS
- Lycoreia

APOLLO MALEATES
- Epidaurus
- Malea (prom.)
- Sparta

APOLLO MALLOEIS
- Lesbos

APOLLO MOIRAGETES
- Delphi

APOLLO NOMIUS
- Arcadia
- Peloponnesus

APOLLO ONCAEATES
- Onceium
- Thelpusa

APOLLO PAGASAEUS
- Pagasae

APOLLO PARNOPIUS
- Athens

APOLLO PARRHASIUS
  Cretea
  Lycaeus
APOLLO PATROUS
  Athens
  Attica
APOLLO PROSTATERIUS
  Megara
APOLLO PTOUS
  Acraephnium
  Boeotia
  Ptoum
APOLLO PYTHAEUS
  Argos
  Asine
  Thornax (Lac.)
APOLLO PYTHIUS
  Athens
  Delphi
  Gortyna
  Laconia
  Mantineia
  Megara
  Oenoe (Att.)
  Paros
  Pheneus
  Pythium
  Rhodes
  Sicinos
  Tegea
  Thasos
APOLLO SALGANEUS
  Salganeus
APOLLO SELINUNTIUS
  Orobiae
APOLLO SITALCUS
  Delphi
APOLLO SMINTHEUS
  Ceos
  Chryse
  Crete
  Lindus
APOLLO SPODIUS
  Thebes
APOLLO TARRHAEUS
  Tarrha
APOLLO TEGYREIUS
  Tegyra
APOLLO TEMPEITES
  Tempe
APOLLO TENEATES
  Tenea
APOLLO THEARIUS
  Troezen

APOLLO THEOXENIUS
  Pellene
APOLLO THERMIUS
  Thermum
APOLLO THYMBRAEUS
  Chryse
APOLLO ZOSTERIUS
  Attica
  Zoster
APOTROPAEI
  Sicyon
ARAETHYREA
  Araethyrea
  Phlius
ARAS
  Araethyrea
  Phlius
ARCAS (s. Lycaon)
  Trapezus
ARCAS (s. Zeus)
  Arcadia
  Delphi
  Maenalus (mt.)
  Mantineia
  Tegea
ARCESILAUS
  Boeotia
  Lebadeia
ARCHELAUS
  Aegae (Mac.)
ARCHEMORUS (See OPHELTES)
ARCHIAS
  Corinth
ARCHILOCHUS
  Boeotia
ARCHITELES
  Calydon
ARDALUS
  Troezen
AREITHOUS
  Arcadia
  Arne (Boeo.)
  Mantineia
ARENE
  Arene
  Lepreum
  Messenia
  Samicum
ARES
  Athens
  Biennus
  Geronthrae
  Ismenus
  Laconia

  Nicopolis
  Olympia
  Olympus
  Patrae
  Salamis
  Sparta
  Tegea
  Thebes
  Thrace
  Tritaea
ARES APHNEIUS
  Cnesius
ARES AREUS
  Sparta
ARES ENYALIUS
  Sparta
ARES GYNAECOTHOENAS
  Tegea
ARES THERITAS
  Laconia
  Sparta
ARETE
  Corcyra
ARETHUSA
  Alpheius
ARGADES
  Athens
ARGALUS
  Laconia
  Sparta
ARGE
  Delos
ARGEIA
  Argos
ARGEUS
  Argos
ARGIOPE
  Parnassus
  Odrysia
ARGONAUTS
  Adriatic Sea
  Aegina
  Anaphe
  Aphetae
  Corcyra
  Crete
  Dodona
  Iolcus
  Lemnos
  Magnesia
  Melantii Scopuli
  Pelion
  Pellene

ARGONAUTS *(cont.)*
    Samothrace
    Tallaeus
ARGUS
    Argolis
    Argos
    Peloponnesus
ARGUS PANOPTES
    Arcadia
    Nemea
ARGYNNUS
    Cephissus (Boeo.)
ARGYRA
    Selemnus
ARIADNE
    Argos
    Crete
    Delos
    Donusa
    Naxos
ARION
    Corinth
    Methymna
    Onceium
    Taenarum
ARISBE
    Arisba
ARISTAEUS
    Adriatic Sea
    Aegean Sea
    Arcadia
    Aristaeon
    Boeotia
    Ceos
    Cos
    Haemus
    Ionian Islands
    Thebes
    Thessaly
    Thrace
ARISTOCRATES
    Arcadia
    Orchomenus (Arc.)
ARISTODEME
    Sicyon
ARISTODEMUS
    Delphi
    Naupactus
    Sparta
    Thebes
ARISTOMACHUS
    Argos
    Peloponnesus

ARMENIUS
    Armenium
    Rhodes
ARNE (d. Aeolus)
    Arne (Boeo.)
    Arne (Thess.)
    Chaeroneia
ARNE (nurse of Poseidon)
    Arne (Arc.)
    Arne (Boeo.)
ARRIBAS
    Epeirus
ARSINOE (d. Leucippus)
    Messenia
    Sparta
ARSINOE (d. Phegeus)
    Psophis
ARTEMIS
    Abae
    Aegina
    Alagonia
    Alpheius
    Amnisus
    Arcadia
    Argolis
    Argos
    Artemisium (Arc.)
    Astypalaea
    Athens
    Aulis
    Brauron
    Calydon
    Cenchreae
    Cirrha
    Cithaeron
    Corinth
    Corinthian Isthmus
    Corcyra
    Crete
    Cyrtones
    Delos
    Dium
    Dreros
    Epidaurus
    Erymanthus (mt.)
    Gargaphia
    Gonnus
    Helos
    Hyampolis
    Icaria (isl.)
    Laconia
    Lilaea
    Maenalus (mt.)
    Mantineia

    Marius
    Megara
    Methone (Mess.)
    Oeantheia
    Olympia
    Olympus
    Orchomenus (Boeo.)
    Orneae
    Paros
    Pellene
    Peloponnesus
    Salamis
    Scillus
    Sicyon
    Sparta
    Tarrha
    Taygetus
    Tegea
    Thasos
    Thebes
    Thermum
    Thrace
    Tisaeum
    Zoetia
    Zoster
ARTEMIS AEGINA
    Sparta
ARTEMIS AETOLE
    Naupactus
ARTEMIS AGROTERA
    Aegeira
    Agrae
    Athens
    Megalopolis
    Megara
ARTEMIS ALPHAEA
    Alpheius
    Elis
    Letrini
ARTEMIS ALPHEIONIA
    Alpheius
ARTEMIS AMARYSIA
    Amarynthus
    Athmonum
    Attica
ARTEMIS AMARYNTHIA
    Amarynthus
    Athmonum
    Attica
ARTEMIS APANCHOMENE
    Caphyae
ARTEMIS APTERA
    Aptera

ARTEMIS ARISTO
   Athens
ARTEMIS ARISTOBULE
   Athens
ARTEMIS ASTRATEIA
   Pyrrhicus
ARTEMIS BRAURON
   Amphipolis
   Athens
   Brauron
   Lemnos
ARTEMIS BRITOMARTIS
   Crete
ARTEMIS CALLISTE
   Arcadia
   Athens
   Cruni
   Megalopolis
   Tegea
ARTEMIS CARYATIS
   Caryae
   Laconia
   Taygetus
ARTEMIS CEDREATIS
   Orchomenus (Arc.)
ARTEMIS CHITONE
   Chitone
ARTEMIS CNACALESIA
   Caphyae
ARTEMIS CNACEATIS
   Tegea
ARTEMIS CNAGIA
   Laconia
   Sparta
ARTEMIS COLAENIS
   Myrrhinus
ARTEMIS CONDYLEATIS
   Caphyae
ARTEMIS CORDACA
   Elis
   Phrixa
ARTEMIS CORYPHAEA
   Coryphum
ARTEMIS CORYTHALLIA
   Sparta
ARTEMIS CYNTHIA
   Cynthus
ARTEMIS DAPHNAEA
   Hypsi
ARTEMIS DELIA
   Delos
ARTEMIS DELPHINIA
   Athens

ARTEMIS DERRHIATIS
   Derrhium
ARTEMIS DICTYNNA
   Dictamnum
   Laconia
   Phalasarna
ARTEMIS DICTYNNAEA
   Anticyra (Phoc.)
ARTEMIS ENNODIA
   Pherae
ARTEMIS EPHESIA
   Alea
   Corinth
ARTEMIS EUCLEIA
   Thebes
ARTEMIS EURYNOME
   Phigalia
ARTEMIS GAEEOCHOS
   Thebes
ARTEMIS HEGEMONE
   Sparta
ARTEMIS HEMERESIA
   Lusi
ARTEMIS HEURIPPE
   Pheneus
ARTEMIS HYMNIA
   Arcadia
   Mantineia
   Orchomenus (Arc.)
ARTEMIS IOLCIA
   Demetrias
ARTEMIS IPHIGENEIA
   Hermione
ARTEMIS ISSORIA
   Sparta
   Teuthrone
ARTEMIS LAPHRIA
   Calydon
   Messene
   Patrae
ARTEMIS LEUCOPHRYNE
   Amyclae
   Athens
ARTEMIS LIMNAEA
   Laconia
   Sicyon
   Sparta
ARTEMIS LIMNATIDES
   Tegea
ARTEMIS LIMNATIS
   Arcadia
   Limnae
   Patrae

ARTEMIS LOCHEIA
   Cynthus
ARTEMIS LOXO
   Delos
ARTEMIS LYCEIA
   Troezen
ARTEMIS LYCOATIS
   Lycoa
ARTEMIS LYSIZONA
   Athens
ARTEMIS MESOPOLITIS
   Orchomenus (Arc.)
ARTEMIS MUNYCHIA
   Peiraeus
ARTEMIS MYSIA
   Sparta
ARTEMIS OENOATIS
   Oenoe (Arg.)
ARTEMIS ORTHIA
   Athens
   Brauron
   Delos
   Elis
   Lemnos
   Orthosium
   Sparta
ARTEMIS PARTHENOS
   Leros
ARTEMIS PATROA
   Sicyon
ARTEMIS PHERAEA
   Argos
   Pherae
   Sicyon
ARTEMIS PITANATIS
   Pitane
ARTEMIS PROPYLAEA
   Eleusis
   Rharian Plain
ARTEMIS PROSEOA
   Artemisium (Eub.)
ARTEMIS PYRONIA
   Pheneus
ARTEMUS RHOCCAEA
   Rhocca
ARTEMIS SARONIA
   Saronic Gulf
   Troezen
ARTEMIS SCIATIS
   Megalopolis
   Scias
ARTEMIS SELASIA
   Sellasia

ARTEMIS SELASPHORA
　Phyla
ARTEMIS SOODINA
　Chaeroneia
ARTEMIS SOTEIRA
　Boeae
　Laconia
　Megalopolis
　Megara
　Pegae
　Pellene
　Phigalia
　Troezen
ARTEMIS STYMPHALIA
　Stymphalus
ARTEMIS TAUROPOLIS
　Amphipolis
　Halae Araphenides
　Macedonia
　Ncapolis
ARTEMIS TRICLARIA
　Patrae
ARTEMIS ZEA
　Peiraeus
ASCALABUS
　Attica
ASCALAPHUS
　Orchomenus (Boeo.)
ASCLEPIUS
　Aegium
　Aliphera
　Ambracia
　Amphissa
　Argos
　Athens
　Asopus (Lac.)
　Astypalaea
　Beroea
　Boeae
　Cenchreae
　Cephale
　Cleitor
　Corinth
　Corone
　Cos
　Crannon
　Cyllene (Elis)
　Cyphanta
　Delos
　Dium
　Dyme
　Elateia
　Eleusis
　Epidaurus

Epidaurus Limera
Gerenia
Gonnus
Gortyna
Gortys
Gythium
Hyperteleatum
Hypsi
Laconia
Las
Leben
Leuctra (Lac.)
Lissus
Melos
Messene
Naupactus
Orchomenus (Boeo.)
Paros
Patrae
Peiraeus
Pellana
Pheneus
Phigalia
Phlius
Prasiae (Lac.)
Sicyon
Tegea
Thebes (Phth.)
Thelpusa
Titane
Titthium
Tricca
Troezen
ASCLEPIUS AGNITAS
　Sparta
ASCLEPIUS AULONIUS
　Aulon
ASCLEPIUS CAUSIUS
　Caus
ASCLEPIUS CYRUS
　Pellene
ASCLEPIUS DEMAENETUS
　Alpheius
ASCLEPIUS PAIDOS
　Megalopolis
　Onceium
ASCLEPIUS PHILOLAUS
　Laconia
ASCRA
　Ascra
ASOPUS
　Asopia
　Asopus (Boeo.)

Asopus (Corin.)
Boeotia
ASPHODICUS
　Thebes
ASPLEDON
　Aspledon
ASTERIA
　Delos
　Olympus
ASTERION
　Argos
　Asterion
ASTERIUS (s. Cometes)
　Asterium
ASTERIUS (s. Teutamus)
　Crete
ASTEROPAEUS
　Axius
　Paeonia
ASTRABACUS
　Sparta
ASTRAEUS
　Caicus
ASTYANAX
　Delphi
ASTYCRATEIA
　Megara
ASTYDAMEIA (wife of Acastus)
　Iolcus
ASTYDAMEIA (d. Amyntor)
　Dolopia
ASTYLUS
　Larissa (Thess.)
ASTYPALAEA
　Astypalaea
ATALANTA (d. Iasus)
　Arcadia
　Calydon
　Cyphanta
ATALANTA (d. Schoeneus)
　Boeotia
　Calydon
　Onchestus
　Schoenus
　Tegea
ATE
　Olympus
ATHAMAS (s. Aeolus)
　Acraephnium
　Athamania
　Athamantius Campus
　Boeotia
　Halus
　Laphystium

ATHAMAS (s. Aeolus) *(cont.)*
  Orchomenus (Boeo.)
  Thessaly
ATHAMAS (s. Oenopion)
  Chios
ATHENA
  Aegina
  Aliphera
  Althepia
  Amphissa
  Andros
  Argos
  Astypalaea
  Athens
  Attica
  Boebe
  Boeotia
  Cameirus
  Cardamyle
  Carthaea
  Chios
  Cleonae
  Corinth
  Corium
  Corone
  Crannon
  Crete
  Cynthus
  Diecterion
  Dium
  Elateia
  Eleusis (Boeo.)
  Elis (city)
  Epidaurus Limera
  Gythium
  Haliartus
  Ialysus
  Ithaca
  Larissa (Thess.)
  Lecythus
  Lessa
  Leuctra (Lac.)
  Maenalus (city)
  Megara
  Neon
  Olympus
  Onugnathus
  Paros
  Pellene
  Pentelicus
  Pleuron
  Rhodes
  Samos
  Scyros

Sicyon
Sunium
Taphiae
Thebes
Thessaly
Titane
Tritaea
Troezen
Zoster
ATHENA AEANTIS
  Megara
ATHENA AETHYIA
  Megaris
ATHENA AGORAEA
  Sparta
ATHENA ALALCOMENEIS
  Alalcomenae
ATHENA ALCIDEMOS
  Pella
ATHENA ALCIS
  Macedonia
ATHENA ALEA
  Alea
  Arcadia
  Mantineia
  Sparta
  Tegea
ATHENA AMBULIA
  Sparta
ATHENA ANEMOTIS
  Methone (Mess.)
ATHENA APATURIA
  Calaureia
  Troezen
ATHENA ARCHEGETIS
  Athens
ATHENA AREIA
  Athens
  Plataea
ATHENA ARISTOBULA
  Athens
  Melite
ATHENA ASIA
  Las
ATHENA AXIOPOENOS
  Sparta
ATHENA BOULAEA
  Athens
ATHENA CELEUTHEIA
  Sparta
ATHENA CHALCIOECOS
  Sparta
ATHENA CHALINITIS
  Corinth

ATHENA CHRYSE
  Chryse
ATHENA CISSAEA
  Epidaurus
ATHENA COLOCASIA
  Sicyon
ATHENA CORIA
  Cleitor
ATHENA CORYPHASIA
  Coryphasium
  Pylus (Mess.)
ATHENA CRANAEA
  Elateia
ATHENA CYDONIA
  Cydonia
  Phrixa
ATHENA CYNTHIA
  Delos
  Paros
ATHENA CYPARISSIA
  Asopus (Lac.)
  Cyparissia
ATHENA ERGANE
  Delphi
  Sparta
  Thespiae
ATHENA HELLOTIA
  Corinth
  Marathon
ATHENA HIPPIA
  Acharnae
  Athens
  Colonus
  Olympia
  Tegea
ATHENA HIPPOLAITIS
  Hippola
ATHENA HYGIEIA
  Acharnae
  Athens
  Delphi
ATHENA ILIAS
  Physceius
ATHENA ISMENIA
  Thebes
ATHENA ITONIA
  Boeotia
  Cierium
  Coroneia
  Iton
  Philia
ATHENA LARISSAEA
  Larissus

ATHENA LINDIA
  Lindus
  Rhodes
ATHENA LONGATIS
  Longas
ATHENA NARCAEA
  Elis
ATHENA NEDUSIA
  Ceos
  Messenia
  Nedon
  Poeeessa
ATHENA NIKE
  Athens
  Megara
ATHENA OLERIA
  Hierapytna
ATHENA ONCA
  Oncae
  Thebes
ATHENA OXYDERCES
  Argos
ATHENA PAEONIA
  Athens
  Oropus
ATHENA PALLENIS
  Athens
  Pallene (Att.)
ATHENA PANACHAEA
  Aegium
  Patrae
ATHENA PAREIA
  Laconia
ATHENA PARTHENOS
  Athens
ATHENA PHRATRIA
  Athens
ATHENA POLIAS
  Athens
  Gonnus
  Hierapytna
  Megalopolis
  Phalanna
  Thebes (Phth.)
  Troezen
ATHENA POLIATIS
  Tegea
ATHENA POLIUCHOS
  Athens
  Dreros
  Halae
  Sparta
  Thasos

ATHENA PROMACHORMA
  Buporthmus
  Hermione
ATHENA PROMACHOS
  Athens
ATHENA PRONAEA
  Delphi
ATHENA SAITIS
  Lerna
  Pontinus
ATHENA SALPINX
  Argos
ATHENA SCILLUNTIA
  Scillus
ATHENA SCIRAS
  Phalerum
  Salamis
ATHENA SOTEIRA
  Asea
  Daulis
  Peiraeus
ATHENA STHENIAS
  Troezen
ATHENA TELCHINIA
  Boeotia
  Teumessus
ATHENA TITHRONE
  Phlya
ATHENA TRITOGENEIA
  Alalcomenae
  Arcadia
  Triton
ATHENA TRITONIA
  Pheneus
ATHENA ZOSTERIA
  Delphi
  Thebes
ATHENAIS
  Alalcomenae
ATHERION
  Patrae
ATLANTIDES
  Samicum
ATLAS
  Amyclae
  Arcadia
ATRAX
  Atrax
ATREUS
  Midea
  Mycenae
ATTHIS
  Athens
  Attica

ATYMNIUS
  Gortyna
AUGE
  Parthenium
  Tegea
AUGEAS
  Alpheius
  Elis
  Ephyra (Elis)
  Peneius (Elis)
AULIS
  Aulis
AULON
  Sparta
AUTESION
  Thebes
AUTOLAUS
  Thelpusa
AUTOLYCUS (s. Deimachus)
  Thessaly
AUTOLYCUS (s. Hermes)
  Eleon
  Ithaca
  Parnassus
AUTONOE
  Boeotia
  Ereneia
  Thebes
AUTONOUS
  Delphi
AUXESIA
  Aegina
  Athens
  Crete
  Epidaurus
  Troezen
AUXO
  Athens
  Attica
AXIEROS
  Samothrace
AXIUS
  Axius
AZAN
  Arcadia
  Azania
AZEUS
  Orchomenus (Boeo.)
AZORUS
  Azorus
BACCHIS
  Corinth
BAETYLUS
  Delphi

BAEUS
  Baea
  Cephallenia
BATON
  Argos
  Thebes
BATTUS
  Thera
BAUBO
  Dium
  Eleusis
BELLEROPHON
  Amyclae
  Argos
  Calydon
  Corinth
  Craneion
  Pleuron
  Tiryns
BENDIS
  Lemnos
  Peiraeus
BENTHESICYME
  Mediterranean Sea
BEROEA
  Beroea
BIAS
  Argos
  Cleitor
  Lusi
  Pylus (Mess.)
BITON (See CLEOBIS and BITON)
BODON
  Bodone
BOEBUS
  Boebe
BOEOTUS
  Boeotia
BOEUS
  Aphrodisias
  Boeae
  Etis
  Side
BOREADES
  Echinades
BOREAS
  Amyclae
  Athens
  Ilissus
  Thrace
BOTACHUS
  Botachidae
BRANCHUS
  Delphi

BRANGAS
  Olynthus
  Thrace
BRAURON
  Brauron
BRIAREUS
  Aegean Sea
  Corinth
BRITOMARTIS
  Aegina
  Argos
  Caeno
  Cephallenia
  Chersonesus
  Crete
  Olus
BRITOMARTIS DICTYNNA
  Dictamnum
BRIZO
  Delos
BUCOLION
  Arcadia
BUDEIA
  Budeion
BUDEIOS
  Budeion
BULON
  Bulis
BUNUS
  Corinth
BUPHAGUS
  Arcadia
BURA
  Bura
BUTES (s. Boreas)
  Naxos
  Thessaly
  Thrace
BUTES (s. Teleon)
  Athens
CAANTHUS
  Ismenus
  Thebes
CABEIRI
  Anthedon
  Arcadia
  Boeotia
  Cabeiraea
  Delos
  Lemnos
  Macedonia
  Pheneus
  Samothrace
  Thebes

CADMUS
  Mycalessus
  Pangaeum
  Rhodes
  Sparta
  Tanagra
  Thebes
  Thrace
CAENIS
  Atrax
CAICUS
  Caicus
CALAICARPUS
  Boeotia
CALAIS
  Strophades
  Tenos
CALCHAS
  Aulis
  Mycenae
CALLIARUS
  Calliarus
CALLIOPE
  Thrace
CALLIPOLIS
  Megara
CALLIRRHOE (d. Achelous)
  Achelous
  Thebes
CALLIRRHOE (beloved of
    Coresus)
  Callirrhoe
  Calydon
CALLISTO
  Arcadia
  Cruni
  Maenalus (mt.)
  Megalopolis
CALOS
  Athens
CALYDON
  Aetolia
  Calydon
CAMEIRUS
  Cameirus
  Rhodes
CAMENAE
  Arcadia
CANACE
  Thessaly
CANETHUS
  Canethus
  Euboea

CANTHUS
    Euboea
CAPANEUS
    Argos
    Delphi
    Thebes
CAR
    Caria
    Corinthian Isthmus
    Megara
CARMANOR
    Crete
    Tarrha
CARMENTA
    Arcadia
CARNUS
    Acarnania
    Naupactus
CARYA
    Laconia
    Taygetus
CARYSTUS
    Carystus
CASSANDRA
    Amyclae
    Athens
    Leuctra (Lac.)
    Mycenae
CASSOTIS
    Cassotis
    Parnassus
CASTALIA
    Castalia
CASTALIDES
    Castalia
CASTALIUS
    Castalia
    Crete
    Crissa
CASTOR
    Gythium
CASTOR and POLYDEUCES (See
    DIOSCURI)
CATREUS (See CRETEUS)
CAUCON
    Eleusis
    Lepreum
    Messenia
CECROPS
    Athenae
    Athens
    Attica
    Eleusis (Boeo.)

Haliartus
Triton
CELEDONES
    Delphi
CELEUS
    Attica
    Eleusis
    Phlius
CENCHRIAS
    Cenchreae
    Corinth
CENTAURS
    Anigrus
    Athens
    Larissa (Thess.)
    Malea (prom.)
    Olympia
    Pelion
    Phigalia
    Pindus
    Samicum
    Thessaly
CENTAURUS
    Larissa (Thess.)
CEPHALUS
    Amyclac
    Athens
    Cephallenia
    Hymettus
    Leucas
    Phocis
    Taphiae
    Thoricus
CEPHEUS
    Arcadia
    Caphyae
    Tegea
CEPHISSUS
    Argos
    Cephissus (Boeo.)
    Oropus
CERAMBUS (See TERAMBUS)
CERAMOS
    Athens
CERBERUS
    Acheron
    Boeotia
    Coroneia
    Hermione
    Laphystium
    Taenarum
    Troezen

CERCOPES
    Oechalia (Eub.)
    Thermopylae
CERCYON
    Alope
    Arcadia
    Eleusis
CERYX
    Athens
    Eleusis
CESTRINUS
    Chaonia
    Cestrine
    Epeirus
CEYX
    Trachis
CHAERON
    Chaeroneia
CHALCIOPE (d. Eurypylus)
    Cos
CHALCIOPE (d. Phalerus)
    Chalcis
CHALCIS
    Chalcis
CHALCODON (a Coan)
    Cos
CHALCODON (s. Abas)
    Chalcis
CHALCON
    Cyparissus
CHARILAUS
    Tegea
CHARITES
    Acidalius
    Argos
    Athens
    Attica
    Cephissus (Boeo.)
    Delos
    Delphi
    Elis
    Hermione
    Laconia
    Mycenae
    Orchomenus (Boeo.)
    Paros
    Sparta
CHARMUS
    Boeotia
CHEIRON
    Amyclae
    Boeotia
    Larissa (Thess.)
    Malea (prom.)

CHEIRON *(cont.)*
Pelion
Thessaly
CHIMAERA
Amyclae
CHIONE
Parnassus
CHIOS
Chios
CHLORIS (d. Amphion and Niobe)
Argos
Olympia
CHLORIS (wife of Neleus)
Orchomenus (Boeo.)
Pylus (Mess.)
CHRYSAOR
Corcyra
CHRYSE
Orchomenus (Boeo.)
CHRYSES (s. Minos)
Crete
Paros
CHRYSES (s. Poseidon)
Orchomenus (Boeo.)
CHRYSIPPUS
Thebes
CHRYSOTHEMIS (d.
Agamemnon)
Mycenae
CHRYSOTHEMIS (s. Carmanor)
Tarrha
CHTHONIA (d. Colontas)
Hermione
CHTHONIA (d. Erechtheus)
Athens
CHTHONIA (d. Phoroneus)
Hermoine
CHTHONIUS (s. Poseidon)
Syme
CHTHONIUS (one of the *Spartoi*)
Thebes
CHTHONOPATRA
Athens
CHTHONOPHYLE
Sicyon
CILLAS
Troezen
CINADUS
Onugnathus
CIRRHA
Cirrha
CISSEUS
Aegae (Mac.)

CITHAERON
Cithaeron
CLEITOR
Arcadia
Cleitor
CLEITUS (beloved of Pallene)
Macedonia
Pallene (Mac.)
CLEITUS (king of Sithones)
Sithonia
Thrace
CLEOBUS and BITON
Argos
Delphi
CLEODAEUS
Peloponnesus
Sparta
CLEODORA
Miletus
CLEOMEDES
Astypalaea
CLEONE
Cleonae
CLEONES
Cleonae
CLEOPATRA
Calydon
CLESO
Megara
CLESON
Megara
CLETA
Sparta
CLIO
Amphipolis
CLONIUS
Boeotia
CLYMENE (d. Creteus)
Crete
CLYMENE (relative of Menelaus)
Sparta
CLYMENUS (s. Caeneus)
Arcadia
Argos
CLYMENUS (s. Cardis)
Olympia
Phrixa
CLYMENUS (s. Oeneus)
Calydon
CLYMENUS (s. Phoroneus)
Hermione
CLYMENUS (s. Presbon)
Orchomenus (Boeo.)

CLYTEMNESTRA
Aulis
Mycenae
Sparta
CLYTIUS
Oechalia (Thess.)
CNAGEUS
Aphidna
Crete
Laconia
CODRUS
Athens
COLAENUS
Colonides
Myrrhinus
COLLYTUS
Athens
COMAETHO (beloved of
Melanippus)
Patrae
COMAETHO (d. Pterelaus)
Taphiae
CONNIDAS
Athens
COPREUS
Mycenae
CORAX
Sicyon
CORESUS
Callirrhoe
Calydon
CORINTHUS
Corinth
COROEBUS
Olympia
CORONIDES
Aonia
CORONIS (nymph)
Naxos
CORONIS (d. Phlegyas)
Dotius Campus
Orchomenus (Boeo.)
CORONIS (d. Phoroneus)
Phocis
CORONUS (s. Apollo)
Sicyon
CORONUS (s. Thersander)
Coroneia
CORYBANTES
Chalcis
Hierapytna
CORYCIA
Corycium
Parnassus

COS
    Cos
COTHUS
    Cerinthus
    Chalcis
COTYS
    Athens
    Corinth
    Thrace
COTYTTO (See COTYS)
CRANAE
    Athens
    Attica
CRANAECHME
    Athens
    Attica
CRANAUS
    Athens
    Attica
    Lamptra
CRANTOR
    Dolopia
CREON (s. Lycaethus)
    Corinth
CREON (s. Menoeceus)
    Taphiae
    Thebes
CRES
    Crete
    Ida
CRESPHONTES
    Abia
    Arcadia
    Messenia
    Stenyclarus
CRETEUS
    Crete
    Cretenia
    Rhodes
CRETHEUS
    Iolcus
    Thessaly
CRETHON
    Pharae (Mess.)
CREUSA
    Athens
    Delphi
CRIASUS
    Argos
CRISUS
    Cirrha
    Crissus
CROMMUS
    Crommyon

CRONUS
    Arne (Arc.)
    Athens
    Cassotis
    Crete
    Delphi
    Elis
    Lebadeia
    Olympia
CROTOPUS
    Argos
    Tripodiscus
CTEATUS
    Cleonae
    Elis
CTESIPPUS
    Same
CTESYLLA
    Cos
CURETES
    Aetolia
    Calydon
    Chalcis
    Clepsydra
    Cnossus
    Crete
    Curetis
    Dicte
    Eleutherna
    Ida
    Messene
    Pleuron
CYAMITES
    Athens
    Eleusis
CYANIPPUS
    Argos
CYATHUS
    Phlius
    Proschium
CYBELE
    Chios
    Dium
    Onchestus
CYCHREUS
    Eleusis
    Salamis
CYCLOPES
    Argos
    Corinthian Isthmus
    Mycenae
    Thrace
    Tiryns

CYCNUS (s. Apollo)
    Aetolia
    Athens
    Calydon
    Canope
    Pleuron
CYCNUS (s. Ares)
    Itone
CYDIPPE (beloved of Acontius)
    Athens
CYDIPPE (priestess of Hera)
    Argos
CYDON
    Crete
    Cydonia
CYLARABES
    Argos
CYLLEN
    Cyllene (Arc.)
CYLLENE
    Arcadia
CYNORTAS
    Laconia
    Sparta
CYNOSURA
    Ida
CYNURUS
    Cynuria
CYNUS
    Cynus
CYPARISSUS (brother of
    Orchomenus)
    Cyparissus
CYPARISSUS (s. Telephus)
    Ceos
CYPSELUS
    Arcadia
    Basilis
CYRENE
    Pelion
CYTHERUS
    Cythera
DACTYLI
    Aptera
    Ellis
    Ida
    Olympia
    Samothrace
DAEDALION
    Parnassus
DAEDALUS
    Aegean Sea
    Athens
    Cnossus

DAEDALUS *(cont.)*
  Corinth
  Crete
  Delos
  Lebadeia
DAEIRA
  Eleusis
DAMASICHTHON
  Boeotia
  Thebes
DAMIA
  Aegina
  Athens
  Crete
  Epidaurus
  Troezen
DAMOPHON
  Corinth
DANAE
  Argos
  Seriphos
DANAIDS
  Argos
DANAUS
  Apobathmi
  Argolis
  Argos
  Cameirus
  Delphi
  Lindus
  Rhodes
DAPHNE (d. Ladon)
  Ladon
  Pisa
DAPHNE (d. Teiresias) (See MANTO)
DARDANUS
  Arcadia
  Crete
  Samothrace
DAULIS
  Daulis
DEIANEIRA (d. Dexamenus)
  Olenus
DEIANEIRA (d. Oeneus)
  Achelous
  Calydon
  Euenus
  Trachis
DEIDAMEIA
  Scyros
DEIMA
  Corinth

DEIMAS
  Arcadia
DEION
  Phocis
  Phthiotis
DEIONEUS
  Oechalia (Thess.)
DEIPHOBUS
  Amyclae
  Olympia
DEIPHONTES
  Argos
  Epidaurus
DEIPHYLE
  Argos
DELIADES
  Corinth
DELPHIS
  Crete
  Crissa
DELPHUS (s. Apollo)
  Delphi
DELPHUS (s. Poseidon)
  Delphi
DEMARMENUS
  Eretria
  Euboea
DEMETER
  Aegila
  Anthedon
  Antron
  Aptera
  Araethyrea
  Argolis
  Argos
  Athens
  Attica
  Buporthmus
  Bura
  Callichorum
  Cephissus (Att.)
  Cleitor
  Colonus
  Copae
  Corinth
  Corinthian Isthmus
  Cos
  Crete
  Delos
  Didymi
  Dium
  Drymaea
  Eleusis
  Enispe

  Gythium
  Halimus
  Lebadeia
  Lepreum
  Lete
  Lilaea
  Megalopolis
  Megara
  Messene
  Messenia
  Mintha
  Olympus
  Onceium
  Paros
  Patrae
  Phalerum
  Phlius
  Potniae
  Proerna
  Pylus (Triph.)
  Pyrasus
  Rharian Plain
  Scolus
  Sicyon
  Thera
  Zoetia
DEMETER ACHAEA
  Athens
DEMETER AMPHICTYONIS
  Anthela
  Thermopylae
DEMETER ANESIDORA
  Phyla
DEMETER CABEIRAEA
  Cabeiraea
  Thebes
DEMETER CARPOPHOROS
  Tegea
DEMETER CHAMYNE
  Elis
DEMETER CHLOE
  Athens
DEMETER CHTHONIA
  Hermione
  Sparta
DEMETER CIDARIA
  Pheneus
DEMETER CORYTHEUSES
  Tegea
DEMETER DELIA
  Delos
DEMETER ELEUSINIA
  Basilis
  Laconia

DEMETER ELEUSINIA *(cont.)*
   Plataea
   Thelpusa
DEMETER EPIPOLE
   Laconia
DEMETER ERINYS
   Onceium
   Thelpusa
DEMETER EUROPA
   Lebadeia
DEMETER HERCYNA
   Hercyna
DEMETER MALOPHOROS
   Megara
DEMETER MEGARA
   Megara
DEMETER MELAENIS
   Arcadia
   Phigalia
DEMETER MYCALESSIA
   Mycalessus
DEMETER MYSIA
   Argos
   Mycenae
   Pellene
DEMETER PANACHAEA
   Achaia (Pelop.)
   Aegae (Ach.)
DEMETER PELASGA
   Argos
DEMETER PROSYMNA
   Lerna
DEMETER STIRIA
   Stiris
DEMETER THERMASIA
   Hermione
DEMETER THESMIA
   Athens
   Megara
   Pheneus
   Troezen
DEMETER THESMOPHOROS
   Argos
   Thebes
DEMO
   Callichorum
DEMODOCUS
   Amyclae
   Corcyra
   Mycenae
DEMOPHON (s. Celeus)
   Attica
   Eleusis

DEMOPHON (s. Theseus)
   Athens
   Attica
   Thrace
DEOMENEIA
   Mantineia
DESPOENA
   Acasesium
   Arcadia
   Lycosura
   Megalopolis
DEUCALION (s. Minos)
   Calydon
   Crete
DEUCALION (s. Prometheus)
   Athens
   Athos
   Cynus
   Delphi
   Locris
   Lycoreia
   Opus
   Othrys
   Parnassus
   Phthiotis
DEXAMENUS
   Bura
   Olenus (Ach.)
DIAS
   Athenae Diades
DICAEUS
   Dicaea
DICTE
   Dicte
DICTYNNA
   Cadistus
   Cydonia
   Dictamnum
   Lissus
   Pergamus
   Polyrrhenia
   Sparta
   Tityrus
DICTYS
   Seriphos
DIOCLES (priest of Demeter)
   Attica
   Eleusis
DIOCLES (s. Orsilochus)
   Pharae (Mess.)
DIOGENEIA
   Cephissus (Boeo.)
DIOMEDE
   Lesbos

DIOMEDES (s. Ares)
   Abdera
   Thrace
DIOMEDES (s. Tydeus)
   Aetolia
   Argos
   Asine
   Attica
   Calydon
   Corinth
   Delphi
   Eion (Arg.)
   Pleuron
   Thebes
   Troezen
DIOMUS
   Athens
   Diomeia
DION
   Laconia
DIONE
   Delos
   Dodona
   Olympus
DIONYSUS
   Acraephnium
   Alagonia
   Alea
   Andros
   Anthedon
   Aphytis
   Arcadia
   Argos
   Athens
   Attica
   Bermius
   Boeotia
   Bryseae
   Callirrhoe
   Ceos
   Cithaeron
   Copae
   Corcyra
   Corinth
   Corinthian Isthmus
   Corone
   Corycium
   Cos
   Crete
   Cyparissia
   Delos
   Delphi
   Dium
   Dodona

DIONYSUS *(cont.)*
  Donusa
  Dracanum
  Edonis
  Eleutherae
  Elis
  Elis (city)
  Epidaurus
  Eretria
  Gythium
  Hebrus
  Helicon
  Heraea
  Icaria (Att.)
  Icaria (isl.)
  Larissa (Thess.)
  Las
  Lerna
  Mantineia
  Maroneia
  Megalopolis
  Megara
  Messene
  Naupactus
  Naxos
  Nysa (Thrace)
  Odrysia
  Olympus
  Orchomenus (Boeo.)
  Panaema
  Pangaeum
  Parnassus
  Philippi
  Potniae
  Prasiae (Lac.)
  Rhodope
  Rhodes
  Sicyon
  Sybrita
  Tanagra
  Taygetus
  Tegea
  Thasos
  Thebes
  Thelpusa
  Thera
  Thrace
  Troezen
DIONYSUS ACRATOPHORUS
  Phigalia
DIONYSUS ACROREITES
  Sicyon

DIONYSUS AESYMNETES
  Meilichus
  Patrae
DIONYSUS AGRIONIUS
  Orchomenus (Boeo.)
DIONYSUS AMPHIETES
  Thebes
DIONYSUS ANTHEUS
  Athens
  Patrae
  Phyla
DIONYSUS AROEUS
  Patrae
DIONYSUS BASSAREUS
  Thrace
DIONYSUS BRISAEUS
  Brisa
DIONYSUS CALYDONIUS
  Calydon
  Patrae
DIONYSUS CISSUS
  Acharnae
DIONYSUS COLONATAS
  Sparta
DIONYSUS CRESIUS
  Argos
DIONYSUS ELEUTHEREUS
  Athens
  Eleutherae
DIONYSUS HYGIATIS
  Amphicleia
DIONYSUS IATROS
  Amphicleia
DIONYSUS LAMPTER
  Pellene
DIONYSUS LAPHYSTIUS
  Laphystium
DIONYSUS LARYMNA
  Larymna
DIONYSUS LIMNAEA
  Athens
DIONYSUS LYSIUS
  Corinth
  Haliartus
  Sicyon
  Thebes
DIONYSUS MEILICHIUS
  Naxos
DIONYSUS MELANAEGIS
  Athens
  Eleutherae
DIONYSUS MELPOMENUS
  Acharnae
  Athens

DIONYSUS MESATEUS
  Mesatis
  Patrae
DIONYSUS METHYMNAEUS
  Methymna
DIONYSUS MYSTOS
  Tegea
DIONYSUS NYCTELIUS
  Megara
DIONYSUS NYSAEUS
  Nysa
DIONYSUS OMADIUS
  Chios
DIONYSUS ORTHOS
  Athens
  Attica
DIONYSUS PSILAS
  Amyclae
DIONYSUS SAOTES
  Lerna
DIORES
  Elis
DIOSCURI
  Amphissa
  Amyclae
  Aphidna
  Arcadia
  Argos
  Athens
  Calydon
  Cephale
  Cephissus (Athens)
  Cleitor
  Corcyra
  Croceae
  Delos
  Epidaurus
  Laconia
  Messene
  Messenia
  Peloponnesus
  Pephnus
  Phlius
  Sicyon
  Sparta
  Taygetus
  Thalamae
DIOSCURI AMBULII
  Sparta
DIOSCURI AMPHETARII
  Sparta
DIOSCURI LAPERSAE
  Las

DIRCE
　Cithaeron
　Dirce (river)
　Dirce (spring)
　Thebes
DODON
　Dodona
DODONA
　Dodona
DOLICHOS
　Eleusis
DOLIUS
　Ithaca
DOLOPS
　Magnesia
DORCEUS
　Dorceia
　Sebrion
　Sparta
DORIDAS
　Corinth
DORUS
　Achaia (Pelop.)
　Athens
　Doris
　Parnassus
DOTIS
　Dotius Campus
DRYAS (s. Ares)
　Calydon
　Daulis
DRYAS (s. Lycurgus)
　Edonis
DRYAS (beloved of Pallene)
　Macedonia
　Pallene (Mac.)
　Thrace
DRYOPE
　Oeta
DRYOPS
　Messenia
　Spercheius
DYSAULES
　Eleusis
　Phlius
DYSPONTEUS
　Dyspontium
ECECHEIRIA
　Olympia
ECHEMUS
　Arcadia
　Tegea
ECHEPHRON
　Psophis

ECHEPOLIS
　Megara
ECHEPOLUS
　Sicyon
ECHETLUS
　Marathon
ECHETUS
　Epeirus
ECHION
　Echinus (Acarn)
　Echinus (Phth.)
　Thebes
ECHO
　Arcadia
　Hermione
EILEITHYIA
　Aegium
　Amnisus
　Argos
　Athens
　Bura
　Cleitor
　Cnossus
　Delos
　Delphi
　Hermione
　Inatus
　Megara
　Messene
　Pellene
　Sparta
　Tegea
　Thebes
EILEITHYIA LYSIZONA
　Athens
EIRENE
　Athens
　Calaureia
ELATUS (s. Arcas)
　Arcadia
　Cyllene (Arc.)
　Elateia
　Delphi
　Orchomenus (Arc.)
　Tegea
ELATUS (s. Periphas?)
　Larissa (Thess.)
ELECTRA (d. Agamemnon)
　Delphi
　Mycenae
ELECTRA (d. Agenor)
　Thebes
ELECTRYON
　Boeotia

　Midea
　Mycenae
　Tiryns
ELEIUS (s. Amphimachus)
　Elis
ELEIUS (s. Tantalus)
　Elis
ELEOS
　Athens
ELEPHENOR
　Cerinthus
　Dium
　Eretria
　Euboea
　Euripus
　Oreus
ELEUSIS
　Attica
　Eleusis
ELEUTHER
　Eleutherae
ELLOPS
　Euboea
EMATHUS
　Emathia
ENALUS
　Lesbos
ENAREPHORUS
　Sparta
ENCELADUS
　Delphi
ENDYMION
　Elis
　Olympia
ENIPEUS
　Enipeus
ENUDUS
　Samos
ENYO
　Athens
　Orchomenus (Boeo.)ʹ
　Thebes
EOS
　Amyclae
　Athens
　Hymettus
　Olympia
EPAPHUS
　Euboea
EPEIGEUS
　Budeium

EPEIUS (s. Endymion)
 Elis
EPEIUS (s. Panopeus)
 Argos
 Carthaea
 Panopeus
EPHYRA
 Corinth
EPICASTE
 Calydon
EPIDAURUS
 Argos
 Epidaurus
EPIDOTAE
 Epidaurus
 Sparta
EPIMELIDES
 Corone
EPIPOLE
 Carystus
EPISTROPHUS
 Anticyra (Phoc.)
 Panopeus
 Phocis
EPOPEUS
 Corinth
 Sicyon
 Thebes
ERASINUS
 Arcadia
ERATO
 Acacesium
 Arcadia
ERATUS
 Asine
ERECHTHEUS I
 Athens
ERECHTHEUS II
 Athens
 Attica
 Eleusis
ERESUS
 Eresus
ERGINUS
 Lemnos
 Orchomenus (Boeo.)
ERICHTHONIUS (s. Dardanus)
 Crete
ERICHTHONIUS (s. Gaea) (See
 ERECHTHEUS I)
ERIGONE
 Athens
 Attica
 Icaria (Att.)

ERINYS
 Athens
ERIPHYLE
 Argos
EROS
 Aegeira
 Athens
 Megara
 Samos
 Sparta
 Thespiae
ERYMANTHUS
 Erymanthus (river)
 Psophis
ERYSICHTHON
 Athens
 Attica
 Delos
 Prasiae (Att.)
ERYTHRAS
 Erythrae
ETEARCHUS
 Axus
ETEOCLES (s. Andreus)
 Orchomenus (Boeo.)
ETEOCLES (s. Oedipus)
 Thebes
ETEOCLUS (s. Cephissus)
 Cephissus (Boeo.)
ETEOCLUS (s. Iphis)
 Delphi
ETEONUS
 Eteonus
EUADNE
 Phaesana
EUAEMON
 Dolopia
EUAMERION
 Titane
EUANDER
 Arcadia
 Pallantium
 Pheneus
EUANTHES
 Chios
EUBOEA (d. Asopus)
 Euboea
EUBOEA (d. Asterion)
 Asterion
 Euboea (mt.)
EUCHENOR
 Corinth
 Megara

EUCLEIA
 Athens
 Boeotia
 Locris
 Thebes
EUENIUS
 Apollonia
EUENUS
 Messenia
 Euenus
EUETERIA
 Corinthian Isthmus
EUIPPUS
 Cithaeron
 Megara
EUMAEUS
 Ithaca
 Syros
EUMELUS
 Glaphyrae
 Pherae
EUMENIDES
 Athens
 Colonus
 Megalopolis
 Sicyon
EUMOLPUS
 Athens
 Attica
 Eleusis
 Thrace
EUNEUS
 Lemnos
EUNOMUS
 Calydon
EUNOSTUS
 Tanagra
EUPALMUS
 Athens
EUPEITHES
 Ithaca
EUPHEME
 Helicon
EUPHEMUS
 Hyria
 Panopeus
 Taenarum
 Thera
EUPHORBUS
 Mycenae
EUROPA
 Cos
 Crete
 Gortyna

EUROPA HELLOTIS
  Crete
EUROPS
  Sicyon
EUROPUS
  Europus
EUROTAS
  Arcadia
  Eurotas
  Laconia
  Sparta
EURYALUS
  Argos
  Delphi
  Thebes
EURYCLEIA
  Ithaca
EURYGYES (See ANDROGEUS)
EURYMACHUS
  Thebes
EURYMEDE
  Calydon
EURYMEDON (s. Minos)
  Crete
EURYMEDON (s. Ptolemaeus)
  Mycenae
EURYPYLUS (s. Euaemon)
  Asterium
  Hyria
  Ormenium
  Patrae
EURYPYLUS (s. Poseidon)
  Cos
EURYSACES
  Athens
  Brauron
  Melite
  Salamis
EURYSTHENES
  Laconia
  Sparta
  Thebes
EURYSTHEUS
  Marathon
  Mycenae
EURYTE
  Calydon
EURYTION (s. Actor)
  Phthiotis
EURYTION (s. Irus)
  Calydon
EURYTION (Centaur)
  Olenus (Ach.)

EURYTIONE
  Corinth
EURYTUS (s. Actor)
  Cleonae
  Elis
EURYTUS (s. Melaneus)
  Oechalia (Mess.)
  Oechalia (Thess.)
EUTHYMUS
  Olympia
EUXANTHIUS
  Crete
GAEA
  Athens
  Bura
  Delphi
  Olympia
  Patrae
  Phlya
  Sparta
  Tegea
GAEA CARPOPHOROS
  Athens
GAEA CUROTROPOS
  Athens
GAEA EURYSTERNOS
  Crathis
GALATEIA
  Phaestus
GALINTHIAS
  Thebes
GAMELII
  Athens
GANYMEDE
  Olympus
GELANOR
  Argos
GELEON (See TELEON)
GIGANTES
  Athens
  Olympus
  Pallene (Mac.)
  Pelion
GLAUCE (d. Creon)
  Corinth
GLAUCE (d. Cychreus)
  Salamis
GLAUCIA
  Glaucia
GLAUCOPUS
  Alalcomenae
GLAUCUS (s. Aepytus)
  Messenia

GLAUCUS (s. Anthedon)
  Anthedon
  Delos
  Iolcus
  Syme
GLAUCUS (s. Minos)
  Crete
GLAUCUS (s. Sisyphus)
  Corinth
  Corinthian Isthmus
  Potniae
GORGASUS
  Pharae (Mess.)
GORGE
  Amphissa
  Calydon
GORGO
  Corinthian Isthmus
GORGONS
  Diecterion
GORTYS (s. Stymphalus)
  Gortys
GORTYS (s. Tegeates)
  Gortyna
GOUNEUS
  Cyphus
  Gonnus
GRAECUS
  Hellas
GYRTON
  Gyrton
GYRTONE
  Gyrton
HADES
  Acheron
  Athens
  Attica
  Corinthian Isthmus
  Eleusis
  Elis
  Elis (city)
  Ephyra (Epeir.)
  Hermione
  Mintha
  Olympia
  Phalanna
  Pylus (Triph.)
  Triphylia
HAEMON (s. Creon)
  Thebes
HAEMON (s. Lycaon)
  Haemonia
HAEMON (s. Thoas)
  Calydon

HAGNO
  Arcadia
  Hagno
  Lycaeus
  Megalopolis
HALIA
  Rhodes
HALIACMON
  Haliacmon
HALIARTUS
  Haliartus
HALIRRHOTHIUS
  Athens
HALITHERSES
  Ithaca
HALMUS
  Corinth
  Orchomenus (Boeo.)
HAMADRYADES
  Oeta
HARMONIA
  Samothrace
  Thebes
HARPALYCE (d. Clymenus)
  Arcadia
  Argos
HARPALYCE (d. Harpalycus)
  Thrace
HARPIES
  Crete
  Echinades
  Strophades
HARPINNA
  Harpina
HEBE
  Athens
  Olympus
HEBE DIA
  Phlius
  Sicyon
HECAERGE
  Delos
HECALE
  Hecale
HECATE
  Athens
  Delos
  Eleusis
  Zerynthus
HECATE CERYNTHIA
  Samothrace
HECATE PHERAEA
  Pherae

HECTOR (descendant of
    Amphiclus)
  Chios
HECTOR (s. Priam)
  Thebes
HEGEMONE
  Athens
  Attica
HELEIUS
  Helos
  Taphiae
HELEN
  Aphidna
  Athens
  Cenchreae
  Cranae
  Delphi
  Gythium
  Helena
  Rhamnus
  Salamis
  Sparta
HELEN DENDRITIS
  Rhodes
HELENUS
  Argos
  Chaonia
  Dodona
  Epeirus
HELIADES
  Rhodes
HELICE (d. Selinus)
  Helice
  Achaia (Pelop.)
HELICE (nymph)
  Chios
HELIOS
  Apollonia
  Argos
  Athens
  Corinth
  Corinthian Isthmus
  Delphi
  Elis
  Elis (city)
  Hermione
  Laconia
  Olympia
  Rhodes
  Taenarum
  Taygetus
  Troezen

HELLEN
  Hellas
  Melitaea
  Phthiotis
HELLOTIA
  Corinth
HEMERA
  Amyclae
  Athens
HENIOCHE
  Thebes
HEPHAESTUS
  Athens
  Delphi
  Lemnos
  Olympia
  Sparta
HEPHAESTUS AMPHIGYEEIS
  Olympus
HERA
  Anaurus
  Arcadia
  Argolis
  Argos
  Asterion
  Athos
  Cephale
  Cithaeron
  Cnossus
  Corcyra
  Corinth
  Coroneia
  Delos
  Enipeus
  Epidaurus
  Euboea
  Euboea (mt.)
  Heraea
  Hierapytna
  Ialysus
  Iolcus
  Larissa (Thess.)
  Lebadeia
  Messene
  Mycenae
  Nauplia
  Olympia
  Olympus
  Patrae
  Plataea
  Prosymna
  Rhodes
  Samos
  Sicyon

HERA *(cont.)*
  Sparta
  Thebes
  Thornax (Arg.)
  Tiryns
  Titane
HERA ACRAEA
  Acraea
  Argos
  Corinth
  Corinthian Isthmus
  Mycenae
HERA AEGOPHAGOS
  Sparta
HERA ALEXANDROS
  Sicyon
HERA AMMONIA
  Elis
HERA ANTHEIA
  Argos
HERA ARGEIA
  Argos
HERA BUNAEA
  Corinth
HERA CHERA
  Stymphalus
HERA HYPERCHEIRIA
  Eurotas
  Sparta
HERA IMBRASIA
  Imbrasus
  Samos
HERA PAIS
  Stymphalus
HERA PELASGA
  Iolcus
  Thessaly
HERA PHARYGAEA
  Pharygae
HERA PRODROMIA
  Sicyon
HERA SAMIA
  Samos
HERA TELCHINIA
  Cameirus
HERA TELEIA
  Megalopolis
  Stymphalus
HERACLEIDAE
  Peloponnesus
HERACLES
  Abdera
  Abia
  Acharnae

Achelous
Aedepsus
Aegina
Alcimedon
Alpheius
Alyzia
Amyclae
Amymone
Anticyra (Thess.)
Arcadia
Argolis
Argos
Artemisium (mt.)
Boeotia
Callium
Calydon
Cenaeum
Ceryneia
Chaeroneia
Chryse
Cithaeron
Cladeus
Cleonae
Corinth
Corinthian Isthmus
Coroneia
Cos
Crete
Delos
Delphi
Diomeia
Dodona
Doris
Dryopis
Dyme
Echidorus
Eleusis
Elis
Ephyra (Elis)
Erymanthus (mt.)
Euenus
Gythium
Halimus
Hermione
Hyettus
Hymettus
Icarian Sea
Iphistiadae
Iton
Lampeia
Las
Lerna
Lichades
Lindus

Malea (Arc.)
Malis
Marathon
Messenia
Methana
Molorchia
Myconos
Nemea
Oechalia (Eub.)
Oechalia (Mess.)
Oechalia (Thess.)
Oenoe (Arg.)
Oeta (mt.)
Olenus (Ach.)
Olympia
Olympus
Opus
Orchomenus (Boeo.)
Ormenium
Paros
Peneius (Elis)
Pheneus
Pherae
Proschium
Psophis
Pylus (Elis)
Pylus (Mess.)
Salamis
Samos
Sicyon
Siphae
Sparta
Strymon
Stymphalus
Taenarum
Tegea
Tempe
Tenos
Thasos
Thebes
Thermopylae
Thespiae
Thessaly
Thisbe
Thrace
Thymoetadae
Tiryns
Torone
Trachis
Tretos
Troezen
Xypete

HERACLES (Idaean Dactyl)
   Crete
   Olympia
HERACLES ALEXICACUS
   Athens
   Melite
HERACLES BURAICUS
   Bura
HERACLES CHAROPS
   Laphystium
HERACLES CYNAGIDAS
   Beroea
HERACLES INDEX
   Athens
HERACLES MACISTUS
   Macistus
HERACLES MELAMPYGOS
   Thermopylae
HERACLES MENYTES
   Athens
HERACLES MISOGYNIS
   Phocis
HERACLES RHINOCOLUSTES
   Thebes
HERAEEUS
   Heraea
HERCYNA
   Hercyna
   Lebadeia
HERMAPHRODITUS
   Alopece
HERMES
   Arcadia
   Argos
   Athens
   Attica
   Beroea
   Biennus
   Boeotia
   Corcyra
   Corinth
   Cyllene (Arc.)
   Dreros
   Dium
   Las
   Megalopolis
   Methana
   Nemea
   Olympus
   Parnassus
   Pharae (Ach.)
   Pheneus
   Pieria
   Pylus (Mess.)

   Rhodes
   Samos
HERMES (cont.)
   Sybrita
   Thrace
HERMES ACACESIUS
   Acacesium
   Megalopolis
HERMES AGETOR
   Megalopolis
HERMES AGORAEUS
   Sicyon
   Sparta
   Thebes
HERMES CRIOPHORUS
   Oechalia (Mess.)
   Tanagra
HERMES CYLLENIUS
   Cyllene (Ach.)
HERMES EPIMELIUS
   Coroneia
HERMES NONACRIATES
   Nonacris
HERMES POLYGIUS
   Troezen
HERMES PROMACHUS
   Tanagra
HERMES PSYCHOPOMPOS
   Athens
HERMION
   Hermione
HERMIONE
   Argos
   Delphi
   Sparta
HERSE
   Athens
   Attica
HESTIA
   Andros
   Athens
   Delphi
   Hermione
   Olympia
HESTIA PRYTANITIS
   Athens
HICETAS
   Arcadia
HILAEIRA
   Messenia
   Sparta
HIMERUS
   Megara

HIPPALCIMUS
   Boeotia
HIPPOCOON
   Laconia
   Sparta
HIPPODAMEIA (d. Atrax)
   Atrax
HIPPODAMEIA (d. Oenomaus)
   Cladeus
   Midea
   Olympia
   Phrixa
   Pisa
HIPPOLYTE
   Athens
   Megara
HIPPOLYTUS (s. Rhopalus)
   Sicyon
HIPPOLYTUS (s. Theseus)
   Athens
   Sparta
   Troezen
HIPPOMEDON
   Thebes
HIPPOMENES
   Onchestus
HIPPOTES
   Naupactus
HIPPOTHOON
   Alope
   Athens
   Eleusis
HIPPOTHOUS (s. Cercyon)
   Arcadia
   Trapezus
HIPPOTHOUS (s. Lethus)
   Larissa (Thess.)
HISTORIS
   Thebes
HODOEDOCUS
   Cynus
HOLAIS
   Arcadia
HOMOLOEUS
   Thebes
HOMOLOIS
   Thebes
HOPLES
   Athens
HORAE
   Argos
   Athens
   Corinth

HORAE *(cont.)*
   Olympia
   Olympus
HORME
   Athens
HYACINTHUS
   Amyclae
   Athens
   Laconia
   Sparta
HYADES
   Dodona
   Thebes
HYANTHIDAS
   Corinth
HYDRA
   Amymone
   Argolis
   Argos
   Athens
   Delphi
   Elaeus
   Lerna
HYETTUS
   Hyettus
HYGIEIA
   Argos
   Boeae
   Corinth
   Epidaurus
   Gortys
   Lissus
   Oropus
   Phigalia
   Sicyon
   Tegea
   Titane
HYLAEUS
   Arcadia
HYLAS
   Dryopis
HYLE
   Hyle
HYLLUS
   Arcadia
   Tegea
HYMENAEUS
   Argos
HYPERENOR
   Thebes
HYPERES (s. Melas)
   Hypereia (Thess.)
   Pherae

HYPERES (s. Poseidon)
   Calaureia
   Hypereia (Arg.)
   Troezen
HYPERION
   Megara
HYPERMNESTRA (d. Danaus)
   Argos
   Delphi
HYPERMNESTRA (d. Thestius)
   Argos
HYPEROCHE
   Delos
HYPNOS
   Sparta
   Troezen
HYPNOS EPIDOTES
   Sicyon
HYPSEUS
   Larissa (Thess.)
HYPSIPYLE
   Lemnos
HYPSUS
   Hypsus
HYRIA
   Calydon
   Canope
   Pleuron
HYRIEUS
   Hyria
HYRNETHO
   Argos
   Epidaurus
IACCHUS
   Athens
   Eleusis
IALMENUS
   Orchomenus (Boeo.)
IALYSUS
   Ialysus
   Rhodes
IAMBE
   Attica
IAMIDAE
   Sparta
IAMUS
   Phaesana
   Olympia
IANISCUS
   Sicyon
IASION
   Paros
   Samothrace

IASIUS
   Arcadia
IASO
   Oropus
IASUS (s. Argus)
   Argos
IASUS (s. Triopas)
   Argos
ICADIUS
   Crissa
   Delphi
   Parnassus
ICARIUS (friend of Dionysus)
   Anygrus
   Athens
   Cos
   Icaria (Att.)
ICARIUS (s. Perieres)
   Acarnania
   Pleuron
   Sparta
ICARUS
   Aegean Sea
   Cnossus
   Crete
   Icaria (isl.)
   Icarian Sea
IDA
   Crete
   Dicte
   Ida
IDAEUS
   Samothrace
IDAS (s. Aphareus)
   Messenia
   Sparta
IDAS (hero in war against
   Thebes)
   Onchestus
IDAS (hero in war against
   Thebes)
   Taenarum
IDAS and LYNCEUS
   Aphidna
   Arcadia
   Calydon
   Laconia
IDOMENEUS
   Amnisus
   Cnossus
   Crete
   Lyctos
   Miletus
   Olympia

ILUS
  Ephyra (Epeir.)
IMMARADUS
  Athens
  Eleusis
INACHUS
  Argolis
  Argos
  Inachus
  Leuctra (Lac.)
INO
  Megara
  Megaris
  Oetylus
  Orchomenus (Boeo.)
  Prasiae (Lac.)
  Thalamae
  Thebes
IO
  Arcadia
  Argos
  Dodona
  Euboea
  Ionian Sea
  Nemea
IOCASTA
  Thebes
IOLAUS
  Athens
  Delphi
  Lerna
  Thebes
IOLE
  Oechalia (Mess.)
  Oechalia (Thess.)
ION (s. Apollo)
  Achaia (Pelop.)
  Athens
  Delphi
  Helice
  Potamus
ION (s. Gargettus)
  Cytherus
IONIDES
  Cytherus
IOPS
  Sparta
IPHIANASSA
  Cleitor
  Lusi
  Tiryns
IPHICLES
  Pheneus
  Thebes

IPHICLUS
  Phylace
IPHIGENEIA
  Aulis
  Brauron
  Delphi
  Megara
  Mycenae
  Sparta
IPHIMEDEIA
  Anthedon
  Drius
  Naxos
IPHINOE (d. Alcathous)
  Megara
IPHINOE (d. Proetus)
  Cleitor
  Tiryns
IPHIS (s. Alector)
  Argos
IPHIS (d. Ligdus)
  Phaestus
IPHIS (beloved of Patroclus)
  Scyros
IPHITUS (s. Eurytus)
  Messenia
  Oechalia (Thess.)
  Tiryns
IPHITUS (s. Haemon)
  Olympia
IPHITUS (s. Naubolus)
  Drymaea
  Phocis
IRIS
  Athens
  Olympus
ISCHYS
  Dotius Campus
ISMARUS
  Eleusis
ISMENE
  Thebes
ISMENIUS
  Ismenus
ISMENUS
  Ismenus
  Thebes
ISSA
  Lesbos
ITANUS
  Itanus
ITHACUS
  Ithaca

ITHOME
  Clepsydra
  Ithome (Mess.)
ITONE
  Crete
ITONUS
  Boeotia
ITYLUS
  Thebes
ITYS
  Daulis
IXION
  Larissa (Thess.)
  Thessaly
JASON
  Anaurus
  Corcyra
  Corinth
  Enipeus
  Euenus
  Iolcus
  Lemnos
  Pelion
JASON PAGASAEUS
  Pagasae
JUPITER CAPITOLINUS
  Corinth
LABDACUS
  Thebes
LACEDAEMON
  Laconia
  Sparta
LACESTADES
  Sicyon
LACIUS
  Laciadae
LACON
  Laconia
LADON
  Arcadia
  Ladon
LAELAPS
  Thebes
LAERTES
  Calydon
  Ithaca
  Nericus
LAIAS
  Elis
LAIUS
  Schiste
  Thebes
LAMEDON
  Sicyon

LAMIUS
   Lamia
LANASSA
   Epeirus
LAOCOON
   Calydon
LAODAMAS
   Glisas
   Thebes
LAODAMEIA
   Phylace
LAODICE (d. Agapenor)
   Tegea
LAODICE (Hyperborean)
   Delos
LAODICUS
   Delphi
LAODOCUS
   Curetis
LAPHRIA
   Cephallenia
LAPHRIUS
   Calydon
LAPITHES
   Larissa (Thess.)
   Thessaly
LARISSA
   Larissa (Arg.)
   Larissa (Thess.)
LARYMNA
   Cynus
   Larymna
LAS
   Arainus
   Laconia
LATHRIA
   Sparta
LAVINIA
   Delos
LEADES
   Thebes
LEBADUS
   Lebadeia
LECHES
   Lechaeum
LEDA
   Aetolia
   Rhamnus
   Sparta
LEIMON
   Tegea
LEIS
   Althepia

LEITUS
   Arne (Boeo.)
   Boeotia
   Plataea
LELEX
   Laconia
   Megara
   Sparta
LEOGORAS
   Samos
LEONTEUS
   Larissa (Thess.)
LEOS
   Athens
LEPETYMNUS
   Lepetymnus
LEPREA
   Lepreum
LEPREUS
   Lepreum
LESBUS
   Lesbos
LETO
   Abae
   Amarynthus
   Amphigeneia
   Argos
   Cirrha
   Delos
   Dreros
   Lete
   Sparta
   Zoster
LETO CYNTHIA
   Cynthus
LETO PHYTIA
   Phaestus
LETREUS
   Letrini
LEUCADIUS
   Acarnania
   Leucas
LEUCIPPUS (s. Lamprus)
   Phaestus
LEUCIPPUS (s. Naxus)
   Naxos
LEUCIPPUS (s. Oenomaus)
   Pisa
LEUCIPPUS (s. Perieres)
   Leuctra (Boeo.)
   Messenia
LEUCIPPUS (s. Thurimachus)
   Sicyon

LEUCIPPUS (Rhodian colonist)
   Rhodes
LEUCOPEUS
   Calydon
LEUCOTHEA
   Corinth
   Corinthian Isthmus
LICHAS
   Cenaeum
   Lichades
LICYMNIUS
   Argos
   Midea
   Tiryns
LILAEA
   Lilaea
LINDUS
   Rhodes
LINUS
   Argos
   Chalcis
   Helicon
   Macedonia
   Thebes
LOCRUS (s. Physcius)
   Locris
LOCRUS (s. Zeus)
   Thebes
LOXO
   Delos
LYCAON
   Arcadia
   Lycosura
   Trapezus
LYCASTUS (s. Ares)
   Erymanthus (river)
LYCASTUS (s. Minos)
   Crete
   Lycastus
LYCOMEDES
   Scyros
LYCOPHRON
   Cythera
LYCORUS
   Lycoreia
LYCTUS
   Lyctos
LYCURGUS (s. Aleus)
   Arcadia
   Lepreum
LYCURGUS (s. Dryas)
   Edonis
   Nysa (Thrace)

LYCURGUS (s. Dryas) *(cont.)*
 Pangaeum
 Thrace
LYCURGUS (s. Pheres)
 Nemea
LYCURGUS (s. Pronax)
 Amyclae
 Thebes
LYCUS (s. Hyrieus)
 Eleutherae
 Hyria
 Sicyon
 Thebes
LYCUS (s. Pandion)
 Andania
 Athens
 Messenia
LYNCEUS (s. Aegyptus)
 Argos
 Delphi
 Lyrceia
LYNCEUS (s. Aphareus)
 Messenia
 Sparta
LYRCUS
 Lyrceia
LYSIPPE
 Cleitor
 Lusi
 Tiryns
MACAR (s. Helios)
 Rhodes
MACAR (s. Lycaon)
 Macareae
MACAREUS (s. Aeolus)
 Thessaly
MACAREUS (s. Crineius)
 Lesbos
MACARIA
 Marathon
MACEDON
 Macedonia
MACEDONUS
 Macedonia
MACHAON
 Gerenia
 Ithome (Thess.)
 Messenia
 Tricca
MACISTUS
 Macistus
MAENALUS
 Arcadia
 Maenalus (city)

MAERA (d. Atlas)
 Mantineia
 Tegea
MAERA (dog)
 Athens
 Icaria (Att.)
MAGNES (s. Aeolus)
 Meliboea
MAGNES (s. Argos)
 Magnesia
MAIA
 Arcadia
MALIADES
 Spercheius
MALUS
 Malis
MANTINEUS
 Mantineia
MANTO (d. Polyidus)
 Megara
MANTO (d. Teiresias)
 Corinth
 Delphi
 Peneius (Thess.)
 Thebes
MARATHON
 Marathon
 Sicyon
MARON
 Maroneia
MARPESSA
 Messenia
MARSYAS
 Athens
 Sicyon
MASTOR
 Cythera
MECISTEUS
 Argos
 Thebes
MECON
 Athens
MEDEA
 Athens
 Corcyra
 Corinth
 Crete
 Iolcus
 Tallaeus
 Thessaly
MEDEIUS
 Pelion
MEDEON
 Medeon

MEDON (s. Ceisus)
 Argos
MEDON (herald of Odysseus)
 Ithaca
MEDON (s. Oileus)
 Phylace
MEDUS
 Athens
MEDUSA
 Athens
 Beroea
 Corcyra
 Diecterion
 Eleusis
 Tegea
MEGAPENTHES
 Argos
 Tiryns
MEGARA
 Thebes
MEGAREUS
 Megaris
MEGARUS
 Geraneia
MEGES
 Dulichium
 Echinades
MEILANION
 Arcadia
MEILICHII
 Myonia
MELAMPUS
 Aegosthena
 Alpheius
 Anigrus
 Argos
 Cleitor
 Lusi
 Othrys
 Phylace
 Pylus (Mess.)
 Tegea
 Tiryns
MELAENEUS
 Melaenae
MELANEUS
 Oechalia (Thess.)
MELANIPPE (d. Cheiron)
 Pelion
MELANIPPE (d. Oeneus)
 Calydon
MELANIPPUS (s. Ares)
 Tritaea

MELANIPPUS (s. Astacus)
  Thebes
MELANIPPUS (beloved of
  Comaetho)
  Patrae
MELANIPPUS (s. Theseus)
  Athens
  Melite
MELANTHIUS
  Ithaca
MELANTHUS
  Mclaenae
MELAS (s. Antassus)
  Corinth
  Gonusa
MELAS (s. Porthaon)
  Calydon
MELAS (s. Poseidon)
  Chios
MELEAGER
  Aetolia
  Calydon
  Sicyon
MELEAGRIDES
  Leros
MELES
  Athens
MELIA
  Thebes
MELIADES
  Melas
MELIBOEA
  Meliboea
MELICERTES
  Corinth
  Megaris
MELISSEUS
  Crete
MELISSUS
  Corinth
MELITE
  Athens
  Attica
  Melite
MELITEUS
  Melitaea
MELTAS
  Argos
MELUS (s. Manto)
  Lesbos
MELUS (s. Melus)
  Delos

MEMBLIARUS
  Anaphe
  Thera
MEMNON
  Amyclae
  Athens
  Corcyra
  Olympia
MENELAUS
  Aulis
  Delphi
  Gythium
  Ithaca
  Laconia
  Malea (prom.)
  Mycenae
  Phare
  Sparta
MENEPHRON
  Arcadia
MENESTHEUS
  Athens
MENESTHIUS (s. Areithous)
  Arne (Boeo.)
MENESTHIUS (s. Spercheius)
  Spercheius
MENIPPE
  Aonia
  Orchomenus (Boeo.)
MENOECEUS
  Thebes
MENOETIUS
  Opus
MENTES
  Ithaca
  Taphiae
MENTOR
  Ithaca
MERIONES
  Cnossus
  Crete
MERMERUS
  Corinth
MEROPE (d. Atlas)
  Corinth
MEROPE (d. Cypselus)
  Basilis
  Messenia
MEROPE (d. Erechtheus)
  Athens
MEROPE (d. Oenopion)
  Chios
MEROPE (d. Pandareos)
  Miletus

MEROPS
  Cos
MESSAPUS
  Massapium
MESSENE
  Messenia
METANEIRA
  Attica
  Eleusis
METAPONTUS
  Icaria (isl.)
METHAPUS
  Thebes
METHE
  Elis
METHON
  Methone (Mac.)
METHONE (d. Oeneus)
  Methone (Mess.)
METHONE (mother of
  Philoctetes)
  Methone (Mac.)
METHYMNA
  Lesbos
  Methymna
METIADUSA
  Athens
METIOCHE
  Aonia
  Orchomenus (Boeo.)
METION
  Athens
METOPE (d. Echetus)
  Epeirus
METOPE (d. Ladon)
  Ladon
MIDAS
  Bermius
  Emathia
MIDEIA
  Midea
MIEZA
  Mieza
MILETUS
  Crete
MIMAS
  Delphi
MINOS I
  Crete
  Dictamnum
  Dicte
MINOS II
  Carpathus
  Cnossus

MINOS II *(cont.)*
    Crete
    Cyclades
    Phaestus
    Praesus
    Saronic Gulf
MINOTAUR
    Cnossus
    Crete
MINTHA
    Mintha
    Pylus (Triph.)
    Triphylia
MINYAE
    Lemnos
    Orchomenus (Boeo.)
    Phrixa
    Pyrgus
    Thera
MINYAS
    Minya
    Orchomenus (Boeo.)
MISME
    Attica
MNASINUS
    Amyclae
    Argos
MNEMOSYNE
    Athens
    Lebadeia
    Tegea
MOIRAE
    Arcadia
    Athens
    Calydon
    Corinth
    Delphi
    Megara
    Olympia
    Sparta
    Thebes
MOLORCHUS
    Cleonae
    Molorchia
MOLOSSUS
    Chaonia
    Epeirus
    Ephyra (Epeir.)
MOLPADIA
    Athens
MOLUS
    Crete

MOPSUS
    Oechalia (Thess.)
    Titarus
MOPSUS TITARESIUS
    Titarus
MOTHONE
    Calydon
MULIUS
    Dulichium
MUSAE
    Aganippe
    Ambracia
    Aonia
    Aptera
    Ascra
    Athens
    Castalia
    Corinth
    Delphi
    Dium
    Dorium
    Emathia
    Helicon
    Hippocrene
    Libethra
    Libethrias
    Megalopolis
    Megara
    Olympus
    Parnassus
    Pieria
    Sparta
    Tegea
    Thespiae
    Thrace
MUSAE AGANIPPIDES
    Helicon
MUSAE ARDALIDES
    Troezen
MUSAE ILISSIADES
    Ilissus
MUSAE LIBETHRIDES
    Libethrias
MUSAE PIERIDES
    Pieria
    Thespiae
MUSAE PIMPLEIDES
    Pimpleia
MUSAE THESPIADES
    Thespiae
MYCENE
    Mycenae
MYIAGRUS
    Aliphera

MYLES
    Laconia
MYRINA
    Myrina
MYRMEX
    Athens
    Attica
MYRMIDON
    Thessaly
MYRMIDONS
    Aegina
    Thessaly
MYRTILUS
    Aegean Sea
    Elis
    Geraestus
    Myrtoan Sea
    Olympia
    Pheneus
    Pisa
MYRTO
    Myrtoan Sea
MYRTOESSA
    Megalopolis
MYTILENE
    Lesbos
    Mytilene
MYTON
    Mytilene
NARCAEUS
    Elis
NARCISSUS
    Cephissus (Boeo.)
NAUBOLUS (s. Lernus)
    Tanagra
NAUBOLUS (s. Ornytus)
    Drymaea
NAUPLIUS (father of Palamedes)
    Caphareus
    Euboea
NAUPLIUS (s. Poseidon)
    Amymone
    Argos
    Nauplia
NAUSICAA
    Corcyra
NAUSIMEDON
    Euboea
NAUSITHOUS
    Corcyra
NAXUS
    Naxos
NEAERA
    Alea

NEBROPHONUS
   Lemnos
NEDA
   Arcadia
   Athens
   Clepsydra
   Ithome (Mess.)
   Neda
NEIS
   Thebes
NELEUS
   Corinth
   Corinthian Isthmus
   Iolcus
   Messenia
   Pylus (Mess.)
NEMEA
   Nemea
NEMESIS
   Patrae
NEMESIS ADRASTEIA
   Asopus (Pelop.)
NEMESIS RHAMNUSIA
   Rhamnus
NEOPTOLEMUS
   Cassotis
   Chaonia
   Corcyra
   Delphi
   Epeirus
   Ephyra (Epeir.)
   Phthiotis
   Pyrrhichus
   Scyros
   Sparta
NEPHALION
   Crete
NEREIDS
   Cardamyle
   Corinthian Isthmus
   Mediterranean Sea
NEREUS
   Gythium
   Mediterannean Sea
NERITUS
   Neritus
NESSUS (Centaur)
   Euenus
   Locris
NESSUS (s. Oceanus)
   Nestus
NESTOR
   Aepy
   Amphigeneia

Arene
Calydon
Ceos
Coryphasium
Dorium
Epitalium
Gerenia
Messenia
Poeeessa
Pteleum (Elis)
Pylus (Mess.)
NICOMACHUS
   Pharae (Mess.)
NIKE
   Athens
   Olympia
   Samothrace
NIKE APTEROS
   Athens
NIOBE (d. Phoroneus)
   Argos
NIOBE (d. Tantalus)
   Cithaeron
   Thebes
NIREUS
   Syme
NISUS (father of Amphinomus)
   Dulichium
NISUS (s. Pandion)
   Athens
   Megara
NOMIA
   Nomia
NONACRIS
   Nonacris
NYCTEUS
   Hyria
   Hysiae
   Thebes
NYCTIMENE
   Lesbos
NYCTIMUS
   Arcadia
   Lycosura
NYMPHAE
   Aphytis
   Arcadia
   Athens
   Attica
   Cephissus (Boeo.)
   Corycium
   Cyrtones
   Delos
   Leben

Olympia
Oropus
Othrys
Pentelicus
Sparta
NYMPHAE ACMENES
   Elis (city)
NYMPHAE ANIGRIDES
   Samicum
NYMPHAE DELIADES
   Delos
NYMPHAE IONIDES
   Heracleia
NYMPHAE ISMENIDES
   Phlya
NYSA
   Nysa (Thrace)
NYSEIDES
   Nysa (Thrace)
NYX
   Megara
OCEANIDS
   Arcadia
OCHIMUS
   Rhodes
ODYSSEUS
   Aetolia
   Asea
   Corcyra
   Delphi
   Dodona
   Eleusis
   Ephyra (Epeir.)
   Ismarus
   Ithaca
   Lesbos
   Malea (prom.)
   Messenia
   Parnassus
   Same
   Sparta
   Taphiae
   Zacynthus
OEAGRUS
   Thrace
OEAX
   Euboea
OEBALUS (s. Cynortas)
   Laconia
   Sparta
OEBALUS (s. Telon)
   Taphiae
OECHALIA
   Oechalia (Thess.)

OEDIPUS
- Athens
- Cithaeron
- Colonus
- Corinth
- Schiste
- Tenes
- Thebes

OENOE (sister of Epochus)
- Oenoe (Att.)

OENOE (nymph)
- Tegea

OENEUS (s. Pandion)
- Athens

OENEUS (s. Portheus)
- Aetolia
- Argos
- Calydon
- Oeniadae
- Oenoe (Arg.)
- Pleuron

OENOMAUS
- Cladeus
- Elis
- Harpina
- Olympia
- Pisa

OENOPION
- Chios

OENOTROPAE
- Delos

OEOCLUS
- Ascra

OEOLYCUS
- Sparta

OEONUS
- Sparta

OETYLUS
- Oetylus

OGYGUS
- Achaia (Pelop.)
- Attica
- Thebes

OICLES
- Arcadia
- Argos

OILEUS
- Locris

OLENIAS
- Calydon

OLENUS (s. Zeus)
- Olenus (Aet.)

OLENUS (husband of Lethaea)
- Ida

OLMUS
- Olmones

OLYNTHUS
- Olynthus
- Thrace

OMPHALE
- Ctimene

ONCHESTUS
- Onchestus

ONCUS
- Onceium
- Thelpusa

ONETOR
- Ida

OPHELTES (s. Lycurgus)
- Nemea

OPHELTES (s. Peneleos)
- Boeotia
- Thebes

OPHIUCHUS (See PHORBAS)

OPIS
- Delos

OPUS
- Opus

ORCHOMENUS (s. Lycaon)
- Orchomenus (Arc.)
- Methydrium

ORCHOMENUS (s. Minyas)
- Orchomenus (Boeo.)

OREITHYIA
- Athens
- Ilissus

ORESTES
- Arcadia
- Argos
- Argos Oresticum
- Athens
- Brauron
- Delphi
- Gythium
- Laconia
- Megalopolis
- Mycenae
- Oresthasium
- Phocis
- Sparta
- Tegea
- Thyrea
- Troezen

ORESTHEUS
- Oresthasium

ORION
- Boeotia
- Chios

- Crete
- Delos
- Hyria
- Lemnos
- Tanagra

ORMENUS
- Ormenium

ORNEUS
- Athens
- Orneae

ORNYTION
- Corinth

ORPHEUS
- Cos
- Dium
- Hebrus
- Lesbos
- Libethra
- Olympus
- Pieria
- Pimpleia
- Thrace
- Zone

ORSILOCHUS
- Pharae (Mess.)

ORTHOPOLIS
- Sicyon

ORUS
- Althepia
- Troezen

OTIONIA
- Athens

OTUS and EPHIALTES (See ALOEIDAE)

OXYLUS
- Aetolia
- Calydon
- Elis
- Elis (city)

PAEON
- Paeonia

PALAEMON
- Boeotia
- Corinth
- Corinthian Isthmus
- Schoenus (Corin.)

PALAESTINUS
- Strymon

PALAMEDES
- Euboea
- Geraestus
- Ithaca
- Lepetymnus
- Nauplia

PALLADIUM
  Athens
  Attica
  Olympus
  Samothrace
PALLAS (s. Lycaon)
  Pallantium
PALLAS (s. Pandion)
  Athens
  Pallene (Att.)
PALLAS (giant)
  Pellene
PALLENE
  Pallene (Mac.)
  Macedonia
  Thrace
PAMISUS
  Pamisus
PAMPHYLUS
  Pindus
PAN
  Acacesium
  Anaphlystus
  Arcadia
  Athens
  Cephissus (Boeo.)
  Cnossus
  Corycium
  Heraea
  Homole
  Lycosura
  Marathon
  Megalopolis
  Melpeia
  Nomia
  Olympus
  Oropus
  Parthenium
  Peraetheis
  Same
  Sicyon
  Psyttaleia
  Tegea
  Thasos
  Troezen
PAN LYCAEUS
  Lycaeus
PAN LYTERIUS
  Troezen
PAN MAENALUS
  Maenalus (mt.)
PAN SINOEIS
  Arcadia

PANCRATIS
  Drius
  Naxos
  Phthiotis
PANDAREOS
  Crete
  Miletus
PANDION I
  Athens
  Eleusis
PANDION II
  Athena Aethyia
  Athens
  Megara
PANDORA
  Athens
PANDOROS
  Athens
  Chalcis
  Euboea
PANDROSOS
  Athens
  Attica
PANOPEUS
  Panopeus
  Taphiae
PANOPS
  Athens
PANTHOUS
  Delphi
PARIS
  Cranae
  Gythium
  Salamis
  Sparta
PARIUS
  Paros
PARNASSUS
  Delphi
  Parnassus
PAROREUS
  Paroria
PARRHASIUS
  Erymanthus (river)
  Parrhasia
PARTHENIA
  Samos
PARTHENOPAEUS
  Argos
  Thebes
PARUS
  Paros

PASIPHAE (d. Aeetes)
  Cnossus
  Crete
PASIPHAE (d. Atlas)
  Thalamae
PASITHEA
  Athens
PATREUS
  Mesatis
  Patrae
PATROCLUS
  Athens
  Opus
  Phthiotis
PEDIAS
  Athens
  Attica
PEGASUS
  Corcyra
  Corinth
  Hippocrene
  Olympus
PEIRANTHUS
  Argos
PEIRASUS
  Tiryns
PEIREN
  Corinth
PEREINE
  Corinth
PEIRITHOUS
  Aphidna
  Athens
  Calydon
  Colonus
  Epeirus
  Larissa (Thess.)
  Thessaly
PEIROOS
  Thrace
PEISENOR
  Ithaca
PEISIDICE
  Methymna
PEITHO
  Athens
  Sicyon
PELARGE
  Boeotia
PELASGUS (s. Arestor)
  Arcadia
  Parrhasia

PELASGUS (s. Phoroneus)
  Erasinus
  Hellas
PELASGUS (s. Poseidon)
  Argos Pelasgicum
  Thessaly
PELASGUS (s. Triopas)
  Argos
  Larissa (Arg.)
PELASGUS (s. Zeus)
  Peloponnesus
PELEGON
  Axius
PELEUS
  Aegina
  Calydon
  Ctimene
  Iolcus
  Pelion
  Phthiotis
  Sepias
  Thessaly
  Trachis
PELIADES
  Mantineia
PELIAS
  Iolcus
PELLEN
  Pellene
PELOPS
  Arcadia
  Charadra
  Cladeus
  Elis
  Euboea
  Geraestus
  Letrini
  Leuctra (Lac.)
  Olympia
  Olympus
  Peloponnesus
  Pelopis Insulae
  Phlius
  Pisa
  Thalamae
PELOR
  Thebes
PENEIUS
  Larissa (Thess.)
  Peneius (Thess.)
PENELEOS
  Arne (Boeo.)
  Boeotia

  Hyria
  Thebes
PENELOPE
  Acarnania
  Ithaca
  Mantineia
  Sparta
PENTHEUS
  Cithaeron
  Parnassus
  Thebes
PENTHILUS
  Thrace
PERAETHUS
  Peraetheis
PERATUS
  Sicyon
PERDIX
  Athens
PERGAMUS
  Chaonia
  Epeirus
PERIBOEA
  Corinth
PERICLYMENUS (s. Neleus)
  Pylus (Mess.)
PERICLYMENUS (s. Poseidon)
  Thebes
PERIERES
  Messenia
PERIPHAS (autochthon)
  Attica
PERIPHAS (s. Lapithes)
  Larissa (Thess.)
  Thessaly
PERIPHAS (s. Oeneus)
  Calydon
PERIPHETES (s. Copreus)
  Mycenae
PERIPHETES (s. Hephaestus)
  Epidaurus
PERSEPHONE
  Aptera
  Arcadia
  Athens
  Attica
  Buporthmus
  Cabeiraea
  Corinth
  Corinthian Isthmus
  Cos
  Crete
  Eleusis
  Ephyra (Epeir.)

  Erineus
  Halimus
  Hercyna
  Lebadeia
  Lerna
  Lete
  Megalopolis
  Megara
  Mintha
  Nysa (Boeo.)
  Oechalia (Mess.)
  Pallantium
  Patrae
  Phalanna
  Pheneus
  Pisa
  Potniae
  Scolus
  Sparta
  Tegea
  Thebes
  Thelpusa
  Thera
PERSEPHONE CARPOPHOROS
  Tegea
PERSEPHONE PROTOGONIS
  Phlya
PERSEPHONE SOTEIRA
  Arcadia
  Sparta
PERSEPHONE THESMIA
  Athens
  Megara
  Pheneus
  Troezen
PERSEUS
  Apesas
  Argos
  Diecterion
  Eleusis
  Larissa (Thess.)
  Midea
  Mycenae
  Seriphos
  Tiryns
PETEOS
  Athens
  Stiris
PHAEA
  Corinth
  Crommyon

PHAEDRA
   Athens
   Crete
   Troezen
PHAENNA
   Sparta
PHAESTUS
   Phaestus
   Sicyon
PHAETHON
   Corinth
PHANES
   Sicyon
   Thebes
PHAON
   Mytilene
PHALANNA
   Phalanna
PHALANTHUS
   Phalanthum
PHALCES
   Sicyon
PHALERUS
   Chalcis
   Gyrton
   Phalerum
PHARIS
   Pharae (Mess.)
PHARMACIDES
   Thebes
PHEGEUS
   Argos
   Psophis
PHEIDIPPUS
   Carpathus
   Casus
   Cos
   Nisyrus
   Sporades
PHEME
   Athens
PHEMIUS
   Ithaca
PHENEUS
   Pheneus
PHERES (s. Cretheus)
   Pherae
PHERES (s. Jason)
   Corinth
PHIALUS
   Arcadia
   Phigalia
PHIGALIA
   Phigalia

PHIGALUS
   Phigalia
PHILAEUS
   Brauron
   Philaidae
   Salamis
PHILAMMON
   Parnassus
PHILLO
   Alcimedon
PHILOCTETES
   Chryse
   Lemnos
   Meliboea
   Methone (Mac.)
   Neae
   Oeta
   Olizon
   Thaumacia
PHILOETIUS
   Ithaca
PHILOLAUS
   Crete
PHILOMELA
   Athens
   Attica
   Daulis
   Pegae
PHILOMELEIDES
   Lesbos
PHILONOME
   Erymanthus (river)
PHILONOMUS
   Amyclae
PHINEUS
   Arcadia
PHLEGYAS
   Dotius Campus
   Orchomenus (Boeo.)
PHLIAS
   Araethyrea
   Phlius
PHOCUS (s. Aeacus)
   Aegina
   Phocis
PHOCUS (s. Ornytion)
   Corinth
   Daulis
   Neon
PHOEBE (d. Leucippus)
   Messenia
PHOEBE (d. Tyndareus)
   Sparta

PHOEBE (d. Uranus)
   Delphi
PHOEBUS APOLLO
   Delphi
PHOENIX
   Ctimene
   Dolopia
   Eion (Mac.)
   Ormenium
   Phthiotis
PHOLEGANDROS
   Pholegandros
PHOLUS
   Pholoe
PHORBAS
   Larissa (Thess.)
   Olenus (Ach.)
   Rhodes
   Thessaly
PHORCYS
   Ithaca
PHORMION
   Sparta
PHORONEUS
   Argos
   Hellas
   Peloponnesus
PHRIXUS
   Orchomenus (Boeo.)
PHRONIMA
   Axus
PHTHIUS
   Phthiotis
PHYLACIS
   Elyrus
PHYLACUS (s. Deion)
   Phylace
PHYLACUS (Delphian hero)
   Delphi
PHYLANDER
   Elyrus
PHYLEUS
   Alpheius
   Dulichium
   Elis
   Ephyra (Elis)
PHYLLIS
   Thrace
PHYLLIUS
   Calydon
   Canope
   Pleuron
PHYSADEIA
   Physadeia

POSEIDON *(cont.)*
  Molycreium
  Myonia
  Naupactus
  Nauplia
  Naxos
  Nicopolis
  Nisyrus
  Olympia
  Olympus
  Orchomenus (Arc.)
  Patrae
  Pella
  Pellene
  Peloponnesus
  Poseidonium
  Rhodes
  Samothrace
  Sparta
  Sunium
  Taenarum
  Telos
  Temenium
  Tempe
  Tenos
  Thasos
  Thessaly
  Thrace
  Tricoloni
  Troezen
POSEIDON AEGAEUS
  Aegae (Eub.)
POSEIDON ASPHALEIUS
  Sparta
POSEIDON CUERIUS
  Cierium
POSEIDON DOMATITES
  Sparta
POSEIDON EPACTAEUS
  Samos
POSEIDON EPOPSIUS
  Megalopolis
POSEIDON GAEAOCHUS
  Gythium
  Sparta
POSEIDON GENETHLIUS
  Sparta
POSEIDON HELICONIUS
  Helice
POSEIDON HIPPIUS
  Methydrium
  Pheneus
POSEIDON HIPPOCURIUS
  Sparta

POSEIDON ISTHMIUS
  Corinthian Isthmus
  Sicyon
POSEIDON LECHAEUS
  Lechaeum
POSEIDON ONCHESTIUS
  Haliartus
  Onchestus
POSEIDON PATROS
  Eleusis
  Rharian Plain
POSEIDON PETRAEUS
  Peneius (Thess.)
POSEIDON SAMICUS
  Macistus
POSEIDON SAMIUS
  Samicum
  Samos
POSEIDON TAENARIUS
  Sparta
POTHOS
  Megara
  Samothrace
PRAXIDICAE
  Haliartus
  Tilphossium
PRAXIDICE
  Gythium
PRAXITHEA
  Athens
PREUGENES
  Patrae
PRIAM
  Corcyra
PRIAPUS
  Orniae
PROCLES (s. Aristodemus)
  Laconia
  Sparta
PROCLES (s. Pityreus)
  Samos
  Thebes
PROCNE
  Athens
  Attica
  Daulis
  Pegae
PROCRIS
  Athens
  Crete
  Phocis
PROCRUSTES
  Cephissus (Eleusis)
  Corydallus

PROETUS
  Argos
  Cleitor
  Midea
  Sicyon
  Tiryns
  Titane
PROMACHUS
  Psophis
  Thebes
PROMETHEUS (s. Iapetus)
  Athens
  Boeotia
  Colonus
  Panopeus
  Sicyon
PROMETHEUS (one of the
  Cabeiri)
  Cabeiraea
PRONAX
  Argos
  Nemea
PRONOE
  Calydon
PRONOUS
  Delphi
  Psophis
PROPODAS
  Corinth
PROSYMNA
  Asterion
  Euboea (mt.)
PROSYMNUS
  Lerna
PROTESILAUS
  Antron
  Mende
  Pallene (Mac.)
  Phylace
  Pteleum (Thess.)
  Scione
PROTEUS
  Carpathus
  Pallene (Mac.)
  Thrace
PROTHOENOR
  Boeotia
PROTHOUS
  Pelion
  Spalathra
PROTOGENEIA (d. Calydon)
  Calydon
PROTOGENEIA (d. Deucalion)
  Maenalus (mt.)

PSAMATHE
    Aegina
    Argos
PSOPHIS (s. Arrhon)
    Psophis
PSOPHIS (d. Eryx)
    Psophis
PTERAS
    Aptera
    Crete
    Delphi
PTERELAUS
    Taphiae
PTOLEMAEUS (s. Damasichthon)
    Thebes
PTOLEMAEUS (s. Peiraeus)
    Mycenae
PTOUS
    Acraephnium
    Ptoum
PYLADES
    Mycenae
    Phocis
PYLAEUS
    Larissa (Thess.)
PYLAS
    Megara
    Pylus (Elis)
    Pylus (Mess.)
PYLIA
    Megara
PYRAECHMES
    Amydon
    Paeonia
PYRRHA (d. Creon)
    Thebes
PYRRHA (d. Epimetheus)
    Cynus
    Delphi
    Opus
    Othrys
    Parnassus
    Phthiotis
PYRRHICHUS
    Pyrrhichus
PYRRHUS (See NEOPTOLEMUS)
PYTHIS
    Delphi
PYTHON
    Cassotis
    Delphi
    Parnassus

RHADAMANTHYS
    Crete
    Haliartus
    Ocalea
RHARUS
    Eleusis
    Rharian Plain
RHEA
    Acriae
    Aegeum
    Anagyrus
    Arne (Arc.)
    Asea
    Athens
    Chaeroneia
    Cnossus
    Crete
    Delphi
    Dicte
    Eleusis
    Ida
    Laconia
    Lemnos
    Lyctos
    Megalopolis
    Messene
    Methydrium
    Olympia
    Parrhasia
    Phaestus
    Plataea
    Samothrace
    Sparta
    Tegea
    Thrace
RHEA DINDYMENE
    Thebes
RHESUS
    Thrace
RHODE
    Mediterranean Sea
RHODOS
    Rhodes
RHOEO
    Delos
    Euboea
RHOETEIA
    Macedonia
    Pallene (Mac.)
    Thrace
RHOETUS
    Arcadia
ROMA
    Delos

ROMULUS and REMUS
    Athens
SABAZIUS
    Thrace
SALAGUS
    Chios
SALAMIS
    Salamis
SALMONEUS
    Salmone
    Thessaly
SAMIA
    Samos
SAMUS
    Samos
SAON
    Samothrace
SARON
    Saronic Gulf
    Troezen
SARPEDON (s. Poseidon)
    Thrace
SARPEDON (s. Zeus)
    Crete
SCAMANDER
    Crete
    Glaucia
SCEPHRUS
    Tegea
SCHEDIUS (s. Iphitus)
    Anticyra (Phoc.)
    Panopeus
SCHEDIUS (s. Perimedes)
    Phocis
SCIRON (robber)
    Megara
    Megaris
    Scironian Rocks
SCIRON (s. Pylas)
    Megara
SCIRUS
    Salamis
    Scirum
SCHOENEUS
    Schoenus
SCYLLA
    Saronic Gulf
    Scyllaeum
    Megara
SEBRUS
    Sebrion
    Sparta
SELEMNUS
    Selemnus

SELENE
    Elis (city)
SELINUS
    Achaia (Pelop.)
SEMELE
    Olympus
    Thebes
    Troezen
SIBYLLA
    Delphi
    Samos
SICINUS
    Sicinos
SICYON
    Sicyon
SIDE
    Side
SILENUS
    Bermius
    Cos
    Elis
    Nysa (Thrace)
    Pyrrhicus
SILVANUS
    Ceos
SIMUS
    Arcadia
SINIS
    Corinthian Isthmus
SINOE
    Arcadia
SINOPE
    Boeotia
SIPHNOS
    Siphnos
SIRENS
    Aptera
SISYPHUS
    Corinth
    Corinthian Isthmus
    Thessaly
SITHNIDES
    Megara
SITHON
    Macedonia
    Pallene (Mac.)
    Thrace
SOSTRATUS
    Dyme
SOTERIA
    Patrae
SPARTA
    Amyclae
    Eurotas

    Laconia
    Sparta
SPERCHEIUS
    Spercheius
SPHETTUS
    Sphettus
    Troezen
SPHINX
    Athens
    Boeotia
    Corinth
    Thebes
SPHRAGITIDES
    Cithaeron
STAPHYLUS
    Peparethus
STENYCLERUS
    Stenyclarus
STEROPE (d. Cepheus)
    Tegea
STEROPE (d. Pleuron)
    Calydon
STHENELAS
    Argos
STHENELUS (s. Androgeus)
    Paros
    Thasos
STHENELUS (s. Capaneus)
    Argos
    Thebes
STHENELUS (s. Perseus)
    Argos
    Midea
    Mycenae
STILBE
    Larissa (Thess.)
    Peneius (Thess.)
STROPHIUS
    Cirrha
    Phocis
STRYMON
    Strymon
STYMPHALIDES
    Stymphalus
STYMPHALUS
    Arcadia
    Stymphalus
STYX
    Arcadia
    Nonacris
SYME
    Syme
SYRINX
    Arcadia

TAENARUS
    Sparta
    Taenarum
TALAUS
    Argos
TALOS (s. Perdix) (See CALOS)
TALOS (man of brass)
    Crete
    Tallaeus
TALTHYBIUS
    Argos
    Sparta
TANAGRA
    Tanagra
TANTALUS (s. Thyestes)
    Argos
    Mycenae
TANTALUS (s. Zeus)
    Corinth
    Crete
TAPHIUS
    Taphiae
TARAS
    Taenarum
TAUROPOLIS
    Megara
TAYGETE
    Sparta
    Taygetus
TECTAMUS
    Crete
TEGEATES
    Tegea
TEGYRIUS
    Thrace
TEIRESIAS
    Boeotia
    Cithaeron
    Delphi
    Thebes
    Tilphossium
TELAMON
    Aegina
    Calydon
    Cos
    Corinthian Isthmus
    Salamis
TELCHIN
    Argos
TELCHINES
    Boeotia
    Cameirus
    Crete
    Ialysus

TELCHINES *(cont.)*
    Lindus
    Rhodes
    Sicyon
    Teumessus
TELCHIS
    Sicyon
TELEBOAS
    Acarnania
TELECLUS
    Amyclae
    Sparta
TELEGONUS (s. Odysseus)
    Ithaca
TELEGONUS (s. Proteus)
    Torone
TELEMACHUS
    Asteris
    Ithaca
    Pharae (Mess.)
    Pylus (Mess.)
    Sparta
TELEON
    Athens
TELEPHUS
    Arcadia
    Mycenae
    Parthenium
    Tegea
TELESPHORUS
    Titane
TELESTES
    Corinth
TELONDES
    Cabeiraea
TEMENUS (s. Aristomachus)
    Argolis
    Argos
    Macedonia
    Temenium
TEMENUS (s. Pelasgus)
    Stymphalus
TENERUS
    Thebes
TENES
    Tenea
TERAMBUS
    Othrys
TEREUS
    Daulis
    Megara
    Pegae
TEUCER (s. Scamander)
    Crete

TEUCER (S. Telamon)
    Athens
    Salamis
TEUCRUS
    Xypete
TEUTAMAS
    Larissa (Thess.)
TEUTHRAS
    Teuthrone
THALASSA
    Corinth
    Mediterranean Sea
THALLO
    Athens
    Attica
THALPIUS
    Elis
THALUS
    Chios
THAMYRIS
    Amyclae
    Dorium
    Parnassus
THANATOS
    Sparta
THASOS
    Thasos
THAUMACUS
    Thaumacia
THEBE (d. Asopus)
    Thebes
THEBE (d. Prometheus)
    Thebes
THEIODAMAS
    Dryopis
THEISOA
    Arcadia
    Theisoa
THELPUSA
    Ladon
    Thelpusa
THELXION
    Argos
    Sicyon
THEMIS
    Athens
    Delphi
    Epidaurus
    Olympia
    Olympus
    Rhamnus
    Tanagra
    Thebes
    Troezen

THEMIS ICHNAEA
    Ichnae
THEMISTO
    Athamania
THERAPNE
    Sparta
THERAS
    Sparta
    Thera
THERSANDER
    Thebes
THERSANDRUS
    Corinth
THERSITES
    Calydon
THESEUS
    Achelous
    Acheron
    Aegean
    Aphidna
    Athena
    Attica
    Calydon
    Cephissus (Att.)
    Cephissus (Eleusis)
    Colonus
    Corinthian Isthmus
    Corydallus
    Crete
    Crommyon
    Deceleia
    Delos
    Delphi
    Echinades
    Eleusis
    Epeirus
    Epidaurus
    Genethlium
    Hecale
    Larissa (Thess.)
    Marathon
    Naxos
    Olympia
    Pallene (Att.)
    Prasiae (Att.)
    Scironian Rocks
    Scyros
    Sparta
    Thebes
    Thymoetadae
    Troezen
THESPIA
    Thespiae

THESPIUS
  Thespiae
THESPROTUS
  Thesprotia
THESSALUS (s. Haemon)
  Thessaly
THESSALUS (s. Heracles)
  Cos
  Nisyrus
THESSALUS (s. Jason)
  Corinth
  Iolcus
  Thessaly
THESTIUS
  Aetolia
  Calydon
  Pleuron
  Thestia
THETIS
  Messenia
  Pelion
  Pharsalus
  Sepias
  Sparta
  Thessaly
  Thetidium
THISBE
  Thisbe
THOAS (s. Andraemon)
  Aetolia
  Calydon
  Pleuron
THOAS (s. Dionysus)
  Lemnos
  Sicinos
THOAS (s. Ornytion)
  Corinth
THOAS (s. Zeus)
  Olenus (Aet.)
THOCNUS
  Thocnia
THRASYMEDES
  Pylus (Mess.)
THRIAE
  Parnassus
THURIMACHUS
  Sicyon
THYESTES
  Mycenae
THYIA
  Delphi
  Thyia

THYIADES
  Corycium
  Delphi
  Parnassus
THYMOETES
  Athens
  Thymoetadae
THYONE (See SEMELE)
THYRAEUS
  Thyraeum
THYREUS
  Calydon
THYRIA (See HYRIA)
TILPHUSA
  Tilphossium
TIMAGORAS
  Athens
TIMALCUS
  Megara
TIMANDRA
  Sparta
TIPHYS
  Siphae
TIRYNS (s. Argus)
  Tiryns
  Argos
TIRYNS (d. Halus)
  Tiryns
TISAMENUS
  Achaia (Pelop.)
  Argos
  Helice
  Laconia
  Sparta
  Thebes
TISIPHONE
  Thebes
TITANES
  Cnossus
  Olympus
  Othrys
  Thessaly
TITHONUS
  Athens
TITHOREA
  Neon
  Parnassus
TITYLUS
  Amyclae
  Euboea
  Panopeus
TLEPOLEMUS
  Cameirus
  Ialysus

  Lindus
  Rhodes
TORONE
  Sithonia
  Torone
TRAMBELUS
  Lesbos
TRAPEZUS
  Trapezus
TRICCA
  Tricca
TRICOLONUS
  Paroria
  Tricoloni
TRIOPAS (s. Lapithes)
  Thessaly
TRIOPAS (s. Phorbas)
  Argos
TRIOPAS (s. Poseidon)
  Delphi
  Dotius Campus
TRIPHYLUS
  Triphylia
TRIPTOLEMUS
  Athens
  Attica
  Eleusis
  Rharian Plain
TRITAEA
  Tritaea
TRITON
  Athens
  Corinthian Isthmus
  Mediterranean Sea
  Tanagra
TROEZEN
  Troezen
TROILUS
  Chryse
TROPHONIUS
  Delphi
  Hercyna
  Hyria
  Lebadeia
  Orchomenus (Boeo.)
  Pagasae
  Thebes
TROXEUS
  Calydon
TRYGON
  Thelpusa
TYCHE
  Aegeira
  Athens

TYCHE *(cont.)*
  Corinth
  Delos
  Elis
  Lebadeia
  Megalopolis
  Megara
  Pharae (Mess.)
  Sicyon
  Thebes
TYCHIUS
  Hyle
TYDEUS
  Aetolia
  Argos
  Calydon
  Thebes
TYNDAREUS
  Aetolia
  Amyclae
  Laconia
  Pellana
  Pleuron
  Sparta
TYRO
  Enipeus
  Iolcus
UDAEUS
  Thebes
VENTI
  Athens
  Coroneia
  Sicyon
  Thyia
  Titane
  Thrace
VENUS FORTUNA
  Corinth
XANTHIPPUS
  Daulis
XANTHUS (Boeotian king)
  Melaenae (Att.)
  Thebes
XANTHUS (s. Triopas)
  Argos
  Lesbos
XENOCLEIA
  Delphi
XENODICE
  Crete
XUTHUS
  Achaia (Pelop.)
  Athens

Delphi
Marathon
ZACYNTHUS
  Zacynthus
ZALMOXIS
  Samos
ZARAX
  Eleusis
  Zarax
ZEPHYRUS
  Amyclae
  Athens
  Ceos
  Eleusis
  Thrace
ZETES
  Strophades
  Tenos
ZETHUS
  Cithaeron
  Eleutherae
  Eutresis
  Thebes
ZEUS
  Aegeira
  Aegeum
  Aegina
  Aegium
  Alalcomenae
  Andros
  Anthedon
  Arcadia
  Argos
  Athens
  Attica
  Biennus
  Boeotia
  Chaeroneia
  Cithaeron
  Clepsydra
  Cnossus
  Colonus
  Corcyra
  Corinth
  Crete
  Cretea
  Delos
  Delphi
  Dicte
  Dodona
  Eleutherna
  Elis
  Epeirus
  Euboea

Gortyna
Hierapytna
Ida
Lebadeia
Lycaeus
Lyctos
Megara
Messenia
Neda
Olympia
Olympus
Omphalium
Parrhasia
Phalerum
Physceius
Rhodes
Samos
Sicyon
Stratus
Taygetus
Tegea
Thebes
Theisoa
Thornax (Arg.)
ZEUS ACRAEUS
  Ethopia
ZEUS ACTAEUS
  Pelion
ZEUS AENEIUS
  Aenos
  Cephallenia
ZEUS AETHIOPS
  Chios
ZEUS AGAMEMNON
  Sparta
ZEUS AGETOR
  Laconia
ZEUS AGORAEUS
  Sparta
  Thebes
ZEUS AMBULIUS
  Sparta
ZEUS AMMON
  Aphytis
ZEUS ANCHESMIUS
  Anchesmus
ZEUS APEMIUS
  Parnes
ZEUS APESANTIUS
  Apesas
ZEUS APHESIUS
  Geraneia
  Megaris

ZEUS APOMYIUS
- Alpheius
- Elis
- Olympia

ZEUS ARBIUS
- Arbius

ZEUS AREIUS
- Pisa

ZEUS ASTRAPAEUS
- Athens

ZEUS ATABYRIUS
- Atabyris
- Cretenia
- Rhodes

ZEUS ATHOUS
- Athos

ZEUS BASILEUS
- Lebadeia

ZEUS BOULAEUS
- Athens

ZEUS CAPPOTAS
- Gythium

ZEUS CARAOS
- Astacus

ZEUS CARIUS
- Boeotia
- Thessaly

ZEUS CASSIUS
- Corcyra

ZEUS CATHARSIUS
- Olympia

ZEUS CENAEUS
- Cenaeum

ZEUS CHARMON
- Mantineia

ZEUS CITHAERONIUS
- Cithaeron

ZEUS CLARIUS
- Tegea

ZEUS COCCYGIUS
- Thornax (Arg.)

ZEUS CONIUS
- Megara

ZEUS COSMETAS
- Sparta

ZEUS CROCEATAS
- Croceae
- Gythium

ZEUS CTESIUS
- Phlya

ZEUS CYNTHIUS
- Cynthus
- Delos
- Paros

ZEUS DICTAEUS
- Dicte
- Pothereus
- Praesus

ZEUS DODONAIS
- Dodona
- Epeirus
- Tomarus

ZEUS ELEUTHERIUS
- Athens
- Plataea

ZEUS EPACRIUS
- Hymettus

ZEUS EPIDOTES
- Mantineia
- Sparta

ZEUS EUANEMUS
- Sparta

ZEUS GENETHLIUS
- Lepsia

ZEUS HECALEIUS
- Hecale

ZEUS HECATOMBAEUS
- Crete
- Gortyna

ZEUS HETAEREIUS
- Iolcus

ZEUS HOMAGYRIUS
- Achaia (Pelop.)
- Aegium

ZEUS HOMARIUS (See ZEUS HOMAGYRIUS)

ZEUS HOMOLOIUS
- Orchomenus (Boeo.)
- Thebes

ZEUS HORCEIUS
- Olympia

ZEUS HYETIUS
- Lebadeia

ZEUS HYMETTUS
- Hymettus

ZEUS HYPATUS
- Athens
- Glisas
- Sparta

ZEUS HYPSISTUS
- Beroea
- Cynthus
- Delos

ZEUS ICMAEUS
- Ceos

ZEUS ITHOMATAS
- Clepsydra
- Ithome (Mess.)
- Messenia

ZEUS LAPHYSTIUS
- Boeotia
- Laphystium

ZEUS LARISSAEUS
- Argos
- Larissa (Arg.)

ZEUS LECHEATES
- Aliphera

ZEUS LEUCAEUS
- Lepreum

ZEUS LYCAEUS
- Arcadia
- Eleutherae
- Lycaeus
- Hagno
- Lycosura
- Megalopolis
- Tegea

ZEUS LYCOREUS
- Lycoreia

ZEUS MAEMACTES
- Athens

ZEUS MECHANEUS
- Argos
- Delphi

ZEUS MEILICHIUS
- Argos
- Athens
- Cephissus (Att.)
- Sicyon

ZEUS MESSAPEUS
- Amyclae
- Laconia
- Taygetus

ZEUS MOIRAGETES
- Arcadia
- Delphi

ZEUS MORIUS
- Athens

ZEUS NEMEIUS
- Argos
- Messene
- Nemea
- Oeneon

ZEUS OMBRIUS
- Hymettus
- Parnes

ZEUS OLYMPIUS
- Athens
- Calymna

ZEUS OLYMPIUS *(cont.)*
  Chalcis
  Cynaetha
  Dium
  Elis
  Lechaeum
  Megara
  Olympia
  Olympus
  Patrae
  Sparta
ZEUS PANHELLENIUS
  Aegina
  Panhellenium
ZEUS PARNETHIUS
  Parnes
ZEUS PHYXIUS
  Argos
  Thessaly
ZEUS PHRATRIOS
  Athens

ZEUS PLUSIUS
  Sparta
ZEUS POLIEUS
  Athens
  Delphi
  Ialysus
  Lindus
ZEUS SCOTITAS
  Laconia
ZEUS SEMALEOS
  Parnes
ZEUS SOTER
  Acraephnium
  Argos
  Cleonae
  Corone
  Epidaurus
  Limera
  Laconia
  Mantineia
  Megalopolis

  Messene
  Peiraeus
  Troezen
ZEUS TELEIUS
  Tegea
ZEUS THAULIUS
  Pharsalus
ZEUS THENATAS
  Amnisus
ZEUS TROPAEUS
  Sparta
ZEUXIPPE
  Athens
ZEUXIPPUS
  Sicyon
ZOETEUS
  Zoetia